Law and Institutions of the European Communities

Fifth Edition

D Lasok   LenDr, LLM, PhD, Dr Juris, LLD, Dhc

of the Middle Temple, one of Her Majesty's Counsel,
Emeritus Professor of European Law and former
Director of the Centre for European Legal Studies at
the University of Exeter

J W Bridge   LLB, LLM, PhD

Professor of Public Law
at the University of Exeter

*Scire leges non hoc est verba earum tenere,
sed vim ac potestatem,* Celsus, 1.3.17

London, Dublin, Edinburgh
Butterworths
1991

United Kingdom	Butterworth & Co (Publishers) Ltd, 88 Kingsway, LONDON WC2B 6AB and 4 Hill Street, EDINBURGH EH2 3JZ
Australia	Butterworths Pty Ltd, SYDNEY, MELBOURNE, BRISBANE, ADELAIDE, PERTH, CANBERRA and HOBART
Canada	Butterworths Canada Ltd, TORONTO and VANCOUVER
Ireland	Butterworth (Ireland) Ltd, DUBLIN
Malaysia	Malayan Law Journal Sdn Bhd, KUALA LUMPUR
New Zealand	Butterworths of New Zealand Ltd, WELLINGTON and AUCKLAND
Puerto Rico	Equity de Puerto Rico, Inc, HATO REY
Singapore	Malayan Law Journal Pte Ltd, SINGAPORE
USA	Butterworth Legal Publishers, AUSTIN, Texas; BOSTON, Massachusetts, CLEARWATER, Florida (D & S Publishers); ORFORD, New Hampshire (Equity Publishing); ST PAUL, Minnesota; and SEATTLE, Washington

A CIP Catalogue record for this book is available from the British Library.

ISBN 0 406 60931 4

Printed by Butler & Tanner Ltd, Frome and London

Preface to the fifth edition

Ubi Societas Ibi Jus

This edition remains true to the authors' original intention to provide a projection of the law of the European Communities as a complete system within the compass of one volume. (See the Preface to the first edition, reproduced below.)

In addition to general updating, the work has been revised and enlarged so as to incorporate developments and new departures over the past four years. These include the dramatic political changes in Europe; the impact of the Single European Act, particularly with regard to legislative procedures; the *locus standi* of the European Parliament; the establishment of the Court of First Instance; the continuing effect of membership on the constitution of the United Kingdom; and developments in relation to the environment and consumer protection.

The text, as far as possible, reflects the materials available at the close of January 1991.

D L
J W B
Exeter
Maundy Thursday 1991

Preface to the first edition

Ubi Societas Ibi Jus

To understand the nature of the law one must understand the nature of the society from which it emanates and which it purports to govern.

We are used to the concepts of national and international law. The former is the law of a sovereign state and as such it governs the society comprised in a state that is a group of people living within a defined area under a government which has executive, legislative, judicial and administrative powers. International law, on the other hand, is the body of rules which governs relations between states and such international organizations as are set up and recognized by states as bearers of rights and duties. In exceptional situations individuals may be regarded as subjects of international law. As a body of rules international law is derived partly from custom and state practice, partly from the will of states expressed in treaties and partly generated by institutions (eg the United Nations Organization) set up by states and based on a treaty.

The object of this book is to define and analyse a nascent body of law which can be described as the law of the European Community. It is neither a national nor an international system of law in the accepted sense of these terms but a *sui generis* system emanating from the will to create a European Community. It reflects, of course, the nature of this design. At this stage we can speak of the European Community only in general political terms as an organization with limited, mainly economic objectives and a potential for development towards a federal organization. In strictly juristic, institutional terms we have to speak of the European Communities, that is the European Coal and Steel Community, the European Atomic Energy Community and the European Economic Community and, therefore, a distinction between 'Community' and 'Communities' has to be borne in mind. The law of the European Community, as we understand it, comprises consequently elements of international and national law as well as the rules generated by the Communities, of which the European Economic

Community may be regarded as a cornerstone of future developments. This we shall endeavour to emphasize.

The genesis of this book lies in the authors' experience of teaching European Community Law in the University of Exeter. They wish to express their thanks to their students, both undergraduate and post-graduate, for the patience and forbearance with which they endured the authors' experimental first steps in this field. The authors claim to have written no more than an introduction to the complex system of Community law. In order to explain its working to the reader it was thought necessary to stress the institutional aspects of the Community and matters of principle at the expense of the details of the law of the economy which is still at a formative stage. It is hoped, however, that it is informative and provocative in that by setting out the rudiments it will make the reader aware of the unprecedented challenge facing Europe, the United Kingdom and the citizen, be he lawyer or layman. The aim throughout has been to approach the subject from the standpoint of the United Kingdom joining a continental Community which is already a going concern and this explains the emphasis placed on the political background of the Community and the civil law framework within which it functions. The authors owe a considerable debt to the numerous pioneer writers on the Communities and their law and pay them generous tribute.

This is a joint work. Chapters 1, 3, 4, 10, 11, 13 and 14 were drafted by D Lasok; chapters 5, 6, 7, 8, 9 and 12 were drafted by J W Bridge; chapter 2 was drafted jointly. The work of each author has been subject to the comments and criticisms of the other and both authors are in agreement on and each accepts responsibility for the form and content of the whole book.

The authors' gratitude is due to all the members of the secretarial staff of the Faculty of Law of the University of Exeter who, with their accustomed cheerfulness and efficiency, undertook the typing of the manuscript; to the Publishers; and to their wives and families to whom this book is dedicated.

D L
J W B
Exeter
Michaelmas 1972

Contents

Table of Statutes

References in this Table to *Statutes* are to Halsbury's Statutes of England (Fourth Edition) showing the volume and page at which the annotated text of the Act may be found.

Table of European Communities Legislation

Treaties

Secondary Legislation

DECISIONS

Table of Conventions and Treaties

Table of other Enactments

List of Cases

Decisions of the European Court of Justice are listed both alphabetically and numerically. The numerical Table follows the alphabetical.

PAGE

A

PAGE

PAGE

F

PAGE

M

PAGE

PAGE

T

U

Decisions of the European Court of Justice are listed below numerically.
These decisions are also included in the preceding alphabetical Table.

PAGE

PAGE

List of Cases lxxiii

PAGE

List of Principal Abbreviations

AJCL American Journal of Comparative Law

AJIL American Journal of International Law

Art Article

Benelux Belgium, The Netherlands and Luxembourg

BGB Bürgeliches Gesetzbuch (Germany)

BYBIL British Year Book of International Law

CECA Communauté du Charbon et de l'Acier (see ECSC)

CEE Communauté Economique Européenne (see EEC)

CEEA Communauté Européenne de l'Energie Atomique (see EAEC/ Euratom)

CMLR Common Market Law Reports

CMLRev Common Market Law Review

Comecon Council for Mutual Economic Co-operation

EAEC/Euratom European Atomic Energy Community

ECSC European Coal and Steel Community

EEC European Economic Community

EFTA European Free Trade Association

ERTA European Road Transport Agreement

GATT General Agreement on Tariffs and Trade

Gaz Uff Gazetta Ufficiale (Italy)

ICJ Reports International Court of Justice Reports

ICLQ International and Comparative Law Quarterly

ILO International Labour Organisation

IMF International Monetary Fund

JO Journal Officiel des Communautés Européennes

JORF Journal Officiel de la République Française

LQR Law Quarterly Review

MB Moniteur Belge

MLR Modern Law Review

NATO North Atlantic Treaty Organisation

OECD Organisation for Economic Co-operation and Development

OEEC Organisation for European Economic Co-operation

PCIJ Rep Permanent Court of International Justice Reports

Recueil Recueil de la Jurisprudence de la Cour de Justice des Communautés Européennes

Reg Regulation

RP Rule of Procedure of the Community Court

UNTS United Nations Treaty Series

Part I

The nature of the European Communities and of Community law

Chapter 1

The birth and growth of the European Community

THE FORMATION OF THE EUROPEAN COMMUNITY

The recurrent dream of a unified Europe is part of our cultural heritage. Students of history are familiar with the attempts to create a united Europe mainly by force, for conquest and universalism go often hand in hand. Only within living memory have two powerful ideologies, Communism and Nazism, endeavoured to unify Europe in their own fashion. In August 1920 the advance of the Red Army 'through the heart of Poland to the conquest of Europe and world conflagration'[1] was brought to a halt at the gates of Warsaw in what was described[2] as the eighteenth decisive battle of world history. In 1945 ended the Second World War, unleashed by one Adolf Hitler who dreamed of a millennium of German domination over Europe. After six years of struggle most of Europe was reduced to smouldering heaps of rubble, physically and politically. The old Europe became just a phase in the Continent's saga and history began to work towards a different concept of unification.

Students of political thought are familiar with the rivalries for excellence between the concept of the sovereign state and federal ideas. From the middle ages right up to our time the state was regarded as the ideal self-sufficient unit, capable of securing protection and self-fulfilment of individuals. The 19th and the first half of the 20th centuries witnessed the apotheosis of the sovereign state as the supreme and sublime goal of human organization. Everything was to be subordinated to the state. This Hegelian ideal, no doubt rooted in Plato's philosophy, being an element of the explanation of the universe and of historical determinism, was eagerly adopted by modern dictatorships both of the fascist and communist type and soon brought into disrepute. The Second World War did not solve Europe's problems but resulted in a new

1 General Tukhachevski in an order to his armies quoted by Umiastowski, R, *Russia and the Polish Republic 1918–1941* (1944), p 84.
2 By Lord D'Abernon; Fuller, J F C, *The Decisive Battles of the Western World, 1792–1944*, Vol 2 (1970), p 411.

division based on the conquest of its eastern half and generating mutual distrust between the West and the East. In a sense it contributed to the creation of two European Communities; of the West (which is the subject of the present study) and of the East (the so-called Council for Mutual Economic Co-operation). The two Communities reflected the political reality of the divided Europe and the relationship of the countries they represented. They also depicted a process of integration along different lines. Whilst the East European Community reflected the leading rôle of the Soviet Union and the common political ideology of the bloc, the West European Community reflected, structurally, vague federalist ideas[3] of the 19th and 20th centuries and, politically, the fear of the other side expressed in the statement that Stalin was the chief architect of West European solidarity.[4]

The Second World War demonstrated the futility of conquests and the vulnerability of the sovereign state concept. The sovereign state could no longer guarantee the protection of the citizen and so the traditional concept of allegiance based on a *sui generis* contract broke down. Interdependence of states rather than independence became the key to post-war international relations, and was reflected in current trends of international law, especially in the ideology and structure of the United Nations. The slogan *si vis pacem para bellum* had to give way to the quest for justice among men and nations and *si vis pacem para pacem* had to become the order of the day. An admirable example of co-operation and a practical application of the call for peace is the European Coal and Steel Community built on the premise that, if the basic raw materials for war (coal and steel) are removed from national control, wars between the traditional enemies, France and Germany, will become virtually impossible as long as both are prevented from developing a substantial war industry. A corollary benefit of the international control of these resources, accruing not only to France and Germany but also to the other members of the Community, was brought about by the rationalization of the coal and steel industries and the economic stimulus created by an enlarged market.

With the demise of the state ideology, federalism found a new lease of life. Federal doctrines have, in the past, set their face against the idolatry of the state, but they were Utopian rather than realistic whilst physical, territorial federalism in Western Europe proved politically impossible. Federalism had to search for other, more realistic forms. Harold Laski, in an introduction to his book,

3 Delmas, C, *Le Fédéralisme et l'Europe* (1969).
4 Spaak, H-P, *Combats Inachevés* (1969), pp 249–250.

Liberty in the Modern State,[5] argued that the Second World War
and its antecedents had shown that 'the principle of national sovereignty has exhausted its usefulness'. He wrote further: 'it is
through supranational planning in fields like electric power, or
transport, an integrated economy of coal and steel, that we can best
hope to attain this end [ie to make liberty possible]. It is, of course,
impossible to leave such planning in private hands.' Laski dubbed
his idea 'functional federalism' because he was opposed to the
concept of territorial federation, that is to say a United States
of Europe or a Federal Western Europe, an enlarged version of
Switzerland, which he regarded as both obsolete and impractical.

Whilst 'functional federalism' has been accepted by the architects
of the West European Community, Laski's pessimism about territorial federalism may yet prove unfounded. It is clear that economic co-operation and legal integration will tighten the political
and organizational bonds between states and from this reality new
political forms will emerge. Territorial federalism is not just round
the corner but is not as remote as it may seem. It may well be that
it will not be heralded by political theory but will grow up as a
child of evolution. In the Community institutions, which we shall
examine in detail, the stage seems to have been set for such a
development.

The post-war practical exercise in international co-operation in
Western Europe has proved that nations can live together and work
together, that they can solve their differences amicably and, where
need be, through appropriate legal and judicial process. It has
demonstrated that the concept of a Community is not only viable
but also capable of growth and development. The Community
institutions have already been working for two generations and
their very existence and practical usefulness will inevitably lead to
their refinement.

If we cast our minds back to the early post-war days we will
realize that a Community approach was the practical answer to
many problems. Europe was in ruins politically and economically;
the European colonial empires faced liquidation; the importance
of the single European states which dominated the League of
Nations was diminished; the 'dollar-gap' resulted in great influence
of the United States of America not only as a benevolent saviour
but also as a potential master; an 'iron curtain' was drawn across
Europe and the world cowered in the shadows of great powers: the
United States of America and Soviet Russia facing each other
menacingly across Europe. Only rapid recovery in concert could
restore Europe's self-respect. What is more it became only too

5 Republished in 1948.

obvious that economic reconstruction had to match political aspirations. Thus the idea of a European Community was forced upon Europeans as an economic and political necessity. As for grand designs, the architects of the Community soon realized that great ideologies and elaborate blueprints were of little practical use and that nothing could be achieved at one stroke. Robert Schuman,[6] the great French European, said: 'L'Europe ne se fera pas d'un coup dans une construction d'ensemble, elle se fera par des réalisations concrètes créant d'abord une solidarité de fait . . .'

This factual solidarity can be traced to events of great importance to Europe and the world at large, as the work of world recovery and reconstruction began to create a fabric of international economic co-operation. We should mention, if only briefly, these events and forms of co-operation because they too contributed to European solidarity and in a sense paved the way for the institutional framework of the European Community.

THE INTERNATIONAL MONETARY FUND AND THE WORLD BANK

The IMF was created at a conference at Bretton Woods in 1946, with the object of maintaining the stability of national currencies, reducing restrictions on the currency exchange and helping countries to maintain a balance of payments. The subscribing countries participate on a share basis: USA 28%, USSR 12·5% and Europe only 16%. The size of the share determines the voting power of the subscribers. Countries (including the United Kingdom) often borrow money to maintain their solvency. The World Bank was also created at Bretton Woods. Here again states participate on a share basis. The USA alone provides 38% of the capital. The Bank offers not only financial assistance but also provides experts in various fields. It has been useful to finance projects incapable of being financed otherwise, especially in the developing countries.

THE HAVANA CHARTER AND GATT

Representatives of fifty-five countries, assembled at Havana on the initiative of the USA in 1947–48, drafted a Charter of International Commerce which envisaged a gradual reduction of customs tariffs; proposed suppression of import quotas (except in the case of agricultural produce) and imbalance of payments; prohibited discrimination in commerce (except in the case of former colonies, customs unions and free exchange areas); encouraged investments

---

6 Quoted by Lorette, L de Sainte, *Le Marché Commun* (1961), p 17; Patjin, S, (ed), *Landmarks in European Unity* (1970), p 46.

in the developing countries and suggested an International Trade Organization. Liberia was the only country which ratified the Charter.

The idea of this Charter was nevertheless accepted by 23 countries which in October 1947 signed the General Agreement on Tariffs and Trade (GATT). It is concerned with customs and commercial policy. The Agreement has been in operation without being ratified between 83 countries which subscribe to its principles and a further 28 countries which apply its principles without having formally signed it. Under the auspices of GATT frequent meetings of experts are held and many rules of customs and trade laws have been modified.

The members of GATT have set up a Council of Representatives with a secretariat in Geneva. Moreover, member countries adhere, as a rule, to the principles propounded by GATT in the matter of customs, import quotas and preferences and enter into bi-lateral agreements in these fields. It is significant that the so-called Schuman Plan and the European Economic Community Treaty were submitted to GATT to ensure conformity with its principles. As from 4 May 1964 the EEC, representing the Member States, has been taking part in negotiations within GATT.

THE UN ECONOMIC COMMISSION FOR EUROPE

This Commission was established in 1947 in Geneva for the purpose of exchanging information and statistical data on coal, electricity and transport in Western and Eastern Europe. Twenty-eight countries, including the USA, are involved. The Commission has published analytical studies of the economic situations of several European countries, but as the division between the Western and Eastern blocs deepened, it failed as an instrument of co-operation.

THE MARSHALL PLAN AND THE ORGANIZATION FOR EUROPEAN ECONOMIC CO-OPERATION

In a speech at Harvard on 5 July 1947 General George Marshall, the US Secretary of State, announced a plan for European relief. Instead of loans to individual countries the US offered economic aid on the sole condition that the Europeans work out a common programme for the relief of poverty and for economic reconstruction. His appeal was addressed to Europe as a whole, stating that '... our policy is not directed against any country or against any doctrine but against hunger, poverty, despair and chaos; its aim is the renewal of active economy throughout the world'.[7] The Plan was welcomed in Western Europe and the Foreign Secretaries of France and the United Kingdom invited the USSR to join them. Ten days later Molotov scorned the invitation and enjoined Czechoslovakia, Poland and Finland, who expressed interest, to have nothing to do with the Plan. Subsequently, in January 1949, a specifically East-European regional organization emerged, allegedly not as a response or counterweight[8] to the Marshall Plan but to meet the needs of the region and to 'strengthen the unity and the brotherly alliance of independent and equal socialist countries'.[9] Thus the division of Europe became further accentuated.

Sixteen West European countries participated in the conference and the ensuing Committee of Economic Co-operation which led to the creation of the Organization for European Economic Co-operation[10] in April 1948. More than 13 milliard dollars were poured into Europe out of the American bounty. This was undoubtedly the first substantial move towards economic co-operation in Europe and the Americans quite rightly take pride in their contribution. Indeed European economic cohesion and strength was in the political interest of the USA even if Europe was to become a competitive force to be reckoned with. Thus American willingness to protect Western Europe from communist expansion contributed towards European unity.[11]

At first the OEEC examined the various national plans of economic reconstruction and then worked out a programme of distribution of the American aid. From a legal point of view the important feature of the OEEC was its inter-governmental structure. The sovereignty of each country was safeguarded and no political strings were attached, so much so that even Switzerland, sworn to perpetual neutrality, could participate. The Organization, which consisted of a Council of Ministers, an Executive Committee and a Secretariat, survived the completion of the Marshall Plan. It embraced 18 countries, including West Germany since 1949 and Spain since 1959 and Yugoslavia represented by an observer. The OEEC could take decisions which were binding on members. It endeavoured to co-ordinate national economic policies and provide experts who serve in an advisory capacity in special fields, ie transport, electricity, textiles, etc. It even tried to bring together rival groups like the EEC and the EFTA.

7 Lorette, op cit, p 22.
8 Ciamaga, L, *Od wspolpracy do integracji* (1965), p 13.
9 Fikus, D, *RWPG–Fakty* (1966), p 16.
10 See the Convention of 16 April 1948, TS 59 (1949); Cmnd 7796.
11 Grosser, A, *Les occidentaux, le pays d'Europe et les Etats-Unis depuis la guerre* (1978), p 224.

From its inception the OEEC endeavoured to liberalize European trade. It brought about a reduction of import quotas without tampering with the customs laws, which resulted in a short-lived trade boom. In 1952 the United Kingdom and France, contrary to the OEEC's advice, lapsed into import quotas and so exposed the weakness of the Organization. As new forms of economic co-operation began to take shape, the OEEC exhausted its usefulness. In 1961 it was transformed into an Organization for Economic Co-operation and Development (OECD)[12] for the purpose of assisting the developing countries. The European countries were joined by the USA and Canada as well as the EEC in its corporate capacity, ie independently of its members.

THE COUNCIL OF EUROPE

Parallel to this economic co-operation there was a movement towards political and military integration. The various European movements joined forces in a Congress of Europe held in May 1948 in The Hague under the presidency of Winston Churchill. This resulted in the Council of Europe, inaugurated in 1949 at Strasbourg. It started with the five countries of the Brussels Military Alliance (now the Western European Union), viz the UK, France, Belgium, Holland and Luxembourg, and now embraces 23 countries of Western Europe including Spain and Portugal which were originally excluded, Greece suspended from membership in 1967 and readmitted in 1974 and San Marino which joined in 1989. Political changes in Eastern Europe towards the end of 1989 opened the way for further enlargement and for making the Council of Europe truly 'European'.

The Council of Europe[13] consists of a Consultative Assembly composed of parliamentary delegates of the Member States, a Committee of Ministers and a Secretariat. It has a permanent seat at Strasbourg. As a political design it has proved a failure since it has not developed beyond the nuclear stage of a federal organization. Its main achievements lie in the field of human rights, having established a Commission and a Court of Human Rights. But, above all, it has kept the idea of a United Europe alive.

In the economic field the Consultative Assembly in 1951 formulated proposals to turn Europe into a 'low tariff club' through the lowering of customs barriers. It also put forward, under the name of the 'Strasbourg Plan', ideas for the economic development of the former colonies of the European powers and for the adoption

12 See the Convention of 14 December 1960, TS 21 (1962); Cmnd 1646.
13 See the Statute of the Council of Europe, TS 51 (1949); Cmnd 7778.

of preferential tariffs between these territories; the British Commonwealth on the one hand and the European countries on the other. Further initiatives aimed at the organization of European agriculture (the so-called green pool) and transport.

Whilst the economic initiatives of the Council of Europe have been superseded by the EEC and the political initiatives remain in an embryonic stage, the Council provides a forum for cultural and political contacts extending beyond the membership of the EEC and so preserves the concept of European unity.

THE NORTH ATLANTIC TREATY ORGANIZATION AND TRANSPORT

NATO developed from the North Atlantic Treaty of 1949[14] which was an extension of the Brussels Treaty of 1948.[15] It now embraces all the West European countries (except Austria, Ireland, Sweden and Switzerland) as well as the USA, Canada, Greece and Turkey. France has withdrawn from NATO but remains party to the North Atlantic Treaty. It is important to note that, without a surrender of sovereignty, decisions[16] within NATO are taken collectively and that this co-operation, though confined to military matters, contributes to the cohesion of Western Europe.

In another technical field, that of transport, the Conference of European Ministers of Transport has for some years now achieved rationalization of railway transport and, incidentally, enabled the 17 countries involved to make substantial economies. This means that railway carriages marked EUROP can be used and repaired anywhere within the organization and need not be returned empty to their countries of origin. Complementing EUROP is EURO-FIMA (*Société de financement de matériel ferroviaire*) which by international agreement is entitled to exemption from customs and taxes in respect of railway equipment no matter where it is ultimately used within the organization. The more complex problem of the rationalization of transport by road, sea and air has recently been tackled by the EEC.

However, following the thaw in West–East relations and the mutual reduction of arms programme, NATO is being adapted to a new rôle. When it has outlived its usefulness defence may well fall within the domain of the European Community.

14 See the Treaty of 4 April 1949; TS 56 (1949); Cmnd 7789.
15 See the Treaty of Economic, Social and Cultural Collaboration and Collective Self-Defence of 17 March 1948; TS 1 (1949); Cmnd 7599.
16 NATO Handbook (1978), p 39.

THE BENELUX UNION

For the purpose of customs, the three countries (Belgium, Netherlands, Luxembourg) have become one. This has been achieved by stages in spite of the disparity of their economic systems and policies. As from 1 January 1948 they removed customs barriers between themselves and agreed upon common customs tariffs vis-à-vis the outside world. In 1951 they adopted a common scheme of customs and excise duties, with the exception of excise on alcohol, sugar and petrol. In 1954 they authorized a free flow of capital which meant a freedom of investment and unrestricted transfer of currency within the three countries. Since 1956 they have entered into common commercial treaties with other countries and accepted a free movement of labour. In 1958 they signed a treaty of economic union which came into force on 17 November 1960. As from that date the economy of the Benelux countries was geared to the basic assumptions of an internal market, that is the removal of customs barriers, resulting in a free movement of goods and the free movement of capital and manpower. These three elements were adopted later on for the formation of the EEC by the Treaty of Rome.

The Benelux union did not destroy the national sovereignty of the three countries or affect their identity as subjects of International Law. Though economic integration led inevitably to a greater cohesion in a political and military sense, each country has preserved its political and legal system. The economic integration of the Benelux countries was not a painless operation for there were rival interests of industries across the border. However, as a result, the internal trade of these countries increased by 50% whereas their external trade jumped to fifth place after the USA, the UK, West Germany and Canada, thus surpassing France even though the population of France was twice that of the Benelux countries.

From 1948 to 1956 the national revenue of Belgium and the Netherlands increased considerably and so did their trade with the outside world. This minute Common Market proved to be profitable, not only to the three countries but also to others. Its unqualified success whetted the appetites of neighbouring states and led to the projection of the experiment on a European scale.

THE SCHUMAN PLAN

Robert Schuman and Count Sforza thought that a customs union between France and Italy would be beneficial to both countries. A customs treaty was signed in 1949 but both countries lacked the will to see it through. This failure indicated that a less ambitious approach, limited perhaps to one basic industry, should be attempted. Thus coal and steel was selected as the industry basic to many other industries and one especially relevant to the business of war. If war were to be eliminated coal and steel must be put under international control and if economic progress were to breach the national frontiers this basic industry must be made to serve a community of nations.

This was not a novel philosophy, for back in 1948 the European Movement proclaimed at The Hague the need for an industrial programme especially for the production and distribution of coal. A year later, at Westminster, the European Movement proposed a scheme for several basic industries, ie coal, steel, electricity and transport, envisaging a European Institution responsible for a general policy in respect of each of these four industries especially in the field of investments, the volume of production and prices and a consultative body consisting of employers and employees as well as representatives of the public interest.

This, in turn, led to the so-called Schuman Plan. In May 1950 France, through its Minister of Foreign Affairs, Robert Schuman, proposed to place all the Franco-German production of coal and steel under a common authority and invited other countries to do the same. Schuman declared: '... Par la mise en commun de productions de base et par l'institution d'une Haute Autorité nouvelle, dont les décisions lieront la France, l'Allemagne et les pays qui adhéreront, cette proposition réalisera les premières assises concrètes d'une Fédération Européenne indispensable à la préservation de la paix ...'[17]

THE EUROPEAN COAL AND STEEL COMMUNITY

On 18 April 1951 the Ministers representing France, Germany, Italy, Belgium, Holland and Luxembourg signed in Paris a treaty which established the European Coal and Steel Community (*Communauté Européenne du Charbon et de l'Acier*). The Treaty was ratified, not without national opposition, eg it was ratified by the French Chamber of Deputies by 377 votes against 235 and by the Senate by 182 votes against 32. The industries concerned were unhappy as the Treaty was imposed upon them without prior consultation but it was, no doubt, a wise scheme.

The Treaty of Paris, this first instrument of European integration, consists of 100 articles, three annexes, three protocols and a convention of transitory provisions. The most important feature of the Coal and Steel Community is its supra-national character. It is no longer an inter-governmental but a truly supra-

17 Lorette, op cit, p 38.

national organization. It was aptly described[18] as 'a quasi federation in an important economic sector, the Member States retaining their sovereignty in all other sectors'.

Apart from supra-national organs the Community enjoys a faculty of self-administration manifested in the choice and recruitment of officials, a financial autonomy marked by the power of levying taxes and a measure of self-control vested in a parliamentary assembly.

The Community was endowed with five organs:

(1) an executive, called the High Authority,
(2) a Consultative Committee attached to the High Authority,
(3) a Special Council of Ministers,
(4) an Assembly, and
(5) a Court of Justice.

The High Authority was the permanent executive of the Community. It consisted of nine members, eight chosen unanimously by the six governments and the ninth co-opted by the eight members to emphasize the supra-national character of the Community. A third of the High Authority retired every second year and was replaced by new members irrespective of nationality. The functions of the High Authority included the launching and management of a common market in coal and steel, development and control of investments and scientific research, action to curb unemployment, discrimination and restrictive practices, the imposition of common taxes upon the production of coal and steel; all this without reference to the governments of the Member States, subject only to responsibility to the Court and the Assembly. It is true that the field of independent action of the High Authority was restricted, but where it could act it took decisions which were binding upon the Member States.

The High Authority was assisted by a Consultative Committee consisting of representatives of employers, trade unions and consumers designated by the Special Council of Ministers on the advice of the trade unions and the producer and consumer organizations.

The Special Council of Ministers represented the sovereign power of the Member States. Its function was to harmonize the national economies on the recommendation of the High Authority in the fields of coal and steel. Political control was in the hands of the Assembly of the Coal and Steel Community, which consisted of 68 members, of which France, Germany and Italy provided 18 each and the remaining 24 represented the Benelux countries.

18 By Guy de Carmay, *Fortune d'Europe* (1953).

Members were elected by their national Parliaments though they could have been elected directly. By a two-thirds majority the Assembly could dismiss the High Authority and together with the Member States propose amendments to the Treaty.

The Court consisted of seven members. Its function was to act as a watch-dog over the application of the Treaty, examine the decisions of the High Authority in the light of the Treaty provisions and adjudicate upon the alleged breaches of the Treaty. During the seven years of its existence the Court gave 137 decisions which were of considerable importance to the Community. These decisions had a binding force in the Member States. They are still relevant to Community law.

Several lessons could be drawn from this experiment. It proved that supra-national institutions could function in spite of diverse national interests; that far from being an economic disaster this first European common market greatly contributed to the economic progress of the Member States. The enlarged market activated industries far beyond those directly connected with coal and steel. The greatest benefit accrued to Italy, the economically weakest member. However, all was not well all the time. In 1959 there was a crisis in the coal industry caused mainly by over-production and an increase in the use of oil which rendered coal mines, especially in Belgium and Germany, redundant. The High Authority endeavoured to finance stock-piling, to reduce production and even to lower wages, but the Council of Ministers refused to sanction these measures clearly because national interests were at stake. The High Authority was, therefore, forced to provide a special aid to Belgium, which was hit very badly, for the rehabilitation and retraining of miners and to restrict imports from outside the Community. The very existence of the Community enabled it to relieve at least one country but it also became clear that there must be a common European policy in the field of energy. Whilst the Community was successful in its field it was not able to cope with other economic problems and its limited success certainly did not satisfy those who worked for a United Europe in their lifetime.

TOWARDS THE TREATIES OF ROME

The greater integration of Europe owes a great deal to military considerations for it is evident that military alliances have political and economic consequences.

The problem of the defence of Western Europe, especially the American insistence on the participation of Germany in the defence of the Continent, raised delicate political and economic questions. The Germans were doing well without having to spend vast sums on defence, yet there was an aversion to their having a finger on the common trigger and some fear of the revival of German military might. These fears were assuaged partly by the international control of coal and steel, partly by the pacific stance of the German people. Moreover, in view of the cost of defence, it was quite inequitable that Germany should be shielded by her neighbours at their expense. A German contribution had to be sought within an international framework. France, especially, insisted on a supra-national control of the armed forces and so in 1952 the European Defence Treaty was signed.

The Treaty envisaged a European Defence Community as a kind of federation without a central federal government. The organization was to consist of a Commissariat, an Assembly, a Council of Ministers and a Court of Justice, all modelled upon the Coal and Steel Community. It is interesting to note that whilst internationalist France actively promoted the idea it was nationalist France which wrecked the edifice, as on 30 August 1954 the French National Assembly refused to ratify the treaty already ratified by other countries.

The failure to create a European Army led to the London Conference in September 1954 which resulted in turn in the admission of Italy and West Germany to the alliance by virtue of the Protocols to the Brussels Treaty signed in Paris in October 1954. The Final Act of the London Conference gave birth to yet another organization, ie the Council of Western European Union embracing the United Kingdom, Belgium, Holland, Luxembourg, France, Germany and Italy. It has subsequently passed through certain mutations but achieved no prominence apart from defence in the NATO setting though logically it brought the United Kingdom into the process of West European integration.

For a while the unionist movement lay dormant, though on the Continent there were encouraging stirrings among the various industries, especially agriculture and the trade unions. The idea was resurrected at the meeting of the Foreign Ministers of the six members of the Coal and Steel Community in June 1955 at Messina. They were unanimous in their resolve to pursue the concept of an economic union and they were encouraged to do so by the governments of the Benelux countries.

At the beginning of the Conference the Ministers proclaimed their intention to 'pursue the establishment of a United Europe through the development of common institutions, a progressive fusion of national economies, the creation of a Common Market and harmonization of social policies'.[19] During the Conference the

19 Quoted by Lorette, op cit, p 60.

Ministers became more precise as they considered that a 'constitution of a European Common Market must be their objective' though they realized that this could only be achieved by stages. To do this, again on the advice of the Benelux countries, the Ministers set up an Inter-Governmental Committee to study the various problems. The United Kingdom was invited to attend and indeed a minor official from the Board of Trade took part in the preliminary discussions.

In July 1955 the Committee met in Brussels with the object of co-ordinating the work of the various sub-committees set up to study the problems of investment, social policy, fuel and power, atomic energy and transport. The work continued during the summer and autumn of 1955 and among the sixty or so experts there were representatives of the Coal and Steel Community, the Organization for European Co-operation, the Council of Europe and, for a while, of the United Kingdom. Then followed a period of considerable activity and several meetings of the Foreign Ministers of the six countries. Reports of experts were considered, and finally a treaty was drafted and signed in Rome on 25 March 1957. This was the first Treaty of Rome which established the European Economic Community (the EEC) commonly known as the Common Market. The Treaty consists of 248 articles, 4 appendices, 9 protocols and a convention relating to the association with the Community of the Overseas Countries and Territories which have special relations with Belgium, France, Italy and the Netherlands.

The second Treaty of Rome, setting up the European Community of Atomic Energy (Euratom) was signed on the same day. It consists of 225 articles, 5 appendices and 1 protocol.

Both treaties had to be ratified by the parliaments of the signatory states. The reaction of these parliaments is worthy of a comparison. In Germany both Houses of Parliament ratified the Treaties unanimously. In Belgium in the Chamber of Deputies 174 voted for and 4 against ratification; in the Senate 134 and 2 against. In France in the Chamber of Deputies 342 voted for and 239 against the ratification; in the Senate 222 for and 70 against. In Italy in the Chamber of Deputies 311 voted for and 144 against the ratification; the Senate voted unanimously for ratification. In Luxembourg 46 votes were cast for and 3 against ratification. In the Netherlands in the Chamber of Deputies 114 votes were cast for and 12 against ratification; in the Senate 44 for and 5 against. The numerical opposition in France and Italy is significant but can easily be explained by the existence of large Communist Parties in those countries and the attitude of the mother-country of Communism to European Unity.[20]

20 'Soviet unease over UK entry', *European Community* (February 1972), p 16.

The Treaties became operative on 1 January 1958.

THE THREE COMMUNITIES

The two Treaties of Rome added two new Communities to the Coal and Steel Community.

The European Atomic Energy Community (Euratom) was created as a specialist market for atomic energy. Atomic energy is a relatively new source of power with a virtually unlimited potential. It is hoped, therefore, that it will satisfy the demands of our technological era. In the sixties the Six imported about a quarter of their energy from countries outside the Community. By 1975, it was considered, they would have to import 40% of their needs unless atomic energy took over from the traditional sources of power. However this target was not realized as in 1973 the Community was importing some 63% of its energy and the oil crisis aggravated the situation. A common energy policy embracing the Euratom for which the Community has been striving, albeit without success, has become not only a matter of economic urgency but also a factor in European integration.

The object of Euratom is to develop nuclear energy, distribute it within the Community and sell the surplus to the outside world. In view of the development costs involved the Community must collectively engage in the necessary research and disseminate the accumulated knowledge. It must develop industry in a rational way ensuring a fair distribution within the Community and, finally, it must, as a body, consider the international implications of the pacific use of nuclear energy. In many respects Euratom corresponds to the Coal and Steel Community.

The objectives of the European Economic Community (EEC) are wider than the objectives of the remaining two Communities, for the EEC is not a mere specialist organization but an instrument of progressive economic integration with a corresponding political potential. Therefore, whilst bearing in mind the three separate juristic entities, the EEC is by far the most important and may be regarded as a prototype of an integrated European Community.

THE MERGER OF THE COMMUNITIES

The main institutions of the ECSC as we have seen were five in number: an executive body known as the High Authority; a Consultative Committee; a Special Council made up of the representatives of the governments of the Member States; a Parliamentary Assembly made up of representative parliamentarians of the national parliaments of the Member States; and a Court of Justice. When the EEC and Euratom were established, their institutions were modelled upon those of the ECSC and this naturally suggested the merger of the separate institutions so as to avoid a multiplicity of institutions responsible for the achievement of similar tasks. This merger has taken place in two stages.

A Convention relating to certain institutions common to the European Communities was concluded simultaneously with the Rome Treaties and provided for the establishment of a single Court of Justice and a single Parliamentary Assembly to serve all three Communities. The completion of this process of institutional merger was not immediately realized, with the result that for some years each of the Communities retained its own executive body (High Authority in the case of the ECSC and Commissions in the case of the EEC and Euratom) and Council. This institutional separatism resulted from the adoption of a functional approach to European integration; three Communities were established by separate treaties and charged with the achievement of specific objectives. Further, the role of the Commissions and Councils in relation to the EEC and Euratom differed significantly from that of the High Authority and Special Council in relation to the ECSC, and so in 1957 separate institutions seemed appropriate. In practice this separation was found to be unsatisfactory. Whilst the objectives of each Community are distinct they also overlap and form part of a larger economic whole. In several fields, such as coal and steel and atomic energy, it was desirable for the Communities to coordinate their policy; the existence of separate institutions each with its own personnel with different views and ideas militated against this. Eventually a treaty was signed in May 1965 and took effect on 1 July 1967, providing for further fusion of the Communities.[21] This treaty instituted a single Commission to replace the High Authority of the ECSC and the Commissions of the EEC and Euratom, and a single Council to replace the separate Councils of the three Communities.

This 'Merger Treaty', which completed the institutional merger of the Communities, represents a further step towards the eventual merger of the three Communities to form a single European Community; but this will require the negotiation of a new treaty to replace the Treaty of Paris and the Treaties of Rome. For the time being 'the three Communities can be regarded as facets of one basic

21 The entry into force of this treaty was delayed by the crisis resulting from a clash between France and her five partners over the agricultural policy of the EEC.

experiment, stages in an unfinished process, the future development of which cannot yet be foreseen'.[1]

THE UNITED KINGDOM AND EUROPEAN SOLIDARITY

The United Kingdom has contributed to European solidarity (particularly in the field of military co-operation) but has tended to
remain aloof. It is true that in 1946 in his famous Zurich speech
Winston Churchill urged the establishment of a United States of
Europe based on a partnership between France and Germany. But
the role which he assigned to the United Kingdom was that of a
friend and sponsor of the new Europe, clearly a role which fell far
short of full participation.[2]

Successive British post-war governments adopted a lukewarm
and sceptical attitude towards developments on the Continent.
There were, perhaps, two main reasons for this. In the first place,
unlike her continental allies, Britain had not endured defeat and
enemy occupation. Although she had suffered economically as a
result of the war, British institutions and the British way of life
were not only preserved intact but could in a sense be said to be
triumphant. From such a standpoint the prospect of compromising
British independence in favour of union with continental Europe
was not very attractive. In addition, at that time Britain was still
in possession of a considerable colonial empire to which, as well as
to the independent members of the Commonwealth, she looked
rather than to the Continent. There was also the special relationship
which had been forged between Britain and the United States. The
British attitude to European integration in the years immediately
following the Second World War is, perhaps, summed up by the
reaction of Ernest Bevin, when Foreign Secretary, to the proposal
that Britain should participate in a European Assembly as part of
the Council of Europe: 'I don't like it. I don't like it. If you open
that Pandora's Box you will find it full of Trojan horses.'[3]

By the late 1950s British exclusion from the advantages which
became apparent within the Community and the fear that she
might lose political influence made her realize that the idea of the
European Community, far from being a failure, was a force to be
reckoned with. The United Kingdom never joined the Coal and

---

1 Palmer, M, Lambert, J et al, *European Unity* (1968), p 169. On the background
   to and effects of the Merger Treaty, see Houben, P H J M, 'The Merger of the
   Executives of the European Communities' (1965–66) 3 CML Rev 37 and Weil,
   G L, 'The Merger of the Institutions of the European Communities' (1967) 61
   AJIL 57.
2 Kitzinger, U, *The European Common Market and Community* (1967), p 37.
3 Robertson, A H, *The Council of Europe* (2nd edn, 1961), p 6, n 3.

Steel Community (although she did establish a form of association with it) and cold-shouldered the Common Market negotiations. In 1957 Britain proposed a 'free trade area' (the so called Maudling Plan) and, when this failed, created a rival organization, the European Free Trade Association (EFTA) in 1959. However, in some respects EFTA, which embraced Austria, Denmark, Norway, Portugal, Sweden, Switzerland and the United Kingdom, proved less successful than the European Economic Community and a positive policy towards the European Community emerged.

In 1961 the Macmillan Government applied for membership of the EEC. The negotiations (the British team was headed by the Lord Privy Seal, Mr Edward Heath) dragged on, but when the British side, leaving some problems to further negotiations, was ready to sign in 1963 the French President, General de Gaulle, vetoed the British entry. In 1967 the Wilson Government renewed the application but it was vetoed again by France before negotiations could take place. The third attempt was made by the Heath Government in 1970 and the negotiations for entry were successfully concluded in January 1972.

Grand debates were held in Parliament and elsewhere during the summer and autumn of 1971 and the Government mounted a massive information service. Opinion polls revealed a considerable opposition to British entry into Europe and party politics obscured the discussion on the merits of the entry. It transpired that the Labour Party, who would have been happy to accept the terms of the British accession when in power, was opposed to the terms when in opposition. The declared reasons that the situation had changed and that the country's economy did not warrant accession at this time, though hardly convincing, were vigorously advanced by the Labour Party opposition. Opponents in principle argued that there was anything but advantage in accession to the Community, whilst the surrender of sovereignty was an unforgivable folly. On 28 October 1971 the Government secured a reasonable majority[4] with the support of the Liberals and Labour dissenters from the official party policy who voted for the entry in principle but pledged themselves to oppose the consequential legislation. The historic decision, which merited a national unity, was soured by the antics of party politics. On 20 January 1972 the eleventh-hour attempt to prevent the signing of the Treaty of Accession until the full text 'has been published and its contents laid before the House' failed, but the vote on the motion produced a majority of only 21 for the Government,[5] the Conservative opponents

4 *Hansard, House of Commons* 1970–71, Vol 823, col 2212.
5 Ibid, 1971–72, Vol 829, col 800.

abstaining and the Labour members voting under a three-line whip.

Because of the lack of bi-partisan policy the British participation in the Community depends much upon the party political game. Indeed the Labour Party opposition announced, in its electoral manifesto of 1974, that when returned to power it would embark upon 'fundamental re-negotiations' of the condition of entry.[6] Such negotiations did take place though it was difficult to see the real purpose other than to keep faith with the electorate and to placate the opposition within the Party. The Government advice that, on balance, Britain should remain in the Community was endorsed by a two-thirds majority of the electorate in what became a novel constitutional experiment: a 'consultative referendum' of 1975. However the Party never adopted any constructive attitude whilst the Labour Government failed to play a positive role or to demonstrate a European conviction. Moreover, when, again in opposition, the Party at its annual conferences in 1980, 1981 and 1982 voted for withdrawal from the Community this, according to a Shadow Foreign Secretary in 1981, was to be done without a referendum. Only after the general election of 1983 some leading members of the Labour Party recognized, at the 1983 annual conference, that withdrawal might not be a realistic proposition. Indeed the question of membership was no longer a prominent issue at subsequent conferences, though in 1985 the leader of the 32-strong British Labour Party in the European Parliament declared that 'as a committed anti-marketeer, I will continue to campaign for withdrawal'.[7]

Conservative governments proved more positive though quite reticent on the question of political integration and reluctant, for example, to join the European Monetary System so essential for the achievement of the Common Market. They wrenched out of the Community a correction of the disproportionate British budgetary contribution but managed so far to achieve only a partial reform in the two areas of major British concern: the Community Budget and the Common Agricultural Policy.

The United Kingdom has proved a difficult and somewhat cool partner. Both major political parties are much to blame, primarily for the lack of a national policy for Europe and the lack of a clear vision of the Community as well as the rôle this country ought to play in the European integration.

---

6 Lasok, D, 'Some Legal Aspects of Fundamental Re-negotiations' (1976) 5 EL Rev 375.
7 As reported in *Europe*, 13 June 1985, p 4.

THE TREATIES OF ACCESSION AND BEYOND

In simple legal terms the first Treaty of Accession,[8] signed on 22 January 1972 on behalf of the six Member States, the Communities (represented by Mr Gaston Thorn, Foreign Minister of Luxembourg and President of the Council of Ministers) and the four prospective members Denmark, Ireland, Norway and the United Kingdom, is a Treaty signifying admission of new members to the three Communities. However, only three joined since Norway, in view of the adverse result of the national referendum, was unable to accede. The Treaty, being a prototype of subsequent accession treaties, consists of three articles stating that the new members accede to the existing Communities and accept all their rules. A lengthy Act, signed at the same time, confirmed the results of the negotiations and gave details of what membership entailed. Full membership as from 1 January 1973 was conditional upon the incorporation of the Community Law into the municipal laws of the new members. The period of transition was completed on 1 July 1977 which meant that as from that date the Community of Nine was fully established.

We shall discuss elsewhere the effects of the Treaty for the United Kingdom and the Community. It will suffice to say, at this stage, that neither the texts of the founding Treaties nor the institutions established under these Treaties were radically changed, though they were adjusted to give effect to the enlarged membership.

The second Treaty of Accession[9] heralded the admission of Greece as the tenth member as from 1 January 1981, the period of transition to be completed in the main by 1 January 1986.

The Third Treaty of Accession,[10] signed on 12 June 1985, brought Spain and Portugal into the Community of Twelve. Subject to a complex transitory regime, these two countries, associated with the Community since 1970 and 1972 respectively, became full members as from 1 January 1986.

Over the years the outward expansion of the Community was accompanied by inner growth and consolidation though not at the speed and scale the integrationists would have liked. Indeed the projected evolution from the stage of the Common Market to that of the Economic Union has proved slow and disappointing since not even all the objectives of the Common Market have been achieved to date. The Monetary Policy, mooted as early as 1964[11]

8 TS 16 (1979); Cmnd 7461.
9 OJ 1979, L2 91/9; EC 18 (1979); Cmnd 7650.
10 OJ 1985, L302/1; EC 27 (1985); Cmnd 9634.
11 Council Decision 64/301; OJ 1964, p 1207; (Sp Ed 1963–64, p 143).

and proposed in earnest in 1971 and 1972[12] to be completed by 31 December 1980, failed to produce a European Monetary System indispensable to a coherent policy and economic integration. In 1985[13] the White Paper from the Commission to the European Council drew particular attention to the scale of unachieved Treaty objectives and pointed the way to their achievement by 1992, that is, 35 years since the signing of the Treaty of Rome.

However, on the positive side, there has been a growing awareness of the Community spirit and hitherto unprecedented political co-operation. The constitution of the Community has also experienced change. The decision of the Council of Ministers of 20 September 1976[14] to carry out the Treaty promise of direct elections to European Parliament resulted in 1979 in a fundamental reform of that institution. Instead of being a body of delegates from national legislatures the Parliament is now truly representative of 'Euro-constituencies' and the national political parties. This has enhanced the legitimacy of that institution and, having raised its prestige, opened up the way to a more active and influential participation in the life of the Community.

The process of integration initiated by the institutional merger proved to be a harder task than imagined. An evolutionary approach was advocated in this respect in the Tindemans Report[15] published in January 1976. It postulated a gradual development towards European Union building on the existing institutions and the practices which have evolved outside the Treaty framework. The Report envisaged a closer co-operation between the Member States, notably a co-ordination of their foreign policy and regular meetings of heads of government acting as the 'European Council'. It proposed 'to put an end to the distinction which still exists between ministerial meetings which deal with political co-operation and those which deal with the subjects covered by the Treaty'. It proposed to strengthen the rôle of the European Council by making the Council of Ministers of Foreign Affairs responsible for the preparation of its meetings and by the European Council indicating the institution or organization responsible for the execution of its decisions.

The Report emphasized further the need to develop a common foreign policy along with extended external economic relations and

---

12 Council Resolutions, Compendium of Community Monetary Texts, 1979, pp 25, 30, 33.
13 COM (85) 310 Final.
14 OJ 1976, L278/1.
15 Based on the recommendation of the Heads of State or Government meeting in Paris in December 1974; EC Bull Supp 1/76; Mitchell, J D B, 'The Tindemans Report – Retrospect and Prospect' (1976) 13 CML Rev 455.

a common defence policy and to convert policy commitments into 'legal obligations'. It advocated recourse to majority voting in the Council as a 'normal practice of the Community'. Avoiding any rigid timetable or development by stages the Report suggested a 'two-speed plan of economic integration' in which the so-called 'weaker members', ie Ireland, Italy and the United Kingdom, should proceed at a slower pace than the others. The idea proved quite unrealistic.

The failure of the Tindemans Report prompted the Brussels European Council of 1978 to ask 'The Three Wise Men'[16] to prepare another report on the political reform of the European Community.[17] This Report,[18] presented to the European Council in October 1979, listed the failures of the Community in carrying out its original and new policies. 'The reasons', it held, 'lie rather in political circumstances and attitudes that sometimes produced conflicting conceptions of the right way forward, and sometimes produced no clear conceptions at all ...'[19] Only the European Council had made a significant contribution towards an improvement of the Community decision-making procedure in so far as it became 'an escape from the bureaucracy weighing down the other institutions in order to provide leadership and guidance'.[20] The Three Wise Men thought that 'the principle needs to be affirmed yet again that the Commission is the natural executive organ of the Community'.[1] They rejected the idea of a 'two-speed integration' and appealed for solidarity in face of the economic recession.[2]

These and other initiatives had no real impact but the bold 'Draft Treaty establishing the European Union',[3] adopted by the European Parliament in February 1984, triggered off action which ultimately resulted in the passing of the Single European Act in 1986. The Draft Treaty, also known by its chief architect as the Spinelli Report, revived the idea of European federalism but was clearly ahead of its time. It consisted of 87 articles divided into five parts dealing with the Union; the objectives, methods of action and competences of the Union; institutional provisions; the policies of the Union; and the finances of the Union, respectively. Reflecting a federalist concept, the Draft Treaty purported to move the Community to a status of a European Union envisaged in the Treaties

16 Borend Biesheuval, Edmund Dell, Robert Marjolin.
17 EC Bull 12/78, p 97.
18 Duff, A N, 'The Report of the Three Wise Men', Jo Common Market Studies, Vol XIX (1981), 237 et seq.
19 At p 19.
20 At p 9.
 1 At p 72.
 2 At pp 89–91.
 3 Capotorti, F, et al, *Le Traité d'Union Européene* (1985) (Text and Commentary).

establishing the European Communities and confirmed by the Conference of the Heads of State or Government of 20 October 1972 and in the Solemn Stuttgart Declaration of 19 June 1983. In order to achieve this objective the Draft proposed a redistribution of powers, especially the law-making function, from the Council of Ministers to the Parliament and the Commission, a diminution of the blocking powers of Member States in the decision-making process, and the imposition of sanctions on the Member States for serious and persistent breaches of their duties. The federalist shift was marked by the enhanced status of the Union in relation to the Member States; increased powers of the Parliament; increased supervisory powers of the Court of Justice (including appeals against the decisions of national courts); the adoption of the European Monetary System; a common citizenship of the Union for the citizens of the Member States coupled with effective protection of fundamental rights derived from the common principles of the Member States' constitutions and the European Convention for the Protection of Human Rights and Fundamental Freedoms.

The Draft Treaty was welcomed by six of the ten national parliaments; the Danish Folketing rejected it, whilst a non-committal attitude pending parliamentary scrutiny was adopted in Greece, Ireland and the United Kingdom. At the Fontainebleau European Council in the summer of 1984 two *ad hoc* committees, one on 'institutional affairs' and another on a 'people's Europe', were set up. Known by the names of their chairmen as the Dooge and the Adonnino Committee, respectively, these Committees presented their reports and recommendations to the Milan European Council of June 1985. The former proposed, in particular, that decisions should normally be taken by a qualified or simple majority; that the Commission's powers should be strengthened; that the Parliament should be given a wider rôle in the decision-making process; and that the Court of Justice's extended powers should include the protection of fundamental rights guaranteed within the Community's legal framework. It recommended the convention of an inter-governmental conference 'to negotiate a Draft European Union Treaty'. Despite the British, Danish and Greek opposition the Council decided by a majority to convene such a conference by reference to Article 236 of the EEC Treaty. It also accepted the Commission's White Paper (mentioned above) containing recommendations for the completion of the internal market and the strengthening of Community technological co-operation.

At the General Affairs Council of July 1985 Foreign Ministers agreed the details of the inter-governmental conference under the Luxembourg Presidency with the twin objective defined by the

Milan Council, ie the revision of the Rome Treaties and the drafting of a treaty on political co-operation and European security. However, the results of the many years of debate are disappointing since the Single European Act,[4] which emerged in 1986, far from advancing the federal concept of the Spinelli Report, consists merely of a number of cosmetic reforms.

Since the effects of the Single Act shall be considered in the relevant chapters it will suffice to observe that it is merely one of the landmarks in the long road towards the European Union. Structurally, its main merit is the simultaneous reform of the three Treaties establishing the Three Communities for it further advances the concept of one Community. It affirms the fine resolution to progress towards European unity but it remains silent as regards its meaning and scope and, in its contents, falls short of the Spinelli Report.

However, it makes certain adjustments to the powers and functions of the institutions, lays down a 'co-operation procedure' which enhances the influence of the Parliament on the Council's decisions and, whilst retaining the principle of unanimity, it moves further towards qualified majority in the decision-making process of the Council. It provides for a more efficient functioning of the internal market and lays down foundations for a joint formulation and implementation of European foreign policy.

Clearly it is a compromise on the basis of the lowest common denominator reflecting, on the one hand, the resilience of the sovereign state and a still precarious degree of West European unity, on the other. There is a unity of purpose but no unity of means and no identical perception of the Community. Yet unity, as emphasized in the Tindemans Report, is a 'self-evident good'.

The founding Treaties were amended by the Single European Act 1986 and they are likely to be amended further as a result of the summit meetings held in Madrid (26–27 June 1989) and Dublin (25–26 June 1990) at which it was decided (not without opposition) to move towards the Economic and Monetary Union and to call an inter-governmental conference on the Political Union respectively.

The Madrid meeting revealed considerable disagreement over the Commission's proposals for the Economic and Monetary Union as well as the Social Charter. In view of the British opposition a compromise was reached on the former but the latter was shelved. It was agreed, though, at Dublin, to implement the Economic and Monetary Union by stages and to call two parallel inter-

4 Single European Act and Final Act, European Communities No 12 (1986); HMSO, Cmnd 9578; See H C Foreign Affairs Committee; Session 1985–86; HMSO 442; H L Select Committee on the European Communities, Session 1985–86, 12th Report, HMSO (HL 149).

governmental conferences on 14 December 1990, immediately after the Rome summit: one on the Political Union and the other on the Economic and Monetary Union; both, it was hoped, producing results by the end of 1992.

Discussions about the future of the Community reflect two broad questions, ie whether the Community should continue as an organization of sovereign states or should become a community of peoples disregarding national boundaries and sovereignties and thus adopt a federal form. There is also a question of the method to be applied. Here we can see a sharp conflict between the evolutionary-pragmatic approach rooted in the common law philosophy and a doctrinaire-formalistic approach of the civil law systems. Both reflect different historical experiences and different constitution-making processes. The former insists on a gradual step-by-step development building upon the completion of the programmes laid down in the Treaties, the latter takes a more imaginative view contending that a constitution is not merely a record of achievements but also an expression of a vision and aspirations. Although the former lacks the drama and the rhetoric of the Latin races, it may prove more realistic, because politics is the art of the possible and because behind the smokescreen of idealism there lurks the hard reality of national interests, and the fact that implementation and enforcement of obligations is more onerous than a declaration of intent or expectations.

It is common ground that if, and when, a sufficient degree of integration and unity has been achieved, national sovereignty will lose much of its emotional glamour and practical importance. At that stage a new constitution of the Community will emerge either through the process of adaptation or a solemn proclamation. Only time will tell whether the Community shall continue as an organization of states, albeit a close one, or graduate into a federal structure. Political developments, both internal and external, will, no doubt, influence the process.

Internally the Community shall move of its own momentum since it has an in-built mechanism for development, the pace being determined only by the Member States themselves. External events too will have their effect. Thus the reunification of Germany on 3 October 1990, preceded by the dramatic changes in Eastern Europe towards the end of 1989 and their likely repercussions in the Soviet Union, cannot be ignored. The cold war ended officially on 21 November 1990 with the signing in Paris by 32 European countries, the USA and Canada of the 'Paris Charter' on the occasion of the Conference on Security and Co-operation in Europe. By signing the 45-page Charter the signatories committed themselves to the principles of democracy, human rights, co-operation, social justice and economic freedom. The Charter incorporates also a promise to end coercion and discrimination, a joint effort to combat terrorism and to achieve a mutual and balanced force reduction. All this augurs well for the European Continent though repression in the Baltic States in January 1991 parallel to the United Nations Organization action against Iraq to liberate Kuwait casts a shadow over the European horizon and may affect the progress of the political and economic integration.

However, it is a matter of speculation whether these events will speed up or retard the consolidation of the Community of today or whether they will lead to its enlargement, thus diluting the present concept of the Community with a larger vision of a united Europe from the straits of Gibraltar to the Urals. At present we have the world's largest trading unit with a population of some 340 million, consisting of 12 states of different sizes, common yet diverse cultural heritages, wealth and aspirations, but still a European Community in the making.

Chapter 2

The concept and status of the
European Communities

1 The legal concept of the European Community

The European Community is a result of international solidarity
which we have considered in the light of post-war developments
in international relations, and of the conscious effort to create a
kind of unity in Western Europe. When political unification proved
premature the architects of the Community seized upon the economic elements of inter-state relations and built these into the three
'Communities' (Coal and Steel, Euratom and EEC), so much so
that today within the vague notion of a political Community we
have three legally definable treaty-based 'Communities'. It follows
that in spite of the machinery for defence (NATO), the economic
co-ordination (the three Communities), and a basis of co-operation
in matters of foreign policy[1] (which should not be overrated) the
constitutional structure remains still in the sphere of speculation.
Political scientists[2] offer a variety of ideas but a blueprint which
can become the basis of discussion at a Government level is yet to
emerge. No doubt statesmen have their ideas too but at an official
level less adventurous schemes can be expected. General de Gaulle
spoke of a Europe of States and President Pompidou,[3] speaking
on the challenge of the enlarged EEC spoke guardedly about a
confederation. Occasionally the EEC, is described as a federation
but, as we shall see later, neither the federal nor the confederal
label exactly fits the organization.

(A) FEDERATION OR CONFEDERATION?

In the long history of mankind only a few confederations can be
recorded: Switzerland 1291–1848; the Netherlands 1581–1795; the
USA 1776–1788; Germany 1815–1866. Since these confederations

1 See Single European Act 1986, art 30.
2 For a summary see: Pentland, C C, 'Political Theories of European Integration:
Between Science and Ideology' in Lasok, D and Soldatos, P (ed), *Les
Communautés Européennes en Fonctionnement* (1981), pp 546 et seq.
3 Times, 12 May 1972.

developed either into unitary states or federations it is worthwhile contrasting the confederal with the federal type of constitution. In a federal state the sovereign power is apportioned between a central government and a number of Member States. There are basically two models of power arrangement: from the base to the centre and from the centre to the base. For example, the US Constitution is so arranged that power flows from the state to the federal government which has no powers, apart from those delegated to it by the states. It is more difficult to find a classic example of the opposite though Canada is sometimes quoted as being one where the power flows from the dominion government to the provinces. This was, no doubt, the scheme convenient to a colonial rule and some of the fathers of the Canadian state but constitutional developments, whilst safeguarding the federal 'peace, order and good government', have confirmed that the provinces were created by the UK Parliament with original and sovereign powers. Therefore Canada only partially fits the model of centralized federation. For the purpose of international relations a federal state is represented by a central government. Internally, the legislature, the judiciary, the administration and indeed the law can be divided into federal and state.

In a confederation the sovereignty enjoyed by the individual Member States is said to be complete. It can be defined as a relationship of sovereign states, each Member State retaining its status as a subject of international law. In a federation, on the other hand, the sovereignty of the individual Member States merges into the one sovereignty of the federation. In a confederation the central government acts directly on the Member States but only through the Member States upon individuals. It follows that outwardly each member of a confederation can enter into separate relations with foreign states and, of course, may of its own right be a member of UNO,[4] whereas members of a federation, as a rule,[4] cannot enter into separate relations with foreign states. Inwardly members of a confederation maintain their independent and separate form of government, legislature, judiciary, administration and system of law, their relation to the central government being contractual rather than organic. A confederation has no distinct legal order for it is a political association of states rather than a composite state.

On balance the emerging European Community fits, in the light of the EEC Treaty, better into a federal than confederal form.[5]

Since, of the three Communities, the EEC is the prototype of

---

4 Cf the anomalous position of two member republics of the USSR: Ukraine and Byelo-Russia; Dolan, E, 'The Member-Republics of the USSR as Subjects of the Law of Nations' [1955] ICLQ 629–36.
5 See further Ipsen, H P, *Europäisches Gemeinschaftsrecht* (1972), pp 182 et seq.

the legal structure of the European Community, it is essential to examine its legal status, for it is a *pointer* to the relationship between the Member States inter se, the Member States to the Community and the Community to the outside world. The status of the EEC rests upon its constitution, ie the Treaty of Rome, and the appropriate rules of international law, as well as the constitutional laws of the Member States.

It is clear that the EEC is not a state[6] in a classical sense for it has no territory of its own except as defined in the Treaties for the purpose of their application, no population which is not a citizenry of the Member States, whilst its 'government' has no powers except those defined by the Treaty. However, it would be quite inadequate to define the EEC as the association of states which subscribe to the Treaty of Rome, since the Treaty lays down a foundation for something more than a loose partnership of states involved in a joint economic enterprise. The Treaty is not a mere contractual compact, it is an institutional stage of European unity.

The EEC, though consisting of sovereign states, is a separate, albeit supra-national, entity and, in this respect, it is governed by the law of international institutions in general and its own constitution, in particular. In this context the law of international institutions, an offshoot of public international law, applies to the EEC as a regional arrangement.

It is perfectly legitimate for sovereign states in their capacity as the makers of international law to act in concert in setting up institutions and organizations furthering the interests of mankind. Of these the most impelling precedent is the UN which, though universal in character and purpose, does not exclude regional organizations. Indeed it has been pointed out[7] that the difficulty of developing global institutions raised the hope of a greater success in the field of regional organizations. Unlike its predecessor, the League of Nations, which was conceived merely to be an association,[8] the United Nations Organization[9] has the status of a legal person, ie it is a bearer of rights and duties pertinent to legal

---

6 According to art 1 of the Montevideo Convention of 1933 on the Rights and Duties of States, 'the state as a person of international law should possess the following qualifications: (*a*) a permanent population, (*b*) a defined territory, (*c*) a government and (*d*) a capacity to enter into relations with other states'.

7 Jenks, C W, 'World Organization and European Integration', *European Yearbook*, Vol I, p 173; see also Scheuner, U, 'Europe and the United Nations', *European Yearbook*, Vol VIII, pp 67–90.

8 Although the Covenant did not confer juristic personality upon the League of Nations it was often argued that such personality was necessary for the League to fulfil its functions; cf Jenks, C W [1945] BYIL 267.

9 United Nations Charter, art 104; Advisory Opinion on Reparation for Injuries suffered in the Service of the United Nations, ICJ Reports (1949), p 174.

personality because it was so willed by the founder states. The same is the position of the EEC. In their terse statement that 'the Community shall have legal personality'[10] the founder states unequivocally created a new international entity independent of its component parts and endowed it with the status and attributes of a legal person.

By virtue of customary international law two attributes, viz the treaty-making power and the capacity of sending and receiving envoys, mark out an entity as a sovereign body and a subject of international law. The Holy See[11] was a classic example of this doctrine from 1870 when it lost territorial sovereignty until 1929 when it regained a symbolic territory by the Lateran Treaty. The EEC need not resort to custom to support its claim for the Treaty provides for both the legal personality and the treaty-making power.[12] The capacity to enter into diplomatic relations derives generally from the legal personality of the EEC and specifically from art 17 of the Protocol on the Privileges and Immunities of the European Communities of 1965. By the end of 1990 the EEC as a legal person distinct from its members has established diplomatic relations with more than 130 countries including the Holy See, China and the USSR and maintains a delegation at the UNO. The German Democratic Republic too, in the last days of its life, appointed an ambassador but, as a result of the reunification of Germany, this appointment has lapsed.

The EEC was set up by a treaty of unlimited duration (art 240), and so was the EAEC (art 208), but the ECSC only for fifty years (art 97). By its design the Community is committed to a continuous progress, by its nature it appears irreversible. Theoretically it is possible for a Member State to withdraw as long as it remains sovereign, that is as long as the political integration or transformation of the economic community into a more homogeneous body politic has not materialized. However, in reality the economic structure of the Member States and their national interests may become so intertwined in the course of time that a break-away may prove well-nigh impracticable. On the other hand it is always possible to maintain the status quo and so reduce the Community to political stagnation. The Community itself has a built-in system which may either advance it towards political and institutional integration or preserve the self-contained units of sovereign states

10 EEC, art 210; ECSC, art 6 (1); EAEC, art 184.
11 Kunz, J L, 'The Status of the Holy See in International Law' (1952) 46 AJIL 308 et seq.
12 EEC, arts 113, 114, 131, 228, 237, 238; ECSC, arts 6, 71; EAEC arts 101 and 206. The treaty making power of the ECSC was implicitly recognized by the UK in the agreement of 1954 between the UK and the ECSC, 258 UNTS 322.

whilst developing the economy and creating wealth within the existing institutions. This depends on whether the Community institutions are strengthened at the expense of sovereignty or whether the sovereign element keeps the Community institutions in the servile role of functional bureaucracy.

Article 236 provides for revision[13] of the EEC Treaty. The initiative rests with the government of any Member State or the Commission who may submit to the Council of Ministers proposals for the amendment of the Treaty. The scope seems unlimited including, presumably, the winding-up of the Community. However, amendments must be passed by a unanimous conference of representatives of the governments of the Member States, convened by the President of the Council on the recommendation of the Council, having previously obtained an approval of such conference by the European Parliament and, in unspecified appropriate cases, by the Commission. Moreover, any amendment must be ratified by all the Member States in accordance with their respective constitutions. In this way sovereignty of the Member States has been safeguarded but also changes in the structure of the Community have been made dependent upon the common will of the Member States. It follows that the position of the Member States inter se and vis-à-vis the Community, as stated in the Treaty, will remain static unless there is a unanimous desire for change.

Enlargement of the Community is also subject to a unanimous decision of the Member States followed by amendment of the Treaty duly ratified by all contracting states in accordance with their respective constitutions.[14] This means that the composition of the Community and the conditions of admission of new members are subject to negotiations between the existing Member States and may be vetoed by a single vote of a mighty or not so mighty state.

It follows that the organization as well as the relations between the Community and its members, on the one hand, and the Member States, inter se on the other, are fixed by the Treaty. In a sense this resembles the constitutional position within a composite state.

(B) INSTITUTIONAL FRAMEWORK

The constitution of the EEC has clearly been devised upon a federal pattern. As in a state, the direction of the Community is in the hands of political organs which comprise the Assembly (renamed European Parliament by the Single European Act, articles 4

---

13 ECSC, art 96; EAEC, art 204.
14 EEC, art 237; ECSC, art 98; EAEC, art 205.

(32d), 6 (2) and 26 (140A)), the Council of Ministers and the Commission.

The Parliament consists of 'representatives of the peoples of the States brought together in the Community'[15] but the strength of this representation is weighted in accordance with the size of the population of the Member States. The Parliament exercises a political control and acts as a deliberative and consultative body with a very limited participation in the legislative process. In a sense it is the Parliament, albeit a weak one, of the Community.

Since the passing of the Single European Act[16] which institutionalized the existing practice of Summit Meetings the European Council has become de jure the supreme organ of the Communities representing both the sovereignty of the Member States and the corporate person of each Community. It consists of the Heads of State or of Government of the Member States and the President of the Commission. However it is concerned only with matters of principle and general direction of the Communities whilst the Council of Ministers retains its position as the supreme working organ. It consists of the representatives of the governments,[17] each government sending one delegate to their meetings. The responsibility for the execution of the objectives laid down by the Treaty falls upon this body. It is the Council which takes the most important decisions and co-ordinates the economic policies of the Member States.[18] However, these powers are exercised in conjunction with the Commission.

The Commission is a truly Community institution. Its members are nominated on account of their general competence and independence by Member States, unanimously. Only the citizens of the Member States are eligible but there may be no more than two from one particular state. The powers of the Commission[19] can be described as the powers of initiative, preparation and decision. The Commission formulates recommendations and opinions on matters with which the Treaty is concerned and participates in the work of the Council and the Parliament. It also has certain executive and quasi-judicial powers.

The judicial power of the Community is in the hands of the Court of Justice (ECJ), whose main function is to 'ensure that in the interpretation and application of this Treaty the law is observed'.[20] Composed of thirteen Judges and assisted by six Advo-

---

15 EEC, art 137; ECSC art 20; EAEC, art 107.
16 SEA, art 2.
17 EEC, art 148; ECSC, art 28; EAEC, art 118.
18 EEC, art 145; ECSC, art 26; EAEC, art 115.
19 EEC, art 155; ECSC, art 8, EAEC, art 124; Treaty of Merger, art 9.
20 EEC, art 164; ECSC, art 31; EAEC, art 136.

cates-General chosen from persons of proven independence and qualified to hold the highest judicial offices in their countries, the Court is really not an international court. If anything it resembles more a federal court than the International Court of Justice at The Hague. It is in fact an internal court of the Community. Its jurisdiction, as defined by the Treaty, is not a substitute for the jurisdictions of the national courts of the Member States since it is confined to the administration of Community law. It is, however, a fully-fledged judicial body with the power of arbitration, adjudication, repression and advice. The power of interpretation of the Treaty, of the acts of the Community institutions and of the bodies established by the Council, which is sometimes exclusive, enables the Court to exercise a quasi-legislative function and thus build up a body of case law which, like the continental administrative tribunals, especially the French Conseil d'Etat, contribute to the development of the law. The power of annulment, which is an instrument of the control of the acts of the Council and the Commission, puts the Court into the unique position of authority. The Court is the custodian of the Treaty, the watch-dog of legality within the Community and the executor of the supremacy of the Community law over the national laws of the Member States in case of conflict between the two systems. Indeed the principle of supremacy of Community law is perhaps the most important aspect of the status of the Community vis-à-vis the Member States.

In order to reduce the workload of the ECJ a Court of First Instance (CFI) was created by virtue of the Single European Act.[21] It consists of 12 Judges but has no Advocates-General. However, where appropriate, its Judges will act as Advocates-General. Its jurisdiction comprises adjudication of disputes between the Community institutions, complaints of Community civil servants and, in certain circumstances, applications for damages in competition cases and for damages against the Commission under ECSC Treaty. Appeals lay to the ECJ.

The powers of the Community organs, which we have briefly outlined above, would be quite meaningless if it were not for the corresponding surrender of sovereignty by the Member States. The surrender of sovereignty is only partial and circumscribed by the Treaty obligations, but it is sufficient to mark a relationship between the Member States and the Community. The relationship is based not only on treaty obligations of a contractual type but also on obligations which result in supra-national institutions and a separate body of law. The relationship resembles more a federation than a confederation and the Treaty is the Constitution, as it were,

21 Council Decision, OJ 1988, L319/1.

of the Community.[1] The law of the Community, on the other hand, is a distinct order from the municipal laws of the Member States but it is administered by both the national authorities and the Community institutions. The relationship of Community law to the laws of the Member States resembles that of a federal to national law in so far as it is directly binding within the territory of the Member States though it is not administered exclusively by a Community judiciary. The acceptance of the Treaty, the law enacted by the Community organs, and the obligation to enact municipal legislation in accordance with the Treaty and the directives of the Community organs emphasize still further the federal concept of the Community. All power of the Community flows from the Member States but the Community has in the territory of the Member States no more than the 'most extensive legal capacity accorded to legal persons under their laws'[2] though it is not entitled to foreign sovereign immunity from suit.[3] This is insufficient as a criterion of a federal state, for federal states are based on constitutions which define the apportionment of power in terms of sovereignty. In the terms of the EEC Treaty the states endeavour to build Community institutions and to create a body of law to regulate the economic activities of the members. Although surrender of a certain portion of sovereignty is necessary in order to achieve these objectives the pooling of sovereignty is not explicit enough to create a federal state or a federal government of the Community. Therefore, at this stage of its development, the Community is merely an association of sovereign states with a federal potential.

(C) RELATIONSHIP BETWEEN THE COMMUNITY AND THE MEMBER STATES

(a) *Attributed powers and the occupied field*
The relationship between the Community and the Member States is based on the attribution (or delegation) of state powers to the Community institutions and the division of functions. Thus, within the specific domain of the Community the institutions are provided with exclusive authority whilst outside the domain of the Community the Member States retain their powers and responsibilities.[4] In fact the Community institutions exercise portions of

---

1 Wagner, H, *Grundbegriffe des Beschlussrechts der Europäischen Gemeinschaften* (1965).
2 EEC, art 211; ECSC, art 6 (3); EAEC, art 185.
3 See *Maclaine Watson & Co Ltd v Dept of Trade and Industry, Re International Tin Council* [1988] 3 All ER 257 at 316–320, CA.
4 See case 30/59 *De Gezamenlijke Steenkolenmijnen in Limburg v High Authority* [1961] ECR 1 at 23 (full quotation p 327, infra).

powers originally vested in sovereign states and in that sense act in a subsidiary capacity. However, to the extent of that delegation, by virtue of the Treaty, a common domain has been created and within that domain the Member States' action has been sublimated to that of the Community. This domain, originally delimited in the founding Treaties, tends to expand through the combined effect of the preamble to the EEC Treaty which lists in general terms the political, economic and social objectives of the Treaty and art 235[5] which enables the Council to legislate on the recommendation of the Commission and in consultation with the European Parliament in matters relevant to the Common Market which have not been expressly dealt with by the Treaty. However, quite apart from the express limitation arising from the reference to the Common Market, the function of art 235 is purely residual[6] and it cannot by itself alone provide the necessary authority for specific legislative measures.[7] Within these limitations new policies, ie on energy, industry, regional development, the protection of the environment and of the consumer, science and technology, education and culture, have evolved.[8]

Once delegated the power cannot be withdrawn[9] or, as stated by the ECJ on several occasions,[10] where the Community has acted within its competence the Member States must refrain from taking concurrent action. However, until the Community has claimed its competence by using it the Member States are free to act as sovereign states.[11] This is the doctrine of the 'occupied field' which, recently, has prevented the United Kingdom from enacting legislation which would extend the number of lighting devices compulsory for motor vehicles beyond the list comprised in a Community directive.[12] Thus the Community determines the extent of the legal integration and does not permit the Member States to be out of step either by exceeding the limit or failing to reach it. It will not, of course, interfere in situations wholly internal to a Member State.[13]

---

5 Full text pp 59 and 115, infra.
6 Case 56/88; *United Kingdom v EC Council* [1989] 2 CMLR 789.
7 See Case 45/86: *EC Commission v EC Council, Re Generalized Tariff Preferences* [1987] ECR 1493, [1988] 2 CMLR 131.
8 See Ch 14, infra.
9 Case 24/83: *Gewiese v Mackenzie* [1984] ECR 817.
10 Eg Case 20/70, supra, Opinion 1/75, supra.
11 Cases 3, 4, 6/76: *Officier van Justitie v Kramer* [1976] ECR 1279, [1976] 2 CMLR 440.
12 Case 60/86: *EC Commission v United Kingdom* [1988] 3 CMLR 437.
13 See eg Case 44/84: *Hurd v Jones (HM Inspector of Taxes)* [1986] ECR 29, [1986] 2 CMLR 1; Case 238/82: *Duphar BV v Netherlands, Re regulation of medical prescriptions without discriminating against imports* [1984] ECR 523,

(b) *Member States' duties*
By a net of duties, transcending the contractual obligations of states in international law, the Treaty integrates the Member States and their peoples into the Community. These duties are general and particular, explicit and implicit, horizontal and vertical.

The most important general duties are expressed in forms of solidarity[14] whereby the Member States undertake to take all appropriate measures to promote the objectives of the Treaties and to refrain from any measures which could jeopardize the achievements of these objectives, and non-discrimination on the ground of nationality.[15] The former is often cited in cases where states are prosecuted for the failure to comply with their obligations; the latter, coupled especially with the social provisions of the Treaty, has been developed by case law of the Community Court not only into a shield of protection of the rights of individuals but also as a weapon against discriminatory national legislation.[16]

The duty of solidarity does not permit Member States to adopt measures that could render a Community law impotent[17] or to retain on their statute book a national measure inconsistent with Community law. Thus it is not enough, for example, for the Constitutional Court of a Member State to order the judiciary to disregard statutory provisions of that kind for the state ought to repeal the offending legislation.[18] Similarly a municipal legislative provision cannot be set up against the direct effect of a regulation without compromising the fundamental principle of supremacy of Community law.[19] As for directives, these have to be transposed into national law as binding provisions, not merely as advisory circulars.[20]

[1985] 1 CMLR 256; Case C-333/88: *Tither v IRC, Re income tax mortgage relief* [1990] 2 CMLR 779.

14 EEC, art 5, EAEC, art 192; ECSC, art 86. The Community too is bound by the principle of solidarity enshrined in art 5; see Case C-2/88, *Re Zwartveld* [1990] 3 CMLR 457.

15 EEC, art 7; EAEC, arts 96 and 97; ECSC, art 69.

16 See eg Cases 61/81: *EC Commission v United Kingdom* [1982] ECR 2601, [1982] 3 CMLR 284; 165/82: *EC Commission v United Kingdom* [1983] ECR 3431, [1984] 1 CMLR 44; Case 248/83: *EC Commission v Germany* [1986] 2 CMLR 588; Case 163/82: *EC Commission v Italy* [1984] ECR 3273, [1984] 3 CMLR 169; Case 167/73: *EC Commission v France* [1974] ECR 359; [1974] 2 CMLR 216.

17 See eg Case 231/83: *Cullet v Centre Leclerc* [1985] ECR 305, [1985] 2 CMLR 524.

18 Case 104/86: *EC Commission v Italy* [1989] 3 CMLR 25.

19 Case 34/73: *Variola SpA v Amministrazione Italiana delle Finanze* [1973] ECR 981 at para 15.

20 Case 239/85: *EC Commission v Belgium* [1988] 1 CMLR 248. See also Case C-240/89: *EC Commission v Italy, Re Directive on the Protection of Workers from Asbestos* OJ 1991, C 17/8.

The principle of non-discrimination on the ground of nationality applies to all persons in all situations covered by Community law. Therefore, for example, a British tourist mugged in France could not be denied compensation under the French scheme which provided compensation for the victims of crime but limited it to French citizens only.[1]

Explicit duties are expressed in the form of a command (eg that customs duties must be abolished) whilst implicit duties can be inferred from the provisions of the Treaties which envisage a certain action (eg adjustment of national monopolies or obligations arising from treaties with non-member countries) or the control of the state apparatus in its executive, legislative and judicial functions in order to facilitate the execution of explicit duties.

There is also an implied duty of vigilance exemplified by the right of the Member States to challenge the validity of acts of the institutions even if they are party to the act in question (for example a regulation made by the Council of Ministers). Such challenge can be taken on the grounds of lack of competence, misuse of powers, breach of Community law or of any essential procedural requirement. Recently this enabled the United Kingdom to obtain annulment of two directives, one for the use of certain hormones in livestock farming,[2] and another providing for minimum standards of comfort for battery hens.[3] In both cases the text of the directive differed from the draft on which the vote was taken, the irregularities having been perpetrated in the secretariat of the Council.

Horizontal duties reflect the international law principle of reciprocity coupled with the Community principle of solidarity enshrined in art 5 of the Treaty. Sometimes these duties are expressed in the direct language of command or prohibition, sometimes in the indirect language of a provision which entrusts a specific task to the Community institutions implying that it will be carried out through co-operation between the Member States and reciprocal respect. For example, in the field of the movement of goods there is a duty not to discriminate against foreign goods by hindering their movements,[4] discriminatory taxes, reliance on derogations to protect national products and, even in

1 Case 186/87: *Cowan v Tresor Public* [1990] 2 CMLR 613.
2 Case 68/86: *United Kingdom v EC Council* [1988] ECR 855, [1988] 2 CMLR 543. See also Case C-331/88: *The Queen v The Minister of Agriculture, ex p Fédération Européenne de la Sante Animale and Others* where the ECJ held valid Directive 88/146 prohibiting the use in livestock of hormonal substances, OJ 1990, C 306/5.
3 Case 131/86: *United Kingdom v EC Council, Re Battery Hens* [1988] ECR 905, [1988] 2 CMLR 364.
4 See Lasok, D *The Customs Law of the EEC* (2nd edn 1990) chs 3–6.

Government-sponsored advertising, by exhorting the public to buy national products.[5] In brief a Member State cannot unilaterally opt out of its obligations.[6]

Vertical duties comprise the Member States' duties to the Community itself and to the citizens of all the Member States including their own. Thus the executive of a Member State must adopt the administrative measures necessary to carry into effect the Community policies, the legislature must enact implementing laws and make sure that the national system is in line with the rules of Community law and the judiciary must ensure not only the correct application of Community law but also the legal protection which individuals, irrespective of their nationality, derive from the Community legal order.

The rights of individuals are enshrined not only in the principle of the free movement of persons, ie workers, self-employed persons and the providers of services and their families and the social security protection, but also various other safeguards. These safeguards include equal treatment in the case of similar offences committed by citizens and aliens,[7] due process of the law[8] and the so-called Eurodefences, ie defences from criminal prosecution under national law which is inconsistent with Community law.[9]

(c) *Enforcement of Member States' duties*
The uniqueness of the Community legal order lies in the control and enforcement of legality to which sovereign states together with the institutions and individuals are subject. Member states have undertaken unconditionally the obligation of submitting the differences arising from the interpretation and application of the Treaties to no other method or authority but the Community Court.[10] Having submitted to a compulsory adjudication by the ECJ they have also delegated to the Commission the power of prosecution.[11] This measure of confidence and integration was hailed by the ECJ as 'far exceeding the rules heretofore recognized in classical international law' and the procedure as 'the *ultima*

---

5 Case 249/81: *EC Commission v Ireland, Re buy Irish campaign* [1982] ECR 4005, [1983] 2 CMLR 104.
6 Case 128/78: *EC Commission v United Kingdom* [1979] ECR 419, [1979] 2 CMLR 45 at para 9.
7 Eg Case 8/77: *Germany v Sagulo et Al* [1977] ECR 1495, [1977] 2 CMLR 585. Case 36/75: *Rutili v Ministère de l'Interieur* [1975] ECR 1219 at 1232; [1976] 1 CMLR 140.
8 Eg Case 98/79: *Pecastaing v Belgian State* [1980] ECR 691; [1980] 3 CMLR 685.
9 Eg Case 83/78: *Pigs Marketing Board v Redmond* [1978] ECR 2347; [1979] 1 CMLR 177.
10 EEC, art 219; EAEC, art 193; ECSC, art 87.
11 EEC, art 169; EAEC, art 141; ECSC, art 88.

ratio enabling the Community interests enshrined in the Treaty to prevail over the inertia and resistance of Member States'.[12]

The function of the judicial process in cases against the Member States is to declare the legal position and thus bring the erring state back on the path of legality. It is assumed that, motivated by the rule of law, the states will comply with the judgment. Should they fail to do so the Commission may bring another action, this time for the declaration that the Member State concerned has failed to fulfil an obligation under the Treaty. Should a state once more defy the judgment the judicial process would be exhausted, the ultimate solution being a political one. This is the Achilles heel of the enforcement system because there is no practical way of physical execution of judgments against states.[13]

2 The status of the Communities

(A) CORPORATE CAPACITY

The three Treaties constituting the Communities are identical and quite explicit on the legal status of the Communities in the Member States. Thus art 211 of the EEC Treaty provides that 'in each of the Member States, the Community shall enjoy the most extensive legal capacity accorded to legal persons under their laws; it may, in particular, acquire or dispose of movable and immovable property and may be party to legal proceedings'.

It is clear from the Treaties that it is only the Communities themselves and not their separate institutions which have legal personality. In a case arising under the ECSC Treaty, *Algera v Common Assembly of the ECSC*,[14] the Court of Justice laid it down in as many words: 'only the Community and not its institutions possess legal capacity'. Although the Court in that case was referring to the institutions of the ECSC, it is equally applicable to the merged institutions which serve the three Communities. It is clear that the legal personality and capacity of the Communities, following the classic theory of the personality of corporations, is quite distinct from those of the Member States. In a case before an Italian court in 1963 it was argued that the acts of the ECSC should be regarded by Italian law as the acts of the Italian state so that the

---

12 Case 25/59; *Netherlands v High Authority* [1960] ECR 355.
13 See Case 160/85: *Commission v Italy* [1986] ECR 3245; Cases 227–230/85: *EC Commission v Belgium* [1989] 2 CMLR 797; Case 169/87: *EC Commission v France (No 2)* [1990] 1 CMLR 49.
14 Cases 7/56 and 3–7/57: [1957–58] ECR 39; Valentine, D G, The Court of Justice of the European Communities (1965), Vol 2, p 748; cf Case 63–69/72: *Wilhelm Werhahn Hansamühle v EC Council* [1973] ECR 1229 at 1246.

ECSC could enjoy the preferential status in the Italian law of bankruptcy which is enjoyed by the Italian state. But the Court rejected that argument and held 'that the Community, while it is composed of the Member States is ... a distinct and autonomous corporation which cannot be identified with them ... [It is] a free and autonomous private corporation, under no control from the State institutions'.[15] Despite the Commission's argument to the contrary the principle was affirmed by the ECJ in a similar case.[16]

Whilst the Communities are 'private' corporations in the sense that they are autonomous and quite distinct from the Member States because they regard themselves to be in a similar position towards the Communities as the promoters of a joint stock company towards the company itself, the Court of Justice of the Communities has held that the legal personality of the Communities is governed by public law. Thus in *Von Lachmüller v EEC Commission*[17] the Court stated that the legal personality of the Community is a personality which 'exists in public law by virtue of the powers and functions which belong to the Community'. This statement was made in accordance with the continental practice of classifying corporate bodies. Thus in French law, for example, the category of *personnes morales de droit public* includes the state itself, administrative sub-divisions of the state and state enterprises such as universities, hospitals and nationalized industries. The competence of such corporate bodies is governed by public law and not by the civil law which would govern the competence of *personnes morales de droit privé*, such as commercial companies.[18] In the *Von Lachmüller* case the Court held that contracts of employment between the EEC and its employees were governed by public law and as such were subject to the procedures of administrative law.

This is a distinction quite unknown to English law which has a single concept of contract. Thus in English law whether a contract is between John Brown and Bill Smith or between John Brown and the Department of the Environment or between John Brown and the National Coal Board all will be subject to the jurisdiction of the High Court. But in French law, which makes a distinction between the public sphere and the private, contracts to which at least one of the parties is a *personne morale de droit public* tend to

---

15 *ECSC High Authority v C O Elettromeccaniche Merlini* [1964] CMLR 184 at 194.
16 Case 168/82: *ECSC v Liquidator of Ferrière Sant'Anna SpA* [1983] ECR 1681 at 1696.
17 Cases 43, 45 and 48/59 [1960]: ECR 463; see also Case 1/55: *Kergall v Common Assembly* [1954–56] ECR 151.
18 See Amos and Walton, *Introduction to French Law* (3rd edn 1967), pp 47 et seq.

be subject to the jurisdiction of the administrative courts, whereas contracts between private individuals or *personnes morales de droit privé* are subject to the jurisdiction of the ordinary civil courts. This jurisdictional distinction is thus reflected in Community law.

Since 1 January 1973, and by virtue of s 2 (1) of the European Communities Act 1972, the Communities have enjoyed corporate status under the laws of the United Kingdom. But this was no innovation, for such a status is already enjoyed by other international organisations of which the United Kingdom is a member under the terms of the International Organizations Act 1968. That Act makes it possible for a special statutory status of a body corporate to be conferred upon such organizations.[19]

Given that it is the Communities themselves which possess legal personality and not the individual institutions, this raises the practical question of how the Communities are represented in law. The Treaties answer this question. In the case of the ECSC art 6 of the Treaty provides that 'the Community shall be represented by its institutions, each within the limits of its powers'. This has been interpreted in the sense that the ECSC may be represented by its institutions each within the limits of the field of competence given it by the Treaty. The Court of Justice has also held that the term 'institutions' means the institutions named in the Treaty and does not include the departments into which those institutions may be divided for administrative purposes.[20] In the cases of the EEC and Euratom the position is much simpler since, at art 211 and art 185 of their Treaties respectively, it is stated that 'the Community shall be represented by the Commission'. This is a rôle which the Commission, with its expert Legal Service, is particularly well equipped to fill.[1]

While the Communities enjoy an extensive legal capacity in the territories of the Member States, they also enjoy privileges and immunities of the type usually accorded to the premises and officers of the international organizations. Article 28 of the Merger Treaty provides that the European Communities shall enjoy in the territories of the Member States 'such privileges and immunities as are necessary for the performance of their tasks'. The terms and conditions of those privileges and immunities are set out in a Protocol annexed to the Merger Treaty. The Protocol provides

19 Cf Bridge, J W, 'The United Nations and English Law' (1969) 18 I & CLQ at 694 and 702.
20 Case 66/63: *Netherlands Government v High Authority of the European Coal and Steel Co* [1964] ECR 533, [1964] CMLR 522.
1 See Ch 5, infra.

that the premises, buildings and archives of the Communities shall be inviolable.[2] The assets and revenues of the Communities shall be exempt from taxation.[3] Customs duties and restrictions shall not apply to either goods intended for official use or to Community publications.[4] The official communications of the Communities shall enjoy the treatment accorded to diplomatic missions and shall not be subject to censorship.[5] The members and servants of Community institutions shall be issued with *laissez-passer* for the purposes of travel.[6] The members of the European Parliament shall enjoy freedom of movement to and from the meetings of the Parliament and their opinions expressed or votes cast in the course of parliamentary proceedings shall not be the subject of inquiry or legal proceedings[7] though the privilege belongs to the institution (which can waive it) and not to the individual concerned. Both representatives of the Member States taking part in the work of Community institutions and the officials and servants of such institutions shall enjoy the customary privileges and immunities which include, inter alia, exemption from national taxation of allowances paid to Community officials[8] as well as payments made by the European Parliament to its members.[9] The Community Court, distinguishing between private and official business, held in *Sayag v Leduc*[10] that a Euratom official, not being employed as chauffeur by the Commission, was not entitled to immunity in respect of liability arising from a road traffic accident caused whilst carrying guests of the Commission in his own car.

The diplomatic missions of non-Member States to the Communities shall equally enjoy such privileges and immunities.[11] Finally, the Protocol stresses that all these privileges, immunities and facilities are accorded solely in the interests of the Communities and that immunity should be waived whenever waiver is not contrary to Community interests.[12]

---

2 Protocol on Privileges and Immunities, arts 1 and 2.
3 Ibid, art 3.
4 Ibid, art 4.
5 Ibid, art 6.
6 Ibid, art 7.
7 Ibid, arts 8–10. See Case 149/85: *Wybot v Foure* [1987] 1 CMLR 819.
8 Ibid, art 13; Case 85/85: *EC Commission v Belgium, Re Property Tax on Community Civil Servants* [1986] ECR 1149, [1987] 1 CMLR 787.
9 Case 208/80: *Lord Bruce of Donington v Eric Gordon Aspden* [1981] ECR 2205; [1981] 3 CMLR 506.
10 Ibid, arts 11–16; see Case 5/68: *Sayag v Leduc* [1968] ECR 395; [1969] CMLR 12. Case 9/69: *Sayag v Leduc* [1969] ECR 329.
11 Ibid, art 17.
12 Ibid, art 18. Cf Bridge, op cit, at 694 et seq.

(B) CONTRACTUAL AND NON-CONTRACTUAL LIABILITY OF THE
COMMUNITY

(a) *Contractual obligations*
In its corporate capacity the Community assumes liability for contracts and non-contractual obligations. The EEC and the Euratom
Treaties[13] provide that the Community's contractual liability is to
be governed by the law applicable to the contract in question.
Though the formula begs the question it must be assumed that a
national municipal law rather than a national private international
law is involved. Such contracts may be concerned with the acquisition and disposal of property, as well as goods to be delivered and
work to be carried out. Obligations arising from the employment
with the Community fall into a special category.

The jurisdictional provisions are in this respect contained in
articles 181 and 183 of the EEC Treaty. The former confers jurisdiction upon the Community Court pursuant to an arbitration
clause contained in a contract concluded by or on behalf of the
Community irrespective of whether or not it is governed by public
or private law. The latter confirms jurisdiction of the national
courts in the absence of such a clause.

Since there is no Community substantive law of contract as such
it is assumed that the governing law will be expressly designated
in cases in which the Community is a party; otherwise, in the light
of the provisions of the 1980 Convention[14] one would assume it to
be the municipal law of a Member State with which the contract
is most closely connected.

The case law on the subject remains yet to be developed. In the
Pellegrini[15] case a contract for the expert cleaning of Community
atomic energy installations situated in Italy was expressly subjected
to Italian law and the Commission's claim for breach of the contract
was decided accordingly. The case sets a precedent for the proposition that where the governing law is the law of a Member State
no expert evidence regarding the same shall be called. This accords
with the continental principle that *curia novit jura* reinforced, no
doubt, by the fact that the Community Court consists of judges
eligible to hold the highest judicial offices in their own countries.
Besides, legal points may well be elucidated in the course of the
written procedure and the Court can, of its own motion, enquire

13 EEC, art 215 (1); EAEC, art 188 (1); there is no equivalent provision in the
ECSC Treaty though the Community is contractually liable, see Case 1/55:
Kergall v Common Assembly [1954–56] ECR 151.
14 Convention on the Law applicable to Contractual Obligations; for details see
Lasok, D and Stone, P A, *The Conflict of Laws in the European Community*
(1987), Ch 9.
15 Case 23/76: *Pellegrini v EC Commission* [1976] ECR 1807, [1977] 2 CMLR 77.

about the matter with the Ministry of Justice or an equivalent department of the state concerned.

In a case[16] concerning building contracts brought on the basis of article 153 of the Euratom Treaty and article 181 of the EEC Treaty the ECJ had to decide not only on the merits of the conflicting claims but also whether Belgian law (chosen by the parties for the major aspects of the contract) or Italian law (designated for some minor aspects but claimed to be the 'natural law' of the whole contract) was the governing law. The ECJ held that the law expressly chosen was to be applied whilst the references to Italian law constituted merely a derogation justifiable in the specific circumstances of the contract which was being executed in Italy. In order to determine the Commission's rights arising from the breach of the contract the Commission was required to prove a causal relationship between its loss and the unilateral interruption in accordance with 'the general principles of the law of liability'. The Commission failed under this head though it succeeded under the three remaining heads, ie compensation for the inferior quality of the executed work; the difference between the contract price and the actual value of the executed work; and the cost of bringing the completed work up to the specifications laid down in the contract. The case demonstrates the problem of the choice of law but also demonstrates a tendency to rely on general principles which can be found in the laws of the Member States rather than the technicalities of the governing law.

Of the other recorded cases one[17] entailed a claim against the Commission for reimbursement of certain expenditure on research equipment incurred in the performance of a market research contract in pursuance of a Commission regulation, the other[18] a claim for goods delivered and work carried out for the Commission. The former failed upon the interpretation of the terms of the contract entailing matters of fact rather than the governing law. The latter succeeded in accordance with Belgian law.

In yet another case[19] the Commission, in pursuance of an arbitration clause, successfully claimed damages for non-performance of a contract by a journalist together with interest at the various statutory rates applicable in Belgium at the relevant time.

16 Case 318/81: *EC Commission v CO.DE.MI.SpA* [1982] ECR 1325, OJ 1985, 328/6 and (1987) 3 CMLR 516.
17 Case 251/84: *Centrale Marketinggesellschaft der deutscher Agrarwirtschaft GmbH v EC Commission* [1986] ECR 217, [1987] 2 CMLR 788.
18 Case 220/85: *Fadex NV v EC Commission* OJ 1986, C 318/6.
19 Case 426/85: *EC Commission v Zoubek* [1988] 1 CMLR 257.

(b) *Community servants and others*

Employment[20] with the Community institutions is subject to a special regime governed by the Staff Regulations[1] supplemented by contracts for auxiliary and local staff and massive case law. The Staff Regulations which govern the Community Civil Service, constitute a *sui generis* unitary code of law binding and applicable in all the Member States.[2] Each institution acts as employer and, therefore, has to be sued in that capacity rather than the Commission which represents the Community generally. Thus, eg, the Court librarian sues the ECJ in its administrative capacity and the ECJ in its judicial capacity hears and disposes of the case.[3] All disputes between the Community and its servants including the employees of the European Investment Bank[4] subject to the exclusive jurisdiction of the Community Court.[5] However, the jurisdiction of the ECJ in this field was transferred to the CFI subject to appeals to the ECJ on points of law only. These appeals are governed by the procedure laid down by the ECJ.[6]

A distinction must be made between Community civil servants and auxiliary[7] and local[8] staff. Civil servants enjoy a status entailing a career structure and pension rights governed by the Staff Regulations, the others have contractual rights and obligations governed by the proper (national) law of the contract. Staff Regulations govern the appointment, promotion, working conditions and emoluments, rights and duties (including the duty of confidentiality which extends beyond the period of service) and protection[9] of the servants as well as their discipline (with the right of appeal to the CFI), personal liability and the termination of office. The application of Staff Regulations may, however, lead to the application of national law where, for example, collateral rights are

20 For details see Lasok, D, *The Professions and Services in the European Economic Community* (1986), Ch 7.
1 Enacted in 1968, amended and consolidated in 1981: see Regulations 187/81, 397/81, 2780/81, 3821/81, 371/82, 372/82, 3139/82, 3332/82, 440/83, 1819/83, 2022/83, 2023/83, 2074/83, 3681/83, 420/85, 1578/85, 3856/86, 793/87, 3019/87.
2 See Case 137/80: *EC Commission v Belgium* [1981] ECR 2393.
3 See Case 15/60; *Simon v Court of Justice* [1961] ECR 115; Case 2/80: *Dautzenberg v Court of Justice* [1980] ECR 3107.
4 See Case 110/75: *Mills v European Investment Bank* [1976] ECR 1613.
5 EEC, art 179; ECSC, art 40 (2) (3); EAEC, art 152.
6 OJ 1989, L 241/1.
7 See Case 17/78: *Deshormes v EC Commission* [1979] ECR 189.
8 See Case 105/80: *Desmedt v EC Commission* [1981] ECR 1701.
9 See Case 18/78: *Mrs V v EC Commission* [1979] ECR 2093; see also Case 180/87: *Hamill v EC Commission* [1990] 1 CMLR 982.

concerned. Thus in two cases[10] involving pension rights of the surviving divorced wives reference had to be made to relevant national laws determining the financial effects of the decrees of divorce and, consequently, of the status of the claimant vis-à-vis the deceased Community official. Similarly, where children's rights based on the Staff Regulations are claimed, their status in relation to the parent will have to be determined by the relevant national law.

Where Staff Regulations do not apply the contents of the contract of employment with the Community shall be governed by a national law. Thus, it was held,[11] that where Italian law was the governing law in relation to auxiliary staff recruited locally the applicant was entitled to the full benefits of permanent employment granted by Italian law in the specific circumstances including the pension rights which would have been earned had the Commission paid the appropriate contribution under the Italian social security system. Similarly, in the case of a medical person,[12] who contracted to provide services to the Commission on an hourly basis, the position was governed by Belgian law as designated in the contract and, therefore, in the circumstances the claim to a pension was held unfounded.

(c) *Non-contractual liability*

In the case of non-contractual liability the Treaties[13] provide that 'the Community shall, in accordance with the general principles common to the laws of the Member States, make good any damage[14] caused by its institutions or by its servants in the performance of their duties'. Thus the Court of Justice is required to apply these general principles as an additional source of law in much the same way that the International Court of Justice can resort to 'the general

10 Case 24/71: *Meinhardt v EC Commission* [1972] ECR 269, [1973] CMLR 136; Case 40/79: *Mrs P v EC Commission* [1979] ECR 3299, [1981] ECR 361.
11 Case 109/81: *Pace (nee Porta) v EC Commission* [1982] ECR 2469.
12 Case 123/84: *Klein v EC Commission*, [1985] ECR 1907, [1987] 2 CMLR 799, ECJ.
13 EEC art 215 (2); EAEC art 188 (2) but see a different formulation of the principle in ECSC arts 40 (1) and 34; see also Lord Mackenzie Stuart, 'The Non-Contractual Liability of the European Economic Community' (1975).
14 Cf Cases 5, 7 and 13–24/66 *Kampffmeyer v EC Commission* [1967] ECR 245, (1967–68) 5 CML Rev 208; Case 153/73; *Holtz and Willemsen GmbH v EC Council and EC Commission* [1974] ECR 675, [1975] 1 CMLR 91; Case 169/73: *Compagnie Continentale France v EC Council* [1975] ECR 117, [1975] CMLR 578; Case 74/74: *Comptoir National Technique Agricole (CNTA) SA v EC Commission* [1975] ECR 533. Case 83/76: *Bayerische HNL Vermehrungsbetriebe GmbH & Co KG v EC Council and EC Commission* [1978] ECR 1209, [1978] 3 CMLR 566.

principles of law recognised by civilised nations' as a source of international law.[15]

A fundamental question which arises here is whether in order to be recognised and applied by the Court of Justice such general principles must be known to the municipal laws of all the Member States. Certainly in connection with the International Court of Justice such an exacting condition has not been applied. Sir Hersch Lauterpracht has defined general principles of law as 'those principles of law, private and public, which in contemplation of the legal experience of civilised nations lead one to regard as obvious maxims of jurisprudence of a general and fundamental character'.[16] Thus the International Court of Justice must enquire of 'the way in which the law of States representing the main systems of jurisprudence regulates the problem in the situations in question'.[17]

The ECJ has adopted a similar approach. As one commentator has put it, 'whilst it is not necessary ... that *all* states concerned agree on a certain principle of law, it is equally true that such a principle must not merely exist in the law of one country or only in a minority of legal systems ... [It] is not desirable to have a *brouillard* consisting of diverse national legal systems, but rather an adequate solution which is germane to the legal order of the Communities. This result will be reached only after thorough comparative analysis of the legal systems. To the extent that such research reveals a common core, it is not unlikely that the solutions adopted will readily be approved by the Member States in their national laws as well'.[18] In the words of Advocate-General Lagrange the spirit which has guided the Court has been 'not simply [to] take a more or less arithmetical average of the different municipal solutions, but [to] choose those solutions from among the various legal systems prevailing in the different Member States as, having regard to the objectives of the Treaty, appeared to it the best or, if one may use the word, the most progressive'.[19]

In recent years the ECJ has made a similar use of general principles of law for the interpretation of Community law and the recognition of human rights.[20] The Court has interpreted its duty

15 See art 38 (1) (c) of the Statute of the International Court of Justice.
16 *International Law, being the Collected Papers of Hersch Lauterpracht* (1970), Vol 1, p 69.
17 Ibid, p 71. For an account of the practice of the International Court also, see ibid, pp 68–77.
18 Lorenz, K, 'General Principles of Law: Their Elaboration in the Court of Justice of the European Communities' (1964) 13 AJCL at 9, 10, 11.
19 Case 14/61: *Hoogovens v High Authority* [1963] CMLR 73 at 85, 86, [1963] ECR 231.
20 See generally Pescatore, P, 'Fundamental Rights and Freedoms in the System of the European Communities' (1970) 18 AJCL 343; Zuleeg, M, 'Fundamental

to ensure that the law is observed as permitting it to apply as part of Community law a body of unwritten, fundamental legal principles which are common to the national legal and political systems of the Member States. The function of these fundamental principles in the Community legal order is, in the words of Advocate-General Dutheillet de Lamothe, 'to contribute to forming that philosophical, political and legal substratum common to the Member States from which emerges through the case law an unwritten Community law, one of the essential aims of which is precisely to ensure respect for the fundamental rights of the individual'.[1] The Court has demonstrated its willingness to test the validity of Community acts against such criteria.

The principles
Regarding the principles governing the non-contractual liability of the Community it has to be borne in mind that the concept cannot be construed in the sense of 'tort' or unlawful act of private law giving rise to a civil remedy of damages and/or injunction but has to be seen in the context of the activities of the Community institutions. These activities include the exercise of administrative and legislative functions and, like in any state system, may fall occasionally below the standard of sound and efficient administration expected in the West European political culture. Such malfunctioning would reveal a fault of the system (*faute de service*) for which the state should be responsible. Moreover, in narrowly defined circumstances, the system may be liable in the absence of fault or blameworthiness. Thus, for example, although under French law a statute may not be challenged in the courts, the administration may incur liability in accordance with the principle of '*égalité devant les charges publiques*' if, as a result of a legislative measure, an individual has suffered damage in excess of the sacrifice borne by the citizenry in a comparable situation.[2]

Similarly, under the German *Grundgesetz* the principle of proportionality (*Verhältnismassigkeit*) protects the citizens from excessive burdens without necessarily imputing fault to the state.[3]

Rights and the Law of the European Communities' (1971) 8 CML Rev 446; Bridge, J W, et al, *Fundamental Rights* (1973), Chapter 20.
1 Case 11/70: *Internationale Handelsgesellschaft GmbH v Einfuhr-und Vorratsstelle für Getreide und Futtermittel* [1970] ECR 1125 at 1146, [1972] CMLR 255 at 271.
2 See Cases 9 and 11/71: *Compagnie d'Approvisionnement v EC Commission* [1972] ECR 391, [1973] CMLR 529 (per Adv-Gen Mayras at 422–423) and Case 26/81: *Oleifici Mediterranei SA v EEC* [1982] ECR 3057 (per Adv-Gen Verloren van Themaat at 3089–3090).
3 See Case 11/70: *Internationale Handelsgesellschaft v EVGF* [1970] ECR 1125 (per Adv-Gen Dutheillet de Lamothe at 1146), [1972] CMLR 255; Case 5/73:

Whilst it can be said that the concept of Community liability has been modelled upon that of state liability one would look in vain for a direct reference to a particular system in the judgments of the Community Court, since the Court contents itself with a synthetic and unattributed statement of the general principle. However, the Advocates-General[4] do occasionally, albeit briefly, refer to national laws relevant in this respect.

Institutional liability
In the terms[5] of the EEC and Euratom Treaties the Community must make good any damage caused by its institutions or by its servants in the performance of their duties. The ECSC Treaty requires, in addition, an element of fault. However in practice so far no-fault liability has to be considered only a remote possibility. The question did arise in Cases 9 and 11/71 cited above where compensation was claimed in respect of subsidies on imports of cereals following the devaluation of the French currency in 1969. However the ECJ rejected the claim without addressing itself to the contention of no-fault liability. A decade later, in Case 26/81 cited above, the ECJ was quite prepared to consider the argument but dismissed the claim as arising from a commercial risk rather than the Community rules which purported to reform the organization of the common market in oil and fats. It observed that 'the alleged damage, even assuming it to have been substantiated, is attributable entirely to the applicant's conduct'. The Court took the opportunity of restating the principle that in order to succeed the applicant must prove 'unlawfulness of the conduct of which the institutions are accused, the reality of the damage and the existence of a causal connection between the conduct and the damage in question'.[6] In doing so the Court re-emphasized the requirement of fault which underlies the unlawful nature of the conduct for which the Community is responsible.

The rules were laid down in *Schöppenstedt v EC Council*[7] where

Balkan Import-Export v HZA Berlin-Packhof [1973] ECR 1091; Case 114/76: *Bela-Mühle v Grows-Farm* [1977] ECR 1211, [1979] 2 CMLR 83; Case 116/76: *Granaria v HAP* [1977] ECR 1247, [1979] 2 CMLR 83; Cases 119, 120/76: *Olmühle Hamburg v HZA Hamburg-Waltershof* [1979] ECR 1269, [1979] 2 CMLR 83.

4 See eg Adv.-Gen. Verloren van Themaat in Case 26/81, note 2, supra; Adv-Gen Reischl in Cases 56–60/74: *Kampfmeyer v EC Commission and EC Council* [1976] ECR 711 at 752–753; Adv-Gen Roemer in Case 5/71: *Aktien-Zuckerfabrik Schöppenstedt v EC Council* [1971] ECR 975 at 989; Adv-Gen Gand in Case 4/68: *Firma Schwarzwaldmilch v Einfuhr-und Vorratsstelle für Fette* [1968] ECR 377, [1969] CMLR 406.

5 See note 3, supra.

6 Note 2, Case 26/81 at para 16.

7 Case 5/71 [1971] ECR 975 at para 11.

the ECJ dismissed a claim for compensation for loss of income alleged to have been caused by a Council regulation laying down the measures needed to offset the difference between national and Community sugar prices. Addressing itself to the problem of liability, the Court held that where legislative action involving measures of economic policy is concerned the Community will not incur non-contractual liability for damage suffered by individuals in consequence of such action unless a 'sufficiently flagrant violation of a superior rule of law for the protection of the individual has occurred'. The Court did not elucidate the meaning of the 'superior rule of law' it had in mind. However it drew a distinction between a claim for compensation and an action for annulment of the measure in question and emphasized the autonomous nature of these two remedies. However, as ruled subsequently,[8] the autonomous nature of the claim for compensation is concerned with procedure, ie the action can be brought in its own virtue without it being collateral to the action for annulment. Yet in practice claims for compensation are linked with the illegality of the act complained[9] of as the self-evident proof of wrongfulness or fault of the system.

Failure to act may also provide a cause of action for compensation where the relevant Community institution is in breach of a duty[10] to act and such failure is a direct cause of loss or damage. Here again failure to execute a duty is tantamount to a fault of the system.

8 Cases 197–200, 243 and 245/247/80: *Ludwigshafener v EC Council and EC Commission* [1981] ECR 3211; see also Case 52/81: *Faust v EC Commission* [1982] ECR 3745; Case 256/81: *Pauls Agriculture Ltd v EC Council and EC Commission* [1983] ECR 1707, [1983] 3 CMLR 176.

9 See eg Case 5/71, supra; Case 9 and 11/71, supra; Case 59/72: *Wünsche v EC Commission* [1973] ECR 791; Cases 63–69/72: *Werhahn v EC Council* [1973] ECR 1229; case 153/73: *Holtz v EC Council and EC Commission* [1974] ECR 675, [1975] 1 CMLR 91; Case 74/74: *CNTA v EC Commission* [1975] ECR 533, [1977] 1 CMLR 171; Case 99/74: *Soc Grands Moulins v EC Commission* [1975] ECR 1531; Cases 54–60/76: *Comp Ind et Agri v EC Council and EC Commission* [1977] ECR 645; Cases 83 and 94/76: *Bayerische HNL v EC Council and EC Commission* [1978] ECR 1209, [1978] 3 CMLR 566; Case 238/78: *Ireks-Arkady v EC Council and EC Commission* [1979] ECR 2955; Cases 241, 242 and 245–250/78: *DGV v EC Council and EC Commission* [1979] ECR 3017.

10 See Case 30/66: *Becher v EC Commission* [1967] ECR 285; Case 43/72: *Merkur v EC Commission* [1973] ECR 1055; Case 40/75: *Soc Bertrand v EC Commission* [1976] ECR1, [1976] 1 CMLR 220; Case 90/78: *Granaria v EC Council and EC Commission* [1979] ECR 1081.

Vicarious liability

In the terms of the Treaties the Community is vicariously liable for non-contractual obligations incurred by Community servants in the course of their official duties. This kind of liability is another aspect of the *faute de service* or of the malfunctioning of the system since the Community selects its servants, details their duties and controls their activities. However the act of the servant must be attributable[11] to the Community because the Community is liable only for those acts which are the necessary extension of the tasks given to the institutions.[12] Therefore, should the servant act outside the scope of his duties or engage in activities which are *ultra vires* the institutions, the Community would not be vicariously liable but the servant would be by virtue of *faute personnelle*.

Cases involving the Community in vicarious liability for misdeeds of its servants are rare. In the case of what was described as 'reciprocal assaults'[13] the Commission was condemned to pay a symbolic ECU to a female official in compensation of non-material damage resulting from a failure to investigate her complaints against a male colleague. In another[14] case the indiscretion of an official led to a series of calamities which fell upon a person who supplied information to the Commission in the course of the investigations of breaches of Community competition rules. The information helped to find the undertaking[15] concerned guilty of breaches of Community law but the disclosure of the informer's identity led to the latter's resignation from his employment; prosecution and conviction in Switzerland for offences under Swiss law which prohibits the passing of commercial secrets to an unauthorized body (ie the Commission, *in casu*); his financial ruin and his wife's suicide. The ECJ dismissed a rather extravagant claim against the Commission[16] for its failure to prevent his prosecution and imprisonment in Switzerland but found the Commission liable for the breach of confidentiality by the Commission official and awarded damages for mental anguish and economic loss plus costs without actually identifying the specific heads of damage.[17]

The Community may also be vicariously liable for the acts of an agency or body under its control. However the liability will depend upon the status[18] of the agency or body in question vis-à-vis the

11 Case 9/69: *Sayag v Leduc* [1969] ECR 329.
12 Ibid, at 336.
13 Case 18/78: *Mrs V v EC Commission* [1979] ECR 2093.
14 Case 145/83: *Adams v EC Commission* [1985] ECR 3539; [1986] 1 CMLR 506.
15 Case 85/76: *Hoffman-LaRoche v EC Commission* [1979] ECR 461, [1979] 3 CMLR 211.
16 Case 53/84: *Adams v EC Commission* [1985] ECR 3539, [1986] 1 CMLR 506.
17 Case 145/83; *Adams v EC Commission* [1985] ECR 3539; [1986] 1 CMLR 506.
18 See Cases 32 and 33/58: *SNUPAT v High Authority* [1959] ECR 127.

Community. The *Worms*[19] case illustrates the point. Worms, a scrap-metal agent, sued the High Authority of the Coal and Steel Community for damages, because having exposed fraud in the scrap-metal business, he was ostracized by dealers and consequently himself went out of business. He argued that the High Authority was at fault because it failed to protect him from the boycott which ruined his business or to end the fraud and prosecute the wrongdoers. He failed because the High Authority was not considered responsible for the agencies it established under Belgian law, one to purchase scrap-metal on behalf of the Coal and Steel Community and another to collect the scrap equalization levy imposed upon scrap-metal dealers to subsidize imported scrap. Worms failed because the purchasing agency was said to be an autonomous private body for which the Community was not vicariously liable. He should have sued before Belgian courts, under Belgian law, the persons and bodies responsible for his loss. Thus the Community is not liable for damage caused by national institutions (eg Agricultural Intervention Boards) even if applying Community law.[20]

Proof of damage, causation and remoteness
Since there are no specific Community rules governing the proof and heads of damage, causation or remoteness the Community Court applies what might be termed the general principles of the law of damage common to the Member States. It insists that the claimant proves his claim in the light of the Community obligations drawing a distinction between admissible claims and claims arising from 'commercial risks' for which the Community cannot be liable. It also dismisses 'speculative' claims and, as we have noted in the *Adams* cases, claims which are too remote. The case law, beginning with the Schöppenstedt[1] ruling that 'a claim for an unspecified form of damages is not sufficiently concrete and must, therefore, be regarded as inadmissible', lays down the rules for the practice of the Court:

In *Kampffmeyer v EC Commission*[2] the ECJ held that compensation was payable where, as a result of an unlawful act of the Commission, the claimant sustained losses from cancellation of transactions following the refusal of import licences.

In *CNTA v Commission*[3] compensation for losses following cur-

---

19 Case 18/60: *Worms v High Authority* [1962] ECR 195.
20 Cases 89/86 and 91/86: *L'Etoile Commerciale v EC Commission* [1988] 3 CMLR 564. Cases 106–120/87: *Asteris AE v Greece* [1990] 1 CMLR 575.
1 Case 5/71, supra, at para 9.
2 Cases 5–7, 13–24 and 30/66 [1967] ECR 245.
3 Case 74/74, supra.

rency fluctuations was possible in view of the abolition of monetary compensatory amounts (MCAs) in respect of colza and rape seeds and oils produced therefrom for export. However the claimant produced no proof and the ECJ held that he cannot be regarded as having suffered loss if he was not exposed to any exchange risk at all, or was so exposed but no actual loss occurred.

In *Lesieur v EC Commission*,[4] the claimant failed to make out a case from the abolition of MCAs in the oil and fats sector which, he argued, resulted in the loss of cheap supplies on the international markets and deprived him of the expected profits. The ECJ ruled that, although a sudden abolition of the MCAs constituted an infringement of the principle of protection of legitimate expectations, the object of the measure was to prevent disturbances in the trade, rather than secure profits for traders. Besides, no actual damage was proved.

In *Société Roquette v EC Commission*[5] the claim, based on the loss arising from the fixing of the MCAs in respect of the importation of amyloid products into France contrary to a regulation on the conjunctural policy in agriculture resulting from the widening gaps of currency values, failed. Neither actual loss nor causal connection was proved.

In *Kampffmeyer v EC Commission and EC Council*[6] a claim in respect of anticipated loss in 1975 based on prices and aids for cereals during 1974 failed. The ECJ held that, although it was not prevented from making a declaration regarding future losses, it could not award damages *in casu* since no liability was established.

In *Milch v EC Commission*[7] the claimant obtained export certificates for certain North African countries fixing in advance refunds for the export of butter stored by the German Agricultural Intervention Board. He sold a quantity of the product to his Belgian partner. The German customs authorities paid a part of the refund but rejected further demands on the ground that there was no proof of marketing in the countries concerned. Thereupon he brought an action against the Commission on the ground that the Commission had led him to believe that the payment of the refunds fixed in advance depended merely upon proof that the product had left the country. The ECJ ruled, however, that he had to show that the product not only left the country but was also marketed in the territory for which it was destined.

---

4 Cases 67–85/75 [1976] ECR 391, [1976] 2 CMLR 185.
5 Case 26/74 [1976] ECR 677.
6 Cases 56–60/74 [1976] ECR 711; see Adv-Gen Reischl at 753 on the nature of damage.
7 Case 44/76 [1977] ECR 393.

In *Pool v EC Council*[8] an English cattle breeder, who claimed compensation for the damage caused to him by fixing the conversion rates of the pound sterling applicable specifically to the agricultural sector, failed as his calculations to prove the alleged damage were based on speculative and unrealistic comparisons and did not support his claim.

In *Julius Kind v EEC*[9] a German butcher sought, unsuccessfully, compensation for alleged losses suffered as a result of the market organization for sheepmeat following the Anglo-French controversy in that field. As an importer of meat from Britain, where the prices were lower than elsewhere, he was hit by the claw-back rule to offset the variable slaughter premium which as from 1980 imposed levies upon the British products. He claimed damages as his business declined, especially that he was unable to penetrate the Swiss market. However he proved no actual loss and revealed that he attempted to enter the Swiss market only after the coming into force of the regulation which he blamed for his alleged loss.

Following the earlier *Quellmehl* and *Gritz* cases[10] a successful claim[11] was made in cases where the ECJ held that, by abolishing subsidies for the production of maize gritz used in the brewing industry, whilst maintaining production subsidies for starch used in the bakery industry, the Commission had infringed the principle of equality, ie a 'superior rule of law' for the protection of the individual. In these cases the producers of quellmehl and gritz were entitled to compensation based on the subsidy they would have received had they been treated equally with the producers of starch.

In a recent case[12] the Court reiterated the three conditions of a successful action in this respect, ie unlawful act, damage and causal link connecting unlawfulness with damage, but warned that undue emphasis on illegality of the act without establishing the other factors may be fatal to the action. In other words, the object of the action is not to punish the institution in default but to compensate the claimant for genuine loss directly attributable to such an act.

---

8 Case 49/79 [1980] ECR 569, [1980] 3 CMLR 279.
9 Case 106/81 [1982] ECR 2885.
10 Cases 238/78: *Ireks-Arkady v EC Council and EC Commission* [1979] ECR 2955; Cases 241, 242 and 245–250/78: *DVG v EC Council and EC Commission* [1979] ECR 3017; Cases 261 and 262/78: *Interquell Starke-Chemie and Diamalt v EC Council and EC Commission* [1979] ECR 3045 and [1982] ECR 3271.
11 Joined Cases 64 and 113/76, 167 and 239/78, and 27, 28 and 45/79: *Dumortier Frères v EC Council* [1982] ECR 1733.
12 Case 253/84: *Groupement Agricole v EC Council and EC Commission* [1988] 1 CMLR 677.

In another case[13] the ECJ explained the procedural aspect of claims against the Community. Thus the claimant must have a *locus standi* in accordance with art 173 (2) of the Treaty, ie direct and individual concern, but has also to pursue his claim in the appropriate jurisdiction. In the instant case the Commission refused to make FEOGA reimbursement to a trader in agricultural produce. The Court confirmed this to be correct because art 215 (2) is inapplicable to cases involving damage caused by national institutions even if they apply Community rules. The action lay at home though the ECJ will eventually (presumably in a preliminary ruling under art 177 of the Treaty) examine whether the Community is liable.

In a more recent case[14] the *locus standi* of an importer of Chilean apples was not in question. The suspension by the Commission of import licences without derogation in respect of products en route on the ocean was held to be a breach of the relevant regulation leading to damages under art 215 (2).

Regarding the heads of damage it seems the Court will award damages for actual loss (*damnum emergens*) as well as the consequential loss (*lucrum cessans*) in accordance with the practice established in the Member States. In claims of a personal nature the ECJ may award compensation for material as well as moral damage.[15] The quantum has to be substantiated by the claimant assuming, of course, that he has proved infringement of a substantive right. Where it is in dispute the parties ought to negotiate a settlement but, where they are unable to agree, the Court will appoint expert assessors to assist in the process.

Claims against the Community for compensation arising from non-contractual liability are subject to a limitation period of five years,[16] the time beginning to run from the date on which the event giving rise to damage had occurred.[17] This, in the case of refunds, is the moment of the actual loss, not the date on which the refunds were instituted.[18]

---

13 Cases 89/86 and 91/86: *L'Etoile v EC Commission* [1988] 3 CMLR 564; see also Case 106–120/87: *Asteris v Greece* [1990] 1 CMLR 575.
14 Case C-152/88: *Sofrimport Sarl v EC Commission* [1990] 3 CMLR 80.
15 See Cases 18/78, supra and 145/83, supra.
16 Protocol on the Statute of the ECJ, art 43.
17 Cases 5–7, 13–24 and 30/66, supra; Case 11/72: *Giordano v EC Commission* [1973] ECR 417.
18 Joined Cases 256, 257, 265 and 267/80 and 5/81: *Birra Wührer v EC Council and EC Commission* [1982] ECR 85 at 106; Case 51/81: *De Franceschi v EC Council and EC Commission* [1982] ECR 117 at 134.

3 The external relations of the Communities

(A) THE POWER BASE

It has already been pointed out that the Communities have personality and capacity under international law. Their personality and capacity may be classified as of the functional sort referred to by the International Court of Justice in its advisory opinion in the *Reparation for Injuries* Case arising from the assassination by terrorists of a United Nations' mediator in Palestine.[19] That is to say that the Communities at international law have the degree of personality and capacity which is necessary to enable them to carry out their functions on the international plane. This general view is substantiated by the terms of the Treaties themselves.

Article 6 of the ECSC Treaty states clearly that 'in international relations the Community shall enjoy the legal capacity it requires to perform its functions and attain its objectives'. The EEC and Euratom Treaties, on the other hand, merely state that the Communities have legal personality but do not refer to any specific attribution of capacity in international law.[20] Nevertheless such latter capacity may not only be inferred from the nature of the Communities as the creatures of treaties but it has also been expressly confirmed by the Court of Justice in its judgment in the *Re ERTA, EC Commission v EC Council*.[1] There the Court observed that art 210 of the EEC Treaty, by stating that the Community has legal personality, 'means that in its external relations the Community enjoys the capacity to establish contractual links with non-member States over the whole field of the objectives defined in Part One of the Treaty'.[2]

This, as we shall see later, is merely a power base from which spring the two attributes of legal personality in international relations, ie the treaty-making power (*jus tractatus*) and the capacity to engage in diplomacy (*jus missionis*). Quantitatively, however, the European Community falls short of the powers characteristic of a federal state in this field. In other words, though having an incipient potential for the creation of its own external policy, the Community can act only within the limits of the founding Treaties. However the scope of the action necessary to achieve the Treaty objectives

19 ICJ Reports 1949, 174. See generally Henig, S, *External Relations of the European Community* (1971) and Costonis, J J, 'Treaty Making Powers of the EEC' (1967) *European Yearbook* 31; Coffey, P, *The External Relations of the EEC*, (1976); Soldatos, P, 'La politique extérieure' in Lasok, D and Soldatos, P, *Les Communautés Européennes en Fonctionnement* (1981), pp 477 et seq.
20 EEC Treaty, art 210 and Euratom Treaty, art 184.
1 Case 22/70 [1971] ECR 263, [1971] CMLR 335.
2 Ibid, at para 14.

may require powers which have not been expressly granted, in which case the founding Treaties themselves authorize recourse to implied powers. In the terms of the EEC[3] Treaty 'if actions of the Community should prove necessary to attain, in the course of the operation of the common market, one of the objectives of the Community and this treaty has not provided the necessary powers, the EC Council shall, acting unanimously on a proposal from the EC Commission and after consulting the Parliament, take the appropriate measures'. This, however, is not a blanket provision increasing the existing powers but an auxiliary lever to be operated for the definite purpose of the common market and strictly within the spirit of the Treaty and in accordance with the procedure laid down therein. In the opinion of the ECJ it can be used in the field of external relations.[4]

A new lever has been provided by the Single European Act mainly at the initiative of the British Government which considers a common approach to foreign policy to be one of the mainsprings of European integration. Article 30 of the Act provides for regular quarterly meetings of the Ministers of Foreign Affairs of the Member States within the framework of European Political Co-operation; insists on a joint formulation and implementation of a European foreign policy and consistency of the external policies of the European Community and the policies agreed in European Political Co-operation. It charges the Presidency of the Council (which assumes the function of the Presidency of European Co-operation) with the management of Political Co-operation and with the task of initiating action and representing the positions of the Member States in relations with the outside world as far as the activities of European Political Co-operation are concerned. It provides further for a Secretariat to assist the Presidency and work with the European Correspondents' Groups and Working Groups as regards the preparation of the meetings of Ministers and the monitoring of the implementation of policies decided by Ministers. The new approach to Political Co-operation within the Community and the formulation of external policy involves also the Commission and the European Parliament. The former shall be fully associated with the proceedings of Political Co-operation, the latter will be informed of the issues which are being examined within the framework of Political Co-operation and given an opportunity of presenting its point of view which shall be taken into consideration within the framework of Political Co-operation.

3 EEC, art 235; ECSC, art 95 (1); Euratom, art 203.
4 Case 22/70, supra [1971] ECR 263 at 283, [1971] CMLR 355 at 362; Joined Cases 3, 4, 6/76: *Officier van Justitie v Kramer* [1976] ECR 1279, [1976] 2 CMLR 440; Opinion 1/76, [1977] ECR 741, [1977] 2 CLMR 299.

Next to the Treaty provisions, the provisions of the Single European Act represent a significant stage in the formation of a concept of Community external policy as well as a practical step towards the formulation of such policy. Future events will enable us to evaluate their effect both in the life of the Community and that of the Member States. For the time being external relations of the Community in its own right are carried out by international treaties or agreements in the context of policies defined by the founding Treaties.

(B) *JUS TRACTATUS*

(a) *Community competence*
According to the founding Treaties each Community has the capacity to establish relations with certain international organizations and to conclude certain types of international agreements. Thus each of them is competent to establish relations with the organs of the United Nations[5] and its specialized agencies and the Organization for European Economic Co-operation[6] as well as the Council of Europe.[7] Moreover the EEC and the Euratom can maintain relations with the General Agreement on Tariffs and Trade and also such relations as are appropriate with all international organizations,[8] including the International Labour Office.[9]

Since the treaty-making power is limited to specific types of treaties the Communities may use it only to conclude treaties and agreements envisaged in the founding Treaties. Thus each Community is competent to make accession[10] treaties which have the object of admitting new members; and in the case of the EEC and Euratom,[11] association agreements, which have the object of establishing a special relationship short of full membership of the Community. Moreover, the EEC has power to make trade[12] agreements and Euratom[13] can enter into agreements or contracts with a non-Member State, an international organization or even an individual from a non-Member State in the context of the common market for atomic energy. However the ECSC[14] Treaty

5 EEC, art 229 (1); ECSC, art 93; Euratom, art 199.
6 EEC, art 231; ECSC, art 93, Euratom, art 201.
7 EEC, art 230; ECSC, art 94; Euratom, art 200.
8 EEC, art 229 (1), (2); Euratom, art 199.
9 See Case 217/86: *EC Commission v EC Council*, OJ 1986, C 242/8 (re Council resolution refusing the Commission authority to negotiate an agreement on the use of asbestos).
10 EEC, art 237; ECSC, art 98; Euratom, art 206.
11 EEC, arts 131–136 and 238; Euratom, art 206.
12 Arts 111 and 113.
13 Art 101.
14 Arts 71–75.

limits the Community competence in the context of the common market for coal and steel to a general supervision of the commercial policy of the Member States in this sector, including tariffs and import and export licences, to ensure compliance with the Treaty.

Since the Community competence is a power attributed to it by the founding Treaties at the expense of the Member States we are confronted with interaction between attributed (Community) and original (state) competence. It is, therefore, possible to distinguish in the field of external relations between exclusive Community competence, concurrent competence, and joint competence.[15] However, irrespective of the existence of Community competence, the consequence of attribution is that the Member States, being sovereign, enjoy their original right until the exclusive Community competence has been used.[16]

Accession Treaties, though concluded by the Community, have to be signed by all the existing and the acceding Member States and they can, of course, be aborted by the veto of an existing member. Because of their constitutional nature they are a class apart but from a Community point of view can be regarded as emanating from the joint competence; though from the point of view of the acceding state as well as the existing Member States, they represent an exercise of sovereign power which, in the case of the latter, is not limited merely to a vote.

Association agreements emanate from the exclusive competence of the Community despite the dominant position of the Council in the negotiations of these agreements.

As emphasized in the case law[17] the Community enjoys exclusive competence in the field of commercial policy. The point was made in the Opinion[18] of the ECJ ruling that export credit agreements within the Organization for Economic Co-operation and Development were closely connected with export trade and, therefore, within the EEC Treaty thus disposing of the contention that there may still be a parallel (or concurrent) competence vested in the Member States. Consequently, held the Court, the Member States must refrain from taking concurrent actions.

In its ruling on the Draft Convention of the International Atomic Energy on the Physical Protection of Nuclear Materials, Facilities

---

15 Waelbroeck, M. et al, *Le droit de la Communauté Européenne* (1981), Vol 12, pp 103 et seq.
16 Joined cases 3, 4, 6/76, note 4, supra.
17 See especially Case 22/70, note 4, supra and cases below.
18 Opinion 1/75 [1975] ECR 1355 at 1364, [1976] 1 CMLR 85 at 93; see also Case 41/76: *Criel v Procureur de la Republique* [1976] ECR 1921 at 1936, [1977] 2 CMLR 535 at 551; Case 52/77: *Cayrol v Rivoira* [1977] ECR 2261, [1978] 2 CMLR 253; Case 179/78: *Procureur de la République v Rivoira* [1979] ECR 1147, [1979] 3 CMLR 456.

and Transport[19] the ECJ held[20] that the Community had exclusive competence to join the Convention not only by virtue of its international legal personality and the treaty-making power but also because of the objectives of the founding Treaty. Since the business of the Convention was within the Community competence the Member States no longer had any concurring powers but, in the spirit of Community solidarity, had to co-operate. However there was a practical problem because the Convention had to be implemented through the co-operation between the Community and the Member States. This problem was resolved by apportioning specific tasks as between the Community and the Member States. The Community assumed responsibility for the supply arrangements and management of the common market in nuclear energy as well as the execution of the security provisions and the management of property rights whilst the remaining tasks were undertaken by the Member States.

With the growing integration within the Community the area of concurrent competence has been in decline. However there are still areas of potential exclusive competence which have not been appropriated by the Community. This is so in cases where the financial commitments cannot be discharged from the Community budget and, therefore, call for further participation of the Member States. Besides there are problems with the trade agreements of the Member States where their partners in trade do not recognize the legal personality of the Community or, for reasons better known to themselves, they prefer to deal with the Member States directly.

The ECJ's opinion on the Draft International Agreement on Natural Rubber[1] exemplifies the first problem for, whilst the Community was competent to become party to the Agreement in its own right, the management of the rubber resources, being within the scope of trade or commercial policy, the lack of own funds to contribute towards this expensive international project necessitated an involvement of the Member States in their individual capacity. The second problem is well illustrated in relations with the USSR and the COMECON countries. Despite repeated overtures the two parts of the divided Europe have kept apart. Whilst the COMECON until the Convention of 1985[2] had no autonomous legal personality its members were reluctant to recognize the personalities of the European Communities. As a result trade between

---

19 Vienna and New York Convention of 3 March 1980; Misc 27 (1980); Cmnd 8112.
20 Ruling 1/78 [1978] ECR 2151, [1979] 1 CMLR 131.
 1 Opinion 1/78 [1979] ECR 2871, [1979] 3 CMLR 639.
 2 See Warsaw Convention of 27 June 1985 on the legal capacity, privileges and immunities of COMECON.

the Member States of the EEC and the COMECON countries continued on a bi-lateral basis. This largely prevented the EEC countries from discharging their obligations under article 234 of the Treaty which provides for a transition in this field from Member States' competence to that of the Community. Indeed they are bound to adjust their treaty obligations negotiated before they became members of the Community in accordance with their duties but such adjustment requires the co-operation of their partners in trade. Whilst the period of adjustment is being extended from time to time, concurrent competence continues. And to cope with the continuing problem the Community has imposed certain conditions[3] under which the Member States can trade with the so-called 'state-trading' countries.

A major breakthrough in the West–East relations occurred when, on 25 June 1988, a joint declaration on behalf of the two sides of Europe recognizing each other was signed during the German presidency. It was a diplomatic achievement after 13 years of negotiations though it did not encompass any trade arrangements. These were to be dealt with through bilateral agreements. However, since this occasion occurred in the death throes of the COMECON the declaration may only be of an historical significance. A year later dramatic changes in Eastern Europe have marked the demise of the COMECON and its individual members, in their own capacity, proceeded to fashion their relations with the Community on a bilateral basis.

Certain agreements reflect as their central feature a concept of joint competence of the Community and the Member State. They also reflect various forms of co-operation between the contracting parties. The word 'co-operation' has several meanings and its precise scope has to be examined in the light of the terms of the agreement in question. Thus, for example, the agreement with Canada[4] is a 'framework agreement of commercial and economic co-operation'; the agreements with Sri Lanka, Pakistan and Bangladesh[5] are each a 'commercial co-operation agreement'; agree-

---

3 Ie: Aids for exports (Reg 2603/69 amended by Regs 234/71: 1078/71; 2182/71; 2747/72; 1275/75; 1170/76; 1934/82); Imports (Reg 1439/74); Protective measures (Reg 1439/74); Quantitative restrictions (Reg 1023/70); Anti-dumping (Reg 459/68 now Reg 2423/88, see Ch 14 infra).
4 OJ 1976, L260; Lasok, D, 'Involvement with the European Economic Community: Some Canadian Considerations', 22 McGill Law Jo No 4 (1976) 575.
5 Sri Lanka, OJ 1975, L247/2; Pakistan, OJ 1976, L168/2; Bangladesh, OJ 1976, L319/2 but the new agreement with Pakistan, OJ 1986, L113/86, is a 'commercial economic, development and co-operation agreement', see Council Reg 1196/86, OJ 1986, L108/1 annexed thereto.

ments with the ASEAN[6] Group (ie Indonesia, Malaysia, the Philippines, Singapore and Thailand) refer to 'commercial, economic and development co-operation'; whilst agreements with the Mediterranean[7] countries as well as the 1975 Lomé[8] Convention are simply 'agreements of co-operation'. We should mention in this context the co-operation agreements with two state-trading countries (which were not members of the COMECON), ie Yugoslavia[9] and China.[10] Co-operation agreements enable the Member States to enter into bi-lateral agreements with the Community partners within the scope of these agreements. However, to ensure Community supremacy, they expressly provide that the bi-lateral agreements are subordinate to the framework agreements and the Community text prevails 'even if the terms of the two were identical'.[11] Another feature, exemplified by the EEC–Canada agreement, is the joint Co-operation Committee set up by the EEC and the other party (without a direct involvement of the Member States) to oversee the implementation and, presumably, to deal with conflicts arising therefrom.

We should also mention in the context of competence the so-called mixed agreements,[12] ie international treaties in which the contracting parties comprise the Community and one or more Member States on the one side and one or more non-Community signatories on the other. Such treaties are not expressly provided for in the EEC Treaty but are evisaged in article 102 of the Euratom Treaty, and therefore, acceptable to the whole Community. Such treaties were considered by the ECJ in the Opinion on Natural Rubber[13] which thought that they were particularly useful to embody multilateral arrangements in cases where the subject matter concerned the Community and individual Member States in such a way that it would be impracticable to negotiate a collective agreement and then subdivide it into a number of agreements each relating to a particular party.

The area we have touched upon is vast and still expanding. What needs to be said in conclusion is that, whilst the founding Treaties

6 OJ 1980, L144/2.
7 Algeria, OJ 1978, L263/2; Morocco, OJ 1978, L264/2; Tunisia, OJ 1978, L265/2; Egypt, OJ 1978, L266/2; Lebanon, OJ 1978, L267/2; Jordan, OJ 1978, L268/2; Syria, OJ 1978, L269/2.
8 Ts 105 (1979); Cmnd 7751; OJ 1976, L25/2; see now Lomé IV of 1989; The Courrier, March-April 1990 pp 56 et seq.
9 OJ 1973, L224/1, renewed 1980. See Gen Report 1980, p 276.
10 OJ 1978, L123/1; see also OJ 1985 C250/2; see Kapur, H, *China and the EEC: The New Connection* (1986).
11 EEC–Canada Agreement, art IV.
12 See further O'Keefe, D and Schermers, H G, *Mixed Agreements* (1983).
13 Opinion 1/78 [1979] ECR 2871, [1979] 3 CMLR 639.

provide a framework for Community external relations and lay down rules regarding exclusive Community competence, the process is still evolving and the original competence of the Member States retained outside the founding Treaties remains to a degree relevant to Treaties within the Community competence. The panorama of Community Treaties[14] reflects a variety of relations ranging from bi-lateral to multi-lateral agreements, various forms of co-operation, preferential and non-preferential trade arrangements, comprehensive agreements as well as commodity agreements. The global strategy for multi-lateral agreements reflects trade relations on a regional basis as well as related to groups of countries and other 'Communities'. Hence the European extension of free trade to the European Free Trade Area (EFTA) countries,[15] association agreements with certain Mediterranean countries,[16] co-operation agreements with the Mediterranean countries of Africa and Asia, agreements of the South-East Asian countries (ASEAN) and certain individual Latin American countries and countries associated in the Cartagena Agreement.[17] However the most spectacular in numbers and geographical extension is the Lomé association convention embracing 66 African, Caribbean and Pacific countries (ACP).

The Community is also involved in tariff negotiations within GATT and participates in the work of the OECD, using the world and regional platform for trade in order to promote and defend its interests.

(b) *Treaty-making procedure*
The founding Treaties lay down the procedures for the exercise of the treaty-making power of the Community. These involve interaction of the Community institutions and agreement between the Member States in Council. Bearing in mind the nuances between the three Treaties the position under the EEC Treaty is as follows:

Accession Treaties
Accession[18] of new members is available to European countries

14 See further, Raux, J, *Les accords externes de la CEE* (1977); Flaesch-Mougin, C, *Les accords externes de la CEE, Essai d'une typologie* (1979) and Stanbrook, C and Hawkes, L W N, 'External Relations', Law of the European Communities, Halsbury's Laws of England (4th edn) Vol 51, 477.
15 Austria, OJ 1972, L300/2; Finland, OJ 1973, L328/2; Iceland, OJ 1972, L301/2; Norway, OJ 1973, L171/2; Portugal, OJ 1972, L301/167; Sweden, OJ 1972, L300/97; Switzerland, OJ 1972, L300/189; See General Report 1978, p 264. See Case 218/83: *Les Rapides Savoyards Sarl v Directeur Général des Douanes et Droit Indirects* [1984] ECR 3105, [1985] 3 CMLR 116.
16 Ie Cyprus, Malta, Turkey (Greece 1963–1981).
17 Ie Bolivia, Colombia, Ecuador, Peru and Venezuela, OJ 1964, L153/1.
18 Art 237; ECSC, art 98; Euratom, art 205.

without any further qualifications. However it can be assumed that further (unwritten) conditions apply, viz that the applicant country must be in the eyes of the existing members a parliamentary democracy capable and willing to carry out the Community obligations. This can be inferred from the experience so far suggesting that the admission of Greece, Spain and Portugal was delayed mainly for political reasons and that Turkey is facing similar difficulties. Indeed the negative opinion[19] regarding the latter suggests further qualifications, viz that the applicant's economy has been aligned to that of the Community, that it has a satisfactory record of human rights and no quarrels with the existing Member States.

The procedure for admission begins with an application to the Council which has to be accepted unanimously and referred to the Commission for its opinion. Since the Treaty does not require a positive opinion it seems that the Council may decide to open negotiations despite an adverse opinion of the Commission. Conversely, any Member State may block the proceedings despite a positive opinion of the Commission. Negotiations that follow are conducted by the Commission under the negotiation mandate imposed by the Council. These negotiations may take a long time. Thus the negotiations on the first British application lasted nearly two years only to be vetoed by France when the United Kingdom was prepared to sign. The negotiations with Greece were long and protracted, ending in 1979 and Greece becoming the tenth Member State on 1 January 1981. The negotiations with Portugal and Spain began formally in 1978 and 1979, respectively, after earlier overtures and favourable opinions of the Commission, the two countries becoming members as from 1 January 1986. The results of the negotiations are enshrined in the Act of Accession which accompanies the Treaty of Accession which signifies, on the one hand, the positive decision of the Council and the agreement of the applicant state on the other, and which has to be ratified by all the contracting states in accordance with their respective constitutions. The Treaty is an instrument of international law whilst being at the same time a 'Community act'. The Treaty and the Act of Accession entail also an amendment of the constituent (founding) Treaty and of the Community law as appropriate. Where the ratification is subject to a referendum the Accession Treaty may be frustrated, as it was in the case of Norway, by the adverse decision of the electorate.

Accession is a political act determined by the states themselves[20]

---

19 Press Conference of Sr Matutes on 18 December 1989, announcing the Commission's opinion.
20 See Case 93/78: *Mattheus v Doego* [1978] ECR 2203, [1979] 1 CMLR 551.

and as such it is not open to judicial scrutiny. In this process the Council acts in a dual role, ie that of an institution representing the collective will of the Member States and that of a gathering of Ministers each representing the interests of its own country. The Commission acts as a purely Community institution as the initiator of policy and the executor of the negotiating mandate laid down by the Council. The Parliament is not formally involved in negotiations but its assent is required.

Association agreements

So far two kinds of association agreements have come to light, ie those with European countries and those with non-European countries specifically envisaged in art 131 of the EEC Treaty.

Association with European countries may be expressly designed to lead to full membership or leave the matter open. However, there is no automatic transition from association to accession. Thus association agreements with Greece of 1963 and Turkey of 1964 offered a prospect of membership but the agreements with Malta and Cyprus have not. Greece became a Member State on 1 January 1981 but Turkey's application of 14 April 1987 was turned down on 18 December 1989.[1] Malta and Cyprus are, at present, considering applying for membership.

Although the terms of the European association differ in detail, the object is to create a customs union between the Community and the associated country and to enable the latter to adjust its economy and so to prepare itself for the assumption of duties consequent upon accession.

The object of the other form of association is, according to article 131(2), to promote the economic and social development of certain non-European countries and territories listed in Annex IV to the EEC Treaty which, in view of their former colonial dependency, have retained a special relationship with some of the Member States or, as critics would have it, to promote a form of neo-colonialism.[2] The developments to date negate the latter suggestion. Indeed according to article 131(3) associations shall serve primarily to further the interests and prosperity of the inhabitants of these countries and territories in order to lead them to the economic, social and cultural development to which they aspire. More precisely, in the light of articles 132–135 of the Treaty the object is to create a customs union between the Community and the

---

1 Commission Opinion and Press Conference on 18 December 1989 of Sr Matutes, member of the Commission responsible for the Mediterranean Policy of the EC.
2 Curzon, *Yearbook of World Affairs* (1971), p 118.

associated states, to encourage investment and economic and commercial co-operation and to regulate on a non-discriminatory basis the right of establishment of nationals and corporations.

Referring specifically to this form of association article 136 of the Treaty provides that multi-lateral agreements shall be made by an implementing convention attached to the Treaty for an initial period of five years to be reviewed and renewed from time to time. However this model was replaced by a negotiated one, which took its name from the capital city where it was signed. The process has gone through six stages of development, ie Yaoundé I (1964), Yaoundé II (1969), with modifications for anglophonic countries, Arusha (1968 and 1969), Lomé I (1975), Lomé II (1979), Lomé III (1984) and now Lomé IV (1989).[3] This reflects an evolution of the relationship between the EEC and, as of now, 66 'developing' African, Caribbean and Pacific Ocean (ACP) countries. The trading position has reached, at present, an almost non-reciprocal level, the only restrictions affecting a fraction of agricultural exports to the EEC, from the ACP countries. Apart from that there are no customs duties and no quantitative restrictions on imports or exports between the parties. The sugar-producing countries have a guarantee regarding the volume of exports and the price, thus contributing to stability in this sector. For the purpose of the origin of goods the EEC treats the ACP countries as one trading unit, thus recognizing the principle of cumulative origin in this respect. The ACP countries grant the EEC the most-favoured-nation treatment in trade and undertake not to discriminate between the Member States. The EEC economic aid, mainly in the form of grants to develop small and medium-sized industries and stabilize the export earnings as well as industrial expertise,[4] is channelled through the Convention to individual countries. The ACP countries receive financial aid from the European Development Fund.

The Convention has established three institutions – a Council of Ministers, a Committee of Ambassadors and a Consultative Assembly – to direct the relations between the Community and the associated states. Any disputes arising under the Convention are initially referred to the Council of Ministers and, in the last resort, to a specified arbitration procedure. The organization has certainly stimulated trade and contributed to the stabilization of the export

3 Lomé II TS 105 (1979); Cmnd 7751; The Courrier, No 58, Special Issue Nov 1979; Kirkpatrick, C H, 'Lomé II', (1980) Journal of World Trade, 352; Lomé III EC 19 (1985); Cmnd 9511; The Courrier, Jan–Feb 1985; Lomé IV The Courrier, March–April 1990, pp 56 et seq.
4 See Case 114/86: *United Kingdom v EC Commission, Re Lomé II Service Contracts* [1989] 1 CMLR 32.

earnings of the ACP states by protecting them against fluctuations in commodity prices.

Irrespective of the type of association the procedure for the making of the association agreements is uniform. Such agreements[5] are concluded by the Council acting unanimously and after receiving the assent of the European Parliament which shall act by an absolute majority of its component members. In practice negotiations are conducted by the Commission under the Council's direction. The Parliament takes no part in the negotiations but has to give its assent as in the case of accession of new members.

Trade agreements
The most numerous are, of course, the trade agreements concluded in the context of the Common Commercial Policy and, as observed earlier, there is a great variety of these corresponding to the Community policy and the interests of the other contracting parties. In accordance with article 113(2)(3) of the EEC Treaty, where agreements with third countries have to be negotiated, the Commission shall make recommendations to the Council which shall, in turn, authorize the Commission to open negotiations. These negotiations are conducted by the Commission in consultation with a special committee appointed for the purpose by the Council within the framework of directives issued by the Council. The mandate and the directives require a decision by a qualified majority of the Council. As from the end of the transitional period the agreements resulting from such negotiations are concluded by the Council taking decisions by a qualified majority in accordance with article 114. The Parliament is not involved formally in the formation of trade agreements but, of course, is free to discuss the issues involved and express opinions. It may also question the members of the Commission and of the Council in the context of the political supervision of the working of the Community.

Implied powers
In view of the limited treaty-making power the Community has the capacity to enter into international agreements strictly within the limits of the Treaty, each type of agreement being governed by specified Treaty provisions. However where the relevant article appears insufficient to carry out the intention of the parties article 235 may be called in aid. Thus, for example, the conclusion of the framework agreement with Canada and the international rubber agreement was supported by reference to article 235 under which unanimity is required.

5 EEC, art 238 (2); Euratom, art 206 (2) amended by art 9 of SEA.

Agreements in general: rôles of Council and Commission

Article 228(1) of the EEC Treaty contains a general formula regarding the procedure for the conclusion of agreements between the Community and one or more states or an international organization where such agreements are envisaged by the Treaty. Such agreements are to be negotiated by the Commission and, subject to the powers vested in the Commission in this field, concluded by the Council, after consulting the European Parliament where required by the Treaty. Although the role of the Commission is only subsidiary in the procedure for the admission of new members it enjoys a wider rôle in other cases. However, as exemplified in the negotiations for the EEC-Canada[6] agreement, the Council as the co-ordinator of the general economic policies of the Member States and the representative of the Member States' sovereignty holds the lever of power and, in concrete situations, will lay down the conditions and the negotiating points in order to accommodate the interests of individual Member States and thus bring about the consensus necessary for the conclusion of the agreements but may not frustrate the Commission's power of initiative.[7]

The respective rôles of the Council and the Commission under the terms of article 228(1) have been settled in Court in the ERTA[8] case.

In January 1962, under the auspices of the UN Economic Commission for Europe, a European Road Transport Agreement (ERTA) was signed by a number of European states including five of the members of the Community. That Agreement has not yet come into force because of an insufficient number of ratifications. In 1967 negotiations were resumed to revise the ERTA. In 1969 the Council of the Communities made a regulation dealing with the harmonization of certain social provisions in the field of road transport. In March 1970 at a meeting of the Council the attitude to be taken by the Member States of the Communities in the final stage of the ERTA negotiations to be held in April 1970 was discussed. Those negotiations were then undertaken and concluded by the Member States in the light of that discussion and the Economic Commission for Europe declared that the ERTA would be open for signature from July 1970. In May 1970 the Commission of the Communities instituted proceedings seeking an annulment of the Council's discussion of March 1970 on the grounds that the Council had acted in breach of article 228 of the EEC Treaty. This

---

6 See Lasok, op cit, note 4, p 63; supra at pp 587–589.
7 See Case 217/86, note (9), p 60, supra.
8 Case 22/70: *EC Commission v EC Council, Re European Road Transport Agreement* [1971] ECR 263, [1971] CMLR 335.

challenge raised the wider issue of the relative rôles of Council and Commission in the conduct of the Community's external relations.

The Court stated that under article 228 the right to conclude an agreement with non-Member States lay with the Council, with the Commission cast in the rôle of negotiator. But those institutions could only play those rôles under the authority of either an express Treaty provision or a decision taken under the Treaty. The bulk of the negotiations for the ERTA had been concluded before the Community had a developed transport policy, therefore the Community as such had no authority to negotiate and ratify the ERTA. At the time of the Council discussions which were in issue, the ERTA negotiations had already reached such an advanced stage that it would have jeopardized the whole Agreement to have attempted to reopen them. Thus the Court held that the procedures specified in article 228 were clearly inapplicable. The only obligation on the Member States was to ensure that nothing was done to prejudice the interests of the Community and so that the Council in co-ordinating the attitudes of Member States to the ERTA in the light of Community interests had acted quite properly. Thus even where the provisions of the Treaties are not directly applicable to the external relations of the Member States they are nevertheless under a continuing obligation, under the terms of article 5 of the EEC Treaty, to 'abstain from any measure which could jeopardise the attainment of the objectives of the Treaty'.

(c) *Signing of Treaties*
Community external Treaties or agreements negotiated in accordance with the requisite procedures are signed on behalf of the Community by the President of the Council who is usually the Minister of External Affairs of the Member State holding the presidency at the time of the signing. Accession Treaties and association agreements have to be signed and ratified on behalf of all Member States.

(d) *Judicial control*
The Community Court plays no part in the exercise of the Community treaty-making power though within its overall mission of seeing that the law is observed it has the power of judicial review of the Community acts. Indeed the Council, the Commission or a Member State may obtain from the ECJ an opinion whether an agreement envisaged is compatible with the founding Treaty.[9] Should the opinion be adverse the agreement would enter into force only following an amendment of the Treaty.

---

9 EEC, art 228 (2); Euratom, art 103 (3), see supra.

(e) *Substitution*

The Community may also assume obligations under an international agreement without actually negotiating and signing it. This occurs in International Law by virtue of substitution with the consent of all parties concerned. The example of the GATT springs to mind in this respect as the Community has assumed the rights and duties vested in the Member States of the Community though strictly it is not a member of that organization.[10] Indeed formal accession would reduce its voting power to one whilst in the present situation the Community, being the spokesman for the whole collective, can count on as many as twelve votes. It is arguable that the Community should also become party to the European Convention on Human Rights but there are several obstacles to formal accession, one of which is that the Convention is open only to states and the Community is not a state as yet. However in practice the ECJ will apply the Convention as one of the sources of general principles of law.[11]

(f) *Euratom and ECSC Treaties*

The negotiation and conclusion of Euratom agreements is in the hands of the Commission acting under the direction of the Council[12] which signifies its consent by a qualified majority. However agreements or contracts whose implementation does not require action by the Council and can be effected within the limits of the relevant budget are negotiated and concluded solely by the Commission though the Commission must keep the Council informed.

There are no provisions in the ECSC Treaty regarding the formation of international agreements. In practice the Commission negotiates and concludes such agreements on behalf of the Community within the framework of the Treaty and Part II of the Convention on the Transitional Provisions attached to the Treaty.

(g) *Effects of Community external Treaties*

Effect on the Community legal order
Under the EEC Treaty external Community Treaties are binding upon the institutions and the Member States.[13] Though no such provision can be found either in the Euratom or the ECSC Treaties it is assumed that the EEC formula has a universal application

---

10 See Joined Cases 21–24/72: *International Fruit Co v Produktschap voor Groenten en Fruit* [1972] ECR 1219, [1975] 2 CMLR 1.
11 See infra.
12 Euratom, art 101.
13 Art 228 (2).

within the Community legal order. Consequently there is a duty of compliance with the terms of the Treaties both upon the institutions and the Member States. Thus in ensuring respect for commitments arising from an agreement concluded by the institutions, the Member States fulfil an obligation not only in relation to the non-member country concerned but also for due performance of the agreement.[14]

Community Treaties are published in the Official Journal and, being in the nature of legal acts, they form an integral part of the Community legal order[15] and may be cited before the ECJ as well as the national courts. In the hierarchy of the Community legal norms they can be placed in a middle position between the founding Treaties with which they ought to be compatible and the Community legislative acts over which they may claim superiority by virtue of international law. However their effect depends upon their specific provisions, ie whether or not they are directly applicable. The problem did arise in connection with claims based upon the GATT and association agreements.

Faced with a claim that an EC regulation restricting the importation of fruit from a non-Community country contravened the rules of the GATT the ECJ held that the supremacy of International Law should be respected but concluded that, *in casu*, the relevant provision of the GATT was neither binding nor capable of conferring any directly enforceable rights upon the private party concerned.[16] In such a case any conflict should be resolved between the Community and the GATT institutions. The Court also held in another case[17] that an EC regulation providing for compensatory amounts to offset the fluctuations in the value of currency did not contravene the GATT and, therefore, was valid. Clearly the ruling would have been different had the GATT rules imposed a duty upon the Community and conferred a corresponding right upon the party concerned.

---

14 Case 104/81: *HZA Mainz v Kupfenberg* [1982] ECR 3641 at 3662, [1983] 1 CMLR 1 at 20; see also Case 253/83: *Sektkellerei Kupfenberg v HZA Mainz, Re Sherry Wine from Spain* [1985] ECR 157; [1987] 1 CMLR 36.

15 See Ruling 1/78 [1978] ECR 2151 at 2180, [1979] 1 CMLR 131 at 160. See Case C-182/89: *EC Commission v France*, OJ 1990, C 319/8 where the ECJ held the importation of feline skins in contravention of the Convention on International Trade in endangered species of wild fauna and flora to be a breach of arts 5 and 189 of the EEC Treaty.

16 See Joined Cases 21–24/72, note 10, supra and also Joined Cases 267–269/81: *Amministrazione delle Finanze dello Stato v SPI* [1983] ECR 801, [1984] 1 CMLR 354; Case 266/81: *SIOT v Ministero delle Finance* [1983] ECR 731; [1984] 2 CMLR 231; Case 38/75: *Nederlandse Spoorwegen v Inspecteur der Invoerrechten en Accijnzen* [1975] ECR 1439, [1976] 1 CMLR 167.

17 Case 9/73: *Schlüter v HZA Lörrach* [1973] ECR 1135.

Effect on Member States

Two questions arise as regards the effect upon the Member States of the Community, ie whether in their relations between themselves they can derogate from their duties to the Community by virtue of prior international obligations and whether their existing international obligations to third countries falling within the scope of the founding Treaties have been affected by their Community obligations.

In the *Radio Valves*[18] case Italy claimed that she was free to apply customs duties established under an agreement[19] made within the framework of the GATT and thus evade the duty of reducing the tariff rates imposed by the EEC Treaty. The ECJ ruled that Italy was unable to do so because within its specific domain the founding Treaty takes precedence over agreements concluded between the Member States before they have set up the Community and these include agreements made under the auspices of the GATT. However the scope of this ruling is limited since it applies only to agreements made between the Member States themselves and not between the Member States and non-Community countries. The latter are subject to specific provisions of the founding Treaties.[20]

The *Radio Valves* case has to be distinguished from the *Plants Inspection*[1] case where the Netherlands successfully pleaded the International Plant Protection Convention[2] against the contention that, by imposing phytosanitary inspection of plants exported to other Member States as well as certificates and fees, that Member State has introduced charges having equivalent effect to customs duties prohibited in inter-state trade under the EEC Treaty. Far from being incompatible with the Community law the Convention was considered by the ECJ to perform a function similar to that of the public health and phytosanitary measures adopted by a Community directive whilst the fees were acceptable as long as they did not exceed the actual costs of the operation. Moreover the simultaneous application of the Convention would promote rather than hinder Community trade. However in the *Van Wesemeal*[3] case the Court held that Belgium could not rely on an International Labour Organization Convention[4] sanctioning fee-charging

---

18 Case 10/61: *EC Commission v Italy* [1962] ECR1, [1962] CMLR 187.
19 Geneva Protocol 6 of 23 May 1956.
20 EEC, art 234; but see Euratom, art 106 and ECSC, art 75.
 1 Case 89/76: *EC Commission v The Netherlands* [1977] ECR 1355, [1978] 3 CMLR 630.
 2 Rome Convention of 1951, TS 16 (1954); Cmnd 9077.
 3 Joined Cases 110, 111/78: *Ministère Public v Van Wesemeal* [1979] ECR 35, [1979] 3 CMLR 87.
 4 Convention No 196; Geneva 1949, Cmnd 7852.

employment agencies in order to derogate from the free movement of services in the Community. Similarly, concerning the labelling of cheese in intra-Community trade, the ECJ held that multi-lateral treaties cannot be pleaded against Community law if only the EC Member States are involved.[5] These cases show that in the relations inter se the Member States must give precedence to their Community obligations over the rights they may claim under international instruments.

The answer to the second question is to be found in article 234 of the EEC Treaty which is both a guarantee of stability and a harbinger of change. Stability of the established international relations and respect for vested rights is assured by paragraph 1 which has adopted the principle of *inter alios facta* of classic International Law enshrined in article 30 of the 1969 Vienna Convention on Treaties. Accordingly the membership of the Community leaves undisturbed the rights and obligations arising from Treaties to which the Member States and third countries are parties. Whilst the relations with third parties are safeguarded 'only in matters governed by the EEC Treaty that Treaty takes precedence over agreements concluded between Member States before its entry into force'.[6]

The second paragraph contains a harbinger of change as it enjoins the Member States to adjust their existing international obligations to their duties to the Community and their fellow members. Thus they ought to use their opportunity, eg when such Treaties come up for revision or renewal, in order to eliminate incompatibilities. They are not expected to break their Treaties but to renegotiate their terms and, when doing so, adopt a common stance where appropriate. In this process they are assisted by Council Decision 69/494[7] which provides for the progressive standardization of agreements concerning commercial relations between Member States and third countries and rules on the negotiation of Community agreements. This Decision gives the Commission the necessary supervisory and co-ordinating powers but also enables it to recommend to the Council the express or tacit extension of the existing agreements. It has postulated the replacement of national bi-lateral agreements by Community bi-lateral agreements by the end of 1972. This, however, has proved a forlorn hope since the deadline has already been extended[8] several times and uniformity is not yet in sight. The problem is more difficult than it might seem because trade agreements usually form part of a

5 Case 286/86: *Ministère Public v Déserbais* [1989] 1 CMLR 516.
6 Case 10/61, note 18, supra, at 10.
7 OJ Sp Ed 1969, p 603.
8 Recent extension, Council decision 90/225, OJ 1990, L120/72.

complex package deal and Community obligations cannot be easily isolated.

With reference to article 234 of the EEC Treaty the ECJ[9] conceded that it did not alter the nature of private rights or duties derived from pre-membership or pre-accession Treaties between the Member States and third countries. It held, accordingly, that the London Fisheries Convention of 1964 which governed maritime relations between Ireland and Spain prevailed over Community law. Since, however, the national law was held to be applicable in the circumstances the penalties for illegal fishing prescribed by it and imposed upon a Spanish trawlerman were not incompatible with the interim fishery regime imposed by the Council Regulation 1376/78 designed to promote a framework of the relations between Spain and the Community. As from the accession of Spain the matter has been subject to the Act of Accession.

Effect on individuals

Since the Community embraces not only the Member States but also their citizens Community external treaties affect individuals too. Being part of the Community *corpus juris* these treaties may be pleaded not only before the ECJ but also before national courts and thence referred to ECJ for interpretation should a national court find this necessary. Individual rights depend, of course, upon the nature of the Treaty, ie whether it is an accession or association or trade agreement and also on the specific provision contained therein, that is whether or not it has a direct effect.

Thus a Belgian[10] importer of wine from Greece could not be absolved from the payment of a countervailing charge imposed by Belgian law by virtue of a Community regulation because the association agreement with Greece upon which he relied, although providing for free access of the product to the common market, did not exempt levies designed to eliminate disturbance of the market. Similarly a German[11] importer of tomato concentrates from Greece could not successfully challenge a Community regulation designed to protect the industry in Italy by raising the price since the association agreement allowed the Community to regulate the import and the price of the product. However, a French[12] importer of bananas could rely on the Yaoundé Convention (a predecessor

---

9 Case 812/79: *A-G v Burgoa* [1980] ECR 2787, [1981] 2 CMLR 193.
10 Case 181/73: *Haegeman v Belgium* [1974] ECR 449 at 459, 460, [1975] 1 CMLR 515 at 530.
11 Case 40/72: *Schroeder v Germany* [1973] ECR 125, [1973] CMLR 824.
12 Case 48/74: *Charmasson v Minister of Economic Affairs* [1974] ECR 1383, [1975] 2 CMLR 208.

of the Lomé Convention) not only to have his case referred to the ECJ for a preliminary ruling but also to defeat the preference of his government for suppliers of bananas from former French colonies; and an Italian[13] importer of hide from Senegal was afforded protection under the same Convention from the imposition of health inspection fees chargeable under Italian law. Not so fortunate was a Madagascan[14] lawyer with French professional qualifications as he was unable to practise law at the Paris Bar because the Lomé Convention did not provide for free access to the professions or freedom to offer services in the Community for the nationals of the ACP countries. Similarly unfortunate was a Turkish wife who came to join her husband in Germany but could not rely on article 12 of the Ankara Agreement which provides that the parties are to be 'guided' by the provisions of the EEC Treaty for the purpose of securing freedom of movement for workers. Since the Agreement was not in the nature of 'self-executing treaties' but its efficacy depended upon the decisions taken by the Council of the Association, the provision was held to have no direct effect, ie it created no enforceable rights.[15] Although the decisions of the Council of Association were held to be binding upon the parties their effects upon the individuals were determined by their specific provisions. Therefore, as exemplified in an English reference for a preliminary ruling arising from the EEC–Portugal[16] free trade agreement, it is essential to consider the nature and scope of the agreement in order to ask the Court the relevant questions and, indeed, assess its impact upon the rights of individuals or, as put by the ECJ,[17] account must be taken of the whole agreement in order to focus attention on the real issues before the Court.

In the English jurisdiction judicial notice was taken of the EEC–Portugal Agreement of 1972 as the Court of Appeal[18] held that it was directly applicable by virtue of section 1 (2) of the European Communities Act 1972. However the Court referred to the ECJ the question whether article 14 of the Agreement prohibiting quantitative restrictions on imports and exports had a direct effect so as to prevail over section 16 (2) of the UK Copyright Act 1956. The

---

13 Case 87/75: *Bresciani v Amministrazione delle Finanze dello Stato* [1976] ECR 129, [1976] 2 CMLR 62.
14 Case 65/77: *Re Jean Razanatsimba* [1977] ECR 2229, [1978] 1 CMLR 246.
15 Case 12/86: *Demirel v Stadt Schwabisch Gmünd* [1987] ECR 3719; [1989] 1 CMLR 421; see also Case C-192/89: *Sevince v Staatsecretaris van Justitie* (judgment 20 September 1989 unreported); and *R v Secretary of State for the Home Department, ex p Narin* (*expulsion of a Turkish national from the UK*) [1990] 2 CMLR 233, CA.
16 OJ 1972, L301/165; Council Reg 2844/72.
17 Case 253/83, note 14, p 73 supra, [1987] 1 CMLR 36 at 55.
18 *Polydor Ltd v Harlequin Record Shops Ltd* [1980] 2 CMLR 413.

ECJ,[19] citing its own judgment in the Terrapin[20] case, held that the enforcement by the proprietor of the copyright protected by national law was justified within the terms of article 23 of the EEC–Portugal Agreement which provided that 'The Agreement shall not preclude prohibitions or restrictions on imports, exports or goods in transit justified on grounds of . . . the protection of industrial and commercial property . . .'. Therefore the enforcement did not constitute any restriction on trade envisaged in article 14 (2) of the said Agreement. The reference seemed unnecessary since the relationship between the EEC and Portugal did not create a common market or a custom union and the case had to be so distinguished.

Another aspect of an EEC trade agreement was raised in the English jurisdiction in a case[1] involving the export of oil to a destination inconsistent with the United Kingdom policy. In a contract A agreed to sell to B a quantity of British North Sea crude oil, 'the destination to be free but always within the exporting country's government policy'. When A learned that the oil was intended for Israel A and the supplier refused to load the oil aboard the ship nominated by B on the ground that delivery to Israel was contrary to the UK policy. After arbitration and protracted litigation in the UK during which the EEC law and the EEC–Israel Agreement were considered the matter came before the ECJ for a preliminary ruling. The ECJ held that the Agreement did not prohibit the imposition of new quantitative restrictions or measures having equivalent effect on exports from a Member State to Israel and that the Council Regulation 2603/69 establishing common rules for exports likewise did not prohibit such restrictions. Moreover articles 34 and 85 (concerning exports and restrictive practices, respectively) did not prevent a Member State from adopting a restrictive policy, subject to certain conditions as the trade involved was not a trade between Member States. If the conditions under which restrictions contrary to articles 34 and 85 were not observed, when for example the Member State concerned failed to give notice to the Commission in accordance with the established procedure, such a failure on the part of a Member State would not create individual rights which national courts were required to protect.

As in the previous cases the rights of individuals depend on the terms of the Agreement.

---

19 Case 270/80 [1982] ECR 329, [1982] 1 CMLR 677.
20 Case 119/75: *Terrapin v Terranova* [1976] ECR 1039 at 1061, [1976] 2 CMLR 482 at 526.
 1 Case 174/84: *Bulk Oil (Zug) v Sun International (No 2)* [1986] 2 All ER 744, [1986] 2 CMLR 732.

(c) *jus missionis*

To carry out their functions in the international setting the Communities have to maintain contacts with non-Member States and international organizations. Customarily these contacts are effected through diplomatic missions accredited to foreign sovereigns. Their main task is to represent the sending sovereign and articulate his position, gather intelligence and pass it on to the authorities at home. The *jus missionis*, an attribute of legal personality at International Law, is governed by time-honoured custom supplemented by bi-lateral Treaties and modern Conventions. However the latter are of little use to the Communities because the 1961 Vienna Convention on Diplomatic Relations applies only to states whilst the 1975 Vienna Convention applicable to world organizations only has not as yet been accepted by the Member States of the Community. Therefore the exercise of the *jus missionis* of the Communities rests upon their claim to international legal personality and the recognition by the countries and international organizations with whom they have established relations. International customary and conventional law applies only by analogy whilst the established practice tends to create precedents and rules of conduct.

In the sense of the 'internal' Community law the right to enter into diplomatic relations is based on the Community's legal personality complemented by the Protocol on the Privileges and Immunities of the European Communities attached to the Merger Treaty of 1965.[2] Article 17 of the Protocol provides that the Member States in whose territory the Communities have their seat shall accord the customary diplomatic immunities and privileges to missions of third countries accredited to the Communities. Since diplomatic relations are normally conducted on the basis of reciprocity it is common ground that the countries concerned have not only recognized the legal personality of the Community but will also extend the same courtesy to its representatives who will enjoy diplomatic immunity and rank according to the diplomatic list.[3] In the course of time a network of diplomatic relations has been established either informally or by formal agreements. So far some 137 countries (including the Vatican and the USSR) have established relations with all three or any one of the Communities. Their representatives are stationed in Brussels, the unofficial capital of

---

2 Ie the Treaty of Brussels establishing a Single Council and a Single Commission of the European Communities.
3 See Case 5/68: *Sayag v Leduc* [1968] ECR 395, [1969] CMLR 12; Case 9/69: *Sayag v Leduc* [1969] ECR 329.

the Communities, but most of these are also accredited to Belgium. Therefore Belgium accords them the same status.[4]

The principle applies to Community civil servants. Therefore Belgium[5] was in breach of art 12(b) of the Protocol (and consequently of art 5 of the EEC Treaty) by not taking the necessary measures to ensure that the byelaws of certain municipalities exempt Community civil servants and other officials and the members of their families from the requirement of registration and tax on their properties situated in these municipalities. Similarly, in a subsequent case,[6] Belgium was condemned for refusing to grant reductions in tax on income from immovable property where, by virtue of art 13(2) of the Protocol the tenants or their spouses are exempt from national taxes on salaries, wages and emoluments paid by the Community. However, the denial of mortgage relief (available in the United Kingdom to taxpayers irrespective of their nationality) to Community civil servants who are exempt from UK taxation and so ineligible for mortgage relief, does not constitute a breach of EC privileges and immunities.[7]

Historically the United Kingdom and Sweden in 1952 were the first countries to send a permanent delegation to the High Authority of the ECSC,[8] followed by Japan in 1954. The United States Ambassador was the first diplomat accredited to the EEC[9] in 1958.

The procedure of accreditation is at present governed by the Accords de Luxembourg.[10] The decision to establish diplomatic relations is taken by the Council unanimously, each Member State having a right of veto regarding every mission and every individual representative. The letters of credence are submitted separately to the President of the Council and the President of the Commission. The doyen of the diplomatic corps accredited to the Community is the Apostolic Nuncio as has been the tradition in relations between Christian countries.

The representatives of the Community abroad have no uniform status; even their official titles and the designation of the missions differ from country to country. The first mission was installed in London following the agreement with the ECSC in 1955 though

4 Virally, M, Gerbet, P, Salmon, J, *Les missions permanentes auprès des organisations internationales* (1971), p 722.
5 Case 85/85: *EC Commission v Belgium (Re registration of Community officials for municipal tax on residencies)*, [1986] ECR 1149; [1987] 1 CMLR 787 at para 27.
6 Case 260/86: *EC Commission v Belgium* [1988] ECR 955; [1989] 3 CMLR 103 at para 12.
7 Case C-33/88: *Tither v IRC* [1990] 2 CMLR 779.
8 First General Report ECSC, points 14 and 15.
9 First General Report EEC, point 168.
10 Ninth General Report, EEC, pp 31–33; EC Bull 3/66.

the first diplomatic representative of the three Communities was accredited to the United Kingdom only in 1968. The second mission was set up in Washington in 1972 and then in 1974 in Tokyo by virtue of a formal agreement between the Commission and Japan.

The first mission to an international organization was installed in Geneva in 1964 to cover the GATT, the ILO, the United Nations Economic Commission for Europe and later UNCTAD. The originally unofficial mission to the United Nations Organization HQ in New York has enjoyed diplomatic status since 1976. There is also a mission to OECD and UNESCO in Paris and to the International Atomic Energy Agency in Vienna.

The existence of diplomatic missions has not only enhanced the international status of the Community and facilitated the negotiations of trade agreements but also contributed to the development of the base for the Community external relations.

Chapter 3

The nature and challenge of Community law

1 The meaning of Community law

It is axiomatic that a body which itself is a distinct legal entity will have its own law either infused into its forms by a superior legislator or generated by its organs or both. In the Community legal order both elements are present: the law of the Treaty and the law generated by the Community organs. Moreover, a certain area of the law will be enacted by the Member States themselves in accordance with the Treaty and, although this law is, strictly speaking, a product of the sovereign legislatures of the Member States it should be included in the wider concept of Community law.[1] These are the dimensions of Community law in the light of its sources. However, before analysing the sources of Community law it seems necessary to consider its nature and scope. This is particularly important from a British point of view, bearing in mind that at accession there was a wholesale reception of Community law and that since accession we have participated in a legislative process which differs considerably from our own.

Community law defies the accepted classifications of law; it is both international and municipal, public and private, substantive and procedural, enacted and formulated in precedents. It is a *sui generis* law and must be treated as such. Therefore it has to be studied in its international setting with due attention to its impact upon the laws of the Member States and the quasi-autonomous law-making capacity of the Community organs.

The three Communities, being a result of Treaties, are subject to public International Law but constitute their own legal order. The treaty obligations are defined in terms of duties of states vis-à-vis the contracting parties and the Community itself, whilst the rights and obligations of individuals derive directly from the

---

1 The Second European Conference of Law Faculties held in April 1971 in Strasbourg under the aegis of the Council of Europe recommended that the authorities in Member States be urged to introduce or reinforce the teaching of (1) the law of European Organizations, (2) the substantive law created by or within European Organizations, and (3) the law of European States.

Treaties. Therefore Community Law is to the Member States both 'external' (ie derived from outside) and 'internal' (ie in force in their territories).

The execution of the Treaties is in the hands of the Community organs and the Community Court has the exclusive power of authoritative interpretation of the Treaties (art 177(1)).[2] Disputes between states (art 182) and complaints against states (arts 169 and 170) are resolved judicially in a manner appropriate to inter-state relations rather than relations between private parties where the court exercises a sovereign authority. In other words, unlike individuals who have no choice, states submit to the jurisdiction of the Court either by agreement (art 182) or by virtue of treaty obligations. Indeed article 219 expressly provides that disputes between the Member States arising from the interpretation and application of the Treaty must be resolved according to the methods provided in the Treaty. In adjudicating upon disputes in which states are involved the Court, like the International Court of Justice, determines the legal position of the parties and recommends, rather than orders, the state in default to take the necessary measures to comply with the judgment (art 171). The sanctions are also limited (arts 169 and 171) and appropriate to the status of states at International Law. The cardinal rule of public International Law that states, large and small, are equal applies in principle within the Community though in the decision-making process of the Community consideration is given to the size of the Member States.

However, the Community, as stated by the Community Court,[3] 'constitutes a new legal order in International Law for whose benefit the states have limited their sovereign rights, albeit within limited fields, and the subjects of which comprise not only the Member States but also their nationals'. It corresponds to the territorial law of a state.

By incorporation of the Treaties into the municipal law of the Member States Community law becomes part of the internal legal structure of the Member States. Moreover, in the process of the approximation of laws a wide area of economic law will, in due course, become uniform throughout the Community. However, although Community measures enacted into the national systems are both Community and municipal law the ECJ[4] insists that they must not lose their identity, and their Community character in

2 Unless otherwise stated references are to articles of the EEC Treaty.
3 In Case 26/62: *Van Gend en Loos v Nederlandse Administratie der Belastingen* [1963] ECR 1 at 29, [1963] CMLR 105 at 129.
4 See Case 34/73: *Variola SpA v Amministrazione delle Finanze dello Stato* [1973] ECR 981 at para 11.

the process for, should this happen, the ECJ's power to give a preliminary ruling upon the validity or interpretation of a measure 'lost' in the national system, would be frustrated.

It is apposite to mention in this context the conflict of laws or private International Law. It is a system of rules designed to facilitate enforcement of foreign judgments and to solve problems which involve a foreign element and, therefore, in justice and convenience cannot be left to the exclusive power of domestic law. Each country has its own conflict rules. However, the primary object of the Community is cohesion. This is achieved partly by incorporation of Community law into the municipal systems and partly by approximation of laws in the areas of a specific Community interest. In this way it is expected conflicts will be eliminated. Outside the scope of Community law the Member States are left to their own devices as to how to solve the problems arising from the co-existence of several systems of law, though the Community promotes a rational approach to jurisdiction and the enforcement of foreign judgments in the territory of the Member States (art 220).[5] A process of approximation of substantive rules of the Conflict of Laws has begun with a Draft Convention on the Law applicable to Contractual and Non-Contractual Obligations[6] but so far resulted in the 1980 Convention on the Law applicable to Contractual Obligations,[7] the provisions regarding Non-Contractual Obligations having been abandoned in the process. Approximation in other fields has been slow and haphazard.[8]

The once (so it seemed)[9] clear-cut distinction between public and private law has been blurred in the course of time. If we consider that public law is concerned with the organization of the state and the relations between the citizen and the state whilst private law governs relations between individuals and/or corporations we shall observe that Community law contains both elements. It has an impact upon the constitutions and public powers of the Member States, it is concerned with the creation of

---

5 Cf Convention on Jurisdiction and the Enforcement of Judgments in Civil and Commercial Matters 1968; original text OJ 1978, L304/36; amended text OJ 1983, C97/2; see Lasok, D and Stone, P A, *Conflict of Laws in the European Community* (1987), Appendix I.

6 Lando, O, et al, *European Private International Law of Obligations* (1975).

7 Original text [1979] 2 CMLR 776; final text OJ 1980, L266; Lasok and Stone, op cit, Appendix III.

8 See Lasok, D *The Law of the Economy in the European Communities* (1980), pp 393 et seq.

9 Publicum jus est, quod ad statum rei Romanae spectat, privatum quod ad singulorum utilitatem: sunt enim quaedam publice utilia, quoadem privatim, *Digesta* 1, 1, 1, 2; cf Llewellyn, K, *The Bramble Bush* (1960), p 18.

a supra-national organization out of the pooled sovereignty of the Member States and brings the citizen politically and in his economic activities face to face with a supra-national authority and a new 'European' allegiance. Private law relations (and here we can safely discard the controversy whether 'commercial law' is 'private law' or a separate branch of the law) are affected too but only to a degree, that is to say in so far as the economic policies enforced by Community law impinge upon such relations. As legal machinery is used for the execution of the economic policies enshrined in the Treaty some aspects of Community law can be described for the want of a better term as 'economic law' or the law of the economy. This phenomenon, characteristic of the Community, will be considered in detail.[10] The bulk of private law relations comprised in the law of contract, tort, property, family relations (though family status determined by national law is relevant to immigration and social security rights) and succession remains outside the scope of Community law. So does criminal law, though criminal sanctions will have to be developed in order to check abuses of the Community system.[11]

True to the civil law tradition the corpus of Community law has been laid down in treaties and derivative legislation but it would be a mistake to assume that precedent plays no active role in the Community law-making process. We shall discuss the sources of Community law in detail and it may suffice to say that the Community Court, like the French Counseil d'Etat to which it has some resemblance, often has an opportunity of explaining the law and laying down rules in precedents and it has not refrained from using this power. As practice develops the Community Court tends to follow its own decisions in the spirit of *jurisprudence constante*[12] but will not hesitate to deviate for good reason.[13] And so the Court considers itself free to decide in a different way the same legal point if it arises between different parties and in a different context.[14]

Without attempting a definition of Community law (which, incidentally, cannot be found in the Treaties) we should reiterate that

10 See Part IV, below.
11 See Bridge, J W, 'The European Communities and the Criminal Law', *Criminal Law Review*, February 1976, p 88; Wood, J, 'The Communities and the Criminal Law', in *In Memoriam J D B Mitchell* (1983), pp 211 et seq; Lasok, D *The Customs Law of the European Economic Community* (2nd edn 1990) Ch 7.
12 Eg Case 32/58: *Aciéries du Temple v High Authority of the European Coal and Steel Community* [1959] ECR 127.
13 Eg Case 48/72: *Brasserie de Haecht v Wilkin-Janssen* [1973] ECR 77, [1973] CMLR 287.
14 Eg Cases 28–30/62: *Da Costa en Schaake NV v Nederlandse Administratie der Belastingen* [1963] ECR 31, [1963] CMLR 224.

Community law consists of that portion of public international law which governs treaties and international institutions, of the Treaties and their Annexes, of the rules generated by the Community organs and those portions of the municipal laws of the Member States which they are bound to enact in the execution of their obligations. These are not distinct branches but merely the dimensions of Community law.

2 The challenge of Community law

Community law is a new legal order but to a British lawyer it is also an alien order because it has emanated from the civil law systems and, despite the British participation in the legislative process, remains under the civil law influence. This does not necessarily mean that it is inferior or oppressive, as has been suggested from time to time in the passion of debate, but that it is simply different from ours. It should be borne in mind that in its background lies the philosophy of sophisticated, long-established legal systems and the will to create a Community through legal integration of which the enacted law is the preferred instrument. Being intertwined with the legal systems of the founder states Community law cannot be isolated from these but historically and philosophically has to be seen as a child of civil law and as more civil law countries join the Community its influence continues and grows.

In order to make a valid comparison between civil law and common law and thus elicit some general features of the Community legal system it will first be necessary to debunk some popular myths. There is in England some, albeit unfounded, aversion to codes of law and even the Code Napoléon, of which the French are justly proud, does not escape criticism as if no branch of English law had been codified or codification had not been the long-term aim of the Law Commission. Critics believe that codes of law stultify the growth of the law and turn it into a pool of stagnant water whilst common law for ever remains a stream of fresh water. Forgetting that codes are essentially a work of compromise they assume that they are the tools of autocracy. Moreover, it is readily assumed that, whilst in this country we are governed by the wisdom of judges contained in precedents, the continentals are denied this privilege and, because of their rejection of *stare decisis*, suffer from the uncertainty of the law. It would be futile to recite the various misconceptions in order to rebut them. What has to be recognized is the fact that despite their common Romano-Christian roots the evolution of the civil law and common law systems happens to differ and that as a result two different legal styles have developed. Comparative studies help one to understand these differences but, not being engaged in a comparative study, we have to content ourselves with a few generalities. Because we have joined the Community as a going concern, with a legal system well on its way, the British lawyer has to face the unprecedented challenge of the continental legal style.[15]

Codes of law are not mere comprehensive, systematically arranged statutes. In a sense they are also codes of morals for in their legal institutions, especially general principles of the law, they offer guidelines to a way of life. The law tends to proceed from general principles to particular rules of conduct and so the administration of justice tends to be deductive rather than inductive. Contrast the British fragmentary legislation and tightly drafted statutes which, according to Lord Scarman,[16] 'are elaborate to the point of complexity; detailed to the point of unintelligibility; yet strangely uninformative on matters of principle'. The English administration of justice tends, therefore, to be inductive, so much so that one can say that we have a system of remedies established by precedent and statute rather than a plain statement of rights and duties from which remedies can be deduced. Community law follows this latter style as it tends to prescribe the right conduct for governments and individuals and grants remedies in the event of deviation.

The codes of law, being systems of generalities, provide but a façade for case law, because decided cases are the real witness of the living law. However, in view of the supremacy of legislation and the constitutionally limited power of judges to adjudicate not *legislate*, precedents have only a persuasive authority and cannot be cited as the source of law or superior authority. The theory that codes have no gaps enables the courts to legislate by way of extensive interpretation from analogy or simply through *equitas*. The European Court of Justice is in a similar position though its scope for legislative activities is wider than that of the civil courts of the Member States.

In England the judge comes, as a rule, from the Bar and remains a member of his Inn of Court even when elevated to the Bench. On the Continent the judge is a product of special training and a judicial career, he stands aloof from the Bar and resembles more an academic lawyer than an advocate. The English administration

---

15 See Lord Denning MR in *H P Bulmer Ltd v J Bollinger SA* [1974] 2 All ER 1226 at 1231–1232, [1974] 2 CMLR 91 at 119 and 120; Scarman, Sir Leslie, *English Law: The New Dimension*, Hamlyn Lectures, Twenty-sixth Series, 1974, pp 21 et seq.
16 BBC Third Programme, *The Listener*, 9 January 1969, pp 44–46.

of justice has a strong personal flavour because as a rule the judge sits alone and delivers a personal judgment of 'his court'. In the Court of Appeal or the House of Lords, though no longer alone, he still delivers his personal, concurring or dissenting, judgment which often conceals an advocate in judicial robes. The continental judge, as a rule, sits as a member of a team, does not deliver his individual judgment whether or not he agrees with the judgment of his brethren and so preserves a kind of judicial anonymity. The European Court of Justice is a 'continental' court in all respects, sits as a team and delivers a single judgment. It is assisted by Advocates-General (an office unknown in this country), whose functions shall be considered elsewhere.[17]

The style of the administration of justice is greatly influenced by the scope and rules of judicial interpretation. As compared with their continental brethren and the European Court, English judges seem to have a narrower scope in the field of interpretation. The *Bosch*[18] case is a good illustration. Whilst our judges are not allowed to study the '*travaux préparatoires*', that is the materials and debates in Parliament leading to the passing of legislation, in order to find out the mind of the legislature, the continental judges are allowed to do so and base their judgment on their study. The *Bosch* case was concerned with restrictive practices contrary to article 85(1) of the EEC Treaty but the question was whether the said article could be applied before the enactment of the procedural rules envisaged by article 87. Pending such enactment national law was to apply. The Dutch court of the first instance ruled that article 85 was not operative before Regulation 17 of 1962 was made; the Court of Appeal referred the case to the Community Court under EEC article 177 and the plaintiff appealed to the Dutch Supreme Court which upheld the reference. The final ruling of the Community Court was that it was the intention of the EEC that article 85 shall be operative only in respect of agreements and decisions which the national authorities considered prohibited and incapable of exemption. Other agreements could be saved in accordance with article 5 of the Regulation. An English Court would probably have applied national law by virtue of article 87.

Another attribute of the continental courts is the power to resort

---

17 See Chapter 9.
18 Case 13/61: *Robert Bosch GmbH v Kledingverhoopbedrijf de Geus en Uitdenbogerd* [1962] ECR 45, [1962] CMLR 1; D Thompson, 'The Bosch Case' (1962) 11 ICLQ 721; Case 14/70: *Deutsche Bakels GmbH v Oberfinanzdirektion München* [1970] 2 ECR 1001, [1971] CMLR 188; Case 42/72: *Alfons Lütticke GmbH v Hauptzollamt Passau* [1973] ECR 57 at 74–75, [1973] CMLR 309 at 316–317.

to teleological interpretation of codes and statutes which enables them to apply old law in the context of social change or give the rules of law a dynamic and functional effect.[19] In this country (perhaps with the exception of the House of Lords) courts have no such power and, indeed, should an iconoclast judge venture into such practices he would soon find his judgments overruled by higher courts. The Community Court, it seems, enjoys this attribute of judicial power in the best traditions of continental courts and, having established its authority, does occasionally resort to this kind of interpretation. Unlike literal interpretations the Court puts into the mouth of the legislator the meaning of words he should have used rather than words he has actually used to express his intention.[20]

The Courts' role is much coloured by the rules of procedure. The predominant feature of continental procedural law is the inquisitorial power of the court. This system places a heavy duty on the court to enquire into the facts of the case in order to ascertain the objective truth. Unlike the English judge the continental judge is not an impartial umpire watching the contest of the parties and seeing merely that the rules of the game are observed. This requires a greater involvement of the court which, among other things, manifests itself in the examination of witnesses and parties by the judge. Although these inquisitorial powers have not been expressly spelt out in the founding Treaties they can be found in the Protocol on the Statute of the Court of Justice[21] and the Rules of Procedure. It is clear that the European Community Court functions like any continental court and this involves a tight control of the proceedings, powers to require parties to produce documents and supply

---

19 Cf Pescatore, P, Interpretation of Community Law and the Doctrine of Acte Clair, in Bathurst, M, et al (eds), *Legal Problems of an Enlarged European Community*, 1972, 27 at pp 32–34.

20 Eg Case 14/63: *Forges de Clabecq v High Authority* [1963] ECR 357, [1964] CMLR 167; Case 9/73: *Schlüter v Hauptzollamt Lorrach* [1973] ECR 1135 at 1153; Case 6/72: *Europemballage Corpn and Continental Can Inc v EC Commission* [1973] ECR 215, [1973] CMLR 199; Case 8/73: *Hauptzollamt-Bremerhaven v Massey-Ferguson* [1973] ECR 897; Case 37–38/73: *Sociaal Fonds voor de Diamant Arbeiders v N V Indiamex and Association defait De Belder*, [1973] ECR 1609; Case 151/73: *Government of Ireland v EC Council* [1974] ECR 285 at 296 and 297; [1974] 1 CMLR 429 at 446–447. Most prominent examples of teleological interpretation include Van Gend, supra; Case 93/71: *Leonesio v Italian Ministry of Agriculture and Forestry* [1972] ECR 287, [1973] CMLR 343; Case 43/75: *Defrenne v SABENA* [1976] ECR 455, [1976] 2 CMLR 98.

21 EEC Statute, arts 21, 22, 26, 28; ECSC Statute, arts 24, 25, 28 (3), EAEC Statute, arts 22, 23, 27, 29; Rules of Procedure, present codified version OJ 1982, C39, arts 47(1), 77, 94. See further Lasok, K P E, *The European Court of Justice: Practice and Procedure* (1984), pp 30 et seq.

the information the court deems necessary as well as the examination of witnesses and parties by the court.

Other salient features of continental procedure are the predominance of written pleadings which contain mainly legal arguments, hence the art of written advocacy somewhat similar to our Chancery proceedings; the absence of drama in court engineered in this country by the public examination and cross-examination of witnesses. Oral procedure consists of the hearing of any witnesses or experts followed by succinct summary of the main points submitted by the advocates of each party to the proceedings. Then follows a collective judgment of the court, after due deliberations in private, usually read in open court on the appointed day together with other judgments. The report of the court is brief and concise based on the draft prepared by the reporting judge. All the features of a civil law court are attributable to the European Community Court and offer a challenge our lawyers have to meet in practice.

Because of its wide dimensions, Community law offers a challenge to three types of lawyers: lawyers in government service, lawyers in commerce and industry, and lawyers in private practice.

Government lawyers of all the Member States together with the Community draftsmen bear co-responsibility for the drafting of the Community legislation. They also play their part in litigation in which the government is involved in cases either before the ECJ or the national courts.

In-house lawyers are particularly concerned with the impact of Community economic law, especially in the field of restrictive practices, intellectual property, corporations, establishment, social security and labour relations, taxation, customs and movement of goods and capital, agriculture in addition to the mass of the Community rules and regulations which affect investments and commercial operations in their various ramifications as well as subsidies to industry, consumer protection and environment.

Lawyers in private practice, both in advice and litigation, face the problem not only of the Community law as such but also of its impact in the various areas of national law, including criminal law. Since by virtue of the European Communities Act 1972 Community law has become part of the British legal system it can no longer be regarded as 'foreign' law left to specialists engaged in marginal practice. Thus expertise in Community law has become an essential ingredient of the quality of legal service; its neglect may result in claims for professional negligence.[1]

---

1 See judgment of the Oberlandesgericht Koblenz in *Re a Lawyer's Professional Negligence* (1990) 3 CMLR 415.

Turning now to a more daunting, though not impossible proposition: article 52 of the Treaty of Rome gives lawyers the 'right of establishment' on the basis of free movement within the Community. So far this right has not resulted in a migration of lawyers within the Community simply because the practice of law is essentially national. However, difficulties have come to light because admission to practise is, in most countries, governed by law and restrictive practices of the profession. In accordance with article 52(2) the Community Court held, in *Reyners v The Belgian State*,[2] that a Dutch national living in Belgium and having appropriate Belgian professional qualifications was unlawfully excluded from the exercise of the profession of *avocat* on the ground that according to Belgian law only Belgian nationals were admitted to practice. The principle was applied to remove a disqualification on the ground of the lack of habitual residence of a Dutch lawyer who lived in Belgium but wished to practise in the Netherlands.[3] The same ruling was made with regard to a Belgian who acquired French professional qualification and wished to practise in Paris.[4] In the *Klopp*[5] case a national rule of practice prohibiting an advocate from maintaining chambers in two different areas was held illegal when applied to a German lawyer wishing to practise in Paris whilst keeping his practice in Düsseldorf, the lawyer being qualified in both countries. The judgment of the ECJ has been applied[6] in France.

Assuming that we continue with the divided profession, there is at present no rule to prevent an alien, as an alien, becoming a member of the Bar. Solicitors, allegedly on the basis of s. 3 of the Act of Settlement 1700 (which declared aliens incapable of enjoying certain offices or places of trust) and a counsel's opinion of some vintage and doubtful weight, had to be British subjects but this discrimination has now been removed.[7] As far as practice is concerned solicitors must observe the general code of their profession whether they handle 'domestic' or 'foreign' business. A foreign lawyer wishing to practise in England and Wales must, subject to

2 Case 2/74: [1974] ECR 631, [1974] 2 CMLR 305.
3 Case 33/74: *J H M Van Binsbergen v Bestuur van de Bedrijfsvereniging voor de Metaalnijverheid* [1974] ECR 1299, [1975] 1 CMLR 298.
4 Case 71/76: *Thieffry v Conseil de l'Ordre des Avocats à la Cour de Paris* [1977] ECR 765, [1977] 2 CMLR 373.
5 Case 107/83: *Ordre des Avocats au Barreau de Paris v Klopp* [1984] ECR 2971, [1985] 1 CMLR 99; see further Lasok, D, *The Professions and Services in the European Economic Community* (1986), pp 161 et seq.
6 *Maitre Cammarata v Conseil de l'Ordre des Avocats au Barreau de Marseille* Court d'Appel, Aix-en-Provence [1988] 1 CMLR 243; *Conseil de l'Ordre des Avocats au Barreau de Nice v Raynel* Supreme Court, [1990] 2 CMLR 190.
7 Solicitors Amendment Act 1974, s 1; Solicitors' Act 1974, s 29.

professional qualifications, elect to practise either as a barrister or a solicitor. He cannot do both. A British solicitor cannot enter into a partnership with a foreign lawyer in England and Wales but may do so abroad subject to local rules. He may however allow his foreign associate to have a seat in his office.[8]

Under the freedom of establishment British lawyers are entitled to set up in practice abroad on an equal footing, their success depending, of course, on their proficiency in foreign and Community law. There is a theoretical and practical side to it. In theory the right of establishment and the principle of non-discrimination apply. By article 52 of the EEC Treaty the freedom of establishment included the right to engage in and carry on self-employed occupation under the conditions laid down by the law of the country of establishment for its own nationals. The treaty is clear – free movement of persons – but how does it affect lawyers? Article 60 (1)(*d*), defining the term 'service', refers to 'liberal professions' and this, traditionally, includes the legal profession. But lawyers are, in some respects, involved in the administration of justice which is a public process and an exercise of the authority of the state, not just commercial enterprise or service with which the Common Market is concerned. English solicitors are designated as 'Officers of the Supreme Court' and barristers are supposed to be 'assisting' the court in its work. German *Rechtsanwälte*, who combine the work of the English barrister and solicitor and are engaged more in litigation than conveyancing, are too 'officers of the court'. The French have a diversified profession but those who are involved in court work are regarded as 'auxiliaries of justice' or of 'tribunals'. The *avocats*, who are the aristocracy of the French legal profession, may be called to the Bench or replace public prosecutors, so there is too a considerable involvement in the administration of justice.

One can, of course, envisage difficulties,[9] eg in France and Germany where only specially appointed lawyers may appear before the Supreme Court; in England the position is rather complicated because of the relations between the two branches of the profession and the existence of Queen's Counsel and Juniors. To face these problems the Bar Council[10] has relaxed the rules by allowing a barrister to accept a brief from a foreign lawyer directly without the intermediary of an English solicitor and a Queen's Counsel to act without a Junior in Community matters. However

---

8 Further details, *Law Society's Gazette*, Vol 70 (1973), p 1568.
9 See Case 138/80: *Re Jules Borker* [1980] ECR 1975, [1980] 3 CMLR 638 and *Public Prosecutor of Cologne v Lischka* (Cologne Court of Appeal) [1981] 2 CMLR 189.
10 *Law Society's Gazette*, Vol 68 (1971), pp 187, 193, 194; Vol 70, p 1568; Vol 71, p 378; *Guardian Gazette*, 27 April 1974, p 114.

these rules apply only to 'foreign work' and are not meant to change the nature of the practice at the Bar in England and Wales or allow the barrister to do the solicitor's work. A barrister may enter into any association including partnership with any lawyer (except solicitors practising in the UK) for the purpose of sharing any office or services abroad but in the UK cannot undertake work not normally performed by a practising barrister in England and Wales, receive or handle client's money or accept the status of an employee or of a commercial agent or business agent.

In December 1975 an agreement[11] between the Paris Bar and the English Bar was made to the effect that members of one may appear and plead before the Courts of the other provided they are led by members of the local Bar. In England and Wales this rule applies to all courts where only barristers may plead. This arrangement may well lead to similar bi-lateral agreements between the English Bar and the corresponding branches of the profession of the remaining Member States of the Community.

Discrimination and restrictive practice apart the stumbling block to the harmonization of the legal profession has been the lack of recognition of professional qualifications obtained abroad. Pending the solution of this problem Council Directive 77/249[12] was passed to 'facilitate the effective exercise by lawyers of freedom to provide services'. However, until the acceptance of mutual recognition of diplomas and professional qualifications the persons to whom the Directive applied had to qualify and obtain the professional title used in the Member State in which they intend to become established. In the spirit of the Directive the Consultative Committee of the Bars and Law Societies of the European Community (CCBE) has introduced, as from October 1978, lawyers' 'Euro-Cards' to enable their holders to identify themselves before the national authorities as persons qualified to practise the law. This was a general rule which did not exclude bi-lateral arrangements across the frontiers. However, the privilege was available only to lawyers established in the EC. Thus an East German lawyer was not eligible, since the GDR was not part of the EC and the Protocol on Internal German Trade, being applicable only to the movement of goods, was irrelevant to the provision of services.[13] The reuni-

---

11 *Times*, December 1975; the relationship between the Paris Bar and the Law Society of England and Wales is governed by an agreement signed on 12 April 1976. In *R v Tymen* [1981] 2 CMLR 544, the British judge expressed his appreciation of the skill with which the French advocate pleaded his case in English.

12 OJ 1977, L 78/17, see European Communities (Service of Lawyers) Order 1978 SI 1978 No 1910.

13 *Re an East German Lawyer*, Supreme Federal Court [1990] 2 CMLR 185.

fication of Germany may well present problems to the other Member States in this respect.

The privilege enabled foreign lawyers to gain access to their clients, provide advice and appear in court in company with a local lawyer. However, warned the ECJ, the requirement that a foreign lawyer must work in conjunction with a local lawyer in relation to court proceedings must not be too restrictive lest the objectives of the Directive become frustrated.[14]

Moreover, the condition was that only lawyers permitted to practise in one Member State could take advantage of the Directive in order to provide service in another Member State. Thus the Directive could not be interpreted in such a way as to enable a lawyer disbarred for reasons relating to 'dignity, good repute and integrity' to gain access to the profession abroad.[15]

However, to ensure complete mobility of lawyers it was essential to establish principles of universal recognition of professional qualifications so that lawyers admitted to practise in one Member State could practise in the entire Community. This was achieved by Council Directive 89/48[16] which completes the work of the ECJ, whose judgments have removed various restrictions based on national laws and practices of the profession.[17] The Directive applies to professions regulated by national laws except those (eg the medical professions) already governed by Community legislation. It is particularly relevant to the legal profession.

The Directive aims at introducing a general system of recognition unrelated to any specific profession. It assumes comparability of educational courses of a university level existing in the Member States. However, such courses should be available only to persons holding a certificate awarded on successful completion of a full-time course of upper secondary education.

The Directive proceeds from a broad definition of professional qualifications consisting of the award of a formal diploma, certificate or equivalent evidence by a competent national authority designated for the purpose by a Member State's laws, regulations or administrative provisions. This award must show that its holder has successfully completed a post-secondary course of at least three years' duration and has also successfully completed the requisite professional training which enables him to take up and pursue a regulated profession in the Member State concerned. This rec-

---

14 Case 427/85: *EC Commission v Germany, Re Lawyers' Services* [1988] ECR 1123; [1989] 2 CMLR 677.
15 Case 292/86: *Gullung v Conseil de l'Ordre des Avocats* [1988] ECR 111; [1988] 2 CMLR 57.
16 OJ 1989, L19/16.
17 See in particular notes 2, 3, 4, 5 supra.

ognition will also be extended to awards obtained in non-Community countries (eg Switzerland), if a Member State, in accordance with recommendation 89/49 appended to the Directive, accords such recognition in its own territory.

Adaptation comprises limited practice under the supervision of a qualified lawyer, possibly accompanied by further training. Aptitude testing, on the other hand, is limited to a test of professional knowledge of the applicant by the competent authorities of the host country with the aim of assessing the ability of the applicant to practise in that country. In principle the host country must give the applicant the right to choose either an adaptation period or an aptitude test. However, for professions whose practice requires knowledge of national law and in respect of which the provision of advice and/or assistance concerning national law is an essential and constant aspect of the professional activity, the host country must decide whether the adaptation or the aptitude test must be applied, though it may not apply both cumulatively. Adaptation has been accepted for the legal profession in the United Kingdom.[18]

Whilst a Member State must recognize professional qualifications obtained in fellow Member States it may also require the applicant for such recognition to provide evidence of professional experience where the duration of his education and training is at least one year less than that required in its territory, or to complete an adaptation period not exceeding three years, or to take an aptitude test where the applicant's education or training differs substantially from those covered by the diplomas required in its own system.

The Directive is limited to the recognition of foreign qualifications necessary for the exercise of the right of establishment leaving to the Member States the details of implementation. However, it reserves to the Member States the right to regulate and to ensure respect of the rules of personal conduct and etiquette of the members of the professions. It also provides for the documentation and proof of good character or good repute.

The Directive came into effect on 4 January 1990. During the subsequent five years its implementation and application will be monitored by the Commission who will report to the European Parliament and the Council of Ministers. Its impact in practice remains to be evaluated as regards both the formation of the legal profession and the practice of the law in the Community.

18 Lasok, D 'Lawyers Facing 1992', Law Society Gazette, 25 October 1989; Wallace, R M M 'Freedom to Practise in the EEC', New Law Journal, vol 139, No 6417 (1989) p 1004.

Practice before the Community Court presents its own problems. The Court was set up largely on the pattern of the World Court and the French Conseil d'Etat. Its jurisdiction includes supervision of the execution of the Treaties, adjudication of disputes between Member States, control of legality of the acts of the Community Institutions and the interpretation of the Treaty and Community legislation. Its procedure is French with some German admixtures. In the main the proceedings are conducted in writing and this emphasizes the importance of the art of 'written advocacy' as a feature of the continental legal style. Since the existing practice was not changed to accommodate British lawyers, new skills have to be learned and unusual difficulties overcome. The case law approach of the Court in developing the Community law is a hopeful sign but should not lull us into a sense of false security.

As for the right of audience before the Community Court, some rules have been laid down in article 17 of the Protocol on the Statute of the Court of Justice. This provides that parties must be represented by a lawyer entitled to practise before a court of one of the Member States and this includes also university teachers if, as in Germany, they have the right of audience before the national courts. The operative words are not very clear: the French version refers to 'avocat inscrit à un barreau de l'un des Etats membres'; the German to 'ein Anwalt, der in einem Mitgliedstaat zugelassen ist'. This would mean that English solicitors could appear before the Court during the whole process, written and oral, provided they have the right of audience before the courts in this country. Since their audience is limited at present, in theory, the question appears open, but in practice solicitors have not been barred from appearing before the Community Court and, indeed, some have made a practice of it.

Finally, academic lawyers, responsible for the formation of the lawyers of tomorrow, have to tune their professional skills and their curricula to the challenge of Community law.

3 The language of Community law

Language is the main tool in the legal workshop and it is common ground that each legal system has its own technical language. So it is with Community law. Within the Community of the Six the problem of the legal language was magnified sixfold as lawyers from the six countries tried first to frame the Treaty and then establish a common interpretation of the texts of Community law. In the enlarged Community the problem has been further magnified and has been complicated through the accession of two common law countries and Denmark with their peculiar legal styles.

The problem of language has a special bearing upon the legislative process, the interpretation and administration of the law and harmonization of national laws. It will be considered in relation to these three areas.

(A) THE TREATY AND COMMUNITY LEGISLATION

The Treaty of Rome was drawn up in a single document in the German, French, Italian and Dutch languages, all four texts being equally authentic.[19] By contrast the ECSC Treaty is in one authentic version in the French language.

The Treaty of Brussels, concerning the accession of Denmark, Ireland, Norway and the United Kingdom, was also drawn up in a single document in the Danish, Dutch, English, French, German, Irish, Italian and Norwegian languages, all texts being equally authentic.[20] The same principle was adopted on the accession of Greece, Greek being the eighth authentic Treaty language and Spain and Portugal, Spanish and Portuguese being the ninth and the tenth authentic languages.

This is an accepted form of a multi-lateral, multi-lingual treaty for which the United Nations Charter is one of the outstanding precedents. The effect of the formula 'equally authentic' is that all texts, having an equal status, can be cited as the authoritative statement of the law and that no one text takes precedence over the others. This does not solve the problem of the discrepancies in the various texts which inter se are nothing but translations. With the greatest care and skill expended on the formulation of treaties discrepancies are inevitable because the translation of a legal text is not merely a matter of language. The question of interpretation of authentic texts which reveal a discrepancy in the meaning of words attributable to legal concepts and institutions resolves itself into the question of the intention of the parties. The rule of International Law, which has evolved to deal with this problem, is that there is a presumption against an interpretation which is contrary to any one of the equally authentic texts. It follows that it is necessary to find a meaning which is compatible with all the texts.

19 Art 248; the languages are listed in alphabetical order in accordance with the French nomenclature of the four countries.
20 Art 3; the languages are listed in alphabetical order according to Cmnd 4862, but since Norway failed to ratify the Treaty there were in the Community seven official languages; see Adaptation Decision, art 2, and ten since the admission of Greece, Spain and Portugal.

In order to achieve this object it is necessary first to establish the meanings of each text and then select the meaning which is not contrary to any particular text. A practical illustration of the application of this rule is the *Mavrommatis* case,[1] in which the Permanent Court of International Justice explained that 'when considering two equally authentic texts, one of which appears to have a wider meaning than the other, it is the duty of the Court to apply the narrower text since such an interpretation is compatible with both texts and, no doubt, corresponds to the common intention of the parties'.

In *Fédération Charbonnière de Belgique* v *High Authority*[2] the Community Court considered the argument that the ECSC Treaty being an international treaty was subject to restrictive interpretation and broadly agreed with the principle, though it considered that rules of interpretation used in both International Law and national laws were perfectly acceptable. However, in later cases a broader formula has evolved. In *Milchwerke Heinz Wöhrmann & Sohn KG v EC Commission*[3] Advocate-General Roemer submitted that where three texts revealed a clear meaning but the fourth was inconsistent with them the latter should follow suit. In *de Geus v Bosch*[4] Advocate-General Lagrange submitted that where all four texts conveyed different meanings the Court should decide the issue according to the spirit of the text. In *Mij PPW Internationaal NV v Hoofdproduktschap voor Akkerbouwprodukten*,[5] concerning the issue of certificates for export refunds, the Court held that no argument could be drawn either from any linguistic discrepancies between the various texts or from the number of the verbs used in one or other version because the meaning of the relevant provisions had to be determined in the light of their objectives.

Moreover in a case[6] concerning the application of rules governing the grant of aid for skimmed milk the ECJ held that 'the elimination of linguistic discrepancies by way of interpretation may in certain circumstances run counter to the concern for legal certainty in as much as one or more of the texts involved may have to be interpreted in a manner at variance with the natural and usual meaning of the words. Consequently it is preferable to explore the possibilities of solving the point at issue without giving preference to

1 [1927] PCIJ Rep Ser A, No 2, p 12.
2 Case 9/55: [1954–1956] ECR 311.
3 Case 31 and 33/62: [1962] ECR 501, [1963] CMLR 152.
4 Case 13/61: [1962] ECR 45, [1962] CMLR 1 at 23.
5 Case 61/72: [1973] ECR 301; see also (re family allowances) Case 6/74: *Moulijn v EC Commission* [1974] ECR 1287.
6 Case 80/76: *North Kerry Milk Products Ltd v Minister for Agriculture and Fisheries* [1977] 2 CMLR 769 at 781.

any one of the texts involved.' However where the word 'spouse' used in all other languages was rendered into Dutch as 'wife'[7] the ECJ preferred a 'sexually neutral construction' meaning either 'wife' or 'husband', as the case may be, thus giving weight to legislative policy rather than language and ensuring at the same time uniformity throughout the Community.

Since the Treaties of Paris, Rome and Brussels are 'self-executing' there is no need of their being 'transformed' by statute into the domestic law of the Member States. Consequently, as far as the authentic texts are concerned, the Treaties have to be taken as they stand. The danger of producing a different text for the purpose of legislation, not uncommon in the process of translation of international conventions, has been excluded. This does not solve the problem of Community law in the countries whose language has not been included in the authentic texts or, as in the case of the United Kingdom, countries which have subsequently adhered to the Treaties. The general rule of international law may be too narrow and so the spirit rather than the letter of the Treaty should prevail.

In their endeavour to give effect to the common intention of the parties comprised in a multi-lingual treaty the draftsmen try to exclude discrepancies and potential conflicts of interpretation but this is a quite impossible task. The end product must be a compromise if not a synthesis of the systems involved. Where this is impossible they have to choose consciously the technical language which seems most appropriate or most commonly used or the language of the legal system which has the greatest influence in the deliberations. The Treaties unmistakably bear the imprint of French law for the French have the uncanny knack of assisting the international law-making process with their texts as the starting point of deliberations and, hopefully, the wording to be adopted.[8] However the ECJ needs not be perturbed by textual discrepancies for, in the best traditions of continental jurisprudence, it can rely on teleological interpretation. In other words, when in doubt, the spirit rather than the letter of the law should prevail, thus giving weight to the legislative policy aimed at by the law-maker. Or, as put by Judge Kutscher[9] 'the difficulties of interpretation arising

---

7 Case 9/79: *Wörsdörfer (née Koschniske) v Raad van Arbeid* [1979] ECR 2717, [1980] 1 CMLR 87.
8 See *Bell Concord Trust Ltd v Customs and Excise Comrs* in which the English Court of Appeal used the French text of the 6th VAT Directive to elucidate the meaning of the Directive and of the English implementing statute [1989] 1 CMLR 845.
9 Kutscher, H, *Methods of Interpretation as seen by a Judge at the Court of Justice*, Judicial and Academic Conference 27–28 September 1976, p 20.

from the multi-lingual nature of Community law are frequently resolved not through a grammatical interpretation but by resorting to an examination of the objects of the provision and its place in the system of the Treaty' ... Indeed committed to a dynamic and evolutionary interpretation of Community law[10] the Court on its own admission 'cannot ... be content with a literal interpretation ...'[11] Moreover the objective envisaged may prompt a liberal interpretation as was, eg the case of 'identification' of persons on social security to their entitlement of butter at reduced price without injury to their pride.[12]

This attitude appears to be reflected in certain dicta of Lord Denning MR[13] who, in his iconoclastic way, may have given the impression that teleological interpretation should be adopted generally, not merely in respect of Community law. When referring to an English statute which incorporated the International Convention on the Carriage of Goods by Road 1956, he said that 'by interpreting the Treaty of Rome ... we must certainly adopt the new approach'.[14] For that he was duly rebuked since 'membership of the EEC does not involve abandonment of national construction of multi-lateral conventions ...'[15] No doubt this is correct as regards international treaties other than the Community Treaties. However, taken out of context, the dictum that ... 'no assistance from methods said to be used in interpreting the Treaty of Rome by the European Court of Justice ...'[16] may become a source of mischief. There is no way of denying that Community law, whether comprised in Treaties or derivative legislation, is a *sui generis* law and has to be interpreted by national courts in the light of the jurisprudence of the Community Court. Should there be a difficulty in this respect the matter ought to be referred to the Community Court for a preliminary ruling under article 177 of the EEC Treaty.

Whilst the Treaty is a 'once and for all' exercise the Community legislation is a continuous process. The techniques have already been perfected through common effort of the Community lawyers and here, perhaps, the lawyer no longer feels a champion of his own system (which, as every lawyer knows, is the best system in the world!) or suffers under the limitations of his national training and the inhibitions acquired from his legal language becoming

10 Ibid, p 39.
11 Case 6/60: *Jean E Humblet v Belgian State* [1960] ECR 559.
12 Case 29/69: *Stauder v City of Ulm* [1969] ECR 419, (paras 4 and 5), [1970] CMLR 112.
13 *H P Bulmer Ltd v J Bollinger SA* [1974] Ch 401 at 419–425.
14 *James Buchanan Co Ltd v Babco Forwarding and Shipping (UK) Ltd* [1977] 2 CMLR 455 at 459, CA.
15 Ibid [1978] 1 CMLR 156 at 161, HL.
16 Ibid.

his second nature. The newcomers to this task are at a certain disadvantage and their contribution initially must perforce be rather limited. This is a special practical challenge to the British civil servant joining the legal service of the Community.

Article 191 (1), (2) of the EEC Treaty provides that 'regulations shall be published in the Official Journal of the Community' and that 'directives and decisions shall be notified to those to whom they are addressed'. At first the *Official Journal* was published in Dutch, French, German and Italian but article 155 of the first Act of Accession, as amended by the Adaptation Decision, provided that 'the texts of the Acts of the Institution of the Community adopted before the accession and drawn up by the Council or the Commission in the Danish and English languages shall, from the date of accession, be authentic under the same conditions as the texts drawn up in the four original languages'.[17] The same principle was adopted in article 147 of the second Act of Accession regarding Greece and article 397 of the third Act of Accession regarding Spain and Portugal.

Since directives and decisions have to be 'notified' but, apparently, need not be 'published' difficulties arose in the past[18] and these prompted the Community Court to suggest that publication be improved. As a result directives and decisions are now, as a rule, published in the *Official Journal*.

Let us turn now to some specific pitfalls of the technical language of Community law, problems known only too well to British translators of the Community texts who soon discovered that 'corresponding' legal terms in two languages seldom correspond *exactly*.[19]

In the drafting of conventions the generalisations about the civil law system are brought to the test and, usually, to grief. Illusions of the oneness of the system based on Roman Law and codes are quickly exposed and we are left with a vague notion of a common core of the law, a common historical heritage, and a similarity of styles. As in a large family there are traces of common genes but also manifestations of mutations and acquired differences. As in a family the stronger members prevail and so one can trace in multilingual texts the influence of a particular system. It is not surprising

---

17 Reg 857/72 of 24 April 1972 establishing special editions of the Official Journal; JO L 101, 1972.

18 Joined Cases 73 and 74/63: *Internationale Crediet-en Handelsvereniging 'Rotterdam' NV v Minister van Landouw en Visserij* [1964] ECR 1 at 13–14 [1964] CMLR 198; Case 69/69: *Alcan v EC Commission* [1970] 1 ECR 385 at 396, [1970] CMLR 337 at 340.

19 Hall, D F, 'Translating the Treaties', *European Review*, Spring Issue 1972; Héraud, G, 'La Communauté Européenne et La Question Linguistique' (1981) 5 *Rev d'Integration Européenne*, 5 et seq.

that the French legal language provides a starting point for the consideration of the problems of language in the Community texts.

The student of Community law must from the start familiarize himself with the problem of language known only too well to the student of comparative law, whilst the practitioner may find support for his argument from a comparison of the texts, bearing in mind that he is confronted with a conceptual rather than purely linguistic problem. Such problems are reflected in the growing volume of case law, examples of which have been listed in the previous editions of this book.

(B) LANGUAGE IN THE INSTITUTIONS

Deliberations within the institutions are conducted in the official languages of the Community which necessitates a system of simultaneous translation and explains the number of interpreters and translators employed by each institution.

(C) LANGUAGE IN THE COMMUNITY COURT

The Community Court, the single court of the three Communities,[20] is a multi-lingual court not only in a linguistic but also a juristic sense.

The requirement that judges must be fit to occupy the highest judicial offices in their respective countries is both an advantage and a handicap. The advantage is obvious in the quality of the judicial body and the potential of having the best legal traditions of the Member States in the service of the Community Court. The handicap is that judges, perhaps more than any other lawyers, are conditioned by their own system. However, until truly Community judges emerge the national judges will continue to enrich and shape the Community judiciary with their native skills and characters. Judge Donner thus summarized the position of the national judge: 'I remember one of my colleagues saying at the end of a long debate in which he had tried to win us over to his national solution on a particular point, "Well, gentlemen, if you do not want to adopt my approach, you will at least have to admit that it is the only reasonable one." '[1]

20 Convention relating to Certain Institutions common to the European Communities of 27 March 1957 annexed to the EEC and EAEC Treaties and amending the ECSC Treaty.
 1 Donner, A M, *The Role of the Lawyer in the European Communities* (1968), p 43.

In order to assist the Court with the linguistic problems the Rules of Procedure[2] enabled the Court to set up a language department consisting of experts, combining the knowledge of several of the official languages of the Court and law (RP 22). Originally the official languages of the Court were French, German, Italian and Netherlands (RP 29 (1))[3] but with the enlargement of the Community the rules of procedure[4] had to be adapted to include the new official languages. At present the official languages of the Court are: Danish, English, French, German, Italian, Netherlands and, since 1 January 1981, Greek and, since 1 January 1986, Spanish and Portuguese; but Irish (though not official) may also be used. These changes resulting in an increased number of the official languages will no doubt further multiply the problems involved.

The present position is that only one of the official languages may be used as the procedural language (RP 29(2)). The choice is, in principle, left to the applicant. However, if the defendant is a Member State or a person or corporation subject to a Member State the procedural language will be the official language of that state. Should there be more than one official language involved the applicant would be able to choose one from these which led the Court to rule that unless the defendant is a Community institution the language of the case is that of the defendant. If the parties to the case so desire, the Court, upon their joint application, may designate the use of another official language as the procedural language. In exceptional circumstances the Court may authorize the total or partial use of another official language as the procedural language if so requested by one of the parties. Such a request has to be considered in the light of the comments by the other party and the Advocate-General but is not open to any of the organs of the Community.

In the proceedings involving a preliminary ruling under EEC article 177[5] on matters of the interpretation of the Treaty, the validity and interpretation of the act of the Community organs and the interpretation of the statutes of bodies established by the Council, the procedural language shall be that of the Court or tribunal which requests the preliminary ruling in question.

The procedural language is used to procure written evidence and

2 These Rules were adopted by the Court on 3 March 1959, in succession to the Treaties of the three Communities and the Statutes of the Courts of Justice envisaged by the Treaties; present codified version OJ 1982, C 39.
3 Dutch, as the language of Holland, is not synonymous with the 'Netherlands language' which is also spoken in certain parts of Belgium. Such Belgians enjoy two 'official languages': French and Netherlands.
4 Case 1/60: *FERAM SpA v High Authority* [1960] ECR 351 at 363; See further Lasok, K P E, op cit, pp 26–29.
5 EEC Statute, art 20; EAEC Statute, art 21; ECSC Treaty, art 41 RP, 29/2.

pleas before the Court. Documents produced in another language must be accompanied by a translation in the procedural language. These documents are regarded as 'authentic' which means in practical terms that they cannot be challenged merely on linguistic grounds (RP 31).

Witnesses and experts ought to use the procedural language or one of the official languages but, if unable to do so the Court will allow them to use another language. The witness or expert is allowed to speak through an interpreter or address himself to a judge of his native language[6] but at the end a record will be made under the direction of the Court's Registrar in the procedural language.

The President of the Court, the Presidents of Chambers when directing the proceedings, the Judge-Rapporteur when making his preliminary report and judges and Advocates-General when asking questions and the Advocates-General when making their submissions may use an official language in preference to the procedural language. However, their utterings will be translated into the procedural language under the direction of the Registrar.

The Registrar will also, on the application of a judge, Advocate-General or one of the parties, ensure that a translation into the official languages of his choice is made of what has been said or recorded during the proceedings before the Court or Chamber (RP 30), is delivered in the procedural language (RP 29 (2)) and then published by the Registrar in all the official languages (RP 68). Since the final version of the judgment will generally be in French the authentic text is usually a translation into the language of the case and it is vetted by a judge whose mother tongue is the same.[7] This may occasionally produce difficulties as eg the inaccurate translation of the German *Gefährdungen der öffentlichen Ordnung* into its French *equivalent des menaces à l'ordre public* into English *breaches of the peace*.[8]

In spite of the tremendous language problem only few cases have so far involved the technical question of the use of language. In *De Gezamenlijke Steenkolenmijnen in Limburg v High Authority*[9] the Court had to rule on the use of the procedural language by an

---

6 Case 18/63, *Wollast (née Schmitz) v EC Commission* [1964] ECR 85, where the witness and the President of the Court were Italians but the counsel was French, and the President acted virtually as an interpreter.

7 Lasok, K P E, 'Practice and Procedure before the ECJ' (1981) ECLR, 89.

8 Case 67/74: *Bonsignore v Oberstadtdirektor der Stadt Köln* [1975] ECR 297, [1975] 1 CMLR 472 and Case 30/77: *R v Bouchéreau* [1977] ECR 1999, [1977] 2 CMLR 800, respectively.

9 Case 30/59: [1961] ECR 1 at 48 but see Case 45/81: *Alexander Moksel Import-Export GmbH v EC Commission* [1982] ECR 1129: procedural language was German but intervener allowed to present submissions at the hearing in English.

intervener. The Court held that 'it is only as from the moment that he is admitted to intervene that the intervener is obliged to use the language required for the procedure in the main action, without prejudice to the application of RP 29 (2) (*c*)'.

In *FERAM v High Authority of the European Coal and Steel Community*[10] the admissibility of documents drawn up in languages other than the procedural language was challenged. The Court held that: 'The documents in question were deposited with the Registry before the close of the oral procedure and consequently were within the cognisance of the Court before it rendered judgment. By a production of a document drawn up in one of the official languages of the Community it is not only its physical existence but also its content which is brought to the cognisance of the Court. Indeed, like all the institutions of the three Communities, the Court is quadri-lingual by virtue of a presumption *juris et de jure*. The provisions concerning the language of procedure cannot be regarded as being of public policy (*ordre public; zwingendes Recht; openbare orde; ordine pubblico*) –

(*a*) because the language of procedure is that of the applicant, unless the defendant is one of the Member States of the three Communities or a legal person subject to the jurisdiction of one of the Member States;

(*b*) because, both on the joint application of the parties and on the application of a single party and without the consent of the other party being necessary, the Court can authorise the use of an official language other than the language of the procedure.

That, therefore, the first fundamental condition required by ECSC article 38 (the discovery of a fact unknown not only to the party that applies for re-consideration, but also to the Court) is not met in the present case. . . .'

The challenge failed.

The rules governing the language of procedure are fairly clear but they do not explain what actually happens when the multi-lingual Court retires for deliberations in private before proceeding to judgment. Judge Donner[11] explained the problems the judges have to face and stressed how difficult it is for a lawyer to shed his second nature acquired in the practice of his national law and to sublimate his experience to a Community concept of law which must perforce savour of a synthesis of the laws of the Member States. No doubt the personality of the individual judge and the authority of his national law play a part in the deliberations.

10 Case 1/60: [1960] ECR 351 at 363–4.
11 Donner, op cit, p 44.

The deliberations are entirely private and in the absence of translators. Practice established French to be the *lingua franca* with the consequent disadvantage to judges whose fluency in French is not as good as might be desired. To get round this difficulty former Judge Riese[12] used to state his position in his native German and then restate it in French. In this way he endeavoured to have his say as best he could first in the legal jargon of his own country, and then give his brethren the benefit of an authentic translation into the 'working' language. It is clear that the Court must live with the problem (further aggravated by the enlargement of the Community) until the relevant portion of the law has become uniform and a new generation of truly Community lawyers has replaced the judges schooled in their native lands.

Still more complex is the jurisprudence of the language of the law. On more than one occasion the Community Court had to turn its mind to the interpretation of technical terms only to confirm that similarities conceal divergencies and nuances in the legal systems. The following examples illustrate the point.

1. *Détournement de pouvoir*[13] – A notion of French administrative law to cover a variety of cases of misuse of power has been before the Court on several occasions. In *Associazione Industrie Siderurgiche Italiane (Assider) v High Authority of the European Coal and Steel Community*[14] Advocate-General Lagrange reviewed painstakingly the concept of the misuse of power in each of the six Member States. In that case an association of Italian steel enterprises complained of being adversely affected by certain decisions[15] of the High Authority of the Coal and Steel Community which concerned the publication of price lists and conditions of sale by the steel industry. The plaintiffs contended that the general decisions of the High Authority in these matters constituted a threat to Italian steel enterprises, and that they were vitiated by the *détournement de pouvoir*. Moreover, since those enterprises which had infringed the previous regulations were not subjected to any sanction, the plaintiffs considered this to be a manifest injustice, and thus a misuse of power in respect of those enterprises which had observed the Treaty. The Court held that since decision 2/54 was annulled by the judgment in the case of *French Government v High Authority of the European Coal and Steel Community*[16] and decision 3/54 repealed by the High Authority it was unnecessary for the Court

---

12 Riese, O, 'Erfahrungen aus der Praxis des Gerichtshofes der Europäischen Gemeinschaft für Kohle und Stahl', *Deutsche Richterzeitung* (1958), 270–272.
13 Ermessemissbrauch, sviamento de potere, misbruik van beveogdheid.
14 Case 2/54: [1954–56] ECR 63.
15 Case 1/54: JO, 13 January 1953, 217; Case 2/54; ibid, 218; Case 3/54, ibid, 219.
16 Case 1/54: [1954–56] ECR 1.

to define *détournement de pouvoir.* Decision 1/54, having been upheld by the Court in the case of *Italian Government v High Authority of the European Coal and Steel Community,*[17] could not be regarded as misuse of power in the absence of new arguments. In the circumstances the Court was able to fall back on the classical dodge of not having to define an awkward concept. The plaintiffs fared no better in their request for an interpretation of the judgment[18] as the Court held that the judgment, being free from obscurities, presented no occasion for interpretation.

The saga of the *détournement de pouvoir* is likely to continue in spite of the attempts by the Court to offer an objective definition of *détournement* as 'the use made by a public authority of its powers for an object other than that for which a power was conferred upon it'[19] simply because of the variations of the use and abuse of public power. The procession of cases continues.[20]

2. *Faute de service* – In several cases the Community Court considered grievances arising from alleged 'default of the administration' (*faute de service*). On one occasion a Belgian corporation[1] complained that it was unable to sell coal in France because of the refusal of a licence by French authorities which, in effect, impeded the free flow of coal within the Community. Repeated requests to the Coal and Steel Community were of no avail and the corporation suffered damage as a result of inaction of the Community. The Court held that the plaintiff was entitled to redress for *faute de service* without insisting that the act complained of had to be annulled first. However, in *Plaumann & Co v EEC Commission*[2] damages were refused in the absence of a declaration of nullity but the decision turned upon different considerations, mainly the *locus standi* of the claimant. In subsequent cases[3] the Court recognized the independent nature of the action in accordance with article 215 (2) and 178, but considered that where a claim is made in respect of injury attributable to a legislative act of the Community involving choices of economic policy the claimant can succeed only if there

17 Case 2/54: [1954–56] ECR 37.
18 Case 5/55: [1954–56] ECR 135.
19 Case 8/55: *Fédération Charbonnière de Belgique v High Authority* [1954–56] ECR 245 at 272–273.
20 See cases under EEC art 215(2) supra.
1 Cases 9–12/60: *Société Commerciale Antoine Vloeberghs SA v High Authority of the European Coal and Steel Community* [1961] ECR 197.
2 Case 25/62: [1963] ECR 95, [1964] CMLR 29. Contrast Case C-229/88 *Cargill BV v EC Commission* [1990] 2 CMLR 753 (reduction of agricultural subsidy) with Case C-152/88: *Sofrimport Sarl v EC Commission* [1990] 3 CMLR 80 (suspension of import licence).
3 Case 5/71: *Aktien-Zuckerfabrik Schöppenstedt v EEC Council* [1971] 2 ECR 975; Cases 63–69/72: *Werhahn v EEC Council* [1973] ECR 1229.

is a 'sufficiently flagrant infringement of a superior rule of law protecting the individual'[4].

Several other cases[5] threw light on the concept of *faute de service* but perhaps the most instructive are the cases involving grievances of Community employees. It was held[6] that failure to renew a contract of employment in an irregular fashion constituted *faute de service* and so would an unlawful activity of an organ of the Community preventing a person from carrying on his normal occupation and causing him material and moral damage.[7]

The many aspects of *faute de service* were considered from a comparative point of view in *Algera v Common Assembly*,[8] a case of disputed validity of the regrading of employees. The Court stated:[9]

'... A study of comparative law reveals that in the six Member States an administrative act creating substantive rights in a particular party cannot in principle be revoked, provided that it amounted to a legal act. In such a case, the substantive right having been acquired, the necessity of ensuring confidence in the stability of the situation thus created outweighs the interest of the administration which might wish to revoke its decision. This applies particularly in the appointment of an official.

If, on the contrary, the administrative act is illegal, the law of all the Member States recognises the possibility of revocation. The lack of an objective legal basis for the act affects the substantive right of the party concerned and justifies the revocation of the said act. It is appropriate to emphasise that this principle is generally recognised and that it is only the conditions for its exercise which vary.

French law requires that the revocation of the illegal act must occur before the expiration of the time limit for bringing an appeal, or if an appeal is brought, before judgment. Belgian, Luxembourg and Dutch law, with certain differences, appear to follow analogous rules.

On the other hand, German law does not recognise a time limit for

4 *Werhahn*, supra.
5 Eg Cases 19/60, 21/60, 2–3/61: *Société Fives Lille Cail v High Authority of the European Coal and Steel Community* [1961] ECR 281 at 295–296, [1962] CMLR 251 at 281–282; Cases 5–7/66, 13–24/66, 30/66: *Firma E Kampffmeyer v EEC Commission* [1967] ECR 245; Case 36/62: *Société des Aciéries du Temple v High Authority of the European Coal and Steel Community* [1963] ECR 289, [1964] CMLR 49 at 56; Case 3/65: *Société Anonyme Métallurgique d'Espérance Langdoz v High Authority of the European Coal and Steel Community* [1965] ECR 1065, [1966] CMLR 146 at 167; 11 Rec. 1321.
6 In Case 1/55: *Kergall v Common Assembly* [1954–56] ECR 151.
7 Cf Case 18/60: *Worms v High Authority of the European Coal and Steel Community* [1962] ECR 195, [1963] CMLR 1 where an independent body was involved and, therefore, the Community was not liable.
8 Cases 7/56, 3 and 757 [1957–58] ECR 39.
9 Valentine, D G, *The Court of Justice of the European Communities*, Vol 2 (1965), pp 757–758.

the exercise of the right of revocation unless such a limit is provided by a special provision. Thus, the Federal law concerning public officials, by article 13 thereof, allows the withdrawal of an appointment only within a period of six months. However, it is generally recognised that the principle of good faith (*Treu und Glauben*) is opposed to an unduly delayed withdrawal ...

... Italian law is particularly precise upon this question. Any administrative act is vitiated by incompetence, violation of the law or ultra vires (*eccesso di potere*) can be annulled *ex tunc* by the administration which enacted it, independently of the substantive rights to which it might have given rise ...

The revocability of an administrative act tainted with illegality is, therefore, recognized in all the Member States ...'

Faute de service was proved and the earlier decision in *Kergall v Common Assembly* was cited with approval.

3. *Exception d'illégalité* – The defence of illegality, which is often resorted to in order to contest the legality of an administrative act, in national jurisdictions can also be pleaded before the Community Court. In a leading case[10] Advocate-General Lagrange thus summarized the contribution of the six legal systems to the concept of *exception d'illégalité*:

'... In three of the Member States, France, Belgium and Italy, this *exception* is freely admitted, being considered as forming part of the normal sphere of application of the claim for annulment. This is due to the fact that in these three countries, rules made by the executive power are considered, as far as the right to appeal against them is concerned, from the formal point of view, that is to say being administrative acts they are liable to be annulled if they are contrary to the law. Given that the direct claim for annulment is possible with regard to them, there is no objection in principle to the [judicial] control of their legality being also exercised when individual claims are made of which they are the object. The advantage is that the *exception* may be set up at any time, even when the time limit for a claim against the regulation or the general decision has expired. On the other hand, if the claim is successful only the individual decision is annulled, which avoids the grave consequences of the annulment of the regulation itself, declared with retrospective effect *erga omnes*.

As far as France is concerned we will cite, among many, two judgments of the Conseil d'État: *Abbé Barthélémy*, 9 July 1926, Recueil 713; *Marcin-Kowsky*, 28 November 1957, Recueil 548. These decisions are interesting because they begin by rejecting as presented out of time

10 Case 15/57: *Compagnie des Hauts Fourneaux de Chasse v High Authority of the European Coal and Steel Community* [1957–58] ECR 155; at 203–205. See also Case 9/56: *Meroni & Co Industrie Metallurgiche SpA v High Authority of the European Coal and Steel Community* [1957–58] ECR 133; Cases 31, 33/62: *Milchwerke Heinz Wohrmann & Sohn KG v EC Commission* [1962] ECR 501, [1963] CMLR 152.

the submissions that the rule should be annulled, and, immediately following, pass judgment on the legality of the very same rule in respect of submissions directed against an individual decision applying the rule. Case law shows, however, that the legality of the rule can only be contested in respect of those of its provisions which provided the basis for the individual decision taken in application of the rule (*Dame Denayer*, 18 February 1949, Recueil 80).

In the three other countries of the Community, Germany, Holland and Luxembourg, there is a strong tendency to remain attached to the material criterion, by virtue of which a regulation is a piece of secondary legislation no different in its legal nature from the law itself. Nevertheless the subordination of the rule to the (general) law remains an established legal principle and, if the former conception causes some hesitation with regard to direct claims for annulment of regulations, the second conception, on the other hand, more readily permits the setting up of the *exception d'illégalité*. In criminal law this *exception* is very freely admitted. The principal difficulties in the latter field lie mainly in determining which judge is competent to rule on the question of legality: that happens, particularly, in France, a country in which the principle of the separation of powers is very strictly applied and where, in consequence, a reference to the administrative court for a preliminary ruling on legality is often made in defiance of the principle according to which the judge in the action is also judge in respect of the *exception*, but such considerations do not arise where, as in the instant case, the same judge has competence.

Are there any special reasons for adopting a different solution for the application of the Treaty? We do not think so. On the contrary, article 41, which confers jurisdiction on the Court – without any restriction as to the nature of the grounds which may be put forward, nor as to the nature of the decision against which the claim is made – to give a preliminary ruling as to the validity of resolutions of the High Authority when the question arises in a dispute the subject of litigation before a national court is an added argument in favour of there being no restrictions, for there is no reason which could justify a more restrictive solution in respect of undertakings having direct access to the Court, than in respect of third parties who may on occasion need the Court's judgment with regard to a decision of the High Authority.'

These examples invite a comparative approach to the interpretation of the Community law concepts. Indeed, as stressed by Advocate-General Roemer,[11] the Court has to 'call upon the law of the different Member States in order to arrive at a meaningful interpretation of Community law'. However, faced with the pluralist linguistic and legal background of the Community legal order the Court has maintained a discreet distance from the national

---

11 Case 6/54: *Netherlands Government v High Authority* [1954–56] ECR 103.

systems.[12] Whilst displaying a certain 'comparative attitude'[13] the Court has in fact embarked on an autonomous interpretation of the Community law emphasizing in this way its autonomous nature. The attractive idea of 'applied comparative law'[14] emerging from Luxembourg remains a theoretical rather than practical proposition.

12 See especially Case 145/83: *Adams v EC Commission* [1985] ECR 3539; [1986] 1 CMLR 506.
13 Pescatore, P, 'Les recours, dans la Jurisprudence de la Cour de Justice des Communautés Européennes, à des normes déduites de la comparaison des droits des Etats Membres', RIDC, 1980, p 337.
14 Cf Jolowicz, A, 'Some Practical Aspects and the Case for Applied Comparative Law', in *New Perspectives for a Common Law of Europe* (ed Cappelletti, M) (1978), pp 237 et seq.

Chapter 4

Sources of Community law

The phrase 'source of law' can be used in several senses. It can mean the causes of law, that is to say the creative elements which contribute to the making of the law and thus can be the law itself. These may be historical facts devoid of any authority or political, social and economic conditions of the society which may, or may not, be regarded by the law as authoritative. The European Community owes its existence to international solidarity and the will to create a better Europe through economic cohesion. As 'causes', or sources of Community law they are rather remote and only of a passing interest to lawyers though lawyers ought to make themselves aware of 'the "grand design" underlying the European construction'[1]. In their work lawyers are concerned more with formal sources, that is authorities which may be cited in court and which are thus judicially cognizable. When analysing these we look to their authors and places where they can be found.

PART ONE
The origins of Community law

Unlike the International Court of Justice at The Hague, which is directed to apply international conventions, international custom, the general principles of law recognized by civilized nations and judicial decisions and the teachings of the most highly qualified publicists of the various nations,[2] the Community Court is left without specific guidance. Each of the relevant Treaties is content with the direction that 'the Court of Justice shall ensure that in the interpretation and application of this Treaty the law is observed',[3] without actually defining the *law* or its sources. In spite of this the Court has functioned vigorously applying Community law from a variety of sources.[4]

1 Pescatore in Bathurst et al, op cit at pp 32–34.
2 Statute of the International Court of Justice, art 38.
3 EEC, art 164; Euratom, art 136; ECSC, art 31 – words 'and of rules laid down for the implementation thereof', added.
4 See Bebr, G, *Judicial Control of the European Communities* (1962), p 26.

In the sense of the author or authority from which Community law is derived we can distinguish between *primary* and *secondary* sources. The distinction is important for theoretical and practical reasons because primary sources, being hierarchically superior, generate derivative (secondary) law and provide the criteria by which the validity of the latter is tested.

Primary sources

(A) CONSTITUTIONAL TREATIES

They are the *Constitutional Treaties* because together they form the organizational law of the Community. They constitute the basis of the Community legal order and the *fons et origo* of all Community law; they are its primary sources.

The primary sources of Community law consist of the three founding Treaties (ECSC, EAEC and EEC) with their Annexes and Protocols, which supplement the Treaties; the Convention on Certain Institutions Common to the European Communities (1957); the Merger Treaty (1965); the Luxembourg Treaty on Budgetary Matters (1970); the first Treaty of Accession and its Annexes (1972); the Second Budgetary Treaty (1975), the Act of the Council concerning direct elections to the European Parliament (1976), the second Treaty of Accession and its Annexes (1979) the third Treaty of Accession and its Annexes (1985) and the Single European Act (1986).

The founding Treaties are 'self-executing'[5] treaties which means that, when ratified, they become law automatically within the Member States. In contrast with 'non-self-executing' treaties (which constitute international obligations but require implementing legislation before they become applicable in internal law), 'self-executing' treaties must be applied directly by the municipal courts as the law of the land. A treaty is, by its nature, a contract between two or more states; it is not a legislative act. However, it may be regarded as a legislative act whenever it is designed by the signatory states as a declaration of their understanding of what a particular rule of law is, or an expressly formulated norm of future behaviour, or a constitution of an international organization. The legislative nature of the EEC Treaty is indicated by its purpose and specific provisions (articles 227 and 247(2)) and confirmed by the 'Act concerning the Conditions of Accession and the Adjustment of the Treaties' (article 2).[6] The status of the Protocols is the

5 On self-executing treaties see the judgment of Chief Justice Marshall in *Foster and Elam v Neilson* 2 Pet 253 (US 1829).
6 Attached to the Treaties of Accession.

same, as by virtue of article 239 they 'form an integral part' of the EEC Treaty.

The content of the EEC Treaty is complex not only because it creates institutions and defines the objectives of the Community, but also because it provides the basis and authority for Community legislation. It provides for an Executive, a Bureaucracy, a Parliament and a Court and charges these institutions with the execution of the Treaty. The Treaty remains a treaty, that is an agreement between the signatory states, but it differs from a classical treaty not only because it creates supra-national institutions but, more importantly, because, unlike a typical treaty, its execution has been taken out of the hands of the parties. The institutions it creates, notwithstanding their imperfections and limitations, can be likened to the corresponding institutions of the internal law. Their strength lies in the fact that certain important powers have been transferred or delegated by the states to these institutions, making them quasi-autonomous. Their weakness lies in the fact that their functioning is contingent upon the continuous discharge of the Treaty obligations by the Member States. Thus, if a country adopts an obstructive attitude the Community will continue to function though its dynamism shall be stunned.[7] If a country withdraws from the Community havoc could be caused but the Community would not come to an end and the institutions would not cease to function. But if a number of states withdrew the Community would cease to be a practical possibility.

If we apply a juristic construction to the Treaty modelled upon internal law it can be argued that the Treaty is the Constitution of the Community[8] or, to use Judge Donner's phrase, that the Member States have undertaken obligations 'not simply on a reciprocal basis but primarily towards the new collectivity they set up'.[9] The authors of this book subscribe to the constitutional theory in spite of arguments advancing an opposite opinion, namely that the Treaty is merely a bundle of contractual obligations.

In addition to the Constitution of the Community the Treaty contains what continental lawyers would term 'ordinary legislation' implying thereby a hierarchy of legal norms.[10] The Treaty 'legislation' is quite detailed in some areas, eg the customs union, and

7 As during the 'constitutional crisis' of 1965, see infra pp 236–240.
8 Eg Wagner, H, op cit, p 24 and Pescatore, P, *L'Ordre Juridique des Communautés Européenes* (1971), pp 36 et seq; for same opinion see German Federal Constitutional Court (First Chamber), Decision of 18 October 1967, [1967] AWD 477–8 (1980) Europarecht, 134–7.
9 'The Constitutional Powers of the Court of Justice of the European Communities', 11 CML Review, 1974, p 128.
10 Ie the Constitution, Acts of Parliament, legislative acts of the Executive and delegated legislation.

only in a general outline in others, eg taxation. The relationship
between 'constitutional' provisions and the 'ordinary legislation'
of the Treaty, obvious to continental lawyers but rather obscure to
British lawyers, who are not familiar with the theory of hierarchy of
legal norms, is of some practical importance as far as the legislative
function of the Community organs is concerned. The point is
whether the Treaty alone can provide sufficient authority for legislation by these organs or whether the growth of Community law
must depend on its original source, ie the power delegated by the
Member States. The answer seems to be in the affirmative, ie that
the Treaty is sufficient for a dynamic and orderly development,
assuming, of course, that the Community organs do not act *ultra
vires*. The Treaty could not have envisaged all the eventualities but
provided[11] a wide scope for Community initiatives, safeguarding
at the same time the principle of legality through the instrumentality of the Court and the vital interests of the Member States
through the instrumentality of the Council. Thus, in order to attain
the Community objectives the Council by a unanimous decision
may take the appropriate measures (which, presumably, include
appropriate legal measures) on the recommendation of the Commission and in consultation with the Parliament. These powers are
wide but circumscribed by the Treaty and so, it was argued[12]
correctly that the provisions of article 235 constitute no blanket
authority for 'implied powers'. The problem did arise under the
ECSC Treaty and the Community Court considered *ultra vires* the
delegation of powers vested in the High Authority to an agency in
Brussels set up for the purpose of operating a system of subsidies
to equalise the cost of scrap iron.[13] More recently the ECJ,[14] ruling
on the validity of a Community action programme for the
vocational training of young people, held (citing its decision in
another case)[15] that the use of article 235 as a legal base for a
measure is justified only where no other provision of the Treaty
gives the Community institutions the necessary power. In the
instant case article 128 of the Treaty provided a sufficient base for
the measure in question.

In order to supplement the powers of the Community organs

11 EEC, art 235; EAEC, art 203; ECSC, art 95.
12 Wohlfarth, E, Everling, H, Glässner, H J, Sprung, R, 'Die Europäische
   Wirtschaftsgemeinschaft', *Kommentar zum Vertrage* (1960), comment (7) on
   art 235.
13 Case 9/56: *Meroni & Co Industrie Metallurgiche SpA v High Authority of the
   ECSC* [1957–1958] ECR 133 at 149–154.
14 Case 56/88: *United Kingdom v EC Council, Re Vocational Training Programme*
   [1989] 2 CMLR 789 at para 5.
15 Case 45/86: *EC Commission v EC Council, Re Generalized Tariff Preferences*
   [1987] ECR 1493; [1988] 2 CMLR 131.

(and thus, presumably, curtail the temptation to rely on 'implied powers') a practice under the ECSC Treaty was established whereby a certain amount of law-making power was exercised by assembled representatives of the Member States.[16] The practice spread to the EEC, the most interesting example of this being the decisions which resulted in the acceleration of the setting up of the customs union.[17] The legal nature of these devices (described as 'acts of representatives')[18] is obscure. They are regarded as 'international agreements in simplified form'[19] and 'borderline of international law and Community law'.[20] These 'acts of representatives', no doubt, contribute to the development of Community policy and law and in a sense provide a substitute for the revision of the Treaty. A further dynamic application of article 235 can be seen in the implementation of the Dublin agreement of 1975 on the adoption of the correcting mechanism in respect of the budgetary obligations of the Member States.[1]

The view that the Treaty provides the Constitution of the Community is fortified by the fact that so far recourse has been taken to the Community Court and Community law rather than international law sources for the purpose of the interpretation of the Treaties and legislative acts made under the Treaties. The Court itself, through the Advocate-General Lagrange,[2] considered the role of general international law as a source of Community law rather limited because:

'... our Court is not an international tribunal, but is concerned with a community which has been created by six states and which resembles more a federation than an international organization ... The Treaty ... although concluded in the form of international treaties and undoubtedly being one, nevertheless also constitutes, from a substantive point of view, the character of the Community and as a consequence the legal

---

16 ECSC, art 69, concerning free movement of skilled labour (JO 586/55 and 1647/63); ECSC, art 70, concerning international railroad tariffs (JO 607/55, 701/55, 130/56 and 431/59); see Kaiser, 'Die im Rat vereinigten Vertreter der Regierungen der Mitgliedstaaten', *Festschrift Ophüls* (1965), pp 107–24.

17 JO 1217/60 and 1284/62.

18 Brinkhorst, L J, 'Implementation of (non-self-executing) Legislation of the European Economic Community, including Directives', *Legal Problems of an Enlarged European Community*, edited by Bathurst, M E, et al (1972), p 72.

19 Pescatore, P, 'La personalité internationale de la Communauté', *Les relations extérieures de la Communauté unifiée* (Liège 1969), p 585.

20 Resolution following the parliamentary report by Burger (EP doc 215/1968–69) concerning collective acts of the Member States of the Community, JO 1969, C.

1 *Bulletin of the European Communities* 1975, No 3, p 6.

2 In Case 8/55: *Fédération Charbonnière de Belgique v High Authority* [1954–56] ECR 245 at 277.

provisions derived from the Treaty must be viewed as the internal law of the Community. . . .'

An international treaty creating rights and obligations of states may be regarded as special law within the general compass of international law. The point which concerns the EEC Treaty as a source of law is whether the obligations contained therein can be derogated from by reference to general principles of international law. One of such general rules (albeit discredited through abuse) is the doctrine of necessity,[3] which suggests that states in cases of extreme emergency may resort to breaches of International Law. As states are rather prone to resort to legal subterfuge under the guise of real or imagined emergency[4] article 226 of the EEC Treaty provides a specific procedure to deal with such situations within the complexity of the Common Market. Accordingly, as decreed by the Community Court,[5] the plea of necessity cannot succeed in face of article 226. Furthermore, having safeguarded certain state interests (eg articles 36, 56(1), 108, 115, 223), the Treaty has reduced[6] the scope of arbitrary 'emergency' action states may be tempted to take in protection of their 'sovereign rights'. Although article 226 was designed to correct matters arising during the transitional period there is no reason why its general principle and mechanism should not be applied in a wider sense.

There is, however, no reason why a rule of International Law recognized by the Member States as a general rule of law should not be applied in the interpretation of the Treaties or Community legislation. Thus, eg, in *Van Duyn v Home Office*[7] the Community Court upheld the principle of International Law that, whilst a state has a duty of receiving its own nationals, it has no such duty in respect of the nationals of another state though Community nationals may claim a right of entry by virtue of a directly applicable provision of the EEC Treaty. In *Nold v EC Commission* the Court considered that 'international agreements in which the Member States have participated or to which they have adhered contain indications which have to be taken into account within the frame-

---

3 Oppenheim, L, *International Law*, Vol 1 (8th edn 1955), pp 297 et seq, and Brownlie, I, *International Law and the Use of Force by States* (1963), pp 40–44.

4 Cf the measures taken by the Labour Government in the UK when coming to power in 1967 which resulted in breaches of several treaties.

5 Case 7/61: *EEC Commission v Government of Italy* [1961] ECR 317 at 328–329, [1962] CMLR 39 at 52.

6 Commission decision of 23 July 1968, No 68/301/EEC, authorizing the French Government to take certain measures under art 108 (3).

7 Case 41/74; [1974] ECR 1337; [1975] 1 CMLR 1.

work of Community law'[8] but in an earlier case[9] the Court held that 'the validity of acts of the institutions within the meaning of article 177 of the Treaty cannot be tested against a rule of International Law unless that rule is binding on the Community and capable of creating rights of which interested parties may avail themselves in a court of law'.

In the light of the above it seems that the Community, being an autonomous organization created within the framework of International Law, is governed by its own law and its Court will apply the rules of International Law only if such rules are relevant to the definition of Community rights[10] or obligations arising from the international status of the Community. Regarding the Member States' position in the Community and vis-à-vis each other they have to bear in mind that, in accordance with International Law (now enshrined in article 30 of the 1969 Vienna Convention on the Law of Treaties), 'by assuming a new obligation which is incompatible with rights held under a prior treaty a State ipso facto gives up the exercise of these rights to the extent necessary for the performance of its new obligations'.[11] Member States are locked in a system of reciprocal duties and duties to the collective which they themselves have created.

(B) DURATION AND AMENDMENT OF THE TREATIES

Whilst the ECSC Treaty (article 97) was concluded for fifty years the EEC (article 240) and the Euratom Treaty (article 208) were concluded for an unlimited period. There is no provision for withdrawal, suspension or expulsion of a Member State. However a precedent for negotiated withdrawal was set up in the case of Greenland which became part of the Community as a Danish dependency but relinquished its privileges on reaching a further autonomy. This necessitated an amendment of the treaties constituting the three Communities.[12]

The Treaties[13] provide a procedure for their amendment which reflects the status of the Community as a creature of International Law and safeguards the sovereign rights of the Member States. Thus an amendment of the ECSC Treaty must be proposed by a

---

8 Case 4/73: [1974] ECR 491 at 507, [1974] 2 CMLR 338 at 354.
9 Case 9/73: *Schlüter v Hauptzollamt Lörrach* [1973] ECR 1135 at 1157.
10 *Van Duyn*, supra; Cases 21–24/72: *International Fruit Co v Produktschap voor Groenten en Fruit* [1972] ECR 1219 at 1226; Case 36/75: *Rutili v Ministère de l'Interieur* [1975] ECR 1219, [1976] 1 CMLR 140.
11 Case 10/61: *EEC Commission v Italy* [1962] ECR 1 at 10, [1962] CMLR 187 at 203
12 Treaty of Brussels, EC 19 (1985); OJ 1985, L29/1.
13 ECSC, art 96; EEC, art 236; Euratom, art 204.

Member State or the High Authority to the Council and if accepted by a two-thirds majority the President of the Council will convene an inter-governmental conference to consider the proposal. Amendments accepted by common accord by the conference become effective when ratified by the Member States in accordance with their constitutions.

A slightly different procedure, entailing the participation of the Parliament, applies to amendments of the two other Treaties. Accordingly a proposal emanating either from a Member State or the Commission goes before the Council and, if the Council after consulting the Parliament and, where appropriate, the Commission, delivers an opinion in favour of calling a conference of the representatives of the governments, such a conference must be convened to determine by common accord the amendments to be made. The amendments enter into force after being ratified by the Member States. The Single European Act, which amended all three Treaties, was enacted in that way, the decision to convene the conference having been reached by a majority of seven to three. The Act was, of course, accepted without dissent.

We should observe in this context that accession of new members entails amendments of the founding Treaties (such amendments being comprised in the Acts of Accession and the relevant Protocols) which require unanimity of decision and ratification by all the contracting states.[14]

Association agreements and other international agreements incompatible with the founding Treaties cannot be entered into unless the Treaty concerned has previously been amended in accordance with the procedure laid down therein.[15]

Whilst the founding Treaties can be amended only in accordance with the procedure laid down therein each Treaty contains a mechanism for minor adaptation through an internal process. These minor adaptations concern the abolition of customs duties and import quotas during the transitional period and the extension of the list of agricultural products under the EEC Treaty;[16] supplies, safeguards, rights of ownership of fissile materials, lists of products and the initial research and training programme under the Euratom Treaty;[17] and the list of coal and steel products under the ECSC

14 ECSC, art 98; EEC, art 237; Euratom, art 205.
15 EEC, arts 228(2) and 238(3); Euratom, art 206(3); see also Opinion 1/73 [1975] ECR 1335, [1976] 1 CMLR 85; Opinion 1/76 [1977] ECR 741, [1977] 2 CMLR 279; Ruling 1/78 [1978] ECR 2151, [1979] 1 CMLR 131; Opinion 1/78 [1979] ECR 2871, [1973] 3 CMLR 639.
16 Arts 14(7), 33(8), 38(3).
17 Arts 76, 85, 90, 92, 215.

Treaty.[18] All three Treaties provide that the Council may, unanimously, at the request of the Court increase the number of judges[19] and Advocates-General.[20] The number of members of the Commission[1] may also be altered by unanimous decision of the Council, presumably at the request of the Commission.

The ECSC Treaty[2] allows an adaptation of the powers of the High Authority to meet unforeseen difficulties affecting the common market in coal and steel without, however, conflicting with the general provisions of the Treaty or disturbing the institutional balance.

Two further adaptations through the internal process are provided for in all three Treaties, ie the introduction of direct elections to Parliament[3] to be recommended to the Member States by the Council at the instance of the Parliament and under the EEC and Euratom Treaties the replacement[4] of the financial contribution of Member States by the Community's own resources to be adopted by the Council on the proposal from the Commission and after consulting the Parliament.

(C) APPLICATION OF THE TREATIES

The founding Treaties,[5] as amended by the Acts of Accession, circumscribe their territorial application thus defining a Community territory. They apply not only to the mass land of the Member States and the territories for which they are internationally responsible (like the self-governing territory of Gibraltar) but also to the territorial waters[6] of the Member States and, presumably, to their contiguous zone and the continental shelf – a matter of great importance not only for fishery rights but also for the exploitation of mineral wealth.

The Protocol[7] on German Internal Trade and Connected Problems granted a special status to the German Democratic Republic (recognizing implicitly the concept of 'one Germany') as a territory which, though not part of the Community territory, was not a non-

18 Art 81.
19 ECSC, art 32(4), as amended by the Convention on Common Institutions, art 4(2)(a); EEC, art 165(4); Euratom, art 137(4).
20 ECSC, art 32(3), amend. as above; EEC, art 166(3); Euratom, art 138(3).
1 Merger Treaty, art 10(1).
2 Art 95(3).
3 ECSC, art 21(3); EEC, art 138(3); Euratom, art 108(3).
4 EEC, art 201; Euratom, art 173.
5 ECSC, art 79(1); EEC, art 227(1); Euratom, art 198(1).
6 See Case 61/77: *EEC Commission v Ireland* [1978] ECR 417 at 446, [1978] 2 CMLR 466 at 513–514; Case 63/83: *R v Kirk* [1984] ECR 2689; [1984] 3 CMLR 522, [1984] 1 All ER 453.
7 Protocol attached to EEC Treaty, art 1.

Member State in relation to the German Federal Republic.[8] The Treaties do not apply to the Faroe[9] Islands or the British sovereign base areas in Cyprus[10] but they did apply to Berlin.[11] Special provisions limiting the effects of the Treaties apply to the French[12] overseas departments, the Channel Islands, the Isle of Man,[13] Mount Athos[14] and the Canary Islands, Centa and Melilla.[15]

The Treaties have also extra-territorial effect, which is especially pertinent to the operation of the Community competition policy. The principle was established by the ECJ in the ICI[16] case in which a British multi-national company, together with its associates, claimed, albeit unsuccessfully, immunity from liability for restrictive practices contrary to article 85(1) of the EEC Treaty on the ground that it had no physical presence in the Community at a time when the United Kingdom was not a member. The jurisdiction over overseas entities can be claimed either in accordance with the so-called 'effects doctrine' favoured by the Commission or the more pragmatic approach of the ECJ which held that the fact that one of the parties to an agreement prohibited by the Treaty is situated outside the Community does not prevent the application of the rules since the agreement is operative in the territory of the Common Market.[17]

(D) CONVENTIONS BETWEEN MEMBER STATES

According to EEC article 220 Member States ought to negotiate conventions to secure for the benefit of their nationals the protection of rights, abolition of double taxation, mutual recognition of companies and reciprocal recognition and enforcement of judgments of municipal courts and arbitration awards. It goes without saying that such conventions shall have the force of treaties and be binding accordingly. By these conventions the Member States can create new laws and, in view of the sovereign power of states, these

---

8 See Case 23/79: *Geflügelschlachterei Freystadt GmbH v HZA Hamburg-Jonas* [1979] ECR 2789.
9 ECSC, art 79(2)(a); EEC, art 227(5)(a); Euratom, art 198(3)(a).
10 ECSC, art 79(2)(b); EEC, art 227(5)(b); Euratom, art 198(3)(b).
11 Declaration, art 1.
12 EEC, art 227(2).
13 Act of Accession 1972, Protocol 3.
14 Act of Accession 1979, Joint Declaration.
15 Act of Accession 1985, art 25, Protocol 2.
16 Case 48/69: *Imperial Chemical Industries Ltd v EC Commission* [1972] ECR 619, [1972] CMLR 557; see also Joined Cases 89, 104, 114, 116, 117 and 125–129/85: *A Ahlstrom Oy v EC Commission, Re Wood Pulp Cartel* [1988] ECR 5193, [1988] 4 CMLR 901.
17 Case 22/71: *Béguelin Import v SA GL Import–Export* [1971] ECR 949 at 959, [1972] CMLR 81 at 95.

laws can go far beyond the scope of the founding Treaties. Should this be the case the Community Court might have to rule whether such laws, being in excess of the founding Treaties, are cognisable by the Court as a source of Community law. Rules seem to be devolving both by the Community Court and the national courts of the Member States. Thus it was held by the Paris Court of Appeal that Community law superseded rights and obligations arising from previous bi-lateral social security conventions between Member States inconsistent with the founding Treaty,[18] though the Community Court[19] held that Community law would not prevent additional social benefits arising under municipal law.

Conventions between Member States subsequent to the founding Treaty were held by the Community Court unable to alter the existing Community law[20] though doubts were cast on the position in the submission of Advocate-General Roemer in *Federal Republic of Germany v EEC Commission*.[1]

Since the position is somewhat uncertain, a cautious approach should be adopted to the problem of conventions between Member States as a source of Community law. If they are within the scope of article 220 no question will arise for the conventions should be regarded as an instrument of harmonization or approximation of national laws. They will be negotiated and concluded within the Community spectrum, the Commission taking an active part in the process. The scope of the conventions envisaged in article 220 is wider than the scope of the harmonization of laws under articles 100–102 of the EEC Treaty. However, little progress has been achieved to date. In fact only four such Conventions have been signed: the 1968 Convention on Jurisdiction and the Enforcement of Judgments in Civil and Commercial Matters, signed in 1969,[2] in force between the original six Member States as from 1 February 1973;[3] the Convention on the Law Applicable to Contractual Obligations,[4] signed in 1980 and in force; the 1968 Convention on the

---

18 *Nani v Caisse d'Assurance Vieillesse des Travailleurs Salariés de Paris* [1964] CMLR 334; 4 CMLRev 70–71.
19 Case 92/63: *Nonnenmacher Moebs v Bestuur der Sociale Verzekeringsbank* [1964] ECR 281, at 288, [1964] CMLR 338 at 347.
20 Case 33/64: *Betriebskrankenkasse der Heseper Torfwerk GmbH v Koster (née van Dijk)* [1965] ECR 97, at 104, [1966] CMLR 191 at 208.
1 Case 24/62: [1963] ECR 63, [1963] CMLR 347 at 361–362.
2 OJ 1972, L299/32, amended final text OJ 1983, C97/2; see Sch 1 to the UK Civil Jurisdiction and Judgments Act 1982; Lasok and Stone, op cit, Chs 5, 6, 7.
3 Denmark, Ireland and the United Kingdom signed the convention on 9 October 1978 (OJ 1978, L304); Greece in 1982, Spain and Portugal to follow suit.
4 OJ 1980, L266 and supplementary Convention on the accession of Greece, OJ 1984, L146; signed by ten Member States final text of 1984, L 146.

Mutual Recognition of Companies and Bodies Corporate, signed in 1968 by the original six Member States but not yet in force;[5] and the European Patent for the Common Market Convention[6] of 1975, signed but not yet in force.

In accordance with the three Acts of Accession the new Member States are bound to accede to the Conventions subject to adjustments which may be necessary in individual cases. Further Conventions, ie on Bankruptcy (1970)[7] and Mergers of Companies (1973),[8] are in a draft form. Originally proposed as a Convention on Know-How, it was enacted in the form of a regulation[9] which entered into force on 1 April 1989.

If the subject matter of a convention is outside the scope of article 220 but nevertheless within the scope of the Community as laid down in the founding Treaties such a convention may well be regarded as a source of Community law. An example to the point is the Luxembourg Convention for the European Patent for the Common Market of 1975.[10] It has been signed, though not yet ratified, by the Member States with the object of creating one patent territory and establishing a uniform legal regime applicable to patents in the whole of the Common Market. It has been actively encouraged by a resolution of the Council of Ministers[11] and the Commission had a hand in it. The Convention, in its preamble, claims to have accomplished one of the Community objectives and, in article 73, enables the national courts to refer matters of its interpretation to the ECJ for a preliminary ruling in accordance with article 177 of the EEC Treaty. Finally it states expressly, in article 93, that none of its provisions 'may be invoked against the application of any provision' of the EEC Treaty.

The Luxembourg Convention (not yet in force) is a companion to the Munich European Patent Convention of 1973[12] which is already in force comprising not only the original Six and the United Kingdom (Denmark, Greece, Ireland, Portugal and Spain to follow) but also a number of other countries, ie Austria, Licht-

5 See EC Bull Supp 2/69; Lasok and Stone, op cit, 89 et seq.
6 OJ 1976, L17/1; Lasok and Stone, op cit, pp 85 et seq.
7 See 1980 Draft, EC Bull Supp 2/82; Lasok and Stone, op cit, Ch 10.
8 Resurrected in the form of the Draft Tenth Directive on Cross-border Mergers; OJ 1985, C23/11; EC Bull Supp 3/85.
9 Regulation 556/89, OJ 1989, L61/7.
10 OJ 1976, L17/1; see Lasok, D, *The Law of the Economy in the European Communities 1980*, pp 269 et seq. See also Community Patent Agreement, OJ 1989, L401/1 and Patent Litigation Protocol, OJ 1989, L401/34; Common Appeal Court Statute, OJ 1989, L401/48 and Common Appeal Court Privileges Protocol, OJ 1989, L401/45.
11 OJ 1976, L17/43.
12 International Legal Materials, Vol XIII (1974), pp 270 et seq.

enstein, Sweden and Switzerland. Both Conventions purport to establish a system of law common to the contracting parties.[13] However European patents, governed by the Munich Convention, except in so far as is otherwise provided in the Convention, have in each of the contracting states for which they are granted the effect of a national patent granted by the state concerned whilst Community patents, governed by the Luxembourg Convention, are to have a unitary character. Having an autonomous character, Community patents are subject only to the Community Patent Convention and to those provisions of the European Patent Convention which are binding upon every European patent. The two Conventions are interrelated but, strictly speaking, only the Luxembourg Convention creating Community patents is a Community legislative act, the Munich Convention not being in a technical sense a Community instrument. However, having said that, one has to bear in mind that the two Conventions have adopted a uniform system for the granting and the contesting of patents but left the enforcement of patent rights to national jurisdictions. This enables the national courts to request preliminary rulings and the Community Court to rule on the interpretation of both Conventions and the validity and interpretation of implementing provisions.[14]

Though a classical instrument of international legislation, conventions have not proved to be an attractive instrument of Community legislation. Ruled by the principles of International Law, they have to be negotiated, signed and, where appropriate, ratified. They may contain a denunciation clause and have to be expressly adopted on accession of new Member States. They are slow to enact, invite reservations and delays in coming into force. They do not seem to have any prominent future in the law-making process of the Community.

(E) COMMUNITY EXTERNAL TREATIES

In addition to Conventions which, as we have noted, represent an internal development of Community law there is a substantial volume of law engendered by Community external treaties.[15] Both sources have an international flavour and both are procedurally linked with International Law but, whilst the former is concerned primarily with the Community internal market, the latter reflects the Community's position as a world trading unit and a power base for the Community's own external policy.

13 Munich Convention, art 1; Luxembourg Convention, art 1.
14 Luxembourg Convention, art 73.
15 See pp 58 et seq, supra.

However, the treaty-making power of the Community, unlike that of a state, is not unlimited, for by virtue of article 228 the Community can enter into agreements with the states and international organizations where so provided by the Treaty. It provides further that such agreements shall be binding upon the Member States if concluded in accordance with the procedure laid down in article 228.

It follows that by submitting to the Treaty the Member States delegate to the Community an important portion of their sovereign power to create international obligations and new laws in as far as the external treaty agreement with a state or international organisation may be a source of law.[16] The delegation is not absolute for it is exercised subject to the participation of each Member State in Council and the recourse to the Court. However, the Court acts as the watchdog of the Community legality but not of the interests of the Member States.

All these agreements, in so far as they shape the trade pattern between the Community and the outside world and thereby affect both the internal arrangement of the Community and the legal obligations of the Member States, can be regarded as a source of Community law from which individual rights may be derived.[17] However both Conventions and external Community treaties or agreements, while sources of Community rights and obligations, defy the classification into primary and secondary sources of Community law and, therefore, should be placed between the founding Treaties and the Community legislation discussed below.

Secondary sources

By secondary sources of Community law we understand the law-making acts of the Community organs which result in a body of law generated by the Community itself in its quasi-autonomous capacity. We regard these sources as secondary because their authority is derived from the provisions of the founding Treaties. Moreover in the hierarchy of legal norms they rank second to Treaty provisions. Their scope is circumscribed and their validity can be tested against the criteria laid down in the Treaties. To all intents and purposes they resemble delegated legislation. The importance of the law-making power of the Community cannot be overemphasized because, as stated by a distinguished jurist, 'the

---

16 Cf Sir Gerald Fitzmaurice, 'Some Problems Regarding the Formal Sources of International Law', *Symbolae Verzijl*, p 160, quot. by Morand, C A, *La législation dans les Communautés Européennes* (1968), p 16.

17 See pp 76 et seq, supra.

first and most essential means by which a supra-national organisation endeavours to carry out its objectives ... resides in the law-making power'.[18]

Legislation denotes rules of law made deliberately in the prescribed form by some competent authority. The founding Treaties carefully avoid the term *legislation* and refer instead to *regulations*,[19] apparently, as has been suggested,[20] to ward off the wrath of the national parliaments likely to be provoked by the suggestion that an outside body shall usurp their legislative function. The Community Court also preferred to refer to *pouvoirs réglementaires*,[1] although on another occasion[2] references were made to *compétence réglementaire* (p 687), *normative* (p 688) and *légiférante* (p 692). Without going into semantic niceties[3] the law-making power of the Community organs can be identified as one corresponding to a generally accepted notion of legislation. This means that it results in rules of conduct addressed to subjects of Community law which emanate from a definite organ, are made in a set form and, by virtue of the authority vested in the organ, have an obligatory character.

(A) OBLIGATORY ACTS

These consist of regulations, directives and decisions made by the Council or the Commission in order to carry out their task in accordance with the Treaty (EEC, article 189).

The nomenclature adopted in the EEC and EAEC Treaties is identical but it differs in the ECSC Treaty. Thus under article 14 of the ECSC Treaty we have decisions, recommendations and opinions. 'Decisions' under the ECSC Treaty correspond to regulations under the remaining two Treaties because they are said to be 'binding in their entirety'. However, the ECJ, depending on the scope of the given act, distinguishes between 'general decisions'[4]

---

18 Guggenheim, P, 'Organisations économiques supranationales, independance et neutralité de la Suisse', *Rev. de droit suisse*, Vol 82 (1963) II, p 247.
19 EEC, art 189(2), EAEC, art 161(2), ECSC, arts 31 and 35(1) and (2).
20 Pescatore, P, 'Les aspects fonctionnels de la Communauté économique européenne', *Les aspects juridiques du marché commun* (1958), p 67; cf Catalano, N, 'La fusion des voies de droit', *Colloquium at Liège* (1965), p 284.
1 Case 15/57: *Compagnie des Hauts Fourneaux de Chasse v High Authority of the ECSC* [1958] ECR 211.
2 Case 20/59: *Italy v High Authority of the ECSC* [1960] ECR 325 terms taken from Rec (1960) 662 at 687, 688, 692.
3 Morand, C A, *La législation dans les Communautés Européennes* (1968), pp 7–17.
4 Case 18/57: *Nold KG v High Authority of the ECSC* [1957] ECR 121; Case 18/62: *Barge v High Authority of the ECSC* [1963] ECR 259, [1965] CMLR 330.

which are equivalent to regulations and 'individual decisions'[5] which are equivalent to decisions under the EEC and EAEC Treaties. 'Recommendations' under the ECSC Treaty correspond to directives under the other two Treaties. 'Opinions' correspond to opinions and, as under the EEC and EAEC Treaties, they have no binding force. Bearing in mind these nuances we shall examine the position in terms of the EEC Treaty.

(a) *Regulations*

Concept and scope   Regulations have a general scope, are 'binding in their entirety' and are 'directly applicable' in all Member States (article 189(2)). The principle applies also to Staff Regulations which, though being a code of employment rules of Community civil servants, have a binding force in the Member States.[6] It follows that, apart from their applicability without the intermediary of the state, regulations are meant to be an instrument of uniformity within the Community. Uniformity is the desired aim but cannot always be achieved and so it may be necessary to leave implementation to the Member States. The agricultural regulations illustrate the point and the problem, for they leave it to each state to execute in its own fashion the system of levies and restitutions, to establish the necessary procedures and impose sanctions. In some cases, eg the free movement of workers[7] and social security of migrant workers,[8] the function of the regulations is to co-ordinate the national systems within the scope of the Treaty provisions regarding the Community rights of free movement or social protection for the Community nationals, their dependants and certain other categories of persons. However these regulations define neither 'workers' nor 'nationality', though both are Community concepts. The former is politically 'neutral' but the latter emanates from the sovereign prerogative of the Member States. It follows that the definition of 'workers' is ultimately a matter for the Community Court[9] but, in the absence of a common Community citizenship, each Member State is free to determine who has the privilege of its citizenship and how its citizenship is lost or acquired.

5 Case 20/58: *Phoenix-Rheinrohr AG v High Authority of the ECSC* [1959] ECR 75; Cases 22 and 23/60: *Raymond Elz v High Authority of the ECSC* [1961] ECR 181; Cases 23, 24, 52/63: *Société Anonyme Usines Émile Henricot v High Authority of the ECSC* [1963] ECR 217, [1964] CMLR 119.

6 Case 189/85: *EC Commission v Germany, Re Family Allowances for Community Officials* [1988] 2 CMLR 86; Case 186/85: *EC Commission v Belgium, Re Family Benefits for Community Civil Servants* [1988] 2 CMLR 759.

7 Reg 1612/68, JO 1968, L 257/2, art 4(12), (13), (15).

8 Reg 1408/71, OJ 1971, L 149/1. Amended and consolidated OJ 1980, C138/1.

9 See Case 75/63: *Hoekstra (neé Unger) v Bestuur der Bedrijfsvereniging voor Detailhanded en Ambachten* [1964] ECR 177, [1964] CMLR 319.

The regulation authorizing Germany to accept the importation of cattle from Denmark, before Denmark joined the Community, exemplifies the use of a regulation otherwise than a general instrument of Community legislation as it concerns one country only and simply gives leave to take measures appropriate to the situation in hand.[10]

The term 'regulation' is also used to describe measures whereby the Commission imposes 'provisional' and the Council 'definitive' anti-dumping duties in specific situations and in respect of individual parties.

Substantive and procedural requirements   In order to constitute a regulation the act of the Community organ must comply with certain conditions. In the first place regulations must rest upon the authority of the Treaty which means that they are made where so provided by the Treaty; if not so provided by the Treaty that act cannot have the character of a regulation.[11] Regulations have to be reasoned (*motivés*) or 'substantiated' in the terms of the Treaty[12] which, in the submission of Advocate-General Lagrange[13] means that they indicate in general terms the aims pursued by the regulations, the reasons which justify the regulations and the outlines of the system adopted.

However, as stated by the ECJ,[14] 'the extent of the requirement laid down by article 190 . . . to state the reasons on which measures are based depends on the nature of the measure in question', which means, in effect, that a statement of the authority and an intelligible exposition of the policy behind the given measure should suffice. In practice regulations (as well as other measures) contain in their preambles not only a recital of the relevant Treaty provisions but also, often, a lengthy statement of the objectives aimed to be achieved.[15] The latter are particularly useful for the analysis of the text.

Since regulations have to be based on specific articles of the Treaty a general reference to the Treaty or to article 235 which deals with the implied powers of the Community,[16] will not suffice.

10 Reg 15/64, JO 573/64.
11 This can be inferred from the judgment of the ECJ Cases 1 and 57, 14/57:
    Société des Usines à Tubes de la Sarre v High Authority of the ECSC [1957–58]
    ECR 105, referring to 'decision' under the ECSC Treaty.
12 EEC, art 190; ECSC, art 15; EAEC, art 162.
13 Case 18/62: *Barge v High Authority of the ECSC* [1963] ECR 259, [1965]
    CMLR 330.
14 Case 5/67: *W Beus GmbH & Co v HZA München* [1968] ECR 83 at 95, [1968]
    CMLR 131.
15 See Cases 154–155/83: *Firma Josef Hoche v Bundesanstalt für
    Landwirtschaftliche Marktordnung* [1986] 2 CMLR 632.
16 See p 37.

This principle was upheld by the ECJ where the Council regulation on Generalized Tariff preferences was challenged by the Commission[17] and where the UK challenged the Vocational Training Programme approved by the Council.[18]

In the former case there was a conflict of opinion between the Commission and the Council, as the Commission wished to enact the measure in question by virtue of article 113 of the Treaty, which meant that it could have been passed by a qualified majority in Council. However, the Council amended the proposal hoping to pass it by virtue of article 235 for which unanimity is required. Since there was no agreement in the Council the regulation was enacted on the basis of a general reference to the Treaty. The ECJ annulled the regulation for lack of substantiation. In its view, the regulation fell squarely within the ambit of article 113 as it was a measure taken in furtherance of the Common Commercial Policy and so article 235 would have been inappropriate. However, without reference to any specific article of the Treaty there was no substantiation which is necessary for derivative legislation.

In the latter case the scheme authorized by the Council fell within the ambit of article 128 and of budgetary appropriations governed by common policies. Therefore the reference to article 235, whose function is 'residual' in the sense that it enables the Member States acting unanimously to supplement insufficient Community powers (as argued by the United Kingdom), would have been clearly inappropriate. Budgetary consideration did not affect the legal basis of the measure involved.

It was held equally inappropriate, or rather, superfluous, to include article 235 where in a matter of tariff classification a combination of articles 28 and 113 was the correct legal basis. However the regulation on harmonized commodity description was not annulled since only a technical defect was revealed.[19]

In this context it is apposite to mention the juxtaposition of general and specific provisions of the Treaty, for it is relevant to the exercise of delegated powers and the substantiation of derivative legislation. In principle *lex specialis derogat legis generali*. Thus, for example, article 100 stands to article 43 as *lex generalis* stands to *lex specialis*. In other words, while article 100 provides the general basis and procedure for the harmonization of national laws, article 43 provides specifically for a common agricultural policy and, within the latter, article 40 for a common organization of agricultural markets. It follows that article 43 provides a sufficient basis

17 Case 45/86: *EC Commission v EC Council* [1987] ECR 1493, [1988] 2 CLMR 131.
18 Case 56/88: *United Kingdom v EC Council* [1989] 2 CMLR 789.
19 Case 165/87: *EC Commission v EC Council* [1990] 1 CMLR 457.

130   *Chapter 4   Sources of Community law*

for consumer protection within the general scheme of agricultural policy,[20] or for animal welfare legislation,[1] while article 40(3) enables the Commission to issue a regulation for the sale of intervention butter cheaply at Christmas even though it undercuts the sales of margarine. Thus the complaint of margarine traders that the regulation is invalid because it is discriminatory cannot be sustained since the common organization of the market for milk (butter) based on intervention is different from that for fats (margarine) based on production aid. On that ground the case can also be distinguished from the Isoglucose cases mentioned below.

The justification for substantiation is clear for it is a safeguard against arbitrary exercise of authority. It is also essential for the parties concerned to know their legal position and to be able to defend their rights. In other words, as explained the ECJ (in a case involving a decision)[2] '... In imposing upon the Commission the obligation to state reasons for its decisions, article 190 is not taking mere formal considerations into account but seeks to give an opportunity to the parties of defending their rights, to the Court of exercising its supervisory functions and to Member States and to all interested nationals of ascertaining the circumstances in which the Commission has applied the Treaty.' What the Court said about the Commission can equally be said about the Council and what can be said about a decision can equally be said about a regulation. Therefore, where, in the circumstances of the case, the reasons turn out to be insufficient, the sanction of nullity may be applied on substantive grounds and also on the ground of the infringement of an essential procedural requirement.[3] Perhaps the most instructive examples of the annulment on that ground are the Isoglucose cases[4] which have incidentally raised important questions concerning the Parliament's (albeit very limited) par-

20 Case 68/86: *United Kingdom v EC Council, Re Agricultural Hormones* [1988] ECR 855, [1988] 2 CLMR 543.
1 Case 131/86: *United Kingdom v EC Council, Re the protection of battery hens* [1988] ECR 905, [1988] 2 CMLR 364
2 Case 24/62: *Germany v EC Commission* [1963] ECR 63 at 69.
3 EEC art 173: Case 18/57: *Nold K G v High Authority of the ECSC* [1959] ECR 41 at 52; Case 6/72: *Europemballage Corpn and Continental Can Co Inc v EC Commission* [1973] ECR 215, [1973] CMLR 199; Case 73/74: *Groupement des Fabricants de Papiers Peints de Belgique v EC Commission* [1975] ECR 1491, [1976] 1 CMLR 589.
4 Joined Cases 103/77 and 145/77: *Royal Scholten-Honig (Holdings) Ltd v Intervention Board for Agricultural Produce and Tunnel Refineries Ltd v Intervention Board for Agricultural Produce* [1978] ECR 2037, [1979] 1 CMLR 675; Case 138/79: *S A Roquette Frères v EC Council* [1980] ECR 3333; and Case 139/79: *Maizena GmbH v EC Council* [1980] ECR 3393; Jacobs, F, *Isoglucose Resurgent: Two Powers of the European Parliament upheld by the Court*, 18 CML Rev (1981), p 219.

Secondary sources 131

ticipation in Community legislation and the right of intervention before the ECJ. At issue was the validity of Council Regulation 1293/79 (OJ 1979, L 162/10) fixing quotas for the production of isoglucose and imposing a tax on this product. The Regulation was successfully challenged by isoglucose producers since it discriminated in favour of sugar producers. However the Regulation was also bad because in the circumstances the essential requirement, ie consultation with Parliament in accordance with article 43(2) of the EEC Treaty, was not observed.

Defective[5] regulations are presumed valid and effective as long as they have not been declared invalid by the Community Court. The temporal effect of the declaration of nullity is within the discretion of the ECJ subject to the guidelines laid down in a case concerning social security rights.[6] In principle, the judgments of the ECJ have a prospective effect but, exceptionally, they may have a retrospective effect.[7]

Regulations have to be published in the Official Journal of the Community. They become binding on the date specified or, in the absence of a commencing date, on the twentieth day following their publication.[8] However, neither the publicity nor the form of the act will be decisive in determining the nature of the act, that is whether or not it is a regulation. The Community Court took the view that it was necessary to consider the contents and nature rather than the form of the act to determine its legal nature.[9] Should this be otherwise, improper acts dressed up as regulations would enable the Community organs to exercise their powers arbitrarily and so would erode the legal protection under the Treaty.

The effect of regulations As we have observed earlier, regulations have a mandatory effect. They bind the states and have the force of law in their territories without the need of transformation or confirmation by their legislatures. Thus it was held by the Com-

5 Case 101/78: *Granaria BV v Hoofdproduktschap voor Akkerbouwprodukten* [1979] ECR 623, [1979] 3 CMLR 124.
6 Case 41/84: *Pinna v Caisse d'Allocations Familiales de la Savoie* [1986] ECR 1, [1988] 1 CMLR 350; see also Case 112/83: *Société de Produits de Mais SA v Administration des Douanes et Droits Indirects* [1985] ECR 719, [1988] 1 CMLR 459.
7 See eg Case 309/85: *Barra v Belgium and City of Liège, Re Education Fees* [1988] 2 CMLR 409.
8 EEC, art 191(1); EAEC, art 163(1).
9 Cf. Cases 16 and 17/62: *Confédération Nationale des Producteurs des Fruits et Légumes v EC Council* [1962] ECR 471 at 478–479, [1963] CMLR 160 at 173–174. Case 250/81: *Greek Canners Association v EC Commission* [1982] ECR 3535, [1983] 2 CMLR 32. Case 26/86: *Deutz und Gelderman v EC Council* [1987] ECR 941, [1988] 1 CMLR 668; Cases 97/86, 193/86, 99/86 and 215/86 *ASTERIS and Greece v EC Commission* [1988] 3 CMLR 493 at paras 13, 14.

munity Court[10] that Council Regulation 1975/69 and Commission Regulation 2195/69, which provided for the payment of a premium in respect of slaughtered dairy cows, were 'directly applicable' and required no domestic provisions to make them effective in Italy so as to create rights vested in the individuals concerned. They left no discretion to Member States. Therefore Italy was in default because she failed to meet her obligation, the inefficiency of the national apparatus affording no defence.[11] In the literature the power to legislate in this way reflects the 'institutional autonomy'[12] of the Community and the concept of 'delegated legislation'.[13] The Member States are at the receiving end and it is their duty to see that the regulation is carried out. 'Consequently', held the ECJ,[14] 'all methods of implementation are contrary to the Treaty which would have the result of creating an obstacle to the direct effect of Community Regulation and jeopardising their simultaneous and uniform application in the whole of the Community.'

Implementation and derogations   The obligatory nature of the regulation and the duty to implement it are well illustrated in the Tachograph[15] case where the British Government unsuccessfully contended that it was free to enact a permissive measure when Council Regulation 1463/70 insisted that the installation of recording equipment in certain vehicles was compulsory and subject to sanction for non-compliance. Holding the United Kingdom liable for a breach of the Treaty the ECJ ruled that it would be inconceivable to allow a Member State to implement a regulation 'in an incomplete or selective manner' ... 'so as to render abortive certain aspects of Community legislation which it has opposed or which it considered contrary to its national interest ...'

Earlier the ECJ[16] defended the integrity of Community law by pointing out that a Member State, when passing a regulation into the national law, must not disguise its Community character by altering, for example, the date on which the regulation came into

10 Case 93/71: *Orsolina Leonesio v Italian Ministry of Agriculture* [1972] ECR 287 at 295, [1973] CMLR 343.
11 Case 39/72: *EC Commission v Italy* [1973] ECR 101, [1973] CMLR 439. See also Case 309/84: *EC Commission v Italy* [1986] ECR 599.
12 Rideau, J *Le rôle des états membres dans l'application du droit communautaire*, AFDI, 1972, p 864 (884–5).
13 Pescatore, P *L'ordre juridiques des Communautés européennes*, 2nd edn 1975, pp 192–3.
14 Note 11, supra, ECR at 114.
15 Case 128/78: *EC Commission v United Kingdom* [1979] ECR 419, [1979] 2 CMLR 45 at para 9, citing its own judgment in Case 39/72: *EC Commission v Italy* [1973] ECR 101, [1973] CMLR 439.
16 Case 34/73: *Variola SpA v Amministrazione Italiane delle Finanze* [1973] ECR 981 at para 15.

force. However for practical reasons, a regulation may have to be implemented in the terms of domestic law (as was, for example, the case of the EEC Egg Marketing Regulations 2772/75 and 95/69 on labelling and quality control) in which case a national measure would be permitted if not incompatible with the terms of the regulation.[17] In other words, in the absence of any provision in the Regulations regarding the purchase of bands and labels to be affixed to egg packs, the Member States are free to make arrangements for the issue of bands and labels and charge for the supervision of the marketing system.

Indeed the regulation may expressly provide for a national implementing measure[18] indicating a time limit for doing so but as repeatedly emphasized by the ECJ it cannot be overridden by national legislation.[19] Although its validity may be challenged albeit indirectly in the course of proceedings at the national level[20] it can be annulled only by the Community Court.[1] However the finding of illegality of a regulation by the ECJ in one case may be relied upon by national courts in other proceedings.[2]

Regulations may be challenged directly before the ECJ under article 173(1) of the EEC Treaty by the Member States, the Council or the Commission but by individuals under article 173(2) only if they are of direct and individual concern to the applicant. Thus in case 138/79,[3] in which the applicant sought the annulment of a Council Regulation fixing a production quota for isoglucose, the respondent unsuccessfully contended that the application was inadmissible because it was directed against a regulation and, therefore, outside the scope of article 173(2). The Court ruled that the

---

17 Case 31/78: *Bussone v Italian Ministry for Agriculture and Forestry* [1978] ECR 2429 at 2444, [1979] 3 CMLR 18 at 30. See also Case 272/83: *EC Commission v Italy, Re Agricultural Producer Groups* [1987] 2 CMLR 426.
18 Eg Reg 1463/70 (OJ 1970, L164/1), art 21(1) – re tachograph.
19 Case 6/64: *Costa Flaminio v ENEL* [1964] ECR 585 at 586–587, [1964] CMLR 425 at 456; Case 43/71: *Politi SAS v Italian Ministry of Finance* [1971] 2 ECR 1039 at 1048–1049, [1973] CMLR 60, *Simmenthal Cases* 35/76; [1976] ECR 1871, [1977] 2 CMLR 1; 106–77 (No 2) [1978] ECR 629, [1978] 3 CMLR 263; 70/77 (No 3) [1978] ECR 1453, [1978] 3 CMLR 670.
20 See Case 199/86: *Raiffeisen Hauptgenossenschaft v Bundesanstalt für landwitschaftliche Marktordnung* [1989] 2 CMLR 999.
1 Cases 119 and 120/76: *Ölmühle Hamburg A-G v HZA Hamburg Waltershof* and *Becher v HZA Bremen-Nord* [1977] ECR 1269, [1979] 2 CMLR 83; see also Case 273/81: *Société Laitière de Gacé SA v FORMA* [1982] ECR 4193, [1984] 1 CMLR 542.
2 See Case 66/80: *International Chemical Corpn SpA v Amministrazione delle Finanze dello Stato* [1981] ECR 1191, [1983] 2 CMLR 593.
3 See note 4, supra; see also Case C-229/88, *Cargill BV v EC Commission* [1990] 2 CMLR 753 (no locus standi), and Case C-152/88, p 57 note 14, supra.

Regulation was a measure in which the undertakings manufacturing isoglucose had a direct and individual concern.

In an earlier case[4] the applicants sought the annulment of Council Regulation 1692/72 concerning protective measures on the importation of motor cycles from Japan but the Court found that it was not of direct and individual concern to them. It would only be so if the applicants, pursuant to that measure, were refused an import authorization. In that case they would be able to raise the matter before the national court, which should, where appropriate, refer the question of its validity to the ECJ by virtue of article 177 of the Treaty. The Court added that 'the possibility of determining more or less precisely the number or even the identity of the persons to whom a measure applies by no means implies that it must be regarded as being of individual concern to them'. Indeed the Regulation could not produce effects in individual cases until it has been implemented by the national authorities. Similarly Council Regulation 3781/85 establishing a system of penalties for infringements of the provisions concerning fishing of the Act of Accession of Spain and Portugal was held to be of no individual concern to an association of fishermen. Its members would be affected only by a national decision which should only be taken if several conditions are complied with, and provided that decision is confirmed by the Commission.[5]

Apart from providing for implementation by national authorities a regulation may provide for derogation, in which case national law will apply in the area specifically reserved for deviation from the general scope of the regulation. A derogation grants the Member States a discretion whether to apply the specific provision of the regulation or substitute for it a national rule. However, derogations have to be construed restrictively and applied strictly within the permissiveness of the regulation. Thus, for example, Regulation 171/83 concerned with conservation of fishery resources provided that although, according to Community rules, fishing for plaice was allowed to the minimum size of 25cm in length of the species, national rules could restrict the size to 27cm. However, complying with the Community rules, a Dutch fisherman was correctly prosecuted for the breach of national rules, such rules being applicable to Dutchmen by virtue of the derogation.[6]

Council and Commission regulations   Since the Council and the

---

4 Case 123/77: *Unione Nazionale Importatori e Commercianti Motoveicoli Esteri (UNICHE) v EC Council* [1978] ECR 845.

5 Case 55/86: *Asociacion Provincial de Armadores de Buques de Pesca de Gran Sol de Pontevedra (Arposol) v EC Council* [1988] ECR 13 at s 13.

6 Case 53/86: *Officier van Justitie v Romkes* [1988] 3 CMLR 126.

Commission are empowered to make regulations a theoretical and practical question as to the standing of the Commission regulations *vis-à-vis* regulations made by the Council may arise. Indeed Advocate-General Roemer argued in a case[7] concerning regulations issued by the Council that they should override regulations issued by the Commission. In principle, where each legislates in its own right, there should be no conflict because the two institutions operate in their respective sphere of competence and one is not hierarchically superior to the other. In practice, however, the Commission exercises substantial powers delegated to it by the Council, notably in the fields of agricultural policy, customs and competition, and makes regulations accordingly. The procedure of delegation itself was challenged, albeit unsuccessfully, in the *Köster*[8] case involving the setting up and operation of management committees to administer the common market in cereals. The objections that, despite the requirement of consulting Parliament under article 43 (2) of the Treaty the Council alone made the relevant regulation and that, by delegating its powers to the Commission, it debilitated its decision-making power, were overruled as the Council retained control and could substitute its own measures for those taken by the Commission. The Court, following an earlier case,[9] held that the delegation did not contravene the Treaty.

Another leading case[10] was concerned with the organization of the common market in sugar. Under the relevant regulation the Commission was empowered to take measures to prevent disturbances in the market resulting from price fluctuations. Its powers were to be exercised under the management committee procedure. However the Commission delegated to Italy the power to control the Italian market and the Italian Government, in turn, enacted a decree imposing a levy on sugar stockholders. The latter challenged the validity of the decree before Italian courts which, on reference, led the Community Court to pronounce upon the validity of the sub-delegation of the Commission's powers to Italy. The ECJ ruled that, whilst the delegation to the Commission was in order, the sub-delegation to Italy was not. It acknowledged the need of 'wide powers of discretion and action'[11] in the hands of the Commission to carry out its mandate but ruled, in effect, that even

---

7 Case 32/65: *Italian v EC Council and EC Commission* [1966] ECR 389 at 415, [1969] CMLR 39 at 46.
8 Case 25/70: *EVGV v Köster* [1970] ECR 1161, [1972] CMLR 255. See also Case 278/84: *Germany v EC Commission, Re Revaluation of the Green Mark* [1988] 1 CMLR 632.
9 Case 9/56: *Meroni & Co v High Authority* [1958] ECR 133.
10 Case 23/75: *Rey Soda v Cassa Conguaglio Zucchero* [1975] ECR 1279, [1976] 1 CMLR 185.
11 At paras 10 and 11.

an extensive interpretation of the task of implementation could not entail a further delegation going out of control of the Council. The principle that *delegatus non potest delegare* has been vindicated.

The third leading case[12] illustrates the operation of delegated powers in the implementation of article 87 of the EEC Treaty concerned with the enforcement of the competition policy. By regulation 17/62[13] the Council provided for the procedure to investigate and adjudicate offences under articles 85 and 86 of the Treaty and laid down sanctions to be administered by the Commission. It delegated to the Commission the power to lay down implementing provisions including provisions governing the hearing of alleged violations before the Commission. The accused firm challenged the legality of such wide powers delegated to the Commission and argued that, since they included the power of legislation, they went beyond the scope of the exercise of powers conferred on the Commission by the Council for the implementation of the rules laid down by the Council by virtue of article 155(4) of the Treaty. The ECJ, explaining the scope of article 155, stressed that the function of implementation entails the taking of the appropriate measures which includes measures of a legislative nature, such as regulations.

The position of delegated legislation has been clarified by article 10 of the Single European Act which, by supplementing the provisions of article 145 of the EEC Treaty, conferred on the Commission, in the Acts which the Council adopts, powers for the implementation of the rules which the Council lays down. The Council may impose certain requirements in respect of the exercise of these powers and may also reserve the right, in specific cases, to exercise directly implementing powers itself. The procedure for the exercise of implementing powers must comply with principles and rules to be laid down in advance by the Council, acting unanimously on a proposal from the Commission and after obtaining the opinion of the European Parliament.

Thus Council regulations and Commission regulations fulfil different functions and their validity has to be tested in the light of the Treaty provisions governing the respective powers and functions of the two institutions. If the Commission issues regulations in its capacity as the executor of the decisions of the Council its regulations have to conform to the letter and the spirit of the delegation but, as can be inferred from the cases mentioned above, the delegated powers have to be wide enough to give effect to the provisions of the Treaty.

12 Case 41/69: *ACF Chemiefarma v EC Commission* [1970] ECR 661.
13 OJ 1959–1962/87.

In exercising its powers, whether original or delegated, the Commission has to act *infra vires* for the measures it enacts will be interpreted narrowly.[14] However, the scope of the delegation will determine the Commission's freedom of action. Thus in the Christmas butter scheme case[15] the relevant regulation was held to be valid because of the wide implementing powers granted to the Commission, while in the tuna case[16] there was no scope for the Commission to use its imagination in providing additional rules. Therefore both the implementing and the tertiary regulation fixing compensation were void.

In the event of conflict between a Council regulation and implementing Commission decision the former (assuming it is valid *per se*) must prevail but the competence to strike out the latter is within the functions of the ECJ. This is an aspect of the exclusive jurisdiction of the Court and of the judicial control of the Acts of the Institutions. Council regulation, which provided that customs duties which have not been recovered because of a mistake of the customs authorities, enabled such authorities to waive the duties if the importer was an innocent party to the mistake. Commission decision regarding the post-clearance recovery of duties provided for a delayed recovery which clearly contradicted the intention of the regulation. A German court faced with the protests of an importer asked the ECJ whether it could, in the circumstances, declare the Commission decision invalid. The ECJ reiterated the principle that only it was competent to exercise the judicial control over Community acts. Thus national authorities must hold such acts valid and, in case of doubt, seek a preliminary ruling from the ECJ.[17]

(b) *Directives*

Concept and scope   As compared with regulations which are, in principle, 'binding in their entirety', directives issued by the Council and the Commission are 'binding as to the result to be achieved, upon each Member State to which they are addressed' and the choice of the method is left to the state concerned (article 189(3), but under ECSC, article 14 recommendations correspond to directives). We can see that, unlike regulations, directives are

14 Case 61/86: *United Kingdom v EC Commission, Re Clawback on Export of Sheep* [1986] 2 CMLR 98; Cases 305/85 and 142/86: *Re Ewe Slaughter Premiums, United Kingdom v EC Commission* [1988] 2 CMLR 169 and Case 162/86: *Livestock Sales Transport Ltd v Intervention Board for Agricultural Produce* [1988] 2 CMLR 186.
15 Cases 279–280/84 and 285–286/84: *Walter Rau Lebensmittelwerke v EC Commission* [1987] ECR 1069, [1988] 2 CMLR 704.
16 Case 264/86: *France v EC Commission, Re Tuna Producers* [1989] 1 CMLR 13.
17 Case 314/85: *Foto-Frost v HZA Lubeck-Ost* [1988] 3 CMLR 57.

not meant to be an instrument of uniformity even if the same objective is aimed at when a directive is addressed to several states simultaneously unless, of course, the wording of a particular directive leaves no discretion.[18] In practice, directives are used mainly to effect approximation of national laws in accordance with article 100. In this respect article 100 delimits both the scope and the methods providing for directives 'for the approximation of such provisions laid down by law, regulation or administrative action in Member States as directly affect the establishment or functioning of the common market'.

Like regulations directives have to be reasoned or 'motivated' and based on the Treaty. Indeed, they are subordinated to the Treaty provisions.[19] They have to be notified to the addressees and will take effect upon such notification.[20] They may be addressed in the language of the addressee state.[1]

Directives must be addressed to states, they cannot be addressed to individuals.[2] Being in the nature of commands directives impose specific obligations upon the Member States. In the first place they have to be implemented completely[3] and in the most effective way. It follows that directives must be implement by 'binding acts', not by 'advisory circulars'. Thus, held the ECJ,[4] 'mere administrative practices which by their nature may be changed at the whim of the authorities and which lack appropriate publicity do not constitute proper implementation . . .' Moreover, the duty to implement is the responsibility of the state or states to which the directive has been addressed even if within that state (or states) the constituent units (eg provinces) have legislative powers.[5]

The duty to implement is enforceable within the discretion of the Commission under article 169 of the EEC Treaty, but not by

---

18 See Case 38/77: *Enka v Inspecteur der Invoerrechten* [1977] ECR 2203. See also Cases 97/86 (ASTERIS) p 131, note 9, ante.

19 Case 103/84: *EC Commission v Italy, Re Subsidy for Municipal Transport* [1986] ECR 1759, [1987] 2 CMLR 825.

20 EEC, art 191(2); EAEC, art 163(2).

1 Council Regulation 1/58, art 3, JO, 6 October 1958, p 385/58 (Sp edn 1952–1958, p 59).

2 Cases 56–58/64: *Consten and Grundig v EC Commission* [1966] ECR 299 at 337, [1966] CMLR 418 at 468.

3 See Case 239/85: *EC Commission v Belgium: Re Toxic and Dangerous Waste* [1988] 1 CMLR 248; see also Case 235/84: *EC Commission v Italy, Re Business Transfer Legislation* [1987] 3 CMLR 115.

4 Case 160/82: *EC Commission v Netherlands* [1984] 1 CMLR 230. See also Case 291/84: *EC Commission v Netherlands, Re Groundwater Directive* [1989] 1 CMLR 479.

5 Case 1/86: *EC Commission v Belgium, Re the Groundwater Directive* [1989] 1 CMLR 474.

a private party. Moreover the Commission cannot be forced to proceed under the pressure of a private party.[6]

It has then been suggested[7] that the choice of the method permitted by article 189 (3) implies the choice of the instrument and the choice of the contents of the instrument. It seems, however, that the choice of the method implies a procedural discretion, ie the choice of the type of instrument or machinery of implementation that suits best the given national system. As regards the contents (or substance) the discretion clearly depends upon the particularity or the degree of detail of the directive in question as well as the state of the existing national law involved. Thus in the eyes of the ECJ[8] it is not sufficient that the existing national law fulfils the aims of the directive for its details must also be implemented if not already covered unequivocally. This does not preclude creation of rights for individuals or pleading the directive before the municipal courts.[9]

Whilst the choice of the method is left to the addressee the Community usually sets a time limit upon the implementation of the directives which, like regulations, emanate either from the Council or the Commission. The reason for this is that time is needed in order to adapt the municipal law accordingly. Even so states are not always able to comply promptly. The speed with which the Value Added Tax was introduced in Italy is a good example of this, showing, incidentally, that a directive is less effective than a regulation in so far as its availability to individuals may depend upon implementation. Therefore many enforcement actions under article 169 of the EEC Treaty are concerned with inadequate or untimely implementation of directives. In most cases a threat of action will suffice and, where the Member State complies, the action will be withdrawn. However no Member State can plead the complexity of the implementation or the necessity of wide consultations in defence of non-compliance,[10] or even a

6 Case 247/87: *Star Fruit Company SA v EC Commission* [1990] 1 CMLR 733.
7 Easson, A J, 'EEC Directives for the Harmonisation of Law', Y E L (1981) p 1 (at 33).
8 Case 91/81: *EC Commission v Italy (Re Collective Redundancies)* [1982] ECR 2133, [1982] 3 CMLR 468.
9 Eg Directive 64/221/EEC, JO 850/64, art 4 (3): 'The Member States cannot introduce new measures or acts which are of a more restrictive nature than those in force at the time of notification of this directive'; Case 41/74: *Van Duyn v Home Office* [1975] Ch 358, [1975] ECR 1337; cf Case 28/67: *Molkerei-Zentrale v Hauptzollamt Paderborn* [1968] ECR 143, [1968] CMLR 187; see also Case 9/70: *Grad v Finanzamt Traunstein* [1970] ECR 825, [1971] CMLR 1 (decision and directives on turnover tax).
10 See Case 58/81: *EC Commission v Luxembourg (Re Head of Household Allowance)* [1982] 3 CMLR 482.

terrorist[11] act if the damage caused thereby had not been repaired with due diligence.

As in the case of regulations only the ECJ is competent to rule on the validity of directives. Therefore, in case of doubt raised within a national jurisdiction, reference to the ECJ for a preliminary ruling ought to be made.[12]

Implementation and derogations   Directives vary considerably in their scope and the precision of their text, especially where they are used as an instrument of harmonization of national laws. There they have to overcome the inbuilt resistance of often well-entrenched national rules. Consequently for political, not legislative reasons, in order to have the measure enacted they often reflect a compromise at the level of the lowest common denominator. Since, unlike instruments of international legislation, they cannot be enacted subject to reservations, they may be riddled with derogations giving effect to the residual force of national law. Here again the doctrine of the 'occupied field' comes to the fore since the scope of a particular directive will delineate the respective Community and national competence. Indeed, if the directive is drafted so tightly that it leaves no doubt as to its scope, and if the business regulated therein is exhaustively treated, there will be no gaps and, therefore, no room for manœuvre, not even for a permissive rule indicating the option of derogation left to Member States.[13] But this may not be so.

Thus, while directives have to be implemented 'completely', their 'complete' implementation in substance may, nevertheless, entrench divisive elements of national laws. This is well illustrated by the directives on consumer protection, for example the directive on the safety of toys[14] and product liability.[15] After nine years of labour in enacting the latter it is obvious that concessions to national laws had to be made. Many other examples can be quoted:

11 Case 101/84: *EC Commission v Italy (Re Failure to provide Transport Statistics due to Destruction of Data Processing Centre)* [1986] 2 CMLR 352.
12 *R v Minister of Agriculture Fisheries and Food, ex p Fédération Européenne de la Santé Animale* [1988] 3 CMLR 207, QB.
13 See eg Case 195/84: *Denkavit Futtermittel GmbH v Land Nordhein-Westfalen (Re Directives on Additives to Animal Foodstuffs)* [1987] 3 CMLR 585; also Case 29/87: *Dansk Denkavit v Landbrugsministeriet* [1990] 1 CMLR 203; Case 130/85: *Wulro BV v Tuchtgerecht van de Stichting Scharreleieren-Controle (Re Labelling of Eggs)* [1988] 1 CMLR 496; Case 306/84: *EC Commission v Belgium* [1988] 1 CMLR 768; Case 60/86: *EC Commission v United Kingdom* [1988] 3 CMLR 437; Case 264/86: *France v EC Commission* [1989] 1 CMLR 13; Case 255/86: *EC Commission v Belgium, Re Labelling of Bulk Fruit and Vegetables* [1989] 3 CMLR 91.
14 OJ, 1988, L187.
15 OJ, 1985, L210.

for example, the directive on the labelling of products distinguishing between dangerous substances and dangerous preparations imposed Community rules with regard to the former but not on preparations containing dangerous substances. In respect of the latter, Member States are free to apply their own laws.[16] Similarly the directives on environmental protection;[17] company law;[18] public works.[19]

A directive may also include a special derogation clause whereby the permissive rule cannot be applied unilaterally but its exercise is conditional upon permission granted by the Council.[20]

Interpretation of directives   Interpretation of directives involves not only the construction of the Community text[1] but also of the national implementing legislation and the residual national law. It is common ground that the implementing legislation ought to be so interpreted as to give effect to the intention of the Community legislator expressed in the directive itself.[2] It is also common ground that derogations must be interpreted strictly otherwise the whole object of the directive might be frustrated.[3] It is interesting to note that the directives to combat sex discrimination have provided a fertile ground for litigation and, consequently, for the interpretation of both the relevant Treaty provisions,[4] the directives themselves and of the implementing legislation. It goes without saying that questions concerning all three aspects are referable to the ECJ for a preliminary ruling, the last one, because

16 Case 187/84: *Italy v Caldana, Re Motor Oil* [1989] 1 CMLR 137.
17 Case 302/86: *EC Commission v Denmark, Re Disposable Beer Cans* [1989] 1 CMLR 619; Case 228/87: *Pretura di Torino v Persons Unknown (Re Purity of Drinking Water)* [1990] 1 CMLR 716.
18 Case 112/86: *AMRO Aandelen Fonds v Inspecteur der Registrar Successie (Re Company Taxation)* [1989] 1 CMLR 789; Case 136/87: *Ubbink Isolatie BV v Dak-en Wandtechniek BV (Re Company Liability to Third Parties)* [1990] 1 CMLR 262.
19 Cases 27–29/86: *Constructions et Entreprises Industrielles SA v Association Intercommunale pour les Autoroutes des Ardennes (Re Tenders Specifications)* [1989] 2 CMLR 224.
20 Case 203/87: *EC Commission v Italy, Re Zero Rating for Earthquake Victims* [1989] 2 CMLR 461.
1 Case 81/87: *R v HM Treasury, ex p Daily Mail and General Trust plc* [1988] 3 CMLR 713; Case C-106/89: *Marleasing SA v La Commercial Internacional de Alimentacion SA* OJ 1990, C 306/8.
2 Case 31/87: *Gebroeders Beentjes BV v Netherlands (Re Public Works Contract)* [1990] 1 CMLR 287.
3 See Case 237/84: *EC Commission v Belgium, Re the Business Transfer Directive* [1988] 2 CMLR 865; see also Case 324/86: *Foreningen af Arbejdsledere i Danmark v Daddy Dance Hall (Re Employees' Rights on Transfer of Undertaking)* [1989] 2 CMLR 517.
4 EEC, arts 7 and 119.

national implementation raises the question of supremacy of Community law in face of its conflict with national law. In the light of their interpretation the effects of the directives are revealed.

The effect of directives   Directives, being commands to Member States, have a direct effect upon their addressees. It is the duty of the latter to give effect to their obligation in this respect. Failure to enact within the specified time or incomplete enactment constitues a breach of article 5 of the Treaty and exposes the state concerned to enforcement proceedings under article 169.[5] Once the obligation has been perfected, for example by the effluction of time, there is no defence except the invalidity of the directive itself (on the ground of procedural or substantive defect), which would have to be declared by the ECJ since Member States have no competence to do so.

The plea that the failure to implement has had no adverse effect on the functioning of the Common Market, tantamount to saying that the directive was superfluous, would be of no avail.[6]

Various other excuses have been offered, albeit without success, for non-implementation of directives, for example: difficulties in appreciating all relevant issues and complexity of national procedures;[7] lack of technical facilities to institute appropriate procedures;[8] the fact that only few combined rail/road and road/inland waterway operations, regulated by a relevant transport directive, occur.[9] It is clear that the burden of proof in showing why the given directive has not been implemented into the national system lies on the defaulting country. Such a burden is not easy to discharge bearing in mind that all the Member States are involved in the legislative process. Since each Member State is responsible for its own default reciprocity is not required. Therefore the fact that some fellow Member State has failed to implement provides no lawful excuse or defence for a state in default.[10]

Rights of individuals   While directives are binding upon the Member States the rights of individuals arising therefrom depend

5 See eg Case 147/77: *EC Commission v Italy (Re Animal Slaughter Directive* [1978] ECR 1307, [1978] 3 CMLR 428; Case 124/81: *EC Commission v United Kingdom Re Ultra Heat Treated Milk* [1983] ECR 203, [1983] 2 CMLR 1.
6 See Case 95/77: *EC Commission v The Netherlands* [1978] ECR 863.
7 Case 390/85 *EC Commission v Belgium: Re Stock Exchange Listing Directives* [1988] 1 CMLR 146.
8 Case 419/85: *EC Commission v Italy, Re the Community Driving Licence* [1988] 3 CMLR 461.
9 Case 420/85: *EC Commission v Italy, Re Combined Transport* [1989] 1 CMLR 490.
10 Case C-38/89: *Ministère Public v Blanquernon* [1990] 2 CMLR 340.

on the scope of any particular directive. By their designation they have, in principle, no direct effect upon individuals unless implemented into national legislation. However, in substance they may well be sufficiently explicit and detailed to make trans-formation (or transposition) a mere formality and thus take effect even in the absence of implementation. In such a case they should have an overriding effect on inconsistent national law. This was the tenor of the decision of the Belgian Conseil d'Etat which held[11] that Directive 64/221 purporting to co-ordinate the special measures concerning the movement and residence of workers on the grounds of public policy, public security and public health, had such effect in Belgium. The ECJ confirmed this principle in the Van Duyn case[12] but a few years later the French Conseil d'Etat denied the direct effect of the same directive.[13] It is not surprising that directives have enriched the case law both at the Community and national level.

In *Grad v Finanzamt Traunstein*[14] the ECJ stated that 'if, in accordance with article 189, regulations are directly applicable and consequently are, by their very nature, capable of producing direct legal effects, it does not follow that the other acts mentioned in this article can never have similar effects' and concluded that 'the provisions of the decision and of the directives, taken together, produce direct effects in the relations between the Member States and their citizens and create for the latter the right to enforce them before the courts'. Grad, a haulage contractor, was caught in a tax law confusion. By Council decision 65/271[15] a uniform turnover tax system to promote competition in transport was introduced. Later two Council directives[16] provided for the introduction of the Value Added Tax as from 1 January 1972. Germany brought the VAT into operation ahead of the Community schedule and as from 1 January 1968 applied it to transport in lieu of the previous tax system. However it imposed a new tax on road transport as from 1 January 1969 providing that it would cease to apply by 31

11 *Corvelyn v Belgium* (7 October 1968, unreported); (1969) Cahiers de droit européen 343, at 345–46.
12 Case 41/74: *Van Duyn v Home Office (No 2)* (direct effect at Directive 64/221) [1974] ECR 1337, [1975] 1 CMLR 1. Case C-188/89: *Foster v British Gas plc* (direct effect of Directive 76/207) [1990] 2 CMLR 833.
13 *Minister of the Interior v Cohn-Bendit* (1979) Dalloz 155, [1980] 1 CMLR 543.
14 Case 9/70: [1970] ECR 825 at 837, see also on turnover tax Case 20/70, *Transports Lesage & Cie v Hauptzollamt Freiburg* [1970] ECR 861, [1971] CMLR 1; Case 23/70: *Haselhorst v Finanzamt Düsseldorf-Altstadt* [1970] ECR 881, [1971] CMLR 1.
15 OJ Sp edn 1965, p 67.
16 Directive 67/227, OJ Sp edn, 1967, p 14 amended by Directive 69/463, OJ Sp edn, 1969, p 551.

December 1970. Grad objected to this new tax which, in turn, raised the question of the effect of the decision in Germany. The ECJ held that the decision was directly applicable and so were the two directives. At the end there was no consolation for Grad because the relevant provision of the decision applied only from 1 January 1972, ie the date of the introduction of the VAT in the Community and, therefore, the internal tax system prevailed in the interim. However the case broke new ground as regards the effectiveness of measures other than regulations.

The second important case in this respect was SACE.[17] In order to accelerate the process of the removal of customs duties ahead of the Treaty schedule directive 68/31[18] required Italy to abolish certain administrative charges imposed on imports by 1 July 1968. The directive was prompted by the Decision 66/532.[19] The point was whether in order to benefit SACE, the combined effect of the decision and the directive overruled the Italian law which authorised the charges imposed after the date fixed by the directive but before the expiry of the transitional period envisaged by the Treaty. The ECJ held that Italy was under obligation to accelerate the process in accordance with the directive and, therefore, SACE had a directly enforceable right in this respect.

In *Re Forestry Reproductive Material*[20] the Court reaffirmed its position saying that 'if in respect of Member States to which it is addressed, the provisions of a directive have no less binding an effect than that of any other rule of Community law, such an effect applies all the more to provisions relating to the time limits for implementing the measures provided for' Further decisions along the same lines followed.

In *Van Duyn v Home Office*[1] the ECJ held directive 64/221 together with article 48(3) as having a direct effect as far as the right of entry of a worker and the derogation on the ground of public policy on the part of a Member State were concerned. Thus the directive explained and complemented the relevant provision of the Treaty.

---

17 Case 33/70: *SACE SpA v Italian Ministry for Finance* [1970] ECR 1213, [1971] CMLR 123.
18 JO 1968, 12/8.
19 JO 1966, 2971.
20 Case 79/72: *EC Commission v Italian Republic* [1973] ECR 667 at 672, [1973] CMLR 773 at 781; see also Case 93/79: *EC Commission v Italy (Re Weighing Machines)* [1980] 2 CMLR 647; Case 91/79: *EC Commission v Italy (Re Detergents)* [1981] 1 CMLR 331; Case 102/79: *EC Commission v Belgium (Re Type Approval)* [1980] ECR 1473, [1981] 1 CMLR 282.
1 Case 41/74: [1974] ECR 1337, [1975] 1 CMLR 1.

In the second *Defrenne* case[2] the combined effect of article 119 of the EEC Treaty (directly applicable as from the end of the transition period) and directive 75/117[3] to implement the principle of equal pay for equal work (laid down in the above-mentioned article) vindicated the right of a Belgian air hostess to an equal treatment with her male colleagues but only as far as their pay was concerned. The decision was much criticized[4] as one stretching the teleological interpretation too far and virtually usurping a legislative function which the Court does not possess but, it seems, it cannot be faulted on that ground. However in subsequent proceedings[5] the Court felt unable to stretch the point to cover all conditions at work. The *Defrenne* case stands out not only as an example of extensive interpretation of a directive made in aid of a Treaty provision but also of direct effect of a directive on the rights of individuals. It has not only exposed sex bias in the employment laws[6] but also led to an enforcement action to eliminate inconsistency of national laws with the Community principle of the equality of the sexes in employment.[7]

The Sex Discrimination (Social Security) directive (79/7) has proved equally effective[8] to extend invalidity care allowance to married women and to eliminate the inconsistency in the UK law that, while non-contributory invalidity pension was denied to women capable of performing normal household duties it was

---

2 Case 43/75: *Defrenne v SABENA* [1976] ECR 455, [1976] 2 CMLR 98. See also Case C-262/88: *Barber v Guardian Royal Exchange Assurance Group* [1990] 2 CMLR 513.

3 OJ 1976, L 39.

4 Hamson, C J, Methods of Interpretation – A Critical Assessment of the Results; *Judicial and Academic Conference*, 27–28 September 1976.

5 Case 149/77: *Defrenne v SABENA* [1978] ECR 1365; [1978] 3 CMLR 312.

6 See Cases: 129/79: *Macarthys Ltd v Smith* [1980] ECR 1275, [1980] 2 CMLR 205; 69/80: *Worringham and Humphreys v Lloyds Bank* [1981] ECR 767, [1981] 2 CMLR; 96/80: *Jenkins v Kingsgate* ibid, 24;12/81: *Garland v British Rail Engineering Ltd* [1982] 1 CMLR 696; 19/81: *Burton v British Railways Board* [1982] 2 CMLR 136; 222/84: *Johnston v Chief Constable of the RUC* [1986] 3 CMLR 240; 152/84: *Marshall v Southampton and South West Hampshire Area Health Authority* [1986] 1 CMLR 688. See also Cases: 14/83: *Von Colson and Kamann v Land Nordrhein-Westfahlen* and Case 79/83: *Hartz v Deutsche Tradux GmbH* [1986] 2 CMLR 430, 170/84: *Bilka-Kaufhaus GmbH v Von Harz* [1986] 2 CMLR 701.

7 Case 61/81: *EC Commission v United Kingdom* [1982] ECR 2601, [1982] 3 CMLR 284; Case 165/82: *EC Commission v United Kingdom* [1983] ECR 3431, [1984] 1 CMLR 44; Case 163/82: *EC Commissioner v Italy* [1984] ECR 3273, [1984] 3 CMLR 169; Case 248/83: *EC Commission v Germany* [1986] 2 CMLR 588.

8 Case 150/85: *Drake v Chief Adjudication Officer* [1986] 3 CMLR 43; Case 286/85: *McDermott and Cotter v Minister for Social Welfare* [1987] 2 CMLR 607.

available to men in similar circumstances.⁹ However, Directive
76/207 was held incapable of extending the benefit of compulsory
maternity leave to fathers.¹⁰

An individual may rely on a directive not only to claim a right
rooted in Community law but also to bring a valid defence to
prosecution under national law which is at variance with it. The
point is well illustrated in the *Ratti* case.¹¹ Ratti was prosecuted
for offences against Italian law in respect of packaging and labelling
of certain products. His defence was that he complied with directive
73/173¹² and directive 77/728¹³ on the packaging and labelling of
solvents and varnishes respectively, neither directive having been
implemented in Italy. He both succeeded and failed. The former
was to be implemented by 8 December 1974, the latter by 9
November 1979 but Ratti anticipated both and in doing so was in
collision with Italian law which remained unamended. On reference for a preliminary ruling the ECJ held that a directive can
become directly effective when the time limit put for its implementation has been reached. Thus Ratti was protected under the former
but not under the latter directive and, therefore, had a defence to
charges in respect of solvents but none in respect of varnishes. The
fact that he imported some of the varnishes from Germany where
the relevant directive had been implemented afforded him no
defence under Italian law. It follows that the date of the entry into
force of the directive according to Community law is decisive.

A private law aspect of a directive came to light in the UHT
milk products case.¹⁴ There, a breach of contract to import these
products was caused by the UK government restrictions because,
inter alia, they were pre-packed in France in metric containers.
The defence, that the traditional pint rather than the continental
litre was the only lawful measure for liquids such as milk, was
successful because the UK had negotiated a temporary stay of the
coming into force of the relevant directives.¹⁵ However, as the
ban continued the Commission brought a successful enforcement

9 Case 384/85: *Clarke v Chief Adjudication Officer* [1987] ECR 2865, [1987] 3
   CMLR 277.
10 Case 184/83: *Hoffmann v Barmer Ersatzkasse* [1986] 1 CMLR 242. See also
   Case 163/82, supra.
11 Case 148/78: *Pubblico Ministero v Ratti* [1979] ECR 1629, [1980] 1 CMLR 96;
   see also Case 79/72: *EC Commission v Italian Republic* [1973] ECR 667 at 672,
   [1973] CMLR 773 at 781.
12 OJ 1973, L 189/7.
13 OJ 1977, L 303/23.
14 Case 244/78: *Union Laitière Normande v French Dairy Farmers Ltd* [1979]
   ECR 2663, [1980] 1 CMLR 314.
15 Ie 71/316, JO 1971, L207/1; 71/354, JO 1971, L243/29; 75/106, OJ 1975,
   L42/1.

action against the United Kingdom in which the defence on the ground of public health failed, whilst the formal defence on the ground of the national market regulation for liquids was no longer available.[16]

The ghost of Grad appeared in a case[17] where a German taxpayer claimed exemption from VAT in respect of credit negotiation transactions based on Directive 77/388 concerning the harmonization of turnover taxes which at that time had not been implemented in Germany. The ECJ, repeating virtually verbatim its dictum on the nature of directives expressed in Grad, concluded that, especially in the light of the Ratti case, the taxpayer may rely on the provisions of a directive if they are unconditional and sufficiently precise. In such a case a state cannot take advantage of its failure to implement the directive. This clarified the law. Such clarification was needed especially that the German Federal Fiscal Court, relying expressly upon the decision of the French Conseil d'Etat in a similar case[18] denied the direct effect of directive 77/388 on the ground that it had not been enacted into a national statute. It thought that whilst the directive was binding upon Member States it could not create 'directly applicable law in those states'.[19]

Next to the question of direct applicability/direct effect is the question of vertical and horizontal effect of directives. Here again the question whether a directive has a merely vertical or also a horizontal effect depends on the intention of the legislator to be divined from its wording. Most of the cases discussed above involve a horizontal effect. However, where vertical effect is concerned a Member State (unless expressly authorized) may not rely on the direct effect against a private party especially in order to increase the existing criminal liability. Thus the interpretation of the national law involved must be carried out within the parameters of the wording and purpose of the directive irrespective of whether or not the national rules have been enacted in order to implement the directive in question.[20]

As mentioned earlier, directives, according to article 189, are meant to be different from regulations. In a sense they are because they allow a defined objective to be achieved by diverse methods.

16 Case 124/81: *EC Commission v United Kingdom* [1983] 2 CMLR 1.
17 Case 8/81: *Becker v Finanzamt Münster – Innenstadt* [1982] 1 CMLR 499 at 512.
18 25.2.1981 (Re la diréctive 77/388) (1981) Dalloz I.R. 33.
19 *Re Value Added Tax Directives* (Case VB 51/80), [1982] 1 CMLR 527 at 529.
20 Case 80/86: *Officier van Justitie v Kolpinghuis Nijmegen BV* [1987] ECR 3969, [1989] 2 CMLR 18; see also Case 14/86: *Pretore di Salo v X* [1987] ECR 2545, [1989] 1 CMLR 71.

However some directives are drafted in considerable detail leaving little discretion for the Member States and, where they provide a blueprint for an entirely novel legislation, they are indistinguishable from regulations. Nevertheless, qualitatively they are distinguishable from regulations in so far as they are addressed to the Member States and not to the whole world generally; they do not rule *erga omnes* but the states; and where they affect individuals they do it by perfecting otherwise imperfect Community rights[1] or affording Community defences against prosecutions by the states in default.[2] In that sense directives are 'indirectly applicable'.[3] However their efficacy depends upon whether they are intended to create a 'direct effect' eg by perfecting the right of establishment of the medical profession through common requirements for medical training and the recognition of professional qualifications, or whether they merely impose an obligation upon the Member States, eg by ordering them to introduce a humane method of animal slaughter.[4] In both cases the directives impose obligations upon the Member States but in the former case the directive differs from a regulation only in form and nomenclature.

Since directives have become the main instrument of harmonization or approximation of national laws their potential as a source of Community Law is quite considerable. However in practice the clear-cut distinction between regulations and directives implied in the Treaty has been blurred.

(c) *Decisions*

Concept and scope   A decision[5] of the Council or the Commission is binding in its entirety upon those to whom it is addressed. It may be addressed either to Member States or to individuals or corporations. It differs from a regulation which is formulated in an abstract manner. However a regulation does not become a decision merely because the addressees can be identified or, in other words, because its scope can be individualized.[6]

Like a regulation or a directive a decision has to be 'substantiated', ie based on a Treaty provision. However, mere references to an article of the Treaty, eg to article 92(1) on state aids,

---

1 Eg *Defrenne*, supra.
2 Eg *Ratti*, supra.
3 Cf Opinion of A G Reischl in *Ratti*, op cit ECR at 1650; Warner, J-P, The Relationship between European Community Law and the National Law of the Member States [1979] 93 LQR 349 at 359; but see Leitao, A R, 'L'effet direct des directives: une mystification?' [1981] RTDE 425.
4 Directive 74/577, OJ 1974, L 316/10.
5 EEC, art 189(4); EAEC, art 161(4); ECSC, art 14(2).
6 Case 789/79: *Calpak SpA v EC Commission* [1981] 1 CMLR 26.

will not suffice.[7] Indeed, it would be against the principle of the due process of law to allow an unsubstantiated decision to have a binding effect. It has to be notified to whom it is addressed though no particular form of notification is needed.[8] It takes effect upon notification.[9]

Unlike a regulation a decision is binding upon the addressee only, but, unlike a directive, it is 'binding in its entirety', leaving no discretion in the manner in which it is to be carried out. However, a decision may be the result of an obligation imposed on the Commission by a regulation.[10] The term 'decision' has of course a special meaning to denote one of the binding Community acts and sometimes a source of Community law. It is not, therefore, a mere conclusion of a process of reasoning or settlement or solution of a problem. Furthermore it is not a mere repetition of an established rule[11] or a stage in internal procedure,[12] or an instruction to an agency set up by the Community.[13] The many cases under article 14 of the ECSC Treaty provided an opportunity for the Community Court to define the meaning of 'decision' and the definition in one of such cases seems apposite to the position under the EEC Treaty. The Court held that a decision must appear as an act originating from the competent organisation intended to produce juridical effects, constituting the ultimate end of the internal procedure of this organisation and according to which such organisation makes its final ruling in a form allowing its nature to be identified.[14]

Whether an administrative act of the organs of the Community is a regulation, directive or decision is determined not by its form but by its content and object,[15] or, as put by Advocate-General

7 Case 248/84: *Germany v EC Commission (Re Regional Aid Plans)* [1989] 1 CMLR 591.
8 Case 6/72: *Europemballage Corpn Continental Can Co Inc v EC Commission* [1973] ECR 215 at 221, [1972] CMLR 690 at 691.
9 Cases 98/78: *Racke v Hauptzollamt Mainz* [1979] ECR 69 and 99/78: *Decker KG v Hauptzollamt Landau* [1979] ECR 101.
10 Case 16/65: *Schwarze v Einfuhr- und Vorratsstelle für Getreide und Füttermittel* [1965] ECR 877, [1966] CMLR 172.
11 Case 9/56: *Meroni & Co, Industrie Metallurgiche SpA v High Authority of the ECSC* [1957–58] ECR 133.
12 Cases 53–54/63: *Lemmerz-Werke GmbH v High Authority of the ECSC* [1963] ECR 239 at 247, 248 [1964] CMLR 384 at 399.
13 Case 21/58: *Felten und Guilleaume Carlswerke Eisen- und Stahl AG v High Authority of the ECSC* [1959] ECR 99.
14 Case 54/65: *Compagnie des Forges de Châtillon, Commentry et Neuves-Maisons v High Authority of the ECSC* [1966] ECR 185 at 195, [1966] CMLR 525 at 538.
15 Cases 16–17/62: *Confédération Nationale des Producteurs de Fruits et Légumes v EC Council* [1962] ECR 471 at 477–479, [1963] CMLR 160 at 173–174.

Roemer,[16] it is the function of the act rather than the process of its formation which should be primarily examined.

Under article 33 of the ECSC Treaty a distinction is made between general and individual decisions depending on the manner in which the addressees are affected.[17] General decisions are 'quasi-legislative acts made by a public authority and having a rule-making effect *erga omnes*'.[18] Individual decisions were held to be decisions in which the competent authority had to 'determine such concrete cases as are submitted to it'.[19]

The EEC and Euratom Treaties distinguish between plain decisions which may be challenged by individuals (or corporations) to whom they are addressed, and decisions in form of regulations which may be challenged by individuals upon proof that they are of direct and individual concern to them. In the latter cases the Court has to examine the substance of the measure to determine its true nature.[20]

Challenging a decision   Decisions, being binding acts, are subject to judicial review at the instance of the Member States, the Council and the Commission within the terms of article 173(1) of the EEC Treaty. Individuals are competent to challenge decisions under the conditions laid down in article 173(2).

The question of the *locus standi* arose recently in a dispute concerning state aids in which the Commission considered a French parafiscal tax unlawful. Challenged by a state-appointed trade association the Commission successfully contended that such a body had no standing to challenge its decision.[1]

The problem under the EEC Treaty is one of 'mixed acts', that is to say acts with the character of regulations[2] and decisions or directives[3] and decisions. Such mixed measures seem impossible

---

16 Case 40/64: In *Sgarlata v EC Commission* [1965] ECR 215 at 231, [1966] CMLR 314 at 318.
17 Case 18/57: *Nold KG v High Authority of the ECSC* [1959] ECR 41 at 49–50; Cases 55–59/63, 61–63/63: *Modena v High Authority of the ECSC* [1964] ECR 211 at 227, 228 [1964] CMLR 401 at 413.
18 *Nold*, supra at 50.
19 Case 20/58: *Phoenix-Rheinrohr AG v High Authority of the ECSC* [1959] ECR 75 at 88–89.
20 Case 101/76: *Koninklijke Scholten Honig NV v EC Council and EC Commission* [1977] ECR 797; [1980] 2 CMLR 669.
 1 Case 282/85: *Comité de Developpement et de Promotion du Textile et de l'Habillement v EC Commission* [1986] ECR 2469, [1988] 2 CMLR 156.
 2 Eg Case 25/62: *Plaumann v EC Commission* [1963] ECR 95; [1964] CMLR 29, where the ECJ held that to be a decision an act ought to be addressed to a particular person and have a binding effect upon that person.
 3 Eg *Consten v Grundig*, p 138, note 2. See also Grad, supra.

under the ECSC Treaty[4] but they came to light under the EEC and the Euratom Treaties. Assuming that such measures are valid per se the practical question of the scope of their application arises or, more precisely, whether they affect individuals apart from states and whether they can be challenged by individuals under article 173(2). It was held[5] that a measure which could be classified as a regulation could contain provisions applicable to individuals and thus enable them to take action under article 173(2). On the other hand, a Commission decision merely to reject a claim for amendment of a regulation will be treated as analogous to a regulation[6] with the result that an individual may not have the necessary *locus standi* under article 173(2).

The problem[7] of a directive and decision was raised by the *Finanzgerichte* (Finance Courts) of Munich (Case 9/70), Baden-Würtemberg (Case 20/70) and Düsseldorf (Case 23/70) which moved the Community Court to rule whether article 4 of *Decision* 65/271/EEC, JO 1500/65, read together with article 1 of the first *Directive* on Turnover Tax, JO 1301/67 'are directly binding in the relations between Member States and private persons and create individual rights which can be invoked before municipal courts'. The Community Court ruled that article 189 does not prevent private individuals from founding their actions before municipal courts upon *Directives* and *Decisions* addressed to Member States. Concluding that these measures can have, in appropriate cases, an internal effect, a learned jurist remarked that, as a result, an important barrier against the legal protection of private parties against these Community measures has been removed.[8]

Terminological confusion In the course of time certain categories of 'decision' having diverse effects have emerged. These include: *Executive decisions*, eg to engage the Community in external relations whether strictly within the Treaty framework (ie trade

4 *Nold*, above, and Case 8/55: *Fédération Charbonnière de Belgique v High Authority of the ECSC* [1954–56] ECR 245 at 247, also Advocate-General Lagrange in Case 30/59: *De Gezamenlijke Steenkolenmijnen in Limburg v High Authority of the ECSC* [1961] ECR 1.
5 In Case 30/67: *Industria Molitoria Imolese v EC Council* [1968] ECR 115, 5 CML Rev 480; see also Case 123/77: *UNICME v EC Council* [1978] ECR 845 at 851.
6 Case 42/71: *Firma Nordgetreide GmbH & Co KG v EC Commission* [1973] CMLR 177.
7 Brinkhorst, L J, 'Implementation of (non-self-executing) Legislation of the European Economic Community, including Directives', *Legal Problems of an Enlarged European Community*, ed by Bathurst, M E et al (1972), p 75; and Mitchell, J D B, 'Community Legislation', ibid, p 100.
8 Brinkhorst, L J, op cit, p 76.

agreements and association agreements) or peripheral to it (eg to take diplomatic initiatives in regard to the Middle East problems taken during the British Presidency of the Community in the latter half of 1981). The former, as we have seen, create rights and obligations vested in the Member States and individuals, the latter do not. In the area of organizational law, eg the Commission by Decision 73/351[9] set up an Advisory Committee on Customs Matters. By a series of Council decisions the monetary policy such as it is has been put into operation. These acts of the Institutions do not resemble exactly the definitions of decisions so far elicited from the judgments of the ECJ mentioned above.

Administrative decisions comprise the internal acts of the Community such as the appointment, promotion and dismissal of officials or the distribution of functions within the Community bureaucracy. They also comprise Commission decisions in the field of dumping, state aids and allocation of funds in the execution of certain policies, eg regional, social.

In the latter context the administration of the European Social Fund came under judicial scrutiny as the United Kingdom complained of the lack of consistency in the execution of the policy.[10] At issue was a Commission decision expressed in the annual declaration of the Fund's assistance to Member States for the ensuing year. Since these decisions have reflected, in the past, a certain consistency, it was argued that a legitimate expectation was created which enabled the Member States to make their commitments. The Commission, having altered the basis of the allocation of assistance after the Member States have made their commitments, was declared to have acted improperly.

Quasi-judicial decisions in their classical forms comprise the decisions of the Commission in a process of adjudication of the behaviour of Member States (ie preliminary to enforcement proceedings) or enterprises in the field of competition (ie negative clearance, exemptions, determination of infringements).

The variety of 'decisions' is confusing for some are, some are not, legally binding. However, a distinction can be made between binding and non-binding decisions. The former are made within the legal framework of the Treaty in the sense of EEC article 189. They are formal acts complying with procedural requirements; they impose rights or obligations upon the Institutions, or the Member States or individuals and are subject to judicial control

---

9 OJ 1973, L 321/37 amended by decision 76/921, OJ 1976, L 362/55.
10 Case 84/85: *United Kingdom v EC Commission (Re the European Social Fund)* [1987] ECR 3765, [1988] 1 CMLR 113.

by the ECJ. The latter do not constitute formal acts of the Institutions, do not comply with strictly legal and formal Treaty requirements and, therefore, are not subject to judicial control. They are taken within the political framework of the Community to conduct or settle Community affairs and, consequently, do not impose rights or obligations upon the Institutions, or the Member States or individuals.

In the light of these criteria the ECJ judgment in Case 114/86,[11] that Commission instructions for nationality quotas for shortlists of tenderers for public service contracts under Lome Convention II were not 'decisions' and, therefore, not subject to judicial review, is rather surprising. These instructions constituted an exercise of power and did affect individual rights as far as the allocation of contracts according to nationality quotas was concerned. It would seem that, rather than dismissing the case for inadmissibility, the Court should have addressed itself to the question whether or not the power was properly exercised. In the light of this case it is not surprising that the Commission was held not to be liable in damages for lost contract to an unsuccessful tenderer for a public contract under Lomé Convention I. The question was, of course, different as the Commission acted according to discretion by giving advice on the selection of the contractors.[12]

Like any other binding Acts, decisions have to be carried out by their addressees. In the case of the Member States, failure to abide by a decision will trigger off an enforcement action under article 169 of the Treaty. Such actions cannot be defended by the plea that the decision in question is unlawful[13] but the ECJ has the inherent power to review the legality of the disputed measure in such proceedings. However, the better view seems that a decision of doubtful character ought to be challenged in attack rather than in defence.

(B) NON-OBLIGATORY ACTS

It is debatable whether recommendations[14] and opinions[15] can be regarded as sources of Community law. These are listed in article

11 Case 114/86: *United Kingdom v EC Commission (Re Lomé II Service Contracts)* [1989] 1 CMLR 32.
12 Case 267/82: *Developpement SA v EC Commission* [1986] ECR 1907, [1989] 1 CMLR 309.
13 Case 226/87: *EC Commission v Greece (Re Public Sector Insurance)* [1989] 3 CMLR 569.
14 Eg *Re Luxembourg Agricultural Policy* 65/300/EEC 26 May 1965, [1965] CMLR 355.
15 Eg Case 7/61: *EEC Commission v Italian Republic* [1961] ECR 317 at 326, [1962] CMLR 39 at 50.

189 of the EEC Treaty as attributes of the power of the Council and Commission[16] necessary for the execution of their task but, unlike regulations, directives and decisions, are said to have 'no binding force'. Unfortunately there is a certain terminological confusion resulting from the interaction of the three founding treaties as the basic sources of Community law. The law-making acts of the ECSC (article 14) differ from those of the EEC (article 189) and EAEC (article 161). The High Authority of the ECSC can make *decisions* which are mandatory in all their aspects and *recommendations* within the scope defined by the Treaty, the choice of the methods of executing recommendations being left to those to whom they are addressed. In this way *decisions* of the ECSC correspond to both *regulations* and *decisions* of the EEC whilst *recommendations* of the ECSC correspond to *directives* of the EEC and EAEC. The High Authority of the ECSC can promulgate opinions which are not binding.

Taking the binding force as a criterion of the authority of the acts of the Community organs *opinions* cannot be regarded as a source of Community law but *recommendations* can only in so far as they are made under the ECSC Treaty. *Recommendations*[17] under the EEC Treaty have no force of law.

The existence of 'non-binding' acts is not exclusive to the European Community. Such acts are typical of international organizations of sovereign states,[18] which in theory cannot take orders from outside. The European Community, in spite of some measure of cohesion, still remains a community of sovereign states and so it has to be recognized that the Community organs have to carry out a variety of functions, some of which call for legislation, others for guidance.[19] Therefore, neither recommendations nor opinions of the Council and Commission should be disregarded. Their role is persuasive and constructive in the formulation and execution of the policies of the Community. Though they cannot be formally cited as sources of Community law they ought to be regarded, in the light of their potential, as auxiliary elements of the law-making process of the Community.[20]

16 See arts 27, 64, 81, 102.
17 Eg recommendation 84/549, OJ 1984, L298/49 for the introduction of services on the basis of common harmonized approach in the field of telecommunications.
18 Cf Sloan, B, 'The Binding Force of a "Recommendation" of the General Assembly of the United Nations', (1948), 25 BYBIL 1; Johnson, D. H., 'The Effect of Resolutions of the General Assembly of the United Nations', (1955–56) 32 BYBIL 97.
19 Cf ECJ judgment in joint Cases 1/57 and 14/57; *Société des Usines à Tubes de la Sarre v High Authority of the ECSC* [1957–58] ECR 105 at 115.
20 Soldatos, P, and Vandersanden, G, 'La recommandation, source indirecte du rapprochement' in De Ripainsel-Landy, D et al, *Les instruments du*

(C) NON-TREATY ACTS

In addition to the listed non-binding acts, various other instruments, such as memoranda,[1] communications,[2] deliberations,[3] programmes,[4] guidelines[5] and resolutions came to light. These are non-Treaty acts descriptive of the various actions or procedures undertaken or carried out in the life of the Community. They have no binding legal effect unless, despite their nomenclature, they meet the criteria laid down in the Treaty for binding Community acts. Such acts must, in the opinion of the Community Court[6] constitute 'the exercise, upon the conclusion of an internal procedure laid down by law, of a power provided for by law which is extended to produce legal effects of such a nature as to affect adversely the interests of the applicant by modifying its legal position ...' Thus 'deliberations' in the Council of Ministers were held to be capable of annulment (though they were valid in the instant case) because in the particular circumstances they were intended to bind the Member States.[7] In *EC Commission v Luxembourg and Belgium*[8] the ECJ held that a resolution of the Council had no binding effect because it was merely an expression of intention. Similarly,[9] the Council Resolution of 22 March 1971, which is primarily an expression of the policy favoured by the Council and Government Representatives of the Member States concerning the establishment of an economic and monetary union within the next ten years following 1 January 1971, cannot for its part, either, by reason of its content, '... create legal consequences of which parties might avail themselves in court ...' Probably in the same

rapprochement des legislations dans la Communauté Economique Européenne (1976), pp 95 et seq.

1 Eg Commission's Memorandum to Council of 18 March 1970 on the establishment of Industrial Policy, Fourth Gen Report 1970 item 205 et seq; Commission to Council on action in the cultural sector EC Bull Supp 6/77, p 5, Commission White Paper 1985; Com (85) 310 Final.

2 Communication by an official: Case 48/69: *Imperial Chemical Industries Ltd v EC Commission* [1972] 2 ECR 619, [1972] CMLR 557; Case 56/72: *Goeth-Van der Schueren v EC Commission* [1973] ECR 181; Commission's Communication to the Council on Admission to Institutions of Higher Education (Com) (78) 468 and 469, both of 22 September 1978.

3 Case 81/72: *EC Commission v EC Council* [1973] ECR 575, [1973] CMLR 639.

4 Eg Council Decision 77/294, OJ 1977, L 101/1 adopting the Fourth Medium-term Programme. Council action programme to implement the Environmental Policy, JO, 1977, C 139/1.

5 Eg Council Resolution laying down guidelines for the Regional Policy, OJ, 1979, C 36/10.

6 Case 182/80: *H P Gauff v EC Commission* [1982] 3 CMLR 402 at para 18.

7 ERTA case, p 70, note 8, supra.

8 Case 90, 91/63 [1964] ECR 625, [1965] CMLR 58.

9 Case 9/73: *Schlüter v Hauptzollamt Lörrach* [1973] ECR 1135 at para 40, supra.

category would be the joint resolution of the Parliament, the Commission and the Council[10] which proclaims that:

'1. The European Parliament, the Council and the Commission stress the prime importance they attach to the protection of fundamental rights, as derived in part from the constitutions of the Member States and the European Convention for the Protection of Human Rights and Fundamental Freedoms.'

'2. In the exercise of their powers and in pursuance of the aims of the European Communities they respect and will continue to respect these rights.'

A resolution may not be binding or creative of rights but, it seems, can be pleaded in support of a Treaty policy. It is doubtful though, whether, like a directive or a regulation, it is a legislative act, but it can convert a programmatic provision of the Treaty into a binding obligation. Such might have been the position in the Manghera case.[11] Manghera, in defiance of a state monopoly for the manufacture, import and sale of tobacco, imported a quantity of the product directly from another Member State without paying the duties due under Italian law. This occurred after a resolution[12] of the Council of Ministers which endorsed the undertaking of two states in default (ie France and Italy) to abolish the existing commercial state monopolies by a certain date. On reference, the ECJ considered that Manghera had a good defence not by virtue of the resolution which the Court found incapable of engendering private rights but by virtue of the direct effect of article 37(1) of the Treaty as from the end of the period of transition.

However the most striking example of a resolution[13] having a binding effect is the Council of Ministers Hague Resolution of 3 November 1976 adopted for the regulation of fishery conservation pending the finalization of the Common Fishery Policy. It provided for consultations with the Commission prior to the enactment of national measures in this field. Unilateral measures taken by the United Kingdom in contravention of the procedural requirement of the said resolution resulted in three enforcement actions: one by France[14] and another two by the Commission.[15] The resolution, like a directive, provided also a valid defence in Community law

10 OJ, 1977, C 103/1.
11 Case 59/75: *Pubblico Ministero v Flavia Manghera* [1976] ECR 91, [1976] 1 CMLR 557.
12 JO 1970, C 50.
13 EC Bull 1976/10 item 1502; summarized in the Irish Fisheries Case 61/77: *EC Commission v Ireland* [1978] ECR 417, [1978] 2 CMLR 466; see further Churchill, R, 'Revision of the EEC's Common Fisheries Policy' (1980) ELRev 3 and 95.
14 Case 141/78: *France v United Kingdom* [1979] ECR 2923, [1980] 1 CMLR 6.
15 Case 32/79: *EC Commission v United Kingdom (Re Fishery Conservation*

for an individual charged with the violation of the UK legislation enacted in contravention thereof.[16]

(D) CONTROL OF THE COMMUNITY LEGISLATION

All the acts of the Community organs are subject to the principle of legality as is the case with the executive and administrative acts of a law-abiding state. This principle imposes a certain limit upon the Community organs as they have to operate within the scope of their organic powers (*infra legem*) or within the scope of their delegated powers. The Treaties are quite explicit in this respect. Article 4 of the EEC Treaty provides that the functions of the Community shall be carried out by the Parliament, the Council, the Commission and the Court of Justice and that 'each institution shall act within limits of the powers conferred upon it by the Treaty'.

If we accept the analogy of the EEC Treaty to a state constitution we can construe a system of control of the acts of the Community organs parallel to that of the acts of state organs. In most systems we can note a triple form of control: constitutional, political (or parliamentary) and judicial, to which we can add for good measure the control by what passes for 'public opinion'.

Thus the constitution (Treaty) sets up the system and defines the functions and powers of the state (Community) organs. The constitutional control is a strictly legal control in so far as it rests upon the assumption that the state itself is governed by law (*Rechtsstaat*, see Bracton on the Rule of Law) and that the machinery of the state operates according to law. Since all the Member States of the Community subscribe to the notion of the *Rechtsstaat* there is no reason to suppose that the Community would be different.

Political or parliamentary control of the executive takes various forms: debate, questions, censure. The legislative acts of the executive are subject to parliamentary scrutiny and where breaches of the constitution are alleged the matter may be considered by a constitutional tribunal or (as in the case of the United Kingdom) parliament itself. This does not preclude a judicial review. The EC Parliament can hardly be regarded as a parliament in the accepted sense of the word. It is a deliberative body and in a limited sense a controlling body. Its control is confined to the control of the Commission as the chief bureaucratic body but, not being a fully-

Measures) [1980] ECR 2403, [1981] 1 CMLR 219; Case 804/79: *EC Commission v United Kingdom* [1981] ECR 1045 [1982] 1 CMLR 543.
16 Case 269/80: *R v Tymen* [1981] ECR 3079, [1982] 2 CMLR 111.

fledged parliament, it neither legislates nor controls the legislative acts of the Community organs.[17]

In the Community the control of legality is in the hands of the Community Court.[18] Thus, apart from the duty of ensuring that the law is observed in the interpretation and application of the Treaty, the Court has the power of judicial review of the legality of acts of the Community Institutions. These include regulations, directions and decisions which are 'binding' but exclude recommendations and opinions which are 'not binding'. The legal status of the Community acts determines the scope of judicial control. It follows that only the 'binding acts' may, in accordance with the Treaties,[19] be subject to judicial control.

Recently various 'Acts' of the European Parliament came under judicial scrutiny, the phenomenon being a reflection of the ascendancy of the European Parliament and of the extent of the judicial control in the Community. While the European Parliament is the master in its own house, ie in control of its own proceedings,[20] certain Acts, particularly those which are not merely regulating procedure and may have legal effects outside the Parliament's domain, have to conform to the principle of legality as understood in the Community system. Thus, in principle, decisions of the European Parliament are subject to judicial review, as, for example, was the resolution to allocate staff, which was *ultra vires*;[1] financial aid to political parties fighting in election to the EC, which was declared to be outside the scope of the Community budget since the matter was exclusively within the power of the Member States.[2] However, the setting up of a parliamentary committee of enquiry[3] or the decisions to hold a plenary session away from Strasburg,[4] though 'decisions' of a kind were not justiciable as they were taken within the notion of parliamentary procedure and were not intended to produce external legal effects.

The making, the notification and the publication of the binding

---

17 However see the *Isoglucose* cases, p 130, supra; see also Case 230/81: *Luxembourg v European Parliament* [1983] ECR 255, [1983] 2 CMLR 726.

18 EEC, art 164, 173, 177.

19 EEC, art 173; EAEC, art 146; ECSC, art 33; but see Case 182/80 p 155, note 6, supra.

20 See Cases 230/81 and 108/83: *Luxembourg v European Parliament* [1983] ECR 255 and [1984] ECR 1945.

1 Case 108/83: *Luxembourg v European Parliament* [1986] 2 CMLR 507.

2 Case 294/83: *Partie Ecologiste, 'Les Verts' v European Parliament* [1987] 2 CMLR 343.

3 Case 78/85: *Group of the European Right v European Parliament* [1986] ECR 1753, [1988] 3 CMLR 645.

4 Cases 358/85 and 51/86: *France v European Parliament, Re Meetings Facilities in Brussels* [1990] 1 CMLR 309.

acts are subject to the Court's scrutiny from the point of view of legality, form and publicity of these acts. The Court has jurisdiction in actions brought by a Member State, the Council or the Commission and may pronounce nullity of the act concerned on grounds of 'lack of competence, infringement of an essential procedural requirement, infringement of the Treaty or of any rule of law relating to its application, or misuse of powers'.[5]

A natural or legal person can also institute proceedings but only for the annulment of a decision addressed to that person or a decision which, 'although in the form of a regulation or a decision addressed to another person, is of direct and individual concern to [the complainant]'.[6] Therefore, held the ECJ,[7] an application for annulment of a decision was unfounded if the applicant had no longer any legally recognised interest in the matter. Indeed it would constitute an abuse of the judicial process to pursue the action when a judgment of the ECJ concerning the same parties and a similar question was already given in another case. Thus the application for annulment of a Commission decision fixing the minimum price of frozen beef put up for sale by the intervention agency had to be dismissed when the applicant having offered a lower price (which was rejected), brought an action for annulment of the decision rejecting his offer.

It must be emphasized that national courts are not competent to rule on the validity of Community Acts. If such Acts are challenged in a national jurisdiction a reference for a preliminary ruling ought to be made but pending such ruling they have to be considered valid. It was so held by the ECJ in a case of attempted post-clearance recovery of customs duties where the imported goods were mistakenly regarded as duty free. The Commission decision ordering recovery out of time was held invalid.[8]

Similarly, while reviewing the Commission decision addressed to a Member State with regard to state aid, the ECJ held that pending the judicial determination the decision had internal validity, was binding on the addressee and had to be complied with unless compliance was impossible or suspended by ECJ's order.[9]

---

5 EEC, art 173(1).
6 EEC, art 173(2).
7 Case 243/78: *Simmenthal SpA v EC Commission* [1980] ECR 593.
8 Case 314/85: *Foto-Frost v HZA Lübeck-Ost* [1988] 3 CMLR 57; see also *R v Minister of Agriculture, Fisheries and Food* [1988] 3 CMLR 207, QB and 661, QB.
9 Case 63/87: *EC Commission v Greece* [1989] 3 CMLR 677.

(E) JUDICIAL LEGISLATION

(a) The powers of ECJ

The Court has the duty of ensuring observance of the law and whilst doing so may explain and complement the Treaties and subordinate Community legislation. This gives the Court an opportunity of laying down or defining Community law. The powers and functions of the Court will be analysed elsewhere[10] and it will suffice here to investigate the ways in which the Court may contribute to the sources of Community law.

The Court, as a fully-fledged judicial body, has the power necessary to carry out its duties as specified in the Treaties. Its jurisdiction is exceptional in the sense that it is not a substitute for the national courts of the Member States. It is exclusive and also circumscribed by the Treaties. In all respects it is the internal Court of the Community and as far as legal style is concerned it is a continental court modelled upon the French Conseil d'Etat.

The jurisdiction of the ECJ combines a variety of judicial functions extending over a number of specialist fields: 'federal' (adjudicating upon the relations between the Member States and the Community), constitutional (on the institutional balance, the institutional competence and the compatibility of Community legislation with the constituent Treaties), administrative (on the validity of administrative orders and decisions), economic and commercial (on the various economic policies of the Community and commercial activities or enterprises) and labour (on the relation between the Community and its servants, now within the competence of the Court of First Instance). The appellate jurisdiction comprises supervision over the quasi-judicial decisions of the Commission (ie in the field of competition, state aids, dumping, economic protective measures, financial sanctions imposed by the Commission under the ECSC Treaty), the jurisdiction of the Common Appeal Court under the Community Patent Agreement[11] and appeals from the judgments of the Court of First Instance.

There are no appeals to the ECJ from national courts which, within their jurisdiction, administer the Community law though it has the power of advising the national courts by means of reference for preliminary ruling on points of Community law.[12]

In so far as the Court has to ensure observance of the law it acts as an instrument of sovereignty; in so far as it has to ensure the correct interpretation and application of the law as regards both the functioning of the Community and the development of the

---

10 See Chapter 9, post.
11 Community Patent Agreement, EEC Member States [1990] 2 CMLR 194.
12 See Ch 10, infra.

Community law, it exercises a law-making function appropriate to a judicial body. We shall address ourselves to the latter.

It is axiomatic that, given the requisite power, the lesser the precision of the law the greater the scope for judicial legislation. The Community Treaties are far from being precise and tightly drafted. In so far as they represent the Community framework it is the task of the Court to complete the system and fill the gaps.

(b) Judicial interpretation

Interpretation is the principal method of laying down judge-made law and since the Court is a continental court it has adopted what we have termed the 'continental style'. In the civil law systems the court has no law-making power and precedent is not regarded as a source of law. However, through the instrumentality of interpretation judges are in the position of filling the gaps in the legal system and, through the definition of rights and duties in judgments, they create a body of rules which, without any statutory authority, has a persuasive force. The Community Court is in a unique position: it is a court of first and last instance, it has the power to review the legality of the acts of the Community organs, has no parliament to look up to as a sovereign source of law and, above all, has to interpret Treaties which comprise general policies alongside precise rules of law.[13] In the circumstances the Community Court cannot help contributing to the growth of Community law.

In the absence of any canons of interpretation[14] the Court is free to draw on rules evolved in the Member States and will do so not only in the spirit of the Community but also for practical reasons, because Community law, in order to command general respect and acceptance, has to be a synthesis of the laws of the Member States and, at every stage of its growth, has to draw strength from the practices and principles already well established.

Literal, or grammatical, interpretation is always the basic method and where the meaning of the text is clear there is no need of interpretation for *clara non sunt interpretanda*. However, in the Community set-up Community legislation must conform to the relevant treaty, so much so that the clear language of an act of a

---

13 Cf opinion of Advocate-General Roemer in Case 13/60: *Ruhrkohlen Verkaufs-GmbH v High Authority of the ECSC* [1962] ECR 83, [1962] CMLR 113 at 125, 128.

14 Kutscher, K, *Methods of Interpretation as seen by a Judge at the Court of Justice* (1976); Slynn, Sir Gordon, Lasok, K P E, Millett, T P, 'The Court of Justice, Law of the European Communities', *Halsbury's Laws of England* (4th edn) Vol 51, 344 et seq.

Community organ must not be allowed to prevail if, in the light of the Treaty, it leads to absurdity.[15]

On the question of linguistic differences and inconsistencies between the different provisions of the Treaty, Advocate-General Roemer submitted in *Internationale Crediet- en Handelsvereniging 'Rotterdam' v Ministry of Agriculture and Fisheries*[16] that the same standard of draftsmanship as that in the national legislation cannot be expected in Treaties.[17] Literal interpretation must take this into account.

Next to literal interpretation comes the logical interpretation which requires the Court to consider the text within the context of the system. In *Simon v Court of Justice of the European Communities*[18] the Court held that where the text is ambiguous the most reasonable solution must be sought, and in *Société Technique Minière v Maschinenbau Ulm GmbH*[19] the Court restricted prohibitions in the Treaty to matters which it considered detrimental to the aims of the Community. In *Federal Republic of Germany v EEC Commission*[20] Advocate-General Roemer submitted that the Court should be guided by considerations which make good sense both politically and administratively, and in *Costa Flaminio v ENEL*[1] Advocate-General Lagrange stated that excessive formalism should give way to the Community spirit in relations between the Community and the Member States. In a more technical sense Advocate-General Lagrange put in a nutshell the purpose of logical interpretation when he stressed in *de Geus v Bosch*[2] that the Court must not be defeated by obscurities or contradictions in the wording of the text for the real meaning can be deduced from the context or spirit of the text. In this vein several

---

15 Case 14/63: *Forges de Clabecq v High Authority of the ECSC* [1963] ECR 357 at 372, 373 [1964] CMLR 167 at 176; Case 2/67: *De Moor v Caisse de Pension des Enployés Privés* [1967] ECR 197, [1967] CMLR 223 at 230–31, 235. See also Case 67/79: *Fellinger v Bundesanstalt für Arbeit* [1980] ECR 535 at 550, [1981] 1 CMLR 471 at 478.

16 Cases 73–74/63: [1964] ECR 1, [1964] CMLR 198 at 206.

17 Cf Lord Denning in *HP Bulmer Ltd v J Bollinger SA* [1974] 2 All ER 1226 at 1231–1232.

18 Case 15/60: [1961] ECR 115 at 125. See also Case 9/70: *Grad v Finanzamt Traustein* [1970] ECR 825 at 839, [1971] CMLR 1 at 25; Case 67/79, supra.

19 Case 56/65: [1966] ECR 235 at 248, 249, [1966] CMLR 357 at 371, 376.

20 Case 34/62: [1963] ECR 131 at 156, [1964] CMLR 369 at 380.

1 Case 6/64: [1964] ECR 585 at 609, [1964] CMLR 425 at 448.

2 Case 13/61: [1962] ECR 45 at 70, [1962] CMLR 1 at 23. See also Case 118/79: *Gebrüder Knauf v HZA Hamburg-Jonas* [1980] ECR 1183 at 1190–1191; Case 143/82: *Lipman v EC Commission* [1983] ECR 1301 at 1310; Case 136/80: *Hudigen Pieters BV v Minister van Landbouw en Visserij* [1981] ECR 2233 at 2241–2242, [1983] 1 CMLR 582 at 593.

cases have been decided illustrating both the technique and law-making potential of logical interpretation.[3]

Courts are notoriously reticent about the use of teleological interpretation which, though basically literal, brings out the intention of the legislature in the light of the conditions prevailing at the time of the judgment.[4] The Treaties have not existed long enough to have, in the absence of a fundamental revision, their lives extended by interpretation, but references to the spirit or the aims of the Treaties[5] enable the Court to fill the gaps in the system and so 'up-date' the text. In doing so the Court has consciously acted not only as the 'Constitutional Court' of the Community but also as an architect of European integration.[6]

The Court does not act arbitrarily but judicially, which means that it has to see that its interpretation reflects the intention of the

3 Eg Case 10/61: *Re Italian Customs Duty on Radio Valves* [1962] CMLR 187 at 201–202; ref. to arts 12, 14 (1) and 19 (2) (III); Case 75/63: *Unger v Bestuur der Bedrijfsvereniging voor Detailhandel en Ambachten* [1964] CMLR 319, ref. to art 51; Case 24/62: *Germany v EEC Commission* [1963] CMLR 347 at 336–367, ref. to arts 25 (3) and 29; Case 10/65: *Deutschmann v Federal Republic of Germany* [1965] CMLR 259, ref to arts 13 and 95; Case 27/67: *Fink-Frucht GmbH v Hauptzollamt München* [1968] CMLR 228 at 299, ref to arts 30 and 95; Case 29/68: *Milch- Fett- und Eierkontor GmbH v Hauptzollamt Saarbrücken* [1969] CMLR 390, ref to arts 9, 12, 13; Case 13/72: *Re Food Aids: Netherlands v EC Commission* [1973] ECR 27 at 40–42; see also the opinion of A. G. Roemer in Case 5/71: *Aktien-Zuckerfabrik Schoppenstedt v EEC Council* [1971] ECR 975 and A-G Warner in Case 81/72: *Re Civil Service Salaries EC Commission v EC Council* [1973] ECR 575 at 595–596, [1973] CMLR 639 at 652–653.

4 See Case 33/69: *EC Commission v Italy* [1970] ECR 93 at 101, [1971] CMLR 466 at 475; Case 43/75: *Defrenne v SABENA* [1976] ECR 455 at 472, [1976] 2 CMLR 98 at 123–124.

5 Eg Case 56/65: *Société Technique Minière v Maschinenbau Ulm GmbH* [1966] ECR 235, [1966] CMLR 357; Case 34/62: *Federal Republic of Germany v EEC Commission* [1963] ECR 131, [1963] CMLR 369; Case 6/64: *Costa Flaminio v ENEL* [1964] CMLR 425; Case 13/61: *de Geus v Bosch* [1962] ECR 45, [1962] CMLR 1; Case 6/54: *Netherlands Government v High Authority* [1954–56] ECR 103; Case 6/60: *Jean E Humblet v Belgian State* [1960] ECR 559; Case 8–11/66: *Re Noordwijks Cement Accoord* [1967] CMLR 77 at 104–105; Case 8/55: *Fédération Charbonnière de Belgique v High Authority of the ECSC* [1954–56] ECR 245; Case 16/61: *Modena v High Authority of the ECSC* [1962] CMLR 221 at 241; *Continental Can*, supra [1973] ECR at 243–245; [1973] CMLR at 223–225, 233–235; Case 151/73: *Ireland v EC Council* [1974] 1 CMLR 429 at 446–447. Ormand, R, 'L'utilisation particulière de la méthode d'interpretation des traites selon leur "effet utile" par la Cour de Justice' 12 RTDE (1976) pp 624 et seq; Bleckmann, A, 'Teleologie und dynamische Auslegung der Europaischen Gemeinschaftsrechts' 14 EuR (1979) pp 239 et seq; Mortelmans, K, 'Les lacunes provisoires en droit communautaire' 17 CDE (1981) pp 410 et seq.

6 Schermers, H, 'The European Court of Justice: Promoter of European Integration' 22A JCL (1974) pp 459 et seq; Lasok, D, 'La Cour de Justice, instrument de l'integration communautaire' Rev d'integration européenne, II (1979) pp 391 et seq.

parties to the Treaties and the *ratio legis* of the text.[7] In tracing the intention the Court is free to consult materials extraneous to the Treaty. These consist of the *travaux préparatoires* leading to the conclusion of Treaties and statements on behalf of the Community. The former are the various publications which reflect the substance of the negotiations and the attitudes of the negotiating parties from the inception to the conclusion of the Treaties. One could single out in this context official communiques and minutes of meetings, should these be available, and the official views of the negotiating governments. In view of the nature of the negotiations and the way governments work in their international relations the materials are not readily available. They have, according to a learned jurist,[8] 'a certain value, though their precise juristic meaning is arguable'. So far the Court does not seem to have taken much notice of the *travaux préparatoires* though the Advocates-General have referred to these in their submissions.[9]

Statements on behalf of the Community may[10] elucidate the Community legislation but the views of the Community officials on the interpretation of the Treaties are hardly relevant.[11] They are equally ineffective as far as the interpretation of the Community legislation is concerned.[12]

It follows that *travaux préparatoires*, as explained by Advocate-General Lagrange[13] have no compulsory place in the interpretation of Treaties, but it is universally accepted that judges may turn to them for information in order to clarify the thoughts of the legis-

7 Case 6/60: *Jean-E Humblet v Belgian State* [1960] ECR 559, supra at p 1154.
8 Reuter, P, *La CECA* (1953), p 30.
9 Cf Lagrange in Case 8/55: *Fédération Charbonnière de Belgique v High Authority of the ECSC* [1954–56] ECR 245; Roemer in Case 6/54: *Netherlands Government v High Authority of the ECSC* [1954–56] ECR 103; Cases 90–91/63: *Re Import of Milk Products* [1965] CMLR 58 at 65; Case 13/60: *Ruhrkohlen-Verkaufs-GmbH v High Authority of the ECSC* [1962] CMLR 113 at 146; Cases 73–74/63: *Internationale Crediet- en Handelsvereniging 'Rotterdam' v Minister von Landbouwen Visserij* [1964] CMLR 198 at 207; Case 26/68: *Caisse Régionale de Securité Sociale du Nord v Torrekens* [1969] CMLR 377 at 382–383; and in Case 38/69: *Re Customs Duties on Lead and Zinc* [1970] CMLR 77 at 85; Case 42/72: A G Roemer in *Alfons Lütticke GmbH v Hauptzollamt Passau* [1973] ECR 57 at 74–75, [1973] CMLR 309 at 316–317.
10 Cases 2–10/62: *Societa Industriale Acciaierie San Michele v High Authority of the ECSC* [1964] CMLR 146 at 165.
11 A-G Roemer in Cases 90–91/63: *Re Import of Milk Products* [1965] CMLR 58 at 65; Cases 8–11/66: *Re Noordwijks Cement Accoord* [1967] CMLR 77 at 87.
12 Cases 53–54/63: *Lemmerz-Werke GmbH v High Authority of the ECSC* [1964] CMLR 384 at 398.
13 Case 8/55: *Fédération Charbonnière de Belgique v High Authority of the ECSC* [1954–56] ECR 245.

lator. The judges are entirely free in their evaluation of these materials.

Preparatory materials are more likely to be used in the interpretation of Commission legislation[14] or a Convention[15] since these are often preceded by working papers or explanatory memoranda accessible to the public.

In addition to interpretation in a technical sense further elements play an auxiliary part in the development of Community law. Of these we shall mention briefly references to the municipal laws of the Member States, references to general principles of law and references to learned writings.

The Treaties, like the rules of public international law, are influenced by the rules of municipal law. More than that they are derived from the laws of the six founding states. It is natural, therefore, that the Community Court should turn for guidance to the laws of the Member States. As submitted by Advocate-General Roemer[16] the Court has to 'call upon the law of the different Member States in order to arrive at a meaningful interpretation of our Community law'. As a result some early cases comprise a detailed comparative study. Perhaps the best examples are the cases involving misuse of power and withdrawal, with retrospective effect, of an illegal administrative act.[17]

In the latter case the Court came to the conclusion that 'a study of comparative law shows that whenever an administrative act is wrong in law, the laws of the Member States admit the possibility of revocation', and in accordance with this finding decreed that such an act was revokable with a retrospective effect. It does not follow, however, that the laws of all the Member States must be consulted. If the problem is peculiar to two countries a consideration of the two systems will be sufficient,[18] and on occasions

14 Case 29/69: *Stauder v Stadt Ulm* [1969] ECR 419 at 425, [1970] CMLR 112 at 118; Case 83/78: *Pigs Marketing Board v Redmond* [1978] ECR 2347, [1979] 1 CMLR 177; Case 107/80: *Adorno v EC Commission* [1981] ECR 1469 at 1484, [1983] 2 CMLR 310 at 325; Case 38/81: *Effer SpA v Kantner* [1982] ECR 825 at 834, [1984] 2 CMLR 667 at 674–675.
15 Case 14/70: *Deutsche Bakels v Oberfinanzdirektion München* [1970] ECR 1001; Case 30/71: *Kurt Siemers v HZA Bad Reichenhall* [1971] ECR 919, [1972] CMLR 121; Case 159/80: *Wünsche v Bundesanstalt für landwirtschaftliche Marktordnung* [1981] ECR 2161 at 2175.
16 Case 6/54: in *Netherlands Government v High Authority of the ECSC* [1954–56] ECR 103.
17 See also Cases 7/56 and 3–7/57: *Algera v Common Assembly* [1957–58] ECR 39; Case 14/61: *Hoogovens v High Authority of the ECSC* [1963] CMLR 73 at 90–91, 96; further examples: Campbell, A, *Common Market Law* (1969), Vol I, 7.258, pp 531–532.
18 A-G Lagrange in Case 5/55: *Associazione Industrie Siderurgiche Italiane v High Authority of the ECSC* [1954–55] ECR 135.

reference to one country only may suffice.[19] The other extreme, which the Court is free to adopt, is that sometimes a national system cannot be regarded as apposite.[20] More intriguing is the possibility of reference to the law of a non-Member State, but this must be regarded as a special case.[1] Indeed the Community law of monopolies and restrictive practices, being modelled upon American law, invites such a reference.[2] Before the British accession the English law of estoppel[3] was considered whilst Advocate-General Warner made a significant British contribution to the discussion of natural justice.[4] More recently the meaning and scope of professional privilege[5] applicable to lawyers in the process of investigation of the alleged breaches of competition rules was defined by reference to national systems.

However reference to national laws is exceptional and for a purely auxiliary purpose. It is not normally made without express direction[6] to that effect. Moreover a concept of Community law must be construed in the context of the Community system by reference to national legislation rather than judgments of national courts[7] and in a manner compatible with the objectives of the

19 French law: Cases 7 and 9/54: *Groupement des Industries Siderurgiques Luxembourgoises v High Authority of the ECSC* [1954–55] ECR 175; Case 12/74: *EC Commission v Federal Republic of Germany* [1975] ECR 18 at 209; German law: Case 18/57: *Nold KG v High Authority of the ECSC* [1959] ECR 41 pp 110–111; Cases 17 and 20/61: *Kloeckner Werke und Hoesch v High Authority of the ECSC* [1962] ECR 325 at 351–353.

20 Eg Case 1/64: *Glucosiéries Réunies v EEC Commission* [1964] CMLR 596 at 599.

1 See eg Case 12/73: *Muras v HZA Hamburg-Jonas* [1973] ECR 963 at 974.

2 Case 13/60: A.G. Roemer in *Ruhrkohlen-Verkaufs-GmbH v High Authority of the ECSC* [1962] CMLR 113 at 141; Case 16/61: *Modena v High Authority* [1962] CMLR 221 at 229–230, 232.

3 A-G Roemer in Cases 41 and 50/59: *Hamborner Bergbau AG v High Authority of the ECSC* [1960] ECR 493. Cf Case 48/72: *Brasserie de Haecht v Wilkin-Janssen* [1973] ECR 77 at 87, [1973] CMLR 287 at 302; Case 84/85: *United Kingdom v EC Commission (Re European Social Fund)* [1987] ECR 3765, [1988] 1 CMLR 113.

4 Case 17/74: *Transocean Marine Paint Association v EC Commission* [1974] ECR 1063, [1974] 2 CMLR 459.

5 Case 155/79: *A M & S Europe Ltd v EC Commission* [1982] ECR 1575 at 1610–1612, [1982] 2 CMLR 264 at 322–324.

6 Case 51/76: *Verbond van Nederlandse Ondernemingen v Inspecteur der Invoerrechten en Accijnzen* [1977] ECR 113 at 124–125, [1977] 1 CMLR 413 at 427; Case 154/80: *Staatssecretaris van Financien v Cooperatieve Aardappelen-vewaarplaats GA* [1981] ECR 445 at 453, [1981] 3 CMLR 337 at 345; Case 64/81: *Corman et Fils SA v HZA Gronau* [1982] ECR 13 at 24.

7 Case 1/77: *Robert Bosch GmbH v HZA Hildesheim* [1977] ECR 1473 at 1481, [1977] 2 CMLR 563 at 578.

Community measure in question.[8] Consequently the process may not result in a restrictive interpretation of Community law.[9]

Echoing article 38 of the Statute of the International Court of Justice the Community Court also refers to 'general principles of law'. These can be traced to doctrines developed within the context of public International Law[10] or the municipal law of the Member States, but others remain untraceable.[11] No doubt the reference to 'general principles of law' has a certain scope as such principles may mean general doctrines of the law, eg justice, the right to be heard, etc., or rules of law expressed in general terms, eg contractual freedom, liability for wrongful act, non-discrimination, etc. Learned commentators[12] recognize the competence of the Court to take recourse to 'general principles of law'. Their views have been summarized as follows: 'il semble que lorsqu'une notion juridique existe, identique, dans le droit interne de tous les Etats membres, celle-ci s'impose aux organes de la Communauté comme un principe général qui doit être appliqué sous peine de la violation d'une règle de droit relative à l'application du traité'.[13]

Finally we should note the contribution of learned writers (the so called *doctrine*) to the *Jurisprudence*[14] of the Community Court. Here again an analogy to article 38 of the Statute of the

---

8 Case 75/63: *Hoekstra (nee Unger) v Bestuur der Bedrijfsvereiniging voor Detailhandel en Ambachten* [1964] ECR 177 at 184–185; [1964] CMLR 319 at 347.

9 Case 149/79: *EC Commission v Belgium* [1980] ECR 3881 at 3903, [1981] 2 CMLR 413 at 435.

10 Eg on equality and discrimination, A-G Lagrange in Case 13/63 *Re Electric Refrigerators* [1963] CMLR 289 at 303, on the status of international administrative tribunals; A-G Roemer in Case 1/56: *Bourgaux v ECSC Common Assembly* [1954–56] ECR 361.

11 Eg on the meaning of 'discrimination' and 'comparable price conditions to consumers in comparable circumstances' in Cases 3–18, 25, 26/58: *Barbara Erzbergbau v High Authority* [1960] ECR 173.

12 Reuter, P, 'Le recours de la Cour de justice des Communautés européennes à des principes généraux de droit', in *Mélanges Henri Rolin* (1964), p 263.

13 Mathijsen, P, *Le droit de la CECA* (1958), p 142.

14 A-G Roemer in Case 13/60: *Ruhrkohlen-Verkaufs-GmbH v High Authority of the ECSC* [1962] CMLR 113 at 159, on oligopoly by a 'noted author'; in Cases 106–107/63: *Toepfer KG v EEC Commission* [1966] CMLR 111 at 118, on the power of intervention of the Council of Ministers by Wohlfart, E, Everling, U, Glaesner, H J, and Sprung, R, 'Die Europäische Wirtschaftsgemeinschaft', *Kommentar zum Vertrag* (1969); AG Lagrange in Case 67/63: *Sorema v High Authority of the ECSC* [1964] CMLR 350 at 352, on the definition of an association of undertakings by Reuter, P, *La Communauté Européenne du Charbon et de l'Acier* (1953); AG Warner in Case 31/74: *Filippo Galli, Preliminary Ruling* [1975] ECR at 70 on the direct applicability of regulations by J A Winter in 9 CML Rev, 1972 p 425 at 435–436; A-G Reischl in Case 72/74: *Union Syndicale, Service Public Européen v ECC Council* [1975] ECR 401 at 416 cites several writers on Administrative Law.

International Court of Justice comes to mind where reference is made to 'the teachings of the most highly qualified publicists'. Continental courts are familiar with the contribution of learned writers to the development of the law and these, to command authority, need not necessarily be dead. Community law is still a relatively undeveloped system, a law in books rather than fully entrenched in life and, therefore, offers a challenge and scope for creative comments. *Doctrine* represents, of course, well-founded opinions on what the law should be, not any piece of 'creative writing', by those who have established a reputation in their field. Its influence should not be exaggerated but viewed from the perspective of the standing of the academic lawyer in the civil law countries and the closer affinity of continental judges to the academic world rather than the Bar. The fact that, in spite of the abundance of academic writings on Community law, the Court only in few cases, albeit through the Advocates-General, referred to juristic writings indicates both the scope and limitations of their contribution.

(c) Community precedents[15]

Since *Jurisprudence* represents the body of case law evolved through interpretation of the texts a few comments on the role of precedents in the Community system seem necessary. The judgment of the Court can be divided into two parts: the *motifs* (reasons) and the *dispositif* (the ruling). From the parties' point of view the ruling is of a primary interest because, after all, it decides the issue. Indeed, under the doctrine of *res judicata* the judgment is binding upon the Court where there is an identity of parties, cause and object.[16] Apart from *res judicata* the Court is not bound by its previous decisions but this does not mean that precedents are ignored.

In the eyes of the continental lawyer precedents have only a persuasive force in the sense that they reflect the application of the law in practice. However they must be taken into account when assessing the likely impact of arguments in court or prognosticating the outcome of litigation. Assuming that courts do not administer justice in an erratic manner the concept of *jurisprudence constante* suggests that their decisions provide a reliable guide. Under the doctrine of separation of powers the judges have no law-making function and indeed by article 5 of the French Civil Code they are prohibited from deciding cases in a general and rule-making manner. Their decisions must be based on the law, not on pre-

---

15 G Koopmans, T, '*Stare Decisis* in European Law', in O'Keefe and Schermers (ed) *Essays in European Law and Integration*, (1982), pp 11–27.
16 Cases 28–30/62: *Da Costa en Schaake NV v Nederlandse Administratre der Belastingen* [1963] CMLR 224; A-G Lagrange at 229–233.

viously decided cases. Should the latter be the case the decision in France would probably be quashed by the Cour de Cassation because of *défaut de base légale*.[17] However, there is no harm in considering cases and citing precedents in the *motifs* of the judgment. Judges who study reports of cases cannot fail to notice the interpretation adopted by the Courts.

They have the benefit of learned comments and opinions expressed in the *doctrine*, and during oral arguments counsel do not neglect the opportunity of impressing upon the Court the fact that a certain decision was reached on similar facts in previous cases. However, by tradition, when deciding a case judges must arrive at the particular interpretation by themselves just in case the Court which decided the previous case made a mistake. Therefore, judgments are substantiated by reference to the law comprised in codes and statutes. In the absence of a code or statute the case will be decided according to custom and in the absence of custom according to 'equity, reason, justice, tradition', but never according to 'precedent'.[18]

The scope for the persuasive influence of precedent is very great indeed in the uncodified areas of the law, notably administrative law. Here in addition to statutes the 'general principles of the law' play a considerable part and these, in turn, can often be found applied in precedents. The French Conseil d'Etat not only administers a body of law derived from precedents but also endeavours to relate its decisions to the pattern of case law.

The Community Court, modelled upon the Conseil d'Etat, fulfils a similar function and relies on its own decisions in a similar manner. On several occasions it either followed or referred to its previous decisions[19] in the *motifs*, which correspond to the *ratio decidendi* of the Common Law doctrine of precedent. There is a growing tendency of citing precedents not only by the Court but also, and to a greater extent, by the Advocates-General.[20]

17 David, R, *Le Droit Français* (1960), p 161.
18 Ibid, p 162.
19 Cases 28–30/62: *Da Costa en Schaake NV v Netherlands Revenue Department* [1963] ECR 31, [1963] CMLR 224; Case 44/65: *Hessische Knappschaft v Maison Singer* [1965] ECR 965, [1966] CMLR 82; Case 28/67: *Mölkerei-Zentrale Westfalen-Lippe GmbH v Hauptzollamt Paderborn* [1968] CMLR 187 at 216–219; *Filippo Galli*, supra, 123; Case 68/74; *Angelo Alaimo v Préfet du Rhône* [1975] ECR 109, [1975], 1 CMLR 262; Case 12/74: *EC Commission v Federal Republic of Germany* [1975] ECR 181, [1975] 1 CMLR 340; Case 67/74: *Bonsignore v Oberstadtdirektor der Stadt Köln* [1975] ECR 297, [1975] 1 CMLR 472; *Union Syndicale* op cit 123; Case 94/74: *IGAV-Industria Gomma etc v Ente Nazionale etc* [1975] ECR 699 at 701, 705, 708; Case 7/75: *Fracas v Belgian State* [1975] ECR 679 at 684; Case 21/75: *Schroeder KG-Hamburg v Oberstadtsdirektor der Stadt Köln* [1975] ECR 905 at 910 to name some older cases.
20 *Fillipo Galli* at 68; *Angelo Alaimo* at 113; *EEC Commission* at 206 et seq;

Advocate-General Roemer thus stated the position in the Community Court:[1] 'it is in the nature of the development of the Common Market that facts appear, which, by reason of their novelty and the impossibility of foreseeing them, may bring about a revision of well established legal opinions' and concluded that previous decisions cannot have the binding force of precedents. In another case[2] involving the interpretation of EEC Treaty article 85 in which the parties abundantly cited previous decisions, he said: 'It is, therefore, appropriate ... to resort to these decisions with discretion, even where the general terms of propositions suggest their application to problems not arising in the case before the Court when they were formulated.' Indeed the question whether a previous judgment was binding upon another national court would be held inadmissible.[3]

Whilst the judgments of the ECJ are precedents in their own right because they have settled important points of law and in many cases broken a new ground the question arises whether they are *precedents* in the accepted sense of the word or, more precisely, within the Common Law doctrine of *stare decisis*.

The doctrine of *stare decisis* rests upon the hierarchy of courts and the style of judgments and reports. The ECJ is a unique court of first and last instance, but since it has become a court of appeal from the First Instance Court precedents are likely to be more widely used in the Community adjudication system, at least to the extent that the latter may consider itself to be bound by previous judgments of the ECJ. Although it is the internal court of the Community it is not an exact replica of a supreme federal court; still less it resembles the Court of International Justice. However it functions like a supreme court of a federation as well as the only judicial organ of an inter-state organization. In that capacity it has to decide matters of principle and policy. In the latter context the ECJ has been using its Olympian position in furtherance of a legal

Bonsignore at 310; *Union Syndicale* at 708; Case 79/74: *Berthold Küster v European Parliament* [1975] ECR 725 at 734; *IGAV-Industria Gomma etc v ENCC-Ente Nazionale etc* at 715; *Fracas*, supra, at 692; Case 8/75: supra. *Caisse Primaire d' Assurance Maladaise Sélestat (Bas-Rhin) France v Association du Football Club Andlau (Bes-Rhin) France* [1975] ECR 739 at 757; *Schroeder KG* op cit at 915; Case 112/76 *Manzoni v Fonds National de Retraite des Ouvriers Mineurs* [1977] ECR 1647; [1978] 2 CMLR 416 to name only some older cases.

1 In Case 1/64: *SA Glucosiéries Réunies v EEC Commission* [1964] CMLR 596 at 598.
2 Case 23/67: *Brasserie de Haecht v Wilkin* [1967] ECR 407, [1968] CMLR 26.
3 See Case 24/66 (bis): *Gesellschaft für Getreidehandel v EC Commission* [1973] ECR 1599 at 1603; per A-G Reischl at 1606.

integration of the Community.[4] Nevertheless, the ECJ's technique
is to decide each case on its specific merits rather than in the light
of the historical experience enshrined in precedents. Therefore it
avoids using the theory of *acte clair* prefering a fresh approach to
the issues before it. However, in the CILFIT[5] case the Court,
albeit hesitantly, recognized the force of precedent in Community
law, repeating its dictum in an earlier case[6] that '... the authority
of an interpretation ... already given by the Court may deprive the
obligation (to refer under article 177) of its purpose and thus empty
it of its substance ...'
Like a supreme court it is not and cannot be bound by its own
decisions.[7] Indeed in the Community context it is doubtful whether
it has the power, let alone the wish, to declare itself bound by its
own decisions.[8] However it may wish to cite its own decisions either
to indicate a continuing line of reasoning or, simply, to cut corners.
This is a matter of the style of citation.
There is a rather haphazard approach to citation in the ECJ
decisions. Originally, in the few cases in which a previous ruling
was adopted there was no trace of the pedigree of the new ruling.
Whole sentences or paragraphs were incorporated in the judgment
without reference to or acknowledgement of the source. The
famous dictum that 'the Community is a new legal order etc' taken
from the *Van Gend* case appeared often in the report. As of late
the formula[9] 'As the Court has already stated in' ... with reference
to the cited case[10] or words to that effect has been adopted. No

4 Lasok, D, La Cour de Justice, instrument de l'intégration communautaire,
  (1979) *Rev d'intégration européenne*, pp 391 et seq.
5 Case 283/81: *Srl CILFIT v Ministry of Health* [1982] ECR 3415 at para 13;
  [1983] 1 CMLR 472.
6 Cases 28–30/62: *Da Costa v Nederlandse Belastingadministratie* [1963] ECR 31,
  [1963] CMLR 224.
7 See Case 112/76: *Manzoni v Fonds National de Retraite des Ouvriers Mineurs*
  [1977] ECR 1647 at 1662, [1978] 2 CMLR 416 at 429 (per A.-G. Warner).
8 Cf the British House of Lords ruled to be so bound in *London Street Tramways
  Co Ltd v LCC* [1898] AC 375 but discarded the rule per Lord Gardiner L.C.,
  reported at [1966] 3 All ER 77, [1966] 1 WLR 1234.
9 Case 26/62: *Van Gend en Loos v Netherlands Administratie der Belastingen*
  [1963] ECR 1 at 29; [1963] CMLR 105 at 129.
10 Eg Case 70/77: *Simmenthal SpA v Amministrazione delle Finanze dello Stato*
  [1978] ECR 1453 at 1469, [1978] 3 CMLR 670 at 684; Case 50/76: *Amsterdam
  Bulb BV v Produktschap voor Siergewassen* [1977] ECR 137 at 146, [1977] 2
  CMLR 218 at 240; Case 128/78: *EC Commission v United Kingdom, Re
  Tachograph* [1979] ECR 419 at 428, [1979] 2 CMLR 45 at 55; Case 153/78: *Re
  Health Control on Imported Meat: EC Commission v Germany* [1980] 1 CMLR
  198 at 207; Cases 66/79, 127–128/79: *Amministrazione delle Finanze v
  Meridionale Industria Salumi SRL* [1980] ECR 1237 at 1261 [1981] 1 CMLR
  1 at 17; Case 811/79: *Amministrazione delle Finanze dello Stato v Ariete SpA*
  [1980] ECR 2545 at 2553, 2555, [1981] 1 CMLR 316.

doubt this is an improvement but we still have to wait for the Court's express acknowledgement[11] of the persuasive authority of its own decisions and for the Court distinguishing rulings inconsistent with the previous ones and giving the reasons for the distinction. So far the Court has tended to ignore previous decisions from which it has deviated.[12] However it did not hesitate to apply the tenor of its judgment in an enforcement action[13] to a subsequent reference[14] arising from a prosecution under national law regulating the advertisement of alcoholic beverage inconsistent with Community law. Yet, in the terms of the judgment it was not a question of applying a precedent but of interpreting the relevant Community law as well as the judgment which explained that law. However, more recently the Court disposed of a case which revealed no new issues simply by reference to its earlier decisions.[15]

The doctrine of precedent must be supported by a comprehensive system of law reporting. The decisions of the ECJ are reported systematically whether in the private collections (eg CMLR) or the Court's own Reports (ECR). However not all cases are so reported and the ECR, though an official publication of the Court, does not carry the seal of authenticity. Probably no such guarantee can be given in view of the linguistic problems of translations but, in view of the quality of the reports, there is no reason to suppose that they are not a faithful reproduction of the Court's records.

There is no hierarchical relationship between the national judiciary and the ECJ. Even in the field of reference for preliminary rulings the ECJ does not operate as a court of appeal or review but simply as a court of reference, albeit with the unique and supreme power of interpretation. Therefore the essential condition upon which the doctrine of *stare decisis* rests is not present. The judgments of the ECJ are not subject to appeal or *exequatur* within national jurisdictions and their executive authority, except in the

---

11 In this respect Case 54/80: *Procureur de la République v Wilner* [1980] ECR 3673, [1983] 2 CMLR 444, at paras 6 and 7, appears unique as the ECJ cited its judgment in Case 65/79: *Procureur de la République v Chatain* [1980] ECR 1345, [1981] 3 CMLR 418 as a source of Community law. See also Case 283/81, note 5, supra.

12 However, in Cases 240–242/82, 261–262/82 and 268–269/82 *Stichting Sigarettenindustrie v EC Commission* [1985] ECR 3831, [1987] 3 CMLR 661, the ECJ distinguished its judgment in Cases 209–215 and 218/78: *Heintz van Landewyck Sarl v EC Commission* [1980] ECR 3125; [1981] 3 CMLR 134.

13 Case 152/78: *EC Commission v France* [1980] ECR 2299, [1981] 2 CMLR 743.

14 Joined Cases 314–316/81 and 83/82: *Procureur de la République v Waterkeyn* [1982] ECR 4337, [1983] 2 CMLR 145.

15 Cases 271–274/84 and 6–7/85: *Procureur de la République v Chiron* [1986] ECR 529, [1988] 1 CMLR 735.

case of judgments against the Member States, is assured by Treaty provisions.[16] However since their status ranks no higher than a *res judicata* it depends upon the given national system whether they are treated as precedents or otherwise. Thus the curious result of section 3(2) of the European Communities Act 1972 is that their status in the United Kingdom appears to be higher than that in the Civil Law countries.[17]

Despite the arguments against the '*government of judges*'[18] the status of preliminary rulings appears to be different from the judgments in contentious proceedings. Here the Court makes a ruling on an abstract point of law which, in a sense, becomes the property of the whole Community in view of the procedure in which the Commission and all the Member States may participate and the general interest the point should have for the entire Community legal system. Therefore, as argued Advocate-General Warner,[19] these rulings should have effect *erga omnes*. In reality they can be so regarded despite the fact that national courts are free to raise similar if not identical questions repeatedly and that the ECJ too is free to change its mind.

In conclusion the creative role of the ECJ in the interpretation and formulation of the principles of Community law has to be recognized without necessarily ascribing to its case law the status of a formal source of law.

(d) Basic doctrines
In furthering 'the intention of the contracting states ... to create a Community designed for progressive integration[20]' the Court developed certain doctrines which characterize the Community legal order as an original system and determine its relationship to the municipal law of the Member States:

(i) *Unity*. From an early stage the Court advanced the idea of a functional unity of the three Communities[1] which, in the jur-

---

16 EEC, arts 187 and 192(2); ECSC, arts 44 and 92; EAEC, arts 159 and 164.
17 Wall, E A, European Communities Act 1972, (1973) p 28.
18 *Lecourt, R, Le juge devant le marché commun*, (1970), p 57; *L'Europe des Juges*, (1976).
19 Case 112/76: *Manzoni v Fonds National de Retraite des Ouvriers Mineurs* [1977] ECR 1647 at 1661–1663, [1978] 2 CMLR 416 at 429–430. See also Joined Cases 28–30/62: *Da Costa en Schaake NV v Nederlandse Belastingadministratie* [1963] *ECR* 31 at 38, [1963] CMLR 224 at 235–236; Case 283/81: *CILFIT Srl v Minister of Health* [1982] ECR 3415 at 3429–3430, [1983] 1 CMLR 472 at 477–478; Case 112/83: *Société des Produits de Maïs SA v Administration des Douanes* [1985] ECR 719, [1988] 1 CMLR 459.
20 Kutscher, op cit p 32.
1 Colin, J-P, *Le gouvernement des juges dans les Communautés Européennes* (1966) 74 et seq.

isprudence of the Court, meant that one founding Treaty should be interpreted with the aid of the others.² Of these cases one involving a Community official merits a special attention.³ Sr Campolongo, who was employed by the High Authority of the Coal and Steel Community, was discharged and took up an appointment with the European Investment Bank instituted under the EEC Treaty. He claimed various benefits including a reinstallation allowance, but the Court decreed that he was not entitled to it because the 'functional unity' of the Communities does not permit accumulation of payments due on the termination of employment with one and commencement of employment with another institution of the Communities. The Court recognized the separate legal personalities of the Communities according to articles 6, 210 and 184 of the Treaties which founded the ECSC, EEC and EAEC, respectively, but emphasized that through the Treaty of Merger a strong legal bond between the Communities has been established. Advocate-General Roemer, whose submissions in this respect were followed by the Court, stated that 'the European Treaties are nothing but a partial implementation of a grand general programme, dominated by the idea of a complete integration of the European States'.

The idea of unity in the uniform interpretation and application of the Community and the equal acceptance of Treaty obligations by the Member States was emphasized by the Court on several occasions. In the *Gingerbread*⁴ cases the Court underlined the unitary and mandatory nature of Community law without which it would be impossible to establish the Common Market. This theme was followed in the *Costa*⁵ case where, inter alia, the compatibility of the nationalization of Italian electricity industry with the EEC Treaty was raised and cases in which the Court insisted that certain key terms of Community law such as, *scrap equalization charge;*⁶ *rediscount rate;*⁷ *public policy;*⁸ to give just a few examples,

2 Case 6/60: *Humblet v Belgian State* [1960] ECR 559; Case 30/59: *De Gezamenlijke Steenkolenmijnen* in *Limburg v High Authority of the ECSC* [1961] ECR 1; Case 9/59: (1959), 6 Rec 27; Case 230/81: *Luxembourg v European Parliament* [1983] ECR 255; [1983] 2 CMLR 726.
3 Cases 27/59 and 39/59: *Alberto Campolongo v High Authority of the ECSC* [1960] ECR 391.
4 Cases 2–3/62: *EC Commission v Luxembourg and Belgium (Import Licences for Ginger Bread)* [1962] ECR 425, CMLR 199.
5 Case 6/64: *Costa v ENEL* [1964] ECR 585, [1964] CMLR 425.
6 Case 26/66: *Koninklijke Nederlandsche Hoogovens v High Authority of the ECSC* [1967] ECR 115.
7 Cases 6–11/69: *EC Commission v French Republic* [1969] ECR 523, [1970] CMLR 43.
8 *Van Duyn*, p 143, note 12, supra; Case 30/77: *R v Bouchereau* [1977] ECR 1999, [1977] 2 CMLR 800.

have a 'Community meaning' and must be interpreted and applied
as such. In respect of the Member States' duties the Court stressed
that a state 'cannot ... unilaterally opt out of ... its obligations'
and that 'non-compliance ... strikes at the very root of the Community legal order ...' and ... 'brings into question the equality
of Member States before Community law ...'[9]

(ii) *Autonomy.* The doctrine of the autonomy of Community
law rests, on the one hand, on the concept of unity and on the
principle of the separation of powers or functions, on the other. The
constitutional principle of separation means, in the Community
context, a division of functions between the Community Institutions and the Member States[10] and, in the administration of
justice, between the Community Court and national courts.[11]

The autonomy of Community law means that it is 'quite independent of the legislation passed by the Member States'.[12] It is
derived from an extraneous source, albeit an organization created
by the Member States themselves, it extends equally and uniformly
over their territories, and has to be applied by their courts in its
original form. The uniformity of its interpretation is assured by
the obligation to seek preliminary rulings from the Community
Court.

The practical application of the doctrine of autonomy has manifested itself in areas where the integrity and efficacy of Community
law has to be safeguarded[13] or where it has to be distinguished from
national law as, for example, in the field of competition where the
two systems overlap.[14] Thus held the ECJ: the efficacy of the Treaty
would be impaired if, in the context of partial integration with
national law, the specific tasks entrusted to the Community were
not interpreted as totally independent.[15] It follows that the Member
States are in no position of taking unilateral measures to carry out
the mandatory provisions of Community law.[16] The concept of the

9 Case 128/78: *EC Commission v United Kingdom, Re Tachographs* [1979] ECR
419, [1979] 2 CMLR 45.
10 ERTA Case, p 70, note 8, para 12, supra; Case 30/59: *Gezamenlijke
Steenkolenmijnen in Limburg v High Authority of the ECSC* [1961] ECR 1 at 23.
11 A-G Roemer in Case 6/54: *Government of the Netherlands v High Authority of
the ECSC* [1954–56] ECR 103.
12 Case 28/67: *Mölkerei-Zentrale Westfalen/Lippe GmbH v Hauptzollamt
Paderborn* [1968] ECR 143 at 152, [1968] CMLR 187 at 217 (this version
differs from ECR).
13 *Variola*, p 132, note 16, supra.
14 Case 14/68: *Wilhelm v Bundeskartellamt* [1969] ECR 1, [1969] CMLR 100.
15 Case 30/59: supra.
16 Eg Case 13/68: *Salgoil Spa v Italian Ministry of Foreign Trade* (*Re Import
quotas*) [1968] ECR 453, [1969] CMLR 181; Cases 90–91/63: *EEC Commission
v Luxembourg and Belgium* (*Re Special Import Licence of Milk Products*) [1964]
ECR 625, [1965] CMLR 58; Case 52/77: *Cayrol v Rivoira and Figli* (*Re import

autonomy of Community law, first mentioned by the ECJ in *San
Michele v High Authority*[17] *of the ECSC*, sets it apart from national
law as a separate and independent legal order yet ruling directly
over the territories of the Member States. It reflects a federal legal
system.

(iii) *Supremacy of Community law.* The supremacy of Community law when in conflict with national law is the logical consequence of the federal concept of the Community.[18] The doctrine
itself is nowhere mentioned in the Treaties but can be deduced
from the Member States' constitutional law,[19] in so far as the
national constitutions[20] and practice recognize the primacy of international obligations without necessarily stating *expressis verbis* that
in the case of conflict Community law prevails, and their readiness
to make the Community function. In other words, since the creation of the Community and the endowment of its Institutions with
executive, legislative and judicial functions implies a delegation of
sovereignty, the Community could not function as a supranational
organisation if the delegated powers were insufficient or capable of
being withdrawn. Therefore supremacy does not reflect any
inherent superiority of Community Law but merely a working
relationship.

Supremacy was first mentioned by the ECJ in a case involving
the effect of the ECSC Treaty on previously enacted Belgian tax
law[1]. On that occasion the Court saw the relationship between the
two systems in the light of the monist theory of International Law.
In *Van Gend*, that most important constitutional case, the Court
saw the 'new legal order' in the light of a federalist concept[2]. Thus
the base of the doctrine was shifted but firmly established in *Costa
v ENEL*[3] in which, inter alia, the question of compatibility of
the Italian decree nationalising the electricity industry with the
Community legal order was raised. The Court held that ... '(The
Treaty) ... has created its own legal system which, on the entry
into force of the Treaty, became an integral part of the legal systems
of the Member States and which their courts are bound to apply
... because of its special and original nature ... (it) could not be
overridden by domestic legal provisions, however framed, without

Licence) [1977] ECR 2261, [1978] 2 CMLR 253; Case 128/78: *EC Commission
v United Kingdom, Re Tachographs* [1979] ECR 419; [1979] 2 CMLR 45.
17 Case 9/65: [1967] ECR 1 at 30.
18 Ipsen, H P, 'Rapport du droit des Communautés Européennes avec le droit
national', *Le Droit des Affaires* (1964), No 47.
19 Cf European Communities Act 1972, s 2(1).
20 See Ch 10, infra.
 1 Case 6/60: *Humblet v Belgian State* [1960] ECR 559 at 569.
 2 [1963] ECR 1 at 12, [1963] CMLR 105.
 3 Case 6/64; [1964] ECR 585 at 593 and 594, [1964] CMLR 425 at 455, 456.

being deprived of its character as Community law and without the legal basis of the Community itself being called into question'.

Commenting specifically on the impact of the Community upon national legislation the Court thought that 'The transfer by the States from their domestic legal system to the Community legal system of the rights and obligations arising under the Treaty carries with it a permanent limitation of their sovereign rights, against which a subsequent unilateral act incompatible with the concept of the Community cannot prevail'.[4]

In the same vein, in the *Second Art Treasures*[5] case, the Court, condemning Italy's attempt to introduce a tax on the export of art treasures, held that ... 'the Member States' assignment of rights and powers to the Community in accordance with the provisions of the Treaty entails a definitive limitation of their sovereign rights against which no provisions of municipal law, whatever their nature, can be legally invoked'.

More recently the Court held that, where the lowest minimum export price of flower bulbs has been fixed by the Community, the exporting country 'may neither adopt nor allow national organisations having legislative power to adopt any measure which would conceal the Community nature and effects' of such provisions, even if the minimum price would render the transaction unprofitable.[6] Implying that a national provision inconsistent with a binding Community role must be void the Court held that such a Community rule would ... 'preclude the valid adoption of new legislative measures to the extent to which they would be incompatible with Community provisions'.[7] ... Addressing itself to the national judicature the ECJ ruled that ... 'A national court which is called upon ... to apply provisions of Community law is under a duty to give full effects to those provisions, if necessary refusing of its own motion to apply any conflicting provisions of national legislation, even if adopted subsequently, and it is not necessary for the court to request or await a prior setting aside of such provision by legislative or other constitutional means.'[8] The ECJ has no express power to declare void national legislation but can achieve the same effect through the doctrine of supremacy since its ruling in this respect may emphasize that it is not sufficient for the national

4 Ibid, ECR at 594.
5 Case 48/71: *EC Commission v Italy* [[1972] ECR 527, para 9, 1972] CMLR 699 at 708.
6 Case 50/76: *Amsterdam Bulb BV v Produktschap voor Siergewassen* [1977] ECR 137 at 151, [1977] 2 CMLR 218 at 243.
7 Case 106/77: *Amministrazione delle Finanze dell Stato v Simmenthal SpA* [1978] ECR 629 at 643, [1978] 3 CMLR 263 at 283.
8 Ibid ECR at 647, CMLR at 283. See also Case C-213/89: *R v Secretary of State for Transport, ex p FACTORTAME* [1990] 3 CMLR 867.

supreme court to disapply inconsistent national law because such law must be specifically repealed by the national legislature. Failure to do so would infringe article 5 of the EEC Treaty.[9]

However the most dramatic assertion of supremacy occurred in the case of an alleged violation of the German Basic Law by a Community regulation.[10] The Court ruled that 'no provision of municipal law, of whatever nature they may be, may prevail over Community law ... lest it be deprived of its character as Community law and its very legal foundation be endangered. The validity of a Community act or its application in a Member State remains, therefore, unimpaired even if it is alleged that the basic rights ... of the national constitution were violated.'

(iv) *Direct applicability and direct effect*. Like the doctrines of autonomy and supremacy the doctrine of direct applicability of Community law has been enunciated in the *Van Gend* case. On that occasion the ECJ held that article 12 of the EEC Treaty was applicable to the Member State and the citizen alike and that it created rights which the citizen could rely on and which his national courts were bound to uphold even against national legislation. The doctrine holds the key to the relationship between Community law and national law and unmistakably points to a federal character of the former because in a federal system federal law bears directly upon the citizens of the component states. We shall see this when assessing the impact of Community law upon the national systems. At this stage it will suffice to consider its theoretical implications. In the literature a distinction is made between 'direct applicability' and 'direct effect' of Community law.[11] This is a valid distinction but not exclusive to Community law. As pointed out by Advocate-General Warner[12] the distinction is known to national statutes 'some provisions of which impose obligations on the State or public authorities without conferring rights on citizens'. Indeed one has to distinguish not only between the contents of legal rules but also between the addressees of these rules. In the *Van Gend* case the argument on behalf of the state concerned (incidentally accepted by Advocate-General Roemer) was that the obligation contained in the relevant Treaty provision concerned the state involved and

---

9 Case 104/86: *EC Commission v Italy, Re Repayment of Illegal Taxes* [1989] 3 CMLR 25, at para 12; see also Case 815/79: *Proceedings against Cremonini and Vrankovich* [1980] ECR 3583 (at 3607); [1981] 3 CMLR 49.

10 Case 11/70: *Internationale Handelsgesellschaft mbH v Einfuhr-und-Vorratsstelle für Getreide und Futtermittel* [1970] ECR 1125 at 1127, [1972] CMLR 255 at 283.

11 Winter, J, 'Direct Applicability and Direct Effect: Two Distinct and Different Concepts in Community law' (1972) CML Rev p 425; Wyatt, D, 'Directly applicable Provisions of EEC law' (1975) 125 NLJ, pp 458, 575, 669, 793.

12 In case 31/74: *Filippo Galli* [1975] ECR 47 at 70, [1975] 1 CMLR 211.

did not give rise to any claim on behalf of the importer. However the Court, in its famous dictum, enclosed both the state and the importer and concluded that the provision was applicable in litigation before national courts and that, because of its content and purpose, it generated remedies available to the importer. In other words, a directly applicable provision had, as its effect, an enforceable Community right.

The doctrine, as we shall see later, is of an immense practical importance as far as individuals are concerned. It also strengthens the federal concept of the Community.

(v) *General principles of law.* Next to the basic doctrines the Court has to be credited with the development of general principles of Community law. To these we have already alluded in the context of interpretation. It remains now to discuss these in the context of the legal integration through the Court's jurisprudence.

By a doctrine, as distinguished from a principle or a rule of law, we understand a general proposition or guidance relating to a fundamental issue such as eg the nature of Community law or the conflict between the Community and national law. A principle, or a rule of law, on the other hand, can be construed more narrowly as a rule of conduct prescribed in the given circumstances and carrying a sanction for non-compliance. Thus a principle or rule of law consists of a hypothesis, a disposition and a sanction. The hypothesis postulates a factual situation which ought to be responded to in accordance with the disposition or prescribed conduct. The law as a normative system is vindicated by the appropriate sanction which is, on the one hand, civil ie nullity of the act in question, damages or both and, punitive, on the other. A punitive sanction often serves to vindicate a civil obligation.

Codified systems consist of general and particular rules. The former come close to doctrines in the sense the term has been used above. However, though they can be vindicated like any particular rule, they serve a dual purpose: as pointers to interpretation by the courts and as indications of policy to legislators. Thus such general rules as eg public policy or equality indicate the limits of interpretation in particular cases and also enable the courts to fill the gaps which are not supposed to exist in codes of law but, in reality, do become exposed because life is more imaginative than the most astute legislator. With reference to the same examples a particular application of public policy or equality may be subject to separate legislation, eg to restrict the sale of firearms or combat racial or sex discrimination, or, simply, a general principle to be further developed in the code.

The above-mentioned legislative techniques are well exemplified in the text of the EEC Treaty. There we find general principles such as the principle of solidarity (article 5) which governs the relationship between the Member States and the Community and the principle of non-discrimination on the ground of nationality (article 7) applicable to matters governed by the Treaty. In these two articles the Court found a powerful support in the interpretation of the Treaty provisions as well as a formal source to complement inadequately expressed intentions of the makers of the Treaty.

The principle of the freedom of movement of persons (article 48) within the Community has been not only partly elaborated in the Treaty but also carried into effect in considerable detail by derivative legislation comprising rules on migration and social security. The right of establishment of liberal professions (article 52) too has been developed partly in the text, partly outside the text of the Treaty by derivative legislation. The same technique has been adopted to all Treaty policies, some of which remain still in their embryonic stage.

Faced with this kind of enacted law the Court, in the absence of interpretation clauses, has to resort to every method of interpretation known to national judiciaries. It also has to dip into the treasury of national tradition in order to adopt for the Community some well-established and universally recognized principles of national law. In the EEC Treaty there is only one reference to 'general principles common to the laws of the Member States' in article 215(2) according to which the non-contractual liability of the Community should be judged. However, in practice, the Court may take recourse to article 173(1) which enables it to annul Community acts which 'infringe the Treaty or any rule of law relating to its application'. These other 'rules of law' begin to emerge as follows:

(a) *Due process and natural justice.* In civilized societies the existence and observance of procedural rules provide a safeguard and protection of substantive rights. The making and enforcement of rules of conduct have to conform to a notion of 'due process' where the authorities do not act arbitrarily but give reasons for their acts,[13] and the accused is informed of his charges, has a right to be heard and represented by an independent advocate.

Thus the sanction of nullity applies to Community acts made in contravention of 'an essential procedural requirement'.[14] The Court, following the Advocate-General's strong plea for the recognition of the principle *audi alteram partem* even in the absence

13 See eg Case 248/84: *Germany v EC Commission (Re Regional Aid Plans)* [1989] 1 CMLR 591; Case 45/86: *EC Commission v EC Council (Re Generalized Tariff Preferences)* [1987] ECR 1493, [1988] 2 CMLR 131.
14 EEC, art 173(1).

of express legislation to that effect, held in a competition case[15] that 'a person whose interests are perceptibly affected by a decision taken by a public authority must be given the opportunity to make his point of view known'.[16] This implies that the party concerned must be informed of the conditions under which the Treaty has been applied.[17]

The right of defence also implies the right to be represented by counsel even in disciplinary proceedings where parties need not and are not normally represented.[18] The principle of *non bis in idem* applies not only in the case of two disciplinary sanctions for a single transgression but also to multiple disciplinary proceedings following a single occurrence.[19] It does not apply to parallel proceedings in competition cases under two different systems.[20]

Double jeopardy was pleaded, albeit unsuccessfully, in respect of forfeiture of returnable deposits.[21] In view of the failure to export in time, forfeiture of two deposits was: one for exportation and another for advance-fixed refund. The ECJ held both forfeitures correct and lawful since they resulted from an administrative procedure which was well founded and the sanction was proportionate to the failure of the applicant. Although it is in the nature of penalty a forfeiture bears no criminal features and, therefore, does not attract criminal safeguards. The principle of double jeopardy does not apply.

The Commission's investigative powers do not override the protection afforded by the privilege of confidentiality of communications between an independent lawyer practising in the Community and his client relating to a case investigated by the Commission.[1]

---

15 Case 17/74: *Transocean Marine Paint Association v EC Commission* [1974] ECR 1063 at 1079, [1974] 2 CMLR 459 at 477.
16 See also Case 75/77: *Mollet v EC Commission* [1978] ECR 897.
17 Case 24/62: *Germany v EEC Commission* [1963] ECR 63 at 69, [1963] CMLR 347; see also Case 34/77: *Oslizlok v EC Commission* [1978] ECR 1099; Case 85/76: *Hoffmann-La Roche v EC Commission* [1979] ECR 461, [1979] 3 CMLR 211. Joined Cases 209–215, 218/78: *Heintz van Landewyck Sarl v EC Commission* [1980] ECR 3125 at 3237, [1981] 3 CMLR 134 at 215; Joined Cases 100–103/80: *Musique Diffusion Française SA v EC Commission* [1983] ECR 1825 at 1880, 1881, 1887, [1983] 3 CMLR 221 at 315, 320; Case 115/80: *Demont v EC Commission* [1981] ECR 3147.
18 Case 115/80: *Demont v EC Commission* [1981] ECR 3147, paras 11 and 12.
19 Joined Cases 18, 35/65: *Gutmann v Euratom Commission* [1966] ECR 103 at 119, [1967] ECR 61.
20 Case 14/68: *Walt Wilhelm v Bundeskartellamt* [1969] ECR 1 at 15, [1969] CMLR 100 at 120–121; Case 7/72: *Boehringer Mannheim GmbH v EC Commission* [1972] ECR 1281 at 1289, [1973] CMLR 864 at 887.
21 Case 137/85: *Maizena GmbH v Bundesanstalt für Landwirtschaftliche Marktordnung* [1987] ECR 4587, [1989] 2 CMLR 336.
1 Case 155/79: *A M & S Europe Ltd v EC Commission* [1982] ECR 1575 at 1610–

(b) *Equality*. Equality before the law is, next to due process, an essential ingredient of justice. In the EEC Treaty equality is to be achieved through suppression of discrimination on the ground of nationality (article 7); as between consumers and producers of agricultural produce (article 40(3)) and as between employees on account of their sex (article 119). The Court, however, deduced from these scanty provisions a general principle of Community law.[2]

In developing the theme the Court made a start under the Coal and Steel Treaty by combating discriminatory practices expressly prohibited by articles 4(b) and 60.[3] More significant is the development under the EEC Treaty where the Court applied the principle of non-discrimination to goods, persons and states. However it made it plain in the case of a discriminatory reception of Italian refrigerators in France[4] that 'the different treatment of non-comparable situations does not lead automatically to the conclusion that there is discrimination'.

Thus the principle of equality in comparable situations forms the basis of the Common Market. Indeed the free movement of goods is assured by enforcing the prohibition of discriminatory measures whether they are equivalent to customs duties[5] or quantitative restrictions[6] or whether they are fiscal measures designed to protect a national produce at the expense of a similar imported one.[7]

Equality of treatment was also vindicated in cases involving subsidies to producers in the context of the Common Agricultural Policy. Thus the Court declared invalid Commission regulation

1613, [1982] 2 CMLR 264 at 322–325; Duffy, P J, 'Legal Privilege and Community Law' 132 NLJ (1982) 580–582.

2   See Case 1/72: *Frilli v Belgian State* [1972] ECR 457, [1973] CMLR 386; Case 152/73: *Sotgiu v Deutsche Bundespost* [1974] ECR 153.

3   Eg Case 8/57: *Haute Fourneaux et Aciéries Belges v High Authority of the ECSC* [1958] ECR 245 at 256.

4   Case 13/63: *Italy v EEC Commission* [1963] ECR 165, [1963] CMLR 289.

5   See Ch 13, post.

6   See Ch 13, post.

7   Eg Cases 52 and 55/65: *Germany v EEC Commission (tax on imported meat)* [1966] ECR 159, [1967] CMLR 22; Case 28/67: *Mölkerei-Zentrale Westfalen-Lippe GmbH v Hauptzollamt Paderborn (powdered milk)* [1968] ECR 143, [1968] CMLR 187; Case 232/78: *EC Commission v France (Sheepmeat)* [1979] ECR 2729, [1980] 1 CMLR 418; Case 168/78: *EC Commission v France (tax on alcoholic drinks)* [1980] ECR 347, [1981] 2 CMLR 631; Case 169/78: *EC Commission v Italy (tax on alcoholic drinks)* ECR ibid 385, CMLR ibid 673; Case 171/78: *EC Commission v Denmark (tax on alcoholic drinks)* ECR ibid 447, CMLR ibid 688 but see also Case 140/79: *Chemical Farmaceutici SpA v DAF SpA* [1981] ECR 1, [1981] 3 CMLR 350; Case 46/80: *Vinal SpA v Orbat SpA* [1981] ECR 77, [1981] 3 CMLR 524.

563/76 which, in order to reduce the stocks of skimmed milk powder, obliged animal feed producers to purchase skimmed milk powder instead of soya used as protein ingredient with the consequent result that the cost of animal feed had increased and upset farmers. The Court held the regulation contrary to the principle of equality in so far as it made the producers purchase skimmed milk powder 'at such a disproportionate price that it was equivalent to a discriminatory distribution of the burden of costs between the various agricultural sectors'.[8]

A similar attitude was adopted in the *quellmehl and gritz*[9] cases. Quellmehl is a product of maize or wheat used in the production of bread, gritz is a product of maize used in brewing. A Community subsidy was provided in order to enable starch to compete with synthetic products. However the unexpected result was that subsidized starch (because it is up to a point interchangeable with quellmehl and gritz) had obtained an unfair advantage over these products and began to replace quellmehl in bakeries and gritz in breweries. To even up the competitive position subsidies were extended to quellmehl and gritz. However, subsequently, by a resolution the Council withdrew the subsidies from quellmehl and gritz but not from starch. The quellmehl and gritz producers obtained a judgment against the Council on the ground of discrimination[10] but subsidies were reinstated only as from the date of the judgment. The claim for compensation under EEC Treaty article 215(2) covering the period during which subsidies were withdrawn was recognized by the Court on the ground that the producers of quellmehl and gritz were a small, clearly definable, group and that the loss they suffered exceeded the normal risk pertinent to their business. Therefore they were entitled to compensation based on the subsidy they would have received had they

---

8 Cases 83, 94/76: *Bayerische HNL Vermehrungsbetriebe GmbH & Co KG v EC Council and EC Commission* [1978] ECR 1209, [1978] 3 CMLR 566; see also Case 114/76: *Bela-Mühle KG v Grows-Farm GmbH* [1977] ECR 1211, [1979] 2 CMLR 83; Case 116/76: *Granaria BV v Hoofdproduktschap voor Akkerbouw-Produkten* [1977] ECR 1247, [1979] 2 CMLR 83; Cases 119, 120/76: *Ölmühle Hamburg AG v Hauptzollamt Hamburg Waltershof (First Skimmed Milk Powder Cases)* [1977] ECR 1269, [1979] 2 CMLR 83.

9 Cases 64, 113/76, 167, 239/78, 27, 28, 45/79: *Dumortier Frères SA v EC Council* [1979] ECR 3091; Case 238/78: *Ireks-Arkady v EC Council and Commission* [1979] ECR 2955; Cases 241, 242, 245–250/78: *DGV v EC Council and Commission* [1979] ECR 3017; Cases 261, 262/78: *Interquell Stärke-Chemie GmbH & Co KG and Diamalt AG v EC Council and Commission* [1979] ECR 3045.

10 Cases 117/76, 16/77: *Firma Albert Ruckdeschel & Co v Hauptzollamt Hamburg-St Annen* [1977] ECR 1753; [1979] 2 CMLR 445; Cases 124/76, 20/77: *Moulins et Huileries de Pont-a-Mousson SA v Office National Interprofessionnel des Céréales* [1977] ECR 1795, [1979] 2 CMLR 445.

been treated equally with the producers of starch. The quantum (left to be determined in later proceedings) was to be reduced by the proportion of the loss they were able to pass to their customers.

The third instance of equal treatment of products is exemplified by the *Isoglucose*[11] cases which, as noted elsewhere,[12] have released potential powers of the European Parliament. Again, to reduce the surplus of sugar, a substantial levy was imposed by regulation on isoglucose, a recently produced sweetener in heavy competition with sugar. According to the complainants this levy was of such a deterrent proportion that it would have made the production of isoglucose uneconomical. The Court restored the balance between the competing products on the ground that discriminatory regulation offended the principle of equality. The levy was eliminated with retrospective effect. However the claim for compensation failed, the Court in an almost perfunctory manner concentrating on the nature of the offending legislation rather than the consequential loss suffered by the producers of isoglucose.[13]

There is as yet no equality between Community citizens in a general sense but only in the context of the freedom of movement of workers and the right of establishment and in the context of enforceable Community rights. As held in the *Van Duyn*[14] case a Member State cannot, in accordance with the rules of International Law, refuse entry to its own citizens but may do so according to the EEC Treaty to the citizens of the fellow Member States only if the Community right of entry falls within the exception of public policy. However once admitted a Community citizen must not be discriminated against whether it concerns his freedom of movement;[15] employment;[16] or the whole variety of social rights including the rights under a national scheme for the protection of the

---

11 Cases 103, 145/77: *Royal Scholten-Honig (Holdings) Ltd and Tunnel Refineries Ltd v Intervention Board for Agricultural Produce (first Isoglucose cases)* [1978] ECR 2037; [1979] 1 CMLR 675; and *Second Isoglucose Cases* 116, 124/77: *Amylum NV and Tunnel Refineries Ltd v EC Council and Commission* [1979] ECR 3497; Case 143/77: *Koninklijke Scholten Honig NV v Council and Commission* [1979] ECR 3583.

12 See p 130, supra. See also Jacobs, F, Isoglucose Resurgent: 'Two Powers of the European Parliament,', 18 CMLRev (1981), 219.

13 *Second Isoglucose Cases*, supra, note 11.

14 Case 41/74: *Van Duyn v Home Office* [1974] ECR 1337, [1975] 1 CMLR 1.

15 Eg Case 36/75: *Rutili v Ministère de l'Interieur* [1975] ECR 1219; [1976] 1 CMLR 140.

16 Eg Cases 44/72: *Marsman v Rosskamp* [1972] ECR 1243, [1973] CMLR 501; 152/73: *Sotgiu v Deutsche Bundespost* [1974] ECR 153; 15/69: *Württembergische Milchverwertung-Südmilch AG v Ugliola* [1969] ECR 363, [1970] CMLR 194; 36/74: *Walrave and Koch v Association Union Cycliste Internationale* [1974] ECR 1405, [1975] 1 CMLR 320; 13/76: *Dona v Mantero* [1976] ECR 1333; [1976] 2 CMLR 578.

victims of crime.[17] A mere threat of discrimination contained in national law is incompatible with Community rules.[18]

The hard-won Community right to equal pay within the national systems[19] has provided an opportunity for broadening up national rules in the name of equality between the sexes.[20] Some problems involving sex equality arose in connection with employees of the Community but these cases had to be decided in the light of the interpretation of contractual rights. Thus an Italian official of the European Parliament who married a Luxembourg national was to be deprived of an expatriation allowance unless she was the head of the family. The Court refused to accept the principle that the entitlement should depend on sex and annulled the decision depriving her of the allowance.[21] Similarly an expatriation allowance of a Belgian employee at a Euratom centre in Italy, who married an Italian and thereby automatically acquired Italian citizenship without relinquishing her Belgian citizenship, was preserved since citizenship acquired involuntarily should not be the determining factor.[1] However in a slightly different situation, where a French Community official working in Belgium married a Belgian citizen

17 Case 186/87: *Cowan v Tresor Public* [1990] 2 CMLR 613.
18 Case 167/73: *EC Commission v French Republic* [1974] ECR 359; [1974] 2 CMLR 216.
19 Case 43/75: *Defrenne v SABENA* [1976] ECR 455; [1976] 2 CMLR 98. See also Case 109/88: *Handels-Og Kontor-Funktionaerernes Forbund I Danmark v Dansk Arbejdsgiverforening, ex p Danfoss A/S* [1991] 1 CMLR 8; Case 9/88: *Da Veiga v Staatssecretaries van Justitie* [1991] 1 CMLR 217; Case 33/88: *Allue and Coonan v University of Venice, Re Employment of Foreign Language Teachers* [1991] 1 CMLR 283.
20 Eg Cases 129/79: *Macarthys Ltd v Smith* [1980] ECR 1275, [1980] 2 CMLR 205; 69/80: *Worringham and Humphreys v Lloyds Bank Ltd* [1981] ECR 767, [1981] 2 CMLR 1; 96/80 *Jenkins v Kingsgate (Clothing Productions) Ltd* [1981] ECR 911, [1981] 2 CMLR 24; *Garland v British Rail Engineering Ltd* (reference to ECJ) [1981] 2 CMLR 542; Case 12/81: (ECJ) [1982] 1 CMLR 696; *Burton v British Railways Board* (reference to ECJ) [1981] 3 CMLR 100. Case 152/84: *Marshall v Southampton and South West Hampshire Area Health Authority* [1986] 1 CMLR 688; Case 150/85: *Drake v Chief Adjudication Officer* [1986] 3 CMLR 43. Case 262/84: *Beets-Proper v F. Lanschot Bankiets* [1987] 2 CMLR 616. Case 237/85: *Rummler v Dato-Druck GmbH (Re Sex Discrimination)* [1987] 3 CMLR 127; Case 286/85: *McDermott and Cotter v Minister for Social Welfare* [1987] ECR 1453, [1987] 2 CMLR 607; Case 262/84: *Beets-Proper v Lanschot Bankiers NV* [1986] ECR 773, [1987] 2 CMLR 616; Case 384/85: *Clarke v Chief Adjudication Officer* [1987] ECR 2865, [1987] 3 CMLR 277; Case 157/86: *Murphy v Bord Telecom Eireann* [1988] 1 CMLR 879; Case 312/86: *EC Commission v France, Re Protection of Women* [1989] 1 CMLR 408; Case C-262/88: *Barber v Guardian Royal Exchange Assurance Group (Re Occupational Pension Scheme)* [1990] 2 CMLR 513.
21 Case 20/71: *Sabbatini v European Parliament* [1972] ECR 345, [1972] CMLR 945.
1 Case 21/74: *Airola v Commission* [1975] ECR 221.

and would not have acquired Belgian citizenship if she had made a declaration that she wished to retain her old one, the inaction on her part was interpreted as her acquiescence. Therefore she had to take the consequences, the Court saying that 'there are no reasons associated with equal treatment why her Belgian nationality should not be taken into account in applying the provision concerned'.[2]

Even computerized rules of procedure are not allowed to discriminate since access to the summary proceedings for the prosecution of debts expressed in foreign currency cannot be denied to a creditor resident in another Member State if such claims can be pursued in ordinary legal proceedings.[3]

In matters involving the conduct of the Member States the Court has often emphasized their duties vis-à-vis each other and the Community they have created, such duties being a reflection of equality and reciprocity. A breach 'strikes at the very root of the Community legal order' and 'brings into question the equality of Member States before Community law and creates discrimination at the expense of their nationals'.[4]

However the principle does not apply in Community trade relations with third countries and individuals or corporations cannot demand equal treatment in that respect.[5]

(c) *Fundamental human rights.* Fundamental human rights whether expressed in a solemn declaration (French system), a constitutional guarantee (German system) or case law (British system), whether extensive or fragmentary, form part of West European heritage. This heritage was enriched by the European Convention on Human Rights of 1950 to which all the Member States of the Community adhere in principle though not in every detail. The Community itself, through a joint declaration of the Commission, Council of Ministers and Parliament[6] of 5 April 1977, echoed by the European Council[7] on 7/8 April 1978, proclaimed its respect for fundamental human rights and postulated their observance in the work of its institutions though the Community is not subject to the jurisdiction of the European Commission on Human Rights.[8] Human rights and representative democracy,

---

2 Case 37/74: *Van den Broeck v EC Commission* [1975] ECR 235.
3 Case 22/80: *Boussac Saint-Frères SA v Gerstenmeier* [1982] 1 CMLR 202.
4 ECJ Court in the *Tachograph* case, p 175, note 9, at para 12, supra.
5 Case 55/75: *Balkan-Import-Export GmbH v HZA Berlin-Packhof* [1976] ECR 19 at 31–32; Case 52/81: *Faust v EC Commission* [1982] 3745 at 3762; Case 245/81: *Edeka Zentrale v Germany* [1982] ECR 2745 at 2756.
6 OJ 1977, C 103/1; EC Bull 3/1977, p 5.
7 EC Bull 3/1978, p 5. Forman, J, 'The Joint Declaration on Fundamental Rights', 2 E L Rev (1977) pp 210 et seq.
8 *D v Belgium and the European Communities, Re the European School in Brussels* [1987] 2 CMLR 57.

stressed the European Council, are the essential conditions of the membership of the Community. In 1979[9] the Commission urged the Community to adhere to the Convention in its corporate capacity. It participated in the Helsinki discussions on human rights. The Helsinki Final Act was signed by Aldo Moro as the President of the Council on the basis of the Community competence in the field of commercial policy.[10] Irrespective of the formal position the Court held: 'In fact, respect for fundamental rights forms an integral part of the general principles of law protected by the Court of Justice. The protection of such rights, whilst inspired by the constitutional traditions common to the Member States, must be ensured within the framework of the structure and objectives of the Community.'[11] However, despite the emotive sound of 'fundamental human rights' the Court, probably because of the nature of its business, had so far few genuine cases involving such rights and putting its sincerity to the test.

In *Stauder v Stadt Ulm*[12] the ECJ rejected as unfounded the claim of a German citizen that the Community scheme to provide butter at a reduced price to certain persons was invalid because, having required him to reveal his identity, it hurt his dignity and this constituted an infringement of his fundamental human rights. The Court held that the Community scheme did not insist that his identity must be revealed and suggested that the clumsy method of proving the entitlement, for which the national authorities were responsible, could have been replaced by a more sophisticated code.

In *Nold v EC Commission*[13] the Court was at pains to show its faith in fundamental human rights but refused to annul a Commission decision on the marketing of coal which, in effect, denied direct access to source of supply to wholesale dealers whose turnover fell below the minimum laid down by the Commission. The plea of discrimination and of the denial of economic opportunities made no impact upon the Court when measured against market rationalization pursued under the Coal and Steel Treaty.

In *National Panasonic (UK) Ltd v EC Commission*[14] the Court, citing Nold, held that there was no violation of the right to privacy

9 EC Bull 4/1978, p 16 and Commission Memorandum on the Accession to the European Convention on Human Rights, EC Bull Supp 2/1979, pp 5 et seq.
10 The European Parliament and the World at Large (Feb 1981), p 5 (18).
11 Case 11/70: *Internationale Handelsgesellschaft* [1970] ECR 1125 at 1134, [1972] CMLR 255 at 271; see also Cases 25, 26, 30/70; *Einfur-und Vorratsstelle etc v Köster, Berodt & Co; Henck und Scheer* [1970] ECR 1161, [1972] CMLR 255 (para 22).
12 Case 29/69: [1969] ECR 419, [1970] CMLR 112.
13 Case 4/73: [1973] ECR 491, [1974] 2 CMLR 338.
14 Case 136/79: [1980] ECR 2033, [1980] 3 CMLR 169.

guaranteed by the Convention in the Community procedures governing search and seizure for the purpose of enforcing the Community competition law. It is clear that a human rights argument cannot be allowed to frustrate the legal process necessary for the enforcement of Community obligations of a corporation engaged in restrictive practices.

In FEDETAB[15] the ECJ, rejecting an application for the annulment of a competition decision, denied the suggestion that the Commission failed to apply article 6(1) of the Convention stressing that 'the Commission is bound to respect the procedural guarantees provided for by Community law and has done so ...'

In *Prais v EC Council*[16] the Court, whilst acknowledging the freedom of religion guaranteed by the European Convention, refused to annul a process of selecting Community employees in favour of a person who complained of unfair treatment because the selection process, held simultaneously in the Community capital cities, happened to coincide with a holy day in the calendar of her religious persuasion.

In *Hauer v Land Rheinland-Pfalz*[17] the Court, following *Nold*, drew a distinction between rights to property guaranteed by the Convention and the EEC Treaty and the exercise of such rights which can be interfered with by virtue of the Protocol to the Convention, the Community law as well as the Constitutions of the Member States. In the circumstances it refused to annul a Council regulation concerned with agricultural planning the effect of which was a restriction on the planting of vines for commercial purposes. However in another case[18] the special position of a farmer engaged in farming as his main occupation was recognized but it was emphasized that corporate entities would not be able to benefit from such concession.

In Valsabbia[19] reference was made to the first Protocol of the Convention as well as the *Nold* case when the Court explained that the minimum price system was not an infringement of property rights and that the Community guarantee cannot be extended to cover commercial risks.

In two cases involving the Member States' rights to control the movement of persons within the Community system the ECJ ignored the plea of a 'right to privacy' without reference to the

15 Cases 209–215/78: *FEDETAB v Commission* [1980] ECR 3125, [1981] 3 CMLR 134.
16 Case 130/75: [1976] ECR 1589, [1976] 2 CMLR 708.
17 Case 44/79: [1979] ECR 3727, [1980] 3 CMLR 42.
18 Case 312/85: *Villa Banfi SpA v Regione Toscana* [1988] 1 CMLR 72.
19 Cases 154, 205, 206, 226–228, 263, 264/78; 39, 31, 83, 85/79: *Ferriera Valsabbia SpA v EC Commission* [1980] ECR 907, [1981] 1 CMLR 613.

Convention. In order to enjoy their right of free movement the persons concerned had to comply with the rules for the control of foreign nationals, the sanctions for the breach of such rules being proportionate to the gravity of the offence.[20]

However in two other cases involving the expulsion and prohibition of re-entry on the ground of public policy of certain ladies of alleged loose morals the ECJ declined to comment on the Convention right of access to courts and fair hearing because such rights were already safeguarded in the Community system.[1] Dealing specifically with the question of public policy it held that, given the procedural safeguards, the Member State was within its rights to take certain anti-prostitution measures even though prostitution as such was not a criminal offence, provided that certain public manifestations of the trade were prohibited and that these measures were applicable to Belgian nationals as well.

In a reference from a French court the ECJ held that an order confining an Italian trade union agitator to a certain area was contrary to Community principle of the equality of treatment and free movement. Referring specifically to certain provisions of the Convention it concluded: 'no restrictions in the interests of national security or public safety shall be placed on the rights secured by the above quoted articles other than such as are necessary for the protection of those interests in a democratic society . . .'[2]

Referring again to fundamental human rights, the ECJ interpreted a provision of the Community Social Security Regulation to the effect that such rights were not violated when three Italian unemployed workers had forfeited their right to unemployment benefit because in their search for employment abroad they were absent from their host country for a period longer than that allowed by the Regulation. The rule was reasonable and they were informed of the position in their own language.[3]

However, citing the right to family life enshrined in article 8 of the European Convention on Human Rights, the ECJ considered that a Member State had a duty under article 9 of Regulation 1612/68 to provide housing accommodation to family members of a migrant worker who were allowed to join him. The proviso that such duty was conditional upon the availability of accommodation

---

20 Case 118/75: *Re Watson and Belmann* [1976] ECR 1185, [1976] 2 CMLR 552; Case 48/75: *Re Royer* [1976] ECR 497, [1976] 2 CMLR 619.
1 Case 98/79: *Pecastaing v Belgium* [1980] ECR 691, [1980] 3 CMLR 685; Cases 115 and 116/81: *Rezguia Adoui and Dominique Cornuaille v Belgium* [1982] 3 CMLR 631, [1982] ECR 1665.
2 Case 36/75: *Rutili v Ministère de l'Interieur* [1975] ECR 1219 at 1232, [1976] 1 CMLR 140.
3 Cases 41, 121 and 796/79: *Testa v Bundesanstalt für Arbeit* [1981] 2 CMLR 552 at 578, [1980] ECR 1979.

was valid only on first entry. Such right could not be lost if the housing position had subsequently deteriorated.[4]

The Court has heard so far not only actions against the Community alleging breaches of fundamental human rights including trade union rights[5] and the protection from expropriation without compensation[6] but also actions against the Member States alleging breaches of Community rights through non-observance of fundamental human rights.[7] However no Community measure has been struck down to date. No doubt this reflects the weakness of the claims but also, some may fear, the readiness of the Court to assert the supremacy of Community law. Indeed, dismissing as unfounded the argument that regulations which imposed a forfeitable deposit for the grant of export licences had violated fundamental rights (ie the right of economic freedom and proportionality) guaranteed by the German Constitution, the Court held that 'no provisions of municipal law, of whatever nature they may be, may prevail over Community law ... lest it be deprived of its character as Community law and its very legal foundations be endangered. The validity of a Community act or its application in a Member State remains, therefore, unimpaired even if it is alleged that the basic rights ... of the national constitution were violated'.[8]

This dictum has to be seen in the context of a weak case in which the Court, nevertheless, like in Stauder and later in *Nold* and *Hauer* repeatedly asserted its adherence to fundamental human rights as 'the general principles of law ... which should be followed within the framework of Community law'.[9] However the ECJ operates under the limitations of its own status and functions in so far as it has to consider the argument of non-conformity of Community measures with fundamental human rights in the light of Community law and not in the light of national constitutions.[10] The

---

4 Case 249/86: *EC Commission v Germany, Re Housing of Migrant Workers* [1990] 3 CMLR 540, at paras 10, 11, 12.

5 Cases 175/73: *Union Syndicale etc, Massa and Kortner v EC Council* [1974] ECR 917, [1975] 1 CMLR 131; 18/74: *Syndicat Général du Personnel des Organismes Européens v EC Commission* [1974] ECR 933, [1975] 1 CMLR 144.

6 Cases 56–60/74: *Kampffmeyer v EC Commission and Council* [1976] ECR 711.

7 Rutili, supra; Case 149/77: *Defrenne v SABENA* [1978] ECR 1365, [1978] 3 CMLR 312 – sex discrimination contrary to EEC art 119, the ILO Convention No 111 of 1958 and the European Social Charter of 1961; Case 98/79: *Pecastaing v Belgian State* [1980] ECR 691, [1980] 3 CMLR 685 (fair hearing in deportation proceedings).

8 *Handelsgesellschaft*, p 178, note 10, supra [1970] ECR at 1127, [1972] CMLR at 283.

9 See *Nold* p 187, supra at ECR 507.

10 Cases 41, 121, 796/79: *Testa, Maggio and Vitale v Bundesanstalt für Arbeit* [1980] ECR 1979, [1981] 2 CMLR 552 at para 18.

ECJ is not a court of human rights as such but the Court of the Community whose law has been fashioned according to the laws of the Member States. Since the Community legal order, albeit limited in its scope, is derived from a delegation of sovereignty, it is, as pointed out by Advocate-General Warner,[11] unthinkable that the delegation would exceed the powers contained in their constitutions. It follows that fundamental rights so guaranteed must be respected in the Community. However for the time being they cannot rank higher than 'general principles of law' which have to be asserted in individual cases without the benefit of a charter of fundamental rights entrenched in the system.

Even if we postulate a charter of fundamental rights for the Community such a charter, at present, can only reflect the current structure and objectives of the Community. These objectives revolve around the economic–social concept of the Community (the political goal being still on the horizon) and, therefore, arguments based on human rights have to be related to the economic activity of the Community. Such arguments evoke little sympathy, generally. Thus, for example, human rights pleas directed against Community rules on the labelling of wine[12] can be easily dismissed on the ground that the use of the labelling terminology has been exhaustively regulated and that the prohibition of any innovative terminology constitutes no infringement of the freedom of commerce guaranteed by the national constitutional law. Similarly it is futile to argue that the organization of agricultural markets, which can operate unfairly against the interest of individual traders, infringes their fundamental rights (ie the right to property and the freedom of commerce) when, in fact, traders have to take ordinary commercial risks foreseeable in the course of their business.[13] Therefore, rather than resorting to the emotive invocation of human rights, it would seem more apposite to appeal to equitable principles which the Court has been developing and which, in the discretion of the Court, may mitigate the harshness of the law.

(d) *Protection of vested rights.* The protection of 'vested rights' has a long tradition in Western Europe. It is based on certain premises such as the impartiality and independence of the judiciary, the running of the affairs of the state according to law and non-retrospective legislation. In exercising its general function the ECJ has endeavoured to incorporate these postulates into the Com-

---

11 Case 7/76: *IRCA v Amministrazione delle Finanze dello Stato* [1976] ECR 1213 at 1237.
12 Case 234/85: *Staatsanwalt Freiburg v Keller* [1986] ECR 2897, [1987] 1 MLR 875.
13 Case 59/83: *Biovilac SA v EC Commission* [1984] ECR 4057, [1987] 2 CMLR 881.

munity legal order and in doing so protect vested rights by recourse
to certain general principles of law.

Vested rights, that is rights acquired within the society's legal
framework and according to legal process, need a climate of legal
certainty. This means, on the one hand, stability of the legal system
and predictability, on the other. One ought to know one's legal
position and, when a change occurs in the law, one should not be
affected adversely as far as one's existing rights are concerned. In
more technical terms one's rights should not be taken away or
forfeited by retrospective legislation and one's legitimate expectations, built upon the existing legal system, should not be frustrated.

Thus, in principle, Community law is not retrospective. Where
it is retrospective it has to be expressly stated to be so and justified
on the ground that the legitimate objective could not be attained
otherwise.[14] It is not quite clear what the legitimate objective means
in abstract. It seems to mean an objective of the Treaty as a superior
rule of law which has to be carried into effect by subordinate
legislation. Such legislation may, therefore, have to be enacted with
a retrospective effect. The position remains yet to be clarified by
the ECJ since the judicial authority on the subject is still rather
scanty and ambiguous.[15] It seems that the need for a retrospective
measure has to be substantiated by the legislator and, where questioned, approved by the Court within its power of review of the
legality of Community acts. In brief, it has to be justified con-
vincingly on the ground of common good.

There appear to be two safeguards of the non-retrospective
principle: interpretation and the protection of legitimate expectations. Thus, in the absence of a clear provision to the contrary,
legislation is presumed to regulate future relations, that is, not to
be retrospective.[16] The principle is well illustrated in a case involving the operative date of a regulation.[17] On 30 June 1976 the
Commission passed a regulation curtailing the right of exporters
of sugar to have their export licences cancelled. The regulation was
to enter into force on 1 July 1976. However the publication of the
measure in the Official Journal was delayed until 2 July. On 1 July

14 Case 98/78: *Racke v Hauptzollamt Mainz* [1979] ECR 69; 99/78: *Decker KG
   v Hauptzollamt Landau* [1979] ECR 101. See also Case 159/82: *Verli-Wallace
   v EC Commission* [1983] *ECR* 2711 at 2718–2719.
15 See Case 37/70: *Rewe-Zentrale des Lebensmittel-Grosshandels GmbH v
   Hauptzollamt Emmerich* [1971] ECR 23, [1971] CMLR 238.
16 See Case 100/63: *Kalsbeek v Sociale Verzekeringsbank* [1964] ECR 565 at 575;
   see also A-G Mayras in case 70/72: *EC Commission v Germany* [1973] ECR
   813 at 844 and A-G Warner in case 7/76, note 11, supra; see also *Rewe-Zentrale*,
   supra, *Racke*, supra, *Decker*, supra.
17 Case 88/76: *Exportation des Sucres v EC Commission* [1977] ECR 709.

the applicant applied for cancellation of licences he held at that time but this was refused by virtue of the regulation. Therefore he moved for the annulment of the regulation. This the Court found unnecessary holding that the regulation must be construed to have come into force on the date of its publication, ie 2 July, and thus protecting the rights vested in the applicant. The Court inferred that the Commission did not intend the regulation to have a retrospective effect.[18]

A prudent person's reliance on the certainty of the law ought to be rewarded by the protection of his confidence in the system.[19] Hence the principle of 'legitimate expectations'[20] derived from German law.

The principle was first applied in the *Staff Salaries*[1] case where the Commission sought annulment of a Council decision which reversed a previous decision fixing criteria for the remuneration of Community civil servants and substituting a new formula. The previous decision was a result of negotiations and was to remain in force for three years. It created a legitimate expectation that the Community would pay its employees according to the agreed scales. The Court upheld this contention and annulled the offending measure but ruled, in accordance with EEC article 174(2), that it should remain in force until a new one has been enacted, thus safeguarding the interim pay regime.

The most illuminating examples of the application of the principle can be found in the jungle of the Common Agricultural Policy. To begin with the *Deuka*[2] case: in order to reduce the surplus of wheat and yet maintain the market prices the Commission adopted a system of premiums to encourage the process of denaturing, ie rendering the produce in question unfit for human consumption. The amount of the premium was fixed for each crop on an annual basis subject to adjustments in response to market fluctuations. To qualify for a premium the processor had to obtain a prior authorization from the relevant authority, carry out the process and prove its completion. By a new regulation coming into force on 1 June 1970 the Commission abolished the relevant regulation, which provided for an increased premium for the denaturing of wheat of a certain grade.

---

18 See also Case 112/77: *Töpfer & Co GmbH v EC Commission* [1978] ECR 1019.

19 Vertrauensschutz, protéction de la confiance légitime. See Case 289/81: *Mavridis v European Parliament* [1983] ECR 1731 at 1744.

20 Usher, J A, The Influence of National Concepts on Decisions of the European Court, [1976] 1 ELRev 359 at 363, note 28.

1 Case 81/72: *EC Commission v EC Council* [1973] ECR 575, [1973] CMLR 639.

2 Case 78/74: *Deuka etc v Einfuhr-und Vorratsstelle für Getreide und Futtermittel* [1975] ECR 421, [1975] 2 CMLR 28.

During June and July 1970 Deuka had denatured a quantity of wheat which the company had purchased before 1 June 1970. It then claimed the increased premium in accordance with the now abolished regulation arguing that the new regulation was invalid. On reference from a German court the ECJ did not annul the regulation but, in the name of legal certainty, held that it ought to be so interpreted as to make the increased premium payable even if the denaturing process occurred after 1 June, provided that the wheat was purchased and the authorization to process it was obtained before 1 June. Deuka had embarked on a venture which had the backing of the law and its expectations had to be protected.

The stress is, therefore, on the requirement that the expectation is 'legitimate',[3] that is, conceived in the mind of a prudent person who acts according to the letter and the spirit of the law in confidence that his fidelity to the law will be reciprocated. Mere speculation will not do. This is illustrated by the *Mackprang*[4] case. In the spring of 1969 the fall in the forward rate of the French franc opened up a prospect of a profit on the exchange rate to dealers in cereals who purchased the produce in France and sold it to the German Agricultural Intervention Agency (EVGF). Under the CAP such national agencies are bound to purchase agricultural produce. The intensified market activities posed a threat to the German intervention system as well as the storage capacity of the Agency. In the circumstances the Commission by Decision 69/138[5] authorized the German Government to restrict intervention purchases to wheat and barley grown in Germany. Identical decisions were adopted for Belgium and the Netherlands. The Decision was issued on 8 May 1969, took effect on the same day but exempted offers made before that date. On 6 May Mackprang, a German dealer in cereals, offered to the EVGF eight lots of wheat purchased in France stating that the produce was situated in various parts of Germany whilst in actual fact it was still in transit from France to Germany. On 8 May the EVGF accepted the offer but subsequently

---

3 Eg Cases 95–98/74, 15, 100/75: *Union Nationale des Coopératives Agricoles de Céréales v EC Commission* [1975] ECR 1615; 44–51/77: *Union Malt v EC Commission* [1978] ECR 57, [1978] 3 CMLR 702; 78/77: *Lührs v Hauptzollamt Hamburg-Jonas* [1978] ECR 169, [1979] 1 CMLR 657; 130/78: *Salumificio di Cornuda SpA v Amministrazione delle Finanze dello Stato* [1979] ECR 867, [1979] 3 CMLR 561; Case 12/78: *Italian Republic v EC Commission* [1979] ECR 1731, [1980] 2 CMLR 573 (*Re Monetary Compensatory Amounts for Durum Wheat*); and Case 84/78: *Tomadini SNC v Amministrazione delle Finanze* [1979] ECR 1801, [1980] 2 CMLR 573; 49/79: *Pool v EC Council* [1980] ECR 569, [1980] 3 CMLR 279.
4 Case 2/75: *Einfuhr-und Vorratsstelle für Getreide und Futtermittel v Mackprang* [1975] ECR 607, [1977] 1 CMLR 198. See also Case 49/79, supra.
5 OJ 1969, L 112.

declined to accept deliveries to its warehouses. Mackprang's claim to compensation on the ground of a legitimate expectation failed. The ECJ, on reference, conceded that the Decision being a derogation from the relevant Regulations had to be interpreted in the light of the objectives pursued by those Regulations but held it was 'a justified precaution against purely speculative activities'.[6] Therefore it did not constitute an infringement of the principle of protection of legitimate expectation. Advocate-General Warner, holding that the transaction was 'subversive to the intervention system', thus disposed of the argument: 'No trader who was exploiting that situation in order to make out of the system profits that the system was never designed to bestow on him could legitimately rely on the persistence of the situation. On the contrary, the only reasonable expectation that such a trader could have was that the competent authorities would act as swiftly as possible to bring the situation to an end. Nor ... could he expect particular tenderness at their hands.'

If a loss occurs as a result of frustrated legitimate expectations an action for damages may be brought under EEC article 215 (2). In such a case the claimant must prove not only that he had such an expectation on which he had acted reasonably but also a causal link between his loss and the relevant Community act. The case of *CNTA v EC Commission*[7] provides an interesting example. By Regulation 974/71 the Council had established a system of monetary compensatory amounts in order to make good losses arising from fluctuations in exchange rates. The system was extended to colza seed by Commission Regulation 1471/71, further extended to France by Commission Regulations 17/72 and 144/72. By Regulation 189/72 made on 26 January 1972 the Commission abolished the system as from 1 February 1972. The CNTA (a French company) was in the colza business which was covered by both Regulations. Before the second Regulation was enacted the CNTA made a number of export contracts which were to be performed after the scheme had been abolished. It claimed that it had suffered loss as a result of the sudden and unexpected abolition of the scheme without there being any provision in respect of transactions entered into during the lifetime of the scheme. CNTA's claim was further strengthened by reference to a scheme of export refunds whose rates fluctuated but could be fixed in advance in respect of any particular transaction. To that end the exporter had to lodge a deposit which would be forfeited if he failed to export as arranged. CNTA, having obtained advance fixing of the refunds in respect

6 Case 2/75, supra, para 4.
7 Case 74/74: [1975] ECR 533, [1977] 1 CMLR 171 and [1976] ECR 797.

of certain transactions before 26 January, claimed that it entered these on the assumption that monetary compensatory amounts would be payable and calculated its profits accordingly.

In order to establish liability under article 215(2) CNTA had to prove that 'in accordance with general principles common to the laws of the Member States', the Commission had acted wrongly. CNTA argued, accordingly, that Regulation 189/72 constituted an act envisaged by the said article because it infringed the principle of legal certainty and frustrated its legitimate expectations. The Court conceded the force of this argument and held that: 'In these circumstances, a trader may legitimately expect that for trans-actions irrevocably undertaken by him because he has obtained, subject to a deposit, export licences fixing the amount of the refund in advance, no unforeseeable alteration will occur which could have the effect of causing him inevitable loss, by re-exposing him to the exchange risk.'

'... The Community is therefore liable if, in the absence of an overriding matter of public interest, the Commission abolished with immediate effect and without warning the application of com-pensatory amounts in a specific sector without adopting transitional measures which would at least permit traders either to avoid the loss which would have been suffered in the performance of export contracts, the existence and irrevocability of which are established by the advance fixing of the refunds, or to compensation for such loss.'

'... In the absence of an overriding matter of public interest, the Commission has violated a superior rule of law, thus rendering the Community liable, by failing to include in Regulation 189/72 transitional measures for the protection of the confidence which a trader might legitimately have in the Community rules.'[8]

Having said that the Court did not declare Regulation 189/72 invalid. Thus the wrongful act was not the Regulation itself but the omission to issue a warning to traders and to institute a transitional regime to protect transactions already in progress. This omission constituted a violation of a 'superior rule of law', ie the protection of legitimate expectations.

Turning to the question of damages the Court held that, in the circumstances, the Community was not liable to compensate the claimant for all the losses incurred. It held that 'it is necessary to take into consideration the fact that the maintenance of the compensatory amounts was in no way guaranteed ... and that it could not therefore legitimately expect under all circumstances to

8 Ibid, paras 42–44; see also Case 12/78: *Re Monetary Compensatory Amounts for Durum Wheat*, p 194, note 3, supra.

make the profits which would have accrued to it from the contract under the system of compensatory amounts' ... 'The protection which it may claim by reason of its legitimate expectation is merely that of not suffering loss by reason of the withdrawal of those amounts.'[9]

In subsequent proceedings to determine the actual damages the claimant was unable to prove any loss arising from the withdrawal of the scheme within the limits stated above because payments for the shipments were made in French currency. Any loss of anticipated profits was covered by the commercial risk involved.[10] However the principle of the protection of legitimate expectations has been established.

Other examples of frustrated legitimate expectations: in Case 120/86[11] by a milk regulation the Commission withdrew non-marketing premiums for five years including the reference year for the calculation of milk quota. The applicant, who planned his production on the basis of the existing quota, was disappointed when allotted a nil quota. The ECJ thought to rectify the position by allowing him to receive his quota from the national reserve for the year in question.

In another case,[12] where the state aid involved was not duly notifed, the Commission delayed for twenty-six months the decision to declare the aid illegal and to order repayment of the aid. However, the recipient had the decision annulled for breach of his legitimate expectation.

(e) *Equity.* It seems convenient to group under a general title of Equity several principles which have been applied or put forward in order to mitigate hardship arising from a strict application of the law. Apart from this common feature these principles can be traced to the municipal law of one or several Member States.

Good faith was pleaded in *Meganck v EC Commission*[13] where a temporary official drew certain family allowances to which strictly he was not entitled. When faced with the demand for repayment he claimed, successfully, that he received these in good faith not knowing from his salary slips that he was in fact overpaid.

Fairness or equity appeared in several cases. Mr Costacurta's[14] application for admission to internal competition for a position in

9 Ibid, paras 45–46.
10 Case 74/74, note 6, supra, [1976] ECR 797.
11 Case 125/86: *Mulder v Minister for Agriculture and Fisheries* [1989] 2 CMLR 1.
12 Case 223/85: *Rijn-Schelde-Verolm Maschinefabrieken en Scheepswerven NV v EC Commission* [1987] ECR 4617, [1989] 2 CMLR 259.
13 Case 36/72: [1973] ECR 527 at 534. See also Case 92/82: *Gutmann v EC Commission* (Re Resettlement Allowance) [1983] ECR 3127.
14 Case 31/75: *Costacurta v EC Commission* [1975] ECR 1563 at 1570.

the Community service was rejected without sufficient reasons being given by the relevant selection board. The ECJ annulled the decision of the board on the ground that in the circumstances, it was *unfair* to the official.

In the *Reich*[15] case the claimant failed to observe the time limit provided for in a licence for the importation of maize from a Member State. He argued that this was due to *force majeure*, ie the delay in importation due to a fault of the railway authority and not his own. The ECJ held that, since *force majeure* was a valid excuse under the regulation governing imports from non-Community countries, there was no reason why *in equity* this principle should not apply to imports from a Member State of the Community.

Lührs,[16] an exporter of potatoes to Sweden, who in the circumstances, could not rely on the plea of legitimate expectations, claimed that he was nevertheless unfairly treated because of the uncertainty inherent in the regulations governing the exchange of the tax on exports into national currency. The ECJ held that *natural justice* required that of the two rates of exchange which could have been applied in his case the one, which at the material time was less onerous to the taxpayer, should be applied.

Force majeure was pleaded both in the *Handelsgesellschaft*[17] and the third *Kampffmeyer* case.[18] Both were concerned with the operation of the system of export/import licences and advance fixing certificates for agricultural produce. The issue of licences was subject to a forfeitable deposit in the event of the authorization to export/import not being exhausted within the stated period. If, as a result of *force majeure*, the transaction was not completed the national authority operating the system could either refund the deposit or extend the period for completion. The system was challenged in the *Handelsgesellschaft* case on several grounds including *force majeure* in so far as the referring court enquired whether, on the proper construction of the regulation in question, the forfeiture of the deposit was excluded only in cases of *force majeure*. Should this be the case the ground would be too narrow to do justice to the appellant. The ECJ answered in the negative but gave a broad definition of *force majeure*. It held: 'The concept of *force majeure* is not limited to absolute impossibility but must be understood in the sense of unusual circumstances outside the control of the

---

15 Case 64/74: *Reich v Hauptzollamt Landau* [1975] ECR 261, at 268, [1975] 1 CMLR 396 at 405.
16 Case 78/77: *Lührs v Hauptzollamt Hamburg-Jonas* [1978] ECR 169 at 180, [1979] 1 CMLR 657.
17 Case 11/72, p 178, note 10 and p 190, note 8, supra.
18 Case 158/73: *Kampffmeyer v Einfuhr-und Vorratsstelle für Getreide und Futtermittel* [1974] ECR 101.

importer or exporter, the consequences of which, in spite of the exercise of all due care, could not have been avoided except at the cost of excessive sacrifice. The concept implies a sufficient flexibility regarding not only the nature of the occurrence relied upon but also the care which the exporter should have exercised in order to meet it and the extent of the sacrifice which he should have accepted to that end' (at para 23).

In the *Kampffmeyer* case the issue was whether the loss of an import licence following despatch by non-registered letter constituted *force majeure* so as to absolve the trader from the forfeiture of his deposit. It was basically a matter of fact, that is, whether a diligent trader fulfils his duty of care in the context of his business and the Community licensing system if he sends his licence by ordinary post. Holding that 'in the absence of any express provision of Community law, it is for the national court to say whether such a trader has or has not exercised all reasonable care', the ECJ ruled that the matter was one of application, not of interpretation and left the decision to the referring court. In German law the responsibility lay with the trader.

Another abortive attempt to take advantage of *force majeure* occurred in *IFG v Commission*[19] where a trader sought from the Community compensation in respect of a transaction which, due to floods in Rumania, was not completed within the period of his import licence. His claim was supported by the argument that due to a change in the Community law his legitimate expectations were frustrated. The ECJ, whilst recognizing *force majeure* to be a cause 'of derogation from the strict requirements of the law', could not find any reason why the Community should be liable under EEC article 215(2) in the present case. Indeed, held the Court, remedy should be sought from the other contracting party.

However a French exporter of wheat to the United Kingdom was successful.[20] His cargo perished in the North Sea but his claim for 'accession compensatory amounts' due under Regulation 269/73 was refused on the ground that he was unable to prove that the goods had reached their destination. The Regulation, unlike Regulation 192/75 governing export refunds for agricultural produce, did not contain the *force majeure* formula. Therefore, on reference, the ECJ rectified the position by applying by analogy Regulation 192/75. It held that 'Regulation 269/73 is to be interpreted as meaning that where goods exported from an old Member State to

19 Case 68/77: *Intercontinentale Fleischhandelsgesellschaft mbH & Co KG v EC Commission* [1978] ECR 353, [1978] 2 CMLR 733.
20 Case 6/78: *Union Française de Céréales v Hauptzollamt Hamburg-Jonas* [1978] ECR 1675.

a new Member State have perished in transit as a result of *force majeure*, the exporter is entitled to the same compensatory amounts as would have been due to him if the goods had reached their destination and if import formalities had been completed there.'[21] Thus the Court not only applied an equitable general principle to mitigate hardship but also in doing so filled a lacuna in the Community system.

Another French[1] exporter dealing in animal feed had not received back from the British customs authorities the original T5 control form which would enable him to claim monetary compensation amounts from the French authorities. Instead he claimed on the ground of *force majeure* and proportionality. However the ECJ found the refusal of the French authorities to entertain his claim justified, pointing out the procedural remedies available for such maladministration of customs formalities.

Force majeure was pleaded unsuccessfully by an Irish exporter of agricultural intervention produce which was stolen from the company's depot in England while on its way out of the Community. The exporter suffered forfeiture of security for non-performance. Since exportation of the procedure was the exporter's principal obligation the forfeiture of the security was not held   disproportionate while the loss of the goods was not regarded as being due to *force majeure*. Moreover, the innocence or non-negligence of the exporter was held irrelevant.[2]

Similarly the inability to export because the purchaser's refusal to take delivery of the goods was not regarded as *force majeure*. Consequently, forfeiture of the deposit to secure export licence was held justified.[3]

Holding that the undertaking not to produce milk runs with the farmland the ECJ ruled that a forced sale of the farm by the mortgagee did not absolve the original farmer from the duty of repaying the whole of the non-marketing premium. In the circumstances the loss of his farm was not caused by *force majeure* which would justify him not facing the penalty for the breach of his obligation.[4]

Greece was also unsuccessful in claiming that the payment of her contribution to the Community budget was prevented by *force*

---

21 Ibid, para 6.
1 Case 266/84: *Denkavit France Sarl v FORMA* [1987] 3 CMLR 202.
2 Case 296/86: *Anthony McNicholl Ltd v Minister for Agriculture* [1988] 2 CMLR 275.
3 Case 109/86: *Ioannis Theodorakis Viomikhania Eleou A E v Greece* [1989] 2 CMLR 166.
4 Case 199/87: *Mads Peder Jensen v Landbrugsministeriet* [1989] 3 CMLR 64.

majeure, ie a strike at the Bank of Greece. The Community was entitled to moratory interest.[5]

Belguim fared no better when she blamed *force majeure* for delayed payments of the monetary compensatory amounts. The complexity of Community legislation was not so unusual as to provide an excuse while the sudden increase in applications was due to the Belgian administration which reintroduced the MCAs. The resulting staffing problem was a matter for Belgian policy and could not be attributed to *force majeure.*[6]

We can conclude, therefore, that the ECJ had adhered to the classic concept of *force majeure* as 'unusual circumstances outside the control' of those who plead it defined in Case 68/77.[7]

The principle of *proportionality,* which is an aspect of the Aristotelian distributive justice, embodied in the German Constitution, made an early debut[8] before the Community Court but was most dramatically, though unsuccessfully, pleaded in the *Handelsgesellschaft* case. In simple terms the principle means that social burdens should be distributed fairly according to the capacity of the members of the society. According to Advocate-General Dutheillet de Lamothe[9] it means that such burdens may be imposed only for the purposes of the public interest to the extent that is strictly necessary for the attainment of such purposes.

Dealing with the argument that forfeitable deposits instituted under Regulation 120/67 infringed the principle of proportionality (as persistently claimed by the trader and maintained by the Verwaltungsgericht at Frankfurt) the ECJ held that it was a matter of Community law which could not be overridden by principles of national law even of a constitutional character. The system itself was justified as it served the purposes of the Treaty in supporting the common organization of agricultural markets.

The system was more positively defended by the ECJ in another case,[10] since the burdens it imposed were not 'manifestly out of proportion to the object in view'[11] whilst 'the competent authorities must be in a position constantly to follow trade movements in order to assess market trends and apply the measures laid down in the

5 Case 70/86: *EC Commission v Greece* [1989] 1 CMLR 441.
6 Case 145/85: *Denkavit Belgie NV v Belgium* [1988] 2 CMLR 679.
7 Supra p 199.
8 Case 8/55: *Federation Charbonnière de Belgique v High Authority of the ECSC* [1954–56] ECR 292 at 299.
9 Case 11/70: *Internationale Handelsgesellschaft,* [1970] ECR 1125 at 1146.
10 Case 5/73: *Balkan-Import-Export GmbH v Hauptzollamt Berlin-Packhof* [1973] ECR 1091 at 1112.
11 See also Cases 119 and 120/76: *Ölmühle Hamburg AG v Hauptzollamt Hamburg Waltershof and Becher v HZA Bremen-Nord* [1977] ECR 1269, [1979] 2 CMLR 83.

Regulation'.[12] However whilst the forfeiture of a deposit for not complying with the licensing system is fully justified[13] it is not so justified on the ground of failing to comply with purely bureaucratic requirements such, for example, as the delay in submitting a proof of imports of tomato concentrates.[14] The principle of proportionality has been applied with diverse results in several other cases dealing with such problems as: the movement of goods[15] and persons[16] and state responsibility for the implementation of the CAP.[17]

Proportionality continues to be a favourite plea in order to save the forfeiture of deposits under the Community regulations. We have seen it above coupled, albeit unsuccessfully, with *force majeure*. The question which arose was whether in Case 38/86 (No 2) forfeiture was a proportional penalty.[18] Forfeiture of security for non-completion of sales of intervention produce was disputed as the purchaser repudiated the contract in order to benefit from the new exchange rate of 'green' currency. However, the ECJ held that the vendor had to bear the consequences which were not out of proportion to his failure to conclude the sales. However, in an earlier case[19] only partial forfeiture was held to be justified on the principle of proportionality. It appears in a rather confused factual situation that the carrier of intervention food aid to Ethiopia had not complied with the tender requirements. His ships sailed later than the deadline and they were more than 15 years old. The main question was whether compliance with the time limit for sailing was the principal obligation since no ships used for the purpose were close to the required category. As the latter was regarded to be secondary obligation only partial forfeiture of the security seemed justified. Still in the maze of the CAP, a dairy company, supplying skimmed milk as animal feed for calves lost only a part of the

12 ECJ reciting a preamble to Regulation 120/67 in the third *Kampffmeyer* case, p 198, note 18, supra.

13 Case 85/78: *Bundesanstalt für Landwirtschaftliche Marktordnung v Jacob Hirsch & Sohne GmbH* [1978] ECR 2517, [1979] 2 CMLR 631.

14 Case 122/78: *Buitoni SA v Fonds d'Orientation et de Regularisation des Marches Agricoles* [1979] ECR 677, [1979] 2 CMLR 665.

15 Case 62/70: *Bock KG v EC Commission* [1971] ECR 897 at 909, [1972] CMLR 160; Case 52/77: *Cayrol v Rivoira and Figli* [1977] ECR 2261 at 2281, [1978] 2 CMLR 253.

16 Case 36/75: *Rutili v Ministère d l'Intérieur* [1975] ECR 1219, [1976] 1 CMLR 140; Case 8/77: *Re Sagulo, Brenca and Bakhouche* [1977] ECR 1495 at 1506, [1977] 2 CMLR 585. Case 30/77: *R v Bouchereau* [1977] ECR 1999.

17 Case 166/78: *Italy v EC Council* [1979] ECR 2575 at 2601.

18 Case 38/86: *Firma Karl-Heinz Neumann v Bundesanstalt für Landwirtschaftliche Marktordnung (No 2)* [1988] 1 CMLR 523.

19 Case 21/85: *A Maas & Co v Bundesanstalt für Landwirtschaftliche Marktordnung* [1986] ECR 3537, [1987] 3 CMLR 794.

subsidy involved. It was duty bound to keep accurate records and submit these to the authority promptly since the amount of the subsidy depended upon the maximum number of calves on individual holdings during the relevant month. Since a number of customers of the dairy company were in default the repayment of the subsidy in full was considered disproportionate.

Finally, the derogation clauses: *public policy;*[20] *public morality;*[1] *public security;*[2] and *public health*[3] which enable the Member States to limit the freedom of movement of persons and goods. All these principles, taken from national laws, form part of the Community system. However in view of their nature and function they have to be interpreted restrictively so as not to become the tools of legal subterfuge. The ECJ, whilst insisting on a uniform interpretation of these principles, has not as yet offered an authoritative definition of any of them. Speaking of public policy it conceded that it is necessary 'to allow the ... national authorities an area of discretion within the limits imposed by the Treaty'.[4]

While it is an open question how far equitable principles can be developed to enrich the Community legal system, it has to be appreciated that the CAP has proved to be one of the main areas of their application. A reform of the CAP into a more rational system might have a sobering effect. The ECJ too has shown concern that the development does not get out of hand. Dealing once more with the plea that forfeiture of a deposit under the CAP in respect of intervention sales was an excessive penalty the Court refused to recognize the principle of 'objective unfairness'[5] (apparently derived from the German system) holding it to be non-existent in the Community law. It stressed that a principle of national law has no obligatory application in the Community system while the uniform application of Community rules throughout the Community is an overriding feature of the Community system. A national judge hard pressed by arguments from the national jurisdiction ought to take refuge in the procedure for a

20 Cases *Van Duyn,* supra; 30/77: *R v Bouchereau* [1978] QB 732, [1977] ECR 1999; 7/78: *R v Thompson* [1978] ECR 2247, [1979] 1 CMLR 47.
1 34/79: *R v Darby, R v Henn* [1979] ECR 3795, [1980] 1 CMLR 246. Case 121/85: *Conegate v HM Customs and Excise* [1986] 1 CMLR 739.
2 See Irish case *McAfee v Smyth and Quigley* [1981] 1 CMLR 410. *R v Goldstein* [1982] 3 All ER 53, [1982] 2 CMLR 181, CA; affd [1983] 1 CMLR 252, HL.
3 Eg Cases 35/76: *Simmenthal SpA v Italian Ministry of Finance* [1976] ECR 1871 at 1876, [1977] 2 CMLR 1; 153/78: *EC Commission v Federal Republic of Germany* [1979] ECR 2555, [1980] 1 CMLR 198.
4 *Van Duyn* op cit, para 18; see also *Bouchereau,* para 34, *Rutili* para 26; *R v Henn, R v Darby,* para 15.
5 Case 299/84: *Firma Karl-Heinz Neumann v Bundesanstalt für Landwirtschaftliche Marktordnung* [1985] ECR 3663, [1987] 3 CMLR 4.

preliminary ruling thus leaving to the ECJ the task of ensuring the uniformity within the Community system.

Reflecting on the use and development of general principles of law at the hands of the Community Court one should not underestimate their potential for the interpretation of Community law and for the closing of gaps which the system reveals in practice. However one should not overestimate this potential or attribute to it the character of a Community 'common law' system[6] implying thereby a new body of rules superimposed upon the law derived from the Community Treaties.

(vi) *Opinions of the Advocates-General.* The Advocate-General participates in every case before the ECJ[7] and his opinion forms an obligatory part of the adjudicating process though not of the judgment itself. In the light of his function and the nature of the Community Court the Advocate-General can be likened to a judge of a first instance court within the Community administration of justice. Therefore, if he is followed by the Court his opinion may be regarded as a concurring judgment by analogy to individual judgments of a collegiate common law court. If he is not followed, by the same analogy, his opinion may be regarded as a dissenting judgment.

In the common law system dissenting and concurring judgments are studied with equal interest since at the ultimate instance a dissent in a court below may become the final ruling. Even without that change of fortune a dissenting judgment may be used in argument on another occasion in the hope that a fresh approach may sharpen its force. In the Community system, on the other hand, the opinion of the Advocate-General has to be seen as a personal judgment and an invitation to the Court to follow suit. It is fully reasoned and it tends to relate the proposed solution to the pattern of case law established by the Court. One can therefore discern a greater appreciation of Community precedents in the opinions of Advocates-General than in the judgments of the Court.

The Advocates-General have made a significant contribution to the development of Community law. Their opinions, in view of their personal style, appear by and large to be more readable than the judgments of the Court. However, no matter their weight as a persuasive force or part of dynamic jurisprudence, they lack the authority of the *res judicata*.

6 As suggested by Hartley, T C, *The Foundations of European Community Law*, 1981, p 144, and Wyatt, D, and Dashwood, A, *The Substantive Law of the EEC*, 1980, p 47; see also A-G Dutheillet de Lamothe in the *Handelsgesellschaft* case, supra, at 1141.

7 There are no Advocates-General in the First Instance Court but judges may act as such where appropriate.

PART TWO
Where to find Community law

I   Treaties and related instruments

The authentic and official English texts of the Community Treaties
are available in a variety of forms:

1. Editions published by the Community:

(i) *Treaties establishing the European Communities: Treaties amending these Treaties: Documents concerning the Accession* (European
Communities Office for Official Publications, 1978). This volume
contains all the Treaties and their annexes in force on 1 July 1978.

(ii) *Documents concerning the accession of the Hellenic Republic to
the European Communities (Official Journal of the European Communities, 1979*, L291).

(iii) *Documents concerning the accession of Spain and Portugal* (OJ
1985, L302).

(iv) *Collected agreements concluded by the European Communities*
(12 volumes published to date). These volumes contain the texts
of agreements with non-Member States and international organizations during the years 1958–1982.

2. HM Stationery Office Editions of the Treaties are also available
as follows:

(i) *Treaty establishing the European Coal and Steel Community,
Paris 18 April 1951* (Amended text: Cmnd. 7461). The sole authentic text of this Treaty is in French which is printed together with
an English translation; the latter has no official standing.

(ii) *Treaty establishing the European Economic Community, Rome
25 March 1957; Treaty establishing the European Atomic Energy
Community, Rome 25 March 1957* (Amended text: Cmnd. 7460).

(iii) *Treaty concerning the Accession of the Kingdom of Denmark,
Ireland, the Kingdom of Norway and the United Kingdom of Great
Britain and Northern Ireland to the European Economic Community
and the European Atomic Energy Community and Decision of the
Council of the European Communities concerning the Accession of the
said States to the European Coal and Steel Community, Brussels 22
January 1972* (Amended text: Cmnd. 7463).

(iv) *Single European Act 1986* (Cmnd 9758).

3. The texts of the principal Treaties and of some other Community instruments are also available in Sweet and Maxwell's *European Community Treaties* (4th edn, 1980). Rudden and Wyatt's *Basic Community Laws* (2nd edn, 1986) is an excellent compilation for students which contains excerpts from the major Treaties and the texts of basic secondary legislation.

4. Annotated texts of the Treaties and of related Community instruments are to be found in *Halsbury's Statutes of England* (3rd edn), Volume 42A, European Continuation Volume 1, 1952–72 and in Sweet and Maxwell's *Encyclopedia of European Community Law*, Volumes BI, II and III. Both of these works are kept up to date by Supplements.

II Community legislation

The legislation of the Communities, ie decisions and recommendations in the case of the ECSC and regulations, directives and decisions in the cases of the EEC and Euratom, are published in the *Official Journal of the European Communities*. This appears, almost daily, in each of the official languages of the Communities. An English edition has been published since 9 October 1972. Since 1968 the *Official Journal* has appeared in two series: one devoted to secondary legislation (the 'L' series), the other containing non-normative communications and information (the 'C' series).

Authentic English texts of pre-accession secondary legislation have been published in *Special Editions of the Official Journal of the European Communities* covering the period 1952–72. The same texts have also been published by HM Stationery Office in 42 volumes arranged under subject headings under the title *Secondary Legislation of the European Communities: Subject Edition*. Annotated texts of Community secondary legislation are to be found in *Halsbury's Statutes of England* (3rd edn), Volume 42A and Supplements and in the *Encyclopedia of European Community Law*, Volumes CI to VI. Community and national legislation relating to economic activities is summarized in *European Law Digest* (1973 and continued). The T.M.C. Asser Institute's *Guide to EEC Legislation* (1979), in two volumes with an annual cumulative supplement, provides an invaluable subject index to past and current Community legislation.

III Case law

The texts of its judgments and opinions with the submissions of the Advocates-General are published in periodical parts by the Court of Justice in each of the official languages of the Communities. The version in the procedural language in respect of a particular case is the only authentic version. The French version, which was commonly used in the United Kingdom before accession, is entitled *Recueil da la Jurisprudence de la Cour*. An English version entitled *European Court Reports* has been published in periodical parts since 1973. English translations of the pre-accession volumes of reports of cases before the Court from 1953 to 1972 have been published.

Since 1962 English translations of the judgments of both the Court of Justice and of some of the courts of the Member States on points of Community law and decisions of the Commission on restrictive practices have been published under the name *Common Market Law Reports*. Since 1970 these Reports have also included the texts of the judgments in the procedural language. English translations of the judgments of the Court of Justice prior to the commencement of the *Common Market Law Reports* are to be found in Volume 2 of Valentine's *Court of Justice of the European Communities* (1965).

English translations of the judgments of the Court of Justice are also to be found in *Common Market Reports* published by the Commerce Clearing House Inc. of Chicago. Since May 1972 leading cases have been published in the *Times* newspaper. Community and national case law relating to economic activities is summarized in *European Law Digest* (1973 and continued). Eversen, Sperl and Usher's *Compendium of Case Law relating to the European Communities* covers the years 1973–1976 and has been replaced by a *Digest of Case Law* prepared under the auspices of the Court of Justice.

IV Subsidiary sources

(i) *Official papers of Community institutions*. There is a vast amount of such material covering all the activities of the Communities. It ranges from general reports and journalism to highly specialized monographs on detailed aspects of Community activity. Most of this material appears in all the official languages and some of the pre-accession papers are also available in unofficial English versions. From the lawyer's point of view the most significant and informative include the following:

Reports and opinions of the Commission and the consultative committees published in the *Official Journal*. Discussion documents and draft legislative proposals are available in mimeographed form with the prefixes COM (for Commission) and SEC (for Secretary General).

The Debates and Working Documents (*Documents de Séance*) of the European Parliament. The Debates are published as an annexe to the Official Journal and the Working Documents are published individually by the Parliament itself.

The Bulletin of the European Communities published in periodical parts by the Secretariat of the Commission. In addition to giving a monthly account of current activities and developments the Supplements to the *Bulletin* are convenient sources of the texts of important reports and proposals for legislation.

The annual *General Report on the Activities of the Communities* submitted by the Commission to the Assembly. The General Secretariat of the Council also publishes an annual *Review of the Council's Work*.

(ii) *Journals.* There are four English-language journals devoted to Community matters. The *Common Market Law Review* (1963/1964 and continued), the *European Law Review* (1975/1976 and continued) and *Legal Issues of European Integration* (1974 and continued) are all concerned with the law. There are also specialist journals: *European Competition Law Review, European Intellectual Property Review* and *European Taxation*. The *Journal of Common Market Studies* (1962 and continued) is not exclusively legal and also covers economic and political aspects of Community activities. Articles on Community legal topics are also to be found in the *International and Comparative Law Quarterly*, the *British Yearbook of International Law* and the *Journal of Business Law*.

(iii) *Treatises.* The companion volume to this work, Lasok's *The Law of the Economy in the European Communities* (1980) is a comprehensive study of the substantive law of the Community. A full and scholarly treatment of Community law will also be found in both Lipstein's *Law of the European Economic Community* (1974) and Kapteyn and Verloren Van Themaat's *Introduction to the Law of the European Communities* (1973) edited and revised by L W Gormley (1989). Collins' *European Community Law in the United Kingdom* (3rd edn, 1984) is a valuable study of structural and procedural aspects of Community law in the context of the law of the United Kingdom. The role of the Court of Justice is comprehensively treated in Schermers' *Judicial Protection in the European Communities* (3rd edn, 1983) K P E Lasok's *The European Court of Justice, Practice and Procedure* (1984), and Toth's *Legal Protection of Individuals in the European Communities*, 2 volumes (1978). *Halsbury's Laws of England* (4th edn) Vol 51, *Law of the European Communities* (edited by D. Vaughan) (1986) (2nd edn,

1991), contain 21 contributions covering the whole area of Community Law.

Among the large quantity of continental literature Gide, Loyrette and Nouel's *Dictionnaire du Marché Commun* in four large loose-leaf volumes, Megret's[8] *Le Droit de la Communauté Economique Européenne* (15 volumes published to date), Groeben, Boeckh, Thiesing and Ehlermann's *Kommentarzum EWG-Vertrag* (3rd edn, 1983) and E Grabitz and Others *Kommentar zum EWG-Vertrag* (2nd edn, 1987) are particularly valuable and so are the large loose-leaf volumes of Smit and Herzog's *The Law of the European Community: A Commentary on the EEC Treaty.*

---

8 Waelbroeck, M, Louis, J-V, Vignes, D, Dewast, J-L.

Part II

The law of the institutions

Chapter 5

The Commission of the European Communities

I Introduction

It has already been pointed out that the European Communities were brought into existence by means of multi-lateral treaties between sovereign states signed and ratified in accordance with their customary constitutional procedures. These original treaties, subject to subsequent amendments,[1] are the source of the constitutional law of the Communities. They set out the objectives and purposes of the Communities, create the institutions of the Communities, define the powers of those institutions and regulate their relations both inter se and with the Member States. In superficial form the Communities are cast in the classic mould of international organizations which has been so frequently used in modern times: the creation, by means of a multi-lateral treaty, of an organization which possesses a distinct legal personality and which acts through the agency of institutions set up and regulated under the terms of the constituent treaty. In possessing these characteristics the European Communities fall within a recognizable and well-defined pattern. But despite this superficial identity which the European Communities have with other international organizations both universal and regional, the Communities may also be said to be unique; this uniqueness lies in their institutions. Not, it is true, in the existence of those institutions as bodies independent and autonomous of the Member States for such institutions are commonly and necessarily found in international organizations. Nor does this uniqueness lie in the capacity of the institutions to impose obligations on the Member States for that is a power possessed, for example, by the Security Council of the United Nations. The uniqueness of the Communities stems from the deep involvement of their institutions in matters traditionally within the

---

1 Notably by the Merger Treaty 1965, the Budgetary Provisions Treaty 1970, the Treaty of Accession 1972 concerning Denmark, Ireland and the United Kingdom, the Financial Provisions Treaty 1975, the Direct Election Decision 1976, the Treaty of Accession 1979 concerning Greece, the Greenland Treaty 1984, the Treaty of Accession 1985 concerning Spain and Portugal and the Single European Act 1986.

exclusive control of each individual state and their capacity to make rules directly and automatically binding not only on the Member States themselves but also on individuals and corporate bodies within those states. Thus the unique character of the Communities lies in the degree of their penetration into the internal legal relations of the Member States, whereas classical international organizations tend to be involved merely with the external legal relations of their members.

The institutions of the European Communities fall into two main categories. In the first place there are institutions vested with a variety of political, legislative, executive and administrative functions and powers. These are the Commission, the Council and the European Parliament, assisted by a number of ancillary organs. Institutions in this category defy more precise classification for two main reasons. One is that these institutions cannot be said to be exclusively executive, administrative, legislative or political but each possesses more than one of these attributes. The other is that in functional terms the Treaties conceive of these institutions not only co-operating but indeed working as a team so that the role and significance of any one of them cannot fully be appreciated in isolation. In the second place there is the Court of Justice and the Court of First Instance, the judicial organs of the Communities.

The institutions will be treated in the above order.

II The Commission of the European Communities

(A) COMPOSITION AND APPOINTMENT

The Commission of the European Communities is composed of seventeen members chosen on the grounds of their general competence.[2] The Treaties provide that the Commissioners must be persons whose independence can be fully guaranteed. They are required to act with complete independence in the performance of their duties solely in the interests of the Communities and they must neither seek nor take instructions from any national government or other body. Each Member State, for its part, pledges to respect the independence of the Commissioners and not to seek to influence them in the performance of their duties. During their term of office Commissioners may not engage in any other occupation, paid or unpaid.[3] When entering upon their duties they give a

---

2 Merger Treaty, art 10 (1), as amended by the Act concerning Spanish and Portuguese Accession 1985, art 15 (the Third Act of Accession hereafter).
3 Ibid, art 10 (2).

solemn undertaking before the Court of Justice of the Communities that they accept the obligations of their office.

The Commissioners must be nationals of the Member States. Each Member State must have at least one but may not have more than two of its nationals on the Commission.[4] The present practice is for each of the larger Member States, viz France, Germany, Italy, Spain and the United Kingdom to have two Commissioners and for the Benelux countries, Denmark, Greece, Ireland and Portugal to have one each. In the case of the United Kingdom the Commissioners have always been nominated so as to reflect the two dominant political parties.[5] The Commissioners are appointed by mutual agreement between the Member States. They hold office for renewable periods of four years.[6] The President and the six Vice-Presidents of the Commission are appointed by the same process and hold office for renewable periods of two years.[7]

A Commissioner's term of office may be terminated by death in office or by resignation. A Commissioner may resign voluntarily; but if he no longer fulfils the conditions required for the performance of his duties or if he has been guilty of serious misconduct he may be compulsorily retired by the Court of Justice upon the application of either the Commission itself or the Council.[8] The whole Commission may be compelled to resign if the European Parliament passes a motion of censure upon it by a two-thirds majority of the votes cast, representing a majority of the European Parliament's members.[9] The power of parliamentary censure has yet to be invoked.

Prior to the accession of Denmark, Ireland and the United Kingdom the Commission was composed of nine members. The enlargement of the Communities raised the question of the representation of the new Member States on the Commission by persons of their nationality. In strict law, since the Commissioners are not national representatives but independent individuals, there was no necessity to increase the membership of the Commission

4 Ibid, art 10 (1).
5 See Times, 15 October 1980.
6 Merger Treaty, art 11.
7 Ibid, art 14, as amended by the Third Act of Accession, art 16 which also authorises the Council, acting unanimously, to amend the provisions concerning Vice-Presidents.
8 Ibid, art 13. A Commissioner has been compulsorily retired because of a permanently incapacitating illness; see *Bulletin of the European Communities* (1976), Part 7/8, points 2.4.41 and 2.4.43 and Decision 76/619, OJ 1976, L201/31. A Commissioner has also been asked by the European Parliament to answer allegations of misconduct; see *European Parliament—EP News* 22–26 October 1990, p 2.
9 Eg EEC Treaty, art 144; also see p 253, infra.

to accommodate new Member States. In reality it would have been impractical to adopt such a legalistic approach. The negotiations over the membership of Denmark, Ireland, Norway, the United Kingdom, Greece, Spain and Portugal proceeded on the basis that if new members were admitted the membership of the Commission would be increased so as to accommodate the new members and maintain the existing level of representation of the original members.[10] This was in fact done by the Council exercising its power under article 10(1) of the Merger Treaty to increase the number of members of the Commission.[11]

(B) ORGANIZATION

The Commission functions as a collegiate body in the sense that the Commission collectively and not the Commissioners individually bears responsibility for the acts of the Commission.[12] The Commission acts by a majority vote.[13] Its rules of procedure provide that the quorum of members is nine and that the conclusions of the Commission shall be final when they receive at least nine votes in support.[14] There is, nevertheless, an inevitable degree of subject specialization as far as individual Commissioners are concerned. It is now an established practice for special responsibilities to be allocated to each Commissioner.[15] There is a temptation to compare these responsibilities, by analogy, with the portfolios given to members of a national government. However, the analogy is imperfect since unlike a member of a national government a Commissioner bears no personal responsibility for his portfolio.

Although the Commission is collectively responsible for its acts, it may authorize its members to take agreed action on its behalf. This practice is provided by article 27 of the *Règlement Intérieure*

---

10 See the Commission's report *The Enlarged Community* (1972), para 36, the White Paper, *The United Kingdom and the European Communities* (Cmnd 4175), para 71, *The Second Enlargement of the European Community* (European Documentation 5/79, p 31) and *Bulletin of the European Communities*, Supplement 2/78, Part 2, para 24.

11 By a decision of 1 January 1973, the Second Act of Accession, art 15 and the Third Act of Accession, art 15.

12 See *Règlement Intérieur de la Commission*, 63/41/CEE, art 1, JO, 31 January 1963, and the Commission's Provisional Rules of Procedure, 67/426/EEC, art 1, OJ 1967, L147.

13 Merger Treaty, art 17 (1).

14 Provisional Rules of Procedure, 67/426/EEC, art 2, as amended by Decision 73/1, OJ 1973, L7, Decision 81/2, OJ 1981, L8 and Decision 86/61, OJ 1986, L72. Many decisions of the Commission are in fact unanimous.

15 See Vacher's *European Companion*, No 73, pp 45–46.

de la Commission[16] and was approved by the Court of Justice in *Re Noordwijks Cement Accoord* (1967).[17] Further, to prevent the principle of collective responsibility from imposing unnecessary delays on the Commission's work, considerable use is made of the so-called written procedure in accordance with the terms of article 11 of the *Règlement Intérieure*. By this procedure draft decisions are circulated among the Commissioners and if no amendments or objections are made within a fixed period the draft is deemed to have been adopted by the Commission as a whole. Where amendments or objections are made or where a Commissioner specifically requests further discussion drafts will be considered at a full meeting of the Commission. This written procedure was not questioned by the Court in *Re Noordwijks Cement Accoord* and so its legality appears to have been accepted.[18]

Each Commissioner is assisted by a *cabinet* in the French sense of a private office or departmental staff whose members tend to be of the same nationality as the Commissioner they serve. A *chef de cabinet* or principal private secretary may deputize for his Commissioner at Commission meetings. In addition to the *cabinets* of the Commissioners the Commission has a staff of some 10,400 divided between the various Directorates-General (D-G) and auxiliary services of the Commission. Each D-G is presided over by a Director-General who is responsible to the Commissioner whose 'portfolio' includes that D-G.[19] The Directors-General are always of different nationality from the Commissioners they serve. On the lower levels of the administrative hierarchy the aim is to have an equitable representation of all the nationalities of the Communities. In view of the multi-lingual nature of the Communities with nine official languages, viz Dutch, French, German, Greek, Italian, Danish, English, Portuguese and Spanish, linguists play a vital role in the activities of the Communities; there are well over 1,600 translators and interpreters on the Commission's staff.[20]

---

16 *Loc cit* in note 13 above. Also see Decision 72/21, OJ 1972, L7 on delegation of signature, Decision 74/55, OJ 1974, L34, on the exercise of certain powers in respect of Community revenue and expenditure and Decision 75/461, OJ 1975, L199 on the taking of measures of management and administration.

17 Cases 8–11/66: [1967] ECR 75, [1967] CMLR 77. In 1987 over 11,000 measures were taken in this way; see Noel, E, *Working Together: The Institutions of the European Community* (1988), p 42.

18 In 1987 the written procedure was used on 2,870 occasions. See Noel, E, op cit, p 42.

19 There are 23 Directorates-General in addition to the Secretariat-General, the Legal Service, the Spokesman's Group, the Statistical Office and some other general services: see Vacher's *European Companion*, No 73, pp 46–71.

20 The official languages of the Communities are determined by Regulation 1 of 15 April 1958, OJ 17, 6 October 1958, p 385/58 (Sp edn 1952–1958, p 59) as

There are also arrangements for the reciprocal secondment of staff between the Commission and the government departments of the Member States.[1]

(C) FUNCTIONS AND POWERS

The Merger Treaty provides in article 9 that the Commission shall exercise the powers and competences bestowed by the Community Treaties upon the High Authority of the ECSC and the Commissions of the EEC and Euratom. The functions and powers of the Merged Commission thus vary from Treaty to Treaty. But despite these differences it is possible to categorize the functions and powers of the Commission into three broad groups: it is an initiator and co-ordinator of Community policy; it is the executive agency of the Communities; it is the guardian of the Community Treaties.

As an initiator of policy the scope of the Commission differs in relation to the ECSC and Euratom on the one hand and the EEC on the other. The ECSC and Euratom Treaties are *traités-lois* in that they lay down codes of specific rules relating to the relatively limited fields of concern of those Communities. In such a context the opportunities for formulating policy are limited since the policy decisions and the rules implementing them were largely taken at the time those Treaties were negotiated and were incorporated into the Treaties themselves. But the EEC Treaty with its more wide-ranging concern with the entire economies of the Member States is a *traité cadre* and sketches in bolder strokes the main lines which are to be followed in achieving an economic union. Thus the EEC Treaty leaves the details of the policies to be followed in the attainment of that goal to be worked out by the institutions of the Community. In this task the Commission plays a major and perhaps its most significant role by participating 'in the shaping of measures taken by the Council'.[2]

In assisting in the formulation of policy the Commission first engages in consultations with interested parties at the political, civil service and trade union levels. Then, with the assistance of its own specialist Directorates and advised by its Legal Service,[3] it

amended by the first Act of Accession, art 29 and Annex I, point XIV, para 1; the Adaptation Decision of 1 January 1973, OJ 1972, L2, the Second Act of Accession, art 21 and Annex I, point XVI, para 1, and the Third Act of Accession, art 26 and Annex I, point XVII.

1 See *Twenty-third General Report on the Activities of the European Communities* (1990), p 40.
2 EEC Treaty, art 155, third provision.
3 See Ehlermann, C-D, *The Role of the Legal Service of the Commission in the Creation of Community Law* (University of Exeter, 1981), pp 6–10.

proceeds to the consideration, often prolonged, of policy proposals until it reaches its final position which is submitted to the Council. It was in this way, for example, that the Commission prepared its opinion on United Kingdom membership of the Communities and its proposals on the agricultural policy of the Communities. After the main lines of policy have been finally agreed the Commission embarks on a consideration of the practical details of the implementation of that policy. The Directorates of the Commission concerned with a particular policy convene meetings with experts from the Member States for the purpose of working out the practical implications of the policy. The experts are invited from the national civil services of the Member States and although they have no brief to commit their respective governments they will be aware of their wishes and so will be in a position to advise the Commission on the acceptability of the Commission's proposals to the governments of the Member States.[4] By this process the Commission formulates its proposals for submission to the Council. As an indication of the scale of this aspect of the Commission's work, during 1989 it sent 624 proposals to the Council plus 214 memoranda and communications.[5]

The merged Commission is also the co-ordinator of policy as between the three Communities. Prior to the merger such co-ordination was virtually impossible because the Communities were institutionally separate. Since the merger the Commission has been able to take steps towards the formulation of common policies in such fields as industry, energy, research and technology which cut across the boundaries of the individual Communities. This co-ordination of policy may be regarded as a further stage in the process leading to a complete merger of the three Communities.

The Commission as the initiator and co-ordinator of policy also gives expression to the interests of the Communities; in this role we see the Commission as the conscience of the Communities. The Member States despite their acceptance of the obligations of membership are apt to be deflected by national interests. Thus it is for the independent Commission constantly to remind both the Communities and the Member States of the fundamental objectives of the Communities and to seek the achievement of those objectives to the fullest extent.[6] This was clearly expressed by the President of the Commission, in a statement to the European Parliament in

---

4 The Commission is indeed under an obligation not to seek or take instructions from any Government; see Merger Treaty, art 10 (2).
5 *Twenty-third General Report on the Activities of the European Communities* (1990) p 39.
6 See *Premier Rapport Général sur l'activité de la CEE* (September 1958), para 8.

September 1970: 'The Commission is, at one and the same time, the guardian of the Treaties and the motive force of integration, capable of accepting with courage the dialectic consequences which go with its twofold task—exercising the vigilance that is needed to preserve us from risks run by the venturesome and acting to correct any excess of vigilance which would inevitably lead to stagnation.'[7] In this role the Commission's views of the Communities have not infrequently differed from those of the governments of the Member States. Over the enlargement of the Communities, for example, the Commission produced a reasoned opinion in 1967 in favour of the admission of the United Kingdom, Ireland, Denmark and Norway to the Communities subject to certain conditions and recommended the opening of negotiations with those countries. That recommendation was not adopted because of the opposition of the French Government at that time to British entry in particular and to the enlargement of the Communities in general.

Secondly, the three Treaties confer upon the Commission a wide range of legislative and executive powers and functions.

Under article 8 of the ECSC Treaty the Commission has the duty of ensuring 'the attainment of the objectives set out in this Treaty, under the conditions laid down herein'. This and many other articles of the Treaty give the Commission wide rule-making powers. For example, article 60 of the ECSC Treaty gives the Commission the power to define practices which come within the prohibition on unfair competitive prices which might tend towards the creation of a monopoly. Similarly article 155 and article 125 of the EEC and Euratom Treaties respectively confer upon the Commission the authority to see 'that the provisions of [the] Treaty and the measures pursuant to it taken by the institutions are carried out'. Thus, for example, article $48(3)(d)$ of the EEC Treaty enables the Commission to make regulations laying down the conditions under which workers have a right to live in a Member State in which they have been employed. During 1989 the Commission adopted no fewer than 5,737 instruments (Regulations, Decisions, Directives, Recommendations and Opinions).[8]

In addition to such powers specifically conferred upon the Commission by the Treaties the Commission may also be invested with powers to ensure the enforcement of decisions made by the Council. This is of particular significance in the EEC where, in connection with the Common Agricultural Policy, the Council has delegated wide rule-making powers to the Commission under the authority

---

7 *Statement to the European Parliament* (15 September 1970), p 22.
8 *Twenty-third General Report on the Activities of the European Communities* (1990), p 39.

of the final provision of art 155 of the EEC Treaty.[9] As a measure of the degree of importance which these powers occupy in the Commission's work, of the more than 2,000 regulations and decisions made by the Commission during 1987 the vast majority related to the Common Agricultural Policy.[10] The role of the Commission as the delegate of the Council for the purposes of law-making has recently been reinforced and systematized by an amendment introduced by the Single European Act 1986.[11] A new provision establishes a general rule that the Council shall confer powers on the Commission to implement general rules laid down by the Council. It also requires the Council to establish an overall framework for such delegation rather than making *ad hoc* arrangements in each case.[12] Acting under this authority, the Council has adopted the so-called 'comitology' decision which lays down the procedures for the exercise of these new implementing powers.[13] That Decision contemplates that the Commission will act either alone or by one of three committee procedures: advisory, management or regulatory. The latter two procedures are subject to variants and the Council has also inserted a safeguard clause. In the event, the anticipated simplification of decision-making procedures has not been realized and there has been a marked reluctance on the part of the Council to grant the Commission implementing powers.[14]

The executive authority vested in the Commission is that of ensuring that the rules of the Treaties are applied to particular cases, whether concerning the government of a Member State or a commercial undertaking. Under the ECSC Treaty the Commission deals directly with coal and steel enterprises. Article 54 of that Treaty, for example, enables the Commission to promote and co-ordinate the capital spending of coal and steel enterprises and it has the power to prohibit the financing of any programme put forward by an enterprise which conflicts with the rules of the Treaty. Under the Euratom Treaty the Commission has responsibilities of a supervisory nature in relation to the protection of the health of workers in the nuclear industry and the supply and use of fissile material.[15] In the EEC Treaty similar powers are conferred

9 Also see Ch 8 (D), infra.
10 Noel, E, op cit, p 19.
11 Art 10 amending EEC Treaty, art 145.
12 See *Twentieth General Report on the Activities of the European Communities* (1987), pp 35, 36.
13 Decision 87/373, OJ 1987, L197/33.
14 See *Twenty-second and Twenty-third General Reports on the Activities of the European Communities* (1989) and (1990), at pp 33 and 31–32 respectively. For further discussion see Ch 8 (D), infra.
15 See Euratom Treaty, Title Two, Chapters 3 and 6.

upon the Commission particularly in relation to the prohibition of restrictive practices and the control of state subsidies.[16] In 1985 the Commission made novel use of its general authority to ensure that the provisions of the EEC Treaty are applied[17] by itself legislating with respect to cereal prices after a failure by the Council to reach a decision on the matter.[18] In the Commission's view such action was necessary to ensure the continuity of the Common Agricultural Policy in the cereals sector. It invoked the failure of the Member States to honour their obligations under article 5 of the Treaty as justifying its action and triggering its own responsibilities under the Treaty. The Court of Justice has sanctioned this recourse to implied powers in terms that 'the Council's failure to act cannot discharge the Commission from its duty to take the necessary steps, using its powers under article 155 of the Treaty'.[19]

The Commission is also given a number of representative, financial and administrative functions. The Commission represents the legal persona of the Communities.[20] It represents the Communities in negotiations with non-Member States and international organizations.[1] The Commission is responsible for the administration of Community funds. In the ECSC a levy on coal and steel production is paid to the Commission direct.[2] In the EEC and Euratom the Commission is charged with giving effect to the budgets of the Communities as adopted by the European Parliament.[3] The EEC and Euratom were originally financed out of contributions from the Member States. But under the terms of a Council Decision of 1970[4], since 1 January 1975 the Communities have been very largely financed out of their own resources, the main sources of which are customs duties, agricultural levies and a proportion of the VAT levied throughout the Community. The Commission also administers four special funds which form part of the Communities' budget: the European Social Fund which is used to redeploy and retrain workers and to promote social welfare;[5]

16 See EEC Treaty, Part Three, Title 1.
17 Under the first provision of EEC Treaty, art 155.
18 See Commission Regulation 2124/85, OJ 1985, L198, p 31.
19 Joined Cases 47 and 48/83: *Pluimveeslachterij Midden-Nederland BV* [1984] ECR 1721, at p 1739.
20 Eg EEC Treaty, art 211.
 1 Eg EEC Treaty, arts 228 et seq.
 2 ECSC Treaty, art 49.
 3 EEC Treaty, art 205; Euratom Treaty, art 179.
 4 Decision 70/243, OJ L94, 28 April 1970, p 19 (Sp edn 1970 (I) p 224). Also see Council Regulation 2/71 applying that Decision, OJ L3, 5 January 1971, p 1 (Sp edn 1971 (I), p 3). The Community's system of own resources is now operated under the authority of Council Decision 88/376, OJ 1988, L185. For further discussion see Ch 7 (C), infra.
 5 EEC Treaty, Part Three, Title 3, Chapter 2.

the European Development Fund which makes grants and loans to overseas territories and countries associated with the Communities;[6] the European Agricultural Guidance and Guarantee Fund which is used to cover agricultural market support costs and to assist farm modernization schemes;[7] and the European Regional Development Fund which has been set up to correct regional imbalances within the Community.[8] Under the terms of article 18 of the Merger Treaty the Commission is also required to publish an annual general report on the activities of the Communities.

Lastly, the Commission as the guardian of the Treaties acts as a watch-dog to ensure that treaty obligations are observed. If an allegation is made that there has been an infringement of Treaty obligations it is for the Commission, as an impartial body, to investigate that allegation, reach a conclusion and notify the action necessary to correct the error. In the case of such an error in respect of the ECSC Treaty, article 88 authorizes the Commission to take steps to ensure that Member States fulfil their obligations under the Treaty. Where a Member State will not voluntarily carry out its obligations the Commission may, with the concurring vote of a two-thirds majority of the Council, withhold from the defaulting Member State sums of money which the Commission may owe that state under the Treaty and authorize the other Member States to withhold certain benefits under the Treaty from the defaulting state as a sanction for its wrongdoing. If these measures prove ineffective the Commission shall bring the matter before the Council. This procedure may be subject to review by the Court of Justice of the Communities.[9] Also under the ECSC Treaty the Commission has the power to impose a monetary penalty on any coal and steel undertaking which acts contrary to its obligations under the Treaty.[10]

The provisions of the ECSC Treaty authorizing action to be taken against a Member State were found to be complex and cumbersome and have been seldom used in practice. Partly because of this experience the equivalent provisions of the EEC and Euratom Treaties are simpler and more effective. Article 169 of the EEC Treaty lays down a general procedure for dealing with breaches of treaty obligations by Member States. It provides that

6 See Implementing Convention of the Association of the Overseas Countries and Territories with the Community 1957, annexed to the EEC Treaty and the Fourth Lomé Convention, Part Three, Title III, *The Courier*, No 120, March–April 1990, pp 56 et seq.

7 This fund was established by Council Regulation No 25 of 4 April 1962, OJ 1962, p 991/62 (Sp edn 1959–1962, p 126).

8 See Regulation (EEC) 1787/84, OJ 1984, L169.

9 See Chapter 9, below.

10 Eg arts 64–66.

where 'the Commission considers that a Member State has failed to fulfil an obligation under the Treaty, it shall deliver a reasoned opinion on the matter after giving the state concerned the opportunity to submit its observations. If the state concerned does not comply with the terms of the opinion within the period laid down by the Commission, the latter may bring the matter before the Court of Justice,'[11] In 1989, 664 letters of formal complaint were sent to Member States, 178 reasoned opinions, and actions before the Court were brought in 97 cases.[12] This reflects a tendency for Member States to rectify infringements at an early stage in the complaints procedure and underlines the important role played by the Commission in this regard. In earlier years most of the infringements concerned customs duties and quotas but latterly the cases have involved a wider range of Treaty provisions, notably the non-implementation or incorrect implementation of directives and the infringement of the basic provisions relating to the free movement of goods.[13] In addition to this general procedure the Treaties also confer authority on the Commission to deal with special infringements. For example article 89 of the EEC Treaty authorizes the Commission to investigate suspected infringements of the Community's rules of competition. If the suspicion is well founded and if the infringements are not brought to an end the Commission may direct the Member States to take the steps necessary to remedy the situation.

(D) PROPOSED REFORMS

Suggestions have been made from time to time concerning the composition, structure and working methods of the Commission. At the time of the First Accession, for example, there was criticism of the increase in the size of the Commission on the grounds that a larger body would be unwieldy and less effective.[14] In 1976, in his Report on European Union, Mr Tindemans proposed that the European Parliament should be given a role in the appointment of the President and Members of the Commission.[15] More recently attention has again been focused on the size of the Commission and its method of working.

---

11 Also see Euratom Treaty, art 141 and Chapter 9, below.
12 *Twenty-third General Report on the Activities of the European Communities* (1990), p 406.
13 Ibid.
14 See *Problems of British Entry into the EEC* (PEP European Series, No 11, 1969) p 101.
15 See *Bulletin of the European Communities*, Supp 1/76, pp 31, 32.

Two independent studies authorized by the Commission[16] and the Council[17] in 1979 both agreed that in recent years the Commission has tended to become a less effective institution. The increase in the size of the Commission together with the difficulty of giving equally meaningful portfolios to each Commissioner have been identified as contributing to the loss of collegiality in the Commission. The desirability of the four larger Member States having two Commissioners of their nationality was also questioned. It was said that such an arrangement runs counter to the independent nature of the Commission and that national interests are properly and adequately protected by the system of weighted voting in the Council[18] and the distribution of seats in the European Parliament.[19] Both of these studies recommend a smaller Commission of one member for each Member State, and that the departments and services of the Commission should be reorganized so that each Commissioner has a portfolio of equal weight.[20] The Commission itself, while accepting that efficient functioning should be the guideline for its future composition, has acknowledged that the burden of work in an enlarged Community justifies a Commission of the present size.[1]

The theme of reform has also been taken up by both the European Parliament and the European Council. The former, in the context of the Draft Treaty on European Union which it adopted in 1984,[2] saw the Commission as an executive body with real authority. That document proposed that the President should be appointed by the European Council and that he would then form his Commission in consultation with that body.[3] Once constituted the Commission would submit its programme to and be invested by the European Parliament[4] to which it would also be responsible.[5] Similar proposals, additionally recommending that the Commission should not include more than one national of any Member State, were made by the Dooge Committee[6] in its report to the European Council in 1985.[7] The Commission, through its current President,

16 *Proposals for Reform of the Commission of the European Communities and its Services (Spierenburg Report)* (1979).
17 *Report on European Institutions (Three Wise Men's Report)* (1979).
18 See Chapter 6, infra.
19 See Chapter 7, infra.
20 *Spierenburg Report*, para 43 and Table I; *Three Wise Men's Report*, pp 67, 68.
1 See *Bulletin of the European Communities* Supplement 2/78, Part 2, para 24.
2 OJ 1984, C77, p 33.
3 Ibid, art 25.
4 Ibid.
5 Ibid, art 29(1).
6 Ie, the Ad Hoc Committee for Institutional Affairs.
7 See EC Commission, *An Ever Closer Union* (1985) Annex II, pp 338, 339.

has clearly indicated its support for the proposition that it 'should be turned into a proper executive answerable for its actions' and appointed democratically.[8] The realization of such schemes as these is, it is submitted, intimately linked to the Community's attitude and progress towards some form of political union.[9]

8 In an address to the European Parliament on 17 January 1990; see *Bulletin of the European Communities*, Supplement 1/90, 'The Commission's Programme for 1990' at pp 12–13.

9 See Ch 1, supra.

Chapter 6

The Council and the European Council of the European Communities

(A) COMPOSITION OF THE COUNCIL

The Council is made up of one representative of the government of each of the Member States.[1] The composition of the Council varies depending upon the subject matter to be discussed. A basic distinction is drawn between so-called General Council meetings and Specialized Council meetings. The former are attended by Foreign Ministers and the agenda may include not only matters relating to external affairs but also matters of general Community concern such as those relating to the institutions. The latter are attended by those ministers whose portfolios relate to the specific subject on the agenda, for example agriculture, finance, industry or transport.[2] In practical terms the Merger Treaty had very little effect on the working of the Council. Because of the common identity of membership there had been virtually a de facto merger of the separate Councils since 1958. The Merger Treaty formalized this arrangement and provided for unified rules of procedure.[3] The office of President of the Council rotates among the members for terms of six months in the following sequence: Belgium, Denmark, Germany, Greece, Spain, France, Ireland, Italy, Luxembourg, Netherlands, Portugal and the United Kingdom for the years 1987–1992 inclusive and Denmark, Belgium, Greece, Germany, France, Spain, Italy, Ireland, Netherlands, Luxembourg, United Kingdom and Portugal for the years 1993–1998 inclusive.[4] The Council meets in private and its meetings are convened upon the initiative of the President or at the request of either a member or of the Commission.[5]

1 Merger Treaty, art 2.
2 On some occasions joint Council meetings are held attended by ministers with different responsibilities in order to deal with problems extending over a range of sectors of the economy. See *Tenth General Report on the Activities of the European Communities* (1977), p 33. Also see *Twenty-seventh Review of the Council's Work* (1980), pp 9, 10.
3 Merger Treaty, art 5. For the text of the Rules of Procedure see Council Decisions 79/868, OJ 1979, L268; and 87/508, OJ 1987, L291/27.
4 Ibid, art 2 as amended by the Third Act of Accession 1985, art 11.
5 Merger Treaty, art 3 and Council's Rules of Procedure, arts 1 and 3, loc cit, in n 3 supra.

(B) THE POWERS OF THE COUNCIL AND ITS RELATIONSHIP WITH THE
COMMISSION AND THE EUROPEAN PARLIAMENT

As in the case of the Commission, the Council exercises the powers
conferred by the Community Treaties upon the former separate
Councils.[6] One of the most interesting features of the constitution
of the Communities is the relationship between the Council and
the Commission. This has already been adumbrated in an earlier
reference to the role of the Commission in the formulation of policy
and as the exponent of the interests of the Communities. There is,
however, a noticeable difference in this relationship between the
ECSC and Euratom on the one hand and the EEC on the other.
The ECSC and Euratom Treaties, at articles 26 and 115 respectively, stress the Council's harmonizing and co-ordinating role in
relation to the policies of the Member States; the EEC Treaty at
article 145 specifies in addition a power to take decisions. In general
terms, under the ECSC Treaty it is the Commission which has the
power to take decisions subject to consultation with the Council;
under the EEC Treaty the power of decision largely lies with the
Council usually acting upon a proposal from the Commission.
These differences appear to indicate that the Commission has more
power under the ECSC Treaty than it has under the EEC Treaty
and that the supra-national character of the Commission in the
ECSC is not enjoyed in relation to the EEC. In fact, the importance
of these formal differences is more apparent than real. We have
already seen that in the ECSC the opportunities for the Commission to initiate policy are limited because of the essential character of the treaty as a *traité-loi*. This gives the Commission powers
of a largely executive character to give effect to the rules already
laid down in the Treaty. The Commission has similar but less
extensive powers under the EEC Treaty itself. But that Treaty's
essential character is that of a *traité cadre* which, as we have seen,
gives the Commission an important role in initiating and formulating policy, subject to the final decision of the Council. Once
such a policy decision has been taken, as in the case of agriculture
for example, the Council confers upon the Commission the necessary executive powers to implement such policy. This role of the
Commission has been enhanced by an amendment mentioned in
the previous chapter which gives general authority to the Council
to confer implementing power on the Commission.[7] Further, whilst
the Commission under the ECSC Treaty has in law wide powers
of independent decision, in practice it has made a point of seeking
the opinion and approval of the Council even in cases in which this

6 Merger Treaty, art 1.
7 See Single European Act, art 10 amending EEC Treaty, art 145.

was not strictly necessary.[8] Bearing in mind the different character of the ECSC and EEC Treaties, the powers of the Commission are broadly of the same order in each with the important addition that under the EEC Treaty the Commission has a vital role in the formulation of policy.

The Commission's initiative in policy-making is enhanced by the fact that in exercising its power of decision under the EEC Treaty the Council can in general act only upon a proposal from the Commission. The Council may amend a Commission proposal only by unanimous vote.[9] Failing that it can accept it, reject it or return it to the Commission for reconsideration. Thus the text of a Commission proposal tends to go through many drafts passing between the Council and the Commission until a final version is agreed. The Commission's position in this process is further strengthened by the rules of voting in the Council. Whilst the normal rule of voting in the Council is by a simple majority,[10] in fact most of the law-making powers of the Council have to be exercised by a qualified majority. For this purpose a system of weighted voting is employed: France, Germany, Italy and the United Kingdom have ten votes each; Spain has eight; Belgium, Greece, Netherlands and Portugal have five; Denmark and Ireland have three; and Luxembourg has two.[11] Where a Council decision is required to be taken upon a proposal from the Commission, for example under article 94 of the EEC Treaty for the application of the rules concerning aids granted by states, a qualified majority of any 54 of the available 76 votes will suffice. In such a case France, Germany, Italy and the United Kingdom who together command a total of 40 votes could not impose their will on the other eight members. In other cases in which the Council can act on its own initiative the qualified majority of 54 must be cast by at least eight Member States, for example under article 6 of the Merger Treaty where the Council may determine the salaries of the Commissioners and the Judges and officers of the Court of Justice. Here again the four larger members cannot dictate to the other members and a clear majority of members is required. Thus the Treaty introduces a system of checks and balances into the decision-making powers of the Council so as to ensure that a decision taken by a qualified majority reflects a broad consensus among the Member States.

8 See von Lindeiner-Wildau, K, *La Supranationalité en tant que Principe de Droit* (1970), pp 104, 105.
9 EEC Treaty, art 149 (1); also Euratom Treaty, art 119.
10 EEC Treaty, art 148 (1); also Euratom Treaty, art 118 (1).
11 EEC Treaty, art 148 (2) and Euratom Treaty, art 118 (2) as amended by the Third Act of Accession 1985, art 14.

A major change in the exercise of the Council's powers has been introduced by the Single European Act 1986. This provides for a new 'co-operation procedure'[12] involving the European Parliament to be used for legislation with respect to the elimination of discrimination on grounds of nationality, free movement of workers and establishment, free movement of services, and harmonization measures relating to the establishment and functioning of the Community's internal market.[13] When this new procedure applies the Council will not be able to proceed to a final decision on the Commission's proposal, having consulted the European Parliament, but must at that stage adopt a 'common position' by qualified majority. Such common position will then be referred to the European Parliament which is given a three-month period during which it may do any one of four things: (i) approve the Council position; (ii) take no decision on the Council position; (iii) amend the Council position by absolute majority; or (iv) reject the Council position by absolute majority. If the European Parliament takes either of the first two steps, the Council will proceed to act on its common position. If the last step is taken the Council may only act on its common position by unanimity. If the third step is taken, the Commission is given one month to consider the amendments proposed by the Parliament with a view to amending its own proposal. Thereafter the Council may do any one of four things during a further period of three months:[14] (i) adopt the Commission's revised proposal by a qualified majority; (ii) adopt Parliamentary amendments not approved by the Commission by unanimity; (iii) itself amend the Commission proposal by unanimity; or (iv) fail to act. The Commission's proposal will in any event lapse if the Council has not acted within the prescribed period.[15] This procedure, which adds a form of second reading to the legislative process in the relevant fields, clearly gives the European Parliament a greater opportunity to influence the Council; but the Council does still have the last word. As for the Commission, it retains the right to amend its proposal or to withdraw it at any stage thus retaining its power to influence events.[16] General satisfaction has been expressed with the operation of this new procedure and the

---

12 Single European Act, art 7, amending EEC Treaty, art 149.
13 Ibid, art 6 (1). It remains to be seen whether this procedure will become a permanent feature of the Community's decision-making process once these objectives of the Single European Act have been achieved.
14 This period may be extended by a maximum of one month by common accord between the Council and the European Parliament; see EEC Treaty, art 149 (2) (g).
15 Ibid, art 149 (2) (f).
16 Ibid, art 149 (3).

overall results have indeed been encouraging.[17] A co-operative and beneficial working relationship seems to be developing, with amendments proposed by the European Parliament attracting support and often having a significant impact on the final outcome. As the Commission has reported, '[t]he inclusion of Parliament in the decision-making process appears to have improved the texts and not disturbed the procedure'.[18]

(C) THE COMMITTEE OF PERMANENT REPRESENTATIVES

The common experience of European organizations set up since 1945 has been that where they have institutions made up of ministerial representatives of governments which, because of other demands on their time and attention, can only meet infrequently, a permanent representative body of ambassadorial rank is necessary not only to carry out routine matters of administration but also to undertake preparatory work for meetings of the ministers and supply an element of continuity in their work. This has been the experience of the OEEC, the Council of Europe, the Western European Union and NATO.[19] In view of this experience it is somewhat surprising to find that the ECSC Treaty made no provision for the Special Council of Ministers to be assisted by a committee of permanent representatives. But by 1953 the need for such assistance had become apparent and the Special Council used its general power to establish committees to set up the so-called Co-ordinating Committee made up of senior officials of the national administrations of the members to prepare material for Council meetings and to undertake *ad hoc* tasks at the Council's request.[20]

This practice prompted the incorporation in the EEC and Euratom Treaties of provisions to the effect that the Council's Rules of Procedure 'may provide for the setting up of a committee consisting of representatives of Member States' the tasks and powers of which shall be determined by the Council.[21] This power was used to establish a Committee of Permanent Representatives, who were in practice the ambassadors of the Member States accredited to the Communities, to carry out work preparatory to Council meetings and any other specific tasks.[22] The Merger Treaty

17 See *Twenty-second and Twenty-third General Reports on the European Communities* (1989) and (1990), at pp 32 and 31 respectively.
18 *Twenty-third General Report* ibid.
19 See the account of these organizations in Palmer, M, et al, *European Unity* (1968).
20 See *Les Novelles: Droit des Communautés européennes* (1969), pp 241 et seq.
21 EEC Treaty, art 151; Euratom Treaty, art 121.
22 See Noel, E, 'The Committee of Permanent Representatives', 5 *Journal of Common Market Studies* (1967), pp 219, 220.

institutionalized this arrangement providing, in article 4, that 'a committee consisting of the Permanent Representatives of the Member States shall be responsible for preparing the work of the Council and for carrying out the tasks assigned to it by the Council'.[1] Thus in effect the ECSC's Co-ordinating Committee was abolished and the EEC/Euratom Committee of Ambassadors extended to the ECSC. This Committee is commonly known as COREPER, an acronym derived from its French title: *Comité des Représentants Permanents*.

The Permanent Representatives were originally regarded as merely the servants, the eyes and the ears of their governments.[2] But in the course of time the Committee has acquired a Community character and has come to play a distinctive and important role in the affairs of the Communities. At first the establishment and institutionalization of this Committee was treated with suspicion. Its German title *Ständige Vertreter* (Permanent Representatives) was for a time parodied as *Ständige Verräter* (Permanent Traitors) because it was feared that it might endanger the Community's institutional balance.[3] The specific fear was that the Commission/Council dialogue might become gradually replaced requiring the Commission to deal with a group of subordinate Permanent Representatives rather than with the ministers themselves. This would erode the supra-national role of the Commission and would effectively place more power in the hands of the Council. In 1958 when the EEC/Euratom Committee of Permanent Representatives was set up the Commission asked the Council for an assurance that there was no intention of delegating the Council's powers of decision to the Permanent Representatives. This assurance was unanimously given by the Council.[4] The Committee of Permanent Representatives is not a Committee of Minister's Deputies. The power of decision and responsibility for decisions remains where the Treaties put it with the Council and the institutional balance resulting from the dialogue between Commission and Council appears to have been preserved.[5]

This assurance paved the way for the establishment of a fruitful relationship between the Permanent Representatives and the Commission. This has resulted in the settlement of problems which

---

1 Also see Council's Rules of Procedure, art 16, OJ 1979, L268/3.
2 See Noel, E, op cit in note 22, above, at p 223.
3 See Mayne, R, *The Institutions of the European Community* (1968), p 37.
4 See Noel, E, op cit in note 22, above, at pp 228, 229.
5 The limited role of the Committee is confirmed by the Council's Rules of Procedure, art 16, OJ 1979, L268/3. But cf Salmon, J J A, 'Le rôle des representations permanentes', *La Décision dans les Communautés Européennes* (1969), pp 57 et seq.

would otherwise waste the time of Ministers and the joining of support for Commission proposals in the face of initial hesitation on the part of the governments of the Member States. In practice the functions and services of the Committee of Permanent Representatives fall into three main categories:

(*a*) liaison between national administrations and Community institutions and the mutual supply of information;

(*b*) participation in the working out and co-ordinating of national attitudes; and

(*c*) direct involvement in work of the Community institutions.[6]

In addition to the Committee of Permanent Representatives, the Council is also assisted by a General Secretariat.[7] This has its own Legal Department and seven Directorates-General each covering a homogeneous group of Community activities.[8] While the General Secretariat reflects the civil service structure of the Commission, it only has a staff of some 2,000 because of the heavy reliance which the Council places on civil servants in the national administrations of the Member States.

(D) THE COUNCIL'S WORKING METHODS

When the Council receives a proposal from the Commission the invariable procedure is to refer it, in the first instance, to an appropriate committee or working party made up of civil service experts. Each of the fields of activity of the Communities is covered by such committees and working parties who advise the Council and whose work is co-ordinated by the Committee of Permanent Representatives. The Commission is represented at these preparatory meetings and may amend its proposals in the light of the discussion, although it is under no obligation to do so.

When the Council meets to consider Commission proposals its agenda is divided into so-called 'A' items and 'B' items,[9] a procedure based on the practice of the French Council of Ministers. 'A' items are those upon which provisional agreement has been reached in the course of the preparatory meetings and 'B' items are those on which there is still disagreement. 'A' items have of course to be formally approved by the Council but they are usually settled

6 See Noel, E, op cit in n 22, above, at pp 223 et seq and Noel, E and Etienne, H, 'The Permanent Representatives Committee and the "Deepening" of the Communities', 6 *Government and Opposition* (1971), p 447.
7 Council's Rules of Procedure, art 17, OJ 1979, L268/3.
8 See Vacher's *European Companion*, No 73, pp 40–44.
9 Council's Rules of Procedure, art 2 (6), OJ 1979, L268/1.

quickly. 'B' items occupy most of the business of Council meetings.[10] Members of the Commission take part by invitation in Council meetings[11] which are otherwise held in private. The role of the Commissioners at these meetings is that of mediator and honest broker. Whilst the Commission is anxious for an agreement which is in tune with Community interests it can also amend its proposals at any time and may thus be able to suggest a compromise which may be acceptable to all sides. The texts of acts adopted by the Council become final upon signature by the President-in-Office at the time of their adoption and by the Secretary-General. No editorial changes may be made thereafter by the General Secretariat, except in relation to simple spelling and grammar.[12]

At the Paris Summit Meeting in October 1972 the Heads of State or Government of the enlarged Community pledged themselves to improve the Council's decision-making procedures and the cohesion of Community action.[13] As a result, during 1973 and 1974 the Council adopted a number of measures designed to achieve those objectives.[14] These measures were largely of a practical nature and did not introduce any new matters of principle. They include: advance planning of the timetable for Council meetings; co-ordination of national cabinet meetings so as to make ministers available for Council meetings; the circulation of papers at least a week before a meeting; more careful planning of the agenda in consultation with the President of the Commission; an agreement that the instructions of the Permanent Representatives should give them wider scope for negotiation so that whenever possible agreement may be reached at the level of the Committee of Permanent Representatives. The Council's Rules of Procedure provide an expedited procedure for handling urgent matters by enabling Acts to be adopted by a written vote. The decision to use this procedure must first be agreed by all the Member States, a requirement which is mandatory and not merely directory.[15] The Rules have also been further amended in the context of the implementation of the Single European Act in respect of the arrangements for calling a vote.

---

10 See Torrelli, M, *L'Individu et le droit de la CEE* (1970), p 60; Noel, E and Etienne, H, 'Quelques aspects des rapports et de la collaboration entre le Conseil et la Commission' and Salmon, J J A, op cit, both in *La Décision dans les Communautés Européennes* (1969), at pp 43 and 67 respectively.
11 Council's Rules of Procedure, art 3 (2), OJ 1979, L268/1.
12 See Council's Rules of Procedure, art 9, OJ 1979, L268/2 and Case 131/86: *United Kingdom v EC Council* [1988] ECR 905, [1988] 2 CMLR 364.
13 See *Sixth General Report of the Activities of the Communities* (1973), pp 15, 16.
14 See *Bulletin of the European Communities* (1973), Part 7/8, p 76, (1974), Part 2, pp 103, 104 and Part 6, p 122.
15 See Council's Rules of Procedure, art 6, OJ 1979, L268/2 and Case 68/86: *United Kingdom v EC Council* [1988] ECR 855, [1988] 2 CMLR 543.

The President of the Council, in addition to calling for a vote on his own initiative, must now also do so at the request of either a member of the Council or of the Commission provided that a majority of the Council's members approve.[16] This change is in the spirit of the Single European Act's advocacy of majority voting.

But, as the *Three Wise Men's Report* has shown, the internal problems of the Council which detract from its efficiency and effectiveness as a Community institution remain unsolved. The principal issues are the burden of business and the way in which it is handled.[17] As the *Report* noted, the key to these matters lies in the Presidency of the Council which has failed to provide a coherent pattern of work.[18] While the six-month rotating term of office is accepted as having advantages over any other system, the *Report* recommended that the authority and organizational support of the Council be strengthened and that more matters be delegated to the Commission and devolved on the Committee of Permanent Representatives.[19] The Dooge Committee[20] has also drawn attention to the need for greater cohesion and internal efficiency within the Council. It criticized the increasing bureaucratic influence which the national authorities of the Member States exercise over the Council. In order to overcome this problem it suggested that the authority of COREPER over Council working parties should be strengthened so as to improve the preparation of the Council's decisions and thus enable it to concentrate on major issues.[21] COREPER now meets in two parts made up of the Permanent Representatives and their Deputies respectively and items for consideration are divided between the agendas of each part.[22]

The solution of particularly difficult problems has been achieved as a result of the famous marathon sessions of the Council.[23] The longest of these concerned the making of regulations to implement the agricultural policy; it took place during December 1961/January 1962 and lasted almost three weeks. During the course of these marathons the Council may attempt to reach the unanimity necessary to amend the Commission's proposal. The Commission will suggest its own counter-amendments. Adjournments may be granted in an attempt to enable the Commission to

16 See Council Decision 87/508, OJ 1987, L291/27 and p 241, infra.
17 *Report on European Institutions* (1979), pp 32–34.
18 Ibid, pp 35 et seq.
19 Ibid, pp 45 et seq.
20 Ie, the Ad Hoc Committee for Institutional Affairs.
21 See EC Commission, *An Ever Closer Union* (1985) Annex II, pp 337, 338.
22 See *Guide to the Council of the European Communities*, (1990), pp 39–43.
23 See Alting von Geusau, F A M, 'Les sessions marathons du Conseil des ministres', *Le Décision dans les Communautés Européennes* (1969), pp 99 et seq.

work out a package-deal which may be acceptable to the Council, and so on.

Although most decisions of the Council are reached by the process described above and are based on an initiative of the Commission, in some the Council has sought to exercise a power of initiative of its own. In so doing it has claimed that it is acting in accordance with article 152 of the EEC Treaty which provides that 'the Council may request the Commission to undertake any studies which the Council considers desirable for the attainment of the common objectives and to submit any appropriate proposals'. On the face of it this is an innocuous provision which was probably intended to provide a safeguard in two senses. First, to enable the Council to spur the Commission to action should it appear to be neglecting its duty in any respect and, secondly, to enable the Council to suggest possible lines of enquiry to the Commission. In either case provided the actual terms of any proposal inspired by article 152 emanate from the Commission itself the basic relationship between Commission and Council will be preserved. But when the Council purports to act under article 152 it tends to go far beyond making a general request to the Commission to consider a particular matter, but it has indicated to the Commission the precise terms its proposal should take.[1] This is quite clearly a distortion of the relationship between Commission and Council as established by the Treaties and an abuse of article 152.

In practice the Commission has co-operated with the Council in such cases and has supplied proposals in the terms suggested. It has probably done this for the reason that when the Council has resorted to article 152 it has presented a united front to the Commission and so the matter is cut-and-dried and the Commission has little, if any, room to negotiate.[2]

(E) THE CONSTITUTIONAL CRISIS OF 1965 AND ITS AFTERMATH

In some cases the problems facing the Communities have proved insoluble, even after recourse to a marathon session. Intransigence on the part of one or more of the Member States may provoke a constitutional crisis in the Communities, as in 1963 resulting from the French veto on British membership[3] and again in 1965. The

1 On this use of art 152 see Torrelli, op cit, pp 42, 43, and Louis, J V, *Les Règlements de la Communauté Economique Européenne* (1969), pp 6–8 and notes. Also see Megret, J, *Le Droit de le Communauté Economique Européenne*, Vol 9 (1979), pp 149–151.
2 Clearly if the Council is unanimous it would be able to amend any counter-proposal from the Commission.
3 See *Sixth General Report on the Activities of the EEC* (1963), introduction.

latter crisis has had a significant effect on working relations between the Council and the Commission and on the Council's voting procedure.

The 1965 crisis arose in the following way.[4] After the 1963 crisis, relations between France and the other members remained strained and instead of all members working harmoniously to solve problems in the light of the interests of the Communities each side was only prepared to reach agreement if its own interests were safeguarded. In 1965 the Commission, in an attempt to solve a number of outstanding problems, suggested a package-deal embracing three unconnected items: (i) the completion of the farm price regulations, which was sought by France in particular; (ii) a Commission proposal for the independent financing of the Communities out of their own resources instead of relying on contributions from the Member States; and (iii) the granting of greater budgetary powers to the European Parliament which was being demanded by the Parliament itself with the support of the Netherlands. This package-deal was opposed by France ostensibly on the ground that the Commission had made the details of its proposals known to the European Parliament before the French Government had had an opportunity to consider them.

The other Member States were willing to consider the package deal as a whole, but France insisted that only the farm finance question should be settled. A deadline of 30 June 1965 had been fixed by the Council for the settlement of this issue and when no agreement had been reached by midnight on that date the French Foreign Minister, who happened to be the current President of the Council, refused to over-run the time-limit and, despite protests, brought the meeting to an end. Thereafter for seven months France refused to take part in any meeting of the Council designed to advance the purposes of the Communities whilst continuing to observe existing Community policies and regulations. The Council continued to meet in the absence of the French representative and called upon France to resume her place. The French Government urged the *révision* of the institutional structure of the Communities. Both sides in the dispute maintained their positions and eventually France was induced to attend a special private meeting of the Council held in Luxembourg partly, no doubt, because of the possibility that the five might use their power of decision in the absence of France.

The formula worked out at the Luxembourg meeting and known as the Luxembourg Accords was really little more than an agree-

<hr>

4 See *Ninth General Report on the Activities of the EEC* (1966), Chapter 1.

ment to disagree.[5] On the one hand the five, whilst refusing to permit any restriction on the Commission's powers under the Treaties, accepted a number of relatively minor points concerning Council/Commission relations designed to facilitate their co-operation without compromising their respective competences and powers. It was agreed that before adopting any particularly important proposal the Commission should establish appropriate contacts with the Permanent Representatives without compromising the Commission's right of initiative. And that proposals and any other official acts which the Commission submits to the Council and to Member States should not be made public until the recipients have had formal notice of them and are in possession of the texts.[6] On the question of voting in the Council it was agreed that, where a decision may be reached by the qualified majority vote on a proposal of the Commission, the Council should endeavour to reach such a decision unanimously in all cases where very important interests of one or more of the Member States are involved. France further insisted that where very important interests are involved the discussion should be continued until unanimous agreement is reached; but the Council failed to produce any agreed policy on what should be done in the event of a failure to reach a unanimous agreement.

This crisis brought to the surface the latent conflict between opposed views on the form which economic union should take: the advocates of integration and ultimate political union on the one hand (represented by the five) and the advocates of national sovereignty and looser political links on the other (represented by France). The 1965 crisis and its resolution illustrates the interdependence of the Member States within the Communities. This is an example of what has been called the process of *engrenage*. Literally this term means 'gearing' or 'meshing' but in this usage it refers to the process whereby as soon as a state becomes involved in the machinery of economic integration it is progressively drawn further into the machine so that matters which in the past were within the sole competence of national governments gradually and irrevocably became part of the Community's decision-making process.[7] This is perhaps the beginning of the replacement of traditional international diplomacy by European constitutional law.

In constitutional terms the legal validity of the Luxembourg Accords is highly suspect. They cannot be regarded as an amendment of the EEC Treaty. Article 236 lays down the procedure for

5 *Ninth General Report on the Activities of the EEC* (1966), pp 31–33.
6 This met the French complaint that the European Parliament was informed of Commission proposals before the Council and Member States.
7 Mayne, R, *The Institutions of the European Community* (1968), p 50.

such amendment; that procedure, which was followed in the cases of the Merger Treaty, the Treaty of Luxembourg 1970 and the Single European Act 1986, was not followed in this case, nor have the Accords been ratified in accordance with the constitutional processes of the Member States. Equally, the Accords cannot be regarded as resolving disputed questions of treaty interpretation, for under article 219 of the EEC Treaty the Member States undertake not to submit a dispute concerning the interpretation or application of the Treaty to any method of settlement other than those provided for therein, in other words such disputes must be referred to the Court of Justice of the Communities. Thus, in so far as the Luxembourg Accords require the Council to be unanimous in cases in which the Treaty, in accordance with the terms of article 148, merely requires a majority, they are constitutionally invalid. They are in direct conflict with the obligation imposed by article 4 (1) of the EEC Treaty that 'each institution shall act within the limits of the powers conferred upon it by [the] Treaty'. Although the Accords have not been formally considered by the Court of Justice, the above stated conclusion is supported by its case law on the extent of the authority of the institutions of the Community. The Court has, for example, stressed that the institutional balance established by the Treaties must not be disturbed.[8] Similarly, it has held that attempts by the Council to act in derogation from the express provisions of the Treaties can have no legal effect.[9]

The Commission, for its part, whilst it has never expressly approved of the Accords, has nevertheless acquiesced and cooperated in their implementation. It would be open to the Commission to challenge before the Court acts of the Council taken under the terms of the Accords but it has not done so.[10] This is no doubt largely due to the acceptance of the view that in the light of the attitudes of the Governments of some of the Member States further achievement of the aims of the EEC is only possible within the terms laid down by the Accords. Treaty amendment is also impracticable because of the lack of unanimity in the Council on this issue.

Although the Accords have not affected the legal relations and powers of the Commission and Council, in practice they have had a limiting effect on the life of the Communities. This has been

---

8 See Cases 25/70: *Einfuhr-und Vorratsstelle für Getreide und Füttermittel v Köster* [1970] ECR 1161 and Opinion 1/78: *International Agreement on Natural Rubber* [1979] ECR 2871.
9 See Case 59/75: *Pubblico Ministero v Manghera* [1976] ECR 91, [1976] 1 CMLR 557 and Case 43/75: *Defrenne v SABENA* [1976] ECR 455, [1976] 1 CMLR 98.
10 Under the terms of EEC Treaty, art 173.

expressed by the Commission in no uncertain terms.[11] In 1969 the Commission expressed its concern and referred to the efficacy of the Council's decision-making methods as being a major problem in the institutional life of the Community largely as a result of the application of the unanimity rule in cases where the Treaties do not require it[12]. This has had the result of slowing down and sometimes completely blocking the progress of integration.

The Commission has frequently stressed that its own right of initiative, independence and authority are of absolutely basic importance for the efficient functioning of the Community. The conviction was expressed that 'it is only by returning to respect for both the letter and the spirit of the institutional arrangements laid down in the Treaty, by ensuring that they operate efficiently and by strengthening them in the light of developments and the requirements of Community life, that the Community will be able to accept in security the risks involved in enlargement'.[13] The Commission has drawn attention in particular to the dangers of insisting on unanimity in the Council, with the consequent power of veto, in an enlarged Community. It has urged that these dangers should be obviated by the acceptance and implementation of two principles: (i) that decisions by majority vote should again be the normal practice of the Council except where the Treaties provide otherwise; and (ii) that where unanimity in the Council is required it should only apply to outline policy decisions and majority voting should then be the rule in connection with the decisions necessary to implement such policies.[14] These principles received a measure of recognition by the Council in 1982. The Commission had produced a proposal for fixing farm prices which was acceptable to nine of the ten Member States. The United Kingdom opposed it for reasons connected with the budgetary problem and invoked the Luxembourg Accords. But the Belgian President of the Council concluded, without a vote, that the conditions laid down in the Treaty for taking a decision had been reached and the Council proceeded to adopt the proposal by qualified majority.[15] This was

---

11 Cf *Second General Report on the Activities of the European Communities* (1969), pp 14 et seq. Some obstacles have since been overcome as a result of The Hague Conference of December, 1969; see *Fourth General Report on the Activities of the European Communities* (1971), pp x et seq.
12 See *Bulletin of the European Communities* (1969), No 9/10, Supplement, pp 33, 34.
13 See *Bulletin of the European Communities*, Vol 2 (1969), No 9/10, Supplement, p 34. Similar recommendations are contained in the *Vedel Report*, Chapters 3 and 7.
14 Also see *Bulletin of the European Communities* (1974) Part 1, p 5 and *Eighth General Report on the Activities of the European Communities* (1975), p 9.
15 See *Bulletin of the European Communities* (1982) Part 5, pp 7, 8.

an important event for two reasons: it was the first time that farm prices had not been fixed by unanimous vote,[16] and it showed that the Council acknowledged that the vital interests at stake were those of the Community itself and the credibility of its decision-making process.

In 1974 the Heads of Government of the Member States declared publicly that 'it is necessary to renounce the practice which consists of making agreements on all questions conditional on the unanimous consent of the Member States'.[17] There is, indeed, evidence that that was more than a mere declaration of intent. It is now standard practice for the *tour de table* procedure[18] to be followed and majority voting is being used increasingly in Council decision-making.[19] Member States have clearly become more willing to abstain rather than to insist on exercising a power of veto.[20] They have also indicated their increased willingness to act by majority through the provisions of the Single European Act aimed at completing the Community's internal market by 1992 which relax the Treaty's requirement for unanimity in favour of a qualified majority.[21] Indeed, this has resulted in a considerable and continuing improvement in the Council's decision-making procedure. The Commission has reported that the now fully accepted possibility of adopting acts by a qualified majority has introduced an element of flexibility on the part of Member States as they strive for consensus. But, this welcome new dynamism has not yet extended to those areas of decision-making in which unanimity is still required.[1] The incident involving farm prices illustrates that it has been the practice for the question of a vote to be left to the President of the Council. But, as we have seen, the Council's rules for calling a vote have recently been amended so as also to enable a vote to be called by a member of the Council or of the Commission.[2] The amendment also requires the issues on which votes are to be taken to be specified on the agenda which must be

---

16 See *Thirtieth Review of the Council's Work* (1984), p 175.
17 See *Eighth General Report on the Activities of the European Communities* (1975), p 298.
18 Council members vote in alphabetical order of the Member States starting with the member who, in that order, follows the member holding the Presidency. See Council's Rules of Procedure, art 5 (1), OJ 1979, L268/2.
19 See *Eleventh General Report on the Activities of the European Communities*, (1978), p 23.
20 See Noel, E, *Working Together: The Institutions of the European Community* (1988), p 27.
21 See Single European Act, arts 13–19.
1 See *Twenty-second and Twenty-third General Reports on the Activities of the European Communities* (1989) and (1990), at pp 32 and 30–31 respectively.
2 See Council Decision 87/508, OJ 1987, L291/27.

sent to members 15 days before the meeting. These changes should also facilitate recourse to majority voting and not simply at the discretion of the President-in-Office. But while progress has been made, the Accords have not yet been abandoned completely. *The Three Wise Men's Report* regarded an insistence on unanimity as available to a Member State when, in its judgment, its very important interests are at stake.[3] As far as the United Kingdom is concerned, the Foreign Secretary has declared that as a last resort the Luxembourg Accords remain in place untouched and unaffected by the Single European Act.[4]

(F) THE EUROPEAN COUNCIL AND THE POLITICAL FUTURE OF THE COMMUNITY

It is clear that whilst the immediate aims of the Communities are economic, their long-term aims are political. The preamble to the EEC Treaty expresses the determination 'to lay the foundations of an ever closer union among the peoples of Europe' and article 2 of the Treaty itself refers to the establishment of closer relations between the Member States. During recent years the questions of political co-operation and political union of the Member States have been the subject of active consideration.

When, in 1969, it was announced that a Summit Conference of the Heads of State or Government was to be held at The Hague in December both the European Parliament and the Commission took the opportunity of expressing the hope that the Conference would take steps to ensure that progress will be made towards political union.[5] In their Final Communique the Heads of State or Government reaffirmed their belief in the political objectives of the Community and took the modest step of instructing their Foreign Ministers to study and make proposals for the achievement of progress in the matter of political unification in the context of an enlarged Community.[6] The Foreign Ministers requested a Committee made up of senior officials of their Ministries and presided over by M Davignon, Director of Political Affairs in the Belgian Foreign Ministry, to prepare a draft report on this matter. The

3 *Report on European Institutions* (1979), p 51.
4 See *House of Commons Debates*, 6th series, 1985–86, Vol 96, col 320. Even the European Parliament's Draft Treaty for a European Union proposed the retention of a national right of veto for a transitional period of ten years; see EC Commission, *An Ever Closer Union* (1985) Annex I, p 312, art 23 (3) of the Draft Treaty.
5 See the European Parliament's Resolution and the Commission's Memorandum reproduced in an annex to the *Third General Report on the Activities of the European Communities* (1970), at pp 482 and 484 respectively.
6 Reproduced ibid, see paras 4 and 15, at pp 487 and 489 respectively.

resulting document, the Davignon Report, was approved by the Foreign Ministers on 20 July 1970.[7]

In the Davignon Report the desire is expressed to make progress towards political unification through co-operation on foreign policy. The object of this co-operation is to achieve a better mutual understanding on major problems of international policy and to strengthen the sense of common purpose by harmonising ideas, concerting attitudes and taking common action whenever this is possible and desirable.[8] To those ends it was proposed that the Foreign Ministers of the Member States should meet regularly at least at six-monthly intervals.[9] Preparations for these meetings should be undertaken by a Political Committee made up of the Heads of the Political Departments of the respective Foreign Ministries, the Committee itself should meet at least four times a year and may set up working groups responsible for specific tasks.[10] The Report also proposed that if the circumstances are sufficiently grave or the subject matter sufficiently important a ministerial meeting may be replaced by a conference of Heads of State or Government.[11] These proposals were implemented and a regular pattern of ministerial meetings in May and November of each year was established.[12] At these meetings such matters as East–West relations, the European security conference and the Middle East were discussed.

At the Paris Summit Meeting in October 1972, in the context of their declared aim to achieve European Union by 1980, the Heads of State or Government agreed to intensify the level of political consultation and asked their Foreign Ministers to prepare a further report on methods to improve political co-operation.[13] That report was completed in July 1973 and subsequently approved by the Heads of State or Government.[14] As a result the Foreign Ministers of the Member States have met regularly at least four times a year.

7 The Report is reproduced in the *Bulletin of the European Communities*, Vol 3 (1970), No 11, at pp 9 et seq. Also see the *Report of the Political Affairs Committee on the Political Future of the European Community* (European Parliament Working Document 118/70).
8 *Davignon Report*, Part Two, sections I and IV.
9 Ibid, section II.
10 Ibid 3 sections II (3) and III. In practice the Political Committee meets much more frequently; see Annex to the Second Report on European political co-operation, *Seventh General Report on the Activities of the European Communities* (1974) at p 509.
11 Ibid, section II (1) (*b*).
12 Meetings were held in May and November commencing in November 1970.
13 See the Declaration issued at the end of the Summit Meeting, paras 14 and 15, *Sixth General Report of the Activities of the European Communities* (1973) pp 15, 16.
14 The Report is printed in *Seventh General Report of the Activities of the European Communities* (1974) at p 502.

The report also confirmed the role of the Political Committee and established the so-called 'Group of Correspondents' to assist it in its work.[15] The machinery for political consultation between the Member States of the Community was given a further dimension by a decision of the Heads of Government at their meeting in Paris in December 1974 to meet regularly three times a year accompanied by their Foreign Ministers.[16] These institutionalized summit meetings are known as meetings of the European Council and quickly became a regular feature of Community life.

The European Council has been hailed as an example of 'the Community's capacity for self-renewal in difficult circumstances'.[17] By the early 1970s a new political impetus was needed as the Community moved from the shelter of the Treaties into largely uncharted waters. It is the European Council's role to supply that impetus. As the *Three Wise Men's Report* has observed,[18] the European Council (i) provides a forum for free and informal exchange of views between the Heads of Government; (ii) it can range over matters of Treaty competence, of political co-operation and of common concern to the Member States; and (iii) it can generate an impetus for the progressive development of the Community.

By the creation of machinery for political consultation distinct from yet parallel to the institutions of the Communities the Governments of the Member States distinguished between matters of international politics on the inter-governmental level on the one hand and the activities of the Communities based on legal obligations contained in the Treaties on the other.[19] Matters of mutual political concern to the Member States which did not directly relate to the Treaties were discussed by the Foreign Ministers outside the Community structure and assisted by the Political Committee; matters which did directly relate to the Treaties were discussed within the Council of the Communities assisted by the Committee of Permanent Representatives. By the same token the European Council was a hybrid which if discussing non-Community matters was no more than a Summit Conference and if discussing Community matters could be regarded as a manifestation of the Council of the Communities.[20] The type of matter

15 See Part II of the Report, ibid at p 504.
16 See the Communiqué issued at the end of the Meeting, para 3, *Eighth General Report on the Activities of the European Communities* (1975) at p 297.
17 *Report on European Institutions* (1979), p 15.
18 Ibid, pp 16, 17.
19 See Second Report on European Political Co-operation, *Seventh General Report on the Activities of the European Communities* (1974) at p 507.
20 There is no reason why the Council should not be made up of Heads of

discussed by the European Council in the field of political co-operation is illustrated by its activities in April 1990.[1] During that month the following items featured on the agenda: the reunification of Germany and relations with Central and Eastern Europe; the relations between Lithuania and the USSR; hostilities in Angola; tension between India and Pakistan; a dispute between Senegal and Mauritania; the threatened use of weapons of mass destruction in the Middle East; the assassination of the President of Colombia; and the civil war in Liberia.

Through these important developments the Community may be seen to have been striving for an external identity in a general political sense over and above its character as a trading bloc. That objective has recently been given a new status and a fresh impetus by the Single European Act. First, the European Council loses its hybrid status and becomes a treaty-based Community institution which brings together the Heads of State or Government and the President of the Commission.[2] It is also provided that the European Council should in future meet at least twice a year.[3] This reduction in the frequency of meetings reflects the Dooge Committee's concern to prevent the European Council from becoming 'simply another body dealing with the day-to-day business of the Community' but rather that it 'should play a strategic role and give direction and political impetus [to] the Community'.[4] Second, on the foundation of existing undertakings and practices,[5] European co-operation in the sphere of foreign policy is also given treaty status and the authority which flows from it. It is now a formal legal obligation of the members of the Community 'to endeavour jointly to formulate and implement a European foreign policy'.[6] Through a process of mutual information and consultation the Member States undertake to maximize the impact of their combined influence on foreign affairs through co-ordination, convergence, joint action and the development of common principles and objectives.[7] It is expressly provided that there must be consistency between the Community's external policies and the poli-

---

Government; see Merger Treaty, art 11. For recent confirmation of this analysis of the European Council as a hybrid see *Report on European Institutions* (1979), pp 17, 18.

1 See *Bulletin of the European Communities* (1990) No 4, points 1.1–1.11 and 1.3.1–1.3.9.
2 Single European Act, art 2.
3 Ibid.
4 See EC Commission, *An Ever Closer Union* (1985) Annex II, p 337.
5 Single European Act, art 1, para 3.
6 Ibid, art 30 (1).
7 Ibid, art 30 (2) and (3) (c).

cies agreed in the field of foreign affairs.[8] Particular emphasis is placed on closer co-operation on the political, economic, technological and industrial aspects of European security.[9] Common positions in relation to international institutions and at international conferences is another aim.[10] Further provisions deal with the institutional arrangements for co-operation in the sphere of foreign policy. The foreign ministers of the Member States are given a new mandate to meet at least four times a year within the framework of European political co-operation with the added authority to discuss foreign policy matters also at the meetings of the Council.[11] Both the Commission and the European Parliament are fully and closely associated with this new dimension of Community activity and the practice of seeking the views of the latter and of keeping it regularly informed on current foreign policy issues are expressly continued.[12] The Presidency for the purposes of European political co-operation will rotate with the Presidency of the Council,[13] assisted by the existing Political Committee[14] and European Correspondents Group.[15] Meetings of either the Political Committee or at ministerial level may be convened within forty-eight hours at the request of at least three Member States.[16] A European Political Co-operation Secretariat is also established in Brussels to assist in preparing and implementing these activities.[17]

These new treaty provisions mark a major advance in the development of the Community as a political force. By removing the earlier distinction between Community matters proper and matters of political co-operation and making the latter legitimate matters of Community concern the Community has signalled its intention to become a full participant in foreign affairs. The opportunity has now been provided to develop a coherent foreign policy consistent with the overall policy objectives of the Community. An opportunity to review progress is provided five years after the entry into force of the Single European Act.[18]

8 Ibid, art 30 (5) which gives the Presidency and the Commission special responsibilities in this respect.
9 Ibid, art 30 (6) without derogation from either the Western European Union or the Atlantic Alliance.
10 Ibid, art 30 (7); as are relations with third countries, regional groupings and international organizations, ibid, art 30 (8) and (9).
11 Ibid, art 30 (3) (a).
12 Ibid, art 30 (3) (b) and (4).
13 Ibid, art 30 (10) (a) and (b).
14 Ibid, art 30 (10) (c) and (f).
15 Ibid, art 30 (10) (e).
16 Ibid, art 30 (10) (d).
17 Ibid, art 30 (10) (g) and (11).
18 Ibid, art 30 (12).

Chapter 7

The European Parliament

(A) COMPOSITION AND ORGANIZATION

Article 137 of the EEC Treaty provides that the European Parliament 'shall consist of representatives of the peoples of the States brought together in the Community'. The European Parliament, which since 1958 has served the three Communities in common,[1] is designed to introduce a democratic element into the workings of the Communities.[2] Through the intermediary of the European Parliament the citizens of the Member States are called upon to co-operate in the functioning of the Communities.[3] At present the European Parliament has 518 members made up in the following way: France, Germany, Italy and the United Kingdom have 81 members each; Spain has 60 members; the Netherlands has 25 members; Belgium, Greece and Portugal have 24 members each; Denmark has 16 members; Ireland has 15 members; and Luxembourg has 6 members.[4]

In very general terms the allocation of the numbers of seats to particular Member States reflects the size of their population. A strictly mathematical proportional representation is not aimed at and would not indeed be practicable because of the vast difference between the population of the smallest member Luxembourg with 350,000 inhabitants and France with some 50 millions. A strictly mathematical exercise would give a derisory number of delegates to the small states and an overwhelmingly large number to the big states.[5] The figures actually employed represent a compromise so as on the one hand to recognize the relative size of population of the Member States, but on the other to ensure that even the smallest member is given a number large enough to enable it to have a reasonably representative delegation. And, at the same time, not to produce an overlarge unwieldy body.

1 Common Institutions Convention 1957, section 1.
2 See Case 138/79: *SA Roquette Frères v EC Council* [1980] ECR 3333 at 3360.
3 See Case 26/62: *Van Gend en Loos v Nederlandse Administratie der Belastingen* [1963] ECR 1 at 12.
4 Decision and Act of the Council concerning Direct Elections, art 2, OJ 1976, L278, as amended by Second Act of Accession, 1979, art 10.
5 On the basis of the figures quoted if Luxembourg had five delegates France would be entitled to some 700.

From the commencement of the European Community in 1952 up to June 1979 the members of the European Parliament were not directly elected. During that period its members were nominated by the national parliaments of the Member States from among their own members.[6] Under the terms of article 138(3) of the EEC Treaty the European Parliament is directed to 'draw up proposals for elections by direct universal suffrage in accordance with a uniform procedure in all Member States'. It is then for the Council, acting unanimously, to lay down the appropriate provisions for adoption by the Member States in accordance with their respective constitutional requirements.[7]

In 1960 the European Parliament acting in pursuance of the mandate given it by the Treaties, submitted detailed proposals for election by direct universal suffrage for the consideration of the Council.[8] The Council studiously ignored the proposals.[9] It was not until after the first enlargement that the governments of the Member States generally made a positive response to the issue of direct elections. During the 1960s (with the exception of the Netherlands) the original Member States, from their entrenched position in the Council, were not favourably disposed towards the matter. This was largely because they were opposed to the possibility of giving more power to the European Parliament, the claims for which would be likely to be strengthened as a consequence of direct elections. However, this hostility gradually disappeared. The Heads of Government of the Member States, at their meeting in Paris in December 1974, not only acknowledged the Treaty objective of direct elections but also urged that it should be achieved as soon as possible.[10]

In January 1975 the European Parliament submitted a new set of proposals for direct elections to the Council.[11] After a prolonged period of consideration the governments of the Member States in September 1976 finally agreed on the Decision and Act concerning

---

6 See ECSC Treaty, art 21; EEC Treaty, art 138 (1) and (2); Euratom Treaty, art 108 (1) and (2); First Act of Accession 1972, art 139 (1).

7 Euratom Treaty, art 108 (3) is to the same effect.

8 For the text of the 1960 proposals see *The Case for Elections to the European Parliament by Direct Universal Suffrage* (European Parliament, 1969), pp 238 et seq.

9 In March 1969 the European Parliament adopted a resolution of protest, ibid, p 277.

10 See *Eighth General Report on the Activities of the European Communities* (1975), p 299. Also see the Green Paper: *Direct Elections to the European Assembly*, Cmnd 6399 (1976), para 1.

11 For the text of these proposals see *Bulletin of the European Communities* (1975), Part I, p 95.

Direct Elections[12] in accordance with which the first direct elections
were held in June 1979. Adjustments have been made to that
instrument in order to accommodate the accession of Greece, Spain
and Portugal.[13]

The Decision and Act concerning Direct Elections not only
specifies the number of representatives to be elected in each
Member State, it also lays down basic rules concerning candidature
and the conduct of the elections. Members of the European Parliament are elected for a term of five years.[14] In principle, anyone
may stand for election. But that principle is subject to a provision
that the holding of certain offices is incompatible with membership
of the European Parliament. Those offices include membership of
the government of a Member State, of the Commission and of
the Court of Justice and employment by an institution of the
Community.[15] Such offices are incompatible in the sense that they
would tend to prejudice either the terms on which they are held or
the individual and non-mandated role of the Members of the
European Parliament.[16] Under the superseded rules governing the
composition of the European Parliament,[17] members had to be
members of their national parliament. Under the rules governing
direct elections, such a dual mandate is simply permissive.[18]

Members of the European Parliament enjoy certain privileges
and immunities.[19] These include freedom of movement when trav-
elling to and from meetings of the Parliament[20] and freedom from
legal process in respect of the opinions expressed or votes cast in
the performance of their duties.[1] During sessions of the European
Parliament they are also entitled to enjoy in their own state the
privileges and immunities accorded to the members of parliament
of that state, and in other Member States immunity from detention
and from legal proceedings.[2]

It has not yet proved possible for the governments of the Member
States to agree on a uniform electoral procedure. The first three
elections in 1979, 1984 and 1989 were therefore held in accordance

12 OJ 1976, L278.
13 Second Act of Accession 1979, arts 10 and 23; Third Act of Accession 1985,
   arts 10 and 28.
14 Decision and Act, art 1.
15 Ibid, art 6 (1).
16 Ibid, art 4 (1).
17 Eg, EEC Treaty, art 138 (1).
18 Decision and Act, art 5.
19 Ibid, art 4 (2).
20 Protocol on Privileges and Immunities annexed to the Merger Treaty 1965,
   art 8.
1 Ibid, art 9.
2 Ibid, art 10.

with the national electoral procedures in each Member State.[3] The European Parliament has been charged with the task of drawing up proposals for a uniform procedure.[4] Any casual vacancies are filled in accordance with procedures to be laid down by each Member State.[5]

In the United Kingdom, effect is given to the Decision and Act concerning Direct Elections by the European Parliamentary Elections Act 1978.[6] In addition to providing that United Kingdom representatives to the European Parliament shall be elected,[7] the Act also establishes constituencies, allocates seats and, pending a decision on a uniform procedure, specifies the methods of voting. For the purpose of direct elections to the European Parliament, the United Kingdom is divided into 79 constituencies: 66 in England; 8 in Scotland; 4 in Wales; and 1 in Northern Ireland.[8] The 81 United Kingdom representatives are allocated so that the English, Scots and Welsh constituencies each return one member and the Northern Irish constituency returns three members.[9] In England, Scotland and Wales, the simple majority system of voting is to be used, and in Northern Ireland the single transferable vote system.[10] By virtue of authority conferred by the Decision and Act concerning Direct Elections,[11] the Act generally disqualifies from membership of the European Parliament persons who are disqualified from membership of the British House of Commons.[12] But that disqualification is subject to an exception in the case of peers, ordained clergy and ministers of religion. Provision is also made for the holding of by-elections.[13] As a result of the 1989 election the distribution of United Kingdom representatives in terms of national political affiliation was as follows: Labour Party 45; Conservative Party 32; Scottish National Party, Democratic Unionist

---

3 Decision and Act, art 7 (2).
4 Ibid, art 7 (1). A major obstacle is the commitment of both major British political parties to the simple majority system, whereas in the other Member States forms of proportional representation are favoured. See *Seventeenth General Report on the Activities of the European Communities* (1984), pp 23, 24 and *Bulletin of the European Communities* (1984) Part 6, p 13.
5 Decision and Act, art 12.
6 1978, c10; originally cited as the European Assembly Elections Act but renamed by the European Communities (Amendment) Act 1986, s 3 (2) as a consequence of the adoption of 'European Parliament' as the official title of this institution under the terms of the Single European Act, art 3 (1).
7 Section 1.
8 Sch 1, para 1, and Sch 2.
9 Section 2.
10 Section 3 and Sch 1, para 2.
11 Art 6 (2).
12 Sch 1, para 5.
13 Sch 1, para 3.

ow

Party, Social Democratic and Labour Party, and Official Unionist Party 1 each.[14]

Although, as we shall shortly see, the European Parliament is more of a deliberative and consultative body than a parliament in the true sense, it has nevertheless parliamentary pretensions. In the first place although up to 1987 the Treaties still referred to it as the Assembly, since 1962 it has formally adopted the title European Parliament[15] and it is invariably referred to by this name in Community circles and Community documents. European Parliament became its official title by virtue of article 3(1) of the Single European Act. Secondly, it has organized itself as if it were a legislative and not a consultative body. The members are not seated in national groups but sit in multi-national political groups. The Rules of Procedure of the European Parliament provide a procedure for the recognition of political groups. In particular minimum numbers are laid down: 23 if the members come from one Member State; 18 if they come from two Member States; 12 if they come from three or more Member States.[16] Thus in the European Parliament we find the nucleus of European political parties made up of individuals of differing nationality linked by common political beliefs. At present there are ten political groups in the European Parliament: the Socialists with 180; the European People's Party (Christian Democrats) with 121; the Liberals, Democrats and Reformists with 49; the European Democrats (Conservatives) with 34; the Greens with 30; the European Unitarian Left with 28; the European Democratic Alliance with 20; the European Right with 17; Left Unity with 14; and the Rainbows with 13. In addition there are ten non-attached members. In this Parliament the Greens appear as a group for the first time and the former Communists and Allies Group has split to form the European Unitarian Left and the Left Unity Groups. No fewer than 93 national political parties are represented within the Parliament. Of the United Kingdom representatives, the Labour and Social Democratic and Labour members have joined the Socialist Group, the Conservatives have formed their own group (European Democrats) which includes two Danish Conservatives, the Official Unionist has joined the European People's Party, the Scottish Nationalist has joined the Rainbows, and the Democratic Unionist remains non-attached.[17]

The European Parliament is organized in 18 standing committees

14 *European Parliament – EP News*, 25–28 July 1989, p 2.
15 See Resolution of 30 March 1962, JO 1962, 1045.
16 Rule 26; see European Parliament, *Rules of Procedure* (4th edn, 1987), p 25.
17 This information is taken from Vacher's *European Companion*, No 73, pp 74–76, 82–84.

each specializing in an aspect of the Communities' activities, eg Economic and Monetary Affairs, Budgets, External Economic Relations, Legal Affairs, etc.[18] These committees were originally set up to draft reports upon the basis of which the general debate in a plenary session of the European Parliament could take place. This is a procedure based on continental parliamentary practice whereby a debate before the whole house is invariably preceded by an examination of the subject of the debate by a committee of the house. The debate then proceeds on the basis of that committee's report.[19] In practice the committees of the European Parliament have come to play an independent Community role largely because an international body like the European Parliament cannot meet as frequently as a national parliament. Therefore, the committees have not only prepared reports for debates in the European Parliament, but have also maintained contact with the Commission and Council in the interim between parliamentary sessions. Thus the committees act as a safeguard for the continuity and effectiveness of parliamentary control. As standing committees they can meet at any time at the request of their chairman or the President of the European Parliament[20] and so by this means the European Parliament is kept abreast of developments within the Communities as they occur and not after the event.

One final point concerning the organization of the European Parliament, in which it differs from a national parliament, is that it is not of course divided into government and opposition parties. The European Parliament is not organized or run by any particular political group represented within it. Its officers and the composition of its committees reflect both political and national representation.[1]

Practical questions concerning the organization of the European Parliament are in the hands of the Bureau of Parliament which is elected for a term of two and a half years and consists of the President and fourteen Vice-Presidents advised by five Quaestors.[2] The latter have particular responsibility for administrative and financial matters directly concerning members.[3] The details of sessions of the European Parliament and its agenda are worked out by the so-called Enlarged Bureau which consists of the Bureau and the chairmen of the political groups.[4] In these administrative and

---

18 See *Rules of Procedure*, Chapter XII and Annex VI.
19 See Rule 36.
20 See Rule 124.
 1 Rules 12 and 110.
 2 See Rules 21 and 22.
 3 Rule 20.
 4 Rules 23 and 24.

organizational chores the European Parliament is assisted by a Secretary-General and a Secretariat of some 3,000 persons[5] divided into seven Directorates-General. The rôle of the Secretary-General is similar to that of the Clerk of the British House of Commons.[6]

The European Parliament holds a number of part sessions each year. During 1986 it held 11 part sessions, passed 605 resolutions and produced 2,199 working documents.[7] It may also meet in extraordinary session at the request of a majority of its members or of the Council or Commission.[8] Between sessions each Committee will meet at least once. Commissioners and members of the Council may make statements to the Parliament and may also be invited to take part in meetings of its committees.[9] The committees follow the working of the Council and Commission closely and they are able to keep the European Parliament as a whole well informed of activities and developments within the Communities.

(B) THE FUNCTIONS AND POWERS OF THE EUROPEAN PARLIAMENT AND ITS RELATIONS WITH THE COMMISSION AND THE COUNCIL

As has already been mentioned, while the European Parliament participates in law-making it is in no sense a legislative body; its functions are of a supervisory and advisory nature. As a supervisory body it possesses a power of censure over the Commission. If a motion of censure is passed by a two-thirds majority of the votes cast, which also represents a majority of the total membership of the European Parliament, the entire Commission must resign and be replaced.[10] Although motions of censure have occasionally been tabled, none has ever been carried.[11] On the face of it this is a far-reaching power; a power which is found in no other international organization. The power of censure does have its limitations, however. In the first place the European Parliament has no direct voice in the nomination of Commissioners to replace a censured Commission. But, more important than that, the power of censure over the Commission is somewhat inappropriate since in general

---

5 See *Twentieth General Report on the Activities of the European Communities* (1987), p 39.
6 Rules 107 (4) and 133.
7 See *Twentieth General Report on the Activities of the European Communities* (1987), pp 38, 39.
8 See EEC Treaty, art 139 and Rule 9 (5).
9 See Rules 56 and 124.
10 EEC Treaty, art 144 and Rule 30.
11 For an analysis of the use of the motion of censure see Herman, V and Lodge, J, *The European Parliament and the European Community* (1978), pp 48 et seq. Also see European Parliament *Forging Ahead: European Parliament 1952–1988* (3rd edn, 1989), pp 141–142.

both the European Parliament and the Commission share a common European attitude to Community matters and tend to be both ranged against the Council as the exponent of national interests. That is not to say of course that the views of the European Parliament and the Commission are naturally identical. They can and do differ, particularly in terms of tactics: the Commission may be prepared to make concessions in the face of the views of the Council in an attempt to reach a workable compromise and the European Parliament may be inclined to take a harder line. But in any event the mere existence of the power of censure does enhance the authority and influence of the European Parliament in that it is a force to be reckoned with and not to be ignored.[12]

Secondly, the European Parliament has the means of exercising a degree of supervision over the day-to-day activities of the Communities through its power to ask questions.[13] This is a procedure reminiscent of the British member of parliament's right to question ministers. Written questions can be put to the Commission and to the Council and ample use is made of this procedure. Written questions and the replies to them are published in the Communities' *Official Journal*. Oral questions may also be put to Council or Commission during a plenary session of the European Parliament and these may be followed by debate. In addition, at each part-session of the European Parliament a period is set aside for Question Time during which oral questions, may be put. This provides an opportunity for short, pointed questions to be put followed by supplementary questions thus enabling a dialogue to take place between the members of the Parliament and the members of the Commission and the Council. During 1989 the Commission replied to 1,711 written questions, the Council to 144 and the Foreign Ministers in the context of political co-operation to 114; oral questions numbered 581, 172 and 130 respectively.[14]

This right to ask questions enables an eye to be kept on developments in Community policy both generally and in relation to particular topics, including matters of political co-operation discussed by the Foreign Ministers of the Member States.[15] Thus the European Parliament is able to comment on issues more or less as they arise, rather than becoming involved in the more protracted

12 Cf the *Vedel Report*, Chapter 3, section II (4); see *Bulletin of the European Communities*, Vol 5 (1972), Supplement to No 4.
13 Eg EEC Treaty, art 140. Also see Rules of Procedure, Chapter VI, section 2 and Annex II.
14 *Twenty-third General Report on the Activities of the European Communities* (1990), p 38.
15 *Fourteenth General Report on the Activities of the European Communities* (1981) at p 28.

procedure of the Parliament's Committees investigating a certain matter and then reporting back. A further example of the supervisory powers of the European Parliament lies in the debates which are held on the Commission's Annual Report on Activities in the Communities. This enables the European Parliament to discuss and comment upon the whole field of Community activity.[16] It has also become the practice for the Commission to present an Annual Programme to the European Parliament. After such a Programme has been the subject of a debate, the Commission and the Parliament draw up an agreed legislative programme and timetable for the year in question.[17] Such agreements are designed both to stress inter-institutional co-operation and to promote efficient and speedy discussion of Community legislation. Initial experience of this procedure has been positive with the timetable being observed in 75% of cases.[18]

As an advisory body the most important of the European Parliament's powers lie in its right to be consulted over major policy proposals in the EEC and Euratom.[19] This process of consultation may take place at either or both of two stages in the decision-making process: the Council may consult the European Parliament after it has received a proposal from the Commission; the Commission itself may consult the European Parliament when it is in the process of drafting its proposals. The Commission has frequently sent its proposals to the European Parliament at the same time as it has sent them to the Council. It will be recalled that one of the contributing factors to the 1965 crisis was the French accusation that the Commission had made its views known to the European Parliament before it communicated them to the governments of the Member States. At the Luxembourg meeting in 1966 it was therefore agreed that proposals and other official acts which the Commission submits to the Council and to the Member States are not to be made public until the recipients have had formal notice of them and are in possession of the texts.

In this consultative role the European Parliament acts largely through its committees. A given proposal will be submitted to the appropriate committee which will produce a report containing a draft opinion. That draft will then be debated by the full Parliament and the final agreed version will be communicated to the Council or Commission as the case may be. This right of consultation is

16 EEC Treaty, art 143 and rule 29.
17 See rule 29 (4).
18 See European Parliament *The Work of the European Parliament: July 1988– June 1989* (1989), p 13.
19 EEC Treaty, arts 43, 54, 56, 87, Euratom Treaty, arts 31, 76, 85, 90 and rule 36.

not a power of decision: the Council is not in any way bound by nor is the Commission obliged to pay heed to, a Parliamentary opinion. But, as the European Court has pointed out, where the Treaties require the Council to consult the European Parliament before an act is adopted, the opinion of the European Parliament must be sought and obtained before an act can be lawfully adopted. If, in such a case, the Council purports to adopt an act without consultation, such an omission would supply grounds for seeking the annulment of the act because an essential procedural requirement had been infringed.[20]

In practice the influence of the European Parliament has tended to vary depending on the subject matter. The explanation of these variations appears to be that the European Parliament's influence is greater where matters can be decided relatively quickly and its influence decreases as negotiations between Council and Commission become more prolonged. In the context of a marathon session where there is a sharp difference of view between Council and Commission, the object of the marathon is to find a solution which both sides can accept and in such a context it is more likely that the European Parliament's opinion will be disregarded. In studies published in 1983 and 1988 the European Parliament reviewed the effectiveness of its activities on the policies of the Community.[21] Both studies report that the Commission has generally shown its readiness to respond to parliamentary opinions at all stages of the legislative process. With regard to the Council, it was found to be difficult to gauge the impact of Parliament because it is often unclear what influences (and from what sources) have been brought to bear during the legislative procedures in the Council. But, the increased use of qualified majority voting under the new co-operation procedure within the framework of the Single European Act[1] has clearly given Parliament more leverage over the Council. On average the Council is accepting 50% of parliamentary amendments at the first reading stage and 25% at the second reading stage of the co-operation procedure. Given that the Parliament attaches more significance to the first reading stage, these percentages are seen as encouraging[2]. In those cases in which it does influence the final outcome, the European Parliament can

20 See Case 138/79: *SA Roquette Frères v EC Council* [1980] ECR 3333. Also see Ch 9 (II) (B), infra.
21 *The Impact of the European Parliament on Community Policies* (Research and Documentation Papers, Political Series No 5, 1983 and Action Taken Series No 3, 1988).
 1 See Ch 6 (B), supra.
 2 See European Parliament *The Work of the European Parliament: July 1988– June 1989* (1989) p 12.

perhaps legitimately claim to be a co-legislator. The positive working relationship between Commission and Parliament, which can place parliamentary amendments in a strong position before the Council, is seen as the principal factor contributing to this development.[3]

In the interests of promoting co-operation between the Council and the European Parliament in matters of decision-making, a conciliation procedure has been established. In 1975 in a Joint Declaration,[4] the Parliament, the Council and the Commission agreed on a procedure which may be invoked in certain cases in which the Council intends to depart from the opinion of the European Parliament. The procedure applies to Community acts of general application which have appreciable financial implications. The Council, together with representative parliamentarians,[5] acts as a Conciliation Committee. The Commission also participates in this process. The aim is to seek to reach agreement, normally within a three-month period. While, in the Council's view, the conciliation procedure has 'brought a new dimension to the role of the Parliament in the Community legislative process',[6] in practice it is a device of limited scope which cannot resolve deeply seated differences.[7] Although some successes in the use of the procedure can be reported,[8] a proposal to broaden its scope to include acts without financial implications has met with some opposition in the Council.[9] More recently, the European Parliament has both renewed its call for this procedure to be extended to all major Community legislation and suggested that it be combined with the new co-operation procedure with the aim of achieving compromise over parliamentary amendments before the Council adopts its common position.[10] While awaiting the Council's response to this initiative, the Parliament has itself decided to make increased use of the conciliation procedure.[11]

---

3 Ibid.
4 OJ 1975, C89.
5 Rules of Procedure of the European Parliament, rule 43 (3).
6 *Twenty Sixth Review of the Council's Work* (1979) at pp 12, 13.
7 See *Report on European Institutions* (1979), Annex 3.
8 Eg the reform of the European Regional Development Fund in 1984; see Regulation (EEC) 1787/84, OJ 1984, L169 and European Parliament Resolution of 30 February 1985, OJ 1985, C72. Also see Berger, C 'Un exemple de concertation réussi: Le Règlement No 3972/86 du Conseil' (1987) *Revue du Marché Commun* (No 305), p 161.
9 See European Parliament, *Progress Towards European Integration, July 1984 to June 1985* (1985), p 25.
10 See *Report on the Conciliation Procedure* PE Doc A 2-351/88, pp 12–15.
11 See European Parliament Resolution of 16 February 1989, OJ 1989, C 69/161.

(C) BUDGETARY POWERS OF THE EUROPEAN PARLIAMENT

The European Parliament has long had pretensions towards becoming a truly parliamentary body and it has been particularly insistent that its control not only over its own budget but also over the budget of the Communities as a whole should be increased.[12] In the first place it has always had the power to draft its own estimates and to debate the Community budgets. But apart from that the budgetary powers of the European Parliament differed originally as between the ECSC on the one hand and the EEC/Euratom on the other. In the case of the former, where funds were paid direct to the Community in the form of levies, the Parliament had virtually full power over its budget and had in practice (although not by virtue of any Treaty provision) acquired advisory rights over the whole of the ECSC budget. In the case of the EEC/Euratom, where finances used to derive from contributions from Member States, the European Parliament had no power at all and it was the Council which had a decisive voice over both the Parliament's budget and the Communities' budgets generally. Since the European Parliament received one-third of its budget from each Community this meant that it had no direct control over the allocation of two-thirds of its budget.

The question of enlarging the European Parliament's powers was discussed in 1964 in connection with the Merger Treaty but no action was taken. It will also be recalled that a proposal that the Communities be financed independently out of their own resources instead of out of contributions from the Member States was part of the proposed package-deal which was the focus of the constitutional crisis of 1965. When the matter was considered by the Council prior to the crisis there was a general consensus in favour of postponing the establishment of direct revenues until 1970 and all members except France were in favour of firmly linking the question of direct revenues with that of increasing the European Parliament's powers. After the crisis it was agreed to postpone these matters until the end of the Communities' transitional period.

Consideration was resumed at the Summit Meeting held at The Hague in December 1969. At that meeting it was agreed that with effect from 1 January 1971 the Communities would progressively draw a greater proportion of finance directly from the revenue of customs duties and levies on agricultural imports. From 1 January 1975 all such duties and levies have been paid direct to the Com-

---

12 On this topic see *Les ressources propres aux Communautés européennes et les pouvoirs budgétaires du Parlement européen* (European Parliament, 1970).

munities subject to 10% rebate to cover collection costs. The balance of the revenue necessary for the Communities is made up out of not more than 1.4% of a Value Added Tax which is in force in the Member States.[13] The system of own resources was amended in 1988. While revenues from customs duties, agricultural levies and the Value Added Tax remain, a new fourth resource has been introduced based on the sum of all the Member States' gross national product at market prices defined in accordance with Community rules. In addition, the new system also provides that in each year from 1988 to 1992 the amount of own resources may not exceed a ceiling figure represented by a stated percentage of the gross national product of the Community.[14] It is anticipated that these arrangements will provide the Community with sufficient and secure resources over the period in question.[15]

The Member States at The Hague Summit in 1969 also drew up the Budgetary Treaty which amended certain budgetary provisions of the Treaties. These included the conferment upon the European Parliament of increased budgetary powers over part of the Communities' budget, the so-called non-compulsory part, which deals with the functioning of the Communities' institutions. During the period 1971–74 the European Parliament's budgetary powers were strengthened by making it more difficult for the Council to reject amendments proposed by the Parliament. Since 1 January 1975 the European Parliament has had complete control over that part of the budget including the power to amend it.[16] The non-compulsory part of the budget amounts, in practice, to between 20 and 30%.[17] The political importance of this control may outreach the amount of money actually involved. Control over the non-compulsory part of the budget gives the European Parliament important powers in relation to the administrative costs of the institutions and such operational expenditure as the Social and Regional Funds.

As far as the remaining part of the budget is concerned the European Parliament has not been given the last word in this field. This is called the compulsory part of the budget in that it is the

13 See Council Decision 85/257/EEC, Euratom, OJ 1985, L128 repealing and replacing Council Decision 70/243.
14 The new system has been set up and is being implemented by Council Decision 88/376, OJ 1988, L185/24 and Council Regulations 1552/89 and 1553/89, OJ 1989, L155/1 and 9. The rules for compiling the gross national product of the Member States are set out in Council Directive 89/130, OJ 1989, L49/26.
15 See *Twenty-second General Report on the Activities of the European Communities* (1989), p 60.
16 Budgetary Treaty 1970, arts 1–9.
17 See Noel, E, *Working Together: The Institutions of the European Community* (1988), pp 33, 34.

automatic consequence of Community rules, most notably the cost of implementing the agricultural policy. In respect of this part of the budget the European Parliament may only propose modifications to the Council which has undertaken to give its reasons to the Parliament if it does not accept such modifications.[18]

At the time the Budgetary Treaty was signed in 1970 the Commission undertook to draft proposals to increase further the budgetary powers of the European Parliament.[19] After some delay, occasioned by the membership negotiations and the enlargement of the Community, the Commission eventually submitted its proposals in June 1973 in the form of a draft Treaty to amend further the budgetary provisions of the Community Treaties.[20] On the basis of those proposals, the governments of the Member States eventually agreed and accepted the Financial Provisions Treaty of 1975,[21] which came into force on 1 June 1977. The principal changes brought about by that Treaty were (i) to give the European Parliament the exclusive authority to adopt the annual budget and to give a discharge to the Commission in respect of its implementation; (ii) the creation of an independent Court of Auditors as a new Community institution to replace the Audit Board;[22] and (iii) that the so-called 'inverted majority rule' be applied to some proposed modifications to the compulsory part of the budget, ie that those proposals should be deemed to have been adopted unless expressly rejected by the Council. In order to promote co-operation on budgetary matters between the Council and the European Parliament a special conciliation procedure has been established under the terms of a Council Resolution of 22 April 1970.[23]

The role of the European Parliament in the budgetary procedure as amended by the Budgetary and Financial Provisions Treaties, may be described as follows.[24] The financial year of the Community is the calendar year. Each year, as a preliminary step, the Commission establishes by reference to such factors as gross natural

18 Eg Budgetary Treaty 1970, art 4.
19 *Sixth General Report on the Activities of the European Communities* (1973), pp 5, 6.
20 See *Bulletin of the European Communities* (1973), Supplement 9/73.
21 OJ 1977, L359.
22 See Ch 8 (E), infra.
23 For the text of the Resolution see *Treaties Establishing the European Communities* (1978 edn), at p 885. This conciliation procedure is quite distinct from that which was created in 1975 in connection with decision-making: see p 257, supra. Also see Council Decision 88/377 and the annexed Inter-institutional Agreement on budgetary discipline and improvement of the budgetary procedure, OJ 1988, L185/29.
24 See EEC Treaty, art 203, as amended and Rules of Procedure of the European Parliament, Rule 66 and Annex IV.

products and inflation the maximum rate by which expenditure in the coming year may be increased. Once that rate has been fixed it may be exceeded only by agreement between the Council (acting by qualified majority) and the European Parliament (acting by a majority of its members and 3/5 of the votes cast).[1] Within that framework, each institution draws up estimates of its expenditure and sends them to the Commission by 1 July. The Commission collates these estimates and forwards them to the Council by 1 September as a preliminary draft budget. This will be the subject of the so-called 'first reading' by the Council. On the basis of the preliminary draft and acting by a qualified majority[2] the Council will establish the draft budget. By 5 October the draft budget must be placed before the European Parliament for its 'first reading'. This gives the Parliament the opportunity, during the ensuing 45 days, to adopt the budget or to make amendments by majority vote to non-compulsory items and to propose modifications by an absolute majority to compulsory items.

If such amendments are made and/or modifications proposed, the draft budget thus revised is sent back to the Council for a 'second reading'. At this stage the Council, acting by a qualified majority, can in its turn modify any of the European Parliament's amendments to non-compulsory items. As far as the Parliament's proposed modifications to compulsory items are concerned, the Council can accept or reject them by a qualified majority. But that basic rule is subject to important qualifications, depending whether the effect of the European Parliament's proposed modifications is simply to reallocate sums of expenditure within the total sum established in the draft budget, or whether it is to increase the size of that total sum. In the former case, the European Parliament's modifications will stand as accepted in the absence of a Council decision to reject them; in the latter case, the European Parliament's modifications will stand as rejected in the absence of a Council decision to accept them. If, at this stage, the Council should accept the modifications proposed and amendments made by the European Parliament, the draft budget is deemed to be adopted. If not, the draft budget will be returned for a 'second reading' by the European Parliament. At this final stage the Parliament has no further specific powers in respect of items of compulsory expenditure. The European Parliament does however have the last word on items of non-compulsory expenditure. The European Parliament can further amend these; for example it may reinstate its own 'first reading' amendments which may have been changed by

1 EEC Treaty, art 203 (9).
2 In accordance with EEC Treaty, art 148 (2), as amended.

the Council at its 'second reading'. For this purpose the Parliament must act by a majority of its members and 3/5 of the votes cast. A period of 15 days is allocated for this.

When this complex procedure has run its course, it is for the European Parliament formally to adopt the budget, ie to transform it from a draft to an operational budget for the coming year. But if there are, in the opinion of a majority of the members of the European Parliament and 2/3 of the votes cast, 'important reasons'[3] why the budget should not be adopted as it stands, the Parliament may reject it and ask for a new draft budget to be submitted to it. If, as a result of such a rejection, no budget has been adopted at the beginning of the next financial year, the Community is financed on the 'provisional twelfths' basis. Until a budget is adopted, an amount not exceeding one-twelfth of the previous year's budget may be spent during each month.[4]

The European Parliament has shown that it is prepared to reject a draft budget if it is not satisfied with it. During the consideration of the draft budget for 1980 the European Parliament made it clear that its adoption of the budget would depend, inter alia, on the Council's acceptance of increases in non-compulsory items and the implementation of measures to curb agricultural expenditure.[5] A lengthy use of the conciliation procedure[6] failed to secure the Council's agreement, particularly in relation to the latter point. The European Parliament therefore rejected the budget on 13 December 1979 because the conditions which it had set had not been satisfied.[7] The budget for 1980 was not finally agreed and adopted until 9 July 1980,[8] the date on which the Commission completed its preparation of the preliminary draft budget for 1981![9] Thus the European Parliament 'demonstrated its determination to exercise its budgetary powers to the full'.[10]

---

3 See EEC Treaty, art 203 (8).
4 See EEC Treaty, art 204.
5 See *Bulletin of the European Communities*, 1979 – 11, pp 86, 108.
6 See *Thirteenth General Report on the Activities of the European Communities* (1980), pp 46, 48.
7 See *Bulletin of the European Communities*, 1979 – 12, p 120.
8 See *Fourteenth General Report on the Activities of the European Communities* (1981), p 47.
9 Ibid, pp 47, 48.
10 See *Thirteenth General Report on the Activities of the European Communities* (1980), p 24. Also see Sopwith, Sir C, 'Legal Aspects of the Community Budget' (1980), 17 CML Rev 315 and Pipkorn, J 'Legal Implications of the Absence of the Community Budget at the Beginning of a Financial Year', (1981) 18 CML Rev 141. The 1985 budget was also rejected; see European Parliament *The Impact of the European Parliament on Community Policies* (Research and Documentation Papers, Action Taken Series No 3, 1988), at pp 16–17.

While the European Parliament now has real budgetary powers they are clearly not without limitation. Although its President alone has the power to adopt the budget it is clear, as the European Court has recently pointed out,[11] that during the budgetary procedure the European Parliament must act in partnership with the Council under the terms laid down in the Treaty. In 1985 the Commission for the purposes of the 1986 budget fixed the maximum rate of increase for non-compulsory expenditure at 7.1%.[12] In establishing the draft budget for 1986 the Council provided for a 7.05% increase for non-compulsory expenditure. During the course of the budgetary procedure the European Parliament argued for a greater rate of increase. After recourse to conciliation the Council proposed a new maximum rate of 14.6%. The European Parliament did not agree and after further conciliation the Council proposed an increase of 17.02%, subject to acceptance by the European Parliament. Without making a direct response to that proposal the Parliament proceeded to resolve to increase non-compulsory expenditure by 19.5%. The Council whereupon withdrew its proposal, but the President of the Parliament nevertheless declared the budget to be adopted and so informed the Council. These events prompted actions in the European Court to annul the 1986 budget and/or its final adoption.[13] Following its own previous case law the Court had no hesitation in accepting the admissibility of the action.[14] On the merits the Court held that since the Treaty laid down no criteria for increasing the maximum rate fixed by the Commission but made it a matter for agreement between the Council and the Parliament, an agreement of such importance may not be inferred from the presumed intention of one or other of those institutions.[15] It therefore concluded that at the time the President purported to adopt the budget the budgetary procedure had not in fact been completed since there was no agreement on the maximum rate of increase. Therefore the adoption of the budget was vitiated by illegality.[16] In an interim order the Court had already authorized the implementation of the 1986 budget to the

11 Case 34/86: *EC Council v European Parliament* [1986] 3 CMLR 94.
12 The facts are conveniently set out ibid, at 96–101.
13 Individual actions were first brought by Luxembourg, the Netherlands, France, Germany and the United Kingdom but it was agreed to proceed with the Council's action. See Case 23/86R: *United Kingdom v European Parliament* [1986] 3 CMLR 82 and Case 34/86: *EC Council v European Parliament* [1986] 3 CMLR 94.
14 See Case 294/83: *Parti Ecologiste Les Verts v European Parliament* [1986] ECR 1339, [1987] 2 CMLR 343.
15 [1986] 3 CMLR at p 149.
16 Ibid, at p 150.

extent that its legality was not being challenged.[17] In its final judgment it did not order the budgetary procedure to be reopened from the beginning, but that it resume at the point at which the Parliament adopted an excessive rate of increase.[18] Within one week of the judgment agreement was reached by Council and Parliament. The budget which was formally and legally adopted a week later ironically exceeded that which the Court had annulled.[19]

Against this background of repeated conflict and crisis which dates back to the early 1980s, it is encouraging to be able to report that the budgets for 1989 and 1990 were adopted on time and in compliance with the Inter-institutional Agreement between the Commission, the Council and the Parliament on budgetary discipline and improvement of budgetary procedure of 1988.[20] That Agreement and its associated Council Decision,[21] which incorporate budget forecasts and a financial perspective for the period 1988 to 1992, seems to be having a positive and beneficial effect on the budgetary process.[22] The Agreement will be reviewed in 1991 and amended, if necessary, in the light of experience.

(D) A FULL LEGISLATIVE ROLE FOR THE EUROPEAN PARLIAMENT?

The general question of the future rôle of the European Parliament was taken up by the Commission in July 1971. It set up an *ad hoc* Working Party of independent experts to examine the whole corpus of problems connected with the enlargement of the Parliament's powers. In its wide-ranging report the Working Party proposed that the powers of the European Parliament should be increased by means of a two-stage plan.[23]

During the first, transitional, stage it was proposed that the European Parliament should have a power of co-decision with the Council in four matters referred to as list A, viz the revision of the Treaties; decisions to give the Communities any necessary new powers; the admission of new members; and the ratification of international agreements concluded by the Communities. In such

---

17 Cited ibid, at pp 101–102.
18 Ibid, at pp 150–152.
19 See *Twentieth General Report on the Activities of the European Communities* (1987), pp 54, 57 and Table 1 on p 55.
20 See *Twenty-second and Twenty-third General Reports on the Activities of the European Communities* (1989) and (1990), at pp 66–71 and 69 respectively.
21 OJ 1988, L185/24 and 33.
22 See European Parliament *The Work of the European Parliament: July 1988– June 1989* (1989), at pp 19–23.
23 *Vedel Report*, Chapter 4, sections I and II.

cases it was proposed that decisions of the Council would take effect only after receiving the approval of the Parliament. Also during this first stage the consultative powers of the Parliament would be extended to cover additional matters, referred to as list B, which would include the Common Agricultural Policy, harmonization of laws and taxes, the common transport policy and the mutual recognition of diplomas. In connection with these and other matters it was proposed that the European Parliament should be given a suspensive veto. In the event of a difference of opinion between the Council and the European Parliament on any of these matters it would enable the Parliament to suspend the decision for one month and require the Council to reconsider the matter. The Council's second decision, whether amended or not, would be final. During the second stage, the Parliament's power of co-decision would be extended to all matters in list B. The matters in list A were chosen because they cover questions which materially involve either the constitutive powers of the Communities or their relations with other international persons. The matters in list B are largely those which involve harmonization measures of one sort or another. Because of the importance of these matters to the life of the Communities and the obligations which they will impose on Member States it was thought appropriate to involve the European Parliament in their determination initially in the form of consultation supported by the suspensive veto and eventually by co-decision with the Council.

The Working Party also made a number of other recommendations designed to increase the democratic control exercised by the European Parliament. The report commented that as European integration extends to include new sectors national parliaments will gradually become less able to exercise their traditional democratic control over legislation affecting their countries. It was suggested that this should be corrected by increasing the powers of the European Parliament.

This general theme has been taken up subsequently by the Commission and the European Parliament itself. Following the Vedel Report, the Commission made a strong recommendation to the governments of the Member States that the European Parliament should participate in the legislative process of the Community and should have the last word on such matters as the approximation of legislation.[1] Later, during the debate on European Union, the Commission advanced the view that in the longer term the legislative power of the Community should be exercised by a bi-cameral Parliament composed of a 'Chamber of Peoples'

---

1 *Sixth General Report on the Activities of the European Communities* (1973), p 5.

and a 'Chamber of States'.[2] The European Parliament in its own contribution to that debate resolved that it should 'participate on at least an equal footing in the legislation process, as is its right as the representative of the peoples of the Union'.[3] Indeed, now that the European Parliament is directly elected its claims for an increased legislative role are clearly strengthened. As President Ortoli observed: 'If the elected Parliament is to be true to its calling, it must be given legislative power.'[4]

In 1984, in its own Draft Treaty for a European Union,[5] the European Parliament revived the idea of legislative authority being exercised jointly with the Council with active participation by the Commission.[6] The essence of the procedure proposed is that both the European Parliament and the Council would be required to act on legislative proposals within specified time limits after the passing of which the respective institutions would be deemed to have approved the proposal in question.[7] Such an arrangement would not only give the Parliament a direct voice in legislation but it would also deprive the Council of the ability to block progress by inactivity. That latter objective would also be reinforced by majority voting becoming the general rule in the Council.[8]

Little has been done in practice to implement any of these far-reaching proposals. The conciliation procedure and the new co-operation procedure fall very far short of giving the European Parliament a legislative role, although as has been seen it may to some extent claim a de facto role as a co-legislator. It is perhaps more significant that while the Dooge Report lends its support to joint decision-making,[9] strong reservations were entered by the British and Greek members of the Ad Hoc Committee[10] who favoured the improvement and extension of the existing conciliation procedure.[11] The political will is still clearly lacking to transform the European Parliament into a full parliamentary legislature.

---

2 *Report on European Union, Bulletin of the European Communities,* Supp 5/75, pp 30–34.
3 *Report on European Union, Bulletin of the European Communities,* Supp 9/75, p 11.
4 *Ninth General Report on the Activities of the European Communities* (1976), p xx.
5 See EC Commission, *An Ever Closer Union* (1985) Annex I.
6 Art 36, ibid, p 315.
7 Art 38, ibid, p. 316.
8 Art 23 (1), ibid, p 312.
9 Ad Hoc Committee for Institutional Affairs, Report to the European Council (March 1985), section III (c), ibid, p 339.
10 Mr Malcolm Rifkind and Mr Ioannis Papantoniou, ibid, p 342.
11 Section III (c) of the Report, notes 33–35, ibid, p 339.

Chapter 8

Ancillary Community institutions

In addition to the subsidiary bodies already mentioned there are a number of ancillary institutions which either advise on or otherwise participate in the activities of the Communities. Some of these owe their origin to the Treaties themselves; others have been established in the light of experience.

(A) CONSULTATIVE BODIES

Of all the ancillary institutions, pride of place should perhaps be given to the Consultative Committee of the ECSC and the Economic and Social Committee which serves both the EEC and Euratom. Both of these advisory bodies consist of representatives of the various sections of economic and social life in the Communities. Thus the Consultative Committee, appointed under the terms of article 18 of the ECSC Treaty,[1] consists of not fewer than 72 and not more than 96 members including an equal number of producers, workers, consumers and dealers in the coal and steel industries. At present it has 96 members allocated as follows: Germany 19, the United Kingdom 18, France 13, Italy 9, Belgium and Spain 8 each, the Netherlands 5, Luxembourg 4, and Denmark, Greece, Ireland and Portugal 3 each.[2] The Economic and Social Committee, appointed under the terms of articles 193 and 198 of the EEC Treaty, articles 165 and 169 of the Euratom Treaty[3] and article 5 of the Common Institutions Convention, consists of 189 persons representing producers, farmers, carriers, workers, dealers, craftsmen, professional occupations and the general public. The 189 members are allocated on a national basis as follows: France, Germany, Italy and the United Kingdom have 24 each, Spain has 21, Belgium, Greece, the Netherlands and Portugal have 12 each, Denmark and Ireland have 9 each and Luxembourg has 6.

1 As amended by the First Act of Accession 1972, art 22, the Second Act of Accession 1979, art 138 and Third Act of Accession 1985, art 22.
2 See *Yearbook of the European Communities* (10th edn, 1990), at pp 245–250.
3 As amended by the First Act of Accession, art 21, the Second Act of Accession, art 17 and Third Act of Accession 1985, art 21.

In the case of both Committees although the members are appointed by the Council they are appointed in their private capacity and are expressly forbidden to act on any mandate or instructions from the bodies nominating them. There is also an obligation on the Council to consult the Commission on appointments to the Economic and Social Committee and it may also obtain the opinion of European organizations representing particular economic and social sectors of interest. Subject to such considerations, the Council has a wide discretion. Given the limited number of places on the Economic and Social Committee, it is not possible for each category of activity to be represented by nationals of each Member State; the Committee's representative character is to be achieved at the Community level. It is the responsibility of the Council to ensure this.[4] The Committee itself is divided into three groups[5] each representing a particular set of interests: Group I, the Employers' Group, is made up of representatives of employers' organizations and chambers of commerce; Group II, the Workers' Group, is made up of representatives of trade unions; and Group III, the Various Interests' Group, which includes representatives of small businesses, the co-operative movement, consumer and family organizations, the environmental lobby, the professions and local government.[6] It is the practice of the Committee, rather like that of the European Parliament and its political groups, for its members to vote by group and not by nationality.

The role of these Committees is an advisory one. They may be consulted by the Commission or Council whenever it is thought appropriate and in some cases consultation is obligatory. Under article 60(1) of the ECSC Treaty, for example, the Commission may define unfair competitive pricing practices after consulting the Consultative Committee and the Council and similarly under article 75 of the EEC Treaty the Council, on a proposal from the Commission, may lay down common rules applicable to international transport between or across the territories of Member States after consultation with the Economic and Social Committee. Thus these Committees provide a sounding board for informed and general opinion on matters relating to the policies of the Communities, roughly on a parallel with the practice in the United Kingdom of consulting interested parties prior to the making of legislation whether parliamentary or subordinate.

Although the opinions of these consultative committees are in

---

4 See Case 297/86: *Confederazione italiana dirigenta di azienda v EC Council* [1988] ECR 3531, at pp 3354–3355.
5 Referred to as 'sections' in the Committee's Rules of Procedure; see Decision 86/605, OJ 1986, L354/1, arts 10 and 11.
6 See Economic and Social Committee *Annual Report 1989* Ch IV.

no way binding they are not without their influence. The suggestion has been made that they may be more influential than the opinions of the European Parliament since they are the informed views of those involved in activities likely to be affected by the policies of the Communities.[7] The Commission appears to treat their views with respect and the Economic and Social Committee has certainly tended to support the Commission's proposals. The Council in the past adopted a more restrictive attitude.[8] More recently, the Committee has had some success in developing more systematic contacts with the Council. In 1987 for the first time the President-in-Office of the Council addressed the Committee on matters to be discussed at a forthcoming meeting of the European Council.[9] Indeed, since that time a pattern has developed of ministers from the Member State occupying the presidency addressing meetings of the Committee.[10] Steps have also been taken to improve co-operation between the two institutions, in particular by ensuring that the Committee's Opinions are received by the Member States as soon as they are issued and by monitoring that due account is taken of such Opinions.[11] Since 1972 the Committee's right to advise on its own initiative on all matters affecting the Community has been recognized and regular use has been made of this right.[12]

(B) TECHNICAL COMMITTEES

There are numerous agencies and committees of experts relating to specific areas of Community activity; some of the more important of these are as follows. A Monetary Committee set up under the terms of article 105 of the EEC Treaty to keep the monetary and financial position in the Member States under review. The Committee appointed by the Council under the terms of article 111 of the EEC Treaty to assist the Commission in tariff negotiations with non-Member States. The Scientific and Technical Committee set up under the terms of article 134 of the Euratom

7 See Torelli, M, *L'Individu et le Droit de la CEE* (1970), at p 58, and Zellentin, G, 'The Economic and Social Committee' (1962), 1 *Journal of Common Market Studies* 22. For a review of the influence of the Committee's Opinions, see *Annual Report 1988*, Table C, p 107 et seq.
8 See Palmer, M, et al, *European Unity* (1968), at p 186.
9 See *Annual Report 1987*, p 9.
10 See *Annual Reports 1987, 1988 and 1989*, at pp 9, 10 and 11–12 respectively.
11 See *Annual Reports 1988 and 1989*, at p 11 and Annex B respectively.
12 See *Sixth General Report of the Activities of the European Communities* (1973) at p 16; Economic and Social Committee *The Right of Initiative of the Economic and Social Committee* (1977); and the Committee's Rules of Procedure, Decision 86/605, OJ 1986, L354/1, art 20, 4th para. The monthly *Bulletin* and the *Annual Report* of the Committee record this and other aspects of its activities.

Treaty. The Administrative Commission for the Social Security of Migrant Workers which supervises the social security arrangements for citizens of community members working in a country other than their own. The Short Term and Medium Term Economic Policy Committees: the former assists in the co-ordination of day-to-day economic policies; the latter studies the likely development of the Community's economy over a five-year period. The membership of these Committees is commonly drawn from the national administrations of the Member States and their rôle is purely advisory.

(C) EUROPEAN INVESTMENT BANK

The European Investment Bank is an independent institution, established by article 129 of the EEC Treaty and endowed with legal personality. The members of the Bank are the Member States of the Community. The task of the Bank, as set out in article 130, is to contribute, by means of its own resources and access to the capital market, to the balanced and steady development of the Common Market. To that end the Bank, operating on a non-profit-making basis, is empowered to grant loans and to give guarantees to facilitate the financing of three types of project in all sectors of the economy: (i) projects for developing the less developed regions of the Community; (ii) projects for modernizing or converting undertakings or for developing fresh activities called for by the progressive establishment of the Common Market; and (iii) projects of common interest to several Member States. In the cases of the latter two types of project, the Bank's assistance is limited to projects which are of such a size or nature that they cannot be entirely financed by the various means available in the individual Member States.

The organization, function and powers of the Bank are set out in detail in a separate Statute annexed to the EEC Treaty. The Bank was originally set up with a capital of 1,000 million European Currency Units (ECU) subscribed by the Member States.[13] Over the years the total capital of the Bank has been increased. At the accession of Spain and Portugal it was set at 28,800 million ECU; the largest contributions are those from France, Germany, Italy and the United Kingdom at 5,508 million each ranging down to Luxembourg at 38 million.[14]

The seat of the Bank is in Luxembourg. The Bank is directed and managed by a Board of Governors, a Board of Directors and

13 Statute of the Bank, art 4 (1). For the method of calculating the value of the European Currency Unit see Regulation 1971/89, OJ 1989, L189/1.
14 See Third Act of Accession 1985, Protocol 1, art 2.

a Management Committee.[15] The Board of Governors consists of the Ministers of Finance of the Member States. The essential role of the Board of Governors is to lay down directives for the credit policy of the Bank and to ensure that those directives are implemented.[16] The system of voting which is provided for the Council by article 148 of the EEC Treaty also applies to the Board of Governors.[17] The Board of Directors consists of 22 directors with 12 alternates. They serve five-year renewable terms and are appointed by the Board of Governors. Three directors are nominated by each of France, Germany, Italy and the United Kingdom; two directors are nominated by Spain; one director is nominated by each of Belgium, Denmark, Greece, Ireland, Luxembourg, the Netherlands, Portugal and the Commission. Germany, France, Italy and the United Kingdom nominate two alternates each; the Benelux countries by common accord, Denmark, Greece and Ireland by common accord and Spain and Portugal by common accord nominate one alternate each, as does the Commission.[18] It is the task of the Board of Directors to manage the Bank in accordance with the Treaty and Statute and the general directives laid down by the Board of Governors. It has the sole power to grant loans and guarantees and to raise loans and it fixes the interest rates and commission payable on loans and guarantees respectively.[19] The current business of the Bank is in the hands of the Management Committee consisting of a President and six Vice-Presidents. These are appointed for six-year renewable terms by the Board of Governors upon a proposal from the Board of Directors. The Management Committee acts under the authority of the President and the supervision of the Board of Directors. Its functions are to prepare the decisions of the Board of Directors on both the raising of loans and the granting of loans and guarantees and to ensure the implementation of those decisions.[20] The President, or in his absence one of the Vice-Presidents, acts as non-voting Chairman of the Board of Directors.[21]

The Bank obtains its funds primarily from loans floated on the capital markets of the world. During 1989 the Bank signed loan

---

15 Statute of the Bank, art 8. Privileges and immunities are enjoyed by the members of the organs, the staff of the Bank and the national representatives on the Bank under the terms of the Protocol on Privileges and Immunities 1965, art 22.
16 Statute of the Bank, art 9.
17 Ibid, art 10.
18 See Third Act of Accession 1985, Protocol 1, art 5.
19 Statute of the Bank, arts 11 and 12.
20 Ibid, art 13.
21 Ibid, art 11 (2).

contracts to the combined value of over 11,600 million ECU.[22] This included loans for projects in the United Kingdom totalling 755.7 million ECU.[23] Although most loans and guarantees are in connection with projects within the territories of the Member States, it has also been empowered to assist overseas territories and states associated with the Community.[24]

Under the terms of article 180 of the EEC Treaty the Court of Justice of the Communities has jurisdiction over certain types of dispute concerning the Bank. In particular the Board of Directors enjoy the powers conferred on the Commission by article 169 of the EEC Treaty in connection with the non-fulfilment by Member States of obligations under the Statute of the Bank; also under the terms of article 173 of the EEC Treaty any Member State, the Commission or the Board of Directors may challenge measures adopted by the Board of Governors and similarly any Member State or the Commission may challenge measures adopted by the Board of Directors. No proceedings appear to have been brought under any of these heads. Article 29 of the Statute of the Bank provides that disputes between the Bank and its creditors and debtors shall be decided by the competent national courts unless jurisdiction has been conferred on the Court of the Justice of the Communities.

(D) MANAGEMENT AND REGULATORY COMMITTEES

We have already seen that with the development of the common policies of the Communities into new areas, particularly agriculture, the Council has delegated to the Commission considerable law-making powers. Under the terms of the Treaties the Commission is not in a subordinate position to the Council, and so if this delegation took the form of empowering the Commission to act independently it would remove such matters entirely from the control of the Council. Further, since these powers would have been transferred to the Commission by the Council upon the Commission's proposal, it is believed that the Commission could only be deprived of such powers by the same process, namely on the Commission's initiative. The member governments wished to avoid these consequences of delegation which might prove disadvantageous to themselves. In addition, particularly in the field of agriculture, it was practically desirable that the process of implementing the common policies should be carried out in close con-

22 See *Twenty-third General Report on the Activities of the European Communities* (1990), at p 76.
23 Ibid.
24 Ibid, at pp 354–360.

sultation with the governments of the Member States. The system of Management Committees was devised to achieve those objectives.

The management committee procedure was introduced by Regulation 19 of 1962.[1] Article 25 of that Regulation established a Management Committee for Cereal Products made up of representatives of the Member States and presided over by a representative of the Commission. Similar management committees have since been set up for each of the main categories of agricultural products. The chairman of a management committee is a member of the staff of the Commission, usually the head of the Department which covers the products dealt with by the Committee. The chairman has no vote. The procedure is for the Commission to submit a draft implementing measure to the appropriate management committee for its opinion. The management committee employs the system of weighted voting used in the Council itself. The management committee's opinion is not binding on the Commission. The Commission may modify its draft in the light of the opinion or adhere to its original proposal. In either event the Commission's decision, after submission of its proposal to the management committee, will have the immediate force of law. But if there is a conflict between the views of the Commission and the opinion of the Committee and if that opinion has received the qualified majority of 54 votes, the matter must be referred to the Council which may within a period of one month reverse the Commission's decision. If, on the other hand, the Commission's draft is acceptable to the Committee or if the Committee is opposed to it but cannot muster the qualified majority or if the Committee fails to respond to the request for an opinion,[2] the Commission's decision is not subject to an appeal to the Council.

It is generally agreed that the management committee procedure works well in practice. In 1989 as a result of 318 meetings of management committees 1,449 favourable opinions were expressed, no opinion was expressed in 133 cases, and an unfavourable opinion was expressed in only one case.[3] This is a typical situation and it testifies to the degree of co-operation and mutual confidence between the Commission and the Member States which has been engendered by this procedure. When the Commission differs from a committee opinion given by a qualified majority, which happens

1 JO No 30 of 4 April 1962, p 933/62, since replaced by Regulation 2727/75, OJ 1975, L281.
2 See Case 35/78: *N G J Schouten B V v Hoofdproduktschap Voor Akkerbouwprodukten* [1978] ECR 2543 at 2558.
3 See *Twenty-third General Report on the Activities of the European Communities* (1990), Table 14, at p 258.

infrequently, the procedure operates as an alarm mechanism and gives a clear indication of a serious problem which can be effectively resolved only by the Member States acting through the Council. The original intention was that this procedure should only be resorted to during the transitional period of the Community's development but because of its success it has been expressly continued in existence for an indefinite period.[4]

Another development has been the application of a similar procedure to areas of community activity other than the agricultural, with a result that committees of government representatives have been set up to assist in the implementation of the common customs tariff and in connection with the control of standards in relation to food and animal health.[5] These latter committees, whilst they are manifestations of the management committee procedure, are usually distinguished from the management committees properly-so-called and are referred to as regulatory committees. In connection with these committees the powers delegated by the Council to the Commission are more circumscribed. The Commission's proposal only has immediate binding effect if it is approved by the committee. If the committee disapproves of a proposal by an opinion reached by the qualified majority, or if no opinion is forthcoming because of the committee's inability to reach the qualified majority, then the Commission must refer its proposal to the Council for acceptance by a qualified majority vote. There is a final rider to this procedure, however, and that is if the Council in such a case has failed to take a decision within three months then the Commission itself may adopt the proposed measure and it will thereby acquire the force of law. In Community jargon this is known as the 'net' or '*filet*' procedure. The management committee procedure is also incorporated into the machinery for administering the European Regional Development Fund.[6]

The constitutional validity of the management and rule-making committee procedures has been questioned in the past.[7] The crux of the question is the vagueness of the Treaty provisions relating to the delegation of powers by the Council to the Commission. Article 155 of the EEC Treaty in its final provision states that the Commission shall 'exercise the powers conferred on it by the

---

4 See Regulation 2602/69, JO 1969, L324.
5 Eg the Committee on Origin, established by Regulation 802/68, JO 1968. L148; the Standing Veterinary Committee established by Council Decision 68/361, JO 1968, L255; and the Common Customs Tariff Nomenclature Committee established by Regulation 97/69, JO 1969, L14.
6 Regulation 1787/84, arts 39–42, OJ 1984, L169.
7 Eg Schindler, P, 'The Problems of Decision-Making by way of Management Committee Procedure in the EEC' (1971) 8 CMLRev 184.

Council for the implementation of the rules laid down by the latter'. It has been argued that the force of that provision is to enable the Council to confer upon the Commission powers which are materially identical with the powers possessed by the Council itself. Thus, where under article 43(2) of the EEC Treaty the Council has the power to adopt regulations for the implementation of the Common Agricultural Policy, if the Council purports to delegate that power to the Commission it may only do so absolutely and not conditionally. By imposing the management committee procedure upon the powers delegated it has been suggested that the Council is making an unlawful change in the decision-making powers of the Commission. In other words the suggestion is that the management committee procedure depends on political expediency within the Communities rather than on constitutional authority under the terms of the Treaty.

The view taken by both the Commission and Council in support of the management committee procedures is that they are perfectly compatible with the Treaties. The view of these institutions was clearly put by the Commission in its *Second General Report on the Activities of the Communities* (1968).[8] There it is pointed out that whilst article 155 of the EEC Treaty does not prevent the Council from exercising its implementing powers itself, it is clear that any implementing powers not retained by the Council may only be delegated to the Commission. Further the Council is, in any event, bound to observe the institutional balance of the Communities.

As early as 1958 in the case of *Meroni & Co v High Authority*[9] the Court of Justice commented on the general concept of delegated powers in the Communities. In its judgment in that case the Court stressed the necessity of preserving the balance of powers which is a characteristic of the institutional structure of the Communities and concluded that any delegation of a discretionary power upon institutions different from those established by the Treaties would be invalid.[10] These principles laid down in the *Meroni* case underlie the judgment of the Court in three cases decided in December 1970 in which the validity of the management committee procedures was directly challenged.[11]

Part of the Community's agricultural policy takes the form of

---

8 Paras 639–42. Also see *Rapport sur les procédures communautaires d'exécution du droit communautaire dérivé* (European Parliament, Document de Séance, No 115/68).

9 Case 9/56; [1957–58] ECR 133.

10 Ibid at 150. Also see Case 23/75: *Rey Soda v Cassa Conguaglio Zucchero* [1975] ECR 1279 at 1300.

11 Cases 25, 26 and 30/70: *Einfuhr-und Vorratsstelle für Getreide und Füttermittel v Koster, Berodt & Co*, [1970] ECR 1161, [1972] CMLR 255.

regulations to forestall unexpected movements of agricultural products which, if permitted, would threaten the common organization of markets in those products. To that end the Commission has made regulations providing for compulsory import and export certificates to be obtained by those who wish to make imports or exports of particular agricultural products. It is further required that such certificates should be supported by the payment of a security which will be forfeit if the imports or exports were not made during the period of the certificate's validity. In these cases the legality of this system of certificates was challenged on the ground, inter alia, that the management committee procedure which had been employed in the making of the regulations was contrary to the EEC Treaty.

The arguments against the legality of the management committee procedure were that it permitted the management committees to interfere in the legislative activities of the Commission, that it gives to the Member States a right of appeal to the Council against a Commission regulation, thus derogating from the role of the Court, and that consequently it disturbs the institutional balance of the Community. The Council expressed the contrary view in terms which have already been outlined above. The Court supported the Council's view. It held that article 155 which authorizes the Council to delegate rule-implementing powers to the Commission must be understood as permitting the Council to lay down provisions and procedures whereby its own policy decisions may be implemented. The management committee procedure was held to come within the modalities upon which the Council is allowed to make such an authorization of the Commission dependent. Further, the allegation that the management committees interfere in the legislative activities of the Commission was not substantiated since the rôle of a management committee is merely to give opinions and it has no power to make decisions. Its views may influence the Commission but, subject to one proviso, the power of decision remains with the Commission. As far as the proviso is concerned, which involves the allegation that the management committee procedure gives a right of appeal to the Council from a decision of the Commission, this the Court also held to be unsubstantiated. The management committee procedure merely enables the Council to take action instead of the Commission where the committee hands down a negative opinion. Practice has shown these cases to be exceptional and in any event whether the final decision is made by the Commission or Council the powers of the Court to review such decisions are left unimpaired.

Finally, the Court said that there is no question of this procedure disturbing the institutional equilibrium of the Communities. The

Council has in effect delegated powers to the Commission subject to the condition that the opinion of the appropriate management committee is sought. Regardless of the contents of that opinion the Commission has the power to make binding decisions. In the event of an adverse opinion the Commission is obliged to refer its decision to the Council which may then choose to substitute its own decision for that of the Commission. Thus the Council is merely reserving to itself the freedom to use its own rule-making power in circumstances in which there is a substantial difference of opinion between its delegate, the Commission, and the representatives of the Member States. Since the rôle of the management committees is essentially consultative and since, subject to the power to delegate, the rule-making powers are conferred by the Treaty upon the Council, the institutional order was held to be unaffected. It is submitted that these conclusions apply equally to rule-making committees.

There is general agreement that the management committee procedure works well. Not only has it been decided to retain it indefinitely but more use is likely to be made of it in future in view of the Council's decision to make wider use of its powers under the last paragraph of article 155 of the EEC Treaty.[12] In delicate areas of Community policy which impinge on individual national interests the management committee procedure has made it possible for considerable progress to be made in the implementation of that policy. But for the introduction of management committee procedures which provide a means for close consultation between the Commission and the governments of the Member States, the Council would probably have been reluctant to transfer wide-ranging legislative powers to the Commission. As a result the Commission's authority within the EEC has tended to be strengthened. Thus the political significance of the management committee procedures must not be overlooked. As one commentator has observed, it has enabled the wills of the Member States to be joined in common activity, thus achieving one of the basic aims of the Communities.[13]

The conferment on the Commission of power to implement rules laid down by the Council has been given a further boost and its utility given further recognition by an amendment introduced by the Single European Act 1986.[14] This new provision gives general

---

12 See *Bulletin of the European Communities* (1974), Part 6, p 122. Also see comments on the role of management committees in *Report on European Institutions* (1979) at pp 47, 48.
13 Bertram, C, 'Decision-making in the EEC: the Management Committee Procedure' (1967–68), 5 CML Rev 264.
14 Art 10, amending EEC Treaty, art 145.

authority to the Council to confer such powers on the Commission in accordance with principles and rules which are to be determined in advance. The Council is authorized to lay down procedures for this purpose on the basis of a Commission proposal and after obtaining the opinion of the European Parliament. At the Inter-governmental Conference which preceded the adoption of the Single European Act the discussion of possible procedures included not only the existing management and regulatory com-mittee procedures but also an advisory committee procedure of an entirely consultative nature. The Conference also requested that for the purposes of completing the internal market priority should be given to that latter procedure.[15] The Commission, with the general support of the European Parliament, drew up an appro-priate proposal incorporating the three types of procedure and referring to the preferred use of advisory committees.[16] The decision which the Council took under these powers, known as the 'comitology' decision, departs significantly from those proposals.[17] It provides that implementing powers conferred on the Com-mission shall be exercised either independently, or by one of the advisory, management or regulatory committee procedures, or by a special emergency procedure in relation to safeguard measures.[18] There are in fact seven possible procedures since both the man-agement and regulatory procedures are each subject to two variants. The Council, for reasons which it has not divulged, deliberately omitted to specify which form of procedure should be used for any given purpose.[19]

The 'comitology' decision has provoked criticism and challenge. Attention has been focused in particular on the variants in procedure, which effectively enable the Council to block imple-menting action, and the Council's express reservation of the right to exercise executive action itself. The Commission's criticisms were recorded in the minutes of the Council meeting which adopted the decision in terms that the decision would impose restraints on the Commission's freedom of action and that it contained no general guarantee of implementing action being taken.[20] Initial experience has tended to confirm such fears: the Council has not

15 See 'Declaration on the powers of implementation of the Commission' adopted by the Inter-governmental Conference and annexed to the Single European Act.
16 For the Commission's proposal, see COM(86) 35 final; for the opinion of the Parliament, see PE DOC A2-138/86.
17 Council Decision 87/373, OJ 1987, L197/33.
18 Ibid, arts 1–3. Art 4 makes it clear that existing procedures for the exercise of conferred powers by the Commission remain in force until amended.
19 See *Thirty-fifth Review of the Council's Work* (1988), p 15.
20 See *Bulletin of the European Communities* (1987), Part 6, point 2.4.14.

given priority to the advisory committee procedure; it has made increasing use of the variant of the regulatory committee procedure which allows it to block Commission proposals by a simple majority; and it has kept implementing powers to itself in some cases.[1] A request from the Commission to the Council to take steps to improve the situation has not so far elicited any response.[2] Attempts to challenge the legality of the 'comitology' decision and the Council's use of it have also been unsuccessful. An action by the European Parliament contending that the decision was unlawful was ruled to be inadmissible on the ground that the Parliament lacks the necessary locus standi to bring such an action.[3] An action by the Commission challenging recourse to the management committee procedure on a matter over which it claimed exclusive competence was dismissed on the merits.[4]

(E) THE COURT OF AUDITORS

The Court of Auditors was established in 1977 under the terms of the Financial Provisions Treaty 1975.[5] The Court of Auditors replaced the two former audit bodies of the Communities: the ECSC Auditor and the Audit Board which served the EEC and Euratom. The decision to set up this new body was linked with the decision to grant to the European Parliament the sole responsibility of discharging the Commission of its responsibility concerning the accounts of the Community. The European Parliament for several years had been urging the reform of the Community's auditing arrangements.[6] It was therefore felt that the new financial arrangements introduced by the 1975 Treaty 'should be accompanied by an intensification of control and audit and this could best be achieved by the creation of a new instrument, the Court of auditors'.[7]

In some respects the rules governing the membership of the Court of Auditors are similar to those governing the Court of

---

1 See *Twenty-third General Report on the Activities of the European Communities* (1990), pp 31–32.
2 Ibid, p 32. The Council is required by art 5 of the 'comitology' decision to review the procedures it provides on the basis of a Commission report before the end of 1990.
3 Case 302/87: *European Parliament v EC Council* [1988] ECR 5615.
4 Case 16/88: *EC Commission v EC Council*, Judgment of 24 October 1989, not yet reported: for information about the case see *Proceedings of the Court of Justice of the European Communities*, No 22/89, p 2.
5 Financial Provisions Treaty, 1975 art 15, replacing EEC Treaty, art 206. Also see Financial Regulation of 21 December 1977, Title VI, OJ 1977, L356.
6 See European Parliament, *The Case for a European Audit Office* (1973).
7 Report of the Court of Auditors for the Financial Year 1977, OJ 1978, C313, at p 5, para 1.3.

Justice.[8] The Court of Auditors is composed of twelve members appointed by the Council in consultation with the European Parliament for renewable terms of six years. The Court elects a President from amongst its members for a renewable term of three years. Members of the Court are chosen from persons who have had relevant auditing experience. They must not only be independent, but must also act at all times in the interest of the Community. They may be removed from office, but only if the Court of Justice is satisfied that the conditions and obligations of office are no longer being met. They enjoy the same privileges and immunities as members of the Court of Justice.

While the Court of Auditors is charged with the responsibility of examining the legality and regularity of the accounts of the Community and presenting an annual report,[9] that is not its only responsibility. It is also part of its task to assess financial management within the Community. In other words, it not only assesses the financial soundness of operations actually carried out, but also judges whether the means employed are the most economic and efficient. The extent of its authority is perhaps best conveyed in the terms of its own first Annual Report:[10]

> 'The principal distinctions between the Court and its predecessors are that the Court enjoys a quasi-institutional status, its members are full-time, it has enhanced powers especially as regards the auditing of all Community income and expenditure (whether budgetized or not), it may start its work immediately expenditure has been committed, ie it need not wait until the accounts are closed, it is entitled to carry out on-the-spot audits in the Member States on its own initiative, it can make observations at any time on specific questions of its own choosing, it gives opinions on financial legislation and it publishes its reports in the Official Journal.'

The institutions of the Community have the right to seek the opinion of the Court of Auditors on specific questions.[11] The European Parliament, in particular, regards this as a means of reinforcing its own authority over Community resources and expenditure. In a resolution on parliamentary control of Community finances which it adopted in 1976, it declared its intention 'to make use of the close and permanent assistance of the Court of Auditors'.[12]

---

8 EEC Treaty, art 206, amended by Second Act of Accession 1979, art 18 and Third Act of Accession 1985, art 20.
9 Ibid, art 16, adding art 206a to the EEC Treaty.
10 OJ 1978, C313, p 6, para 1.5.
11 Financial Provisions Treaty, 1975, art 16 (art 206a (3)).
12 OJ 1976, C159, at p 16. For a list of the reports and opinions adopted by the Court of Auditors over the period 1985–1990, see *Report of the Court of Auditors for the Financial Year* 1990, Annex I, OJ 1990, C313, Vol II, at p 47.

Chapter 9

The Court of Justice and the Court of First Instance

I The Court of Justice

(A) COMPOSITION AND PROCEDURE

1. *Composition and organization*[1]

The Court of Justice of the Communities, as we have seen, has its origins in the Court which was originally set up under the ECSC Treaty. In the words of the EEC Treaty the role of the Court is to 'ensure that in the interpretation and application of [the] Treaty the law is observed'.[2]

The Court is composed of thirteen judges unanimously elected by the Governments of the Member States. In practice each Member State has a judge of its nationality on the Court.[3] It has been agreed that the thirteenth judgeship will be held in rotation by nationals of the five larger Member States. They hold office for six-year renewable terms. The Treaties provide that the judges must be chosen 'from persons whose independence is beyond doubt and who possess the qualifications required for appointment to the highest judicial office in their respective countries or are jurisconsults of recognized competence'.[4] In practice the Bench has been made up of a mixture of professors of law, judges, lawyers in private practice and government legal advisers.

The judges enjoy the usual guarantees of independence and impartiality. They enjoy immunity from suit and legal process during their tenure of office and they retain that status after ceasing

---

1 See EEC Treaty, arts 165–168 (as amended by the adjusted First Act of Accession 1972, arts 17–19, Second Act of Accession 1979, arts 16 and 135, Third Act of Accession 1985, arts 17–19 and 384 and Single European Act, arts 11 and 12) and Protocol on the Statute of the Court of Justice, Titles I and II.

2 Article 164; see also ECSC Treaty, art 31 and Euratom Treaty, art 136.

3 The present United Kingdom judge is Sir Gordon Slynn, formerly a judge of the Queen's Bench Division of the High Court and President of the Employment Appeal Tribunal. From 1981–1988 he was an Advocate-General of the Court.

4 EEC Treaty, art 167. Lasok, K P E, *The European Court of Justice: Practice and Procedure* (1984), pp 4 et seq; Pavlopoulos, A J, *The Advocate General's Office* (1986).

to hold office in respect of acts done in the performance of their duties. This immunity may, however, be suspended by the Court itself in plenary session.[5] The judges also enjoy privileges and immunities in respect of taxation, currency and exchange regulations. They may not hold any office of an administrative or political nature nor engage in any occupation or profession paid or unpaid, although in the case of the latter in an exceptional case permission may be given by the Council.[6]

Judges may resign or be removed from office. To resign, a judge must inform the President of the Court who in turn notifies the President of the Council which latter act creates the vacancy. A judge may be removed from office if, in the unanimous opinion of his brethren, he no longer fulfils the conditions required or meets the obligations resulting from his office. The Court's decision to remove a judge must be communicated to the President of the European Parliament and the President of the Commission and must be notified to the President of the Council. The latter notification produces a vacancy.[7]

The President of the Court is appointed by the judges from among their own number by an absolute majority vote in a secret ballot. A President holds office for a three-year term which may be renewed. The Court may sit for certain purposes in chambers and so there are four Presidents of Chambers to preside over them. They are elected for one-year renewable periods by the same process used to elect the President.[8] The number of judges may, at the request of the Court, be increased by a unanimous decision of the Council.[9]

The judges of the Court are assisted by six Advocates-General who must possess the same professional qualifications as the judges and are also appointed for a six-year renewable term by a unanimous decision of the Council.[10] Each of the four larger Member States has an Advocate-General of its nationality. The fifth and sixth posts of Advocate-General are to be held in rotation by nationals of the smaller Member States.[11] One of their number is designated annually by the Court as First Advocate-General.[12] The

---

5 Protocol on the Statute of the Court, art 3.
6 Ibid, art 4.
7 Ibid, arts 5 to 7.
8 Rules of Procedure of the Court, art 10.
9 EEC Treaty, art 165.
10 EEC Treaty, arts 166, 167; as amended by the Council Decision of 1 January 1973 increasing the number of Advocates-General, OJ 1973, L2 and Decision 81/209, OJ 1981, L100.
11 The present British Advocate-General is Francis Jacobs, QC, formerly Professor of European Law in the University of London.
12 Rules of Procedure of the Court, art 10.

office of Advocate-General is one which has no precise parallel in the English legal system. The institution of Advocate-General, like much of the procedure of the Court itself, is largely derived from French law. The function of the Advocate-General is similar to that of the *Commissaire du Gouvernement* at the French *Conseil d'Etat*. It is the rôle of the *Commissaire du Gouvernement* to act as what has been called 'the embodied conscience of the Court'.[13] He is required to consider the issues in a case impartially and individually and to reach his own personal conclusion as to what in law and justice should be done. Before the *Conseil d'Etat* considers its judgment the *Commissaire*, orally and in public, states the facts and the law as he sees them and suggests the principles in accordance with which he thinks the case should be decided. The *Commissaire* does not participate in the giving of judgment, still less is he the representative of or subordinate to the government. His purpose is to act as an entirely uncommitted and fearless defender of the law and justice. Similarly, in the case of the Advocates-General of the Court of Justice of the Communities, the Treaties require them to 'make reasoned submissions in open court, with complete impartiality and independence', on cases before the Court.[14] Their task is a threefold one: to propose a solution to the case before the Court; to relate that proposed solution to the general pattern of existing case law; and, if possible, to outline the probable future development of the case law. The Advocates-General therefore represent neither the institutions of the Communities nor the public; they function only as the spokesmen of the law and justice in the context of the Treaties.

As in the case of the submissions of the French *Commissaires du Gouvernement* so the submissions of the Advocates-General are in no way binding on the Court. But their submissions are invariably published with the judgment of the Court and where, as often happens, the Court agrees with the Advocate-General, the Advocate-General's full consideration of the wider aspects of the case not only throws valuable light on the Court's comparatively brief judgments, but also act as an indicator of the direction the jurisprudence of the Court is likely to take in the future. In this way the Advocates-General are in a position to influence the development of Community law[15].

As has been said there is no precise parallel in the English legal system to the office of Advocate-General. The Attorney-General does have a role as guardian of the public interest or protector of

13 Hamson, C, *Executive Discretion and Judicial Control* (1954), p 80.
14 Eg EEC Treaty, art 166.
15 See Brown, L N and Jacobs, F G, *The Court of Justice of the European Communities* (3rd edn, 1989), chapter 4.

public rights, eg as a party in civil proceedings for an injunction or declaration in cases of public nuisance and his appearance before public tribunals of inquiry as a spokesman for the public interest. Similarly, in matrimonial proceedings, the Queen's Proctor has a right of intervention to prevent a decree nisi being made absolute on the ground, for example, that material facts have not been put to the court. A court may also ask the Official Solicitor to instruct counsel to ensure that all points of view on matters of law are fully before the court. But in these cases the rôles of the Attorney-General, the Queen's Proctor and the Official Solicitor are limited and special whereas that of the Advocates-General is unlimited and general.[16] The rôle of the Advocate-General is a hybrid in that it has both advocatory and judicial characteristics. As an independent advocate of the legal interests of the Community, he may be regarded as a sort of institutionalized *amicus curiae*. As a person appointed with the same qualifications and on the same conditions as the judges and whose views have a formative influence on the law, he may be regarded almost as a first instance judge whose opinions are never decisive but are always subject to review by the Court.[17] Advocates-General may retire and be removed by the same procedure as in the case of judges and they enjoy similar privileges and immunities. The Treaties are silent on the nationality of the judges and Advocates-General but in practice they are always of the nationality of one of the Member States.

The seat of the Court is in Luxembourg and, subject to public holidays and the usual vacations, it is in permanent session. In case of urgency the President may convene the Court during vacations.

The day-to-day administration of the Court is in the hands of the Registrar and his staff. The Registrar is elected by the judges by majority vote after consultation with the Advocates-General. The Registrar's term of office is six years and he is eligible for re-election. The Court may dismiss him if he no longer complies with the obligations of his office.[18]

Each judge and Advocate-General is assisted by three legal secretaries. The legal secretaries are normally of the same nationality as their masters and are required to have legal training. Their main tasks are to prepare pre-trial studies on the legal questions involved in a case before the Court and to assist in the drafting of opinions

---

16 See Edwards, J LlJ, *Law Officers of the Crown* (1964), Chapter 14; *Rayden on Divorce* (13th edn, 1979), pp 477–479; *Halsbury's Laws of England* (4th edn), Vol 10, para 950.

17 Cf. Warner, J-P, 'Some Aspects of the European Court of Justice' (1976), 14 JSPTL (NS) 15, pp 17–19.

18 See Rules of Procedure of the Court, Title 1, Chapter 3; Lasok, op cit, pp 9–10 and 14–21.

and judgments. They thus provide a service similar to that of the Law Clerks to the Judges of the United States Supreme Court.[19]

In principle the Court sits in plenary session with a quorum of seven, but it is enabled to set up separate chambers and has established four chambers of three judges and two chambers of six judges each presided over by a President of Chamber. It is the function of these chambers, at the request of the Court, to undertake preliminary examinations of evidence in particular cases. They can also hear and decide cases brought by one of the officials of a Community institution against that institution, references for preliminary rulings and any actions brought by natural or legal persons the nature or circumstances of which do not necessitate a hearing by the full Court. If a Member State or a Community institution is party to the latter type of action it can insist on a hearing by the full Court.[20] Each chamber is assisted by an Advocate-General.[1]

2. *Practice and procedure*
The practice and procedure of the Court are based on a code of Rules of Procedure drawn up by the Court.[2] The procedure of the Court is divided into three stages: a written stage; a preparatory enquiry stage; and an oral stage. As soon as a written application is filed with the Registrar, the President appoints one of the judges as judge-rapporteur. The task of the judge-rapporteur is to prepare a preliminary report on the case for the consideration of the Court. This is followed by the First Advocate-General assigning one of his colleagues to the case.[3]

The written stage takes the form of pleadings. The plaintiff in his application will set out his claim against the defendant and the grounds upon which it is made. The defendant will then be notified of the application and will be given the period of one month within which to prepare and submit to the Court a statement of defence. The plaintiff may make a written reply to the defence and the defendant may then also make a final rejoinder. This exchange of submissions comprises the written stage in the proceedings. It should be pointed out that these written submissions go far beyond the scope and purpose of English pleadings. The arguments of the

---

19 For comment see Feld, W, *Court of the European Communities* (1964), p 27 and Brown and Jacobs, op cit, pp 17–18.
20 See Rules of Procedure, art 95, as amended in 1979. See OJ 1979, L238, p 3.
1 See Rules of Procedure of the Court, art 10.
2 The Rules require the unanimous approval of the Council; EEC Treaty, art 188. The present Rules were approved on 26 November 1974; see OJ 1974, L350. For subsequent amendments see OJ 1979, L238, OJ 1981, L199, OJ 1987, L165 and OJ 1989, L241.
3 See Rules of Procedure of the Court, arts 9 and 10 and Title 2.

parties are set out fully together with the nature of the evidence upon which reliance is placed. This form of documentary advocacy has the effect of stressing the written stage at the expense of the other two stages.[4]

The judge-rapporteur then examines the pleadings and considers whether the case requires a preparatory enquiry, ie a proof-taking stage which is a familiar part of continental legal procedure. The judge-rapporteur reports to the Court on whether a preparatory enquiry is necessary and after the Court has also heard the Advocate-General on this point it will decide whether to proceed to a preparatory enquiry. If the Court decides that a preparatory enquiry is necessary it can be held before the full court, before one of the chambers of the court or it may be entrusted to the judge-rapporteur himself. In any event, the preparatory enquiry may take the form of a personal appearance of the parties and their witnesses for oral examination, the production and inspection of documentary evidence, experts' reports or an inspection by the Court of the place or thing in question. This procedure of preparatory enquiry is principally conducted not by the lawyers representing the parties, but, following continental practice, by the Court, chamber or judge-rapporteur as the case may be. The Advocate-General may also participate in the preparatory enquiry. The representatives of the parties may only question witnesses 'subject to the control of the President.'[5] In addition to witnesses who are called at the request of the parties, the Court and the Advocate-General also have the power to summon witnesses. Evidence is given on oath sworn either in accordance with the laws of the state of the witness's nationality, or alternatively in the form set out in the Rules of Procedure. The Court has the power to exempt a witness from taking the oath.[6] At the end of the preparatory enquiry the Court may allow the parties to submit written observations on matters which have arisen in the course of the preparatory enquiry.

After the conclusion of the preparatory enquiry, or, if there has been no preparatory enquiry,[7] at the end of the written proceedings, the oral stage takes place before the court. Immediately prior to the oral stage the judge-rapporteur will issue his report for the hearing which will outline the case, summarize the arguments of the parties and make a statement on the facts of the case on the basis of the evidence presented during the written and preparatory enquiry stages. This will be followed by oral argument on behalf

---

4 For example, in 1971 the Court gave judgment in 60 cases in which the written procedure totalled 18,000 pages; Campbell, op cit, Vol 3, para 7.23.
5 Rules of Procedure, art 47 (4).
6 Rules of Procedure, arts 47 (5) and 110.
7 As is usually the case. See Brown and Jacobs, op cit, p 229.

of the parties. There is no hearing of witnesses or oral examination at this stage. The parties must be legally represented during the oral stage.[8]

Members of the Court and the Advocate-General may put questions to agents and counsel during the oral proceedings. The Court may also at this stage order a further preparatory enquiry to be held either by a chamber or by the judge-rapporteur. At the conclusion of the case the parties' representatives make closing speeches to the Court: plaintiff first, followed by defendant. The Advocate-General then presents his opinion which brings the oral proceedings to a close. There is usually an adjournment between the speeches by counsel and the Advocate-General's delivery of his opinion.

The judges withdraw to deliberate in private without the participation of Advocates-General, legal secretaries or interpreters. In the course of their deliberations they may reopen the oral proceedings if they so wish. These deliberations finally result in the Court's judgment which is drafted by the judge-rapporteur. Judgment is delivered in open court. Again, following continental practice, the court renders a single collegiate judgment; separate or dissenting opinions are not permitted. Even if the judgment is based on a majority decision that fact, let alone the nature of the majority, is not disclosed.[9] It has already been pointed out that in the vast majority of cases the Court accepts the conclusions of the Advocate-General. But in those cases where the Court has not followed the Advocate-General, his opinion can in a sense be regarded as a dissenting judgment.

The languages of the Court are the official languages of the Communities, viz. Danish, Dutch, English, French, German, Greek, Italian, Portugese and Spanish; Irish may also be used although it is not an official language.[10] French has become the working language of the Court and it is the language in which the Court's deliberations are conducted. Only one of the Community languages may be used as the procedural language in a given case. The basic rule is that the choice of procedural language is made by the plaintiff where one of the Communities' institutions is the defendant, on the basis that the representatives of the Communities

---

8 Member States and Community institutions must be represented by an agent who may be assisted by a lawyer entitled to practise before a court of a Member State. Corporate bodies and individuals may also have an agent but they must be represented by a lawyer entitled to practise before a court of a Member State. See Protocol on the Statute of the Court, art 20. Lasok, op cit, pp 66 et seq.

9 For comment on the practice of single collegiate judgments see Bebr op cit, p 24 and Feld, op cit, p 99.

10 Rules of Procedure, art 29 (1).

are well versed in all the official languages. But where the defendant is one of the Member States or the court of a Member State is seeking a preliminary ruling then the procedural language must be the language of that state. The Court's judgments, together with the report for the hearing and the opinion of the Advocate-General, are published in each of the official languages; the copy in the procedural language of a given case being regarded as the authentic and definitive version.[11]

The Court's judgments have binding force from the date of their delivery.[12] As far as the enforcement of the Court's judgments is concerned the position varies depending on the outcome of the case and the identity of the defendant. If the Court upholds or declares invalid an act of a Community institution then either that act may be implemented or not depending upon the decision of the Court; in such cases there is no question of enforcing the judgment in the strict sense. If the Court gives judgment against a Member State under the ECSC Treaty enforcement is achieved by enabling the Commission, acting jointly with the Council, to impose sanctions on the defaulting member. This procedure is not reproduced in the Treaties of Rome which contain no enforcement measures for use against Member States. The Rome Treaties merely provide that the Member State in question is required to take the measures necessary to execute the Court's judgment. Lastly, if the Court gives judgment against a corporate body or individual in the form of a fine, such judgment debts are enforceable without further formality by the national courts of the Member States.[13]

3. *Revision and interpretation of judgments*

The decisions of the Court are final and are not subject to appeal; it is not open to a national court when called upon to enforce a judgment of the Community Court to challenge that judgment in any way. The only possible course of action open to an unsuccessful litigant is to request a revision of the Court's judgment.[14] Such a request may be made on the ground of the discovery of a fact likely to prove of decisive importance which, before judgment, was unknown both to the Court and to the party requesting revision. Two periods of limitation apply to requests for revision: the request must be made within ten years of the date of the judgment and within three months of the date on which the new fact became

11 See Rules of Procedure arts 29, 30 and 31. On the problems of multi-lingual judicial deliberations see Feld, op cit, pp 100, 101 and Hartley, T C, *The Foundations of European Community Law* (2nd edn, 1988), pp 66–73.
12 Rules of the Court, art 65.
13 EEC Treaty, arts 187, 192.
14 See Protocol on the Statute of the Court, art 41 and Rules of Procedure of the Court, art 98 to 100.

known to the applicant. If these conditions are satisfied, and without prejudice to the merits, the Court hears the Advocate-General and considers the parties' written submissions before deciding whether the alleged new fact does exist and whether it justifies revision. If the Court decides that the request is admissible then it proceeds to consider the merits of the case and this can, if necessary, involve a completely new trial. In *Acciaieria di Roma v High Authority of the ECSC* (1960) the Court made it clear that the newly discovered fact must have been unknown both to the Court and to the party, and that knowledge of it prior to judgment by either Court or a party will make the request inadmissible.[15] In *Fonderie Acciaierie Giovanni Mandelli v EC Commission* (1971), the Court refused an application for revision in a similar case in which a relevant document could have been obtained by the applicant either at the time of the commencement of the original action or at the enquiry stage.[16] The Court regards the procedure for revision as an exception to the doctrine of *res judicata*. As such it interprets the conditions for revision strictly and will not allow the procedure to be used for the purpose of bringing an appeal.[17]

A final point concerning the practice of the court relates to the possibility in case of difficulty as to the meaning or scope of a judgment of asking the Court to interpret its judgment.[18] Such a request may be made by any of the parties to the case or by a Community institution which can show that it has an interest in the decision. The only part of a judgment which may be the subject of a request for interpretation is the operative part or what we would call the *ratio decidendi*. As the Court itself put it in *Assider v High Authority of the ECSC* (1955)[19] 'the only parts of a judgment which can be interpreted are those which express the judgment of the Court in the dispute which has been submitted for its final decision and those parts of the reasoning upon which this decision is based and which are, therefore, essential to it ... the Court does not have to interpret those passages which are incidental and which complete or explain that basic reasoning'.

In the later case of *High Authority and European Court v Collotti* (1965)[20] the Court considered the nature of the 'difficulty' necessary to justify a request for an interpretation. In the *Assider* case the court had said that it was sufficient for the parties to give different

---

15 Case 1/60: [1960] ECR 165.
16 Case 56/70: [1971] ECR 1.
17 Case 116/78 Rev: *Bellintani v EC Commission* [1980] ECR 23.
18 See Protocol on the Statute of the Court, art 40 and Rules of Procedure of the Court, art 102.
19 Case 5/55: [1954–56] ECR 135.
20 Case 70/63 A bis: [1965] ECR 275.

meanings to the judgment. In the *Collotti* case the Court defined
the nature of the difficulty more precisely. The Court held: 'In
order to be admissible, an application for interpretation ... must
not raise the possible consequences of the judgment in question
on cases other than the one decided, but only the obscurity and
ambiguity of the meaning and scope of the judgment itself in
relation to the case decided by the judgment in question.' An
application for interpretation may concern the effect of the judgment on the legal relations of the parties to the case, but not
the application of the judgment nor the consequences which flow
from it.[1]

(B) CONTENTIOUS JURISDICTION[2]

The Court is the creature of the Community Treaties and so its
jurisdiction derives exclusively from those Treaties. Any attempt
to attribute other jurisdiction to the Court will fail. In the case of
Schlieker v High Authority of the ECSC (1963)[3] the plaintiff alleged
that through the inactivity of the High Authority she had suffered
loss. It was argued on behalf of the High Authority that the right
to bring proceedings before the Court based on the inactivity of a
Community institution was limited by the Treaty to Member
States, other Community institutions and undertakings and associations. Frau Schlieker argued in reply, upon analogy with German
municipal law, that the Court had a residual jurisdiction to enable
it to protect the interests of individuals where the Treaty texts are
silent. This view was rejected both by the Advocate-General and
the Court. The Advocate-General observed that 'the Treaty system
... does not in a general clause guarantee legal protection without
any gaps. Reference to ... the Basic Law (*Grundgesetz*) of the
Federal Republic of Germany cannot lead to any other solution,
for the Court can define the limits of its supra-national legal protection only by using the text of the Treaty and not by following
national law.'[4] The Court agreed with this submission and held
that: 'Whatever may be the consequence of a factual situation of
which the Court may not take cognizance, the Court may not depart
from the judicial system set out in the Treaty'. Thus in interpreting
the Treaties the Court is bound to adhere strictly to the provisions

1 Case 9/81: *EC Court of Auditors v Williams* [1983] ECR 2859.
2 The Court's jurisdiction to give preliminary rulings at the request of the courts
   of the Member States will be discussed later in connection with the relationship
   between Community law and municipal law; see Chapter 11.
3 Case 12/63: [1963] ECR 85, [1963] CMLR 281.
4 Unwritten rules of Community law for the protection of fundamental rights
   may, however, be derived from national law; see Chapter 2, supra.

of the text, and, being the creature of the Treaty, it has no power other than that conferred by the Treaty.[5]

The jurisdictional provisions of the Treaties are somewhat complex; as one commentator has observed, 'No international tribunal has ever been equipped with so varied a jurisdictional competence as has the Court of the European Communities.'[6] The contentious jurisdiction conferred upon the Court by the Treaties falls under two main heads which will be treated in the following order:

(a) Actions against Member States; and
(b) Actions against Community institutions.

1. *Actions against Member States*

Actions against Member States take two forms:

(i) Actions by Member States against Member States.

(ii) Actions by Community institutions against Member States.

(i) All the Treaties confer upon the Court a compulsory jurisdiction to decide disputes between Member States concerning the application of the terms of the Treaties and a permissive jurisdiction, based on the consent of the parties, over disputes between states related to the object and purpose of the Communities in general. Thus the EEC Treaty provides first at article 170 that 'A Member State which considers that another Member State has failed to fulfil an obligation under this Treaty may bring the matter before the Court of Justice.'[7] Secondly, the EEC Treaty provides ✗ at article 182 that 'The Court of Justice shall have jurisdiction in any dispute between Member States which relates to the subject-matter of this Treaty, if the dispute is submitted to it under a special agreement between the parties.'[8] The Court's jurisdiction over both of these types of dispute is exclusive; recourse by Member States to other means of settlement is expressly forbidden by the Treaties. Article 219 of the EEC Treaty provides that 'Member States undertake not to submit a dispute concerning the interpretation or application of this Treaty to any method of settlement other than those provided for therein'.[9] This insistence on referring inter-state disputes to the Court of Justice underlines one of the major purposes of the Court and that is to guarantee uniformity of interpretation and application of the law of the Communities.

Under the terms of article 170 of the EEC Treaty, before one

---

5 See Case 66/76: *CFDT v EC Council* [1977] ECR 305, [1977] 1 CMLR 589.
6 Bowett, D W, *Law of International Institutions* (3rd edn 1975), p 278.
7 Cf ECSC Treaty, art 89, and Euratom Treaty, art 141.
8 Cf ECSC Treaty, art 89, and Euratom Treaty, art 154.
9 Cf ECSC Treaty, art 87, and Euratom Treaty, art 193.

Member State brings another before the Court the matter must be referred to the Commission. This gives the Commission an opportunity to deliver a reasoned opinion on the alleged breach of Treaty in the light of observations made by the Member States in dispute. This procedure seems to be designed for the purpose of promoting the resolution of the dispute without resort to litigation. But whether or not the Commission delivers such an opinion, the Member State making the allegation can insist on proceeding with the action. In general, Member States prefer to resolve their disputes outside the courtroom; only one article 170 action has so far been heard. In that case[10] France alleged that the United Kingdom's fishery conservation measures were contrary to Community law. The Commission delivered an opinion in support of the French view. The European Court agreed with that opinion and gave judgment against the United Kingdom.[11]

(ii) By virtue of article 88 of the ECSC Treaty the Commission is given the power to decide whether a Member State has failed to comply with its obligations under the Treaty. If it so decides in relation to a given Member State the Commission must invite that state to express its views on the matter. The Commission may then record the state's wrongdoing in a reasoned opinion and give the state a limited time within which to take steps to fulfil its obligations. The purpose of this process is to enable both the Commission and the Member State to exchange views in the hope that the issue may thereby be settled. If it is not, it is open to the Member State in question to bring proceedings before the Court challenging the Commission's decision. Although such litigation takes the form of a Member State bringing proceedings against the Commission, in substance the issue before the Court is an alleged breach of Treaty obligations by a Member State; the Treaty places the onus of challenging that allegation upon the Member State. In the EEC Treaty by virtue of article 169 a somewhat different procedure is followed.[12] There if the Commission considers that a Member State has failed to fulfil any of its obligations under the Treaties then it shall issue a reasoned opinion after giving the state concerned the opportunity to submit its comments. If the Member State does not comply with the terms of such opinion within the

10 Case 141/78: *France v United Kingdom* [1979] ECR 2923; [1980] 1 CMLR 6. Also see p 365 post.
11 Disputes between Member States may be at the root of litigation between the Commission and a Member State. See Case 232/78: *EC Commission v France* [1979] ECR 2729 where the dispute had earlier been the subject of an art 170 action brought by Ireland against France (Case 58/77: OJ 1977, C142) which was later withdrawn (OJ 1978, C76).
12 Also Euratom Treaty, art 141.

period laid down by the Commission the Commission may bring the matter before the Court of Justice. Thus, whilst in the ECSC the Commission has the power to determine finally a Member State's breach of obligations subject to the Member State's right to appeal to the Court, in the EEC and Euratom the Commission can only provisionally determine the breach of obligation and it must apply to the Court for that determination to be confirmed. A similar right of action by the Commission against a Member State is given by article 93(2) of the EEC Treaty in the context of the rules concerning state aid. If the Commission finds that financial aid granted by a Member State is incompatible with the Treaty it shall require that Member State to abolish or alter such aid. If the Member State does not comply within the prescribed period, the Commission may refer the matter to the Court direct.

The Commission has brought over seven hundred actions[13] against Member States under the terms of articles 169 and 93(2), the overwhelming majority of cases arising under article 169. Proceedings will lie against Member States not only for any acts on the part of a Member State but also for omissions, including administrative failures to implement Community law.[14] This reflects the dual duty which article 5 of the EEC Treaty imposes on Member States: to take all appropriate measures to ensure the fulfilment of Treaty obligations and to abstain from any measure which could jeopardize the attainment of Treaty objectives. These actions not only serve the narrow purpose of enforcing the obligations of Member States in specific cases, but they also provide the Court with a vehicle for elaborating more broadly the nature of the Treaty obligations of Member States.

In one of the early cases, the Commission brought actions against Belgium and Luxembourg in which it alleged that a tax which those Member States were imposing on import licences for dairy products was contrary to the EEC Treaty.[15] The defendant governments argued that a Council resolution of 1962 which had not yet been implemented would have justified the tax. They maintained that the Commission had no authority to require the abolition of a tax which but for the failure to implement the Council resolution would be part of Community policy. But the Court held that, except for cases expressly authorized by the Treaty, Member States are prohibited from taking justice into their own hands. Therefore

13 See *Twenty-third General Report on the Activities of the European Communities* (1990), Table 2, p 437.
14 See Case 31/69: *EEC Commission v Italy* [1970] ECR 25, [1970] CMLR 175.
15 Cases 90–91/63: *EEC Commission v Luxembourg and Belgium* [1964] ECR 625, [1965] CMLR 58.

a failure by the Council to carry out its obligations could not excuse the defendant Member States from carrying out theirs. Similarly, in a later case against Italy the Court rejected an attempted defence which was based on the fact that Member States other than Italy had also failed to carry out the obligation in question by the required date.[16]

In other cases in which a Member State has failed to fulfil its Treaty obligations the Court has not been moved by pleas that such failure is attributable to the special characteristics of the legal and constitutional order of a Member State or to prevailing political or economic conditions. Therefore, a political crisis in Italy which paralysed Italian legislative processes was not accepted as a defence to an article 169 action.[17] In the same way the Court rejected a plea by the United Kingdom that its refusal to comply with a Community obligation was justified for economic and practical reasons including opposition by Trade Unions.[18] As the Court said in that latter case, 'practical difficulties which appear at the stage when a Community measure is put into effect cannot permit a Member State unilaterally to opt out of fulfilling its obligations'.[19] Partial and idiosyncratic implementation of Community obligations will not satisfy the Court.[20] Nor can a Member State avoid an article 169 action by delaying taking implementing measures until the particular obligation has been revoked.[1] Community law must apply in each Member State independent of its unilateral will.

The case law on article 169 of the EEC Treaty also throws some light on the nature of the reasoned opinion which the Commission must make concerning the alleged breach of Treaty obligations. In *EEC Commission v Italy* (1961)[2] the Commission wrote a letter to the Italian Government, after giving the Government an opportunity to make its observations, stating that a particular Italian decree was contrary to the Treaty. The Government was asked to end the alleged infringement within one month. This letter did not contain a full review of the situation of the Italian market nor whether that situation justified the decree. Italy did not comply

---

16 Case 52/75: *EC Commission v Italy* [1976] ECR 277, [1976] 2 CMLR 320.
17 Case 30/72: *EC Commission v Italy* [1973] ECR 161.
18 Case 128/78: *EC Commission v United Kingdom* [1979] ECR 419, [1979] 2 CMLR 45.
19 Ibid at 429. Also see Case 102/79: *EC Commission v Belgium* [1980] ECR 1473 at 1487.
20 Case 39/72: *EC Commission v Italy* [1973] ECR 101, [1973] CMLR 439.
 1 Ibid. In the context of art 169 and 93 (2) actions, interim measures may be taken against a Member State in emergency situations; see Cases 31, 53/77R: *EC Commission v United Kingdom* [1977] ECR 921.
 2 Case 7/61: [1961] ECR 317, [1962] CMLR 39.

with the Commission's request within the stated period and so the Commission instituted proceedings under article 169. Italy challenged the admissibility of these proceedings on the ground, inter alia, that the Commission's letter was not a reasoned opinion within the meaning of article 169. The Court rejected that argument and said that an opinion is considered to be reasoned 'when it contains, as in the present case, a coherent statement of the reasons which convinced the Commission that the state in question had failed to fulfil one of its obligations under the Treaty'. This was also the view expressed by the Advocate-General in his submissions where he said that 'no formalism is required ... because ... the reasoned opinion is not an administrative act, checked by the Court as far as its legal character is concerned. There is no question here of "insufficient reasons" giving rise to a formal defect. The only purpose of the reasoned opinion is to specify the point of view of the Commission in order to inform the Government and, possibly, the Court.' Thus, if a purported reasoned opinion did not coherently express the Commission's viewpoint that would be a ground on which the Court might dismiss the Commission's case.[3]

In the case of article 88 of the ECSC Treaty if the Member State does not appeal to the Court or if it loses its appeal, the Commission may, subject to a concurring two-thirds majority of the Council, impose on the Member State the sanctions mentioned earlier. In the cases of the EEC and Euratom Treaties no such sanctions are available. Both article 171 of the EEC Treaty and article 143 of the Euratom Treaty state that, if the Court of Justice finds that a Member State has failed to fulfil any of its obligations under the Treaty, such state shall take the measures required for the implementation of the judgment of the Court.[4] Thus in such cases the Court's judgments are essentially declaratory in nature indicating that in the last analysis the success of the Communities depends upon the good faith of Member States. A Member State's failure to implement a judgment given against it would also be likely to have an unfavourable political effect on its relations with its fellow members.[5]

---

3 Another essential part of the pre-litigation procedure under art 169 is the giving of a Member State an adequate and realistic opportunity to make observations on an alleged breach of treaty obligations; Case 31/69, *EC Commission v Italy* [1970] ECR 25, [1970] CMLR 175.
4 A failure by a Member State to execute a previous judgment of the Court will constitute an infringement of EEC Treaty, art 171; Case 48/71: *EC Commission v Italy* [1972] ECR 527, [1972] CMLR 699.
5 On the effectiveness of art 169 proceedings see *Hartley*, op cit, pp 313–315.

2. *Actions against Community institutions*

We have already seen that French law has exerted a strong influence on the procedure of the Court of Justice of the Communities. This is also true of the jurisdiction of the Court to exercise control over the acts of the institutions of the Communities. French administrative law traditionally recognizes two main categories of litigation: the *recours de la légalité* and the *recours de pleine juridiction*. The former is a kind of judicial review of the legality of administrative acts in which the Court is merely asked to annul, ie declare void, an administrative act on one of a number of specified grounds. In such a case if the Court finds that a given act is unlawful on one of those grounds it can merely give judgment to that effect; it cannot substitute its own decision on the merits for that of the institution whose act has been challenged, nor can it award any other remedy such as damages. In addition to *recours de la légalité* French administrative courts may also hear *recours de pleine juridiction*. In such cases those courts are not limited to controlling the legality of acts on specific grounds but they are free to pronounce on the actual merits of the parties' case and to substitute their own decision for that of the administrative authority. Such jurisdiction is *pleine*, ie full or plenary, in the sense that when exercising it the court has the complete powers of a civil court to award compensation for damage. These two types of administrative jurisdiction are possessed by the Court of Justice of the Communities and the following discussion will be in terms of that classification:

(a) *Actions concerning legality (recours de la légalité)*

(i) *Actions for annulment.*—The acts of the institutions of the Communities take a variety of forms but not all of them are susceptible to challenge. Only those acts which are binding in law are susceptible to challenge. Under the ECSC Treaty the Commission may act in three forms: decisions, recommendations and opinions. Of these decisions and recommendations are legally binding whilst opinions have no binding force; thus article 33 gives the Court jurisdiction to hear actions for the annulment of such decisions and recommendations. Under the EEC and Euratom Treaties the acts of the Commission and the Council may take five forms: regulations, directives, decisions, recommendations and opinions; of these the first three are legally binding and are susceptible of an action for annulment. Thus the Court has declined to entertain an action for annulment in connection with any act which is not designed to produce binding legal effects. In *Sucrimex SA and Westzucker GmbH v EC Commission* (1980)[6] the Court rejected

6 Case 133/79: [1980] ECR 1299, [1981] 2 CMLR 479.

an action challenging the legality of a telex message from the Commission to the authorities of a Member State. In accordance with Community rules Sucrimex had exported a quantity of sugar to Westzucker. When the appropriate national authority was asked to pay the export refunds in respect of that transaction, payment in full was refused in accordance with the terms of the Commission's telex message. In dismissing the action, the Court held that under Community law the application of provisions concerning export refunds was a matter for the appropriate authorities of the Member States. In these matters the Commission had no power of decision, but it could express an opinion. This was confirmed by the contested telex message which did not disclose any intention to produce binding legal effects. The Court does, nevertheless, adopt a flexible approach to this issue. It will look to the substance of an act rather than to its form. Therefore, if an act is in the form normally used for non-binding acts, but in the view of the Court it does in fact create binding obligations, such an act would be actionable despite its apparent informality.[7] There is recent authority for the proposition that even a decision communicated orally during a conversation may be an act which is susceptible to an action for annulment.[8] It has also been held that certain acts of the European Parliament are open to challenge. Thus by invoking article 38 of the ECSC Treaty which provides, inter alia, that on the application of either a Member State or the High Authority, an act of the European Parliament may be held void, the Court has claimed jurisdiction to review a decision of the European Parliament concerning its seat.[9] More generally the Court has held that acts of the European Parliament, at least in the budgetary field, which are intended to have legal effects on third parties are susceptible to an action for annulment under article 173 of the EEC Treaty.[10]

Actions may be brought not only by Member States and by Community institutions but also by private parties. In the first place, article 173(1) of the EEC Treaty states that the legality of measures taken by the Council or by the Commission may be challenged in proceedings instituted by a Member State, the Council or the Commission.[11] In general terms only a party which

7 See Case 22/70: *EC Commission v EC Council* [1971] ECR 263, [1971] CMLR 335.
8 See Cases 316/82 and 40/83: *Kohler v EC Court of Auditors* [1984] ECR 641.
9 See Cases 230/81 and 108/83: *Luxembourg v European Parliament* [1983] ECR 255 and [1984] ECR 1945.
10 See Case 34/86: *EC Council v European Parliament* [1986] 3 CMLR 94; and Case 294/83: *Parti Ecologist 'Les Verts' v European Parliament* [1987] 2 CMLR 343.
11 Cf ECSC Treaty, arts 33 and 38, and Euratom Treaty, art 146.

can show sufficient legal interest in a case can institute proceedings before the Court, but such is the nature of the Communities that all Member States are deemed to have an interest in the legality of all Community acts. Thus, for example, in the *Netherlands v High Authority of the ECSC* (1964)[12] the Netherlands was permitted to challenge a decision of the High Authority which was in fact addressed to some German coal enterprises on the ground that it conflicted with the terms of ECSC Treaty. The unfettered nature of the right of Member States to challenge Community acts is illustrated by a case in which Italy sought the annulment of a regulation for which it had voted in the Council. The Court rejected the Council's plea that the action was inadmissible. It held that every Member State has the right to challenge every Council regulation 'without the exercise of this right being conditional upon the position taken up by the ... Member States ... when the regulation in question was adopted.'[13]

It is clearly possible under the Treaties for one Community institution to challenge an act of another Community institution. To date this has not happened very often.[14] In his submissions in the first of those cases the Advocate-General referred to the novelty of the proceedings and attributed this to the fundamental harmony which reigns between these two institutions. Be that as it may, in that action the Commission challenged certain activities of the Council in the field of the external relations of the Communities. In March 1970 the Council discussed the attitude to be taken by the members of the Communities at a meeting to be held in April of that year to conclude the negotiations for a European Road Transport Agreement (ERTA) under the auspices of the UN Economic Commission for Europe. At that April meeting the members of the Communities negotiated and concluded the Agreement in accordance with the terms of the Council's discussion. The Commission challenged the validity of that discussion on the ground that it involved violation of Treaty provisions, particularly since under article 228 the Commission is given the task of negotiating agreements between the Community and non-Member States subject to the approval of the Council. The Council challenged this action on the grounds of its admissibility and its merits. On the question of admissibility the Advocate-General submitted that,

---

12 Case 66/63: [1964] ECR 533, [1964] CMLR 522.
13 Case 166/78: *Italy v EC Council* [1979] ECR 2575 at 2596.
14 See Case 22/70: *EC Commission v EC Council* [1971] ECR 263, [1971] CMLR 335; Case 81/72: *EC Commission v EC Council* [1973] ECR 575, [1973] CMLR 639, Case 70/74: *EC Commission v EC Council* [1975] ECR 795, [1975] 2 CMLR 287, and Case 218/82: *EC Commission v EC Council* [1983] ECR 4063, [1984] 2 CMLR 350.

whilst in principle the action was admissible because the discussion in issue was an official discussion of the Council, upon analysis that discussion was not a legally binding act of the Council as defined by the Treaty and so was not susceptible to challenge. The Court disagreed with the Advocate-General on this point and held that the action was admissible. The Court pointed out that article 173 of the EEC Treaty specifically excluded recommendations and opinions from review by the Court. Not only was this discussion neither a recommendation nor an opinion, it had definite legal effects on the Member States since during their negotiations on the ERTA they consistently acted in accordance with the conclusion of the Council discussion. But although the Court differed from the Advocate-General on the question of admissibility they both agreed that the action should be rejected on the merits.[15]

The question has arisen whether the European Parliament may challenge acts of the other institutions under article 173 of the EEC Treaty, despite the fact that it is not named as a potential plaintiff. In 1987 the Parliament tested its claim by seeking the annulment of a Council decision on grounds that it had unlawfully failed to delegate authority to the Commission and had thereby deprived the Parliament of its prerogative of exercising political control over the Commission.[16] In response to the Council's plea that the action was inadmissible, the Parliament argued that given that the Treaty had been liberally interpreted to recognize the Parliament as a defendant under this article[17] it should be similarly interpreted to recognize it as a plaintiff, particularly bearing in mind its Treaty right to challenge inaction.[18] The need for the Parliament to be able to protect its prerogatives was also stressed. The Court declared the action inadmissible.[19] It rejected the submission that there should be parallelism between the active and passive role of Parliament in proceedings under article 173, noting that that article had not been amended by the Single European Act which, inter alia, was concerned with the Parliament's powers. Regarding any possible encroachment by the Council on the Parliament's prerogatives, the Court took the view that it was the responsibility of the Commission under article 155 of the EEC Treaty to ensure that such prerogatives were respected.[20] This rebuff to the European Parliament's hopes has more recently been partially redressed by the

---

15 The merits of this case have already been discussed in connection with the external relations of the Communities; see pp 70–71 supra.
16 Case 302/87: *European Parliament v EC Council* [1988] ECR 5615.
17 See p 297, supra.
18 See p 310, infra.
19 [1988] ECR, at pp 5636–5644.
20 As to art 155, see Ch 5, II(C), supra.

judgment in another case.[1] There it sought to challenge a Council regulation on the ground that it was based on a Commission proposal which failed to respond to the Parliament's disagreement with the legal base chosen for the regulation in the context of the co-operation procedure.[2] The Court agreed that in such a situation the Parliament clearly could not rely completely on the Commission to safeguard its prerogatives. In such circumstances the action by the Parliament was admissible.

Secondly, actions may be brought against acts of Community institutions by private parties, that is to say by individuals or corporate bodies.[3] The *locus standi* of private parties differs somewhat as between the ECSC on the one hand and the EEC on the other. In the ECSC undertakings or associations of undertakings may challenge acts of Community institutions where either those acts apply to them individually or, although acts of a general nature, nevertheless involve a misuse of powers affecting them.[4] *Groupement des Industries Sidérurgiques Luxembourgeoises v High Authority* (1956)[5] is a clear illustration of this. The plaintiffs were manufacturers of steel and the main industrial consumers of coal in Luxembourg. They challenged the refusal of the High Authority to declare illegal a Luxembourg levy on coal for industrial use. The Luxembourg government intervened in the proceedings and argued that the plaintiffs' action was inadmissible on the ground that they were steel producers and the action was solely concerned with coal. But the Court held that the Treaty did not limit actions relating to coal undertakings and, since prima facie this levy was detrimental to the plaintiffs, their right of action could not be denied. In the EEC, on the other hand, the right of action is not limited to undertakings but is available to any individual or corporate body against either a decision directed to him or it or a decision which, although in the form of a regulation or a decision addressed to someone else, is of direct and individual concern to him or it.[6]

Certain points of principle concerning the *locus standi* of private parties to challenge acts in the context of the EEC are clear. The Treaty does not recognize an *actio popularis* but requires the party bringing the action to have sufficient legal interest in the issue.

---

1 Case C-70/88: *European Parliament v EC Council*, Judgment of 22 May 1990, not yet reported.
2 As to this procedure, see Ch 6(B), supra.
3 The novelty of this right of audience is fully justified by the fact that Community law applies directly to private parties which art 173 refers to as natural and legal persons.
4 Eg ECSC Treaty, arts 33 (2) and 80.
5 Cases 7 and 9/54: [1954–56] ECR 175.
6 EEC Treaty, art 173 (2); also see Euratom Treaty, art 146 (2).

This is comparable to the notion of sufficient interest in English administrative law[7] and to the French maxim *pas d'intérêt, pas d'action.*[8] A right of action is admitted against three types of act: decisions addressed to the party bringing the action; decisions in the form of regulations addressed to other persons; and decisions addressed to other persons. In the last two cases the party bringing the action must be able to satisfy the Court that the decisions affect him directly and individually. Despite dicta in some cases in which a generous interpretation of these provisions has been suggested,[9] the Court has tended to interpret them restrictively and the resulting case law has not yet evolved an entirely consistent line of authority.

Least difficulty arises where the act challenged is a decision expressly addressed to the private party bringing the action, such as in connection with the Community's rules on competition. In such cases there appears to be a conclusive presumption that the plaintiff has *locus standi.*[10] On the question whether a given act is a decision, particularly in the context of decisions in the form of regulations, the Court looks to the object and content of the act rather than to its form.[11] A distinction is drawn between acts which apply to a limited, identifiable number of designees and acts of a normative character which apply to categories of persons envisaged in the abstract and as a whole; the former are decisions, the latter regulations.[12] Thus the Court has held that a regulation relating to the manufacture of a particular product by a limited number of producers is nevertheless a regulation because of its objective, normative character.[13] Whereas a regulation which was only concerned with import licences which had been sought before that

7 Wade, H W R, *Administrative Law* (6th edn 1988), pp 688 et seq.
8 See Brown, L N and Garner, J F, *French Administrative Law* (3rd edn 1983), pp 102, 103.
9 See Case 25/62: *Plaumann & Co v EEC Commission* [1963] ECR 95 at 106, 107; and Case 69/69: *S A Alcan Aluminium Raeren v EC Commission* [1970] ECR 385 at 393.
10 Eg Case 48–57/69: *Imperial Chemical Industries Ltd v EC Commission* [1972] ECR 619, [1972] CMLR 557; Case 6/72: *Europemballage Corpn and Continental Can Co Inc v EC Commission* [1973] ECR 215, [1973] CMLR 199, and Cases 6 and 7/73: *Istituto Chemioterapico Italiano SpA and Commercial Solvents Corpn v EC Commission* [1974] ECR 223, [1974] 1 CMLR 309.
11 Cases 16–17, 19–22/62: *Confédération Nationale des Producteurs de Fruits et Légumes v EEC Council* [1962] ECR 471 at 478.
12 Ibid at 478, 479.
13 Case 6/68: *Zuckerfabrik Watenstedt GmbH v EC Council* [1968] ECR 409, [1969] CMLR 26. Also see Case 123/77: *UNICME v EC Council* [1978] ECR 845 and Case 101/76: *Koninklijke Scholten Honig NV v EC Council and EC Commission* [1977] ECR 797.

regulation was made was, in fact, a bundle of individual decisions.[14] This distinction between regulations and decisions also impinges on the requirement that decisions addressed to other persons[15] must be of both direct and individual concern to the party bringing the action. The Court has tended to reverse the order of these two conditions as they are set out in the Treaty on the ground that if the applicant is not individually concerned by the decision, it becomes unnecessary to enquire whether he is directly concerned.[16] In *Plaumann & Co v Commission* (1964) the Court defined individual concern in the following terms: 'Persons other than those to whom a decision is addressed may only claim to be individually concerned if that decision affects them by reason of certain attributes which are peculiar to them or by reason of circumstances in which they are differentiated from all other persons and by virtue of these factors distinguishes them individually just as in the case of the person addressed'.[17] In applying that definition the Court has declined to find individual concern where a decision is addressed to an abstractly defined category of persons even where in reality the decision only affects an ascertainable number of such persons.[18] Such a decision potentially affects an indeterminate number of persons. But where, on the other hand, at the time a decision is made the number of persons affected by it is already finitely determined, eg if the decision is retroactive or if it refers to certain persons by name, then those persons are individually concerned.[19] The Court's approach to the question of direct concern appears to depend on whether the party to whom the decision was addressed had a discretion to implement it. If there was no discretion then,

---

14 Cases 41–44/70: *N V International Fruit Co v EC Commission* [1971] ECR 411, [1975] 2 CMLR 515. Also see Case 138/79: *SA Roquette Frères v EC Council* [1980] ECR 3333.

15 'Other persons' includes Member States; see Case 25/62: *Plaumann & Co v EC Commission* [1963] ECR 95 and Case 730/79: *Philip Morris Holland BV v EC Commission* [1980] ECR 2671, [1981] 2 CMLR 321. It may also include other private parties; see Case 26/76: *Metro-SB-Grossmärkte GmbH & Co KG v EC Commission* [1977] ECR 1875, [1978] 2 CMLR 1.

16 Case 25/62: *Plaumann & Co v EEC Commission* [1963] ECR 95 at 107.

17 Ibid.

18 Eg Case 1/64: *Glucoséries Réunis v EEC Commission* [1964] ECR 413; Case 38/64: *Getreide-Import Gesellschaft v EEC Commission* [1965] ECR 203, [1965] CMLR 276; and Case 63–65/69: *Compagnie Française Commerciale et Financière SA v EC Commission* [1970] ECR 221, [1970] CMLR 369.

19 See Cases 106–107/63: *Alfred Toepfer and Getreide-Import Gesellschaft v EEC Commission* [1965] ECR 405, [1966] CMLR 111; Case 62/70: *Bock v EC Commission* [1971] ECR 897, [1972] CMLR 160; and Cases 41–44/70: *NV International Fruit Co v EC Commission* [1971] ECR 411, [1975] 2 CMLR 515; Cases 113/77: *NTN v EC Council and EC Commission* [1979] ECR 1185, [1979] 2 CMLR 257.

subject to the other criteria, the decision is of direct concern; if there was a discretion then it is not. In *Alfred Toepfer v EEC Commission* (1966)[20] the plaintiff's application for a licence to import maize was rejected by the German authorities on 1 October 1963, because of protective measures which they were taking under the terms of the EEC Regulation No 19. On the same day the German authorities notified the Commission of those measures which were subject to confirmation, amendment or rejection by the Commission within four days of notification. On 3 October the Commission made a decision authorizing the German authorities to maintain the protective measures in force between 1 to 4 October inclusive. The plaintiffs challenged that decision. The Court of Justice held that they had the necessary *locus standi*. The decision concerned them directly because it was immediately enforceable and left no discretion with the German authorities; it concerned them individually because the number and identity of the persons affected was determined before 3 October.

There is clearly a close relationship between the notion of a decision as an act which determines what is to happen in a limited number of particular cases and the notions of direct and individual concern. In one case the Court apparently assumed that if an act affects persons directly and individually then that act is a decision.[1] The Court adopted this approach expressly in *UNICME v EC Council* (1978)[2] in which the annulment of a regulation was sought. This is possible at the suit of a private party only if the act in question is a decision in the form of a regulation. But the Court observed: 'It is unnecessary to consider whether the contested measure may be regarded as a regulation and it is sufficient to establish whether it is in fact of direct and individual concern to the applicants.'[3] The Court has also accepted the possibility that a provision in a regulation may, at the same time, be both general and specific: general as far as most of those affected by it are concerned, but of direct and individual concern with respect to some. In such a situation the latter, but not of course the former, would have *locus standi* to challenge that provision.[4]

On the question of the grounds of action all three Community Treaties mention the same four grounds which are derived from French administrative law, viz:

20 Loc cit in previous note.
1 Case 100/74: *Société CAM SA v EC Commission* [1975] ECR 1393 at 1402, 1403.
2 Case 123/77: [1978] ECR 845.
3 Ibid, at 851.
4 See Cases 239, 275/82: *Allied Corporation v EC Commission* [1984] ECR 1005, [1985] 3 CMLR 572.

(i) lack of competence, or

(ii) infringement of an essential procedural requirement, or

(iii) infringement of the Treaties or of any rules of law relating to their application, or

(iv) misuse of powers.[5]

(i) Lack of competence is broadly comparable to the English doctrine of substantive *ultra vires*. 'Each institution,' in the words of article 4 of the EEC Treaty, 'shall act within the limits of the powers conferred upon it ...' Therefore, if a Community institution acts without authority that act may be declared void on the ground of lack of powers. Lack of competence covers situations in which the Communities have no power, have power but invoke the wrong Treaty provision,[6] or in which the Communities have power but it has been exercised by the wrong body. Thus in *Meroni v High Authority* (1958)[7] the plaintiff challenged certain levies imposed by the High Authority on the basis of decisions taken by subordinate bodies to whom the High Authority had purported to delegate certain powers. The Court held that those subordinate bodies lacked the power to take such decisions since the Treaty did not authorize the High Authority to delegate its decision-making power. Other areas in which questions of lack of competence have arisen are where an institution has claimed implied powers or the authority to extend its jurisdiction beyond the territorial limits of the Community. While the Court has acknowledged the existence of implied powers in relation to the EEC,[8] there are clearly limits to such powers. If those limits should not be respected, a plea of lack of competence could be raised.[9] In the context of the Community's rules on competition,[10] on several occasions the Commission has imposed penalties for breach on corporations based outside the Community. Pleas by such corporations that the Commission lacked competence to impose those penalties have so far failed. The Court has been satisfied that the penalties related

5 ECSC Treaty, art 33; EEC Treaty, art 173; Euratom Treaty, art 146.
6 See Case 68/86: *United Kingdom v EC Council* [1988] ECR 855, [1988] 2 CMLR 543.
7 Case 9/56: [1957–58] ECR 133.
8 See Case 22/70: *EC Commission v EC Council* [1971] ECR 263, [1971] CMLR 335.
9 Cf Case 8/55: *Fédération Charbonnière de Belgique v High Authority* [1954–56] ECR 245.
10 EEC Treaty, arts 85–90.

to activities carried on within the Community.[11] But here again there is clearly a limit to the Commission's authority which if exceeded would justify a plea of lack of competence.[12]

(ii) Infringement of essential procedural requirements also has an equivalent in English law, viz procedural *ultra vires*. But, as in the case of both English and French administrative law, the Court of the Communities will not annul an act merely because some minor and unimportant procedural rule has not been observed; an action for annulment on this ground will only be granted when the procedural rule which has been infringed is an essential rule in the sense that it is substantial or basic. Such procedural requirements can be imposed either by the Treaties or by secondary legislation. An example of the former is provided by the case of *Germany v EEC Commission* (1963).[13] Prior to the establishment of the EEC Germany used to import cheap wines for the production of 'Brennwein'. In 1961 it asked the Commission for a tariff quota of 450,000 hectolitres of wine for this purpose. The Commission granted a quota of only 100,000 hectolitres. Article 190 of the EEC Treaty requires that the Commission's decisions shall 'state the reasons on which they are based'. Germany challenged the partial rejection of its request on the ground that that decision was insufficiently reasoned. The Commission had merely said that its decision was based on 'information that has been gathered' which indicated 'that the production of wines of this nature within the Community is amply sufficient'. The Court agreed with the Advocate-General that the Commission's decision should be annulled on the ground that it gave inadequate reasons and thus infringed an important procedural rule. The Court said 'In imposing upon the Commission the obligation to state reasons for its decisions, article 190 is not taking mere formal considerations into account but seeks to give an opportunity to the parties of defending their rights, to the Court of exercising its supervisory functions and to Member States and to all interested nationals of ascertaining the circumstances in which the Commission has applied the Treaty. To attain these objectives, it is sufficient for the decision to set out, in a concise but clear and relevant manner, the principal issues of law and of fact upon which it is based and which are necessary in

11 Eg, Case 48/69: *Imperial Chemical Industries v EC Commission* [1972] ECR 619, [1972] CMLR 557 and Cases 6–7/73: *Istituto Chemisterapico Italiano SpA and Commercial Solvents Corpn v EC Commission* [1974] ECR 223, [1974] 1 CMLR 309.
12 See Joined Cases 89, 104, 114, 116, 117 and 125 to 129/85: *A Åhlström Osakeyhtiö v EC Commission* [1988] ECR 5193.
13 Case 24/62: [1963] ECR 63, [1963] CMLR 347. Also see Case 73/74: *Groupement des Fabricants de Papiers Peints de Belgique v EEC Commission* [1975] ECR 1491, [1976] 1 CMLR 589.

order that the reasoning which has led the Commission to its decision may be understood.'[14] This the Court held, the Commission's vague statements failed to do.[15] In *Transocean Marine Paint Association v EC Commission* (1974)[16] the procedural requirement arose under a Regulation. In 1967 the plaintiff had been granted an exemption from applicability of the Community's rules on competition under the terms of article 85(3) of the EEC Treaty. In 1972 the exemption came up for renewal. The Commission refused to renew it on the original terms and imposed additional conditions because of changes which had occurred in the competitive situation. The plaintiff found one of the additional conditions particularly onerous and sought its revocation on the ground that no notice was given of it nor any opportunity to comment. The Court held that the Regulation under which the Commission had acted incorporated 'the general rule that a person whose interests are perceptibly affected by a decision of a public authority must be given the opportunity to make his point of view known'.[17] That obligation had not been fulfilled in this case and so the Commission's Decision was, to that extent, annulled.[18]

(iii) Infringement of the Treaty or of any rule of law relating to its application is a ground broad enough to embrace the other three more specific grounds of challenge. Indeed, cases brought on any of those grounds could equally be brought under this. In practice however this general ground has by no means been superfluous. Its broad formulation has provided the juridical basis upon which the Court has developed the Community concept of legality beyond the terms of the Community Treaties and secondary legislation to general principles of law recognized by the Member States. An illustration is provided by *August Töpfer & Co GmbH v EC Commission* (1978).[19] The plaintiff held a number of export licences for sugar. In accordance with Community rules the amount of export refund he would receive in respect of such transactions was fixed in advance. In principle, if the value of such refunds changes as a result of currency fluctuations before the transaction is carried out, the licence holder may apply to have the licence cancelled. In this

---

14 [1963] ECR at 69.
15 A failure to consult the European Parliament when required so to do by the Treaty is also a violation of an essential procedural requirement; see Case 138/79: *SA Roquette Frères v EC Council* [1980] ECR 3333.
16 Case 17/74: [1974] ECR 1063, [1974] 2 CMLR 459.
17 Ibid at 1080.
18 As to the consequences of a failure by the Council to follow its own rules of procedure, see Case 68/86: *United Kingdom v EC Council* [1988] ECR 855, [1988] 2 CMLR 543 and Case 131/86: *United Kingdom v EC Council*, ibid at 905.
19 Case 112/77: [1978] ECR 1019.

instance this basic scheme was varied by a Commission Regulation which withdrew the plaintiff's right of cancellation and substituted the payment of compensation. This was financially disadvantageous to the plaintiff and so he sought the annulment of the Regulation. He alleged that the Regulation breached a general principle of law, namely the principle of legitimate expectation. The plaintiff maintained that by the terms under which his export licences had been granted, he could expect either to receive the export refunds or be able to exercise his right of cancellation. Because of the Commission's intervention that expectation had not been realized. Although the Court dismissed the plaintiff's action on the merits, it did acknowledge expressly that the plaintiff's argument was one which it would entertain. 'The submission that there has been a breach of [the] principle [of legitimate expectation] is admissible in the context of proceedings instituted under article 173, since the principle in question forms part of the Community legal order with the result that any failure to comply with it is an "infringement of this Treaty or of any rule of law relating to its application" within the meaning of the article quoted'.[20] It follows from this that the breach of any principle accepted by the Court as a general principle of Community law may be invoked as a ground for the annulment of a Community act. Such principles are regarded by the Court as forming an integral part of the legal order of the Community established by the Treaties.

(iv) Misuse of powers provides the basis of an action for annulment when it can be shewn that a discretionary power has been used to achieve some object other than that for which the power was conferred. Thus proceedings for an action on this ground involve the Court in determining the object which the act in question was intended to achieve and then to decide whether that object comes within the purpose for which the power was conferred. As the Advocate-General put it in *Fédération Charbonnière de Belgique v High Authority*[1] 'it is a matter of discovering what was the object in fact pursued by the author of the act, when he took the decision, in order to be able to compare it with the object he ought to have pursued and which, unless the contrary is proved, he is deemed to have pursued'. The question is, therefore, whether the author of the act really had an illegal or legal object in view at the time he took the act. It is not necessary for an illegal objective to have been actually achieved, it is sufficient that the motive behind the act was illegal. Further, if an act achieves a legal object but also incidentally achieves other illegal objects that will not be a misuse of power,

---

20 Ibid, at 1033.
1 Case 8/55: [1954–56] ECR 245.

provided that the legal object is the dominant object. In *France v High Authority* (1954),[2] for example, the High Authority, purporting to act under article 60 of the ECSC Treaty, made a number of decisions authorizing steel enterprises to deviate from their published prices provided that such deviations did not constitute discrimination which is forbidden by the Treaty. The French Government challenged those decisions alleging that the High Authority had no power to achieve those particular aims under article 60 but should have acted under articles 61 and 65 for the real object of those decisions was to lower steel prices generally and prevent price agreement and this could only be done under those latter articles. Therefore it was asserted that by issuing those decisions under article 60 it had misused its powers. But the Court held that in fact there had been no misuse of powers, for even if those decisions had in fact been made to achieve an unjustified object the decisions would not be vitiated provided the essential object of the power was achieved. The Court held that was so in this case. Misuse of powers has a particular significance under the ECSC Treaty since it is the ground upon which coal and steel undertakings may challenge Community acts which are general in character.[3] In the other two Communities this ground has had little significance.[4]

An action for annulment must be brought within limited periods of one month under the ECSC Treaty and two months under the EEC and Euratom Treaties.[5] These periods are necessarily short since the economic regime set up by the Treaties is a dynamic thing which it would be impossible to alter long after the event by actions against decisions taken. In the case of regulations, which must be published in the Official Journal, time begins to run from the fifteenth day after publication. In the case of directives and decisions, which do not have to be published but must be notified to their addressees, time runs from the day after the date of notification[6] or if there has been no notification from the day after the date upon which the decisions or directives came to the knowledge of the addressees.[7]

In general the effect of an annulment is quite simply to declare the Community act in question to be void and this is the basic rule

2 Case 1/54: [1954–56] ECR 1.
3 ECSC Treaty, art 33 (2).
4 But see Cases 18, 35/65: *Gutmann v EAEC Commission* [1966] ECR 103 and Case 105/75: *Guiffrida v EC Council* [1976] ECR 1395 concerned with the terms of appointment of Community officials.
5 ECSC Treaty, art 33; EEC Treaty, art 176; Euratom Treaty, art 146.
6 Rules of Procedure of the Court, art 81 (1).
7 See Case 6/72: *Europemballage Corpn and Continental Can Co Inc v EC Commission* [1973] ECR 215 at 241.

to be found in all three treaties.[8] In the ECSC the Commission is required to take steps to give effect to the annulment and to compensate for any loss suffered as a result of the annulled act. The EEC and Euratom Treaties simply require the institution whose act has been annulled to take the necessary steps to comply with the Court's judgment. Thus, subject to compensation under the ECSC Treaty, which in any event is awarded by the Commission, annulment has a purely negative effect. But the annulment may not affect the whole of the act against which an action has been brought. Article 174 of the EEC Treaty enables the Court to confirm particular parts of a regulation which it has otherwise annulled. Thus in a case in which a regulation concerned with the price of fruit and vegetables was challenged, the Court declared void that part of the regulation which related to tomatoes.[9] The EEC Treaty itself does not expressly extend this possibility of partial annulment to acts other than regulations, but nevertheless we find the Court in *Consten and Grundig v EEC Commission* (1966)[10] annulling a decision in part In that case Consten and Grundig entered into a contract whereby Consten became the sole agent for the distribution of Grundig products in France. Other firms selling Grundig products in France complained to the Commission that this contract was contrary to article 85 of the EEC Treaty, which controls restrictive practices. The Commission issued a decision which stated that the contract did violate article 85. Consten and Grundig then brought these proceedings challenging the decision and the Court held that certain elements in the contract infringed the Treaty and certain others did not, therefore the decision was partially annulled and partially upheld. This is an example of the flexible approach which the Court adopts towards the question whether a particular administrative act is a regulation or a decision. Indeed there would seem to be no reason in principle why a process of partial annulment should not be applied in appropriate cases to acts other than regulations *stricto senso*.[11] The Court's willingness to do this is illustrated by the *EC Council v European Parliament*[12] in which the decision to annul the declaration by the President of the European Parliament that the

8 ECSC Treaty, art 33; EEC Treaty, art 174; Euratom Treaty, art 147.
9 Case 151/73: *Ireland v EC Council* [1974] ECR 285, [1974] 1 CMLR 429. In Case 138/79: *SA Roquette Frères v EC Council* [1980] ECR 3333 the Court declared an entire regulation void despite the fact that the private plaintiffs sought only its partial annulment and that they only had *locus standi* in respect of those parts of the regulation which concerned them directly and individually.
10 Cases 56 and 58/64: [1966] ECR 299, [1966] CMLR 418.
11 Also see Case 17/74: *Transocean Marine Paint Association v EC Commission* [1974] ECR 1063, [1974] 2 CMLR 459.
12 Case 34/86: [1986] 3 CMLR 94.

1986 budget was adopted was expressly held not to affect the validity of payments already made and commitments already entered in implementation of the budget. Indeed, the Court held that the annulment was operative prospectively from the point in the budgetary procedure at which the illegality occurred. It also appears that in cases in which a regulation is declared to be void on the ground that it invoked the wrong Treaty provision, the Court will order that the effects of such regulation shall remain in force until new measures taken in compliance with its judgment have entered into force.[13]

(ii) *Actions against inactivity.*—The second main category of actions concerning legality is the action against inactivity. Where the Treaties impose a duty to act on the Council or Commission and they fail to act then an action may be based on a violation of the Treaty through inactivity. The inactivity must first be brought to the attention of the institution concerned and if it has not taken satisfactory steps to remedy or justify its inactivity an action may be instituted.[14] Under the ECSC Treaty such actions may be brought against the Commission either by Member States, or by the Council or by undertakings or associations of undertakings. Under the EEC and Euratom Treaties while the Member States and the other Community institutions (including the European Parliament) have a general competence to challenge the inactivity of either Commission or Council, individuals and corporate bodies may only do so if they can shew that one of those institutions has failed to address an act (other than a recommendation or opinion)[15] to him or it.[16] Such an action under the ECSC Treaty is *Groupement des Industries Sidérurgiques Luxembourgeoises v High Authority* (1956).[17] The Luxembourg Government imposed a levy on coal intended for industrial use for the purpose of subsidizing the price of household coal. The plaintiffs, who were the main users of industrial coal, alleged that this levy was contrary to the ECSC Treaty and requested the High Authority to use its powers to require the Luxembourg Government to abolish the levy. During the two months following this request the High Authority did nothing and the plaintiffs brought an action under article 35 of the ECSC Treaty and the Court held that the action was admissible. Cases brought by private parties under the EEC Treaty show that

---

13 See Case 275/87: *EC Commission v EC Council* [1989] ECR 259.
14 ECSC Treaty, art 35; EEC Treaty, art 175; Euratom Treaty, art 148.
15 See Case 6/70: *Borromeo Arese v EC Commission* [1970] ECR 815, [1970] CMLR 436.
16 See Case 103/63: *Rhenania Schiffahrts-und Speditions-Gesellschaft mbH v EEC Commission* [1964] ECR 425 per Advocate-General Roemer at 431, 432.
17 Cases 7 and 9/54: [1954–56] ECR 175.

an article 175 action will fail if the act sought is one which cannot be properly addressed to the plaintiff. In one case a complaint that the Commission had failed to issue a decision amending the rules concerning intra-Community trade was dismissed since the proper addressees of such a decision would have been the Member States.[18] Similarly, where a plaintiff's claim could only be met by making a regulation the action was dismissed since a regulation cannot be described 'by reason either of its form or of its nature' as an act which could be addressed to the plaintiff.[19] An article 175 action will also fail if the allegedly defaulting institution has 'defined its position' within two months of being called upon to act. Thus in *Alfons Lütticke GmbH v EEC Commission* (1966)[20] the action was held to be inadmissible since within that two-month period the Commission had declared its position and had made clear its attitude to the matter in question. This clearly falls far short of compelling the performance of a specific act. The Court also distinguishes between a failure to act and a refusal to act. While the former prima facie comes within the scope of article 175, the latter does not since it is regarded as constituting a negative decision. A refusal by the Commission to revoke an allegedly illegal act has been held not to be actionable under article 175.[1] In the same way, if, when called upon to act, the Commission adopts a measure other than that sought by the plaintiff the action will fail.[2] In such cases the appropriate remedy is to seek the annulment of the act in question under the terms of article 173. It is also clear that where the Council or Commission adopts the measure requested after the action has been brought but before judgment has been given, the Court will take the view that the action no longer has any substance and a decision is therefore unnecessary.[3] The only successful action to date under article 175 is the *European Parliament v EC Council*[4] in which the Court condemned the Council's failure to introduce a common transport policy as required by article 75(1) of the EEC Treaty. The Court held, notwithstanding Parliament's omission to specify the measures which should have been taken, that the Council had failed to carry

18 Case 15/71: *Firma C Mackprang, Jr v EC Commission* [1971] ECR 797, [1972] CMLR 52.
19 Case 90/78: *Granaria BV v EC Council and Commission* [1979] ECR 1081 at 1093.
20 Case 48/65: [1966] ECR 19, [1966] CMLR 378.
1 Cases 10 and 18/68: *Società 'Eridania' Zuccherifici Nazionali v EC Commission* [1969] ECR 459.
2 Case 8/71: *Deutscher Komponistenverband eV v EC Commission* [1971] ECR 705, [1973] CMLR 902.
3 See Case 377/87: *European Parliament v EC Council* [1988] ECR 4017.
4 Case 13/83: [1985] ECR 1513, [1986] 1 CMLR 138.

out, by the Treaty deadline, measures which were sufficiently precise so as to ensure the provision of services in the field of international transport and to fix conditions under which non-resident carriers might operate within a Member State.

(iii) *The plea of illegality.*—We have seen that a restrictive period of limitation is applied to actions for annulment with the general result that if an act is not challenged within that period the act becomes unassailable. But a situation may arise in an action before the Court under some Treaty article other than that which provides for actions for annulment in which the illegality of an unchallenged act may be in issue. If the period of limitation were to be applied strictly such an issue could not be raised outside the period, but to overcome such a possible result all three Treaties make it possible for such a question of illegality to be raised in such proceedings;[5] this again is a form of procedure known to French law. Under the ECSC Treaty both types of binding act, namely decisions and recommendations, may be challenged by this procedure. But under the EEC and Euratom Treaties only regulations are open to challenge. This provision can only be relied upon as a defence; it does not of itself give rise to an independent cause of action.[6] If such a plea of illegality is successfully invoked its technical effect will not be to declare the act in question illegal in terms of its general application but only in so far as it applies to the plaintiff. This is made clear by the case law. In *Meroni & Co v High Authority* (1958)[7] the High Authority requested Meroni to pay a levy on the authority of earlier decisions of a general nature which it had taken. Meroni declined to pay and challenged the High Authority's request on the ground that the general decisions on which it was based were illegal. The High Authority argued that such a plea was inadmissible since the time limit for the challenge of those decisions had expired. The question therefore arose whether Meroni could rely on the defence of illegality. The Court held that he could and in its judgment considered the nature of this defence: 'An applicant's right, after the expiration of the period prescribed [for actions for annulment] . . . , to take advantage of the irregularity of general decisions or recommendations in support of proceedings against decisions or recommendations which are individual in character cannot lead to the annulment of the general decision, but only to the annulment of the individual decision which is based on

---

5 ECSC Treaty, art 36; EEC Treaty, art 184; Euratom Treaty, art 156.
6 Cases 31 and 33/62: *Milchwerke Heinz Wöhrmann and Sohn KG v EEC Commission* [1962] ECR 501, [1963] CMLR 152 and Joined Cases 275/80 and 24/81: *Krupp Stahl AG v EC Commission* [1981] ECR 2489.
7 Case 9/56: [1957–58] ECR 133.

it.'[8] In view of the limited right which individual and corporate bodies have to sue for the annulment of general decisions this defence of illegality is important since it widens the legal protection of such parties.

It does not immediately appear from the wording of article 184 of the EEC Treaty in what precise context the illegality of a regulation may be pleaded. When attempts were made to use this procedure to challenge regulations directly and in isolation, the Court elaborated on the view which it had earlier expressed in the *Meroni* case[9] and made it clear that a regulation may only be challenged by virtue of article 184 when it provides the legal basis of an act which is the primary objective of the action. For example, in *Italy v EEC Council and EEC Commission* (1966)[10] the primary objective of the action was to challenge a 1965 regulation. In addition the Italian Government invoked article 184 and asked that two 1962 regulations be declared inapplicable. The action was dismissed on the ground that the 1962 regulations did not provide the legal basis of the 1965 regulation, so that if the former were declared inapplicable they would in no way affect the authority of the latter. The Court said that the intention of article 184 'is not to allow a party to contest at will the applicability of any regulation in support of an application. The regulation of which the legality is called in question must be applicable, directly or indirectly, to the issue with which the application is concerned'.[11] Another uncertainty concerns the meaning of 'regulation' in relation to article 184; is the plea of illegality available in respect of a Community act which is not a regulation in form but is in substance a general act which determines rights and obligations objectively and in advance? Consistent with its approach to the distinction between general and individual acts, the Court has held that an act which is general in substance but not in form shall be treated as a regulation for the purposes of article 184.[12]

Article 184 of the EEC Treaty refers to 'any party' being able to invoke this plea and the question has been raised whether this expression includes Community institutions and Member States as well as individuals and corporate bodies. As far as Community institutions are concerned it is generally agreed that the plea is not available on both legal and practical grounds. In the first place the plea is designed to protect the private interests of a party which may be affected by an illegal general act, but a Community insti-

---

8 Ibid, at 140.
9 Case 9/56: [1957–58] ECR 133.
10 Case 32/65: [1966] ECR 389.
11 Ibid, at 409.
12 See Case 92/78: *Simmenthal SpA v EC Commission* [1979] ECR 777 at 800.

tution has no private interests only a share in the general interests of the Communities. Further, Community institutions have no restrictions on their right to challenge a general act and so, unlike the case of individuals and corporate bodies, there is no reason to extend the period of limitation in this way. Secondly, it is difficult to envisage in practice a situation in which, say, the Council would direct an individual decision to the Commission requiring it to respect a Council regulation. As far as Member States are concerned there are also reasons in principle why the plea should not be available. Member states, as in the case of institutions, have no restrictions on their competence to challenge acts provided they do so within the period of limitation and so in their case also there would appear to be no reason to make the defence of illegality available. Secondly, the Member States wield political influence over Community acts through the Council and this influence plus the general right of challenge should give ample protection to their interests.[13]

For some time it was believed that the Court supported the view that Member States could plead the plea of illegality. In *Italy v EEC Council and EEC Commission* (1966)[14] the Italian Government had relied on article 184 and although, as we have seen, the plea was dismissed the Court did not question its admissibility. But in the light of a more recent case, the better view probably is that article 184 is only available to private parties. In an enforcement action brought by the Commission against Belgium under article 93(2) of the EEC Treaty,[15] Belgium maintained that the decision which had been addressed to it under that article had no legal basis. The legality of the decision had not been challenged under article 173, but on analogy with article 184 Belgium pleaded the illegality of that decision. The action could have been disposed of on the sole ground that the act in issue was an individual decision, but the Court considered the case on a broader basis. It referred to the right which Belgium had to challenge the decision under article 173 and to the period of limitation in that article being intended to safeguard legal certainty. It then observed: 'It is impossible for a Member State which has allowed the strict time limit laid down ... in article 173 to expire without contesting by the means available under that article the legality of the Commission decision addressed to it, to be able to call in question that decision by means of article 184 of the Treaty.'[16] While the Court addressed itself expressly to the individual decision in issue, its reasoning is equally applicable

13 See Bebr, op cit, pp 141 et seq.
14 Case 32/65: [1966] ECR 389, [1969] CMLR 39.
15 Case 156/77: [1978] ECR 1881.
16 Ibid, at 1896.

to any act, including a regulation, which a Member State could have challenged under article 173. This would certainly be in keeping with the Court's own view that the purpose of article 184 is 'to provide those persons who are precluded ... from instituting proceedings directly in respect of general acts, with the benefit of a judicial review of them at the time when they are affected by implementing decisions which are of direct and individual concern to them.'[17]

(b) *Plenary jurisdiction*
In addition to its jurisdiction to declare actions of Community institutions to be null and void the Court has a plenary jurisdiction in certain cases. This enables the Court in those instances to go into the merits of the parties' cases and to substitute its own judgments for those of the Communities' institutions. We have in fact already dealt with one example of this plenary jurisdiction in connection with violations of the Treaties by Member States. In addition there are three other instances of plenary jurisdiction.

In general the liability of the Communities in contract falls under the jurisdiction of municipal courts, unless in accordance with article 181 of the EEC Treaty the contracting parties agree to the contrary.[18] Article 183 of the EEC Treaty provides that, subject to the powers of the Court of Justice, there is nothing to prevent a case to which the Community is a party from being determined by the domestic courts of the Member States.[19] But jurisdiction over non-contractual (tortious) liability on the other hand has been conferred upon the Court of the Communities. Under article 34 of the ECSC Treaty an action for damages will lie where the Commission fails to comply within a reasonable time with a judgment declaring a decision or recommendation to be void. Article 40 of the ECSC Treaty provides for liability for wrongful administrative acts in terms that an action will lie in respect of damage resulting from acts or omissions on the part of the Community or its servants. The EEC and Euratom Treaties do not expressly distinguish between legislative and administrative wrongdoing as grounds for seeking damages. Articles 178/215 and 151/188 respectively provide generally for non-contractual liability in the context of damage caused by the institutions or servants of the Communities in the performance of their duties in accordance with the general principles common to the laws of the Member States. Under all three Treaties the extent of this non-contractual liab-

17 Case 92/78: *Simmenthal SpA v EC Commission* [1979] ECR 777 at 800.
18 Euratom Treaty, art 153 is to the same effect; see Case 23/76: *Pellegrini and CSAS v EC Commission* [1976] ECR 1807, [1977] 2 CMLR 77.
19 Also see ECSC Treaty, art 40 (3) and Euratom Treaty, art 155.

ility is in practice in terms of the distinction known to French law as that between *faute de service* and *faute personnelle.*[20] A *faute de service* occurs where damage results from the malfunctioning of Community institutions or Community servants; there is said to be a *faute personnelle* when the damage results from some personal wrongdoing on the part of a Community official which is in no way linked with his official position. In the case of a *faute de service* the Communities are liable; in the case of a *faute personnelle* the individual wrongdoer alone is personally liable. This distinction is comparable, although not identical, with the distinction well known to English law between a servant acting in the course of his employment and a servant on a frolic of his own. The non-contractual liability of the Community is that of a public authority. It is not liable for what may be termed ordinary torts committed in the course of Community activities, but only in respect of wrongs arising out of activities which form a necessary part of its official activities as defined in the treaties, ie the legislative and administrative acts of the Institutions and their officials. In accordance with this view, the Community was not held liable for injuries resulting from a road accident caused by a Euratom engineer who was driving his own car in the course of his work: 'the Community is only liable for those acts . . . which . . . are the necessary extension of the tasks entrusted to the institutions.'[1] Within those limits actual liability under the EEC Treaty is in accordance with the general principles common to the laws of the Member States. This involves the Court in a comparative study of the relevant national laws in order to pick out the decisive elements which may reflect a trend. National law is not analysed in order to produce a principle acknowledged by all the Member States. Such an exercise would be unlikely to produce a workable legal principle. The aim is to identify trends generally, but not necessarily universally, recognized and to use them as the juridical basis for the development of particular rules of Community liability.[2]

The relationship between the action for damages and the actions for annulment and inactivity has caused the Court some difficulty. When first confronted with this question the Court expressed the view that the action for damages was quite distinct both by reason of its object and the grounds upon which it can be brought.[3] But when, later, an action for damages arose out of an allegedly unlawful act which had not been annulled, the Court changed its mind and

20 See Brown, L N, and Garner, J F, op cit, pp 99 et seq.
 1 Case 9/69: *Sayag v Leduc* [1969] ECR 329 at 336.
 2 Ibid, at 340, per Advocate-General Gand.
 3 Cases 9 and 12/60: *Société Commerciale Antoine Vloeberghs SA v High Authority of the EEC* [1961] ECR 197.

held that 'An administrative measure which has not been annulled cannot of itself constitute a wrongful act on the part of the administration inflicting damage upon those whom it affects. The latter cannot therefore claim damages by reason of that measure.'[4] More recently, against the background of strong criticism,[5] the Court has reverted to its original view. In *Alfons Lütticke GmbH v EC Commission* (1971)[6] it observed that the action for damages is an independent action having its own special purpose and subject to conditions which were designed for that purpose. It would be contrary to the independence of this right of action if its exercise was made subject to other Treaty provisions designed for different purposes. This view has been reiterated in a series of subsequent cases which appears now to represent the *jurisprudence constante* of the Court.[7] Where an action for damages is brought in respect of a legislative act which involves choices of economic policy the Community will only be liable if the individual plaintiff can prove that there has been a sufficiently serious breach of a superior rule of law protecting him.[8] Such a rule could be either a rule in the Treaty such as the prohibition on discrimination[9] or one of the unwritten rules of Community law, such as the principle of legitimate expectation, which the Court draws from the rules of the constitutions of the Member States which are designed to protect individual rights.[10] That the alleged breach of such a rule has to be sufficiently serious is in practice a very difficult condition to satisfy. The Court has taken the view that liability in these cases will not be incurred unless the defendant institution has manifestly and gravely disregarded the limits of its powers to such a degree that its conduct verges on the arbitrary.[11] The plaintiff in an action for

---

4 Case 25/62: *Plaumann & Co v EEC Commission* [1963] ECR 95 at 108.
5 Eg Advocate-General Roemer's submissions in Case 5/71: *Aktien-Zuckerfabrik Schöppenstedt v EC Council* [1971] ECR 975 at 990 et seq.
6 Case 4/69: [1971] ECR 325.
7 See Case 5/71: *Aktien-Zuckerfabrik Schöppenstedt v EC Council* [1971] ECR 975; Cases 9 and 11/71: *Compagnie d'Approvisionnement de Transport et de Crédit SA and Grands Moulins de Paris SA v EC Commission* [1972] ECR 391, [1973] CMLR 529; Case 43/72: *Merkur Aussenhandels GmbH v EC Commission* [1973] ECR 1055.
8 Eg Case 153/73: *Firma Holtz and Willemsen v EC Council and EC Commission* [1974] ECR 675 at 692 and Cases 83 and 94/76, 4, 15 and 40/77: *Bayerische HNL Vermehrungsbetriebe GmbH & Co KG v EC Council and Commission* [1978] ECR 1209 at 1224.
9 Eg Cases 4451/77: *Groupement d'Intérêt Economique 'Union Malt' v EC Commission* [1978] ECR 57, [1978] 3 CMLR 702.
10 See eg Case 74/74: *Comptoir National Technique Agricole SA v EC Commission* [1975] ECR 533.
11 See, for example, Case 238/78: *Ireks-Arcady GmbH v EC Council and EC Commission* [1979] ECR 2955 and Cases 116, 124/77: *GR Amylum NV v EC Council and EC Commission* [1979] ECR 3497.

damages must, of course, establish a causal connection between the injury and the act or omission on the part of the Community and the quantum of damages must be ascertainable and not speculative.[12] Problems about the appropriate forum for claims for damages against the Community are likely to arise in some circumstances. Where the alleged wrong results from the act of a Community official acting in that capacity, the action will lie in the European Court.[13] But where, as is common, the act is that of an authority in a Member State, a complex body of case law has developed on the question whether in such cases the action should lie in the courts of the Member State, in the European Court, or in both. The precise nature of the claim is a crucial factor in such cases. If the claim is for a liquidated sum, such as for repayment of a sum paid to a national authority or for payment of a sum due from a national authority under Community law, the action will lie in the relevant national court.[14] But if the claim is for an unliquidated sum to compensate for harm caused by a national authority in implementing a Community act, the action may be brought in the European Court notwithstanding the concurrent availability of a national remedy.[15]

The Court's plenary jurisdiction also extends to the settlement of disputes between the Communities and their employees over contracts of employment. The terms of service are set out in the Communities' Staff Regulations, and article 179 of the EEC Treaty, for example, provides that the Court shall be competent to adjudicate in any dispute between the Community and its servants within the limits and under the conditions laid down by their service regulations or conditions of employment. Actions concerning contracts of service cannot be lodged directly with the Court of Justice. Claims must first be made to the appointing body via an hierarchical administrative process. If the dispute is not resolved by this process then a right of action lies to the Court of Justice which has the power to consider the dispute in its entirety and to settle it by its judgment. This is a fairly fertile source of litigation before the

12 See Cases 5, 7 and 13–24/66: *Firma E Kampffmeyer v EEC Commission* [1967] ECR 245 and Case 30/66: *Kurt A Becher v EC Commission* [1967] ECR 285, [1968] CMLR 169.

13 See Case 145/83: *Adams v EC Commission* [1986] 1 CMLR 506.

14 See Case 132/77: *Société pour l'Exportation des Sucres SA v EC Commission* [1978] ECR 1061, and Case 133/79: *Sucrimex SA v EC Commission* [1980] ECR 1299. Where there is no national remedy available a claim will lie in the European Court: Cases 197–200, 243, 245, 247/80: *Ludwigshafener Walzmühle Erling KG v EC Council and EC Commission* [1981] ECR 3211.

15 See, for example, Cases 261, 262/78: *Interquell Stärke-Chemie GmbH & Co KG v EC Commission* [1979] ECR 3045.

Court but it is somewhat specialist and it is neither appropriate nor practicable to discuss it in the present context.[16]

Lastly the court has plenary jurisdiction to hear appeals against fines and other pecuniary penalties. The Court not only has jurisdiction to quash a penalty of this sort but it may also lower or increase this penalty when in the Court's view it is either unacceptable or inappropriate.[17] An example is provided by article 17 of Regulation 17 which authorizes appeals against fines and periodic penalty payments imposed by the Commission for breaches of the Community's rules on competition.[18]

II The Court of First Instance

For some time the Court has been faced with an ever-increasing work-load.[19] Over the period 1980 to 1987 the annual number of new cases lodged with the Court increased from 279 to 395. In 1987 the Court and its Chambers combined delivered 422 judgments, while in the same year 208 cases were still pending before the Court and another 181 before its Chambers. The average length of proceedings before the Court has also steadily increased over the same period and in 1987 it was twenty months for direct actions and eighteen months for preliminary rulings. Various factors have contributed to this situation. There has long been a general trend as the Community develops for more and more cases to be brought. This trend has been strongly reinforced by the doubling of the numbers of the Member States with all the resulting new opportunities for direct actions and requests for preliminary rulings. The Court has done its best to improve the situation by simplifying, improving and making more efficient its working methods; the steady increase in the number of judgments delivered annually testifies to this.[20] But the scale of the problem had become such as to call for more drastic measures in order to ensure the proper administration of justice.

16 See pp 47, 48 supra. For further information, see Brown & Jacobs, op cit, chapter 9. Since November 1989 these cases must initially be brought before the newly-established Court of First Instance subject to a limited right of appeal to the Court of Justice. See below for an account of this new Court.
17 ECSC Treaty, art 36 (2); EEC Treaty, art 172; Euratom Treaty, art 144.
18 Eg Case 41/69: *ACF Chemiefarma NV v EC Commission* [1970] ECR 661 and Case 7/72: *Boehringer Mannheim GmbH v EC Commission* [1972] ECR 1281, [1973] CMLR 864.
19 The statistics which follow have been taken from *Synopsis of the work of the Court of Justice of the European Communities in 1986 and 1987* (1988), Section I, 1, A.
20 Ibid, Graph No 4, at p 19.

In the past proposals for reform largely focused on the Court's jurisdiction over staff cases, ie disputes between the Community and its employees, which often involve complex issues of fact and occupy a disproportionate amount of the Court's time. In other international organizations, notably the United Nations, the International Labour Organization, and other UN agencies, such disputes are referred to special Administrative Tribunals. In 1978 the Commission proposed the establishment of a similar body to deal with Community staff cases but no action was taken on it.[1] More recently discussion has centred on the establishment of a more general first instance tribunal to relieve the burden on the Court and its Chambers. This has borne fruit in that the Single European Act 1986 has amended the EEC Treaty[2] so as to authorize the Council, acting unanimously, at the request of the Court and after consulting the Commission and the European Parliament, to 'attach to the Court of Justice a court with jurisdiction to hear and determine at first instance, subject to a right of appeal to the Court of Justice on points of law only ..., certain classes of action or proceeding brought by natural or legal persons'.[3] It is further expressly provided that the new court 'shall not be competent to hear and determine actions brought by Member States or by Community institutions or questions referred for a preliminary ruling'.[4]

In accordance with the above procedure, in November 1988 the Council took the decision to establish a Court of First Instance (CFI) which became operational on 1 November 1989.[5] The CFI consists of twelve judges appointed by common accord by the Governments of the Member States from persons of undoubted independence who possess the ability required for appointment to judicial office.[6] The judges are appointed for six-year terms and

1 See Commission Proposal for a Council Regulation establishing an Administrative Tribunal for the European Communities, OJ 1978, C222, at p 6. For a discussion of that proposal, see House of Lords, Select Committee on the European Communities, Session 1978/79, 17th Report.
2 Single European Act, art 11 adding art 168A to the EEC Treaty and making an addition to art 188.
3 EEC Treaty, art 168A (1).
4 Ibid.
5 Decision 88/591, OJ 1988, L319/1 as corrected at OJ 1989, L241/4. For background to this Decision see: the Proposal by the Court of Justice at [1988] 1 CMLR 185; House of Lords Select Committee on the European Communities, Session 1987/88, 5th Report; and European Parliament, Document A2-107/88.
6 Decision 88/591, art 2. In practice there is one judge of the nationality of each of the Member States. The United Kingdom judge is David Edward, QC, formerly Salvesen Professor of European Institutions in the University of Edinburgh.

are eligible for reappointment. They elect their President from among their own number for a term of three years. No Advocates-General are appointed to the CFI but the judges of the CFI may themselves be called upon to act in that capacity when their task is the same as in the case of the Court of Justice. The CFI generally sits in chambers of five or three judges, although it may provide for plenary sessions in its Rules of Procedure.[7] The jurisdiction of the CFI consists of categories of action which have been transferred to it by the Court of Justice. In such cases the jurisdiction of the CFI is exclusive, subject to a right of appeal to the Court of Justice on points of law. The heads of jurisdiction of the CFI are:

(i) disputes between the institutions and their employees (staff cases);

(ii) actions against the Commission by undertakings concerning levies, production, prices, restrictive agreements and concentrations in the context of the ECSC Treaty; and

(iii) actions against the Commission by private parties for annulment or for failure to act relating to the implementation of the competition rules under the EEC Treaty.[8]

In the last mentioned class of case, claims for compensation for damage may also be entertained. The Council has reserved the right to confer on the CFI jurisdiction with regard to dumping and subsidies.[9] A decisive factor in transferring these matters to the CFI is that they all typically involve the investigation of facts, often of a complex nature, which is perhaps better suited to a specialist tribunal. Matters excluded from the CFI are cases brought by Member States and institutions, all references for preliminary rulings from the courts and tribunals of the Member States, and all actions arising under the Euratom Treaty.

Decisions of the CFI on both substantive and procedural issues are appealable to the Court of Justice on points of law within two months of the notification of the decision.[10] Three grounds of appeal are available: lack of competence of the CFI; a breach of procedure which adversely affects the interests of the applicant; and an infringement of Community law by the CFI.[11] In all except

---

7 The Rules of Procedure have yet to be made and in the meantime the CFI uses the Rules of the Court of Justice. The enabling Decision has added a new Title concerning the CFI to the EEC Statute of the Court of Justice, art 46 of which governs procedure. A draft of the proposed rules is currently before the Council; see OJ 1990, C136.

8 Decision 88/591, art 3 (1) and (2).

9 Ibid, art 3 (3). Arrangements to ensure that each court is properly seised with actions falling within its jurisdiction are provided by EEC Statute, art 47.

10 EEC Statute, art 49.

11 Ibid, art 51.

staff cases, Member States and institutions may lodge an appeal even where they were not interveners in the action before the CFI.[12] Procedure on appeal before the Court of Justice consists of written and oral stages, although the latter may be dispensed with.[13] If an appeal is allowed the decision of the CFI will be quashed. Final judgment may then either be given by the Court of Justice or the case may be referred back to the CFI; the latter is likely where complex facts need to be taken into consideration. Where there is a reference back, the CFI is bound by the judgment of the Court of Justice on points of law.[14] It may also be presumed that the CFI is under a general obligation to follow and apply the case law of the Court of Justice and that a failure to do so would justify an appeal on the ground of an infringement of Community law.

In the short term the CFI should be able to contribute to the easing of the problems which have confronted the Court of Justice in recent years. While it is premature to attempt any assessment of its impact in the longer term, some doubts may be raised. The range of cases transferrred to the CFI is small and may well prove to be outweighed by the additional appellate function conferred on the Court of Justice. Further, it seems likely that the number of Community actions will continue to increase and the prospect of additional Member States after 1992 will add a further dimension to the rate of increase. Time may show that further reforms to the judicial arrangements of the Community may prove to be necessary.[15]

12 Ibid, art 49, para 3.
13 Ibid, art 52.
14 Ibid, art 54.
15 For early views on the CFI see Kennedy, T, 'The Essential Minimum: The Establishment of the Court of First Instance', (1989) 14 EL Rev 7 and Toth, A-G, 'The Court of First Instance of the European Communities', in White, R and Smythe, B, (eds) *Current Issues in European and International Law* (1990), at 19.

Part III

The relationship between Community law and the municipal law of the Member States

Chapter 10

Implementation of Community law in the legal systems of the Member States

I INTRODUCTION

The most intricate and complex aspect of Community law is its relationship to the municipal law of the Member States. Conceptually Community law, like public International Law, feeds upon the internal law of states, but once emancipated and worked into a system, Community law emerges as a different, autonomous body of law.

Volumes have been written on the subject from a theoretical and practical point of view not only because the growth of the Community law is symptomatic of the growth of the Community but also because of the theoretical and practical consequences of conflicts between Community law and the municipal law of the Member States. At a theoretical level the starting point of a discussion on the relationship between Community law and the municipal law of the Member States, that is between an 'external' and an 'internal' system of law, is the doctrine of sovereignty; at a practical level it is the Treaty obligation and the resulting status of Community law in the territory of the Member States.

Sovereignty is a conceptual chameleon: it can be seen in different colours and be described in different ways. In classic terms Jean Bodin (1530–96) wrote that 'it is the distinguishing mark of the sovereign that he cannot in any way be subject to the commands of another, for it is he who makes Law for the subject, abrogates Law already made, and amends obsolete Law. No one who is subject either to the Law or to some other person can do this. That is why it is laid down in the civil Law that the prince is above the Law, for the word *Law* in Latin implies command of him who is invested with sovereign power ...'[1] For the purpose of our discussion sovereignty may be described in positive terms as the oneness of the legal system within the territory of a state. Oneness does not exclude plurality of laws within the system (as is, eg, the

---

1 *Six Books of the Commonwealth*, Book I, Chapter 8.

case in the United Kingdom or the USA) but implies one supreme source of law embodied in the constitution of the state; in other words the jurisdiction over the territory is in the hands of one authority (eg government in Parliament) which is supreme. In negative terms sovereignty means a system of law and admin- istration of justice which is free from outside interference. Pro- ceeding from the assumption of the oneness of the legal system the Member States of the Community are not entirely sovereign for, by Treaty, they have delegated a portion of their law-making power to an external authority (the Community) and at the same time consented to abide by the law so made. In the field of the admin- istration of justice they recognize the authority of the Community Court over matters and persons in their territory falling within the jurisdiction of that Court and also consent to their municipal courts taking judicial cognizance of Community law. In theory, therefore, as long as the state remains a member of the Community there should be no conflict between the municipal (internal) law of the Member States and the Community (external) law because the latter becomes part of the former. In fact, however, conflicts do arise and this raises the question of the supremacy of the one over the other. Reduced to a practical level sovereignty means the ultimate authority in respect of a particular matter and raises the question whether the Community or the state law governs a par- ticular situation.

Another digression into the theory of relations between external and internal law leads us to the consideration of two rival doctrines, dualism (parallelism) and monism,[2] which purport to explain the basis of legal obligation. According to the positivist philosophy of law, the relationship between the law of a sovereign state and the law of mankind, reflected in the law generated by agreements between states, has been expressed in the dualist (parallelist) doctrine. In simple terms this doctrine presupposes the existence of two separate systems of law: international and national, co- existing side by side as it were in watertight compartments. Though International Law is the universal law of mankind it stops at the door of the sovereign state and remains outside unless admitted to the territory of the state. It means that International Law binds states in their relations with each other but has, subject to few exceptions, no binding force in the territory of the state unless transformed or translated into rules of municipal law. This doctrine, favouring sovereignty, is still the reigning theory and the United Kingdom is among its adherents.

---

2 Starke, J G, 'Monism and Dualism in the Theory of International Law' (1936) 17 BYBIL 66.

Monism is the rival doctrine propounding the existence of a single system of norms or legal rules binding states and individuals alike. States are, after all, nothing but forms of organization or legal fictions whilst the individual is the ultimate subject of law. Both international and municipal law are only parts of the same structure and their rules are interrelated. Consequently monism cuts across sovereignty bringing the individual face to face with international law and relieving the state of the task of transforming it into rules of domestic law. The origins of monism can be traced to the medieval concept of the unity of law as Natural Law was considered to be a reflection of the wisdom of God through the reason of man. It ceased to be fashionable when the theory of Natural Law was superseded by the theory of Positive Law. The 20th-century revival of the monist doctrine in its positivist rather than naturalist garb is a reaction against the 19th-century apotheosis of the sovereign state degenerating into nationalism which saw International Law solely as a product of the 'will' of states.

The legal concept of the European Community reflects a monist approach. Therefore, to understand the relationship between the Community law and the law of the Member States it is unhelpful to think in terms of sovereignty (nationalism) versus collectivity (internationalism). We have to formulate instead a functional approach which in practical terms reconciles the need of a Community law with the aspiration of states to be supreme within their territories. Once this is appreciated the question of the supremacy of one system or the other resolves itself into a division of labour or functions of the respective bodies of rules within a unitary concept of law. Within its respective sphere each system is supreme as stated by the Community Court:[3]

'... The Community is founded on a common market, common objectives, and common institutions ... Within the specific domain of the Community, ie for everything which relates to the pursuit of the common objectives within the common market the institutions [of the Community] are provided with exclusive authority ... Outside the domain of the Community, the governments of the Member States retain their responsibilities in all sectors of economic policy ... They remain masters of their social policy; the same undoubtedly holds true for large segments of their fiscal policy ...'

Ten years later, in the ERTA Case which was, inter alia, concerned with the treaty-making power of the Community and the Member States the Court held that

---

3 Case 30/59: *De Gezamenlijke Steenkolenmijnen in Limburg v High Authority of the ECSC* [1961] ECR 1 at 23.

'... By the terms of article 5, the Member States are required on the one hand to take all appropriate steps to ensure the carrying out of the obligations arising out of the Treaty ... and on the other hand to abstain from any steps likely to jeopardise the attainment of the purposes of the Treaty. If these two provisions are read in conjunction, it follows that to the extent that Community rules are promulgated for the attainment of the purposes of the Treaty, the Member States cannot, outside the framework of the Community institutions assume obligations likely to affect such rules or alter their scope ...'[4]

These two dicta delimit the respective spheres of the Community and the Member States both in the 'internal' and 'external' aspect of sovereignty.

Let us turn now to the founding Treaties, especially the EEC Treaty, which is a unique treaty. It cannot be compared with traditional international treaties which set out the obligations of the parties and, in most cases, leave the implementation and enforcement of the obligations to the forces which make International Law effective. It is a self-executing treaty. The EEC is, by the will of the founding states, a separate legal entity, a new subject of law and, although it takes life from the agreement of states, it has a quasi-independent existence. Being a subject of law it enjoys the treaty-making power and the power of diplomatic representation but, above all, it has its own institutions and a law-making power. Community law is therefore an autonomous legal order binding not only the Member States but also their citizens directly and immediately.

The EEC Treaty itself has a legal framework – actually two such frameworks – the constitutional framework which we have already analysed and the economic framework which we shall consider later on. What we must discuss now is the impact of the Treaty and the Community legislation on the legal systems of the Member States. In doing so we should bear in mind[5] that '... the Community constitutes a new legal order of international law, in favour of which the States within certain areas have limited their sovereign rights ...' because it reflects the difficulties inherent in the 'dualist' thinking which has so far dominated the European legal scene. Indeed some of the constitutions of the Member States had to be amended in order to ease the process of assimilation of international obligations inherent in the Community Treaties into the law of the

4 Case 22/70: *EC Commission v EC Council* [1971] ECR 263 at 275, [1971] CMLR 335 at 355; at paras 21 and 22; see also Opinion 1/75: *Re the OECD Understanding on a Local Cost Standard* [1975] ECR 1355, [1976] CMLR 85.
5 Case 26/62: *Algemene Transport- en Expeditie Onderneming van Gend en Loos NV v Nederlandse Tariefcommissie* [1963] ECR 1 at 12, [1963] CMLR 105 at 129; see also Case 6/64: *Costa v ENEL* [1964] ECR 585 at 594, [1964] CMLR 425 at 456.

land. In this respect the United Kingdom is not in a unique position. However, with the continuing growth of Community law expanding into most areas legal sovereignty may soon become an outmoded concept relegated by political and economic integration into the historical museum of the European continent.

II CONSTITUTIONS OF THE MEMBER STATES AND TREATY OBLIGATIONS

The admission of external law to the territory of a state raises a constitutional problem of transmission, on the one hand, and supremacy in the case of a conflict with municipal law, on the other. A further problem, as far as the countries with written constitutions are concerned, arises from the internal relationship between the constitution and the ordinary law of the land. The constitution, as the basic law of the land, consists not only of the rules which organize the political framework of the state but also of the general principles on which rests the whole edifice of law and order. It follows that there is a hierarchy of legal norms or in Pound's rather inelegant phrase, 'authoritative starting points for legal reasoning'[6] which, in the event of a conflict with external law, raises the question whether external law is superior/subordinate to the law of the Constitution and the ordinary law of the land alike or whether the hierarchy of legal norms will affect the issue.

In view of the diversity of the legal systems involved it seems necessary to investigate the position in each Member State.

(a) *Ratification of the EEC Treaty*

According to the constitutions of the original six Member States treaties are made and ratified by the Head of State.[7] However in the case of especially important treaties these Constitutions require a parliamentary approval in the form of either a resolution or a special law. In France, Italy, Germany and the Netherlands a special Act enabling the Head of State to ratify and thus commit the country internationally was necessary.[8] Accordingly these laws were passed during 1957.[9]

The position in Belgium and Luxembourg is somewhat different. The effect of the law passed by reference to article 37(1) of the

---

6 Pound, R, 'Hierarchy of Sources and Forms in Different Systems of Law' [1933] *Tulane Law Review* 475 at 483.

7 Belgium, art 68; France (Constitution of 1946 which was in force at that time), art 31, Constitution of 1958, art 52; Federal Republic of Germany, art 59; Italy, art 80; Luxembourg, art 37; the Netherlands, art 50 (in force at that time).

8 France, art 27; Italy, art 80; Germany, art 59 (2); the Netherlands, art 60 at the time of the signing of the Treaties.

9 France, 8 August 1957, Germany, 27 July 1957, Italy, 14 October 1957, the Netherlands, 5 December 1957.

Constitution of Luxembourg, which enables the Grand Duke to conclude treaties, is to exercise parliamentary control over the acts of the executive.[10] The interpretation of the Belgian Constitution was subject to controversy as to the rôle of Parliament in this matter[11] but Parliament approved the Treaty by the Law of 22 December 1957 and so according to custom the Treaty may '*sortir son plein et entier effet*'.[12]

In the United Kingdom treaties are made and ratified by the Crown,[13] so much so that the battle about the membership of the Community was fought in the political arena of the House of Commons rather than the courts of law. Formally the Treaty obligations were implemented by the European Communities Act 1972, as subsequently amended, which has the effect of both a 'constitutional' and an 'ordinary' law.

In Ireland treaties are made by the government and ratified by Parliament.[14] Every treaty has to be laid before the lower house (Dáil Eireann) and if a charge on public funds is involved the terms must be approved by the Dáil. However, if the treaty is to be part of domestic law it can only be such as determined by the Oireachtas,[15] ie the body composed of the President of the Republic and both houses (ie the Dáil and the Senate). Such determination cannot take effect otherwise than by legislation.[16] However in order to enable the country to accede to the Communities a bill was passed by the Oireachtas in 1971 adding subsection 3 to article 29.4 of the Constitution and a Referendum was held in 1972.

Constitutional problems arising in connection with ratification of the Single European Act 1986 were aired before the Irish High Court and the Supreme Court.[17] They decided that the Bill to ratify the Act was not unconstitutional. The amendments of the founding Treaties such as the changes in the voting system of the Council, the extension of the Community domain into the protection of the environment and the establishment of the Court of First Instance were held to be within the scope of the amend-

---

10 Law of 30 November 1957; Pescatore, P, *Introduction à la Science du Droit* (1960), pp 170 and 175.
11 Constantinides-Mégret, C, *Le Droit de la Communauté Economique Européenne et l'Ordre Juridique des Etats Membres* (1967), pp 14–15.
12 Constantinides-Mégret, op cit, p 15.
13 *Blackburn v A-G* [1971] 1 WLR 1037 (see Lord Denning MR at 1040). Also see Chapter 12 infra.
14 Constitution of 1937 (as amended in 1941, and 1972), art 29, which deals with international relations, and art 28 under which executive powers in this respect can be conferred upon the government.
15 Ibid, art 29 (6).
16 Kelly, J M, *The Irish Constitution* (1980), pp 155–156.
17 *Crotty v An Taoiseach* [1987] 2 CMLR 666.

ments of the Irish Constitution necessitated by the accession to the Community. However, Title III of the Single European Act (which is in reality a separate Treaty), which includes provisions on European Co-operation in the Sphere of Foreign Policy and thus impinges upon the freedom of the Member States in the conduct of their external affairs, was considered not ratifiable without a referendum and amendment of the Irish Constitution.

According to the Danish Constitution of 1953 (article 19) the Monarch acts in international affairs on behalf of the Kingdom but without the consent of the Folketing cannot commit the country to any obligations of importance or for which parliamentary approval is necessary. Therefore in practice treaties are negotiated and ratified by the Executive subject to parliamentary approval. Accession to the Communities was approved by the Folketing and a referendum held in 1972. Attempts to have the procedures leading to the accession declared unconstitutional[18] and the 'signatures on the treasonable document declared void and unauthorised whereby our Queen may be saved from the biggest swindle in the history of Denmark'[19] were dismissed by the courts on the ground that the Head of State could not be held to account before her courts.

In Greece too treaties are negotiated by the Executive subject to parliamentary approval.[20]

Under the Spanish[21] Constitution of 1978 (article 63(2)) the power to make international treaties belongs to the Crown, but since the King is a constitutional monarch the negotiations are in the hands of the government and the conclusion is subject to parliamentary control. Certain treaties require prior authorization of the national parliament (Cortes Generales). In this way the Cortes Generales give authorization to the King to give his assent to the treaty negotiated by the government. The King signs the instrument of ratification.

Article 95(1) provides for prior constitutional amendment to enter into treaties which contain provisions contrary to the Constitution. Community treaties, limiting the sovereign power of the state, fall into that category. However the necessity of constitutional amendment can be overcome by virtue of an 'organic law' enacted by the Cortes Generales under article 93 which provides that 'authorisation may be granted for concluding treaties by which

18 *Tegen v Prime Minister of Denmark* [1973] CMLR 1.
19 *Aggergren v The Queen and Prime Minister* [1973] CMLR 5.
20 Act No 945 (Official Gazette Part I No 170 of 27 July 1979), Roucounas, E, 'Pour le dialogue entre droit communautaire et droit grec' (1980) *Rev Hellenique de Droit International* 11 at 15.
21 Aurrecoechea, J, 'Some Problems concerning the Constitutional Basis for Spain's Accession to the European Community' (1987) 1 ICLQ, 14 et seq.

powers derived from the Constitution shall be vested in an international organization or institution'. Such authorization was granted by Organic Law 10/1985 of 2 August 1985.[1]

By virtue of article 138(b) of the Constitution of Portugal of 1976 international treaties are negotiated by the Government and ratified by the President after having been duly approved by the appropriate body, ie the Government, the Constitutional Court or the National Assembly, depending on the type of treaty in question. Treaties involving participation in international organizations, treaties of peace and defence and those affecting the frontiers of the state as well as treaties submitted by the Government have to be approved by the National Assembly. The act of approval takes the form of a statute. Clearly Community Treaties fall into that category. Such a law was passed in 1982.

(b) *Incorporation of the Treaty into municipal law*
The method of incorporation depends on whether a country follows the monist or the dualist doctrine. Among the original Six, France and Italy represent the two extremes: the former is monist, the latter is dualist, whilst the remaining four occupy a middle position with a distinct dualist leaning. Denmark, Ireland, Greece and the United Kingdom fall into the dualist category.

The French Republic started with a dualist posture but by article 26 of the Constitution of 1946 reversed the tradition and turned monist. Article 26 provided that Treaties duly ratified by the Head of State and published have the force of law even if they are inconsistent with French law 'without there being any need of resorting to any legislative measures other than those necessary to secure ratification'. The Constitution of 1958, now in force, not only adopted the position but article 55, as if to confirm the supremacy of Community law, provided that Treaties or Agreements ratified or approved 'have an authority superior to that of laws'. It follows that Treaties are not subject to transformation into the rules of French municipal law but take their place automatically by virtue of the Constitution in the internal legal order, subject to reciprocity and the sovereign will of the French people. However in the case of the EEC Treaty the condition of reciprocity is satisfied in the light of article 170 which contains Community remedies to enforce it.[2]

The Italian Constitution of 1948 contains no reference to the incorporation of treaties into Italian law. Article 11 permits a

---

1 Ibid, at 22.
2 *Administration des Douanes v Société Cafés Jacques Vabre et J Weigel et Compagnie Sarl, Cour de Cassation* [1975] 2 CMLR 336, 13 CMLR Rev 128–32.

delegation of national sovereignty to international organizations but fails to deal with the problem of treaties. Accordingly a practice has been established in accordance with the hierarchy of legal rules: if the treaty affects a law the execution of the treaty takes the form of a law, if it affects merely administrative rules a decree of the Executive will take care of the situation. Reflecting this formula the law of ratification of the two Treaties of Rome passed on 14 October 1957 provided in article 2 that 'the agreements specified in article 1 will receive full and complete execution'. In this way the act of ratification became the act of execution or incorporation of the Treaties into Italian law. The consequences, as far as supremacy is concerned, are quite significant because, being equal to an internal legislative act, the Treaty, in principle, assumes no higher or lower rank than the corresponding piece of Italian legislation. Conflicts with domestic law are implicitly avoided in accordance with the principle that *lex posterior derogat priori*.[3] In practice, as we shall see later, difficulties arise.

In Germany, the general view is that the act of ratification signifies not only the approval of the Treaty but also incorporation.[4] Article 24 of the Federal Constitution provides for the transfer of sovereign powers to intergovernmental institutions. Article 25, on the other hand, provides that the 'general rules of international law shall form part of federal law; they shall take precedence over the laws and create rights and duties directly applicable to the inhabitants of the territory of the federation'. This has been interpreted restrictively to include the general customary rules of international law but to exclude the conventional rules.[5] It follows that international treaties have the force of a federal law, that is, ordinary *law*, not constitutional law. Being no more than *law* in the hierarchy of legal rules they can derogate from a preceding federal law or the law of the *Länder* but cannot override a constitutional rule of the Federation or (presumably) the *Länder*. This was at the heart of the controversy over the alleged breach of the German *Grundgesetz* by Commission Regulations instituting a system of forfeitable

---

3 Cf the decision of the Italian Constitutional Court of 7 March 1964 in *Costa v ENEL* [1964] CMLR 425 at 456; *Frontini v Ministero delle Finanze* No 183/1973 [1974] 2 CMLR 372, Const Court Menis, C, *Traité CEE et Ordre Juridique Italien*, 2–3 (1983) CDE, 120 et seq.

4 Seidl-Hohenveldern, I, 'Transformation or Adoption of International into Municipal Law' (1963) 12 ICLQ, pp 101 et seq.

5 Bebr, G, 'Law of the European Communities and Municipal Law' (1971) 34 MLR 481 at 487 quoting Mangeldt-Klein, *Das Bonner Grundgesetz* (1957) 675–677; Carstens, K, 'Der Rang europäischer Verordnungen gegenüber deutschen Rechtsnormen', *Festschrift für Otto Riese* (1964) 65, 75. See also Bundesverfassungsgericht, 14 May 1968 (Regel des Völkerrechts) BVerfGe 23, 288 at 316.

export/import deposits. On that occasion[6] the Bundesverfassungsgericht held that: '... Article 24 does not actually give authority to transfer sovereign rights, but opens up the national legal system (within the limitations indicated) in such a way that the Federal Republic of Germany's exclusive claim to rule is taken back in the sphere of validity of the Constitution and room is given, within the State's sphere of rule, to the direct effect and applicability of law from another source.' Addressing itself specifically to the sensitive issue of conflicts between the guarantees of fundamental rights and the Community legislation the Federal Constitutional Court held that the reservation derived from article 24 shall apply as long ('*so lange*') as the Community integration has not resulted in a directly elected legislative assembly and a charter of fundamental rights. However, while keeping an open mind to this particular reservation[7] the Bundesverfassungsgericht had no hesitation in recognizing the binding force of ECJ's rulings under article 177.

According to a 1970 amendment of the Constitution of Belgium[8] article 25 bis provides that 'the exercise of powers may be conferred by a Treaty or by Law on institutions of Public International Law'. This formula resembles the delegation of powers under the Italian Constitution and certainly confirms the dualist approach to treaties which are denied the authority of superior law. Amidst the discussions[9] on the relations between the constitution and Treaty law the Belgian Cour de Cassation struck a valiant blow for the recognition of the supremacy of the Treaty law in the judgment of 27 May 1971.[10] The Constitution of Luxembourg was amended in a similar way, article 49 bis providing for a delegation of legislative and administrative powers to international organizations.[11]

The effect of the delegation of sovereignty in these three constitutions seems to provide room for the recognition of the binding force of the Community law enshrined in treaties whilst retaining

---

6 Case 52/71 *Internationale Handelsgesellschaft mbH v Einfuhr- und Vorratsstelle für Getreide und Futtermittel* [1974] 2 CMLR 540 at 551–552. Majority decision of Federal Constitutional Court of 29 May, 1974.

7 See Bundesverfassungsgericht in *Steinike und Weinling v Ernährung und Forstwirtschaft* [1980] 2 CMLR 531 at para 12.

8 Law of 18 August 1970; Louis, J V, 'L'article 25 bis de la constitution belge' [1970] *Rev du Marché Commun* 136, 410–416.

9 Ganshof van der Meersch, W J, 'Le juge belge à l'heure du droit international et du droit communautaire' (1969), 84 *Journal des Tribunaux* 4671, 537–551; Waelbroeck, M in Donner, A M, et al, *Le juge devant le droit national et le droit communautaire* (1966) at pp 29 et seq.

10 *Etat Belge v SA Fromagerie Franco-Suisse le Ski* (1971) RTDE 494.

11 Pescatore, P, 'L'autorité en droit interne des traités internationaux selon jurisprudence luxembourgeoise' (1962) 18 *Pasicrisie Luxembourgeoise* 99–115.

at the same time the sovereignty of parliament. It now remains to be seen whether the formula is sufficiently wide to read into it the supremacy of Community law necessary for the functioning of the Community as a supranational organization.

To meet this situation the amendment of the constitution of the Netherlands of 1956[12] provided that international treaties and agreements shall be the supreme law of the land (article 68). The Constitution of 1983 further accentuates the monist approach. It provides in article 92 that legislative, administrative and judicial powers may be conferred on international organisations by, or in virtue of, a treaty. Article 93 rules that provisions of treaties and of decisions of international organizations, the contents of which may be binding on anyone, shall have this binding effect as from the time of publication. This means that both precedent and subsequent national laws are overridden by international obligations as was already the position under the 1956 amendment. Article 120 also confirmed the principle that courts are not competent to judge the constitutionality of laws and international treaties.

According to article 96(1) of the Spanish Constitution treaties once officially published form part of the internal legal order. This means that formal incorporation is required. They then rank as statutes.[13] By this device Spain adopted the Community Treaties and the existing volume of Community law but has not solved the problem of supremacy.

The three members admitted in 1973 proceed from a dualist position. In the United Kingdom it was necessary to pass the European Communities Act 1972[14] in order to transform the Treaty obligations into domestic law, to adopt the so-called 'enforceable Community rights' and to set up machinery for the implementation of the remaining rules of Community law. In Ireland, too, this object was achieved by the European Communities Act 1972, which provided, inter alia, that 'from the first day of January 1973, the Treaties governing the European Communities and the existing and future acts adopted by the institutions of those Communities shall be binding on the state and shall be part of the domestic law thereof under the conditions laid down in those Treaties'. In Denmark the law of 11 October 1972 expressly adopted the Treaties enumerated therein and made provision for the delegation of sov-

12 Van Panhuys, H F, 'The Netherlands Constitution and International Law' (1964), 58 AJIL 88–108; Van Dijk, P, 'The Implementation and Application of the Law of the European Communities within the Legal Order of the Netherlands' (1969) 6 CML Rev 283–308.
13 Judgment of Supreme Court of 12 December 1980, quoted by Aurrecoechea at 28, supra.
14 See Chapter 12, below.

ereign powers to the Communities and for the adoption of Community acts directly applicable by virtue of Community law.

The Greek Constitution of 1975 enacted in anticipation[15] of admission to the Community provides (article 28) for the limitation of the exercise of national sovereignty subject to safeguards of human rights, democratic government and the principle of equality and reciprocity with her partners. The same article (28) guarantees incorporation and supremacy of international law and international conventions duly ratified under the condition of reciprocity. However article 93(4) which governs the review of the constitutionality of laws states that courts are not bound to apply laws which are contrary to the constitution. This is a potential source of conflict with Community law.

In terms similar to article 25 of the German Constitution the Constitution of Portugal (article 8) provides that the principles of customary International Law form part of the Portuguese legal order. There is no automatic reception of international conventional law. Moreover articles 7 and 9 charge the state with the duty of safeguarding national independence and provide that Portugal must, in her international relations, always respect the Constitution. It means, in effect, that the Constitution overrides treaty obligations. Therefore it was necessary in 1982 to amend article 8 of the Constitution which provides, in paragraph 4, that the rules enacted by the competent institutions of international organizations to which Portugal is a party are directly applicable in the internal order as long as this is expressly provided for in the corresponding treaties. This has effectively dealt with the problem of Community treaties and the direct applicability of Community law but has left open the problem of supremacy.

This brief survey of the constitutional scene of the Member States shows not only a diverse approach to the status of the Treaties but also indicates a cautious commitment of the majority of these states to the Community rather than a formal and irrevocable abdication of their national sovereignty.

III INCORPORATION OF THE COMMUNITY LEGISLATION

(a) *Reception of Community law*
The logic of the acceptance of Treaty obligations demands an unconditional reception not only of the primary but also of the derivative rules of Community law. Article 5 of the EEC Treaty reminds the Member States that they must 'take all appropriate measures, whether general or particular, to ensure fulfilment of the

---

15 Roucounas, op cit, p 13.

obligations arising out of this Treaty or resulting from action taken by the institutions of the Community. They shall facilitate the achievement of the Community tasks. They shall abstain from any measure which could jeopardise the attainment of the objectives of the Treaty.' Moreover, the Member States must 'in close co-operation with the institutions of the Community, co-ordinate their respective economic policies to the extent necessary to attain the objectives of the Treaty' (article 6 (1)). Since policies are enforced through the instrumentality of the law, the Member States must adapt and modify their laws in order to bring about harmony within the Community and, above all, remove the legal barriers to the creation and working of the Community. Since the EEC is concerned with customs duties, movement of goods, persons, services and capital, agriculture and fisheries, transport, competition and restrictive practices, state aid to industry, taxation, and social security, and whilst the ECSC and Euratom are concerned with coal, steel and nuclear energy industries, the Member States undertake a considerable number of specific obligations. These obligations are in many respects regulated by Community legislation whose scope ranges from relatively trivial provisions like the calculation of the compensation for hatching eggs[16] to the most solemn historical provisions regarding the establishment of the Community.

In the case of the new members, the accumulated volume of Community law became the object of a wholesale reception at the time of their accession. By article 2 of the 1972 Act of Accession they became subject to 'the provisions of the original Treaties and the acts adopted by the institutions of the Communities' whilst by article 149 they were considered 'as being addressees of and having notification of directives and decisions within the meaning of article 189 of the EEC Treaty and of article 161 of the EAEC Treaty, and of recommendations and decisions within the meaning of article 14 of the ECSC Treaty, provided that those directives, recommendations and decisions have been notified to all the original Member States'. The same principles govern the position of Greece, Portugal and Spain subject to specifically negotiated derogations.

The impact of Community law upon the laws of the Member States depends on two principles: the direct applicability and the supremacy of Community law. The former is relevant to the implementation, the latter to the enforcement of Community law.

---

16 Article 77 (2) of the 1972 Act of Accession provides that 'the compensatory amount per hatching egg shall be calculated on the basis of the compensatory amount applicable to the quantity of feed grain required for the production in the Community of one hatching egg'.

Apart from a reference to the direct applicability of regulations, the Treaties do not contain a detailed exposition of these principles, which are essential to the Community, therefore they had to be elaborated by the Court of Justice of the Communities.

(b) *Directly applicable rules of Community law*
Depending on their nature and function the rules of Community law are either 'directly' or 'indirectly' applicable. In this context a distinction should be made between rules which are 'directly applicable'[17], that is rules becoming automatically upon their enactment part of the *corpus juris* of the Member States and rules 'directly enforceable' that is rules having a 'direct effect' as far as rights and obligations of the citizen are concerned.[18] In other words 'directly applicable' rules concern the state, whilst 'directly enforceable' rules concern the rights of individuals. The former imply state duties, the latter citizens' rights flowing from state duties to implement and enforce Community law.

Despite the subtle distinction between 'direct applicability' and 'direct effect', the ECJ has not been using these terms consistently. Thus, for example, it held that 'article 52 of the Treaty is a directly applicable provision'[19] and that 'in such a situation, at least, article 119 is directly applicable and may thus give rise to individual rights which the Courts must protect'.[20] In the *Van Gend* case,[1] on the other hand, it decreed that 'article 12 must be interpreted as producing direct effects and creating individual rights which Courts must protect' and on another occasion[2] stated that in 'applying the principle of co-operation laid down in article 5 of the Treaty, it is the national courts which are entrusted with ensuring the legal protection which citizens derive from the direct effect of the provisions of Community law ...' However, despite this dictum, it should be borne in mind that article 5 is addressed to the Member States alone, stating their general obligation to further the objectives of the Treaty. In that sense it is directly applicable to the states but not to individuals since it is incapable of generating

---

17 'Enforceable Community rights' according to s 2 (1) of the British European Communities Act 1972.
18 See Winter, J, 'Direct Applicability and Direct Effect – Two Distinct and Different Concepts in Community Law' [1972] CML Rev 425; Wyatt, D, 'Directly Applicable Provisions of EEC Law' [1975] 125 NLJ, pp 458, 575, 669, 793.
19 Case 2/74: *Reyners v Belgium* [1974] ECR 631, [1974] 2 CMLR 305.
20 Case 43/75: *Defrenne v SABENA* [1976] ECR 455, [1976] 2 CMLR 98.
1 Op cit [1963] ECR 1 at 13, [1963] CMLR 105 at 130, 131.
2 Case 33/76: *Rewe-Zentralfinanz eG v Landwirtschaftskammer für das Saarland* [1976] ECR 1989, [1977] 1 CMLR 533.

subjective rights and thus cannot be said to have a direct effect as
far as individuals are concerned.[3]

It seems accordingly that 'directly applicable' provisions take
force in the territory of the Member States without further enactment whilst provisions having a 'direct effect' are capable of creating enforceable Community rights. The latter follows from the
former. These rights are created either by the Treaty directly
or, as stated the ECJ[4] 'also by reason of obligations which the
Treaty imposes in a clearly defined way upon individuals as
well as upon the Member States and upon the institutions of the
Community'.

The notion of 'direct applicability' is derived from the monist
concept of International Law and the self-executing nature of
certain Treaties or Treaty provisions. It, therefore, enables the
rules of Community law, despite their extraneous source, to become
automatically part of the *corpus juris* of the Member States. The
notion of 'direct effect', on the other hand, is derived from the
judicial interpretation of the will of the legislator who decides
whether a provision is merely programmatic[5] or constitutes a
command to its subject,[6] or a right vested in an individual,[7] or an
obligation imposed upon him.[8] Thus, whilst the distinction
between 'direct applicability' and 'direct effect' appears of little
significance in the eyes of the Community Court, its jurisprudence,
through the instrumentality of the doctrine expressed by both
terms, has advanced the rights of individuals grounded in Community law.

The doctrine of direct effect can be traced to certain leading cases.
In the *Van Gend* case the ECJ held that there was an unconditional
obligation on the part of the Member State to refrain from introducing new customs duties which, in turn, created a corresponding
right in favour of the citizen. The alternative to the direct effect,
thought the Court, 'would remove all direct judicial protection of

3 See Case 9/73: *Schlüter v Hauptzollamt Lörrach* [1973] ECR 1135; Case 44/84:
  Hurd v Jones (HM Inspector of Taxes) [1986] ECR 29, [1986] 2 CMLR 1;
  Case C-333/88: *Tither v IRC* [1990] 2 CMLR 779.
4 *Van Gend*, supra at p 12.
5 Eg EEC, art 74: 'The objectives of this Treaty shall, in matters governed by
  this Title, be pursued by Member States within the framework of a common
  transport policy.'
6 Eg EEC, art 72: 'Member States shall keep the Commission informed of any
  movements of capital to and from third countries which come to their
  knowledge.'
7 Eg EEC, art 175 (3): 'Any natural or legal person may ... complain to the
  Court.'
8 Eg EEC, art 86: 'Any abuse ... of a dominant position within the common
  market ... shall be prohibited.'

the individual rights'. In *Alfons Lütticke v Hauptzollamt Saarlouis*[9] the Court held that a Member State must not impose on the product of another Member State any internal tax in excess of that applicable to similar domestic products and this safeguarded the importer's interests. In *Salgoil SpA v Italian Ministry of Foreign Trade*[10] the ECJ confirmed that a Member State had no discretion in the application of the Treaty provisions governing import quotas within the Community. In the *Van Duyn* case the freedom of movement was recognized as an enforceable right though, in the circumstances, it was curtailed by the application of a derogation clause. Both the right and the exception were held to be 'directly applicable'.[11] The right of establishment of a lawyer who, though not a national, was qualified according to the law of the host state, was deduced from article 52[12] and Italy was held to be in breach of the same article for having failed to remove a nationality quali- fication in respect of customs agents[13] and persons employed in tourism, journalism and retail pharmacies.[14] In the much cri- ticized[15] *Defrenne* case a Belgian air hostess was able to vindicate her right to equal pay by virtue of EEC article 119 which (coupled with a directive) was held to have a direct effect as from the end of the period of transition.

However the Community Court has stated the doctrine in a most forthright manner in the second *Simmenthal* case[16] emphasizing that a directly applicable Community rule takes precedence over the national legislation whether antecedent or subsequent to the relevant Treaty provision. Irrespective of the constitutional impli- cations the national courts are bound to give effect to it. The message of the Community Court is that certain provisions of the Treaty are by their very nature and purpose directly enforceable

---

9 Case 57/65: [1966] ECR 205, [1971] CMLR 674; see also Case 28/67: *Mölkerei- Zentrale Westfalen/Lippe GmbH v Hauptzollamt Paderborn* [1968] ECR 143, [1968] CMLR 187.

10 Case 13/68: [1968] ECR 453, [1969] CMLR 181.

11 Cf the opposite decision of the French Conseil d'Etat in the *Cohn-Bendit* case, Dalloz 1979, J155.

12 Case 2/74: *Reyners v Belgian State* [1974] ECR 631, [1974] 2 CMLR 305; see also Case 71/76: *Thieffry v Conseil de l'Ordre des Avocats à la Cour de Paris* [1977] ECR 765, [1977] 2 CMLR 373.

13 Case 159/78: *EC Commission v Italy* [1979] ECR 3247 at 3264, [1980] 3 CMLR 446 at 463.

14 Case 168/85: *EC Commission v Italy* [1986] ECR 2945; [1988] 1 CMLR 580.

15 Hamson, C, 'Methods of Interpretation – a Critical Assessment of the Results', *Reports of the Judicial and Academic Conference Luxembourg* (1976).

16 Case 106/77: *Amministrazione delle Finanze dello Stato v Simmenthal SpA* [1978] ECR 629, [1978] 3 CMLR 263. See also Case 158/80: *Rewe Handelsgesellschaft v HZA Kiel* (Re direct application of directive) [1981] *ECR* 1805, [1982] ICMLR 449.

in national courts. As they affect private interests they create Community rights which, as a corollary, correspond to Community obligations imposed upon the Member States. These, as confirmed by the Community Court, and national courts, include the following:

(1) Article 7 which prohibits discrimination on grounds of nationality;[17]
(2) Articles 9 and 11 on the customs union as from the end of the transitional period;[18]
(3) Article 12 which forbids new customs duties or similar charges;[19]
(4) Article 13 (2) on the abolition of charges having an equivalent effect to customs duties on imports;[20]
(5) Article 16 on the abolition of customs duties on exports;[21]
(6) Articles 30 and 31 which forbid quantitative restrictions and measures having equivalent effect;[1]
(7) Article 32 (1), (2) on the abolition of quotas in trade between Member States;[2]
(8) Article 36 as far as 'disguised restrictions on trade' are concerned;[3]
(9) Article 37 (1) and (2) which forbids measures likely to restrict

---

17 Case 1/78: *Kenny v Insurance Officer* [1978] ECR 1489, [1978] 3 CMLR 651. Case 45/75: *Rewe-Zentrale v HZA Landau-Pfalz* [1976] ECR 181, at 198, [1976] 2 CMLR 1 at 25. Case 22/80: *Boussac v Gerstenmeier* [1980] ECR 3427, [1982] 1 CMLR 202.

18 Case 33/70: *SACE SpA v Italian Ministry of Finance* [1970] ECR 1213, [1971] CMLR 123. Case 18/71: *Eunomia di Porro & C v Italian Ministry of Education* [1971] ECR 811, [1972] CMLR 4; Case 251/78: *Denkavit v Minister für Ernährung* [1979] ECR 3369 at 3384, [1980] 3 CMLR 513.

19 Case 26/62: *Van Gend,* supra.

20 Case 77/72: *Capolongo v Azienda Agricolo Maya* [1973] ECR 611 at 622, [1974] CMLR 230. Case 63/74: *W Cadsky SpA v Instituto Nazionale per il Commercio Estero* [1975] ECR 281, [1975] 2 CMLR 246; Case 94/75: *Süddeutsche Zucker v HZA Mannheim* [1976] ECR 153; [1976] 2 CMLR 54.

21 Case 48/71: *EC Commission v Italy* [1972] ECR 527, [1972] CMLR 699. Case 45/76: *Comet BV v Produktschap voor Siergewassen* [1976] ECR 2043, [1977] 1 CMLR 533.

1 Case 13/68: *Salgoil SpA v Italian Ministry of Foreign Trade* [1968] ECR 453, [1969] CMLR 181. Case 12/74: *EC Commission v Federal Republic of Germany* [1975] ECR 181, [1975] 1 CMLR 340. Case 74/76: *Iannelli and Volpi SpA v Meroni* [1977] ECR 557, [1977] 2 CMLR 688; Case 251/78, supra; Case 124/81: *EC Commission v United Kingdom* [1983] ECR 203, [1983] 2 CMLR 1; Case 42/82: *EC Commission v France* [1983] ECR 1013; [1984] 1 CMLR 160; Case 16/83: *Re Prantl* [1984] ECR 1299; Case 207/83: *EC Commission v United Kingdom* [1985] 2 CMLR 259.

2 Case 13/68: *Salgoil,* supra.

3 Case 78/70: *Deutsche Grammophon GmbH v Metro-SB-Grössmärkte GmbH & Co KG* [1971] ECR 487, [1971] CMLR 631. Case 192/73: *Van Zuylen Frères v Hag AG* [1974] ECR 731, [1974] 2 CMLR 127. Case 29/72: *Marimex SpA*

the abolition of customs duties and quantitative restrictions
between Member States or adjustment of state monopolies;[4]
(10) Article 48 (2) on discrimination between workers on the
ground of nationality;[5]
(11) Article 48 (3); Regulations 15 and 38/64; Directive 64/221 on
the restrictions of the freedom of movement;[6]
(12) Article 52 concerning the right of establishment;[7]
(13) Article 53 which forbids new restrictions on the right of
establishment;[8]
(14) Articles 59 and 62 on the freedom to provide services;[9]
(15) Articles 85 and 86 on competition;[10]

v Italian Finance Administration [1972] ECR 1309, [1973] CMLR 486. Case
21/75: *Firma I Schröeder KG v Oberstadt-direktor der Stadt Köln* [1975] ECR
905, [1975] 2 CMLR 312.
4 Case 59/75: *Pubblico Ministero v Flavia Manghera* [1976] ECR 91, [1976] 1
CMLR 557; Case 148/77: *Hansen v HZA Flensburg* [1978] ECR 1787, [1979]
1 CMLR 604.
5 Case 167/73: *EC Commission v French Republic* [1974] ECR 359, [1974] 2
CMLR 216. Case 41/74: *Van Duyn v Home Office* [1975] Ch 358, [1974] ECR
1337, [1975] 1 CMLR 1. Case 13/76: *Dona v Mantero* [1976] ECR 1333, [1976]
2 CMLR 578; Case 152/73: *Sotgiu v Deutsche Bundespost* [1974] ECR 153;
Case 36/75: *Rutili v Ministère de l'Interior* [1975] ECR 1219, [1976] 1 CMLR
140.
6 Case 67/74: *Bonsignore v Oberstadtdirektor der Stadt Köln* [1975] ECR 297,
[1975] CMLR 472. Case 41/74: *Van Duyn v Home Office*, supra; Case 36/75,
supra; Case 48/75: *Re Royer* [1976] ECR 497, [1976] 2 CMLR 619; Case
118/75: *Re Watson and Belmann* [1976] ECR 1185, [1976] 2 CMLR 552.
7 Case 2/74: *Reyners v Belgian State* [1974] ECR 631, [1974] 2 CMLR 305. Case
33/74: *Van Binsbergen v Bestuur van de Bedrijfsvereniging voor de
Metaalnijverheid* [1974] ECR 1299, [1975] 1 CMLR 298. Case 11/77: *Patrick
v Ministère des Affaires Culturelles* [1977] ECR 1199, [1977] 2 CMLR 523.
8 Case 6/64: *Costa v ENEL*, supra; Case 96/85: *EC Commission v France* [1986]
3 CMLR 57.
9 Case 33/74: *Van Binsbergen*, op cit; Case 36/74: *Walrave and Koch v Union
Cycliste Internationale* [1974] ECR 1405, [1975] 1 CMLR 320. Case 39/75:
Coenen v Sociaal Economische Raad [1975] ECR 1547, [1976] 1 CMLR 30.
Cases 110 and 111/78: *Ministère Public and Chambre Syndicale des Agents
Artistiques et Impresarii de Belgique, ASBL v van Wesemael* [1979] ECR 35,
[1979] 3 CMLR 87; Case 13/76: *Donà v Mantero* [1976] ECR 1333; Case
71/76: *Thieffry v Conseil de l'Ordre des Avocats à la Cour de Paris* [1977] ECR
765: Case 107/83: *Ordre des Avocats au Barreau de Paris v Klopp* [1984] ECR
2971, [1985] 1 CMLR 99; Case 90/76: *Van Ameyde v UCL* [1977] ECR 1091;
Case 15/78: *Soc. Gén. Alsacienne de Banque v Koestler* [1978] ECR 1971;Case
115/78: *Knoors v Secretary of State for Economic Affairs* [1979] ECR 399; Case
136/78: *Ministère Public v Auer* [1979] ECR 437, [1979] 2 CMLR 373; Case
271/82 *Auer v Ministère Public* [1985] 1 CMLR 123; Case 52/79: *Procureur du
Rui v Debauve* [1980] ECR 833.
10 Case 13/61: *Kledingverkoopbedrijf de Geus en Uitdenbogerd v Robert Bosch
GmbH* [1962] ECR 45, [1962] CMLR 1. Case 127/73: *BRT v SABAM* [1974]
ECR 51 and 313, [1974] 2 CMLR 238; Case 37/79: *Marty v Lauder* [1980]
ECR 2481, [1981] 2 CMLR 143 and subsequent cases.

(16) Article 90 (2) on revenue-producing monopolies;[11]
(17) Article 93 (3) concerning aids by states;[12]
(18) Article 95 (1) which prohibits internal taxation of products of other Member States.[13]
(19) Article 119 on equal pay for men and women.[14]

It goes without saying that the majority of articles 137–248 representing the 'organizational law' of the EEC are 'directly applicable' though by their nature and function they do not constitute rights enforceable by individuals.[15]

The list is by no means complete as certain provisions of the Treaty remain yet to be considered judicially. As for the criterion of direct enforceability, the Community Court[16] held as follows:

'... The Treaty's objective of establishing a common market the functioning of which affects the subjects of Member States entails that the Treaty is something more than an agreement creating obligations between state parties alone. The Community is a new legal system, in support of which the Member States have limited their sovereign rights in certain fields, and the subjects of the new legal system are not only the Member States but their inhabitants as well. Community Law, being independent of the legislation passed by Member States, therefore, creates rights as well as duties for individual persons who are subject to the legal order of Member States. These rights and obligations arise not only when they are expressly provided for in the Treaty, but also as a result of the duties imposed by it in a clearly defined manner upon nationals of Member States, the States themselves and the institutions of the Community ...'

Advocate-General Mayras, quoting several precedents in the *Van Duyn* case,[17] thought that '... the provision must impose on the Member State a clear and precise obligation; it must be unconditional, ie not accompanied by any reservation ..., and the application of the Community rule must not be conditional on any subsequent legislation whether of the Community institutions or

11 Case 155/73: *Italy v Sacchi* [1974] ECR 409, [1974] 2 CMLR 177.
12 Case 120/73: *Lorenz v Federal Republic of Germany* [1973] ECR 1471; Case 6/64, supra; Cases 91/83 and 127/83: *Heineken v Inspecteur der Vennootschapsbelasting* [1984] ECR 3435, [1985] 1 CMLR 389.
13 Case 57/65: *Lütticke v HZA Saarlouis* [1966] ECR 205, [1971] CMLR 674; Case 28/67: *Mölkerei-Zentrale Westfalen/Lippe GmbH v Hauptzollamt Paderborn* [1968] ECR 143, [1968] CMLR 187; Case 216/81: *Compagnia Generale Interscambi SpA v Amministrazione delle Finanza dello Stato* [1983] 1 CMLR 685.
14 Case 43/75: *Defrenne v SA SABENA* [1976] ECR 455, [1976] 2 CMLR 98 and subsequent cases; p 183, supra.
15 For exceptions, see EEC arts 173, 184, 215.
16 Case 28/67: *Mölkerei-Zentrale Westfalen/Lippe GmbH v Hauptzollamt Paderborn* [1968] ECR 143 at 152, [1968] CMLR 187 at 217.
17 Supra, ECR at p 1355; CMLR at p 8.

of the Member States; and must not lead to the latter having an effective power of discretionary judgment as to the application of the rule in question'.

The test of direct effect is, therefore, primarily the capacity of the text to produce rights and obligations which individuals may seek to enforce against the state. The national law should not bar the enforcement of such rights and obligations,[18] even though the enforcement may in the context of national law present considerable technical difficulties. However, as indicated by decisions arising from the application of EEC article 85 and article 86, a text may, even indirectly, give rise to directly enforceable rights and obligations.[19] In this sense the nature of a specific provision may have to be inferred from its purpose and the intention of the authority which brought into being such a provision (ie whether the Treaty or Community legislation).

To what extent procedures prescribed by the Treaty may give rise to directly enforceable rights and obligations remains to be seen. Procedural law is, in many respects, the guarantor of substantive rights. Where the prescribed procedures are not observed, the individual may suffer and should, in justice, be entitled to relief.[20] This, among other things, seems to have been in the mind of the Giudice Conciliatore Fabbri in *Flaminio Costa v ENEL*[1] when he referred to the ECJ a complaint that the Italian decree nationalising the electricity industry, passed in the absence of consultation with the Commission (articles 101 and 102), distorted the conditions of competition and infringed the rights of the individual. Although the Community Court held that article 102 created no directly enforceable rights, the general question seems to remain open.

To take another example Article 177 is surely directly applicable but has no direct effect in so far as it does not create directly enforceable rights. However it is also capable of creating an expectation in the minds of litigants that their case will be heard by the Community Court. However the procedure for the preliminary ruling is governed entirely by the national systems[2] which may,

18 *Salgoil SpA*, supra.
19 Eg Case 48/72: *Brasserie de Haécht v Wilkin-Janssen* [1973] ECR 77, [1973] CMLR 287; Case 127/73: *BRT v SABAM* [1974] ECR 51, [1974] 2 CMLR 238.
20 Cf World Court in *The Free Zones Case* [1932] PCIJ Rep Ser A/B, No 46; *Wimbledon Case* [1923] PCIJ Rep Ser A No 1; *German Settlers Case* [1923] PCIJ Rep Ser B No 6.
1 Case 6/64, supra.
2 Eg Case 36/80: *Irish Creamery Milk Suppliers Association v Ireland* [1981] ECR 735, [1981] 2 CMLR 455. Case 244/78: *Union Laitiere Normande v French Dairy Farmers* [1979] ECR 2663, [1980] 1 CMLR 314. Case 146/73:

through cumbersome procedures or appeals on the point whether or not to refer, frustrate that expectation. In the opinion of the ECJ a state policy to restrict the reference would amount to a breach of the Treaty[3] and so would procedural discrimination against a person endeavouring to assert a Community right[4]. Whilst the ECJ made it plain that '... in the absence of Community rules on this subject it is for the domestic legal system of each Member State to designate the courts having jurisdiction and to determine the procedural conditions governing actions at law intended to ensure the protection of the rights which citizens have from the direct effect of Community law'[5] it would be a rather tenuous proposition that procedural safeguards implicit in the enforcement of Community rights do themselves constitute 'enforceable Community rights'.

The principle of direct applicability of Treaty provisions defined by the Community Court applies also to secondary legislation. Regulations[6] fall into that category unless they give the Member States discretion in their implementation.[7] If they do not allow any discretion an action, as in the slaughtered cows case,[8] may be brought against the state by the individual whose Community right has been impaired through the deficiency of the national system. Moreover, in such a case, the state in default will be exposed to enforcement proceedings.[9]

Directives, as we have observed earlier,[10] may give a direct effect creating thereby enforceable Community rights. However they have also another potential since '... the individual invokes a provision of a directive before a national court in order that the competent national authorities, in exercising the choice which is

---

Rheinmühlen-Düsseldorf v Einfuhr-und Verratsstelle für Getreide und Futtermittel [1974] ECR 139, [1974] 1 CMLR 523.
3 Case 77/69: *EC Commission v Belgium* [1970] ECR 237.
4 Case 33/76: *Rewe Zentralfinanz eG and Rewe Zentral AG v Landwirtschaftskammer für das Saarland* [1976] ECR 1989, [1977] 1 CMLR 533 (limitation of actions).
5 Ibid.
6 See pp 127 et seq. See also Case 83/78: *Pigs Marketing Board v Redmond* [1978] ECR 2347, [1979] 1 CMLR 177.
7 Eg Reg 15/64/EEC (JO 573/64) concerning the import of cattle from Denmark to Germany; See also Case 31/74: *Re Galli* [1975] ECR 47, [1975] 1 CMLR 211.
8 Case 93/71: *Leonesio*, supra.
9 Case 39/72: *EC Commission v Italy* [1973] ECR 101; [1973] CMLR 439; Case 309/84: *EC Commission v Italy (Re Non-Payment of Premium for Renunciation of re-planting of Vines under Reg 456/80)* [1986] ECR 599.
10 Case 51/76; *Verbond van Nederlandse Ondernemingen v Inspecteur der Invoerrechten en Accijnzen* [1977] ECR 113 at 127, [1977] 1 CMLR 413: See also Case 21/78: *Delkvist v Anklagemijndigheden* [1978] ECR 2327 at 2340.

346   Chapter 10   Implementation of Community law

left to them as to the form and the methods for implementing the directive, have kept within the limits as to their discretion set out in the directive...'¹¹

(c) *Indirectly applicable rules of Community law*
In addition to provisions which contain rules of law directly applicable in the territory of the Member States the founding Treaties comprise a number of policies or general provisions which have to be implemented by state legislation. The former are cognisable by the national courts and for all intents and purposes are regarded as having a direct and immediate effect with regard to persons and things in the territory of the Member States. The latter consist of Treaty obligations which by virtue of the Treaty provisions have to be transformed into detailed rules of law. The ECJ expressly ruled that certain provisions of the EEC Treaty have no direct effect. These include the Community 'solidarity principle' expressed in article 5;¹² articles 32 (2) and 33¹³ concerning quotas in inter-state trade; articles 67 and 71¹⁴ concerned with the movement of capital; article 90 (2)¹⁵ permitting Member States to grant special or exclusive rights to public undertakings entrusted with the operation of services of general economic interest; article 91 (1)¹⁶ which prohibits aids granted by states save in specific circumstances; article 97 (1)¹⁷ permitting Member States which levy a turnover tax to establish average rates; article 102¹⁸ concerned with consultations between the Commission and any Member States regarding the approximation of laws; article 107¹⁹ concerned with the rates of exchange and articles 117 and 118 concerned with social policy.²⁰ To these we can add the decisions and directives of the Community organs addressed to one or several states which are of a general or mixed character and have to be further elaborated. The rules of

11 Case 51/76: *Verbond van Nederlandse Ondernemingen v Inspecteur der Invoerrechter en Accijnzen* [1977] ECR 113 at 127, [1977] 1 CMLR 413.
12 Case 9/73: *Schlüter v HZA Lörrach* [1973] ECR 1135 at 1162; see also Cases 44/84 and C-333/88, supra.
13 Case 13/68: *Salgoil SpA v Italian Ministry of Foreign Trade* [1968] ECR 453 at 461.
14 Case 203/80: *Re Casati* [1981] ECR 2595 at 2615–2616.
15 Case 10/71: *Minstère Public de Luxembourg v Müller* [1971] ECR 723 at 730.
16 Case 77/72: *Capolongo v Maya* [1973] ECR 611 at 621, [1974] 1 CMLR 230 at 244–245; Case 78/76: *Steinike und Weinlig v Germany* [1977] ECR 595, [1977] 2 CMLR 688.
17 Case 28/67: *Mölkerei Zentrale v HZA Paderborn* [1968] ECR 143 at 156, [1968] CMLR 187 at 221.
18 Case 6/64: *Costa v ENEL* [1964] ECR 585 at 595.
19 Case 9/73, supra, at 1161.
20 Case 126/86: *Gimenez Zaera v Istituto Nacional de la Seguridade Social (Re Pensions of Spanish Civil Servants)* [1989] 1 CMLR 827.

law indirectly applicable have this in common: that they have to be enacted by the Member States to become part of their municipal law and that the Member States have a considerable discretion in the choice of the methods. In most cases the Member States have merely to adapt their existing laws to the overall strategy of the founding Treaties, notably the Common Market in the EEC. However the intensity of the adaptation and the degree of discretion accorded to Member States depend on the Treaty provisions. Thus according to the EEC Treaty three such degrees can be discerned.[21]

Firstly, the states may enjoy complete discretion in the implementation of their obligations. Two examples, discussed by a learned writer,[22] illustrate the point. To implement Regulation No 3 concerning the social security of migrant workers (reference to EEC article 51) Italy set up a special pension for miners;[1] the Netherlands, on the other hand, considered that their existing law was inadequate and took the opportunity of remodelling the system and adapting it to the problems of migrant workers.[2] To implement the EEC agricultural policy France passed a general statute (*loi d'orientation agricole*),[3] whilst Belgium decided to recast the whole system and so repealed the law of 1931 on import, export and transit of goods and substituted for it a new law on agriculture.[4]

Secondly, the states may have a choice of either implementing or not implementing the Community law, but in the exercise of their option they have to act within the scope of authority accorded to them. The following provisions of the EEC Treaty are relevant in this respect:

Article 25, which enables the Council to grant to the Member States, on the recommendation of the Commission, tariff quotas at a reduced rate of duty or duty free;[5]

Article 115, which enables the Commission to authorise the Member States to take protective measures in derogation from the general principles of the commercial policy of the Community;[6]

---

21 Sohier, M, and Megret, C, 'Le rôle de l'exécutif national et du législateur national dans la mise en oeuvre du droit communautaire' *Semaine de Bruges* (1965), op cit, pp 108 et seq; Constantinidès-Mégret, op cit, pp 132 et seq.

22 Constantinidès-Mégret, op cit, p 133.

1 Law of No 5, 3 January 1960, Gaz Uff, No 27, 1960.

2 Law of 13 January 1965; reference to Regulations 15 and 38/64 on the free movement of workers, EEC, art 48.

3 Law of 8 August 1962, JORF, 10 August 1962.

4 Law of 11 September 1962; MB 26 October 1962, p 9491, and Law of 20 July 1962; MB 26 July 1962, p 6218.

5 Eg decisions of the Commission of 9 November 1964 (JO 1964, p 3259) and of 12 November 1964 (JO 1964, p 3549) quoted by Constantinidès-Mégret, op cit, p 134.

6 Eg decision of 21 September 1964 (JO 1964, p 2497, op cit, p 134).

Article 226, which enables the Commission to authorise the Member States to take protective measures during the transitional period in derogation from the rules of the Treaty.[7]

Thirdly, there are measures which the Member States have to take in order to discharge their obligations. In this respect they act merely as agents of the Community instrumental in the execution of the Community law. For example, to carry into effect the CAP Member States have to set up Agricultural Intervention Boards. These are national institutions founded upon Community law. They administer the Community system and collect, inter alia, charges levied by the authority of Community legislation. Should such charges be declared illegal because based upon an invalid regulation the repayment of these charges falls upon national law.[8]

(d) *Techniques of incorporation*

A study of the problem of state legislation turning the rules of Community law indirectly applicable into the municipal law of the Member States reveals not only a diversity of approach, but, above all, a slow progress. Parliaments are far from being eager to act and their procedures are lengthy and cumbersome. As guardians of national sovereignty they seem to resent the intrusion of extraneous law-making authority although they have accepted the Community Treaties. As legislators parliaments, no doubt, do not relish their subordinate position, or having their functions reduced to mere formality, in the matter of Community legislation. As parliament debates seem nugatory in view of clear Treaty obligations to execute Community law, the tendency is to leave the matter in the hands of the Executive.[9]

Should parliament turn perverse and pass a law inconsistent with the Treaty obligations, precious little can be done. Evidently the state concerned could be in breach of the Treaty which in turn would enable the Commission to act under article 169. Should the state be recalcitrant in not heeding the 'reasoned opinion' of the Commission, the matter could be brought before the Community

---

7 Eg decisions of 20 December 1963 (JO 1964, p 145) and of 16 April 1964 (JO 1964, p 1162).

8 Case 130/79: *Express Dairy Foods Ltd v Intervention Board for Agricultural Produce* [1980] ECR 1887, [1981] 1 CMLR 451; See also Case 68/79: *Hans Just I/S v Danish Ministry of Fiscal Affairs* [1980] ECR 501, [1981] 2 CMLR 714; Cases 66, 127 and 128/79: *Amministrazione delle Finanze v SrL Meridionale Industria Salumi* [1980] ECR 1237, [1981] 1 CMLR 1; Cases 205–215/82: *Deutsche Milchkontor GmbH v Germany* [1983] ECR 2633, [1984] 3 CMLR 586; Case 349/85: *Denmark v EC Commission (Re Export Refunds)* [1988] ECR 169.

9 Reports on Constitutional Laws in France (1964–65) by M de Grailly (The House of Deputies) and M Marcilhacy (Senate) quoted by Constantinidès-Mégret, op cit, p 145.

Court.[10] If the Community Court decides against the state, the state is bound to 'take the necessary measures to comply with the judgment' (article 171), which means the repeal of the offending legislation. However, in theory, the game could go on for ever if the government concerned were unable to influence its parliament. Although the Community would be in jeopardy, the Community Court could not strike down the municipal legislation it considers 'illegal' in the eyes of the Community law, simply because the Court has no direct authority in the territory of the Member State. Rather than putting the Community at risk the Member States have evolved a practical, though individualistic, approach to the implementation of Community law. Their solution of the problem depends on the Constitution.

The French Constitution of 1958 sharply distinguishes between legislation by statute (*loi*) and legislation by decree (*décret*). Whatever is not listed in article 34 as being subject to legislation by Parliament falls, by virtue of article 37, into the Government's lap and becomes subject to *pouvoir réglementaire*. In addition the Government may be authorised to make ordinances by statute which is usually of a limited duration but may be renewed. Consequently the French Government appears well equipped constitutionally to deal with Community legislation, assuming, of course, that politically this is acceptable to Parliament. However the government will, if necessary, refer to the *Conseil Constitutionnel* matters which may impinge upon the Constitution. Thus when certain budgetary provisions of the EEC Treaty were modified in 1970, the Government asked the Conseil Constitutionnel to consider whether the new Treaty included any provisions contrary to the Constitution or necessitating an amendment to the Constitution. The answer was in the negative.[11] More recently the Conseil was asked to rule whether the direct universal suffrage to the European Parliament[12] by the French electorate did affect the sovereignty of the French parliament. Here too the answer was in the negative. In *Re Isoglucose*[13] (No 1 and No 2) the Conseil confirmed that Community taxation was directly enforceable in France though when included in the national Budget it had to be distinguished from the national revenue.

On 10 July 1966 the law 'relative to the application of certain treaties' authorized the Government to issue ordinances to ensure the implementation of EEC directives. The government ordinances

10 Cf Case 45/64: *EEC Commission v Republic of Italy* [1965] ECR 857 at 864, 865, [1966] CMLR 97 at 107–108.
11 JCP 1970, II. 16510.
12 [1977] 1 CMLR 121.
13 [1978] 2 CMLR 361 and 364.

are made by the Council of Ministers after advice from the Conseil d'Etat. They come into force on publication but become void if the bill ratifying them is not submitted to Parliament before the date fixed by the enabling statute.[14] Parliament too makes statutes to harmonize French law with Community law.[15] In France the Code of Customs Law enables the Government to take certain measures which have to be approved by Parliament. This method was used in order to carry out the Community customs regulations.[16] The result[17] is a very complex and diverse system of implementation based, in principle, on parliamentary delegation authorized by article 38 of the Constitution and the Government's own power of legislation.

Countries in which the executive cannot rely on a direct constitutional authority in this respect, have evolved a system of delegation of powers. This implies parliamentary approval of the acts of the government which, in practice, is often granted retrospectively, so much so that parliament appears to exercise a merely formal control.

Examples of this practice can be taken from the Benelux countries, notably in the field of customs law and agriculture.[18]

In Belgium the Customs and Excise Law of 2 May 1958, having authorised the King to take measures by decree subject to parliamentary approval, has adopted basically the French solution. A similar law was passed in the Netherlands on 25 June 1960 but it does not require parliamentary sanction for measures taken under the authority of the said law.

The execution of the agricultural policy of the Community in the Benelux countries reveals a more complex picture. Without going into details it may suffice to note that in Belgium under the law of 1962, which replaced the law of 1931 on import, export and transit of agricultural produce, powers were delegated to the King to make decrees relevant to the Community agricultural policy. A similar law was passed in Luxembourg. In the Netherlands, where the agricultural system is quite unique, and complex because it is

---

14 Eg 24 July 1966 on commercial companies; 3 July 1970 on monopoly over all explosives; 22 May 1971 on forestry reproductive materials; 8 July 1971 on customs bonded warehouses.

15 Eg 15 April 1970 on the nationality of public service concessionaries; 11 February 1971 on transport; 22 February 1971 on investments in the Community.

16 Eg the decision of the EEC Council of 4 April 1962 was incorporated in art 19 of the French Customs Code by decree, JO 1962, p 999.

17 For a complete and up-to-date account, see Bailleux A, *Techniques d'application du Droit Communautaire dans l'ordre juridique français*, unpublished doctoral thesis, Nice, 1975.

18 Constantinidès-Mégret, op cit, pp 150–154.

based on a network of 'professional' organizations endowed with a great deal of autonomous power, authority, under the Agricultural Law, is delegated to the Queen to carry out the Community agricultural policy by decree. Summing up the position in the Benelux countries we can say that their governments put into effect Community law by virtue of a general delegation of power.

A system of general delegation can be said to exist also in Denmark by virtue of the Constitution[19] (article 20) and in Ireland and the United Kingdom by virtue of the European Communities Acts 1972, ss 2 and 2 (2) respectively. In Ireland, dissatisfaction with the operation of the 1972 Act led to the enactment of the European Communities (Amendment) Act 1973. Under this Act ministerial regulations have statutory effect but the control over the exercise of this power is in the hands of a watch-dog committee drawn from the Dáil and the Senate. Its function is to monitor all drafts prepared by the Commission and all acts of the Communities as well as all regulations issued by the Irish ministers as a result of the membership of the Communities. It can also make recommendations to Irish Parliament.

An authority for general delegation can be found in article 78 (5) of the Greek Constitution which provides for delegated legislation to carry out 'economic measures within the framework of international relations with economic organisations'. Community legislation prior to accession is to be implemented by presidential decrees on the proposal of competent ministers. Similar instruments are to be used to implement post-accession legislation under parliamentary supervision since, according to article 3 of the Act of Accession, the Government is obliged to submit annual reports on Community affairs. A parliamentary watchdog committee is likely to be established.[20]

A system of specific delegation of legislative power operates in Italy and the German Federal Republic.

Article 76 of the Italian Constitution provides that the exercise of the legislative power may be delegated to the Government for a specific purpose and only for a limited period. On this principle article 4 of the act of ratification of 14 October 1957 authorizes the Government to promulgate by decree having the force of ordinary law, in accordance with the 'general principles enshrined in the EEC Treaty', the necessary rules to:

(i) ensure the execution of the obligations arising from article 11;

---

19 Sørensen, M, 'Compétences supranationales et pouvoirs constitutionnels en droit danois', *Miscellanea W. J. Ganshof van der Meersch* (1972), Vol 2, pp 481 et seq.

20 Evrigenis, D, 'Legal and Constitutional Implications of Greek Accession to the European Communities' (1980) 17 CML Rev, p 157 at 168.

(ii) carry out measures provided in articles 37, 46, 70, 89, 91, 107, 108, 109, 115 and 226;

(iii) carry out dispositions and principles comprised in articles 95, 96, 97 and 98 of the EEC Treaty.

The original delegation expired in 1961 but has been extended quinquennially. By virtue of this delegation several decrees have been passed. However, before taking any measure the Government has to seek advice of a Parliamentary Commission consisting of 15 Members of the House of Deputies and 15 Members of the Senate.

A technique of reproducing Community regulations into national law has caused some confusion between domestic and Community law, the identity of the latter being lost and the law enforcement authorities disregarding the directly applicable force of Community measures. The practice was condemned by the Community Court[1] as well as the Italian Constitutional Court[2] with the result that the normative power of the Community institutions was recognized and Community law assumed its correct position in the Italian legal system.

Article 80 (1) of the Basic Law of the German Federal Republic of 1953 provides for the delegation of legislative power to the Executive by statute which has to determine the context, purpose and extent of the delegation. The law of ratification granted to the Federal Government the power to carry into effect articles 14, 16, 17 (1), and 23 (2) of the EEC Treaty (Customs Provisions) as well as certain provisions of the protocols on mineral oils and bananas. Such decrees could be made without approval of the Federal Parliament (Bundestag) unless the Parliament objected within three weeks from the date when draft decrees were laid before it. No approval of the decrees by the Federal Council (Bundesrat) was required though the Council had fourteen days to make comments on the draft decrees.

The Customs Law of 1957[3] made under the above rules was amended by the Law of 1961[4] which enlarged the powers of the Federal Government. Article 77 of the Law of 1961 is particularly relevant to the implementation of Community law. It concerns measures under EEC article 103 (short-term economic policy) and, more generally, Community legislation. The former will be studied

---

1 See Case 39/72: *EC Commission v Italy* [1973] ECR 101, [1973] CMLR 439 and Case 34/73: *Variola SpA v Ammimstrazione Italiana delle Finanze* [1973] ECR 981.

2 Judgment No 183 of 27 December 1973 in *Re Frontini*, Foro Italiano, 1974, I/314; Judgment No 232 of 30 October 1975 in *Re Industrie Chimiche della Italia (ICIC)*, Foro Italiano, 1975, 2667-2668.

3 Law of 27 July 1957, BGBI II (1957), p 753.

4 Law of 14 June 1961, BGBI I (1961), p 758.

by the relevant parliamentary committee and submitted to the Bundestag which will accept or reject the decrees. The Bundestag cannot approve these by silence. They will also be submitted to the Bundesrat but merely for opinion. Drafts of decrees for the implementation of the Community legislation are laid before the Bundestag and the Bundesrat and the Bundestag is presumed to have approved the decrees if within three months from this submission they have not been formally abrogated by Parliament. The function of the Bundesrat is purely advisory. Customs laws have been modified on several occasions by this process. In the field of agriculture several laws have been passed. Of these the Law of 1964[5] conferred upon the Federal Government the power of legislating by decree in order to put into effect the regulations, decisions and directives of the Council and the Commission of the EEC governing the marketing of cereals, milk products and rice.

It is clear from this brief survey of the methods of implementing Community law that the Member States have retained a measure of parliamentary control in this matter. The problem is by no means simple and in the interests of the smooth running of the Community as well as the efficacy of the Community law in the territory of the Member States, it ought to be studied in depth with a view to formulating a common approach and a uniform procedure.

IV INCORPORATION THROUGH THE COMMUNITY COURT

(a) *The rôle of the ECJ*

We have already considered the meaning and effect of Community legislation as a source of Community law; we should emphasize now the rôle of the Community Court in the process of the incorporation of Community legislation into the municipal laws. The Court has an indirect influence under EEC articles 173 and 177. Under article 173 the Court has the power of annulment and indeed, should the action for annulment be well founded, the Court will strike down the offending piece of Community legislation (article 174). On the other hand whatever is uncontested or declared valid by the Court has the force of law in the territory of the Member States. It is important to note that the decisions of the Court in respect of the validity of the Community legislation have a universal application; they are enforceable *erga omnes* (article 174 (1)).

However, perhaps more significant, from a practical point of view, is the Court's impact through its interpretation of Com-

5 Law of 13 August 1964.

munity law. Where the national court requests interpretation the impact is direct and instructive. It is equally instructive in other cases, though the impact has to be measured through the doctrine of judicial precedent. Here the British and Irish judges are out of step with their continental brethren as they lavishly cite the decisions of the Community Court as well as the judgments of national courts.[6] However a rigid application of the doctrine of *stare decisis* must be discounted simply because the Community Court is not bound by its own decisions and a slavish adherence to a precedent unrecognized on the Continent would lead to serious anomalies and distortions of Community law by British or Irish judges.

In spite of the merely persuasive authority of precedents in continental jurisprudence the decisions of the Community Court are gaining prestige in national jurisdiction. They are being cited[7] and some courts occasionally cite decisions of national courts.[8] They do so not in principle or out of habit but because they appreciate the authoritative exposition of Community law by the Community Court and of the relevant national law by national courts. As for the authority of the Community precedents there is as yet no uniform approach to this matter. Reports indicate that the French Cour de Cassation[9] considered that French courts are generally bound by the rulings of the Community Court and so did the Belgian[10] Cour de Cassation; the German Federal Supreme Court[11] felt that the decisions of the Community Court are binding 'beyond the instant case', whilst the Milan Court of Appeal applied[12] the Community Court's ruling in one case and considered

---

6 See eg *Bulmer v Bollinger* supra.
7 *Fiorini v Société Nationale des Chemin de Fer Français* [1975] 1 CMLR 459; *Re Dry Shavers* [1975] CMLR 550; *Administration des Douanes v Société Cafés Jacques Vabres* [1975] 2 CMLR 336, Paris Court of Appeal.
8 *Francesco Cinzano & Cie GmbH v Java Kaffeegeschäfte GmbH;* [1974] 2 CMLR 21. Bundesgerichtshof.
9 *Garoche v Striker Boats (Nederland), Cour de Cassation* [1974] 1 CMLR 469; *Glinel Case* [1984] 2 CMLR 137 at 151; *Ministère Public v Cambournac* [1984] 2 CMLR 556 at 558 but not so the Conseil d'Etat, see *Cohn-Bendit*, supra.
10 *Procureur du Roi v Debauve* [1984] 2 CMLR 204 at 208; see also Tribunal de Commerce, Liège which emphasized that the rule of precedent is inspired by the Common Law systems (*stare decisis et non quieta movere*) rather than the Civil Law principle of *res judicata*: *AGROTAB v Distrimis SA* [1985] 3 CMLR 294 at 301–302.
11 Case KZR 7/69: *Re Brewery Solus Agreement* [1975] 1 CMLR 611. Same the *Bundesverwaltungsgericht: Rewe-Zentralfinanz GmbH v Landwirtschaftskammer für das Saarland* [1978] 2 CMLR 594 and the *Bundesverfassungsgericht:* Case IZR 114/73: *Terrapin (Overseas) Ltd v Terranova Industrie* [1978] 3 CMLR 102; *Hoffmann-La Roche v Centrafarm* [1984] 2 CMLR 561.
12 *Sirena SRL v EDA SRL* [1975] 1 CMLR 409.

it binding only inter partes, in another.[13] No doubt a trend towards recognition of Community precedents is gaining momentum.

Article 177[14] gives the Community Court the power of interpretation of the Treaty, of the acts of the Community organs and of the statutes of bodies[15] established by the Council in the form of a preliminary ruling. This means that non-Community Treaties of the Member States even though noted in EEC regulations are not included in the interpretative competence of the Court.[16] The Treaty is silent as to the scope of this ruling: is it valid *erga omnes* or only *quoad casum*? Some writers[17] doubt the *erga omnes* effect, others[18] argue that it has this effect. Whether one can go that far, bearing in mind that a national court may repeatedly request a preliminary ruling in similar circumstances and the Community Court, not being bound by its previous decisions, may change its mind, is debatable. However, whatever the effect of the judgment, it is an instrument of integration of Community law with municipal law and of uniformity throughout the Community. Therefore preliminary rulings should have a universally binding effect despite the warning against the spectre of the 'government by judges'.[19] This effect can be inferred not only from the function of the Court but also from the procedure on reference which provides for the intervention of the Member States and the Commission as well as the recent amendment of the rules which allows issues on which there is an established body of law to be decided by a chamber of three judges instead of the whole Court.[20]

If the Court affirmed[1] its adherence to its precedents many a reference for a preliminary ruling would be unnecessary. In this

---

13 *SAFA v Amministrazione delle Finanze* [1973] CMLR 152.
14 ECSC, art 41; EAEC, art 150.
15 See Case 110/75: *Mills v European Investment Bank* [1976] ECR 955 (on admissibility), [1976] ECR 1613 (on merits) and Case 44/84: *Hurd v Jones* (Re tax of English headmaster of a European School in England) [1986] 2 CMLR 1.
16 Case 28/68: *Caisse Regionale de Sécurite Sociale du Nord v Torrekens* [1969] CMLR 377.
17 Eg Catalano, N, *Manuel de droit des Communautés Européennes* (1965) (French Translation), p 88.
18 Eg Zuccala, 'Di una forma d'intepretazione guirisprudenziale autentica delle leggi', Guirisprudenzia Italiana (1959), IV, Coll. 139–144; quoted by Constantinidès-Mégret, op cit, pp 39–40. Trabucchi, 'L'éffet "erga omnes" des décisions préjudicielles rendues par la Cour de Justice des Communautés Européennes' (1974) RTDE 56 quot. with approval by A-G Warner in Case 112/76: *Manzoni v Fonds National de Retraite des Ouvriers Mineurs* [1977] ECR 1647 at 1661–1663, [1978] 2 CMLR 416 at 429–430.
19 Lecourt, R, *Le juge devant le Marché Commun*, (1970), p 57.
20 Rules of Procedure, arts 95, 103 and 104; cf. Case 120/75: *Riemer v Hauptzollamt Lübeck-West* [1976] ECR 1003.
1 In Case 283/81: *CILFIT v Minister of Health* [1982] ECR 3415 at para 13,

context the reply to the question[2] whether, following its judgment[3] in the interpretation of article 2 (1) of the Sixth Council Directive on the harmonization of the turnover taxes, no such tax should be levied on the supply of narcotic drugs within the territory of a Member State, is quite instructive. However the Court may avoid the question related to its previous ruling and simply answer the point as if interpreted anew regarding the reference to precedent inadmissible as it did on a previous occasion.[4]

Article 177 should be read together with article 20 of the Protocol on the Statute of the Community Court which provides for the procedure to be applied when a preliminary ruling is sought. Accordingly when any Court or tribunal of a Member State decides that it cannot proceed to judgment without the elucidation of a point of Community law relevant to the case the proceedings are suspended and the Court or tribunal refers the matter to the Community Court. The decision to seek a ruling is notified by the Registrar of the Community Court to the parties, the Member States and to the Commission, and also to the Council if the act, the validity or interpretation of which is in dispute, originates from the Council. Within two months of this notification, the parties, the Member States, the Commission and, where appropriate, the Council, are entitled to make their submissions or observations to the Court. In this way the matter ceases to be of sole concern to the parties and the adjudicating court; it becomes of common concern to the whole Community. By giving the national judge access to the Community Court, whilst enabling all the Member States and the Community organs to make representations, the Treaty sets the stage for an understanding between the municipal courts and the Community Court and for a development towards a common law of the Community. At the same time the Treaty asserts the superiority or exclusive competence of the Community Court.

(b) *The reference*[5]

Many cases have been submitted for a preliminary ruling and the Court has developed a certain practice in this field and recently

---

[1983] 1 CMLR 472, the ECJ hinted that previous case law may obviate reference.

2 Case 289/86: *Vereniging Happy Family Rustenburgerstraat v Inspecteur der Omzetbelastingen* [1989] 3 CMLR 743; and Case 269/86: *Mol v Inspecteur der Invoerrechten en Accijnzen* [1989] 3 CMLR 729.

3 Case 294/82: *Einberger v HZA Freiburg* (No 2) [1985] 1 CMLR 765.

4 Case 24/66 bis: *Getreidehandel v EC Commission* [1973] ECR 1599 at 1606.

5 Slynn, Sir Gordon, Lasok, K. P. E., Millett, T. P., *Law of the European Communities*, Halsbury's Laws of England (4th edn) Vol 51, pp 278 et seq.

issued certain guidelines[6] to the national courts of final jurisdiction. In the first case[7] under article 177 the Court advised that the referring court is free to adopt a direct and simple form of reference which will enable the Community Court to rule strictly within the limits of its jurisdiction. Thus formalism was dispensed with but at the same time the Court implied that it would not be politic to decide the issue otherwise than in the terms of interpretation of Community law. Furthermore the Court stressed that whilst two different legal orders are involved (national and Community) the national court is about to administer Community law albeit under the guidance of the Community Court.

In the *Van Gend* case[8] the Court observed that the considerations which may guide the national court in the choice of its questions and their pertinence to the issue to be decided are outside the jurisdiction of the Community Court. In this case a Dutch Administrative Tribunal enquired whether article 12 of the EEC Treaty 'entailed internal legal effects, that is whether or not an individual may directly derive rights which have to be protected by his national courts'. Article 12 provides that Member States shall refrain from introducing between themselves any new customs duties on imports or exports, or any charges having equivalent effect, and from increasing those which they already apply in their trade with each other. The question raised a constitutional issue, that is whether the Community Court was really interpreting Community law or whether it usurped the power to interpret the Dutch Constitution (ie the power to levy taxes). The Dutch Government was of the opinion that the Community Court had no jurisdiction in matters involving Dutch customs duties. However the Community Court firmly asserted its jurisdiction and the power to rule in the matter, as it pointed out that article 12 came for *interpretation* not for *application* according to Dutch law. In this delicate situation the Court refrained from ruling upon the conflict between Dutch and Community law but firmly declared that article 12 had a direct effect though the mode of application was left to the internal process of the Netherlands.

Indeed, there must be a question[9] on a point of Community law the answer to which will determine the outcome of the case. In other words there must be a dispute involving aspects of Community law

6 Case 283/81, supra, and infra at paras 17–20.
7 Case 13/61 *Kledingverkoopbedrijf de Geus en Uitdenbogerd v Boschen Van Rijn* [1962] ECR 45, [1962] CMLR 1.
8 Case 26/62: supra; see also Case 56/65: *Société Technique Minière v Machinenbau Ulm GmbH* [1966] ECR 235, [1966] CMLR 357.
9 Advocate-General Lagrange in Case 28–30/62: *Da Costa en Shaake v Nederlandse Belastingadministratie* [1963] ECR 31, [1963] CMLR 224.

and the reference must be necessary to settle the issue. Thus, eg a national ruling that only first-class passengers[10] may use express trains reveals no connection with Community law and, therefore, questions of discrimination and free movement will be inadmissible in the context of the dispute. As in that case, no Community law was involved in the case concerned with the FEOGA accounts[11] and, therefore, the case was not referable. Similarly there was no cause for reference in the matter of agreement between national bureaux of motor insurers.[12] Although the agreement was vital for the implementation and operation of Directive 72/166 on compulsory motor insurance the agreement was not a 'Community Act' within the terms of the first paragraph of article 177, and therefore its interpretation was outside the scope of the ECJ's jurisdiction. Where there is a real dispute involving Community law reference will not be ousted simply because the Commission may embark upon an enforcement action[13] nor will a reference act as estoppel to an enforcement action under article 169 of the Treaty even if the interpretation of Community law in the preliminary ruling has rendered such action unnecessary.[14]

However the relevance of the request is not for the ECJ to determine but for the referring court.[15]

In *Costa v ENEL* the Court held that it had power to select what was relevant from the list of questions imperfectly formulated by the referring court and in this way refused to be drawn into an internal conflict. 'Consequently,' held the Court, 'the decision should be given not upon the validity of an Italian law in relating to the Treaty but upon the interpretation of the above-mentioned articles in the context of the points of law stated by the *Guidice Conciliatore*.'[16]

In *Schwarze v Einfuhr-und Vorratstelle für Getreide und Fut-*

---

10 Case 298/84: *Iorio v Azienda Autonoma delle Ferrovie dello Stato* [1986] 2 CMLR 665.
11 Case 133/84: *United Kingdom v EC Commission* [1987] 1 CMLR 294.
12 Case 152/83: *Demouche v Fonds de Garantie Automobile* [1987] ECR 3833, [1989] 1 CMLR 544.
13 Case 172/82: *Syndicat National des Fabricants Raffineurs d'Huile v Inter-Huiles* [1983] 3 CMLR 485.
14 Case 231/78: *EC Commission v United Kingdom* [1979] ECR 1447, [1979] 2 CMLR 427 following the reference in Case 118/78: *Meijer v Department of Trade* [1979] ECR 1387, [1979] 2 CMLR 398; Case 124/81: *EC Commission v United Kingdom* [1983] ECR 203 [1983] 2 CMLR 1, following the reference in Case 244/78: *Union Laitière v French Dairy Farmers* [1979] ECR 2663, [1980] 1 CMLR 314.
15 Case 232/82: *Baccini v Office National de l'Emploi* [1983] ECR 583, [1983] 3 CMLR 572.
16 [1964] CMLR 425 at 455.

termittel[17] the Court had to decide whether a badly drafted reference should be sent back whence it came as suggested by the French Government. The ECJ refused to do this and held that 'when it appears that questions asked by a municipal court for the purpose of interpretation in reality concern the validity of a Community act, it is for the Court of Justice to enlighten the national court immediately without insisting upon a formalism which would be purely dilatory and which would be incompatible with the true nature of the machinery established by article 177.' Thus the ECJ will, in a helpful manner, assist the referring court in focusing its attention upon the relevant aspects of Community law and will, if necessary, reformulate the reference[18] provided, of course, it is reasonably possible to reformulate the questions.[19] This does not mean that the ECJ will decide[20] the issue for the referring court or become involved in a national controversy.[21]

However, no matter how helpful the Community Court is in the process of the elucidation of the points before it, there is a limit to its competence for the object of the reference is limited to answering questions on issues raised by the referring court.[22] Therefore it cannot be used to apply the Treaty to a particular situation or determine the validity of a national measure,[23] and thus do the work of the referring court.

Nevertheless the ECJ may be able to extract points of Community law from the reference and deal with these as if properly presented.[24] The ECJ sees itself as having a duty to accept the reference without questioning the reasons for it or criticising the referring court.[1] However it is incumbent upon the referring court to determine the facts of the case[2] and therefore reference will be

17 Case 16/65: [1965] ECR 877 at 886, 887, [1966] CMLR 172 at 186–187. See also Case 83/78: *Pigs Marketing Board (Northern Ireland) v Redmond* [1978] ECR 2347, [1979] 1 CMLR 177.
18 Eg Case 78/70: *Deutsche Grammophon GmbH v Metro-SB Grössmärkte GmbH* [1971] ECR 487, [1971] CMLR 631.
19 See Case 14/86: *Pretore di Salo v X* [1987] ECR 2545, [1989] 1 CMLR 71.
20 *Van Gend*, supra.
21 *Costa v ENEL*, supra.
22 Case 51/72: *Fratelli Grassi v Amministrazione delle Finanze* [1973] CMLR 332.
23 Case 20/64: *SARL Albatros v SOPECO (Société de Pétroles et des Combustibles liquides)* [1965] ECR 29, [1965] CMLR 159; Case 100/63: *Kalsbeek v Sociale Verzekeringsbank* [1964] ECR 565 at 572.
24 Case 82/71: *Pubblico Ministero della Repubblica Italiana v SPA Società Agricola Industria Latte* [1972] ECR 119, [1972] CMLR 723.
1 Case 10/69: *Portelange SA v SA Smith Corona Marchant International* [1969] ECR 309, [1974] 1 CMLR 397; Case 155/73: *Italian State v Sacchi* [1974] ECR 409, [1974] 2 CMLR 177; Case 126/80: *Salonia v Poidomani and Baglieri* [1982] 1 CMLR 64.
2 Case 222/78: *ICAP Distribution Srl v Beneventi* [1979] ECR 1163, [1979] 3

rejected if the issue is merely 'academic' in the sense that it does not reveal any real dispute between the parties.[3] Presumably the national court of its own motion will refuse to refer if facts have not been ascertained to its satisfaction[4] or if, despite the arguments to the contrary, it is clear that no point of Community law is involved.[5]

While reference techniques have developed within the national practice the ECJ issued certain guidelines in this respect reiterating the principles involved.[6] Having to decide a dispute over the payment of a fixed health inspection levy on wool from outside the Community the Italian Supreme Court asked the ECJ whether, in the sense of the third paragraph of article 177, the obligation to refer was subject to any conditions. The ECJ replied that the obligation to refer was based on co-operation between national courts and the Community Court. More particularly the third paragraph sought to prevent the occurrence within the Community of divergencies in judicial decisions on questions of Community law. However, article 177 does not constitute a means of redress available to the parties. Therefore the court or tribunal concerned cannot be compelled to refer but may of its own motion do so. Furthermore courts or tribunals envisaged in the second and third paragraph of article 177 'have the same discretion' to ascertain whether a decision on a question of Community law is necessary to enable them to give judgment. 'Accordingly, they are not obliged to refer a question concerning the interpretation of Community law raised before them if that question is not relevant, that is to say, if the answer . . . can in no way affect the outcome of the case.'

Turning to the specific point raised by the Supreme Court the ECJ cited its early ruling[7] to the effect that although the third paragraph of article 177 unreservedly requires court or tribunals mentioned therein to refer questions raised before them,

---

CMLR 475; cf. *Lord Bethell v SABENA* (English Commercial Court) [1983] 3 CMLR 1.

3 Case 104/79: *Foglia v Novello* [1980] ECR 745, [1981] 1 CMLR 45. Case 244/80 *Foglia v Novello* [1982] 1 CMLR 585.

4 *Church of Scientology of California v Customs and Excise Comrs* [1980] CMLR 114; on appeal [1981] 1 CMLR 48, CA.

5 *British Leyland Motor Corpn Ltd v TI Silencers Ltd* [1980] 1 CMLR 598; *Re Virdee* [1980] 1 CMLR 709, English High Court; *Re Budlong and Kember* [1980] 2 CMLR 125; *Surjit Kaur v Lord Advocate* [1980] 3 CMLR 79, Ct of Sess; but see Case 175/78: *R v Saunders* [1979] ECR 1129, [1979] 2 CMLR 216 (which should not have been referred).

6 Case 283/81, supra, paras 17–20.

7 Joined Cases 28–30/62: *Da Costa v Netherlandse Belastingadministratie* [1963] ECR 31, [1963] CMLR 224.

'... the authority of an interpretation under Article 177 already given by the Court may deprive the obligation of its purpose ... Such is the case especially when the question raised has already been the subject of a preliminary ruling in a similar cause.'

However, stressed the Court in the present ruling,

'... in such circumstances national courts and tribunals ... remain entirely at liberty to bring a matter before the Court of Justice if they consider it appropriate to do so.'

'Finally,' ... observed the ECJ,

'... the correct application of Community law may be so obvious as to leave no scope for any reasonable doubt as to the manner in which the question raised is to be resolved. Before it comes to the conclusion that such is the case, the national court or tribunal must be convinced that the matter is equally obvious to the courts of the other Member States and to the Court of Justice. Only if those conditions are satisfied may the national court or tribunal refrain from submitting the question to the Court of Justice and take upon itself the responsibility for resolving it ...'

The guidelines comprise three reasons why the court of the last instance need not refer, ie the question raised is irrelevant, there has already been a ruling of the ECJ on the subject and the position is so obvious as to leave no scope for any reasonable doubt.

(c) *The timing*
The question arises as to when the reference should be made.[8] It goes without saying that a question of Community law must be raised before the national court and that the answer to it must be relevant to the issue, that is, necessary to enable the court to adjudicate. Community law does not determine either the timing or the degree of necessity. All this is left to national procedures. As far as references from the English High Court are concerned it is expressly provided[9] that such an order may be made at any stage of the proceedings. This is correct because the court controls the proceedings from the beginning to the end and the court alone is in the position of judging the timing and the necessity.

A subsidiary question regarding interlocutory proceedings has been raised and answered in the affirmative.[10] The position is covered by article 177 (2) because a problem of Community law may occur at the initial or interlocutory stage of the proceedings

8 See Jacobs F., 'When to refer to the European Court' (1974) 90 LQR 486.
9 RSC Ord 114, r 2 (1).
10 Case 107/76: *Hoffman-La Roche v Centrafarm Vertriebsgesellschaft Pharmazeutischer Erzeugnisse mbH* [1977] ECR 957, [1977] 2 CMLR 334; see Jacobs, F [1977] 2 ELRev 354.

and has to be settled by the court before proceeding further. The court may have to make a ruling which will determine the subsequent course of the action or even dismiss it.

(d) *Multiple and repeated references*
These are admissible[11] and even desirable to save time and expense. In the cited case such a multiple reference gave the ECJ an opportunity of ruling on turnover equalization tax in relation to various groups of products. Perhaps a more interesting variant of multiple reference was the *EMI v CBS*[12] case which was concerned with a trademark dispute between an English and an American company, the matter being litigated simultaneously in England, Denmark and Germany. Since the questions raised in all three countries were basically the same, it was possible to bring these within one reference and dispose of accordingly.

If dissatisfied with the response the referring court is free to try again since repeated references are not prohibited.[13]

(e) *Questions of criminal law*
The enforcement of Community law is in the hands of national authorities. They dispose of coercive rules and of the machinery to apply these. Even in the limited area of direct Community coercion the fines and periodic penalties imposed by the Commission to enforce the rules of competition are, under EEC article 192, executed by the competent national authorities in accordance with national law and procedures.

Where a Community rule has to be supported by a criminal sanction the relevant legislative Community act can merely provide that such sanction will be enacted by the Member States. Failure to enact the sanction would not give rise to a reference to the Community Court so that it could be read into the national legislation in question but rather to an enforcement action as, eg, in the *Tachograph* case.[14] Therefore references involving questions of criminal law are likely to occur in cases where the defendant seeks protection of Community law from the existence or severity of a national criminal sanction. Indeed such references are admissible.[15] In theory where the national law is manifestly incompatible with Community law the doctrine of supremacy should enable the court

---

11 Case 29/68: *Milch-Fett-und Eierkontor GmbH v Hauptzollamt Saarbrücken* [1969] ECR 165, [1969] CMLR 390.
12 Case 51/75: *EMI Records Ltd v CBS (United Kingdom) Ltd* [1976] ECR 811, [1976] 2 CMLR 235.
13 See eg Case 244/80: *Foglia v Novello (No 2)* supra; Case 14/86 supra.
14 See p 132, supra.
15 Case 82/71: *Pubblico Ministero v SPA Societa Agricola Industria Latte* [1972] CMLR 723.

to disregard the offending national law but, in practice, it is more likely that a reference will be made. Indeed the position is not always clear. A few random samples illustrate the point:

A Dutch licensed victualler, prosecuted for selling liquor at prices below the minimum fixed by the national law, successfully pleaded article 30 of the EEC Treaty (movement of goods) in his defence.[16] Similarly, in the *Northern Irish Pigs* case[17] a conviction under the Movement of Pigs Regulations (Northern Ireland) 1972 and forfeiture of the pigs in question were held contrary to Regulation 2759/75 governing the market in pig meat.

However a German baker[18] was unable to persuade the Court that the German bakery law which prohibits baking and deliveries of the product during certain hours at night was contrary to the provisions of articles 7 and 30–34 of the EEC Treaty.

A migrant worker[19] was able to resist an expulsion order served by an administrative authority as an object lesson to other foreigners but not so a rapist.[20] Expulsion was held to be too severe a sanction for a breach of a minor offence against immigration rules.[21] Requirements for a driving licence irrelevant to road safety could not be enforced by criminal sanctions.[22]

Importers of pornographic materials contrary to a national law had their convictions confirmed as falling within the derogation of public policy or public morality notwithstanding the fact that such materials were a merchandise in free circulation in another Member State.[23] Pleas based on the Community principle of the freedom of movement of capital and goods were of no avail to persons convicted according to national rules for the illegal importation of Krugerrands and attempted exportation of silver alloy coins no longer in circulation.[1] Forfeiture of both gold and silver coins followed.[2]

16 Case 82/77: *Openbaar Ministerie of the Netherlands v van Tiggele* [1978] ECR 257, [1978] 2 CMLR 528.
17 Case 83/78: *Pigs Marketing Board (Northern Ireland) v Redmond* [1978] ECR 2347, [1979] 1 CMLR 177.
18 Case 155/80: *Re Sergius Ocebel*, [1981] ECR 1993.
19 Case 67/74: *Bonsignore v Oberstadtsdirektor der Stadt Köln* [1975] ECR 297, [1975] 1 CMLR 472.
20 Case 131/79: *R v Secretary of State for Home Affairs, ex p Santillo* [1980] ECR 1585, [1980] 2 CMLR 308, ECJ; on appeal [1980] 3 CMLR 212; affd [1981] 1 CMLR 569, [1981] 2 All ER 897, CA.
21 Case 157/79: *R v Stanislaus Pieck* [1980] ECR 2171, [1980] 3 CMLR 220.
22 Case 16/78: *Public Prosecutor v Michael Choquet* [1978] ECR 2293, [1979] 1 CMLR 535.
23 Case 34/79: *R v Henn and Darby* [1979] ECR 3795, [1980] 1 CMLR 246 but see Case 121/85: *Conegate v HM Customs and Excise* [1986] 1 CMLR 739.
1 Case 7/78: *R v Thompson* [1978] ECR 2247, [1979] 1 CMLR 47.
2 *Allgemeine Gold und Silberscheideanstalt v Customs and Excise Comrs* [1980] QB 390, [1980] 1 CMLR 488, CA.

Prosecutions arising from breaches of national sea fishery laws have led to references to the ECJ[3] and indeed to a head-on collision between two Member States, one of which suing the other on behalf of one of its citizens convicted of offences against the fishery law of the latter.[4] Whilst holding the defendant state guilty of a breach of the Community law the ECJ lost no time in stressing that: ... 'Where criminal proceedings are brought by virtue of a national measure which is contrary to Community law a conviction in those proceedings is also incompatible with that law'.[5]

These samples confirm that points of criminal law are referable to the Community Court for a preliminary ruling and illustrate the potential of further developments in this field.

The field has recently been widely opened through the prosecution of traders in England and Wales for breaches of the Shops Act 1950. The temptation to trade on Sunday has been sustained by the incongruities of the Act (which does not apply in Scotland), the rise of large diversified trading emporia which combine business with recreational facilities and the lacklustre enforcement of the law. Fines have proved too low to deter the breaches of the Act while the unwillingness to guarantee costs in applications for injunctions have encouraged both trading and defence against prosecutions. Moreover a defence on the ground of the freedom of movement of goods has brought the controversy within the scope of Community law.[6]

(f) *The ruling*
In a sense the rulings of the ECJ under article 177 may be regarded as abstract points of law because the Community Court, content with the definition of the law, leaves its application to the referring national court. This indeed is the message of the *Van Gend* case reflecting a division of functions between the Community and the national jurisdictions. It is, therefore, necessary to distinguish between 'interpretation' and 'application', the former being the

---

3 Eg Cases 3, 4, 6/76: *Officier van Justitie v Kramer* [1976] ECR 1279, [1976] 2 CMLR 440; 812/79: *A-G v Burgoa* [1980] ECR 2787, [1981] 2 CMLR 193; Case 269/80: *R v Tymen* [1981] 2 CMLR 544, CA; [1981] ECR 3079; refd [1982] 2 CMLR 111.
4 Case 141/78: *France v United Kingdom, Re Fishing Net Mesh Sizes* [1979] ECR 2923, [1980] 1 CMLR 6. See also Case 63/83: *R v Kirk* [1984] ECR 2689, [1984 3 CMLR 522.
5 Ibid.
6 See the ambiguous ruling of the ECR in Case 145/88: *Torfaen Borough Council v B & Q plc* [1990] 2 QB 19, [1990] 1 CMLR 337 and the purported interpretation of the ruling in *Council of the City of Stoke-on-Trent and Norwich City Council v B & Q plc* [1990] 2 CMLR 377.

task of the ECJ, the latter of the national court involved.[7] Indeed when concluding, for example, that the national measure which is the subject matter of the reference is contrary to Community law, the ECJ contents itself with saying that it is 'incompatible' with the relevant provision of the Treaty. The obvious inference that it ought not to be applied because it is 'invalid' is left to the referring court. The same, when the prosecution and conviction founded upon national law is declared to be 'incompatible' the inference is that the conviction ought to be quashed by the national court. Sometimes, having stated the principle to be applied, the ECJ refers matters of fact back to the referring court. Eg the question whether a national trade agreement[8] which restricts the supply of national but not of foreign newspapers to retailers does have an effect on inter-state trade was referred back with the reminder that it is for the referring court to decide, as a matter of fact, whether or not it does so.

It is instructive to follow cases through to see how the preliminary ruling was applied but few records are available in this respect. In the British references there has been no reluctance in applying the rulings.[9]

However in the *Santillo* case the Queen's Bench Divisional Court[10] appears to have misinterpreted the ruling but the apparent error was corrected by the Court of Appeal.[11] No difficulty arose in a social insurance case[12] where the National Insurance Commissioner, applying a ruling of the ECJ which he had requested, held that an Irishman claiming British benefits was not disqualified for the period of his imprisonment in Ireland although an Englishman imprisoned in the United Kingdom would be so disqualified.

(g) *Courts and tribunals*
Article 177 is addressed to both the courts and tribunals 'against

7 Case 183/73: *Osram GmbH v Oberfinanzdirektion Frankfurt* [1974] ECR 477 at 485, [1974] 2 CMLR 360 at 366; Case 228/87: *Pretura Unificata di Torino v Persons Unknown (Re Water Pollution)* [1990] 1 CMLR 716.
8 Case 126/80: *Salonia v Poidomani and Baglieri* [1982] 1 CMLR 64.
9 See Case 129/79: *Macarthys Ltd v Smith* [1980] ECR 1275, [1980] 2 CMLR 205; apld [1981] QB 180, [1980] 2 CMLR 217, CA. *R v Thompson*, supra; *R v Henn and Darby* [1979] 2 CMLR 495, HL; *R v Henn and Darby* [1980] AC 850, [1980] 2 CMLR 229, HL, *Pigs Marketing Board v Redmond* [1979] 3 CMLR 118, but see the problem of interpretation raised by the Sunday Trading cases, supra.
10 *R v Secretary of State for Home Affairs, ex p Santillo* [1980] 3 CMLR 212.
11 Ibid [1981] QB 778, [1981] 1 CMLR 569.
12 *Kenny v Insurance Officer* [1978] 1 CMLR 181; Case 1/78: *Kenny v National Insurance Comr* [1978] ECR 1489, [1978] 3 CMLR 651; *Kenny v Insurance Officer* [1979] 1 CMLR 433.

whose decision there is no judicial remedy under national law'[13] and 'any court or tribunal'.[14] The former include, prima facie, the Supreme Courts and the highest specialist courts of the Member States, ie the *Cour de Cassation* and the *Conseil d'Etat* in Belgium and France; the *Corte di Cassazione*, the *Consiglio di Stato* and *Corte Costituzionale* in Italy; the *Bundesgerichtshof*, the *Bundessozialgericht*, the *Bundesverwaltungsgericht*, the *Bundesdisziplinarhof* and the *Bundesfinanzhof* in Germany; the *Hoge Raad*, the *Tariefcommissie* and the *College van Beroep* in the Netherlands; the Supreme Court in Ireland; the *Højesteret* in Denmark; the House of Lords and in some cases the English Court of Appeal, the Scottish Court of Session and the Northern Irish Supreme Court in the United Kingdom. However, in *Costa v ENEL*[15] the Community Court accepted a reference from a *Guidice Conciliatore* of Milan on the ground that because of the small claim involved, the magistrate in question was a court of the first and last instance. The Court's *dictum* that reference can be made from any court whose decisions are final (*sans recours*) has broadened the basis of article 177 (3). The reference to 'any court or tribunal' (article 177 (2)) includes, presumably, apart from the inferior courts of law, any adjudicating body or institution which in the domestic jurisdiction exercise judicial functions,[16] including, of course, the English magistrates' courts but not a professional[17] body like the Paris Bar, private arbitrators[18] or a consultative body.[19]

The position of the National Insurance Commissioner in the British system has posed some questions[20] since his decisions are not subject to appeal though they may be quashed for error of law by the High Court. It seems that he has no obligation to refer[21]

---

13 Dont les décisions ne sont pas susceptibles d'un recours juridictionnel de droit interne; dessen Entscheidungen selbst nicht mehr mit Rechtsmitteln des innerstaatlichen Rechs angefochten werden können; avverso le cui decisioni non possa proporsi un ricorso giurisdizionale di diritto interno.
14 Une juridiction, ein Gericht, una giurisdizione.
15 Case 6/64 [1964] ECR 585, [1964] CMLR 425.
16 See Case 61/65: *Vaassen-Göbbels v Beambtenfonds voor het Mijnbedrijf* [1966] ECR 261, [1966] CMLR 508 and Case 246/80: *Broekmeulen v Committee for Registration of Medical Practitioners* [1982] 1 CMLR 91.
17 Case 138/80: *Re Jules Borker* [1980] ECR 1975, [1980] 3 CMLR 638.
18 Case 102/81: *Nordsee Deutsche Hochseefischerei GmbH v Reederei Mond an Reederei Friedrich*, [1982] ECR 1095.
19 Case 318/85: *Proceedings against Regina Greis Unterweger*, reference by Commissione Consultiva per le Infrazioni Volutarie, JO 1986, C121/3.
20 Jacobs, F, 'Which Courts and Tribunals are bound to refer to the European Court?' (1977) 2 ELRev 119.
21 See Case 4/74: *Re Holiday in Italy* [1975] 1 CMLR 184.

though this can be done by the High Court on an application for judicial review.[1] It can also be done by the Commissioner himself.[2]

Whilst reference from the 'final court' is obligatory[3] it is only discretionary from the other courts or tribunals[4] that is, if the court considers it necessary to enable it to give judgment. However, obligatory reference does not mean that the Supreme Court must in every case involving Community law seek a ruling from Luxembourg. Should it be so the Community Court would become a kind of court of appeal from the national jurisdiction which it was never meant to be, for its jurisdiction under article 177 is limited to interpretation of Community law in cases where such interpretation is requested by national courts. There is, therefore, no automatic reference but a judicial reference which implies uncertainty of the law in the opinion of the referring court and this, to use the expression of Advocate-General Lagrange,[5] embodies *une règle de bon sens et de sagesse*. The point has now been made by the Court itself[6] which emphasized the discretionary power of the courts of the last instance as opposed to the compulsion which might be read into the verb 'shall bring' used in the third paragraph of article 177.

In the same case the ECJ stressed the judicial nature of the reference and added that the national court may, if so inclined, refer of its own motion. This reflects an inquisitorial concept of the judicial process. In the adversarial system the judge may not be so inclined. Indeed, in the absence of a plea he may prefer to resolve the matter according to national law. Thus if neither party argues for reference or if both oppose it, it is unlikely that a reference would be made.[7]

Apart from arguing in court the parties cannot engineer a ref-

---

1 Case 41/77: *R v National Insurance Comr, ex p Warry* [1977] ECR 2085, [1977] 2 CMLR 783; Case 143/79: *Walsh v National Insurance Officer* [1980] ECR 1639, [1980] 3 CMLR 573.
2 *Kenny*, p 326, supra; Case 110/79: *Coonan v Insurance Officer*, [1980] ECR 1445.
3 'That court shall; cette juridiction est tenue; dieses Gericht ist verpflichted; tale giurisdizione è tenuta.'
4 'That court of tribunal may; cette juridiction peut; so kann; tale giurisdizione può.'
5 In Case 28/30/62: *Da Costa en Schaake v Nederlandse Administratie der Belastingen* [1963] ECR 31, [1963] CMLR 224 at 234; See also Lagrange, M, 'The Theory of the Acte Clair: A Bone of Contention or a Source of Unity?' (1971) 8 CMLRev 313.
6 Case 283/81: *CILFIT Srl v Minister for Health* [1982] ECR 3415, [1983] 1 CMLR 472.
7 See *English-Speaking Union of the Commonwealth v Customs and Excise Comrs* [1981] 1 CMLR 581.

erence by inserting into their contract an 'article 177 clause'[8] or
contrive a situation in which there is an apparent conflict but, in
fact, no litigious issue between them[9] or where the object of the
reference is to obtain a ruling concerning the law of a Member
State other than the state for which the question has been raised.
In such cases the ECJ has no jurisdiction since the duty assigned
to it by article 177 is not that of delivering advisory opinions on
general or hypothetical questions but of assisting in the administration of justice in the Member States.[10]

(h) *Acte clair*
This rule of common sense will differ, no doubt, according to the
style of the national judiciary, their sense of independence and
their Community orientation. Since reference under article 177
involves interpretation, perhaps the most vital factor in the decision
whether or not to refer is the confidence of the national court in
the art of the interpretation of Community law. Indeed, if the court
is certain of the position it need not, in accordance with the doctrine
of *acte clair* or *sens clair*, seek the ruling of the Community Court.
Acte clair implies that the legal rule in question is clear and,
therefore, requires no interpretation in accordance with the maxim
clara non sunt interpretanda. However, *certainty* may mean literally
certainty in an objective and undisputed sense. It may also mean
certainty as a form of subterfuge applied to avoid the cumbersome
machinery of preliminary ruling as remarked bluntly by a French
Avocat Général[11] '*bien entendu, la théorie de l'acte clair intervient
essentiellement pour mettre un obstacle au renvoi pour interprétation*'.
Conscious of this tendency the ECJ reminded the national jurisdictions that the doctrine of *acte clair* ought to be resorted to only
with utmost care.[12] On the other hand courts, being well versed in
the art of interpretation, need not be reminded that reference to
Luxembourg should be an exception rather than a rule and that it
should be resorted to out of necessity and not out of habit.[13]

8 Case 93/78: *Mattheus v Doego Fruchtimport und Tiefkühlkost eG* [1978] ECR
   2203, [1979] 1 CMLR 551.
9 Case 104/79: *Foglia v Novello* [1980] ECR 745; [1981] 1 CMLR 45; Case
   244/80: *Foglia v Novello* (No 2) [1981] ECR 3045; 1 CMLR 585.
10 Case 261/81: *Walter Rau v De Smedt PvbA* [1982] ECR 3961; [1983] 2 CMLR
   496; Case 46/80: *Vinal SpA v Orbat SpA* [1981] ECR 77; [1981] 3 CMLR
   524; Case 244/78: *Union Laitière Normande v French Dairy Farmers Ltd* [1979]
   ECR 2663; [1980] 1 CMLR 314.
11 Quoted by Pescatore, P, 'Interpretation of Community Law and the Doctrine
   of "Acte Clair"', *Legal Problems of an Enlarged European Community*, ed by
   Bathurst, M E, et al (1972), p 42.
12 Case 283/81: *CILFIT*, supra, at paras 16 and 17.
13 Cf Graham, J, in *Löwenbräu München v Grünhalle Lager International Ltd*
   [1974] CMLR 1.

(i) *Appeals*

The principle of *acte clair* applies to the inferior as much as to the final courts but in this context a practical question of appeals against the reference from the inferior courts arises. This basically is a matter for each individual country and there is no uniform practice among the twelve. In Germany, Denmark[14] and the Netherlands the reference goes forward to the Community Court whilst in Belgium, the United Kingdom[15] and France the appeal has first to be disposed of. Ireland, however, went further than any other Member State in clearing the way for reference of any court in so far as there is no appeal against the order. In so ruling the Supreme Court held that the constitutional right of appeal available in the domestic jurisdiction must give way to the supremacy of Community law expressed in article 177 of the Treaty.[16] The Community Court, on the other hand, follows its own guidelines which are determined by its function in the Community. This was succinctly stated in the *Bosch* case:[17]

'In fact, just as the Treaty does not prohibit domestic supreme courts from receiving the appeal for annulment, but leaves the examination of its admissibility to domestic law and to the opinion of the domestic judge, the Treaty subjects the jurisdiction of the Court of Justice solely to the existence of a request within the meaning of article 177, without requiring the Community judge to examine whether the decision of the domestic judge is appealable under the provisions of his domestic law.'

However, the spirit of non-intervention has not solved the problem as in two cases involving the same parties the Court was in effect asked to make a ruling on a conflict of opinion between German courts.[18] This conflict was, in the terms of the reference from the *Bundesfinanzhof*, reduced to the question whether an inferior court had an unfettered right of reference to the Community Court or whether article 177 upheld the hierarchy of national courts with the effect that on points of law an inferior court is bound by the ruling of a superior court. The Community Court, addressing itself to the *Hessisches Finanzgericht*,[19] ruled that

14 *Firma Hans Just i/s v Ministeriet for Skatter OG Afgifter* [1980] 1 CMLR 4; (Danish Supreme Court) Decided by ECJ: Case 68/79: *Hans Just I/S v Ministry for Fiscal Affairs* [1980] ECR 501, [1981] 2 CMLR 714.
15 Order 114 (5); see Chapter 12.
16 *Campus Oil Ltd v Minister for Industry and Energy* [1984] 1 CMLR 479 (Irish Supreme Court).
17 Case 13/61: *Bosch en Van Rijn v Kledingverkoopbedrijf De Geus en Uitdenbogerd* [1962] ECR 45 at 50, [1962] CMLR 1 at 26.
18 *Rhein-Mühlen-Düsseldorf v Einfuhr- und Vorratstelle für Getreide und Füttermittel* [1974] ECR 33, [1974] 1 CMLR 523 and 146/73: [1974] ECR 139, [1974] 1 CMLR 523.
19 Case 146/73: [1974] ECR at 147.

article 177 did not preclude an inferior court making its reference to the Community Court whilst the Community Court had no choice but to attend to the questions put before it. Addressing itself to the *Bundesfinanzhof*[20] the Community Court ruled that the existence of a rule of domestic law whereby a court is bound on points of law by the rulings of the court superior to it cannot of itself take away the power provided for in article 177 of referring cases to the Court. If inferior courts were bound without being able to refer matters to the Court, the jurisdiction of the latter to give preliminary rulings and the application of Community law at all levels of the judicial systems of the Member States would be compromised. It seems that the problem is basically a domestic one though for the sake of uniformity and in the spirit of the integration of judicial remedies within the Community a common solution should be found.

The relationship between the Community Court and the judiciary of the Member States is delicately poised between the recognition of the independence of the courts of sovereign states and the need for a uniform application of Community law throughout the Community. It is a problem which, one hopes, will solve itself in the course of time and as a result of the consolidation of the Community, though nuances between the styles of the national judiciaries are bound to remain.

20 Case 166/73: [1974] ECR at 38, 39.

Chapter 11

Enforcement of Community law

ENFORCEMENT OF TREATY OBLIGATIONS

The EEC Treaty is a self-executing treaty, a well-designed instrument of international co-operation. The Member States not only assume the duty of carrying out the measures prescribed by the Treaty and the Community organs but also submit to the judicial authority of the Community. In this way the state acts as an intermediary if not a subordinate instrument of the execution of the Treaty.

The enforcement of the Treaty is safeguarded by political, economic and legal means. The most important weapon, which in classic International Law states may resort to in order to frustrate a treaty, is interpretation. This weapon has been taken away from the signatories of the EEC Treaty and so they cannot resort to legal subterfuge. Though they can defy the Treaty by breaking it they cannot get round it or, under the guise of sovereignty, flout their obligations with impunity. Moreover they cannot claim, as Italy[1] did, the benefit of an 'international agreement' when the Treaty obligations have been further specified by a decision, ie decision 66/532 urging Italy to accelerate the reduction of the import rates on the basis of the continued protection of the Italian lead and zinc industry.

The interpretation of the Treaty has been entrusted to the Community Court (article 164 and 177) but there is a double check because by article 219[2] 'the Member States undertake not to submit any dispute concerning the interpretation or application of the Treaty to any method of settlement other than those provided in the Treaty'. This, in addition to administrative action, establishes a judicial system of settling disputes, the Community Court having a monopolist position.

Restricted in their classic weaponry the Member States may be tempted to flout the Treaty overtly but this too was provided for.

1 Case 38/69: *Customs Duties on Lead and Zinc, EC Commission v Italy* [1970] ECR 47 at 56, 57, [1970] CMLR 77 at 89–90.
2 ECSC, art 87; Euratom, art 193.

The Treaty provides for repressive measures, should this occur. The procedure of repression is gentle and well suited to the type of the likely offender.

Member states can sue one another before the Community Court but before doing so they must bring their complaint before the Commission.[3] In practice the task of suing the defaulter is undertaken by the Commission[4] as the guardian of the Treaties.

The reluctance of states to sue each other is understandable: such actions are invidious and the plaintiff state of today may well be the defendant tomorrow. Moreover a suit by the Commission tends to be technical rather than vindictive and, from a Community point of view, the Commission has the title to represent the Community's objective interests. In the light of this procedure France[5] suing the United Kingdom directly over the arrest of a French trawler exhibited a deviation from the norm understandable perhaps in the atmosphere of the *guerre des moutons.*[6]

Each country[7] has been before the Community Courts on a number of charges which vary so much that it is quite impossible to determine the pattern of state delinquency. Technically we are concerned with failures to carry out the obligations arising from the membership of the Communities. The principal, if not the only, object of the enforcement action is to ensure that these obligations are carried out and thus vindicate the rule of law.

Should a state fail to execute the judgment of the Community Court it may once more be sued, this time for breach of article 171. This procedure has in fact been applied but the Member State in question complied with the original judgment.[8] There is also a precedent that a Member State had refused to comply[9] with the judgment but this is unique.

The efficacy of the enforcement procedure has inherent limitations because a recalcitrant state cannot really be forced to abide by the judgment of the Court though by virtue of article 88 (3) of

---

3 EEC, art 170; ECSC, art 89; Euratom, art 142.
4 EEC, art 169; ECSC, art 88, Euratom, art 141.
5 Case 141/78: *France v United Kingdom (Re Fishing Net Mesh Sizes)* [1979] ECR 2923, [1980] 1 CMLR 6.
6 Case 232/78: *EC Commission v France, Re Restrictions on Imports of Lamb* [1979] ECR 2729, [1980] 1 CMLR 418.
7 Lasok, D 'The United Kingdom before the Community Court' in *Rechtsvergleichung Europarecht und Staatenintegration, Gedächtnisschrift für Léontin-Jean Constantinesco* (ed by Luke, G, Ress, G, Will, M R), 1982, pp 439 et seq.
8 Case 7/68: *EC Commission v Italy (first art treasures case)* [1968] ECR 423, [1969] CMLR 1, and Case 48/71: *EC Commission v Italy (second art treasures case)* [1972] ECR 527, [1972] CMLR 688.
9 Cases 24, 97/80 R: *EC Commission v France (second imports of lamb case)* [1980] ECR 1319.

the ECSC Treaty sanctions of a pecuniary nature and retaliatory measures by way of derogations from the provisions of article 4 of that Treaty in order to correct infringements of Treaty obligations may by applied under the control of the Council of Ministers. Such sanctions have not been applied to date. The lack of sanctions under the EEC and Euratone Treaties may be regarded as a weak point of the system. This indeed is the last vestige of sovereignty. In this respect the Community differs from a federal state which may have federal means at its disposal for the execution of the judgments of the federal court or the decisions of the federal executive. Therefore the ultimate sanction in the EEC is political and economic. The former consists of the pressure of public opinion within the Community and persuasion by the fellow Member States. The economic sanction lies in the common interest inherent in the preservation and improvement of the Community quite apart from any counter-measures which may be taken by the Member States individually or collectively. Though the machinery of enforcement is far from perfect there is no reason to believe that states would wantonly act contrary to the accepted obligations. They are only too well aware that the smooth working of the Community depends on their co-operation and that the economic intertwining cannot be disentangled without self-inflicted hardship.

ENFORCEMENT OF COMMUNITY LAW AT COMMUNITY LEVEL

Away from the lofty stage of inter-state conflicts or internal Community disputes, the enforcement of Community law (including the Treaty) occurs in the more usual setting of disputes in which individuals, corporations and states are involved. Such disputes are decided either at Community or state level bearing in mind that Community law is *state law* and, therefore, subject to the judicial notice of municipal courts.

The underlying philosophy of the Community and, indeed, the practical assurance of the Community development in accordance with the Treaty and the Community legislation is the doctrine of the supremacy of Community law. It is still a theory because in spite of the constitutional adjustments of the Member States there is, generally, a certain amount of hesitation, if not reluctance, to accept the monist doctrine and by-pass national legislatures. At the root of this is not only distrust of the Brussels bureaucrats who are neither directly controlled by nor responsible to the Member States but, more importantly, an instinctive aversion to external laws and authorities invading, as it were, the sacred preserve of sovereign states. These states have a long and proud history and a strong sense of national identity coupled with an individualistic notion of national interest. Therefore psychological barriers have to be removed in order to make the legal obligations enshrined in Treaties and subordinate legislation meaningful and acceptable. In the circumstances it is not surprising that the lead in the process of the enforcement of Community law had to come from the Community Court.

The main difficulty is that, apart from article 189, the EEC Treaty contains no formal and unequivocal assertion of the supremacy of Community law. Yet, it is common ground that the edifice of the Community would collapse if the Community were to degenerate into a legal Tower of Babel. Thus the Community Court in a number of cases formulated and reaffirmed the principle of supremacy. The Court, as the guardian of legality and instrument of cohesion within the Community has, from the start, been in a strong position to define the status of the Community law and to give it precedence when in conflict with the municipal law of the Member States. Most of these cases were brought under article 177 and the Court did not hesitate to use its authority in furthering the aims of the Community.

Whilst the Community Court in its judicial capacity has no rival system of law to administer and is only remotely concerned with the political consequences of its decisions, the municipal courts have to face the juristic and practical problems arising from the conflict between domestic law and Community law forming part of their national system. The theory that Community law is part, albeit autonomous, of national law does not solve these problems.

Indeed municipal courts often have to face the fact that the legislature has not removed from the national statute book measures which have been declared by the ECJ 'incompatible with Community law'. Impliedly such measures are *invalid* but the ECJ has no power to strike them out. It can only expect that they will be either formally repealed by the legislature or disregarded by the municipal courts. At a Community level this is a matter of state responsibility for its legislature and, therefore, a state in default incurs the risk of enforcement action under article 169. At a national level the problem remains unresolved. Therefore, as the Tribunal de Grande Instance recently asked in Paris, 'Are these measures directly and immediately inapplicable?'[10]

The question arose from the prosecution of importers and advertisers of certain apéritifs for offences under the French 'Drinks Code'. Certain provisions of this Code, notwithstanding the health implications, were declared to have breached article 30 of the

10 *Europe*, No 3287; 14 January 1982, p 12.

Treaty and the ECJ[11] condemned France in the stereotyped terms of its judgments in comparable cases, ie: 'The Republic of France, regulating the advertising of alcoholic beverages in a discriminatory manner, thus maintaining obstacles to freedom of intra-Community trade, has neglected to fulfil the obligations imposed on it under article 30 of the EEC Treaty.' However the Republic took no notice of this dictum and the public prosecutor continued his work. The trial court put its problem thus at a knife point: 'It seems that Community law, although possessing authority which is superior to that of French internal law, does not necessarily have to be directly and immediately applicable to the internal code of law. It must be determined then whether Community law such as it has been laid down ... by the Court of Justice, renders directly and immediately inapplicable the articles L1, L17, L18 and L21 of the Drinks Code and the measures against alcoholism in French national Law.'[12]

In response[13] the ECJ recorded the failure of the French Government to remedy the infringments found in its earlier judgment and reiterated the obligation of the national legislature to amend the law in order to render effective the directly applicable provisions of Community law.

However, the fact that municipal courts are not only prepared to follow the Community Court but also to assert independently the supremacy of Community law is quite significant. It shows that they are prepared to follow the rule of law established by the Community Court and in doing so do not hesitate to disregard the possible claim of municipal law or of their national government to confine disputes involving Community matters to domestic jurisdiction and municipal law. The judge sworn to administer the law of his country has to overcome the temptation to give precedence to the law in which he has been trained over the law derived from an external source.

ENFORCEMENT OF COMMUNITY LAW AT NATIONAL LEVEL

The corollary to the incorporation of the Treaties and Community legislation into municipal law is the judicial notice of Community law in the Member States. Community law, being part of the national legal structure, is applicable and enforceable by the municipal courts as the internal law of the states irrespective of its external origin. However, conflicts arise in practice and an analysis

---

11 Case 152/78: *EC Commission v France, Re Advertising of Alcoholic Beverages* [1980] ECR 2299, [1981] 2 CMLR 743.
12 Quot. from Europe, op cit.
13 Cases 314–316/81 and 83/82: *Procureur de la République v Waterkeyn* [1982] ECR 4337, [1983] 2 CMLR 145.

of the decisions of the municipal courts shows, at least during the first decade of the operation of the EEC Treaty, a great deal of confusion and erratic jurisprudence. National judges and lawyers had to settle down to the novel experience and assimilate the challenge of Community law. In this process, the doctrine of supremacy of Community law elaborated by the Community Court and the lessons drawn from preliminary rulings under article 177 had a steadying effect. The recognition by national courts of the direct effect of certain rules of Community law and of its supremacy, is therefore the most important factor in the process of enforcement of Community law at the Member State level.

We have already observed that, in some cases in which a preliminary ruling under article 177 was requested, the national courts were involved in conflicts between Community law and national law. Moreover, conflicts were often made more acute when the Constitution, the highest law of the land, was said to be infringed. The Community Court refrained from entering the lists, confined itself to interpretation of the relevant rule of Community law, but, nevertheless, albeit indirectly, indicated that Community law had to prevail, irrespective of whether the conflict was with the Constitution or the ordinary law of the land.

It seems, in the light of the experience of the founder members of the Community, that once the Treaties have been duly ratified and incorporated into their legal systems, allegations of unconstitutionality of these Treaties can hardly be made an issue of litigation. By the same token, the constitutionality of the Community legislation can *ex hypothesi* hardly be raised because, in order to be 'unconstitutional', the Community acts would have to be inconsistent with Community law and this is a matter for the Community Court. In theory, the Community Court could, by upholding the validity of Community legislation, contribute to a constitutional crisis in a Member State, the outcome of which cannot be predicted. If the supremacy of Community law and the authority of the Community Court were to prevail, the state concerned would have to put its own house in order; if, on the other hand, the authority of the Community Court were to be questioned, the matter would develop into a political crisis within the Community which could be solved only by political means. Putting these highly conjectural questions aside, it seems that more typical is the conflict between Community law and the ordinary law of the Member States. Indeed, as far as the United Kingdom is concerned, it is from this type of conflict that lessons can be learned simply because we do not have an hierarchy of legal norms as our Acts of Parliament have the same status whether they are concerned with the reform of the House of Lords or the reform of the law of illegitimacy.

Arising from Treaties the Community law, notwithstanding its incorporation into the legal systems of the Member States, presents certain problems of enforcement by municipal courts when in conflict with municipal law. According to the prevailing doctrine, International Law takes priority over municipal law in the jurisprudence of the International Court of Justice[14] but there is no uniformity in state practice. France, the Netherlands and Luxembourg admit supremacy of International Law over municipal law, but the other countries treat the rules of International Law on an equal footing with the rules of municipal law. In the British[15] system a distinction is made between customary and conventional rules of International Law. The former are incorporated through the doctrine of precedent, the latter through legislation. The Greek[16] Constitution recognizes supremacy of international conventional law over ordinary non-constitutional enactments but customary rules are on an equal footing with domestic law. However Community law, though generated by Treaties, is not, strictly speaking *International Law* in the traditional sense of the term. Therefore the analogies with International Law which are occasionally raised are not particularly helpful. Being a *sui generis* system it has to be treated as such and its enforcement has to be seen in the light of the practice evolving in the Member States. One starts with International Law as far as the Treaties are concerned but secondary Community law raises specific Community problems. At the basic practical level these problems can be reduced to the application of Community law (including the doctrine of supremacy) and the readiness to seek preliminary rulings from the ECJ.

France

In the light of article 55 of the French Constitution of 1958, Parliament must refrain from passing legislation inconsistent with the international obligations of France since 'a treaty duly ratified has, from the moment of its publication, an authority superior to that of statutes.'[17] Should such a bill be presented to Parliament it

---

14 *The Free Zones Case* [1932] PCIJ Rep Ser A/B No 46; *The Wimbledon Case* [1923] PCIJ Rep Ser A No 1; *German Settlers Case* [1923] PCIJ Rep Ser B No 6.

15 Lasok, D, 'Les traités internationaux dans le système juridique anglais' (1966), *Rev Gén de Droit Int Public*, p 1 (at 3).

16 Evrigenis, D, 'Legal and Constitutional Implications of Greek Accession to the European Communities' (1980), 17 CML Rev, p 157 at 166.

17 *Per* Commissaire du gouvernement Mme Questiaux in *Re Syndicat Général des Fabricants de Semoules Conseil d'Etat* [1970] CMLR 395 Dalloz 285.

could be declared unconstitutional by the *Conseil Constitutionnel* (article 61).[18] The Judiciary and public authorities have to conform. As confirmed by the *Conseil d'Etat* in the *Kirkwood* case[19] an individual may contest the validity of administrative acts of the state on the ground that they violate international obligations. Case law,[20] even under the previous Constitution, conforms to the rule that international obligations have to be honoured by the courts, and judges, through the instrumentality of interpretation, endeavour to avoid conflicts on the assumption that Parliament did not intend to violate International Law.

Relying on the principle of reciprocity the *Conseil Constitutionel* ruled in 1971[1] that the budgetary treaty of 1970 and the decision of the Council of Ministers whereby the Community budget was to be financed by the Community's own resources conformed to the Constitution. It also confirmed that direct elections to the European Parliament[2] did not constitute an unconstitutional transfer of sovereignty. In the *Isoglucose*[3] case the *Conseil* endorsed the direct effect of Community legislation stressing that their binding force is not subject to control of national authorities, notably the French Parliament and that, therefore, subsidies to producers were governed by the relevant regulation issued under article 189 of the Treaty. Finally it ruled that the discriminatory tax on alcoholic beverages, condemned previously by the Community Court[4] as contrary to article 95 of the EEC Treaty, was inconsistent not only with the Treaty but also with the principle of reciprocity enshrined in the Constitution.[5]

The existence of the Community Court with its inherent jurisdiction gave rise to the theory that since the Community Court solely administers Community law, whilst the national courts administer both the municipal law and Community law, the latter is called upon to resolve conflicts between the two systems without reference to the former.[6] In practice French courts have experi-

---

18　Eg *The Abortion Law* held constitutional (1975) II. JCP 180 30 (*Conseil Constitutionnel*) despite the argument that it contravened the European Human Rights Convention.

19　Decided on 30 May 1952, quoted by Constantinidès-Mégret, op cit, at p 85.

20　Cited by Constantinidès-Mégret, ibid, at p 86.

1　Décision recources propres, RGDIP 1971, p 239.

2　Décision Assemblée Européenne, AFDI 1976, p 787.

3　Décision Isoglucose, RTDE 1979, p 142.

4　Case 168/78: *EC Commission v France* [1980] ECR 347, [1981] 2 CMLR 631.

5　Décision Alcools, RGDIP 1981, p 600.

6　See *Riff v Soc Grande Limonaderie Alsacienne*, decided by the Cour de Cassation (Chambre Criminelle), 19 February 1964, [1965] 1 Clunet 85–90; 2 CML Rev 448–449; *Etat Français v Nicolas and Société Brandt*, decided by the Cour d'Appel of Amiens, 9 May 1963; [1963] CMLR 239 at 245; [1964] Clunet 93;

enced some difficulty, probably because 'traditionally French tribunals, at least in the past, regarded foreign legislation and
pronouncements of foreign courts with some mistrust'.[7] Consequently they were rather reluctant to administer Community law.
Thus in *Re Shell-Berre*[8] the *Conseil d'Etat*, applying the doctrine
of *acte clair*, refused to refer to the Community Court the question
whether a law of 1928 which enabled the government to exercise
control over the import and distribution of oil was incompatible
with articles 3, 7, 30, 35, 37, 59, 62, 85, 92 and 96 of the EEC
Treaty. A similar attitude was shown by the first subsection of the
Conseil d'Etat in *Syndicat Général des Fabricants de Semoules*[9]
which held that a French decree introducing an import levy on
semolina inconsistent with Community regulations was to prevail.
It could be said that the case was rather exceptional as it concerned
imports from Algeria which, by virtue of French legislation, were
to remain within the French customs frontiers but, in fact, the
Conseil d'Etat preferred to apply French law to Community law.
The breakthrough came in *Re Syndicat National du Commerce
Extérieur*.[10] In that case a syndicate dealing in cereals requested the
interpretation of the term 'any holder' (EEC regulation 1028/68)
to be referred to the Community Court as it considered itself to
be prejudiced by the narrow interpretation of this term by the
ONIC (ie the National Cereals Board). The *Conseil* agreed that
the Community Court gave a wide interpretation which, in
turn, enabled the *Conseil* to annul the decision of the ONIC in
this respect.

Dealing with the individuals the *Conseil* acted in a rather individualistic manner. It set aside a Prefect's order to deport aliens
who applied for a residence permit in order to establish a production co-operative to be known as a 'Pioneer European Village',[11]
but denied admission to a person who in his youth, a decade earlier,
achieved notoriety during the student troubles.[12] The latter case is
remarkable because the *Conseil* ignored the relevant Community
precedents, refused to make a reference to the Community Court
and ruled that directives (in particular directive 64/221) cannot be
invoked by individuals in national proceedings in order to challenge

upheld on other grounds by the Cour de Cassation (Chambre Criminelle), 22
October 1964, [1965] Clunet 90; 2 CML Rev 449.
7 Simon, M 'Enforcement by French Courts of European Community Law'
(1974) 90 LQR 467 at 471.
8 [1964] CMLR 462, [1964] Clunet 794.
9 [1970] CMLR 395, [1968] Dalloz 285, 6 CML Rev 419.
10 [1971] Dalloz 576 and 645.
11 *Re Hill and Holzappel* [1978] 2 CMLR 554.
12 *Minister of the Interior v Cohn Bendit* [1980] 1 CMLR 543, [1979] Dalloz 155.

an administrative act. Its defiance was extended to the VAT directive 77/388 which it considered to have no direct effect.[13]

The Civil Courts appear to be more favourably disposed towards Community law but they too had their difficulties. In the *Consten*[14] saga involving the validity of an exclusive distribution contract, the Paris Court of Appeal quashed the judgment of a Commercial Court (which effectively denied the application of EEC regulation 17/1962 in this respect)[15] and stayed the action until the Commission had made its decision in the matter. Two years later a Court of First Instance dealing with the same problem[16] noted the Commission decision in the previous case and stayed the action to await the outcome of the proceedings before the Community Court. From that time on the French Civil Courts became quite prepared to resort to the proceedings under article 177, a notable early example being the *Ulm* case.[17] Thus, the Paris Court of Appeal, applying the judgment of the Community Court in the *Beguelin* case,[18] held article 85 and regulations 10/1965 and 67/1967 directly applicable in France with the effect that a contract between a French and a Dutch firm, granting the former exclusive distribution rights, was declared invalid. The decision was confirmed by the *Cour de Cassation*.[19]

The Criminal Chamber of the *Cour de Cassation* also made its contribution. In *Administration des Contributions Indirectes, etc. v Ramel*[20] the *Cour de Cassation* dismissed an appeal against the acquittal of the respondent on the charge of offering for sale inferior wine imported from Italy. The wine was admitted to France under the EEC regulations although its quality did not comply with French law. In the *Republic v Von Saldern et al*[1] the *Cour de Cassation* dismissed an appeal against conviction for breach of exchange control regulations involved in the import of chemicals from the USA. The appeal was based on Community customs regulations concerning the valuation of imported goods which were issued after the alleged offence. Since these regulations were not

---

13 *Re la directive No 77/388* [1981] Dalloz I.R. 331.
14 Cases 56, 58/64: *Consten and Grundig v EC Commission* [1966] ECR 299, [1966] CMLR 418.
15 *Consten v UNEF* [1963] CMLR 176, [1963] Dalloz 189.
16 *Consten v Willy-Leissner, Rev. Trim. de Droit Européen* (1965) 487.
17 Case 56/65: *Société Technique Minière v Maschinenbau Ulm GmbH* [1966] ECR 235, [1966] CMLR 357.
18 Case 22/71 *Beguelin Import Co v SAGL Import-Export* [1971] ECR 949, [1972] CMLR 81.
19 *Entreprises Garoche v Société Striker Boats Nederland* [1974] 1 CMLR 469.
20 [1971] CMLR 315, [1971] Dalloz 211.
 1 (1971) 10 CML Rev 223.

retrospective the appeal had to fail and the question of conflict with national law did not arise. In the *Guerrini* case,[2] concerning a conviction for an offence under a 1939 law laying down standards for the marketing of eggs, the Court of Appeal at Aix disregarded the relevant EEC regulations (122/67 and 1619/68) as it considered itself bound by the unrepealed statute. However the *Cour de Cassation* reversed that decision on the ground that the regulations had a direct effect repealing, as it were, the French legislation from the date on which the regulations came into force.

However, perhaps the most significant case is that of *Administration des Douanes v Société Cafés Jacques Vabre and J Weigel et Cie Sarl*.[3] The central point of that case was whether importers of instant coffee from Holland were legitimately charged with import duties which put them at a disadvantage as compared with French manufacturers of the product and thus suffered discrimination contrary to EEC article 95. The French customs authorities claimed that article 265 of the *Code de Douanes*, being enacted after the French accession to the Community, had to be applied and that article 55 of the Constitution notwithstanding, French courts had no jurisdiction in the matter of the constitutionality of the Code. In the Court of First Instance and the Paris Court of Appeal these arguments were rejected and finally the *Cour de Cassation* decided that the EEC Treaty established a separate legal order which prevails in France even over subsequent legislation. The requirement of reciprocity under article 55 of the Constitution has been satisfied in the Treaty of Rome. It held

'... the treaty which by virtue of the above-mentioned article of the Constitution has an authority superior to that of statutes, established its own juridical order integrated with that of Member States, and by virtue of this special character the juridical system which it has created is directly applicable to the nationals of these states and is binding on their courts; and therefore ... article 95 of the Treaty has to be applied ... to the exclusion of article 265 of the Customs Code, despite the fact that the latter is of a later date.'

Recognizing the supremacy of Community law (ie the right of establishment) the *Cour de Cassation* quashed the judgment of a court of appeal and ruled that a German was entitled to recover his farm from a French tenant on expiry of the lease despite the provision of the *Code Rural* which insists that aliens are not allowed to farm in France without a special permit to that effect. It held that 'the provisions of French internal law which imposed the

2 *Guerrini Case*, 7 January 1972 (JCP 1972, II), 10 CML Rev 451.
3 Court of Appeal, Paris, 7 July 1973, Dalloz (1974) 159, Cour de Cassation, 24 May 1975, Dalloz (1975) 497. [1975] 2 CMLR 336. Also see Simon, M (1976), 92 LQR 85.

requirement of an administrative permit on those who wanted to farm in France have ceased to be applicable'.[4]

In a case concerned with French monetary compensatory amounts, the *Cour de Cassation*[5] quashed a decision of a court of appeal in which the latter decided that in its ruling in Case 145/79[6] the Community Court had exceeded its competence by encroaching upon the jurisdiction of the national judiciary in so far as it ruled upon the consequences of an annulled Commission regulation. Whilst it conceded that the court of appeal was not obliged to seek a preliminary ruling it held that the court of appeal indulged in the interpretation of the Treaty, which it had no power to do, and on that ground quashed the decision. In doing so the *Cour de Cassation* not only affirmed the principle of supremacy of Community law but also the binding force of a preliminary ruling. Moreover it stressed that the extent of the Community competence is a matter of Community law which ought to be defined by the Community Court.

A selection of more recent cases confirms that the French judiciary at all levels strives to uphold Community law. Thus, for example, a *Tribunal de Grande Instance*[7] ruled that, in the absence of a proof of lawful manufacture in the Member State of origin, the import of motor car spare parts produced in breach of an industrial property right (ie design) could be prohibited by virtue of article 36 of the EEC Treaty. This was, no doubt, correct, bearing in mind the case[8] decided by the ECJ that French manufacturers of motor cars had the right to patent certain elements of the bodywork of their product and thus prohibit the manufacture, sale and export of these elements by certain specialists in imitating parts detached from the original model.

The *Cour d'Appel* of Aix-en-Provence, noting that the national law on the minimum petrol prices (already declared illegal by the ECJ)[9] had no hesitation in applying Community law directly on the principle that it was inconsistent with article 30 of the EEC Treaty.[10] The same court, following the ECJ,[11] considered the

---

4 *Von Kempis v Geldof* [1976] 2 CMLR 152, Cour de Cass Civil Chamber, 15 December 1975, Dalloz (1976) 33.
5 Arret No 1096 P of 10 December 1985; See Schermers H G, CLRev (1986) 473 et seq.
6 Case 145/79: *Roquette Frères SA v France* [1980] ECR 2917.
7 *Regie Nationale des Usines Renault v Thevenoux*, Trib de Grande Instance, Roanne [1988] 3 CMLR 686.
8 Case 53/87, para 11, decided on 5.10.1988.
9 See also Cases 271–274/84 and 6–7/85: *Procureur de la Republique v Chiron* [1986] ECR 529, [1988] 1 CMLR 735.
10 *Aldis SA v Chabrand* [1987] 2 CMLR 396.
11 Case 107/83: *Ordre des Avocats au Barreau de Paris v Klopp* [1984] ECR 2971; [1985] 1 CMLR 99.

French domestic rule which prohibits lawyers from Marseille opening offices in Paris and Canakry (Guinea) contrary to the right of establishment enshrined in article 52 of the EEC Treaty and, therefore, inapplicable.[12] In the same field the *Cour de Cassation* confirmed the principle, in another case, declaring that the French rule against multiple chambers (ie prohibiting a French lawyer to open chambers in Brussels unless he leaves the Nice Bar) was a breach of article 52.[13]

A Paris *Cour d'Appel* referred a question arising from the application of the consumer protection directive on door-step selling, ie whether the prohibition of such sales of educational[14] courses was incompatible with article 30 of the Treaty.

The *Conseil d'Etat* refused a residence permit to a German applicant who, though not qualified to practise medicine, wanted to establish himself in such practice.[15] Since he had no right to carry out self-employed activities he was considered not to be entitled to a resident permit. It seems that a reference for a preliminary ruling might have been more appropriate.

The *Conseil* ruled that the grant by statute of voting rights to non-European overseas French citizens in the election to the European Parliament was compatible with article 227 (1) of the EEC Treaty which defines the Community territory. The ruling was based on the principle that the Treaty and other international treaties prevail over subsequent French statutes.[16] The *Conseil* also considered the duty of the state to implement Community directives on VAT. It ruled that it was inappropriate to continue in force or enact national rules incompatible with the objectives of Community legislation. Such national law would be unlawful after the end of the implementation period of the relevant directive. It also annulled the refusal of the executive to legislate in order to repeal the offending national provisions.[17] Exercising its judicial control over executive legislation the *Conseil* annulled a ministerial order fixing the hunting season for water fowl as being incompatible with the Wild Birds Directive (79/409). In doing so it emphasized

---

12 *Maitre Cammarata v Conseil de l'Ordre de Avocats de Marseille* [1988] 1 CMLR 243.
13 *Conseil de l'Ordre des Avocats au Barreau de Nice v Raynel* [1990] 2 CMLR 190.
14 *Ministère Public v Buet and Educational Business Services Sarl* [1988] 3 CMLR 426.
15 *Re Joseph Weber* [1988] 2 CMLR 809.
16 *Re Nicolo* [1990] 1 CMLR 173.
17 *Re Compagnie ALITALIA* [1990] 1 CMLR 248.

the need for national legislation to conform to the provisions of directives.[18]

The *Cour de Cassation*, following the judgment of the ECJ[19] in which the latter held invalid a special provision of Regulation 1408/71 applicable to France which denied children allowances to foreign workers temporarily out of France, held that such allowances had to be paid. Discrimination against migrant workers in France was thus brought to an end.[20] In two cases[1] the *Cour de Cassation* held, following the decisions of the ECJ,[2] that discriminatory taxes imposed on high power cars manufactured in the Community but outside France were illegal and those already paid ought to be repaid.

The Netherlands

Since the amendment of the Netherlands Constitution in 1953 and 1956, there seems to be no doubt that, in principle, Community law should be given precedence before Dutch law. We have already noted the *Van Gend en Loos* case[3] which, prior to coming before the Community Court for preliminary ruling, unfolded as a case involving a conflict between the Constitution and Community law. Similarly in *de Geus v Bosch*[4] the argument that only rules of International Law of a 'universal application' take precedence over national law failed. These decisions had, undoubtedly, a profound effect upon the practice of Dutch courts.

Of more recent cases *Centrafarm*[5] calls for special mention. In that case the *Hoge Raad*, applying the preliminary rulings of the Community Court, refused an injunction to a trademark holder and a patentee which would restrain the marketing in Holland of thus protected pharmaceutical products originating from the United Kingdom.

In *Officer Van Justitie v Adriaan de Peijper, Managing Director of Centrafarm BV*, the *Kantongerecht*[6] at Rotterdam pronounced upon the freedom of movement and parallel imports of phar-

---

18 *Re Rassemblement des Opposants à la Chasse* [1990] 2 CMLR 831.
19 Case 41/84: *Pinna v Caisse d'Allocations Familiales de la Savoie* [1986] ECR 1, [1988] 1 CMLR 350.
20 *Pinna v Caisse d'Allocations Familiales de la Savoie* [1990] 2 CMLR 366.
1 *Directeur General des Impôts v Dubois* [1990] 2 CMLR 823 and *Directeur General des Impôts v Feldain* [1990] 2 CMLR 827.
2 Case 112/84. *Humblot v Directeur des Services Fiscaux* [1985] ECR 1367, [1986] 2 CMLR 338 and Cases 76, 86–89 and 149–87: *Segnela v Administration des Impôts* [1988] ECR 2397, [1989] 3 CMLR 823.
3 Case 26/62 [1963] ECR 1, [1963] CMLR 105.
4 Case 13/61: [1962] ECR 45, [1962] CMLR 1.
5 Case No 10. 712, *Centrafarm BV and De Peijper v Sterling Drug Inc* [1976] 1 CMLR 1.
6 [1976] 1 CMLR 19.

maceutical products but left a question open as to whether certain rules of national law regarding the authentication and certification of such products, imposed by another Member State, were contrary to the EEC principles of the freedom of movement of goods. Applying the ruling of the ECJ[7] the *Kantongerecht* acquitted the importer of drugs therapeutically indistinguishable from approved national products from a charge arising under national drug control legislation which requires certain documentation which could not be procured because the drugs in question were imported.[8]

In the *Ruigrok* case[9] the Supreme Court upheld the conviction for cultivating hyacinth bulbs commercially without a licence. Thus the convicted cultivator had to pay the fine notwithstanding the fact that the relevant Dutch law was inconsistent with Community law as previously decreed by the Community Court. Whilst accepting the ruling of the ECJ as binding (and resulting in the quashing of the conviction in the cited case) the Supreme Court distinguished the present case in so far as it concerned an application to set aside a judgment which had become absolute and this, according to Dutch law, was inadmissible. The conviction was a result of an error of law and not of facts unknown to the court at the time of the conviction and sentence and, therefore, could not be set aside.

Dealing with aliens, the *Raad van State*, without referring the matter to the ECJ, held that a British subject continuously wilfully unemployed was not entitled to have his residence permit renewed.[10] However another,[11] though in irregular employment and guilty of petty offences, was allowed to stay in Holland. More recently the question whether a British wife of a South African citizen[12] was entitled to the status of 'favoured EEC citizen' for the purpose of residence despite the fact that her earnings were below the national subsistence level, was referred to the ECJ. At stake was her status as 'worker'. Advocate-General Sir Gordon Slynn thought that the principal test was not the number of hours worked but whether 'work was the genuine and substantial purpose of the application to reside'. The ECJ concurred. Less fortunate was a Turkish worker who, on reference to the ECJ, was held ineligible

---

7 Case 104/75: *Re de Peijper* [1976] ECR 613, [1976] 2 CMLR 271.
8 *Officer Van Justitie v de Peijper* [1977] 1 CMLR 321.
9 [1977] 1 CMLR 306.
10 *Williams v Secretary of State for Justice* [1977] 1 CMLR 669.
11 *Simbula v Secretary of State for Justice* [1978] 2 CMLR 74.
12 Case 53/81: *Levin v Staatssecretaris van Justitie* [1982] ECR 1035, [1981] 3 CMLR 663.

for extension of a residence permit by virtue of the EEC–Turkey Association Agreement.[13]

The *Raad van State* held inadmissible the appeal against the refusal of the Government to bring before the ECJ an action for annulment of a Council regulation which imposed a levy for the production of the isoglucose. Such a Government decision was not subject to judicial review in accordance with Dutch administrative law and, therefore, a citizen could not force the Government to bring an action in this respect.[14]

Luxembourg

The Constitution of Luxembourg contains no provision regarding the relationship between International Law and municipal law, but the judiciary, in the course of time, has evolved the principle of supremacy of International Law.[15] In this process a judgment of the *Conseil d'Etat* of 1950 and a judgment of the Superior Court of 1954 have a special significance as they established the principle that a rule of International Law will prevail over a rule of national law even if the latter is subsequent to the former.[16]

Belgium

The Belgian Constitution of 1831 has been revised, mainly to accommodate Belgian membership of the European Community. Accordingly article 25 (b) provides that the exercise of certain state powers may be delegated by treaty or by statute to institutions set up under International Law. Since 1925 Belgian courts gave precedence to International Law over national law if the latter was inconsistent with a treaty.[17] This rule was broadened by the *Cour de Cassation* in 1964.[18] The court distinguished between treaties binding the state and treaties creating rights and obligations directly enforceable by individuals. Only the latter, by their very nature, can be in conflict with Belgian domestic law and if they are in conflict they must have precedence over municipal law. This ruling was complemented by a decision of the *Conseil d'Etat* made a month before the decision of the *Cour de Cassation*.[19] In a case

---

13 Case C–192/89: *Sevince v Staatsecretaris van Justitie* (ECJ judgment 20 September 1989, as yet unreported).

14 *Koninklijke Scholten-Honig NV v Minister of Agriculture and Fisheries* [1978] 3 CMLR 251.

15 Pescatore, P, 'Prééminence des traités sur la loi interne: la jurisprudence luxembourgeoise', *Journal des Tribunaux*, 1953, p 445; see also Constantinidès-Mégret, op cit, p 88, 89.

16 Cases cited in *Les Novelles: Droit des Communautés Européennes* (1969), p 67.

17 Ibid, p 63.

18 Ibid, p 63.

19 Ibid, p 64.

brought against the Belgian Ministry of Agriculture, the Treaty of 1953 between Belgium and France concerning the protection of birds was construed as an obligation binding the state alone and having no direct effect upon the rights and obligations of citizens.

It would appear, accordingly, that depending on their classification (ie whether binding the citizen or merely the state) some provisions of the EEC Treaty are directly enforceable by Belgian courts, whereas others are not so enforceable. Following this philosophy the *Tribunal de Commerce de Bruxelles* considered article 85 (1) of the EEC Treaty directly applicable.[20] Being directly applicable, the Treaty may render void a contract valid when made.[1]

No doubt the process of accommodating Belgian traditions to the problem of Community law enforcement was influenced by the two famous cases *Costa v ENEL* and *Van Gend en Loos* which had a considerable impact within the Community. Their influence can be seen in the decision of the Magistrates' Court of Antwerp[2] which, having lavishly cited authorities and juristic opinion, concluded that, should there be a conflict between the EEC Treaty and subsequent Belgian legislation, the former would prevail.[3] The Belgian Government too agreed that the Treaty should be given precedence over any subsequent legislation inconsistent with the Treaty.[4]

In the field of social legislation the District Court of Tongeren has held that article 12 of Council Regulation 3 prevailed over Belgian legislation on industrial accidents in accordance with the principle that *lex posterior derogat priori*.[5]

In the *Corveleyn*[6] case the *Conseil d'Etat* applied the Community directive 64/221 of 25 February 1964 in order to quash a deportation order. But the high water mark of the evolution towards the recognition of the supremacy of Community law was reached in the decision of the *Cour de Cassation* in *Minister for Economic Affairs v SA Fromagerie Franco-Suisse 'Le Ski'*.[7] This case, concerning a claim for money paid by mistake on the ground that, by reason of article 12 of the EEC Treaty, the duties in question did

20 *Van Heuvermeiren v Buitoni* [1967] CMLR 241 at 245, (1966) 1 CDE, 317.
1 *Association Générale des Fabricants de Ciment Portland Artificiel v SA Carrière Dufour* [1965] CMLR 193 at 207–208.
2 *Sociaal Fonds voor de Diamantarbeiders v Chougol Diamond Co* [1969] CMLR 335 at 320–323.
3 The Community Court in another context (effects of the introduction of the common external tariff) involving the same parties, implied the same result; cases 2–3/69: [1969] ECR 211 at 221–224, [1969] CMLR 335 at 349–353.
4 *SPRL Corn and Food Trading Co v Etat Belge* (1968) CDE, 550 at 554.
5 *NV Essimex v J Jans* [1972] CMLR 48.
6 *Corveleyn v Belgium*, 7 October 1968, (1969) CDE 343 at 345–346.
7 [1972] 2 CMLR 330.

not apply to the products imported from Member States of the Community, gave the Procureur-Général Ganshof van der Meersch an opportunity to discuss the nature of the self-executing provisions of the Treaty, the binding force of Community law, sovereignty and the relationship between Community law and the law of Belgium. In his erudite submissions, he reviewed a host of learned writings and 48 cases decided by the Community Court, the Belgian courts and the courts of Luxembourg and Germany.[8] Quoting *Van Gend en Loos* and *Costa v ENEL* he submitted that:

'Community law is integrated in the law of Member States. From its very nature, it follows that a subsequent measure of state legislation cannot be set against it ... As Professor Pescatore has said: "One is entitled to think that the fundamental argument is to be found in this last passage: the very existence of the Community is called in question if the Community legal system cannot be established with identical effects and with uniform effectiveness over the whole geographical areas of the Community ..."[9]

The primacy of the rules of Community law is doubly justified on legal grounds. First by their agreement on the transfer of their rights and obligations under the Treaty to the Community legal system, the states definitely limited their "sovereign rights", or to put it more accurately, "the exercise of their sovereign powers". The Community system implies some surrender of sovereignty and Community law is a specific law which gives effect to this surrender. The integration aim of the Treaties of Paris and of Rome is attained by handing over to the Community institutions powers having as their object and effect the determination of a corresponding limitation of the powers of Member States ...

Thus was created for these states a duty to abstain from action in the fields regulated by the Treaty and a duty to take all complementary steps needed to enforce Community legislation.

Secondly, Community law is a specific and autonomous law which is binding on the courts of the Member States and makes it impossible to set against it any domestic law whatsoever. The very nature of the legal system instituted by the Treaties of Rome confers that primacy on its own foundation, independently of the constitutional provisions in states.[10] The specific character of Community law stems from the objectives of the Treaty which are the establishment of a new legal system to which are subject not only states, but also the nationals of those states. It also stems from the fact that the Treaty has set up institutions having their own powers and especially that of creating new sources of law. From their very structures, these institutions reflect the will of the authors of the Treaty to go beyond the state framework and to impose

8 See, in particular, ibid, pp 351–358.
9 Pescatore, P, *Droit communautaire et droit national* (1969), p 183, quoting from *Costa v ENEL* [1964] CMLR 425 at 455, 456.
10 Quoting Tallon, D, *Le droit communautaire* (1966) 1 *Cahiers de Droit Européen* 571.

obligations directly on individual persons and to confer rights directly on them[11] ... If the Community system is not recognised as superior, rules would not be the same within each Member State, and the consequences would be that such a situation would necessarily give rise to forms of discrimination proscribed by the treaties, that obligations would not bear equally on everybody and that not everyone would derive equal benefit from the rights derived from the treaties ...'

This long passage represents the quintessence of the Belgian and Community *doctrine* and reflects, it seems, the mood within the Community. The Court, on the other hand, in its terse judgment ruled:

'Even if assent to a treaty as required by article 68 (2) of the Constitution, is given in the form of a statute, the legislative power, by giving this assent, is not carrying out a normative function. The conflict which exists between a legal norm established by an international treaty and a norm established by a subsequent statute, is not a conflict between two statutes.

The rule that a statute repeals a previous statute in so far as there is a conflict between the two, does not apply in the case of a conflict between a treaty and a statute.

In the event of a conflict between a norm of domestic law and a norm of international law which produces direct effects in the internal system, the rule established by the treaty shall prevail. The primacy of the treaty results from the very nature of international treaty law. This is a fortiori the case when a conflict exists, as in the present case, between a norm of internal law and a norm of Community law.

The reason is that the treaties which have created Community law have instituted a new legal system in whose favour the Member States restricted the exercise of their sovereign powers in the areas determined by those treaties.

Article 12 of the Treaty ... is immediately effective and confers on individual persons rights which national courts are bound to uphold.

It follows from all these considerations that it was the duty of the judge to set aside the application of provisions of domestic law that are contrary to this Treaty provision ...'[12]

Belgian courts, from the lowest to the highest, are not inhibited either procedurally or psychologically from making references under article 177, the first one occurring in 1967.[13] Recently a problem of the position of road transport services came to light. According to Belgian law a carrier, in order to qualify for a road transport licence, must be established in Belgium. Thus questions

---

11 Quoting his own writings, 'Le droit communautaire et ses rapports avec les droits des Etats membres', in *Droit des Communautés européennes* (1969), Nos 138–139.
12 [1972] CMLR at 372, 373.
13 Case 6/67: *Guerra* [1967] ECR 219.

regarding the status of a company with a real base in the Netherlands but operating from an unmanned and locked-up caravan
were raised. The licence was refused on the assumption that the
refusal did not breach the Treaty provisions on the right of establishment. However the Conseil d'Etat[14] was troubled with the
uncertainty regarding services and referred the matter to the ECJ
whose ruling is pending. The tendency[15] is to accord the judgments
of the Community Court *l'autorité de la chose jugée* and to consider
violations of Community law equivalent to violations of a Belgian
statute.

Federal German Republic

The starting point of the German practice is the strong dualist
tradition of which Triepel[16] was perhaps the most influential
exponent. According to this doctrine a rule of International Law
becomes enforceable only if expressly incorporated into the municipal law. Having been so incorporated, it ranks in the hierarchy of
legal norms among the ordinary rules of internal law (statutes) and
is subject to the principle *lex posterior derogat priori*. However, in
this context, Community law was soon recognised as having a
special status being a *sui generis* law though the courts have, for a
while, followed an erratic course.

Learned writers, especially Ophüls,[17] Ipsen[18] and Wohlfart,[19]
advocated a departure from the tradition arguing that Community
law ought to have precedence over national law. The courts, on the
other hand, had to deduce the rule of supremacy from the provisions of the Federal Constitution which, by article 24 (1), enables
the Federal State to transfer sovereign powers to international
institutions and, in article 25, proclaims that the general rules of
International Law form an integral part of the federal system.
Ipsen[20] called article 24 the *Integrationshebel* (lever of integration)

---

14 *Lambregts Transportbedrijf PVBA v The State (Belgium)* [1989] 2 CMLR 987.
15 Lenaerts, K, *The Application of Community Law in Belgium* (23) CML Rev
    (1986) 253 at 282.
16 Triepel, H, *Völkerrecht und Landesrecht* (1899); *Rec. de Cours de l'Académie
    de la Haye*, 'Les rapports entre le droit interne et le droit international', 1923,
    Vol 1, pp 76 et seq.
17 Ophüls, C F, 'Zwischen Völkerrecht und staatlichem Recht, Grundfragen des
    europäischen Rechts', *Juristen-Jahrbuch*, Vol 4 (1963–64), pp 137–162.
18 Ipsen, H P, 'Rapport du droit des Communautés Européenes avec le droit
    national', *Le Droit et les Affaires* (1964), No 47.
19 Wohlfart, E, 'Europäisches Recht, Von der Befugnis der Organe der
    europäischen Wirtschaftsgemeinschaft zur Rechtsetzung', *Jahrbuch für
    Internazionales Recht*, Vol 9, pp 12–32.
20 Ipsen, op cit, p 26.

and Vogel[1] argued that the legislature must contribute towards European integration. The judges must follow the legislature and give precedence to Community law inconsistent with internal law.[2] The prevailing juristic opinion favoured supremacy of Community law but courts were faced with arguments that Community law was 'unconstitutional' in so far as it contravenes 'fundamental rights'. Under a written constitution which guarantees 'fundamental rights' with little ingenuity any question can be raised to a constitutional issue.

The following are the landmarks on the road to the supremacy rule.

In *Re Tax on Malt Barley*[3] the Federal Constitutional Court (*Bundesverfassungsgericht*) clarified the position of the EEC Treaty Ratification Law and the Community agricultural regulations whose constitutionality was doubted by the *Finanzgericht* of Rheinland-Pfalz. It held:[4]

'Section one of the EEC Treaty Act is based upon the power contained in article 24 (1) of the Constitution, and is within the limits imposed on the transfer of sovereign rights to international authorities by article 79 (3) of the Constitution. A balanced system for the co-operation of the Community's Council, Commission and Parliament guarantees a control of power which is institutionally preserved as effective as the traditional separation of powers. It satisfies the most stringent demands of "the rule of law" ...'

Turning to the Regulation issued under the EEC article 189, the Court declared:

'... Article 189 is of great importance in the framework of the whole Treaty. But it would be wrong to conclude from this that the whole Treaty would be purposeless if article 189 and the regulations passed thereunder were not immediately binding in the Federal Republic. In the Court's opinion, the nullity of one provision does not in principle entail the invalidity of the whole act or law. The whole law would only be void in such a case if on its true construction, the remaining provisions had no significance on their own or if the unconstitutional provisions are part of a self-contained set of regulations which would have no sense of efficacy if one of their constituent parts is taken away.

These provisions apply to Treaty law too. The effect of their application to section one of the EEC Treaty Act is that, even if this provision were to be held unconstitutional in so far as it relates to article 189 of

1 Vogel, K, *Die Verfassungsentscheidung des Grundgesetzes für eine internationale Zusammenarbeit* (1964), p 46.
2 Fuss, E W, 'Rechtsschutz gegen deutsche Hoheitsakte zur Ausführung des Europäischen Gemeinschaftsrechts', *Neue Juristische Wocheinschrift* (1966), p 1782.
3 Case III 77/63 [1964] CMLR 130.
4 2 BvL 29/63: *Re Tax on Malt Barley* [1967] CMLR 302 at 311, 316.

the Treaty, the EEC Treaty Act would still not become totally invalid; the effectiveness of the remaining provisions in the German Federal Republic would not be disturbed ...'

As a result, a substantial body of case law has confirmed the view that article 189 and the Treaty are directly applicable in Germany.[5] On the question of Community law being inconsistent with previous German Law the *Finanzgericht* of Münster held[6]

'... the organs of the Community were given powers of legislation in matters pertaining to the Community and that legislation is binding on the Member States. If those powers are to mean anything Community legislation must have the effect, within its sphere of competence, of amending or repealing, by implication, national legislation which is repugnant to it ...'

The Courts went further because in a number of cases[7] they held that Community law superseded subsequent German legislation.

On the specific question of direct application of the EEC Treaty (article 95 (1)) two cases should be specially noted. In the *Mölkerei* case[8] the Court held that the rate of compensatory tax imposed on an imported agricultural product from another state violated the non-discrimination principle. The Court arrived at this conclusion because '... in so far as the court finds that there is a contravention of that rule of Community law it must take account of the *precedence* of Community law. That is the only way in which the immediate effectiveness accorded to article 95 by the European Court[9] can be interpreted and a corresponding juridical protection be given to the individual subjects of the Member States of the Community ...' In *Re Imported Thai Sand Flower*[10] the *Finanzericht* of Bremen held that imported products had to be classified for the purpose of customs duties according to the EEC Regulations governing the common organization of the market for cereals rather than German rules. The Court ruled that '... to the extent that the Member States have assigned legislative powers in levying tariff matters to the Community in order to ensure the proper operation of the common market for cereals, they no longer have the power to make legislative provisions in this field'. More recently the Federal Supreme Fiscal Court ruled that the increased excise duty rates based on annual total production of source brewery did not infringe

---

5 See cases listed by Campbell, op cit, Vol 1, 1.83 and Supplement No 2, p 15.
6 In Case IVc 20–21/63: *Re Import of Pork* [1966] CMLR 491 at 498–499.
7 See cases listed by Campbell, op cit, Vol 1, 1.103, and Supplement No 2, p 16, Supp 1975, p 43.
8 VII 156/65 *Mölkerei-Zentrale Westfalen/Lippe GmbH v Hauptzollamt Paderborn* [1969] CMLR 300 at 312.
9 In Case 48/65: *Lütticke v EEC Commission* [1966] CMLR 378.
10 [1971] CMLR 521 at 523.

article 95 (1) because the same treatment was applied to foreign and national breweries.[11]

However, in a case[12] involving the validity of export deposits said to be in violation of the German Constitution, the Administrative Court in Frankfurt am Main held that Community law enjoyed only a limited superiority over national law.

The Court reviewed a substantial body of juristic opinion representing inter alia the view that Community law can be scrutinized against the provisions of the Federal Constitution which the Federal legislature has no power to abrogate or restrict. The Court held that article 12 (3) of Regulation 120/67 of the EEC Council of 13 June 1967 and article 9 of Regulation 473/67 of the EEC Commission of 21 August 1967, which require export deposits, constituted an infringement of the Federal Constitution because they infringed the 'freedom of development, economic freedom and the principle of proportionality' and were, therefore, unconstitutional. The Court considered that 'these regulations are not German statutes but legal provisions of the European Economic Community which constitute neither public international law nor national law of the Member States' and concluded that like statutes (*Gesetze*) operating in Germany they are subject to scrutiny against the fundamental principles of the Constitution. However it referred the matter for a preliminary ruling to the Community Court which rejected its argument holding that:[13]

'The validity of acts of the Community institutions may be assessed only by reference to Community law since national legal provisions ... cannot have priority over the law created by the Treaty ... unless its character as Community law is to be denied and the legal basis of the Community itself questioned. The validity of a Community act and its applicability to a Member State cannot therefore be affected by the claim that fundamental rights ... or the principles of its constitution have been infringed ...'

The Administrative Court, not satisfied with the ruling, submitted the case to the Federal Constitutional Court[14] which considered that the contested ruling on deposits did not offend the fundamental rights guaranteed by the German Constitution but affirmed its determination to scrutinize the secondary Community law in the light of the *Grundgesetz*. It also expressed the hope that complete integration of the Community and the development of a

11 *Re Taxation of Imported Beer* [1988] 1 CMLR 482.
12 *Internationale Handelsgesellschaft mbH v Einfuhr- und Vorratsstelle für Getreide und Futtermittel* [1970] CMLR 294.
13 Wording taken from a Note to European Parliament, PE 37.907 (Directorate for Research and Documentation) p 5. Also see [1972] CMLR 255.
14 [1972] CMLR 177.

Community Parliament should bring about a Community Charter of Fundamental Rights. Until this has occurred conflicts between Community law and German Fundamental Rights are not excluded and in such conflicts the German law may claim priority.[15]

The many references to the ECJ noted in the preceding pages demonstrate a liberal application of article 177 by the German courts. However the cases to be especially noted are those involving constitutional issues. Another interesting feature of the German case law is the willingness to acknowledge the persuasive authority of the judgments of the European Court.

Recognizing the implications of the European Convention on Human Rights and the strength of the Community case law in this field the Federal Constitutional Court has dropped its reservations about the ECJ handling of German human rights cases. It also acknowledged the supremacy of Community law in this delicate area as well as the *erga omnes* effect of the ECJ's rulings under article 177.[16] Thus the ghost of the *Handelsgesellschaft* case has been finally laid to rest. Thus the Supreme Federal Administrative Court[17] citing several EEC precedents, saw no contravention of the constitutional guarantee of property rights in the refusal of the National Agricultural Intervention Agency to buy agricultural produce under the CAP system. It also ruled that a retrospective national regulation issued by virtue of a Commission direction restricting subsidies in respect of home-produced wheat was not unconstitutional since the German Constitution does not prohibit legislation having a retrospective effect.

The same court held that a time-barred[18] action could not be revived after the ruling of the ECJ in favour of the appellant.[19] Thus an applicant, who waited until the ECJ had decided in his favour, was unable to obtain reimbursement of illegally levied phythosanitary inspection fees on apples imported from France. The national limitation statute was applied.

The Verwaltungsgericht in Frankfurt am Main,[20] interpreting the CAP rules regarding milk quotas, awarded damages to a former tenant farmer on the ground of maladministration. On surrendering his quota the applicant applied for milk cessation payments but these were refused. No landowner's permission was

15 Note to European Parliament, PE 37.907, p 7. Also see [1974] 2 CMLR 540.
16 *Re the Application of Wünsche* [1987] 3 CMLR 225. Cf *Steinike* case p 334, note 7 supra and p 395, note 6 infra.
17 *Re Intervention Buying* [1978] 2 CMLR 644.
18 Case 71/74: *Rewe-Zentralfinanz v Landeswirtschaftskammer für das Saarland* [1978] 2 CMLR 594.
19 In Case 33/76: *Rewe-Zentralfinanz RG and Rewe Zentral AG v Landswirtschaftskammer für das Saarland* [1970] ECR 1989, [1977] 1 CMLR 533.
20 *Re the Kuchenhof Farm* [1990] 2 CMLR 289.

required and the fact that the reversioner could not claim the quota was irrelevant. Since the tenancy ended before the surrender of the quota and the authorities have not accepted the surrender in time the applicant was a victim of maladministration and, therefore, was entitled to compensation to the extent of the cessation payments which, otherwise, would have been due to him.

The Federal Supreme Court[1] expressly recognized the persuasive authority of a Community precedent[2] in so far as the existence of such a precedent absolved the Supreme Court from the obligation of making a reference under article 177.

The Federal Supreme Court also considered 'reverse discrimination' in relation to the right of establishment of a lawyer to be quite in order since, in this context, inequality of treatment was neither unconstitutional nor prevented by Community law. Citing the *CILFIT* case it refused to make a reference to the ECJ on the basis of *acte clair*.[3] In another case,[4] concerning the position of an East German lawyer, it ruled that the matter was purely internal, ie his right to practise in West Germany was subject to German law rather than Community law since the German Democratic Republic was not part of the Community and, therefore, he could not claim the right of a Community citizen. Therefore the Community rules on establishment did not apply, nor did the Protocol on internal German trade since the latter was concerned solely with the movement of goods.

Ruling in the matter of direct elections to the European Parliament the Federal Constitutional[5] Court held that the European Parliament had functions similar to national parliaments. In European elections the principles of the German electoral law were applicable.

The same court, upholding, no doubt, the principle of the separation of functions between the Community institutions and the national institutions, ruled that the validity of Community legislation applicable in the Member States cannot be reviewed by German courts.[6]

Decisions of inferior courts are also reflective of the general

---

1 *Terrapin (Overseas) Ltd v Terranova Industrie CA Kapferer & Co* [1978] 3 CMLR 102. See also *Re Skimmed Milk Powder for Animal Feed* [1988] 1 CMLR 265 and *Re the 'KLINT' (Trade Marks)* [1988] 1 CMLR 340.
2 Case 119/75: *Terrapin (Overseas) Ltd v Terranova Industrie CA Kapferer & Co* [1976] ECR 1039, [1976] CMLR 482.
3 *Re a German Advocate* [1990] 1 CMLR 254; Case 283/81: *CILFIT v Ministry of Health* [1982] ECR 3415, [1983] 1 CMLR 472.
4 *Re an East German Lawyer* [1990] 2 CMLR 185.
5 *Re the European Elections Act* [1980] 1 CMLR 497.
6 *Firma Steinike und Weinlig v Bundesamt für Ernährung und Forstwirtschaft* [1980] 2 CMLR 531.

mood of compliance. The Kammergericht[7] of Berlin confirmed that Community law prevails in the field of competition where a breach of the national law is justified by a decision of the Commission made by virtue of a binding Council regulation. In such a case the trader is protected even though he is not a direct addressee of the decision in question. If in such a case an interlocutory injunction is called for a reference to the ECJ is either unnecessary or inappropriate.

A Provincial Court of Appeal in Hamburg[8] granted an injunction to a German patent holder to enable him to restrain the importation of a product from an American licensee of an American patent. The product was imported into Belgium where no parallel patent existed and thence to Germany where, however, a parallel patent did exist. There was thus no exhaustion of the patent right and the German patent holder was able to protect his rights.

Also in the field of intellectual property the Hanseatische Oberlandesgericht,[9] dealing with a trade mark, simply followed the Coffee HAG saga[10] and applied a Community precedent,[11] declining to refer the matter to ECJ in accordance with the *acte clair* principle. Thus the German HAG was able to resist the importation into Germany of the Belgian HAG coffee since, following the break in the chain of ownership of the mark through post-war expropriation, the principle of exhaustion governed the issue. Reference to ECJ was refused.

The Court of Appeal in Hamburg,[12] banning the advertising of a Dutch product in Germany, acted in conformity with German law on misleading advertising which it considered, in turn, conforming to the relevant Community directive. The ensuing restriction was held justified on health grounds by virtue of article 36 of the EEC Treaty since attributing health properties to foodstuffs was considered misleading. No reference to ECJ.

Similarly the Court of Appeal in Cologne[13] issued, on the ground of consumer protection, an injunction against the use of German language on labels which concealed the Dutch origin of the product. The injunction did not restrict imports but merely the type of get-up which was considered misleading. No reference to the ECJ was made, judging that no breach of article 30 or 36 was involved.

7   *Verband Sozialer Wettbewerb eV v F Berlin KG* [1987] 3 CMLR 418.
8   *Re Patented Bandaging Material* [1988] 2 CMLR 359.
9   *Re HAG Coffee* [1989] 3 CMLR 154.
10 Case 192/73: *Van Zuylen Frerès v HAG AG* [1974] ECR 731; [1974] 2 CMLR 127.
11 Case 19/84 *Pharmon BV v Hoechst AG* [1985] 3 CMLR 775.
12 *Re Advertising of Dutch Slimming Tea* [1989] 3 CMLR 373.
13 *Re Labelling of Dutch Poultry* [1990] 2 CMLR 104.

One can also cite an example of non-conformity. We have noted earlier the problem of direct applicability of the VAT directive 77/388 which was considered by the Bundesfinanzhof[14] to be of no direct effect but orthodoxy seemed to have been restored when in the *Becker*[15] case the ECJ, on reference from a lower finance court, ruled that direct effect of directives was in appropriate conditions a well-established case law. However the controversy flared up again. In a similar case[16] a lower finance court asked whether the same directive was applicable prior to the time relevant in the *Becker* case to which the ECJ gave an affirmative answer. The referring court duly proceeded to confirm the claimant's exemption from the VAT[17] but the tax office appealed and the Bundesfinanzhof[18] annulled the decision of the finance court. In both cases the Bundesfinanzhof held the directive inapplicable on the ground that it had not been implemented by legislation. Elaborating its judgment in the latter case the Bundesfinanzhof questioned whether the referring court examined correctly the constitutional position, ie whether a sufficient degree of sovereignty was delegated by article 24 of the Constitution to the Community in this respect. It then proceeded to interpret article 189 (3) of the EEC Treaty concluding that, whilst the ECJ had competence to interpret the Community law, it had no competence to interpret its effects in the national systems. Thus the Bundesfinanzhof deviated from the German line of authorities including the decision of the Federal Constitutional Court[19] relevant in this area. This baffling controversy came before the Federal Constitutional Court[20] which decreed that the Bundesfinanzhof was wrong in denying the direct effect of the directive since such a power is vested in the ECJ only. In doubt the national court has to ask the ECJ for a preliminary ruling. However, the rulings of the ECJ are binding upon the German courts and the national law implementing Community

14 Case VB 51/80, 16 July 1981, *Re VAT Directives* [1982] 1 CMLR 527.
15 Case 8/81: *Becker v Finanzamt Münster-Innenstadt* [1982] ECR 53, [1982] 1 CMLR 499 at paras 21–25; see also Case 255/81: *Grendel GmbH v Finanzamt für Körperschaften, Hamburg* [1982] ECR 2301, [1983] 1 CMLR 379.
16 Case 70/83: *Kloppenberg v Finanzamt Leer* [1984] ECR 1075, [1985] 1 CMLR 205.
17 Niedersächsisches Finanzgericht, judgment of 11 May 1984, RIW 85, 234.
18 Judgment of 25 April 1985, EuR 1985, p 191.
19 *Re Lütticke*, BVerfGE 31, 145; 9 June 1971; AWD 1971, pp 418–420; Europarecht, 1972, p 51.
20 For the reaction of German writers see: Schmidt, G, 'Die Durchführung des Europäischen Gemeinschaftsrechts in ther BRD und anderen EG-Mitgliedstaaten', 4/84, *Integration*, pp 205 et seq; Scheuing, D H, 'Rechts-probleme bei der Durchsetzung des Gemeinschaftsrechts in der Bundesrepublik Deutschland', EuR 1985, pp 229 et seq; Tomuschat, C, 'Nein, und abermals nein!' Zum Urteil des BFH vom 25 April 1985', EuR 1985, pp 346 et seq.

directives has to be interpreted in accordance wtih ECJ's interpretation of the directives. The principle of supremacy of Community law applies here. Recognizing the binding force of Community precedents the Bundesfinanzhof paid a compliment to the ECJ for being in tune with the common European traditions and using the case law method in developing the Community law in conformity with practice in the common law and the civil law systems.[1]

The saga ends with the statement of the Bundesfinanzhof that, irrespective of the rulings of the ECJ, the VAT directive applies notwithstanding the lack of its implementation in Germany.[2]

In a case involving the refusal of the Supreme Federal Court to make a reference to the ECJ the Federal Constitutional Court dismissed the complaint for a constitutional review. It recognized the status of the ECJ as a 'statutory court' under the German Constitution. Therefore an arbitrary refusal to make a reference under article 177 (3) of the EEC Treaty would amount to a breach of article 101 (1) of the German Constitution. However the Federal Constitutional Court is not competent to review errors though a deliberate failure to make a reference would amount to an error and would expose the German Republic to an enforcement action at the hands of the European Commission. Since in the case under review there was no arbitrary refusal to proceed with the action, the refusal to refer was not arbitrary.[3] The litigation arose from the importation into Germany of feeding stuffs from the Netherlands which contained additives patented in Germany, though not in the Netherlands which was, apparently, deliberate. The court below found for the German patentee and the Supreme Court refused to take the appeal or to refer the matter to the ECJ. It was within its power to do so and in the eyes of the Constitutional Court there was no breach of the Constitution.

In a rather intriguing case the Federal Constitutional Court declared German tobacco companies to have no *locus standi* in their attempt to obtain a judicial review of the constitutionality of the voting of the German Minister in the Council of Ministers.[4] Leading to an injunction to muzzle him they wished to influence his decision in the adoption of the common position on the draft directive on the labelling of cigarettes which carried a health warning. They argued, albeit unsuccesfully, that the directive, if adopted, would be in conflict with fundamental rights guaranteed by the German constitution, i.e. the freedom of expression, commerce and property rights.

1 In *Re Application of Frau Kloppenburg* [1988] 3 CMLR 1.
2 *Kloppenburg v Finanzamt Leer* [1989] 1 CMLR 873.
3 *Re Patented Feedingstuffs* [1989] 2 CMLR 902.
4 *Bayerische Staatsregierung v Bundesregierung* [1990] 1 CMLR 649.

Italy

In Italy's practice, the dualist doctrine, represented by Judge Anzi-lotti,[5] has left a deep imprint on the relationship between Community law and Italian law. The dualist tradition coupled with a rigid Constitution put the Italian judge in a position which is more difficult than that of the judge in any other country of the EEC. The relevant provisions of the Constitution (articles 10 and 11) state that the Italian legal order conforms to the generally recognized rules of International Law and that Italy will agree, on equal terms with other states, to the limitation of sovereignty necessary to establish a lasting peace and justice among nations. This is hardly conducive to the courts being Community-minded when confronted with the compelling challenge to obey the Constitution.

Italy's problem is well reflected in the *Costa v ENEL* case which, parallel to its career in the Community, had a full run at home. The Constitutional Court, as we have seen, was called upon to decide whether or not the decree nationalizing the electricity industry and establishing a monopoly in the shape of the ENEL as well as certain provisions of the EEC Treaty were contrary to the Constitution. According to the Constitution, the constitutional court has the power to review legislation and declare 'illegitimate' Acts of Parliament and subordinate legislation which do not conform to the Constitution (article 136 (1)). Community law was brought into the contest as it was alleged that articles 37 (2), 53, 93 (2) and 102 of the EEC Treaty, which were relevant to this case, infringed article 11 of the Constitution. In terms of the conflict of legislations, the nationalization decree of 1962 was said to have repealed an earlier (Community) law.

The Court dealt with the problem in a classic dualist fashion: infringement of the Treaty would entail international responsibility of the State of Italy, but would not necessarily affect the validity of the law enacted in contravention of treaty. In this way, the Court, in accordance with the dualist doctrine, accorded to the Treaty no higher rank than that of the ordinary legislation. The problem was reduced to a conflict between two 'internal' laws where the principle *lex posterior derogat priori* should apply. It appears that the position would have been different[6] if the Treaty had been promulgated as a *constitutional law* in accordance with article 138 of the Constitution in which case the nationalization decree would have to be tested in the light of the Treaty. However, article 11 of the Constitution enabled the State of Italy to surrender

---

5 Anzilotti, D, *Corso di Diritto Internazionale*, Vol 1 (3rd edn 1928), pp 51 et seq.

6 Neri, S, 'Le juge italien et le droit communautaire', *Le juge national et le droit communautaire* (1966), p 81.

by treaty some of its sovereign powers to an international institution and this indeed occurred when the EEC Treaty was ratified. The Court recognized this, but concluded that it did not have to discuss the nature of the EEC or the consequences of the ratification of the Treaty, or, indeed, decide whether or not the decree infringed the Treaty.[7]

The decision of the Constitutional Court stimulated the jurists and the lively discussions which followed produced a trend in favour of the supremacy of Community law which was in conflict with Italian law. This has been deduced by Quadri[8] and others from article 10 of the Constitution. They reasoned in their dualist fashion that, transformed into Italian law, a rule of international law is binding: *pacta recepta sunt servanda.*

The second support for the doctrine of supremacy is derived from article 11 of the Constitution. The most plausible is the argument of the former judge of the Community Court, Catalano[9] who sees two effects of article 11: a permissive effect which enables the Italian State to delegate its sovereignty and a dispositive effect which limits the powers of the constitutional organs of the State. He argues further that, although the measure which, in effect, limits sovereignty may take the form of an ordinary law, it differs nevertheless from ordinary law because it has a constitutional effect. If, therefore, a treaty limits the legislative power of the Italian law-making bodies within certain areas, the legislature, acting within the scope of its authority, can no longer exercise its power in these areas.

In *Société Acciaierie San Michele v High Authority of the ECSC*[10] the Constitutional Court recognized the 'permissive' effect of article 11. In this case the appellant, a steel company, contested the constitutionality of a fine imposed by the High Authority of the ECSC for failure to produce invoices relating to the consumption of electricity by the appellant. The Court, in dismissing the appeal, held: '... in recognising the Community order the state was endeavouring not so much to insert the same in its own system, but rather to make way within such system for the international co-operation which the state has as its aim ... the organs of our internal jurisdiction are not qualified to criticise acts by organs of the ECSC because the latter are not subject to the sovereign power of the Member States of the Community, and cannot be found within the framework of any such state. Therefore, their acts can only be

---

7 24 February–7 March 1964, *Foro Italiano* (1964), I, 465.
8 Quadri, R, *Diritto Internazionale Pubblico* (1963), pp 59 et seq.
9 Catalano, N 'La position du droit communautaire dans le droit des Etats membres', *Droit communautaire et droit national* (Bruges 1965), pp 61 et seq.
10 Case 98/65: [1967] CMLR 160, 4 CML Rev 81, [1965] *I Foro Italiano* 569.

subject to a legislative qualification on the part of individual Member States albeit within the limits where there may exist an obligation not to refuse to acknowledge their effects . . .'

Recognizing the 'right of the individual to his jurisdictional protection' the Court acknowledged the power of the Community Court to exercise its jurisdiction and of the Italian subject to plead Community law where appropriate.

The principle of supremacy of Community law was thus accepted, but it fell to a body of jurists assembled in Rome in February 1966 to affirm supremacy not only in respect of previous but also in respect of subsequent Italian legislation. An important exception to the rule *lex posterior derogat priori* was conceded in favour of Community law. But, at the same time, the jurists affirmed the power of the Italian judiciary, especially the Constitutional Court, to scrutinize Community acts and determine whether or not they conform to the Italian Constitution[11].

Developments in the post- *San Michele* period testify to general compliance with the principle. In *Salgoil SpA v Ministry for Foreign Trade*[12] the Rome Court of Appeal, following the ruling of the Community Court in the same case,[13] held that article 31 of the EEC Treaty gave rise to individual rights which can be enforced by national courts, though such rights have to be regarded as rights within the national system of law. The Italian attitude is conveniently summarized in *Frontini v Ministero delle Finanze.*[14] On a reference from the *Tribunale* of Turin the *Corte Costituzionale* confirmed the constitutionality of the Italian EEC Treaty Ratification Act and upheld the supremacy of Community regulations. By the same token the supremacy of the EEC Treaty itself was implicitly recognized. The *Corte Costituzionale* made a significant reservation in connection with human rights. It recognized that the European Court was the guarantor of the rights and interests of individuals in fields of law concerned with economic relations. But, if ever the legislative power of the EEC were to be used to violate the fundamental principles of the Italian Constitution or the inalienable rights of man, then the *Corte Costituzionale* would reserve the right to control the continuing compatibility of the EEC Treaty with such principles and rights.[15]

11 French text of the Jurists' Resolution, Neri, S, 'Le droit communautaire et l'ordre constitutionnel italien' (1966), CDE 363 at 376, 377.
12 [1970] CMLR 314 at 335–336.
13 Case 13/68 [1968] ECR 453 at 462, 463, [1969] CMLR 181 at 196.
14 [1974] 2 CMLR 372. Cf the attitude of the German Constitutional Court discussed above.
15 Cf German Federal Constitutional Court in the *Handelsgesellschaft* case [1974] 2 CMLR 551–552, supra.

The question whether all Italian courts have to refuse to apply national law when inconsistent with Community law or whether this is a matter reserved exclusively for the Constitutional Court (left open in the *Frontini* case) was considered in the ICIC case.[16] Whilst the Italian and the Community texts concerning the application of the import licensing system for cereals were identical there was the technical question whether the Italian text, being the *lex posterior* to the relevant Community regulation, was the governing text to be applied by the courts. There was also a problem of divergent interpretation as between the ECJ and Italian courts. The *Corte Costituzionale* declared the national text unconstitutional saying that: 'There was no reason ... to reproduce the regulations ... in national laws. The adoption of the corresponding Italian law violates the principles of ... the Treaty, whose constitutionality has been accepted ...'. However on the practical point of direct application of the Community law the Court held that: 'the existing legal order does not attribute to the Italian judge any power to refuse the application of subsequent internal rules ... on the ground of the general priority of Community law over national law. ... Therefore the judge is bound to raise the question of the constitutionality of legislative rules which reproduce directly applicable Community regulations and transform them into internal law. ...'

This attitude was in strong terms condemned unequivocally by the Community Court in the *Simmenthal (No 2)* case[17] where it held that:

'... every national court must ... apply Community law in its entirety and protect rights which the latter confers on individuals and must accordingly set aside any provision of national law which may conflict with it, whether prior or subsequent to the Community rule.

Accordingly any provision of a national legal system ... which might impair the effectiveness of Community law by withholding from the national court ... the power to do everything necessary at the moment of its application to set aside national legislative provisions which might prevent Community rules from having full force and effect are incompatible with those requirements which are the very essence of Community law ...'

16 *Industrie Chimiche della Italia v Minister of Foreign Trade*, Constitutional Court, 20, 30 October 1975, No 232 CC III, 1975, 319–327; (1976) RTDE 396–403. Quotations taken from Brinkhorst, L J, and Schermers, H G, *Judicial Remedies in the European Communities* (2nd edn 1977), pp 217–220.

17 Case 106/77: *Amministrazione delle Finanze dello Stato v Simmenthal SpA* [1978] ECR 629, [1978] 3 CMLR 263 at paras 21 and 22.

In the ICIC case the *Corte Costituzionale* hinted at the need of legislation to solve the problem and this seemed to be the only way out of the impasse. However in the absence of such legislation the matter came once more before the courts[18] when an Italian importer claimed restitution of charges for sanitary inspection of poultry levied in accordance with Italian law but contrary to Community law. The question of supremacy was referred by the Milan court to the Corte Costituzionale which by then had the benefit of the ECJ's decision in the *Second Simmenthal* case. The Milan court wanted to know whether to follow the Community or the Italian case law. This was, in effect, an invitation to re-examine the latter. Since the relevant Italian statute was already abrogated the Constitutional Court held that there was no reason why this repeal should not have a retrospective effect in the light of the delegation of sovereignty to the Community by virtue of article 11 of the Constitution. It also confirmed that the relevant Community regulations had the effect of a *lex posteriori* which, in conformity with the Italian Constitution, abrogated the preceding Italian law. In this way supremacy of Community law was put into effect, albeit, in a manner inconsistent with the doctrine established by the Community Court. Thus the problem lingers on unless judges of first instance are accorded the authority of disregarding national *subsequent* law in conflict with Community law.[19]

Other Member States
We shall consider in the following chapter the attitude of the British courts to the challenge of Community law. In Denmark in an action for infringement of a trademark in which Community law was introduced at a late stage, the court decided to hear the arguments and give judgment on the points of Danish law first. Points of Community law were deferred with the possibility of reference to the Community Court.[20]

Direct applicability and supremacy of Community law was recognized by the Irish Supreme Court[1] and references for preliminary rulings, once accepted,[2] present no procedural problem.[3]

18 Case *Società Comavicola v Ministry of Finance*, Corte Costitutionale, 26 October 1981, No 176, GU 4.II.1981, No 304.
19 Menis, C, 'Traité' CEE et Ordre Juridique Italien', 2–3 (1983) CDE, p 320 at 344.
20 *EMI Records Ltd v CBS Grammofon A/S* [1975] 1 CMLR 572.
1 *Pigs and Bacon Commission v McCarren* (Irish Supreme Court), [1981] 3 CMLR 408.
2 Case 812/79: *AH-G v Burgoa* [1980] ECR 2787, [1981] 2 CMLR 193; Case 36/80: *Irish Creamery Milk Suppliers Association v Ireland* [1981] ECR 735, [1981] 2 CMLR 455.
3 *Campus Oil Ltd v Minister for Industry and Energy* (Irish Supreme Court) [1984] 1 CMLR 479.

During recent years the Irish judiciary became more involved. The High Court had several sex discrimination problems to resolve. Having to interpret a national implementing statute[4] it had to consider the relevance of work of 'less value' to 'work of equal value'; it referred the matter to the ECJ, it seems rather grudgingly. It thought in this context that Community law would be irrelevant unless there is ambiguity in the wording of the statute. The question was answered by the ECJ[5] which said, *in casu*, that a comparator's work was of less value than that of the complainant but stressed that article 119 of the Treaty applied just the same. The High Court,[6] applying the ruling it had requested, stressed the supremacy of Community law where conflict with national law has to be resolved.

Still in the field of employment the High Court considered the complaint of discrimination against married women who, on their marriage, were forced to resign from the Irish Airlines. The Court found such employment condition equivalent to sex discrimination and ruled that Directive 76/207 was applicable, the procedures and remedies available under Irish law being in tune with the directive.[7] However, the Court dismissed the complaint of discrimination against men[8] when it ruled that marriage gratuity for female bank staff (but not for men) paid on the basis of seniority not on basis of sex did not infringe the Anti-Discrimination (Pay) Act 1974 but in fact reflected accurately article 119 of the EEC Treaty and the relevant ECJ's case law.

Sex discrimination in the field of social security[9] was brought before the High Court after the EJC found[10] that there was unlawful discrimination, contrary to Directive 79/7, because married women received lesser unemployment benefit than men or single women. The complaint this time was brought on behalf of mothers of dependent children. According to Irish law such mothers were entitled to a special benefit only in the absence of a resident father. This was not a breach of Directive 79/7. A wife is automatically considered to be a dependent adult which enables the husband to claim a special benefit. A husband is not dependent unless he is physically or mentally handicapped. This is discrimination contrary to Directive 79/7. There is, however, no benefit where a

---

4 *Murphy v Bord Telecom Eireann* [1987] 1 CMLR 559.
5 Case 157/86, supra [1988] 1 CMLR 879.
6 Murphy, supra [1988] 2 CMLR 753.
7 *Aer Lingus Teoranta v Labour Court* [1989] 1 CMLR 857.
8 *Governor and Company of the Bank of Ireland v Kavanagh* [1990] 1 CMLR 87.
9 *Cotter v Minister for Social Welfare* [1990] 2 CMLR 141.
10 Case 286/85: *McDermott and Cotter v Minister for Social Welfare* [1987] ECR 1453, [1987] 2 CMLR 607.

husband is not financially dependent on his wife, but there is no remedy in such a case because, in the opinion of the Court, it would be unjust and inequitable for the taxpayer to carry the burden. The Court found Directive 79/7 directly effective in Ireland from the time it came into force, ie since December 1984, but a remedy became available only after the judgment of the ECJ in case 286/85.

Legislation implementing agricultural regulations concerning the milk[11] quota came before the High Court as a constitutional issue involving the guarantee of property rights. The Court ruled that such legislation was necessary in view of the obligations arising from the membership of the Community and, therefore, covered by the constitution. However, it would have to be applied even if contrary to the constitution. Ruling on merits the Court held that the transfer of milk quotas *pro rata* with the transfer of farmland did not constitute a retrospective abridgement of property rights and upheld the validity of the quota reduction arising from the sale of a part of the holding involved.

The High Court acknowledged the twin objective of Directive 75/268 on hill farming[12] as conservation and security of farm incomes, when considering the Irish implementing law. It ruled, however, that while means test and inclusion of a spouse's off-farm income was permissible for the calculation of the subsidy under the directive the provision regarding the inclusion of a spouse's off-farm income was contrary to the Irish constitution. As it constituted a threat to the institution of marriage the implementing legislation had to be, to that extent, declared invalid.

The High Court made a reference for a preliminary ruling[13] on the proportionality of penalty of the forfeiture of an export deposit where the exporter was unable to carry out the contract because of the theft of the product while in England en route to its continental destination. The ECJ[14] considered that the theft of the consignment from the exporter's depot was not caused by *force majeure* and that, therefore, there was no lawful excuse for saving the deposit. Since exportation was the exporter's principal obligation the forfeiture of the whole security was not disproportionate.

Concerning the Spanish crews on board Irish fishing boats in an Irish–Spanish joint venture, the High Court enquired of the ECJ whether the requirement of the Irish law that the crews must be at least 75% Irish nationals was compatible with Community law.[15]

11 *Lawlor v Minister for Agriculture* [1988] 3 CMLR 22.
12 *Greene v Minister for Agriculture* [1989] 3 CMLR 830.
13 *Anthony McNicholl Ltd v Ministry for Agricultural* [1987] 1 CMLR 847.
14 Case 296/86: *Anthony McNicholl Ltd v Ministry for Agriculture* [1988] 2 CMLR 275.
15 *Pesca Valentia Ltd v Minister for Fisheries & Forestry* [1987] 1 CMLR 856.

The ECJ,[16] surprisingly, ruled that this was not a case of discrimination contrary to article 7 of the EEC Treaty. Following this ruling the Irish High Court[17] discharged the interlocutory injunction granted on reference to the ECJ. The ruling of the ECJ is surprising as it sharply contradicts the precedent laid down in Case 167/73[18] where it held that a mere threat of discrimination contained in the maritime law which required that captains, certain officers and a proportion of the crew of French merchant vessels had to be French nationals was incompatible with Community law.

A delicate, controversial issue impinging upon the Irish constitution is at present before the Irish courts.[19] The Supreme Court had to rule on the freedom to receive services, *in casu*, abortion services lawful in the United Kingdom and available generally while the principle of the sanctity of life enshrined in the Irish constitution prohibits such services. The question was whether, in the light of Community law on the movement of persons and the freedom to provide and receive services, information about abortion services available in the United Kingdom can be legitimately prohibited. The Supreme Court answered the question in the affirmative. The matter came once more before the High Court and the Supreme Court[20] which made a reference to the ECJ refusing an appeal against the reference. Ireland is the last bastion against the rising tide of demands for abortion and the powerful industry which has been thriving on the relaxation of the moral code and on the theory which, for social convenience, denies humanity to the unborn. Unless there is a change in the Irish constitution the moral dilemma will continue and with it the question how the economic freedom of the Common Market can outweigh the traditional approach to the sanctity of human life.

Judicial practice in Greece, Portugal and Spain remains yet to be evaluated.

We can say, in the light of this review of practice in the members of the Community, that Community law is enforced as 'Community law', or the 'internal law' and that, in the case of conflict with municipal law, whether previous or subsequent, the Community rule prevails. This situation has not come about without difficulty or heart-searching as the dualist tradition entrenched in the national systems of law had to succumb to the challenge of the Community. In this process, the Community Court acted as the

---

16 Case 223/86: *Pesca Valentia Ltd v Minister for Fisheries & Forestry* [1988] 1 CMLR 888.
17 *Pesca Valentia Ltd v Minister for Fisheries & Forestry* [1990] 1 CMLR 707.
18 Case 167/73: *EC Commission v France* [1974] ECR 359; [1974] 2 CMLR 216.
19 *A-G v Open Door Counselling Ltd* [1988] 2 CMLR 443.
20 *Society for the Protection of Unborn Children (Ireland) Ltd v Grogan* [1990] 1 CMLR 689.

pacemaker and, as we have noted, some of its decisions not only settled matters for the given Member State, but also set a trend within the Community. The Community Court acted as an agent of cohesion and uniformity. However, without the stimulating contribution of jurists the message of Luxembourg would not have been as effective and successful as it was. Here the *doctrine* came into its own as a factor contributing to integration if not an auxiliary source of law. Its power and authority on the Continent should not be underestimated.

Part IV

The law of the economy

Chapter 12

Community law in the United Kingdom[1]

RATIFICATION OF THE TREATIES

By the constitutional law of the United Kingdom treaty-making power is a prerogative power vested in the Sovereign and customarily exercised on her behalf either by her Ministers or by duly authorized plenipotentiaries. Ratification is the formal act whereby the Crown confirms and finally agrees to be bound by the terms of a Treaty. Under the terms of article 2 of the First Treaty of Accession the High Contracting Parties undertook to ratify the Treaty in accordance with their respective constitutional requirements and to deposit their instruments of ratification with the Italian Government by 31 December 1972 at the latest. In the event three of the four applicant states complied with that obligation and the Treaty entered into force on 1 January 1973.[2] By the act of ratification the United Kingdom acceded to the three European Communities. Article 2 of the Act annexed to the First Treaty of Accession thus provides that 'from the date of accession, the provisions of the original Treaties [as defined in article 1] and the acts adopted by the institutions of the Communities shall be binding on the new Member States and shall apply in those States under the conditions laid down in those Treaties and in this Act'.

In the United Kingdom, the Courts, and for that matter Parliament, have no role to play in the negotiation and ratification of treaties. In a case concerning a treaty of 1842 between the Crown and the Emperor of China Lord Coleridge CJ stated that the Queen had 'acted throughout the making of the treaty and in relation to each and every of its stipulations in her sovereign character, and by her own inherent authority; and, as in making the treaty, so in performing the treaty, she is beyond the control of municipal law and her acts are not to be examined in her own Courts.'[3] Thus

---

1 For a more detailed treatment of this topic, see Collins, L, *European Community Law in the United Kingdom* (4th edn, 1990).
2 As a result of Norway's decision not to ratify, the Council used its authority under the Treaty of Accession, art 2, para 3 to make the necessary adjustments; see Adaptation Decision of 1 January 1973, OJ 1973, L2.
3 *Rustomjee v R* (1876) 2 QBD 69, at 74.

when in 1971 a Mr Blackburn applied for declarations to the effect
that by signing the Treaty of Rome Her Majesty's Government
would be irrevocably surrendering part of the sovereignty of the
Queen in Parliament and by so doing would be acting contrary to
law his statements of claim were struck out as disclosing no reasonable causes of action. The Court of Appeal unanimously upheld
Eveleigh J's dismissal of the plaintiff's appeal against the Master's
order. The court applied the dicta of Lord Coleridge CJ cited
above. In the words of Lord Denning: 'The treaty-making power
of this country rests not in the courts, but in the Crown; that is,
Her Majesty acting upon the advice of her Ministers. When her
Ministers negotiate and sign a treaty, even a treaty of such paramount importance as this proposed one, they act on behalf of the
country as a whole. They exercise the prerogative of the Crown.
Their action in so doing cannot be challenged or questioned in
these courts.'[4]

INCORPORATION OF THE TREATIES INTO THE LAW OF THE
UNITED KINGDOM

Although, at least since the time of Blackstone, the customary rules
of International Law have been regarded as part and parcel of the
common law and directly enforceable by English judges, the United
Kingdom adopts a distinctly dualist approach to treaties. A treaty
to which the United Kingdom is a party is, as we have seen, the
result of an exercise of the prerogative and as such is not self-
executing in the sense that the provisions of such a treaty do not
automatically have the force of law in the United Kingdom. The
intervention of Parliament is necessary in order to enable the provisions of such a treaty to be enforced in British courts. The classic
statement of this doctrine is contained in an Opinion of the Judicial
Committee of the Privy Council in 1937:

> 'It will be essential to keep in mind the distinction between (1) the
> formation, and (2) the performance, of the obligations constituted by a
> treaty, using that word as comprising any agreement between two or
> more sovereign States. Within the British Empire there is a well estab-
> lished rule that the making of a treaty is an executive act, while the
> performance of its obligations, if they entail alteration of the existing
> domestic law, requires legislative action. Unlike some other countries,
> the stipulations of a treaty duly ratified do not within the Empire, by
> virtue of the treaty alone, have the force of law. If the national executive,
> the government of the day, decide to incur the obligations of a treaty
> which involve alteration of law they have to run the risk of obtaining

4 *Blackburn v A-G* [1971] 1 WLR 1037 at 1040; Salmon and Stamp LJJ to the
same effect at 1041.

the assent of Parliament to the necessary statute or statutes. To make themselves as secure as possible they will often in such cases before final ratification seek to obtain from Parliament an expression of approval. But it has never been suggested, and it is not the law, that such an expression of approval operates as law, or that in law it precludes the assenting Parliament, or any subsequent Parliament, from refusing to give its sanction to any legislative proposals that may subsequently be brought before it. Parliament, no doubt ... has a constitutional control over the executive: but it cannot be disputed that the creation of the obligations undertaken in treaties and the assent to their form and quality are the function of the executive alone. Once they are created, while they bind the State as against the other contracting parties, Parliament may refuse to perform them and so leave the State in default. In a unitary State whose Legislature possesses unlimited powers the problem is simple. Parliament will either fulfil or not treaty obligations imposed upon the State by its executive. The nature of the obligations does not affect the complete authority of the Legislature to make them law if it so chooses.'[5]

This doctrine applies equally to the Community Treaties so that the mere accession of the United Kingdom to those Treaties did not give them the force of law within the United Kingdom. Legislation was necessary to achieve that result and in the absence of such legislation, as the Court of Appeal has pointed out, the Community Treaties would fall outside the cognizance of British Courts.[6] Thus one of the aims of the European Communities Act 1972 is to give the force of law to those provisions of the Treaties which are intended to take direct effect within the Member States. Section 2 (1) of the Act provides that:

'All such rights, powers, liabilities, obligations and restrictions from time to time created or arising by or under the Treaties, and all such remedies and procedures from time to time provided for by or under the Treaties, as in accordance with the Treaties are without further enactment to be given legal effect or used in the United Kingdom shall be recognised and available in law, and be enforced, allowed and followed accordingly; and the expression "enforceable Community right" and similar expressions shall be read as referring to one to which this subsection applies.'

5 *A-G for Canada v A-G of Ontario* [1937] AC 326 at 347, 348, per Lord Atkin. A similar statement was made in *Legal and Constitutional Implications of United Kingdom Membership of the European Communities* (1967) (Cmnd. 3301), at para 22. Section 6 of the European Parliamentary Elections Act 1978 has introduced a constitutional innovation in that British ratification of any treaty which increases the powers of the European Parliament is subject to the prior approval of the United Kingdom Parliament. For an instance of recourse to that provision see s 3 (4) of the European Communities (Amendment) Act 1986.
6 *McWhirter v A-G* [1972] CMLR 882 at 886, per Lord Denning MR and at 887 Phillimore LJ.

Therefore, what the Act terms 'enforceable Community rights' are to be given direct effect in the United Kingdom. This provision is strengthened by section 3 (2) which provides inter alia that United Kingdom courts shall take judicial notice of Community Treaties, which term is defined by section 1.

IMPLEMENTATION OF COMMUNITY SECONDARY LEGISLATION IN THE UNITED KINGDOM

It has already been pointed out in earlier chapters that Community secondary legislation falls into two categories: that which is and that which is not directly applicable in the Member States. As far as the former is concerned, viz. decisions in the ECSC and regulations in the EEC and Euratom, whilst within the Community legal system they will be binding on the United Kingdom as soon as they are made, they need statutory authority to give them the force of law within the United Kingdom, just as in the case of the provisions of the Treaties themselves. Section 2 (1) of the European Communities Act applies to them also and without further enactment they are to be given legal effect within our domestic legal systems. Thus the entire body of ECSC decisions and EEC and Euratom regulations in force at the commencement of British membership automatically became part of the law of the United Kingdom on 1 January 1973. Similarly all such decisions and regulations made after the commencement of British membership will also automatically become part of the law of the United Kingdom as soon as they are made. In addition those provisions of Community secondary legislation which have direct effect in the legal systems of the Member States constitute 'enforceable Community rights' under section 2 (1) of the European Communities Act and as such are enforceable in the courts of the United Kingdom.

An important issue in connection with directly applicable Community secondary legislation made after British entry is the role of the United Kingdom Parliament. Whilst the actual making of such secondary legislation will be in the hands of the Council or Commission and outside the direct control of Parliament, in the absence of effective democratic control within the Communities themselves it is vital that Parliament should have an opportunity to consider such legislation. By the time, say, an EEC regulation has been made it will be too late for comment for such a regulation will already be part of United Kingdom law. In order to enable Parliament to examine and comment upon proposed Community legislation and thus express views for the guidance of the British representatives on the Council of the Communities, each House has established a select committee to scrutinize Community secondary legislation: the House of Commons Committee on European Secondary Legislation and the House of Lords Committee on the European Communities. Both Committees are concerned with draft Community legislation which has been proposed by the Commission to the Council, but there are differences in approach and in terms of reference. The reports of the Commons Committee express opinions whether the proposed legislation raises questions of legal or political importance and how it may affect matters of principle or policy. The Lords Committee, which is organized into specialist sub-committees, not only reports on matters of policy and principle but also on the merits of the proposed legislation. The Committees are able to confer together. Each is assisted by a legal adviser. Debates are held in each House on the recommendation of its Committee. The procedure is a useful one but there are practical difficulties of timing and of a congested Parliamentary timetable.[7]

In the case of Community secondary legislation which is not directly applicable, such as ECSC recommendations and EEC and Euratom directives, but leaves the choice of the means of their implementation to the individual Member States,[8] there are two possible courses of action. Such Community legislation could be implemented in the United Kingdom either by statute or by subordinate legislation. Whilst the European Communities Act does not expressly rule out the use of statutes for such purposes its emphasis is on the use of delegated legislation. Thus section 2 (2) of the Act confers extensive authority upon Her Majesty in Council and upon Ministers and Government Departments to make subordinate legislation:

'(*a*) for the purpose of implementing any Community obligation of the United Kingdom, or enabling any such obligation to be implemented, or of enabling any rights enjoyed or to be enjoyed by the United Kingdom under or by virtue of the Treaties to be exercised; or

(*b*) for the purpose of dealing with matters arising out of or related to any such obligation or rights or the coming into force, or the operation from time to time, of subsection (1) above.'

7 See Erskine May's *Parliamentary Practice* (19th edn, 1976), at pp 669, 671. For an account of the work of the Scrutiny Committees, see Bates T St JN, 'The Scrutiny of European Secondary Legislation at Westminster' (1975–76), 1 *European Law Review*, p 195 and Fraser, Lord, 'Scrutiny of Community legislation in the UK Parliament', in Bates, St J (ed) *In Memoriam J D B Mitchell* (1983) at 29. The reports of the House of Lords Committee are particularly valuable sources of information and comment on Community affairs.
8 See Chapter 4, supra.

The wide extent of these delegated law-making powers is confirmed by section 2 (3) which lays down that a provision made under sub-section (2) includes 'any such provision (of any such extent) as might be made by Act of Parliament'. In other words the subordinate legislation made under section 2 (2) to implement Community obligations can be used to repeal or amend any past or future Act of Parliament the provisions of which are incompatible with Community law.

But these powers of making subordinate legislation are not entirely without limitation and are subject to Schedule 2 to the Act. That Schedule provides that the powers conferred by section 2 (2) shall not include the power:

'(*a*) to make any provision imposing or increasing taxation; or
 (*b*) to make any provision taking effect from a date earlier than that of the making of the instrument containing the provision; or
 (*c*) to confer any power to legislate by means of orders, rules, regulations or other subordinate instrument, other than rules of procedure for any court or tribunal; or
 (*d*) to create any new criminal offence punishable with imprisonment for more than two years or punishable on summary conviction with imprisonment for more than three months or with a fine of more than level 5 on the standard scale (if not calculated on a daily basis) or with a fine of more than £100 a day.'

These limitations are also given a measure of entrenchment since section 2 (4) states that they shall remain in force unless and until amended or repealed by a subsequent statute. As far as the form and procedure of such subordinate legislation is concerned Schedule 2 states that the power to make regulations shall be exercisable by statutory instrument and that wherever the power is exercised without a draft having been approved by resolution of each House of Parliament, then it shall be subject to annulment in pursuance of a resolution of either House.[9] This gives the Government a choice as to the procedure to be adopted and that choice will no doubt be exercised in the light of the subject matter of the legislation.[10]

Thus under the provisions of section 2 of the Act ample provision appears to have been made for the implementation of Community secondary legislation in the United Kingdom subject to the important constitutional safeguards in Schedule 2. Community law is having an immediate and a continuing impact on the law of the United Kingdom and whilst that impact should not be under-

9 Statutory Instruments made to implement Community obligations are conveniently reproduced in Sweet & Maxwell's *Encyclopedia of European Community Law*, Vols AI and II, Part A3.
10 Sch 2, para 2.

estimated it also should not be exaggerated. In the words of the White Paper reporting on the negotiations 'the English and Scottish legal systems will remain intact. Certain provisions of the treaties and instruments made under them, concerned with economic, commercial and closely related matters, will be included in our law. The common law will remain the basis of our legal system and our courts will continue to operate as they do at present ... All the essential features of our law will remain, including the safeguards for individual freedom such as trial by jury and habeas corpus and the principle that a man is innocent until proved guilty as well as the law of contract and tort (and its Scottish equivalent), the law of landlord and tenant, family law, nationality law[11] and land law.'[12]

ENFORCEMENT THROUGH THE COMMUNITY COURT

The enforcement of Community law through the agency of the European Court is achieved by direct and indirect means. The direct means takes the form of actions against Member States who fail to fulfil their obligations under the Treaties.[13] By means of such actions the Court can directly influence the enforcement of Community law in the national legal orders of the Member States. Thus if the United Kingdom either legislates contrary to Community law or fails to legislate as required by Community law that would amount to a failure to fulfil Treaty obligations and the Commission or another Member State would be able to bring proceedings against the United Kingdom in the European Court.[14] If judgment were given against the United Kingdom there would arise an obligation to take steps necessary to comply with the judgment.[15] Actions have been brought against the United Kingdom both by the Commission under the terms of article 169 of the EEC Treaty and by a fellow Member State under the terms of article 170. Two cases decided in 1979 will serve as illustrations.

The first case concerned potatoes,[16] which are included among the agricultural products which come within the Common Agricultural Policy of the Community. The United Kingdom operated a system for regulating the market in potatoes which included controls on their import and export. In December 1977 the United

11 But on the question of immigration, see Vaughan, D, (ed) *Law of the European Communities* (1986), vol 2, para 15.09.
12 *The United Kingdom and the European Communities* (Cmnd 4715), para 31.
13 See Chapter 9, supra.
14 Eg under the terms of EEC Treaty, arts 169, 170.
15 Eg by virtue of EEC Treaty, art 171.
16 Case 231/78: *EC Commission v United Kingdom* [1979] ECR 1447, [1979] 2 CMLR 427.

Kingdom Government imposed a ban on the import of potatoes until further notice. In the view of the Commission such a ban was contrary to the United Kingdom's obligations under the EEC Treaty. An article 169 action resulted in which the Court gave judgment against the United Kingdom. It held that the import ban was contrary to the Community's freedom of movement of goods between the Member States.[17] The second case concerned measures to conserve fisheries.[18] The Community has authority over all questions relating to the protection of fishing grounds and the conservation of the resources of the sea. In pursuance of that authority the Community resolved that the Member States should not take any unilateral conservation measures without first consulting and seeking the approval of the Commission. In April 1977 the United Kingdom Government, without referring to the Commission, made an order prohibiting the use in British waters of certain small mesh nets. The master of a French trawler was subsequently fined for infringing that order. France (supported by the Commission) complained that this United Kingdom order did not comply with Community policy. In the resulting article 170 action the Court gave judgment against the United Kingdom because of the failure to consult and seek the approval of the Commission.

The European Court also influences the enforcement of Community law indirectly by means of its competence to give preliminary rulings on points of Community law at the request of national courts and tribunals. The provisions of the Treaties which give the right, and in some cases impose the duty, to request preliminary rulings became part of the laws of the United Kingdom by virtue of section 2 (1) of the European Communities Act 1972 which specifically refers to 'remedies and procedures' provided for, by or under the Treaties. This right/duty applies not only to the ordinary courts, from lay magistrates up to the House of Lords, but also to tribunals. Thus all courts and tribunals in the United Kingdom have been able to request preliminary rulings in appropriate cases since 1 January 1973 when the European Communities Act came into force. The unfamiliarity of such a procedure in the United Kingdom prompted the drawing up of special rules of procedure for some, but not all, courts. As far as the English courts

---

17 In particular art 30 of the EEC Treaty which prohibits quantitative restrictions on imports between Member States. For further examples of art 169 actions against the United Kingdom see Cases 128/78: [1979] ECR 419, [1979] 2 CMLR 45; 170/78: [1980] ECR 417, [1980] 3 CMLR 716 and 32/79: [1980] ECR 2403. Also see Collins, L, op cit, at pp 218–219.

18 Case 141/78: *France v United Kingdom* [1979] ECR 2923, [1980] 1 CMLR 6.

are concerned[19] rules have been made for the High Court and Court of Appeal, Civil Division;[20] the Court of Appeal, Criminal Division;[1] the County Court;[2] and the Crown Court.[3] No changes have been made to the Judicial Standing Orders of the House of Lords and it is believed that when requesting preliminary rulings the House makes use of the procedure adopted by the Supreme Court.[4] The rules of magistrates' courts have not been changed, but the attention of magistrates' clerks has been drawn to the possibility of seeking a preliminary ruling by a Home Office Circular.[5] In connection with tribunals, consultation with the responsible government departments led to the conclusion that adequate procedural machinery exists to deal with references to the European Court.[6]

The Rules which have been made for English courts all follow a particular pattern. Orders referring questions to the European Court may be made before, or at any stage during, the trial or hearing of a cause or matter. Such Orders shall be made by the Court requesting the preliminary ruling and shall normally have the effect of staying proceedings pending the ruling. In all cases the transmission of an Order requesting a preliminary ruling to the Registrar of the European Court is undertaken by the Senior Master of the Supreme Court (Queen's Bench Division). Where such an Order is open to appeal the Senior Master must not forward it to the European Court until the time for appealing has expired, or, if an appeal is brought, until the appeal has been settled. It has been argued by some commentators that both the use of the Senior Master as an intermediary between English courts and tribunals and the European Court, and making Orders requesting a preliminary ruling subject to appeal are incompatible with Community law.[7] As far as the transmission of the request for a preliminary

---

19 For Scottish Courts, see SI 1972 No 1981, and SI 1973 Nos 450 and 543. For Northern Irish Courts, see SR & O 1972, Nos 317, 354 and 380.

20 Rules for the Supreme Court (Amendment No 3) 1972 (SI 1972 No 1898 L27) which added Order 114 to the Rules of the Supreme Court.

 1 Criminal Appeal (References to the European Court) Rules 1972 (SI 1972 No 1786 (L25)).

 2 The County Court (Amendment No 2) Rules 1973 (SI 1973 No 847 (L13)).

 3 Crown Court (References to the European Court) Rules 1972 (SI 1972 No 1787 (L26)).

 4 This statement is based on information kindly supplied by the Judicial Office of the House of Lords.

 5 Circular No 149/1973 (CS 18/1973), dated 4 September 1973.

 6 This statement is based on information kindly supplied by the Council on Tribunals and the Lord Chancellor's Office.

 7 See Jacobs, F G and Durand, A, *References to the European Court: Practice and Procedure* (1975), at pp 164, 165, 171, 172 and Advocate-General Warner in Case 166/73: *Rheinmühlen-Düsseldorf v Einfuhr-und Vorretsstelle für Getreide*

ruling is concerned it is the practice of continental courts to deal directly with the European Court, which does, for this purpose, form an integral part of the legal systems of the Member States. On the question of a request for a preliminary ruling being subject to appeal it has already been pointed out that continental practice is not uniform[8] nor has the question been decided conclusively by the European Court.[9] The English rules on appeals may certainly be questioned to the extent that they have the effect of interposing an obstacle between the English courts and the European Court. The use of the Senior Master and the possibility of appeal may also cause unjustifiable delays in the reference procedure.[10]

It has already been pointed out that while courts and tribunals which are not of last instance have a discretion whether to seek a preliminary ruling, courts and tribunals of final instance are under an obligation to do so. Some doubts exist in the United Kingdom concerning which courts and tribunals are those 'against whose decisions there is no judicial remedy under national law.'[11] The position of the House of Lords is clear; subject to the relevant Treaty provisions it will be obliged to request preliminary rulings. The House of Lords has indeed recognized its obligation to refer issues concerning the applicability and interpretation of Community law to the European Court.[12] But the position of the Court of Appeal is not so clear. The Court of Appeal may be a court of final instance in two situations. The Court of Appeal may be declared by statute to be the final court of appeal.[13] If a question of the validity or interpretation of Community law came before the Court of Appeal in such a situation then it would clearly be obliged to seek a preliminary ruling from the Community Court. But rather more problematic may be the commoner situation in which despite the possibility of an appeal to the House of Lords the Court of

---

und Futtermittel [1974] ECR 33 at 47. For a contrary opinion, see Collins, L, op cit, at pp 194–200.

8 See Chapter 10, supra.

9 See the case and literature cited in note 7, supra.

10 These factors may have contributed to the inordinate delay in transmitting to the European Court the first United Kingdom request for a preliminary ruling in *Van Duyn v Home Office*. The Order requesting a preliminary ruling was dated 1 March 1974 (see [1974] 1 WLR at 1118) and it was lodged at the European Court on 13 June 1974 (see [1975] 1 CMLR at 14).

11 This expression replaces 'from whose decisions there is no possibility of appeal under internal law' which was used in the earlier unofficial Foreign Office translation. The new translation certainly seems to be closer to the French 'dont les décisions ne sont pas susceptibles d'un recours juridictionnel de droit interne'.

12 See *R v Henn and Darby* [1979] 2 CMLR 495; *Garland v British Rail Engineering* [1981] 2 CMLR 542.

13 Eg County Courts Act 1984, s 82.

Appeal may be, and indeed usually is, the final court of appeal. Since appeal to the House of Lords is only by leave that leave may either not be sought or may be sought and refused. In such situations it is suggested that the Court of Appeal should be obliged to seek a preliminary ruling in an appropriate case since, although it is not the supreme appellate court, there is no judicial remedy against its decisions in those situations. A similar problem arises in connection with tribunals. Is a tribunal from whose decision there is no appeal but which is open to review by certiorari obliged to seek a preliminary ruling? Certiorari is a form of judicial remedy under national law. But, it is a discretionary and highly technical remedy and in most cases the decision of such a tribunal would be final. It is therefore suggested that, as in the case of the Court of Appeal, such a tribunal should regard itself as under the obligation to request a preliminary ruling.[14] Thus in terms of the dispute in continental legal circles between the 'concrete' and 'abstract' theories of article 177, paragraph 3 of the EEC Treaty the 'concrete' theory is thought to be preferable.[15]

The initial reaction of English courts and tribunals to this question did not, however, reflect this attitude. In the Court of Appeal no general view has yet emerged. In *Bulmer v Bollinger* Lord Denning expressed the opinion that 'short of the House of Lords no other English Court is bound to refer a question to the European Court at Luxembourg'.[16] But in the same case Stamp and Stephenson LJJ refused to commit themselves on that point in the absence of further argument.[17] More recently, conflicting views have been expressed by differently constituted Courts of Appeal. In one case support for a variant of the 'concrete' theory was given in terms that the ultimate court of appeal in England is either the Court of Appeal (if leave to appeal to the House of Lords is unobtainable) or the House of Lords.[18] In another case it was unanimously declared that a court or tribunal below the House of Lords can only be subject to the obligation to seek a preliminary ruling 'where there is no *possibility* of further appeal from it'.[19]

14 Cf Jacobs, F G and Durand, A, op cit at pp 162, 163. Also see Freeman, Elizabeth, 'References to the Court of Justice under article 177' (1975) 28 *Current Legal Problems* 176 at 184–186.
15 See Donner, A M, 'Les rapports entre la compétence de la Cour de Justice des Communautés Européennes et les tribunaux internes', 115 *Recueil des Cours de la Haye* (1965) at pp 42 et seq. Also see case 6/64: *Costa v ENEL* [1964] ECR 585 at 592.
16 [1974] Ch 401 at 420.
17 Ibid, at pp 427, 430.
18 *Hagen v Fratelli D and G Moretti SNC* [1980] 3 CMLR 253.
19 *R v Pharmaceutical Society of Great Britain, ex p Association of Pharmaceutical Importers* [1987] 3 CMLR 951 at 969, emphasis added.

What appears to be common ground between these two views is that in cases where leave to appeal to the House of Lords is not granted the Court of Appeal thereby becomes obliged to seek a ruling. But such a suggestion is clearly fraught with procedural difficulties. Once the Court of Appeal has given judgment in a case it is *functus officio* and if leave to appeal to the House of Lords is not then granted the matter cannot be revived before the Court of Appeal.[20] Nor does this cope with the more typical situation in which leave to appeal from the Court of Appeal is not sought. Similar uncertainty exists regarding tribunals. Lord Denning's view has been echoed in a decision of the National Insurance Commissioner (now the Social Security Commissioner). He held that since his decisions may be set aside by certiorari, he did not 'constitute a tribunal against whose decision there is no judicial remedy under national law, even though an order of certiorari cannot be made without the leave of the High Court'.[1] As far as the Court of Appeal is concerned, a practical solution could take the form of that Court being obliged to give leave to appeal to the House of Lords in a case in which a point of Community law is in issue but the Court of Appeal does not itself seek a preliminary ruling.[2] A simpler solution, and one fully in keeping with the spirit and objectives of article 177, would be for the obligation to refer to arise with regard to courts or tribunals at the point from which a further judicial remedy becomes discretionary.

THE QUESTION OF SUPREMACY[3]

It has been repeatedly laid down by the Community Court and is in general accepted by the original six Member States that the

20 Cf *Magnavision NV SA v General Optical Council* [1987] 1 CMLR 887.
1 *Re a Holiday in Italy* [1975] 1 CMLR 184 at 188.
2 See Jacobs, F, 'Which courts and tribunals are bound to refer to the European Court?' (1977) 2 EL Rev 119.
3 The literature on this topic from the British standpoint includes the following: Martin, A, 'The Accession of the United Kingdom to the European Communities: Jurisdictional Problems' (1968–69) 6 CML Rev 7; Hunnings, N M, 'Constitutional Implications of joining the Common Market', ibid, 50; de Smith, S A, 'The Constitution and the Common Market: a tentative appraisal' (1971) 34 MLR 597; Wade, H W R, 'Sovereignty and the European Communities' (1972) 88 LQR 1; Mitchell, J D B, et al, 'Constitutional aspects of the Treaty and Legislation relating to British membership' (1972) 9 CML Rev 134; Trinidade, F A 'Parliamentary Sovereignty and the Primacy of European Community Law' (1972) 35 MLR 375; Winterton, G, 'The British Grundnorm: Parliamentary Supremacy Re-examined' (1976) 92 LQR 591; Bridge, J W, 'Abstract Law and Political Reality in the Post-European-Accession British Constitution', [1987] Denning LJ 23; and Bradley, A W, 'The sovereignty of Parliament–in perpetuity?' in Jowell, J and Oliver, D (eds) *The Changing Constitution* (2nd edn 1989) at p 25.

Community Treaties have established a new and distinct system
of law, the rules of which have to prevail over the rules of the
municipal laws of the Member States. Thus from the commencement and for the duration of British membership the municipal law of the United Kingdom must yield in cases of conflict to
the superior Community law. To the generations of British lawyers
schooled in the Diceyan orthodoxy such a prospect is no doubt
unthinkable if not impossible; but nevertheless it is one of the
obligations of membership. The implications were clearly summarized in the 1967 White Paper:

> 'The Community law having direct internal effect is designed to take
> precedence over the domestic law of the Member States. From this it
> follows that the legislation of the Parliament of the United Kingdom
> giving effect to that law would have to do so in such a way as to override
> existing national law so far as inconsistent with it. This result need not
> be left to implication, and it would be open to Parliament to enact from
> time to time any necessary consequential amendments or repeals. It
> would also follow that within the fields occupied by the Community
> law Parliament would have to refrain from passing fresh legislation
> inconsistent with that law as for the time being in force. This would not
> however involve any constitutional innovation. Many of our treaty
> obligations already impose such restraints – for example, the Charter of
> the United Nations, the European Convention on Human Rights and
> GATT.'[4]

As far as the body of Community law in force on the eve of
British membership was concerned no difficulty was experienced.
That law, as we have seen, was given legal force in the United
Kingdom by section 2 (1) of the European Communities Act and
will have precedence over prior British law by the simple operation
of the rule *lex posterior derogat priori*.[5] Certain difficulties may arise,
however, in avoiding and resolving conflicts between Community
law and statutes passed after the commencement of United
Kingdom membership. The 1967 White Paper stated that Parliament will have to refrain from passing fresh legislation inconsistent with Community law and remarked this was by no means
an innovation because of existing restraints under other treaties.
But the critical question is whether our doctrine of Parliamentary
sovereignty means that such restraints must always be voluntarily
imposed by Parliament or whether they can be compulsorily
guaranteed.

The application of the orthodox doctrine of the absolute sov-

4 *Legal and Constitutional Implications of United Kingdom Membership of the
European Communities* (Cmnd 3301), para 23.
5 Certain express amendments are in fact made by Part II of the European
Communities Act.

ereignty of Parliament to statutes designed to implement treaty
provisions into United Kingdom law has meant that such statutes
have been regarded as in no way different from ordinary statutes
and may be either expressly or impliedly amended or repealed by
subsequent inconsistent statutes. It is true that there is a legal
presumption that Parliament does not intend to derogate from
International Law, but such a presumption cannot prevail in the
face of an expressly inconsistent subsequent enactment.[6] If this
doctrine were to be applied to Community law it would hardly
satisfy the Communities since there would be no legal guarantee
of Parliament's good behaviour.

There are a variety of possible solutions to this problem. Some
are suggested in the writings of those contemporary constitutional
lawyers who challenge the orthodoxy of Dicey and his followers.
Professor Mitchell has argued that the Act of Union with Scotland
1707 is fundamental law which imposes legal restraints on the
United Kingdom Parliament and just as a new legal order was
established in 1707 so there is no reason why another new legal
order in the context of the Communities should not be created in
1972.[7] Professor Heuston, whilst not denying that Parliament is
sovereign in terms of the area of her power, maintains that limitations may be imposed on the manner and form by which that
power is exercised.[8] Applied to the matter in hand that thesis would
involve the imposition of procedural restrictions on Parliament's
freedom to legislate inconsistently with Community law which
would not absolutely prevent such legislation but would make it
more difficult. But not all of the possible solutions are of such a
fundamental nature. It has been suggested that a formal clause be
inserted in all statutes,[9] or that the enacting formula of all statutes
should be amended,[10] to include a statement that the statute is to
be construed as not conflicting with Community law. Another
commentator has drawn on the experience of the Canadian Bill of
Rights and has suggested that a strongly worded presumption
against anything other than an express derogation from Community law should be written into the enabling act.[11] Yet others
have suggested that reliance should be placed on the gradual emerg-

6 See *IRC v Collco Dealings Ltd* [1962] AC 1, [1961] 1 All ER 762.
7 See Mitchell, J D B, 'What Happened to the Constitution on 1st January 1973?'
  (1980) 11 *Cambrian Law Review* 69. For an even more drastic solution, see
  Hood Phillips, O., *Reform of the Constitution* (1970), Chapter 7.
8 See Heuston, R F V, *Essays in Constitutional Law* (2nd edn), Chapter 1.
9 See Hunnings, N M, loc cit in note 1, supra.
10 See Wade, H W R, loc cit in note 1, supra, and Wade, H W R, *Constitutional
  Fundamentals* (1980), Chapter 3.
11 See de Smith, S A, loc cit in note 1, supra, and *R v Drybones* (1970) 9 DLR
  (3d) 473.

ence of a constitutional convention by which it would be recognized that Parliament could not legislate contrary to Community law.[12]

In dealing with the problem of the supremacy of Community law the European Communities Act adopts a subtle approach which does not incorporate any of the fundamentalist or procedural solutions described above nor is it content to rely on the uncertain emergence of conventional limitations. The Act avoids any outright statement of the supremacy of Community law. It was probably thought that this was unnecessary in view of the practice of the original six Member States. It would also be contrary to the main stream of British constitutional practice and it would in any event have been politically dangerous to have adopted such an approach. The supremacy of Community law in the United Kingdom is effectively guaranteed by the combined operation of provisions of sections 2 and 3 of the Act. As we have seen section 2 (1) gives present and future Community law legal force in the United Kingdom and creates the concept of enforceable Community rights. Thus since the doctrine of the supremacy of Community law is part of that law section 2 (1) makes that doctrine part of the law of the United Kingdom. The effectiveness of that doctrine is guaranteed by two further provisions. First, section 2 (4) provides that, subject only to the limitations specified in Schedule 2, 'any enactment passed or to be passed, other than one contained in this Part of this Act, shall be construed and have effect subject to the foregoing provisions of this section', in other words, subject to the rule of the supremacy of Community law which is an enforceable Community right.[13] Secondly, section 3 (1) provides that:

'For the purposes of all legal proceedings any question as to the meaning or effect of any of the Treaties, or as to the validity, meaning or effect of any Community instrument, shall be treated as a question of law (and, if not referred to the European Court, be for determination as such in accordance with the principles laid down by and any relevant decision of the European Court).'

Thus in all matters of Community law the courts and tribunals[14] of the United Kingdom are to defer to the relevant decisions of the Community Court whether or not such matters have been actually referred to the Community Court. This is a very important factor

---

12 See Martin, A, loc cit in note 1, supra, and cf Lloyd, Lord, *The Idea of Law* (1966) at pp 169, 170.
13 See the statement by the Lord Chancellor, Lord Hailsham, when introducing the Bill in the Lords, *Parliamentary Debates, House of Lords*, Vol 333, No 111, 25 July 1972, col 1230.
14 See *Shields v E Coomes (Holdings) Ltd* [1979] 1 All ER 456 per Lord Denning MR and Case 69/80: *Worringham and Humphreys v Lloyds Bank Ltd* at 461, 462 [1980] 1 CMLR 293 at 300, per Kilner Brown J.

since the doctrine of supremacy has been developed by the Community Court.

The European Communities Act does not therefore seek to guarantee the supremacy of Community law by forbidding Parliament to enact conflicting legislation. Instead the guarantee is provided by denying effectiveness to such legislation within the legal systems of the United Kingdom to the extent that it conflicts with Community law. Thus the ultimate sanction remains an extra-legal one. There is nothing to prevent a future Parliament from repealing the European Communities Act in its entirety. If it chose to do so it would indicate that the political will that the United Kingdom should remain a member of the Communities was lacking and in the last analysis there is nothing which any mere rule of law can do in such a situation. In other words it must be assumed that as long as the United Kingdom is a member of the Communities she will honour the legal and constitutional obligations of membership. The legal guarantees of good faith contained in the Act are adequate, subject to the political will of the Member States that the Community system shall succeed.[15]

The question of supremacy has received some attention from the judiciary. In the pre-accession case of *Blackburn v A-G* Lord Denning observed 'we have all been brought up to believe that, in legal theory, one Parliament cannot bind another and that no Act is irreversible. But legal theory does not always march alongside political reality.'[16] After referring to the practical impossibility that Parliament would legislate contrary to the statutes emancipating the Dominions and Colonies he added, 'Legal theory must give way to practical politics.'[17] He then went on to say that if and when Parliament legislated contrary to Community law 'we will then say whether Parliament can lawfully do it or not'.[18] Since the accession, there has clearly been an awareness of the implications of the doctrine of the supremacy of Community law. In *Esso Petroleum v Kingswood Motors Ltd* Bridge J observed that where Community law 'is in conflict with our domestic law the effect of the [European Communities] Act of 1972 is to require that the Community law shall prevail.'[19] Similarly in *Aero Zipp Fasteners v YKK Fasteners*, Graham J said that the European Communities Act 1972 'enacted that relevant Common Market law should be applied in this country

---

15 Cf Warner, J-P, 'The Relationship between European Community Law and the National Laws of the Member States' (1977), 93 LQR 349 at 364, 365.
16 [1971] 1 WLR 1037 at 1040.
17 Ibid.
18 Ibid.
19 [1974] QB 142 at 151.

and should, where there is a conflict, override English law'.[20] In *R v Secchi* a Metropolitan magistrate has remarked that the effect of making Community law part of English law 'is to make English law, both statute and common law, subject to Community law, in those fields in which Community laws have been passed'.[1] More recently, Hoffmann J has declared that 'The Treaty of Rome is the supreme law of this country, taking precedence over Acts of Parliament'.[2]

For some time the House of Lords has recognized the authority of Community law.[3] In *R v Secretary of State for Transport, ex p Factortame* it was faced with constitutional issues involving the supremacy of Community law. The case arose as a result of changes introduced by the Merchant Shipping Act 1988 whereby the registration of fishing vessels as British was forbidden if the shareholders of the companies which owned them were not British. As a result, fishing vessels owned by British companies with Spanish shareholders did not qualify for registration. They instituted proceedings alleging that the new UK rules on registration contravened Community law, in particular the Common Fisheries Policy. They also sought interim relief in the form of the suspension of the new rules pending a final determination of the action. The Divisional Court of the Queen's Bench Division, by way of interim relief, ordered that the new rules be disapplied to the applicants pending final judgment.[4] The Court of Appeal reversed that decision on the ground that under the UK constitution the courts had no power to disapply Acts of Parliament.[5] On further appeal, the House of Lords confirmed that there was a presumption that an Act of Parliament was compatible with Community law unless and until declared to be incompatible but it held that as a matter of English law there was no jurisdiction to grant the interim relief requested. The House acknowledged, however, that if there was an overriding principle of Community law which required national courts, irrespective of the position under national law, to grant interim relief to protect alleged rights under Community law, then it was under a duty to devise such a remedy. It sought a preliminary ruling on that point.[6] The European Court, invoking its previous

20 [1973] CMLR 819 at 820.
1 [1975] 1 CMLR 383 at 386.
2 *Stoke-on-Trent City Council v B & Q plc* [1990] 3 CMLR 31 at p 34.
3 *R v Henn and Darby* [1979] ECR 3795, [1980] 2 CMLR 229.
4 [1989] 2 CMLR 353. The Divisional Court also sought a preliminary ruling on the substantive questions of Community law: Case 221/89, pending before the European Court. The Commission has also brought proceedings against the United Kingdom arising out of the same issue: Case 246/89. For an interim order in that case, see [1989] 3 CMLR 601.
5 [1989] 3 CMLR 1.
6 [1990] 2 AC 85.

case law that no law of the Member States should compromise the full effectiveness of Community law, ruled that 'a national court which, in a case before it concerning Community law, considers that the sole obstacle which precludes it from granting interim relief is a rule of national law must set aside that rule'.[7] In the light of that ruling the House of Lords unanimously granted the relief sought.[8] On the issue of supremacy, in the words of Lord Bridge, 'under the terms of the [European Communities Act] 1972 it has always been clear that it was the duty of a United Kingdom court, when delivering final judgment, to override any rule of national law found to be in conflict with any directly enforceable rule of Community law.... Thus ... to insist that, in the protection of rights under Community law, national courts must not be inhibited by rules of national law from granting interim relief in appropriate cases is no more than a logical recognition of that supremacy'.[9]

Another related issue which has come before English courts concerns the response, in terms of interpretation, which should be made in the face of incompatibilities between English law and Community law. An approach advocated by Lord Denning has received a measure of support from the House of Lords.[10] That suggests that a distinction should be made between mere inconsistencies on the one hand and deliberate derogations on the other. In the former category of cases, where the incompatibility may be assumed to be inadvertent, it is suggested that the courts are under a duty to apply Community law on the presumption that Parliament intended to fulfil the Treaty obligations of the United Kingdom. But should the incompatibility be deliberate and clearly intended by Parliament, then the courts would be under a duty to apply English law.[11] More recently the House of Lords has been able to examine this issue, taking into consideration the presumption in favour of Community law contained in the European Communities Act.[12] In *Duke v GEC Reliance Ltd*[13] the female plaintiff alleged sex discrimination contrary to Community law in that she had been required to retire at 60 while comparable male colleagues retired at 65. English law in force at the material time did not extend equality between the sexes to retirement ages. In earlier litigation the European Court had held such inequality contrary to Com-

---

7 Case 213/89: [1990] 3 CMLR 1 at 30.
8 [1990] 3 CMLR 375.
9 [1990] 3 CMLR 375 at p 380.
10 See *Garland v British Rail Engineering Ltd* [1983] 2 AC 751 at 771.
11 See *Macarthy's Ltd v Smith* [1979] 3 All ER 325, [1979] 3 CMLR 44 at 47;
   Shields v E Coomes (Holdings) Ltd [1979] 1 All ER 456 at p 460.
12 Section 2 (4).
13 [1988] AC 618.

munity law and had declared that the consequent right to equal treatment had direct effect but only against the state and its agencies.[14] Since the plaintiff could not rely on direct effect, she argued that the incompatible English law should be interpreted in a non-discriminatory way. The House of Lords rejected that argument on the grounds that the presumption of interpretation only applied to statutes which intended to enforce Community law and where the Community right in question had direct effect.[15] In later cases involving sex discrimination the House of Lords has adopted a similar approach. Thus where there has been a conflict between UK regulations intended to implement Community law and the Community law in question, there has been a willingness to interpret such regulations contrary to their literal meaning in the interests of achieving compatibility with Community law.[16] Although this goes a long way towards overcoming inconsistencies by means of interpretative techniques, it must nevertheless be doubted whether the factor of the intention of Parliament may be legitimately taken into account as a matter of Community law. In a recent ruling, the European Court has held that national courts must always interpret national law in the light of the wording and purpose of Community law whatever the date of the national law in question.[17]

COMMUNITY LAW BEFORE UNITED KINGDOM COURTS AND TRIBUNALS

Since the commencement of British membership the courts, tribunals and lawyers of the United Kingdom have been confronted with the 'incoming tide' of Community law.[18] They have been faced with the unprecedented challenge of participating in a novel and unique system of law based on unfamiliar continental legal principles. During this time, points of Community law, of varying degrees of significance, have arisen in numerous reported British cases. All levels of the judicial hierarchy have been involved: Value Added Tax tribunals, industrial tribunals, the Social Security Commissioner, the Special Commissioners for Income Tax, the Employment Appeal Tribunal, magistrates, county courts, crown courts, judges of the High Court, the Queen's Bench Divisional Court, both Divisions of the Court of Appeal and the House of

---

14 See Case 152/84: *Marshall v Southampton and South West Hampshire Area Health Authority* [1986] ECR 723, [1986] 1 CMLR 688.

15 [1988] AC at pp 630, 639–640, per Lord Templeman with the concurrence of the other law lords.

16 See *Pickstone v Freemans plc* [1989] AC 66, [1988] 2 All ER 803; *Litster v Forth Dry Dock and Engineering Co* [1990] 1 AC 546, [1989] 1 All ER 1134.

17 See Case C-106/89: *Maerleasing SA v La Commercial de Alimentacion SA* Judgment of 13 November 1990, not yet reported.

18 Cf Lord Denning in *H P Bulmer v J Bollinger SA* [1974] Ch 401 at 418.

Lords.[19] Earlier in this chapter reference has been made to the light
which these cases throw on the questions of the supremacy of
Community law and the identity of those courts and tribunals
which are under the obligation to request preliminary rulings from
the European Court. In addition the cases reveal the nature and
extent of judicial understanding and assimilation of Community
law in the United Kingdom at present.

The first and obvious question concerns the extent to which the
rules of Community law have become part of the corpus of law
which the courts and tribunals of the United Kingdom themselves
apply. There is clearly a general acceptance that Community law
can now form part of the law of the United Kingdom.[20] As far
as the EEC Treaty is concerned there was initially a mistaken
impression that every provision of the Treaty must now be given
legal effect by United Kingdom courts and tribunals. Lord
Denning was a proponent of that view.[1] His judgments contain
such statements as 'the Treaty is part of our law. It is equal in force
to any statute. It must be applied by our courts'[2] and the Treaty
of Rome 'is by statute part of the law of England'.[3] But the heresy
that all Treaty provisions are part of the law of England and
enforceable by its courts has now been abandoned in favour of
the established view that only those provisions which satisfy the
conditions for direct effect have that status.[4] In the context of the
secondary legislation of the Community there appears to be a
general recognition that regulations are directly applicable in the
United Kingdom. As far as the direct effect of the secondary
legislation of the Community is concerned, after some initial waver-
ing,[5] there now seems to be a general appreciation of the cir-

19 For example see the cases cited in Collins, op cit, at 183–189.
20 Eg *Lerose Ltd v Hawick Jersey International Ltd* [1973] CMLR 83 at 95 per
   Whitford J; *Minnesota Mining Co v Geerpres Europe Ltd* at 95; [1973] CMLR
   259, at 264, 265, per Graham J; *Dymond v G B Britton (Holdings) Ltd* [1976]
   1 CMLR 133 at 135, per Oliver J.
 1 Also see *Esso Petroleum Co Ltd v Kingswood Motors Ltd* [1974] QB 142 at 151,
   per Bridge J.
 2 *Application des Gaz SA v Falka Veritas Ltd* [1974] Ch 381 at 393.
 3 *Schorsch Meier GmbF v Hennin* [1974] 3 WLR 823 at 830. Also see *H P Bulmer
   Ltd v J Bollinger SA* [1974] Ch 401 at 418m 419 and *Re Westinghouse Electric
   Corpn Uranium Contract* [1978] AC 547 at 564. For an early case in which the
   significance of Treaty provisions was clearly appreciated see *Van Duyn v Home
   Office* [1974] 1 WLR 1107 at 1116, per Pennycuick VC.
 4 See, for example, Lord Denning's exposition of the 'direct applicability' of
   Treaty provisions in *Shields v Coomes (Holdings) Ltd* [1979] 1 All ER 456 at
   461.
 5 Compare *H P Bulmer Ltd v Bollinger SA* [1974] Ch 401 at 418, 419 with
   Processed Vegetable Growers Association Ltd v Customs and Excise Comrs [1974]
   1 CMLR 113 at 127, 128.

cumstances in which this applies. For example, under the influence of Vice-Chancellor Pennycuick's judgment in *Van Duyn v Home Office*[6] and the European Court's ruling in that case,[7] it is now accepted that directives can confer rights on individuals which are enforceable by them in English courts and which those courts must protect.[8] The consequences for domestic remedies of directly enforceable Community rights have also been acknowledged. The House of Lords has held that where such rights have been created in favour of individuals, their breach constitutes a breach of a statutory duty which gives rise to liability in damage.[9] It has also been held by the Court of Appeal that a breach of a Treaty provision which confers rights and duties on individuals and Member States respectively is subject to judicial review but will not give rise to liability in damages unless the tort of misfeasance in public office has been committed.[10]

Another matter which emerges from the reported cases is the mode of interpretation of Community law. The unfamiliarity of the style and format of the EEC Treaty and Community secondary legislation have provoked judicial comment. The Treaty 'lays down general principles. It expresses its aims and purposes, all in sentences of moderate length and commendable style. But it lacks precision. It uses words and phrases without defining what they mean. An English lawyer would look for an interpretation clause, but he would look in vain. There is none. All the way through the Treaty there are gaps and lacunae.'[11] The ultimate authority of the European Court on the interpretation of Community law has been acknowledged[12] as also has the necessity of uniform interpretation of that law in all the Member States.[13] As aids to interpretation the case law of the European Court and of the national courts of the Member States has been invoked and some use has been made of the texts of Community instruments other than those in English.[14] But the generality and apparent incompleteness of the texts of

---

6 [1974] 1 WLR 1107 at 1037, 1040.
7 Case 41/74: [1974] ECR 1337 at 1348, 1349.
8 *Shields v E Coomes (Holdings) Ltd* [1979] 1 All ER 456 at 462, per Lord Denning MR.
9 *Garden Cottage Foods Ltd v Milk Marketing Board* [1984] AC 130, [1983] 2 All ER 770.
10 *Bourgoin SA v Ministry of Agriculture, Fisheries and Food* [1986] QB 716, [1985] 3 All ER 585.
11 *H P Bulmer Ltd v J Bollinger SA* [1974] Ch 401 at 425, per Lord Denning. Also see *Application des Gaz SA v Falks Veritas Ltd* [1974] Ch 381 at 393, 394.
12 *H P Bulmer Ltd v J Bollinger SA* [1974] Ch 401 at 419, per Lord Denning.
13 Ibid, at 425. Also see *EMI Records v CBS Ltd* [1975] 1 CMLR 285 at 297, per Graham J.
14 *Re a Holiday in Italy* [1975] 1 CMLR 184 at 190.

Community law has led some English judges to claim the right to play a creative role in interpreting Community law so as to fill gaps in its formal fabric. English courts have been exhorted to 'divine the spirit of the Treaty and gain inspiration from it. If they find a gap, they must fill it as best they can. They must do what the framers of the instrument would have done if they had thought about it'.[15] This is indeed what the European Court does and what national courts guided by the European Court may do. But if that approach is adopted without seeking guidance from the European Court then the integrity and uniformity of Community law may be put at risk. This is particularly so in the case of a Member State whose legal traditions differ in many ways from the continental legal traditions upon which the Community legal order is founded.

At the time of British accession there was an influential body of judicial opinion in England which held that difficulties over the interpretation of Community law will not often arise; in the majority of cases lower courts and tribunals should have no difficulty in interpreting Community law; courts and tribunals should not be too ready to request preliminary rulings from the European Court because of the burden that would place on the Court and because of the increased cost and delay for the litigants.[16] The judgment of Lord Denning in *Bulmer v Bollinger* represents the high-water mark of this approach.[17] Stress was placed on the complete discretion of all courts other than the House of Lords to decide when a preliminary ruling is necessary. Drawing largely upon the national case law of the six original Member States, Lord Denning purported to lay down 'guidelines' to assist English courts in deciding whether a reference is necessary and in exercising their discretion. Quite apart from the fact that the practice of national courts on preliminary rulings is not necessarily an accurate representation of Community law on preliminary rulings, a number of questionable recommendations are contained in the 'guidelines', without qualification. These include recourse to the *acte clair* doctrine; that the facts of a case should always be decided before a decision is taken to request a preliminary ruling; that judges' discretion should be influenced by such factors as time, the burden on the European Court, the nature and importance of the question in issue, expense and the wishes of the parties. All of these

15 *H P Bulmer Ltd v J Bollinger SA* [1974] Ch 401 at 426, per Lord Denning.
16 See Lord Diplock, 'The Common Market and the Common Law' (1972), 6 JALT 3 at 13, 14; Lord Denning in *The Times, Forward into Europe*, Part 1, 2 January 1973 at 11; Lord Hailsham in an extract from a speech to magistrates appended to Home Office Circular No 149/1973 (CS 18/1973).
17 [1974] Ch 401 at 420–425, particularly.

'guidelines' are subject to serious reservations.[18] Lord Denning's assumption that the importance of a question of Community law is directly related to the position in the national judicial hierarchy of the court in which the question arises[19] is not borne out by the experience of the European Court. Questions of fundamental importance to Community law and its development have not infrequently come before the European Court in the form of references from lowly national courts and tribunals.[20] Whenever there is a risk of divergent views on Community law it is in everyone's interest, not least that of actual and potential litigants, to seek a ruling from the European Court at the earliest opportunity.[1]

The threat to the uniformity of Community law posed by national courts and tribunals, when interpreting that law, going on voyages of discovery of their own without taking advantage of the navigational aids provided by the European Court is clearly illustrated by one of the early cases which came before the Court of Appeal. In *Schorsch Meier GmbH v Hennin*[2] the defendant was indebted to the plaintiffs in a sum of German Marks. The debt was not paid and as a result of a fall in the value of sterling the plaintiffs brought an action in the County Court claiming payment in German Marks. The judge rejected the plaintiffs' argument based on article 106 of the EEC Treaty on the ground that the article had no bearing on English law, and a request that the matter be referred to the European Court was refused. The plaintiffs appealed against both of those rulings. In connection with the first, on the assumption that the EEC Treaty has the status of an Act of Parliament, the Court of Appeal unanimously held article 106 to be a rule of law for English courts to apply. No consideration was given to the case law of the European Court concerning the direct effect of Treaty provisions. In the absence of any European or national case law on the direct effect of article 106, no reference was made to scholarly commentaries on the subject.[3] When interpreting article

---

18 For critical comments, see Mitchell, J B D, 'Sed Quis Custodiet Ipsos Custodes?' (1974) 11 CML Rev 351; Jacobs, F G, 'When to Refer to the European Court' (1974) 90 LQR 486; Freeman, Elizabeth, 'References to the Court of Justice under Article 177' (1975) 28 *Current Legal Problems* 176.

19 [1974] Ch at p 421.

20 Eg Case 6/64: *Costa v ENEL* [1964] ECR 585; Case 61/65 *Voor Het Vaasen (née Göbbels) v Beambtenfonds Mijnbedrijf* [1966] ECR 261, [1966] CMLR 508; Case 33/70: *SpA SACE v Ministry for Finance of the Italian Republic* [1970] ECR 1213, [1971] CMLR 123.

1 Cf Case 190/73: *Officer van Justitie v J W J van Haaster* [1974] ECR 1123, at 1136, per Advocate-General Mayras.

2 [1975] QB 416, [1975] 1 All ER 1520.

3 Eg *Les Novelles: Droit des Communautés européennes*, chapter VI; Campbell, A, *Common Market Law*, Vol 3, paras 15.99 to 15.103; Kapteyn, P J G and

106 the Court of Appeal took the lead of Lord Denning who said, 'There is no need to refer the interpretation to the court at Luxembourg. We can do it ourselves'.[4] The Court of Appeal then attempted to divine the purpose and intent of the article. Since it is concerned, inter alia, with the obligation of Member States to authorise payments connected with the movement of goods in the currency of the Member State in which the creditor resides, the Court of Appeal held that the German plaintiffs were entitled to payment in German currency.[5] Beyond that no genuine attempt was made to interpret the article as a whole nor to place it properly in the context of the Treaty. The case raised entirely novel points of some importance and a preliminary ruling from the European Court was manifestly necessary.

Lord Denning's 'guidelines', as might be expected, have exercised some influence on judicial attitudes towards preliminary rulings, particularly in the case of tribunals and the lower courts. A metropolitan magistrate, for example, has observed that Lord Denning has supplied 'the essential guidelines which English courts must follow'.[6] A Value Added Tax Tribunal,[7] the Employment Appeal Tribunal[8] and a High Court Judge sitting in the crown court[9] have all accepted the authority of the 'guidelines'. Under their influence preliminary rulings have not been sought apparently on the simple ground that the parties believed that it would be contrary to their interests.[10] On the other hand, the reported cases also show that English judges and others exercising judicial powers acknowledge the significance and importance of preliminary rulings and demonstrate their willingness to seek the guidance of the European Court. There has been a steady and increasing flow of references on such diverse questions as: the scope

Verloren van Themaat, P, *Introduction to the Law of the European Communities* (1973) at p 222.
4 [1975] QB 416 at 426.
5 Since art 106 appears in the part of the Treaty concerned with economic policy and balance of payments it is probably of public law rather than private law significance, that is concerned with exchange control rather than the currency in which debts may be paid. The relevance of art 106 to judgment debts has been questioned obiter in the House of Lords; *Miliangos v George Frank (Textiles) Ltd* [1975] 2 CMLR 585 at 596, per Lord Wilberforce.
6 *R v Secchi* [1975] 1 CMLR 383 at 386.
7 *English Speaking Union of the Commonwealth v Customs and Excise Comrs* [1971] 1 CMLR 581 at 599.
8 *Burton v British Railways Board* [1981] 3 CMLR 100 at 102.
9 *R v Tymen* [1980] 3 CMLR 101 at 107.
10 *Extrude Hone Corpn v Heathway Machine Sales Ltd* [1981] 3 CMLR 379 at 399 and *English Speaking Union of the Commonwealth v Customs and Excise Comrs* [1981] 1 CMLR 581 at 599.

of the Community's equal pay provisions;[11] the direct effect of directives;[12] uncertainty concerning Community rules on intellectual property;[13] the authority of the United Kingdom to introduce fish conservation measures;[14] the meaning and effect of the free trade agreement with Portugal;[15] whether a self-employed person is a worker for the purpose of the social security provisions of the Community;[16] and the validity and meaning of a regulation concerned with the financial structure of the Common Agricultural Policy.[17] The House of Lords has even obtained a preliminary ruling for the purpose of giving the Criminal Division of the Court of Appeal an elementary lesson in Community law.[18]

After an understandably hesitant start United Kingdom cases reveal no reluctance to consider and apply Community law.[19] United Kingdom courts and tribunals are now, on the whole, adopting a positive and constructive approach to the challenge of this novel body of law. The reasons for this promising outcome lie partly in the clearly observable differences between English and Community law.[20] It is becoming increasingly acknowledged that Community law demands a different approach and this should help to promote a fruitful relationship between the law of the United Kingdom and the law of the Community. The Commission, in a review of the attitudes of national courts to Community law, has expressed general satisfaction with the practice of UK courts both in regard to upholding the primacy of Community law and to frequent use of the preliminary ruling procedure.[1]

---

11 *Macarthys Ltd v Smith* [1979] 3 All ER 325, [1979] 3 CMLR 44.
12 *Burton v British Railways Board* [1981] 3 CMLR 100.
13 *EMI Records Ltd v CBS United Kingdom Ltd* [1975] 1 CMLR 285.
14 *R v Tymen* [1981] 2 CMLR 544.
15 *Polydor Ltd v Harlequin Records Shops Ltd* [1980] 2 CMLR 413.
16 Case 21/5: *Re an illness in France* [1976] 1 CMLR 243.
17 Case 146/77: *British Beef Co Ltd v Intervention Board for Agricultural Produce* [1978] 2 CMLR 83.
18 *DPP v Henn and Darby* [1980] 2 CMLR 229 at 234, per Lord Diplock.
19 The Court of Appeal has even been restrained by the House of Lords for over-enthusiasm. See *James Buchanan & Co Ltd v Babco Forwarding and Shipping (UK) Ltd* [1978] 1 CMLR 156 at 164 per Viscount Dilhorne and *The Siskina* [1978] 1 CMLR 190 at 220 per Lord Diplock.
20 See Bridge, J W, 'National Legal Tradition and Community Law: Legislative Drafting and Judicial Interpretation in England and the European Community' (1981), 19 *Journal of Common Market Studies* 351.
 1 See *Sixth Annual Report to the European Parliament on Commission Monitoring of the Application of Community Law*, COM (89) 411 final, Appendix, pp 31–34.

Chapter 13

The Community law of the economy: The Common Market

An analysis of the EEC Treaty will reveal that, like the Constitutions of modern Germany or Italy, it consists of a political and
economic charter. The former comprises the 'Organizational' or
the 'Constitutional' Law of the Community, the latter the law of
the economy. We have discussed the former in the preceding pages
but to complete the picture it seems apposite to summarize, albeit
briefly, the rudiments of the Community law of the economy. A
more detailed analysis will be found in a work[1] complementary to
this volume.

I The concept of the law of the economy

The economic structure of all the Member States reflects a 'mixed
economy' ie a system based on private enterprise and state control
of the 'basic' industries. Moreover the omnipresent state, through
the instrumentality of the government, purports to direct the economic life of the nation in a variety of ways and in various degrees
of intensity.[2] Thus the national systems subscribe to the theory of
the *économie dirigée* but differ in the details of its application. This,
in turn, is reflected in the lay-out of the Treaty which purports to
create an 'Economic Community' out of the national varieties by
defining common policies and designing the means and ways of
their implementation. Structurally two objectives are envisaged:
an economic integration within the Community and the projection
of the Community as a single trading entity in the world market.

In a historico-political sense the West European Community is
an answer to the challenge of our times[3] but there is also an
economic explanation of its raison d'être.[4] In other words the

---

1 Lasok, D, *The Law of the Economy in the European Communities* (with a Chapter
   on Agriculture by J W Bridge), 1980.
2 Ibid, pp 9 et seq.
3 Soldatos, P, *L'explication historico-politique des la genèse de Communautés
   européennes*, in Lasok, D and Soldatos, P, *Les Communautés Européennes en
   Fonctionnement* (1981), pp 41 et seq.
4 Bourrinet, J, *L'explication economique de la genèse des Communautés Européennes*,
   ibid pp 65 et seq.

creation and continued existence of the Community implies an interaction of politics and economics because the political integration of Western Europe reflects the progress of its economic integration. In this process the law plays a significant part since it binds the Member States together by a system of reciprocal duties[5] and a duty of solidarity towards the collective they have created;[6] it provides the institutional framework of the 'new legal order'[7] and lays down policies as well as the rules for their implementation and enforcement. The dual role of the law as a force of integration is that of organizing the Community and its economy. Therefore the Community law of the economy is the body of rules addressed to the Member States, individuals, and private and public corporations which in their entirety purport to govern the economic life both at a state and individual level. Since the Community can be built only by stages,[8] starting from a broad base of 'European solidarity', the Community law of the economy purports to create first a Common Market and then bind the Member States into an Economic Union of which a Monetary Union forms an intermediate stage.

Whilst the Community legal order supports a unitary economic order in the making it displays certain federalist characteristics. Thus it proceeds from a division of functions between the Community and the Member States and a separation of competences between the Community and national institutions.[9] Its relationship with the national systems, on the other hand, is based on the triple quality of Community law: autonomy, direct applicability and supremacy.

In accordance with article 2 of the EEC Treaty[10] the principal task of the Community is to establish a Common Market and to approximate the economic policies of the Member States. To that end the Treaty lays down the elements of the Common Market and defines policies which, when implemented, will move the Community from the stage of the Common Market to the stage of the Economic Union. Taken together the elements of the Common Market and the common policies constitute the substantive con-

---

5 Lasok, D Duties of Member States in the European Communities, *Fundamental Duties* (ed by D Lasok et al), 1980, pp 16 et seq.
6 Donner, A M, 'The Constitutional Powers of the Court of Justice of the European Communities' (1974) 11 CML Rev 128.
7 Case 26/62: *Van Gend en Loos v Nederlandse Administratie der Belastingen* [1963] ECR 1, [1963] CMLR 105.
8 Schuman, R, Declaration, 9 May 1950, launching the idea of a Coal and Steel Community.
9 See Case 30/59: *De Gezamenlijke Steenkolenmijnen in Limburg v High Authority of the ECSC* [1961] ECR 1 (at 23).
10 See also ECSC, art 2 and EAEC, art 2.

tents of the Community law of the economy. The procedural contents, ie the rules of the Community process of defining, implementing and enforcing the Treaty objectives, complement the Community *corpus juris*.

Whilst priority is given to the development of the Common Market the Treaty envisages a simultaneous development of policies. Therefore a rigid classification into these two segments of economic law would appear rather pedantic if not artificial. However it is made here deliberately in order to identify the legal problems and to mark the developments to date. The Common Market rules are in operation, albeit incomplete,[11] most of the policies are still in the making.

II The Common Market

In a technical sense we have three Common Markets, each conceived by a Treaty founding the Coal and Steel, Euratom and Economic Community, respectively. However the EEC, being the most prominent of the three and virtually all-embracing, is the subject matter of this study.

The Common Market is a single 'internal' market embracing several sovereign states, ie autonomous economic territories. The Common Market territory[12] is marked out by the political frontiers of the Member States subject to special arrangements with regard to certain overseas and European territories for which the Member States are responsible. Within these frontiers the economic forces of supply and demand are allowed to operate freely in the context of 'directed economy'. The chief elements of the internal Common Market comprise the four freedoms, ie the freedom of movement of goods, persons, services and capital as well as the two principal policies, ie the Common Agricultural Policy and the Competition Policy.

The single 'internal' market projects the Community on the world market as a single trading unit. This projection is to be achieved through the Common Customs Tariff and the Common Commercial Policy. The former appears to be completed, the latter, facing world-wide problems and entrenched Member States' obligations, has to be trimmed to the prevailing trade winds.

Though the internal and the external facets form two inseparable characteristics of the single Common Market they have not developed uniformly. This, in a sense, reflects what has been said

11 See Commission White Paper 1985.
12 EEC, art 227.

earlier, that is, that elements of the Common Market and Economic Union do not develop in isolation but tend to overlap. Thus, whilst the 'internal' Common Market (subject to the transitory position of the younger Member States, Greece, Portugal and Spain) has been almost accomplished[13] the 'external' Common Market has been slow on the uptake because of the nature of the Common Commercial Policy. Though affecting the internal market, it forms part of a wider issue and has to be seen both as an element of trade and external relations of the Community. It combines economics and politics.

III The Four Freedoms

(A) MOVEMENT OF GOODS[14]
(i) *Customs disarmament*
Subject to the transitional period[15] completed on 1 July 1968 by virtue of Council decisions of 1960 and 1962[16] the Treaty provides for the elimination of customs duties[17] and quantitative restrictions[18] as well as charges having equivalent effect to customs duties and measures having equivalent effect to quantitative restrictions in trade between the Member States of the Community. Since none of the relevant concepts has been defined by the Treaty it fell upon the ECJ to determine in specific cases whether or not a breach of the Treaty has occurred. In the leading case[19] the Court held article 12 directly applicable and thus afforded an importer protection from national law imposing on a product coming from a fellow Member State its own classification of goods and a duty in excess of the Community rate. Because the obligation to eliminate customs duties is absolute any exception must be clear and unambiguous and has to be interpreted strictly.[20]

---

13 See Commission White Paper (Com (85) 310 Final) for the Milan Summit Conference 28–29 June 1985 listing deficiencies and indicating measures to be taken.
14 For details, Lasok, D, *The Customs Law of the European Economic Community* (2nd edn 1990) Chs 3, 4, 5.
15 EEC, art 8.
16 To be completed by Spain and Portugal by 1 January 1993, Act of Accession, arts 31 and 196 respectively.
17 EEC, arts 9–17.
18 Ibid, arts 30–35.
19 *Van Gend*, supra.
20 Cases 52 and 55/65: *Germany v EEC Commission* [1966] ECR 159, [1967] CMLR 22; Case 199/84: *Procuratore della Repubblica v Tiziano Migliorini Sund (Re Re-export of a Product from Czechoslovakia)* [1985] ECR 3317, [1987] 2 CMLR 841.

Quotas to restrict imports or exports are also abolished. The classic example of this prohibited practice was the suspension of the import of pork products into Italy in which case Italy was held to be in breach of the Treaty.[21] More recent examples of state bans on imports include the British restriction on the import of Dutch potatoes,[22] the French refusal to accept sheepmeat from Britain[23] and the British refusal to accept French UHT milk products[24] and poultry,[1] to name just the most notorious ones. In that respect a previous international[2] agreement provides no defence to a breach of Community law.

Charges having equivalent effect to customs duties have been defined by the ECJ as 'duties whatever their description or technique, imposed unilaterally, which apply specifically to a product imported by a Member State but not to a similar national product and which by altering the price, have the same effect upon the free movement of goods as a customs duty'.[3] They include duties imposed upon import licences,[4] such licences being no longer valid in trade between Member States; tax on the export of objects of art,[5] statistical levies,[6] charges for health inspections,[7] charges on the marketing or processing of already imported goods,[8] storage charges prior to completion of customs formalities,[9] to list only a few examples. However value added tax is not a charge equivalent to customs duty.[10]

21 Case 7/61: *EEC Commission v Italy* [1961] ECR 317, [1962] CMLR 39.
22 Case 231/78: *EC Commission v United Kingdom* [1979] ECR 1447, [1979] 2 CMLR 427.
23 Case 232/78: *EC Commission v French Republic* [1979] ECR 2729, [1980] 1 CMLR 418; Case 171/83 R: [1983] ECR 2621.
24 Case 124/81: *EC Commission v United Kingdom* [1983] ECR 203, [1983] 2 CMLR 1; see Case 153/78: *EC Commission v Germany (Re Health Control of Imported Meat)* [1979] ECR 2555, [1980] 1 CMLR 198.
1 Case 40/82: *EC Commission v United Kingdom* [1984] ECR 283.
2 Case 10/61: *EC Commission v Italy* [1962] ECR 1, [1962] CMLR 187.
3 Cases 2 and 3/62: *EEC Commission v Luxembourg and Belgium* [1962] ECR 425 at 432, [1963] CMLR 199 (Gingerbread).
4 Cases 90 and 91/63: *EC Commission v Luxembourg and Belgium* [1964] ECR 625, [1965] CMLR 58.
5 Case 7/68: *EC Commission v Italy* [1968] ECR 423, [1969] CMLR 1.
6 Case 43/71: *Politi SAS v Italian Ministry for Finance* [1971] ECR 1039, [1973] CMLR 60.
7 Case 29/72: *Marimex SpA v Italian Finance Administration* [1972] ECR 1309, [1973] CMLR 486; Case 39/73: *Rewe-Zentralfinanz GmbH v Direktor der Landwirtschaftskammer Westfalen-Lippe* [1973] ECR 1039, [1977] 1 CMLR 630; Case 158/82: *EC Commission v Denmark* [1983] ECR 3573; [1984] 2 CMLR 658.
8 Case 78/76: *Steinike and Weinlig v Germany* [1977] ECR 595, [1977] 2 CMLR 688.
9 Case 132/82: *EC Commission v Belgium* [1983] ECR 1649, [1983] 3 CMLR 600.
10 Case 39/82: *Donner v The Netherlands* [1983] ECR 19, [1983] 1 CMLR 711.

It should be noted that neither the level and designation of the charge, nor its objective, ie whether or not to benefit the state or whether to protect the competing national product matters, but what does matter is the fact that the charge is imposed on goods crossing the frontier of a state.[11]

In the *Scotch Whisky* case[12] the ECJ offered a rather broad description of measures having equivalent effect to quantitative restrictions saying that these include 'all trading rules enacted by Member States which are capable of hindering, directly or indirectly, actually or potentially, intra-Community trade'. However in the *Second Whisky* case[13] the Court modified its extreme stance holding that the prohibition on marketing the product without documentary proof that it was genuine did not per se constitute an infringement of the Treaty.

Examples of charges equivalent to customs duties and measures equivalent to quantitative restrictions are legion as if the Member States deliberately set out to avoid their Treaty obligations. The *Simmenthal* cases[14] contain both: sanitary inspection procedures of frozen meat and live cattle at the Italian frontier were held to be equivalent to quantitative restrictions and fees charged equivalent to customs duties.

Similarly a national marketing system[15] incompatible with the Community common organization of a market; or excessive checking or inspection of imported goods;[16] or advertising[17] rules designed to champion or protect domestic products at the expense of the imported ones; or a pricing[18] system discriminating against imported goods; or marketing rules under which a particular description[19] or alcoholic strength requirements[20] disqualify

11 Joined Cases 2–3/69: *Sociaal Fonds voor de Diamantarbeiders v SA Ch Brachfeld & Sons* [1969] ECR 211; [1969] CMLR 335.
12 Case 8/74: *Procureur du Roi v Dassonville* [1974] ECR 837, [1974] 2 CMLR 436.
13 Case 2/78: *EC Commission v Belgium, Re Import of Spirituous Drinks* [1979] ECR 1761, [1980] 1 CMLR 216.
14 Case 35/76: *Simmenthal SPA v Italian Minister for Finance* [1976] ECR 1871, [1977] 2 CMLR 1; Case 106/77: *Simmenthal* [1978] ECR 629, [1978] 3 CMLR 263; Case 70/77: *Simmenthal* [1978] ECR 1453, [1978] 3 CMLR 670.
15 Case 83/78: *Pigs Marketing Board (Northern Ireland) v Redmond* [1978] ECR 2347, [1979] 1 CMLR 177.
16 Case 272/80: *Frans-Nederlandse Maatschappij voor Biologische Producten* [1981] ECR 3277, [1982] 2 CMLR 497; Case 124/81, supra.
17 Case 249/81: *EC Commission v Ireland* [1982] ECR 4005, [1983] 2 CMLR 104.
18 Case 65/75: *Tasca* [1976] ECR 291, [1977] 2 CMLR 183; Case 229/83: *Association Leclerc v Au Blé Vert Sàrl* [1985] 2 CMLR 286.
19 Case 12/74: *EC Commission v Germany* [1975] ECR 181, [1975] 1 CMLR 340.
20 Case 120/78 *Rewe v Bundesmonopolverwaltung für Branntwein (Re Cassis de Dijon)* [1979] ECR 649, [1979] 3 CMLR 494.

imported goods, are measures equivalent to quantitative restrictions in Community trade.

However, charges for services rendered such as for example charges levied on oil in transit from Italy to Germany and Austria arising from the use of harbour waters and port facilities are legitimate[21] but not so charges for checks forming part of administrative procedure for the protection of public health and hygiene.[22]

When an inspection of goods is part of an international regulation of trade based on a convention to which the Member States are parties, the charges are justified but, like in cases authorized by Community legislation, the principle of proportionality applies.[23]

Treaty provisions designed to remove trade barriers addressed to the Member States may also be applied to private parties if such parties relying upon rights, such as intellectual property rights, created by national laws aim to divide markets or restrict the movement of goods in the Common Market.[24]

(ii) *Tax aspects*

Member States are often tempted to impose taxes upon foreign goods in order to protect their own products. Such discriminatory taxes are prohibited by article 95 of the EEC Treaty.[1] However it should be borne in mind that article 95 does not purport to regulate both fiscal policy and customs law. Yet it may correct a Member State's behaviour where it impinges upon the movement of goods by applying disparate and discriminate rates to similar domestic and imported products. In such a case a tax would be a charge having equivalent effect to a customs duty.

Whether or not a tax is discriminatory will depend not only on the rate charged but also on a comparison between the products involved. In this respect article 95 lays down a double test. Not

---

21 Case 266/81: *SIOT v Ministero delle Finanze* [1983] ECR 731; [1984] 2 CMLR 231: but see Case 69/84: *Padovani v Amministrazione delle Finanze dello Stato (Re Clearance and Port Charges on Re-exported Goods)* [1987] 1 CMLR 62.

22 Case 314/82: *EC Commission v Belgium* [1984] ECR 1543, [1985] 3 CMLR 134.

23 Case 89/76: *EC Commission v Nederlands* [1977] ECR 1355; [1978] 3 CMLR 630; Case 1/83: *IFG v Freistaat Bayern* [1984] ECR 349; [1985] 1 CMLR 453.

24 Eg Cases 56 and 58/64: *Consten SARL and Grundig Verkaufs v EEC Commission* [1966] ECR 299, [1966] CMLR 418; Case 78/70: *Deutsche Grammophon GmbH v Metro-SB-Grossmärkte GmbH & Co KG* [1971] ECR 487, [1971] CMLR 631; Case 192/73: *Van Zuylen v Hag* [1974] ECR 731, [1974] 2 CMLR 127; Case 15/74: *Centrafarm v Sterling Drug* [1974] ECR 1147, [1974] 2 CMLR 480; Case 119/75: *Terrapin v Terranova* [1976] ECR 1039, [1976] 2 CMLR 482.

1 Case 28/67: *Mölkerei-Zentrale Westfalen-Lippe v Hauptzollamt Paderborn* [1968] ECR 143 at 155, [1968] CMLR 187 at 217; *Tax on Imported Spirits Cases*, supra.

only must there be equality of fiscal treatment between similar imported and domestic products, but the internal taxation must also be such as to avoid indirect protection to other competing products.[2] The ECJ[3] ruled further that not only the rate of direct and indirect internal taxation on domestic and imported products, but also the basis of assessment and rules for levying the tax must be taken into consideration.

Dealing recently with Danish tax on alcoholic drinks the ECJ held that fruit wine and grape wine were similar products but the former was domestically produced whereas the latter was imported. A tax discriminating between these products was, therefore, contrary to article 95.[4] However, fortified fruit wine and whiskey were not similar products and, here again, the former was a domestic product whereas the latter was not. The Danish tax system covered a variety of domestic and imported drinks and, where the products were different, irrespective of their origin, the rate of tax was also different. There was, therefore, no discrimination contrary to article 95.[5]

The conclusion to be drawn from case law is that, while Member States may legitimately distinguish between various alcoholic drinks, they may not use that distinction to justify tax discrimination or to allow tax advantage or confer tax protection to domestic products.[6] The principle applies to all products.

(iii) *Derogations under article 36*

Article 36 allows the Member States to derogate from their obligations on several grounds provided such derogations do not constitute 'a means of arbitrary discrimination or a disguised restriction on trade'. These grounds include 'public morality,'[7]

---

2 Case 27/67: *Fink-Frucht v HZA München* [1968] ECR 223 at 234, [1968] CMLR 187; Case 77/69: *EC Commission v Belgium (Re Duty on Timber)* [1970] ECR 237, [1974] 1 CMLR 203.

3 Case 74/76: *Iannelli v Meroni* [1977] ECR 557 at 579–580, [1977] 2 CMLR 688.

4 Case 106/84: *Re Taxation of Wine, EC Commission v Denmark* [1986] ECR 833, [1987] 2 CMLR 278.

5 Case 243/84: *John Walker v Ministeriet for Skatter* [1986] ECR 833, [1987] 2 CMLR 278.

6 Cases 68/79: *Hans Just I/S v Danish Ministry for Fiscal Affairs* [1980] ECR 501; [1981] 2 CMLR 714; 46/80 *Vinal SpA v Orbat SpA* [1981] ECR 77; [1981] 3 CMLR 524; 216/81: *Cogis v Amm delle Finanze* [1982] ECR 2701; [1983] 1 CMLR 685; 277/83: *Re Marsala Liqueur Wine, EC Commission v Italy* [1987] 3 CMLR 324.

7 *R v Henn, R v Darby* [1978] 3 All ER 1190 CA; affd [1980] AC 850, [1979] 2 CMLR 495, HL; Case 34/79: [1979] ECR 3795, [1980] 1 CMLR 246; but see Case 121/85: *Conegate Ltd v HM Customs and Excise* [1986] 1 CMLR 739.

public policy,[8] and public security;[9] the protection of health[10] and life of humans, animals or plants;[11] the protection of national treasures[12] possessing artistic, historic or archaeological value; or the protection of industrial and commercial property'. Being in the nature of an exception to the rule these grounds have to be construed restrictively.

The case law in the field of derogation has developed considerably.[13] Moreover, attempts have recently been made to justify restrictions on the ground of consumer protection[14] but in such cases the ECJ tends to give credit to the intelligence of consumers and generally counsels to resort to appropriate labelling rather than restrictions on imports.

8 Case 7/78: *R v Thompson* [1978] ECR 2247, [1979] 1 CMLR 47. See also unsuccessful pleas in Cases 95/81: *EC Commission v Italy (Re Advance Payments for Imports)* [1982] ECR 2187 at 2204; 50/83: *EC Commission v Italy* [1984] ECR 1633, [1985] 1 CMLR 777; 154/85: *EC Commission v Italy* [1987] ECR 2717, [1988] 2 CMLR 951.

9 *McAfee v Smyth and Quigley (radios used by terrorists)* [1981] 1 CMLR 410, Belfast Magistrates' Court; *R v Goldstein* [1982] 3 All ER 53, [1982] 2 CMLR 181, affd [1983] 1 All ER 434, [1983] 1 CMLR 252 HL. See also Case 95/81, supra; Case 72/83: *Campus Oil Ltd v The Minister for Industry and Energy (Re Security of Oil Supplies)* [1984] ECR 2727, [1984] 3 CMLR 544.

10 Case 29/72: *Marimex SpA v Ministero delle Finanze* [1972] ECR 1309, [1973] CMLR 486; *Simmenthal Cases,* supra; Case 153/78: *EC Commission v Germany* [1979] ECR 2555, [1980] 1 CMLR 198; Case 788/79: *Re Gilli and Andres* [1980] ECR 2071, [1981] 1 CMLR 146; Case 30/79: *Land of Berlin v Firma Wigei* [1980] ECR 151, [1981] 3 CMLR 746; Cases 141–143/81: *Holdijk* [1982] ECR 1299, [1983] 3 CMLR 635; Case 1/83: *IFG v Freistaat Bayern* [1985] 1 CMLR 453; Case 124/81: *EC Commission v United Kingdom (Re Packaging of UHT Milk)* [1983] ECR 203; [1983] 2 CMLR 1; Case 274/87: *EC Commission v Germany (Re Quality of Sausage)* [1989] 2 CMLR 733.

11 Case 39/73: *Rewe-Zentralfinanze GmbH v Direktor der Landwirtschaftskammer Westfalen-Lippe* [1973] ECR 1039; cf Case 89/76: *EC Commission v Nederlands* [1977] ECR 1355, [1978] 3 CMLR 630. Case 153/78: *EC Commission v Germany* [1979] ECR 2555, [1980] 1 CMLR 198; Case 124/81: *EC Commission v United Kingdom* [1983] ECR 203, [1983] 2 CMLR 1; Case 40/82: *EC Commission v United Kingdom* [1982] ECR 2793, [1982] 3 CMLR 497, and [1984] ECR 283, Case 39/73, supra; Case 89/76: *EC Commission v Nederlands* [1977] ECR 1355, [1978] 3 CMLR 630.

12 Case 7/68: *EC Commission v Italy* [1968] ECR 423, [1969] CMLR 1. Case 18/71: *Eunomia di Porro e C v Italian Ministry of Education* [1971] ECR 811, [1972] CMLR 4.

13 Lasok, op cit, pp 78 et seq.

14 Eg Case 179/85: *EC Commission v Germany, Re Use of Champagne-Type Bottles* [1988] 1 CMLR 135; Case 178/84: *EC Commission v Germany, Re Purity Requirements for Beer* [1988] 1 CMLR 780; Case 174/84: *EC Commission v Greece, Re Beer Purity Standards* [1988] 1 CMLR 813; Case 286/86: *Ministère Public v Deserbais Re Marketing of Cheese* [1989] 1 CMLR 516; Case 261/81: *Rau v De Smedt, Re Marketing of Margarine* [1982] ECR 3961; [1983] 2 CMLR 496; see also Cases 341/82 and 189/83: *EC Commission v Belgium* [1985] 1 CMLR 120.

In a number of cases the Community Court had to grapple with the problem of measures having equivalent effect to quantitative restriction arising from the claims to protection of intellectual property rights. Faced with the argument that these rights are protected under article 36 and article 222 of the Treaty the ECJ distinguished between the existence of such rights and their abuse in order either to impede the movement of goods[15] or frustrate the Community rules of competition.[16] In the ruling of the Court the protection of article 36 can be afforded only for the purpose of ... 'safeguarding rights which constitute the specific subject matter of that property ...'[17] which means that the use of intellectual property rights in contravention of a paramount principle of the Common Market such as the free movement of goods cannot be justified. It cannot be relied on to protect national economic interests or justify economic measures.[18]

(iv) *Derogations under article 115*

Article 115 (1) provides for derogation from the principle of free movement of goods to make it sure that the execution of the Common Commercial Policy is not obstructed by deflection of trade caused by imports of goods from outside the Community or where differences between such measures lead to difficulties in one or more of the Member States. In such cases the Commission has power to authorize protective measures to be taken by the Member States concerned. By Decision 80/47[19] the Commission established a system of intra-Community surveillance where there is a danger that imports of certain products may give rise to economic difficulties.

15 Eg Case 192/73: *Van Zuylen Frères SA v Hag AG* [1974] ECR 731, [1974] 2 CMLR 127; Case 15/74: *Centrafarm BV and De Peijper v Sterling Drug Inc* [1974] ECR 1147, [1974] 2 CMLR 480; Case 3/78: *Centrafarm BV v American Home Products Corpn* [1978] ECR 1823, [1979] 1 CMLR 326; Case 119/75: *Terrapin (Overseas) Ltd v Terranova Industrie CA Kapferer & Co* [1976] ECR 1039, [1976] 2 CMLR 482; Case 102/77: *Hoffmann-La Roche & Co AG v Centrafarm Vertriebsgesellschaft etc* [1978] ECR 1139, [1978] 3 CMLR 217.
16 Cases 56 and 58/64: *Consten and Grundig* op cit; Case 24/67: *Parke, Davis & Co v Probel* [1968] ECR 55, [1968] CMLR 47; Case 40/70: *Sirena Srl v Eda Srl* [1971] ECR 69, [1971] CMLR 260; Case 78/70: *Deutsche Grammophon GmbH v Metro-SB-Grossmärkte GmbH & Co KG* [1971] ECR 487, [1971] CMLR 631.
17 In *Terrapin*, supra, at 505.
18 See Case 238/82: *Durphar BV v Netherlands* [1985] 1 CMLR 256.
19 OJ 1980, L16/14.

(v) *National security safeguards*
Article 223 of the EEC Treaty permits the Member States to withhold information which they consider essential to their security and to take such measures as they deem necessary for the protection of the essential interests of their security connected with the production of or trade in arms, munitions and war materials, but such measures must not adversely affect competition in the Common Market regarding products which are not intended for specifically military purposes.

Article 224 allows for derogations in the event of serious internal disturbances affecting the maintenance of law and order, in the event of war or international tension constituting a threat of war, or in order to carry out obligations for the purpose of maintaining peace and international security.

Both articles have to be interpreted restrictively[20] since they could lead to unilateral action evading the duties imposed by the exigencies of the Common Market. It is interesting to note that no attempt has been made to rely on these derogations in cases where the movement of goods was disturbed by angry mobs resorting to violence.[1] Evidently, as stated by A G Verloren van Themaat[2] local disturbances do not seem to justify measures affecting the freedom of imports or exports unless they are so serious as to necessitate a large-scale intervention of security forces. However, individuals exposed to mob rule (as, for example, experienced by British carriers of lambs and sheepmeat in France during the summer of 1990) would take a different view.

(vi) *Physical and technical barriers to trade*
The physical barriers consist of the national frontiers with the whole apparatus of frontier controls. They are the visible obstacle to the free movement of goods and persons and in a 'People's Europe' constitute an anachronism. The object is not merely to simplify the existing procedures but to eliminate completely the internal frontier control. However, there is an argument for retention of controls in order to combat drug smuggling, terrorism, illegal immigration and international frauds.

So far formalities have been simplified by using a single administrative document[3] in the intra-Community trade and a special transit procedure with EFTA[4] countries. Directives[5] of 1983 and

---

20 See Case 13/68: *Salgoil SpA v Italian Ministry for Foreign Trade* [1968] ECR 453 at 463; [1969] CMLR 181.
1 Case 42/82: *EC Commission v France* [1983] ECR 1013; [1984] 1 CMLR 160.
2 In Case 231/83: *Cullet v Centre Leclerc* [1985] 2 CMLR 524 at 534.
3 OJ 1987, L226.
4 OJ 1987, L157.
5 OJ 1983, L359/8 and OJ 1987, L24/33.

1987 implement the principle of simplified procedure. Council Regulation 4060/89[6] purports to eliminate controls performed at the frontiers of the Member State for road and inland waterway transport. Thus as from July 1990 control takes place 'solely as part of the normal control procedures applied in a non-discriminatory fashion throughout the territory of the Member States'. By 1992 the Commission is due to produce a Code of Practice to be applied uniformly by the national customs authorities. In the meantime the ECJ declared illegal certain practices including double controls, ie controls in the country of export and import of the same product. It ruled, accordingly, in a case concerning fish[7] that it is unnecessary to repeat in the country of destination the checking procedures which have already been carried out in the country of export, though sample checking or checking for the deterioration of certain products during transport or during handling may be justifed.

The removal of technical barriers involves extensive legislation laying down Community standards. At first the Community adopted a one-dimensional approach laying down rules for individual products, for example certain foodstuffs, industrial products, pharmaceutical and agricultural products. This was a slow and laborious process. The new approach, outlined in the White Paper, is a multi-dimensional strategy based on two principles: selective harmonization and mutal recognition. Accordingly a distinction is made between what is essential to harmonize and what may be left to mutual recognition of national standards. Therefore harmonization is to be restricted to those sectors in which it is essential to create a uniform Community market, ie establishing minimum health and safety regulations as a result of which manufacturers who conform to these regulations will have access to the markets of the other Member States.

The principle of mutual recognition in non-essential fields is based on the *Cassis de Dijon* formula[8] which means that the Member States must accept each other's product which may be different in some detail but which, essentially, respond to the same demand. Regarding manufactured goods it means that Member States must accept products from the others which though manufactured to a different design nevertheless perform the same function as those manufactured specifically to national standards.

In order to prevent the Member States from continuing to lay down their own national product standards different from the

6 OJ 1989, L390/18.
7 Case 132/80: *United Foods NV v Belgium* [1981] ECR 995, [1982] 1 CMLR 273.
8 Case 120/78: *Rewe-Zentral v Bundesmonopolverwaltung für Branntwein (Re Cassis de Dijon)* [1979] ECR 649; [1979] 3 CMLR 494.

Community, Council Directive 83/189[9] obliged them to notify the Commission in advance any newly proposed regulations and technical standards. The Commission has power to prevent Member States from implementing these proposals until it has been proved that they do not create any new barriers to intra-Community trade.

The enforcement of the Community customs rules remains in the hands of the national authorities subject to the supervisory function of the Commission and, ultimately, the enforcement procedure against the Member States before the Court of Justice. The administrative and criminal sanctions differ from country to country whilst the Draft Treaty on Common Penal Rules of 1971[10] remains a half-forgotten proposal. However, the principle of proportionality applies to national repressive measures.[11]

State monopolies

State monopolies of 'a commercial character' shall be progressively adjusted in order to eliminate discrimination in the conditions under which goods are procured and marketed between nationals of Member States (article 37).[12] Thus not all the monopolies are incompatible with the Common Market.[13] If a State continues with a monopoly, eg for the manufacture, import and sale of tobacco[14] despite the resolution to abolish it, a party may raise article 37 in defence against prosecution for offences committed in breach of the national monopoly law. Similarly a charge upon imported alcoholic drink levied in order to support the state monopoly in spirits is incompatible with article 37.[15] Should a Member State fail to carry out its obligation or re-establish a monopoly of a commercial character it would face an enforcement action under article 169 of the Treaty.[16]

9 OJ 1983, L109/8.
10 Ibid, pp 141, 142 and EEC General Report 1971, item 176.
11 Case 203/80: *Re Guerrino Casati* [1981] ECR 2595 at 27; [1982] 2 CMLR 365; Case 299/86: *Italy v Drexl (Re Penalty for Smuggling)* [1989] 2 CMLR 241.
12 Spanish and Portuguese state monopolies ought to be eliminated by 1 January 1991 and 1993 respectively.
13 See Case 6/64: *Costa v ENEL* [1964] ECR 585, [1964] CMLR 425.
14 Case 59/75: *Pubblico Ministero v Manghera* [1976] ECR 91, [1976] 1 CMLR 557.
15 Case 45/75: *Rewe-Zentrale des Lebensmittel-Grofshandels GmbH v Hauptzollamt Landau-Pfalz* [1976] ECR 181, [1976] 2 CMLR 1.
16 See eg Case 90/82: *EC Commission v France* [1983] ECR 2011; [1984] 2 CMLR 516; Case 78/82: *EC Commission v Italy* [1983] ECR 1955; Case 161/82: *EC Commission v France* [1983] ECR 2079; [1984] 2 CMLR 296.

(v) *External trade*
The Community external trade is founded upon the twin principles
of Common Customs Tariff (CCT) and the Common Commercial
Policy (CCP). The former is a code of law based on the Treaty[17]
adopted in 1960 and applied at present in its up-dated versions of
1987.[18] The CCP,[19] on the other hand, together with the Conjunctural Policy[20] and the Balance of Payment provisions[1] forms
part of the Community Economic Policy.[2]

COMMON CUSTOMS TARIFF

The CCT consists of the rules on nomenclature or classification of
goods, origin and valuation of goods as well as customs formalities.
It has to be applied uniformly by the national customs authorities
because since its adoption, the Member States can no longer enact
autonomous provisions in this field.[3] In other words the CCT has
replaced the national tariffs.[4] Moreover the Member States are
bound by the CCT nomenclature and explanatory notes and tariff
notices issued by the Customs Co-operation Council.[5]

The initial CCT nomenclature established by regulation 950/68
on the basis of the Brussels Convention is subjected to annual
review the results of which are published in the Official Journal.[6]
However despite the precise description of goods problems of
interpretation arise and these have to be solved ultimately by the
Community Court. In the turkey tails[7] case the ECJ laid down
certain guidelines in this respect saying that 'products which are
not covered by any tariff heading must be classified under the
heading for the products for which they are most analogous' and
this 'should be decided on the basis not only of their physical
characteristics but also of their use and commercial value'. Sub-

17 EEC, arts 18–29.
18 Reg 2658/87, OJ 1987, L256/1 amended by Reg 20/89, OJ 1989, L4/19 and
   Reg 1672/89, OJ 1989, L256/1.
19 EEC, arts 110–116.
20 EEC, art 103.
1 EEC, arts 104–109.
2 EEC Title II.
3 Case 74/69: *HZA Bremen-Freihafen v Waren-Import Gesellschaft Krohn* [1970]
   ECR 451 at 463, [1970] CMLR 466.
4 Case 38/75: *Nederlandse Spoorwegen v Inspecteur der Invoerrechten en Accijnzen*
   [1975] ECR 1439, [1976] 1 CMLR 167.
5 Case 14/70: *Deutsche Bakels GmbH v Oberfinanzdirektion München* [1970] ECR
   1001, [1971] CMLR 188.
6 OJ Sp Ed 1968 (I), p 925. See Commission Reg 646/89, OJ 1989, L71/20.
7 Case 40/69: *HZA Hamburg v Bollmann* [1970] ECR 69 at 81, [1970] CMLR
   141.

stantial case law includes definitions of tapioca,[8] maize groats,[9] diet-mayonnaise,[10] sausage,[11] (which in the instant case was a revolting article manufactured of fat and lowest grade meat offal), glass reflectors,[12] ice cream,[13] laughing device,[14] work of art,[15] books for children,[16] chocolate,[17] and game[18] (which in the instant case concerned caribou meat, the classification into 'wild' or 'domestic' product depending upon the country of origin since these animals roam freely in Greenland but are domesticated in Norway), sports shoes,[19] sailing boards,[20] lithographs,[1] rosé wine,[2] animal waste,[3] other tobacco,[4] and medicinal products,[5] to quote only a few examples.

The declaration of origin is important at least to determine whether the goods originate from the Community or from a third country and, therefore, whether or not they are subject to the free movement or the CCT and the CCP. If they come from outside they become goods in free circulation under article 10 (1) of the EEC Treaty when the formalities have been complied with and the appropriate duty has been paid. The Community rules in this

---

8 Case 72/69: *HZA Bremen v Bremen Handelgesellschaft* [1970] ECR 427, [1970] CMLR 466; Case 74/69, supra.

9 Case 13/71: *Henck v HZA Emmerich* [1971] ECR 767.

10 Case 30/71: *Siemers v HZA Bad Reichenhall* [1971] ECR 919, [1972] CMLR 121.

11 Case 12/73: *Muras v HZA Hamburg-Jonas* [1973] ECR 963.

12 Case 183/73: *Osram v Oberfinanzdirektion Frankfurt* [1974] ECR 477, [1974] 2 CMLR 360.

13 Case 53/75: *Belgiun State v Vandertaelen and Maes* [1975] ECR 1647.

14 Case 22/76: *Import Gadgets v LAMP Spa* [1976] ECR 1371.

15 Case 23/77: *Westfalischer Kunstverein v HZA Münster* [1977] ECR 1985, [1978] 1 CMLR 373; Case 155/84: *Onnasch v HZA Berlin-Packhof* [1987] ECR 1449, [1986] 2 CMLR 456.

16 Case 62/77: *Carlsen Verlag v Oberfinanzdirektion Köln* [1977] ECR 2343, [1978] 3 CMLR 14.

17 Case 77/71: *Gervais-Danone AG v HZA München* [1971] ECR 1127, [1973] CMLR 415.

18 Case 149/73: *Witt v HZA Hamburg-Ericus* [1973] ECR 1587. See also Case 28/70: *Witt v HZA Lüneburg* [1970] ECR 1021, [1971] CMLR 163 (Rock Cornish Game Hens).

19 Case 298/82: *Gustav Schickedanz KG v Oberfinanzdirektion Frankfurt am Main* [1984] ECR 1829.

20 Case 32/84: *Van Gend v Inspecteur der Invoerrechten* [1985] ECR 779.

1 Case 291/87: *Huber v HZA Frankfurt am Main* [1990] 1 CMLR 159.

2 Case 89/84: *Fédération Nationale des Producteurs de Vins v Ramel* [1986] 2 CMLR 529.

3 Case 90/83: *Paterson v Weddel & Co Ltd* [1984] ECR 1567; [1984] 2 CMLR 540.

4 Case 141/86: *R v HM Customs and Excise, ex p Imperial Tobacco* [1988] 2 CMLR 43.

5 Case 35/85: *Procureur de la Republique v Tissier* [1986] ECR 1207, [1987] 1 CMLR 551.

respect are based on the Brussels Convention enshrined in Regulation 802/68.[6] With the reform of the Nomenclature an adaptation of the rules of origin was needed. Thus Regulation 3860/87,[7] with reference to article 15 of Regulation 2658/87 replaced Annex 1 to Regulation 802/68 as amended in the course of time. In its preamble Regulation 3860/87 refers to the Harmonized Commodity Description and Coding System which, as from 1 January 1988, will be applied in the Community by means of the CN. However, the practical question of the definition of origin in specific cases may not always be solved by the CN. Therefore the rules embodied in Regulation 802/68 and the case law remain a practical guide in this respect.

Regulation 1769/89[8] prescribes the standard form and size of the certificate of origin required for customs purposes.

A few problems concerning origin had to be decided by the Community Court. These include poultry products from Poland,[9] synthetic textile fabrics from the Middle East in circulation in Belgium but imported into France,[10] Spanish grapes despatched from Italy to France,[11] milboard sails from Hong Kong,[12] to mention only a few examples. However the greatest difficulties have been caused by products of which the component parts have been manfactured in several countries and products assembled by the so-called 'screwdriver' technique in the Community from components manufactured outside the Community.[13] Subject to special provisions of different trade agreements between the Community and third countries, the goods or produce are deemed to have either originated entirely from the foreign country in question or been imported in parts and processed or treated in the Community in which case they would be in free circulation[14] when the requisite conditions have been satisfied. If the goods were produced

6 OJ 1968, L148/1.
7 OJ 1987, L363/30.
8 OJ 1989, L174/11.
9 Case 9/72: *Firma Georg Brunner v HZA Hof* [1972] ECR 961, [1972] CMLR 931.
10 Case 41/76: *Criel (Donckerwolcke) v Procureur de la Republique* [1976] ECR 1921, [1977] 2 CMLR 535.
11 Case 52/77: *Cayrol v Rivoira* [1977] ECR 2261, [1978] 2 CMLR 253. See also Case 179/78: *Procureur de la République v Rivoira (Re penalty for false declaration)* [1979] ECR 1147, [1979] 3 CMLR 456.
12 Case 385/85: *SR Industries v Administration des Douanes* [1988] 1 CMLR 378 at para 7.
13 See eg Case C-26/88: *Brother International GmbH v HZA Giessen* [1990] 3 CMLR 658; *Japan v European Economic Community (Re Screwdriver Assembly, GATT Economic Panel)* [1990] 2 CMLR 639.
14 Case 179/78, supra; Case 113/78: *NGJ Schouten BV v Hoofdproduktschap voor Akkerbouwprodukten* [1979] ECR 695, [1979] 2 CMLR 720.

partially in the Community they are regarded as originating in the Member State in which the last substantial process or operation was completed.[15] However, new problems have come to light due to the so called 'screwdriver technique', ie importation of components to be assembled in the Community at the minimum effort and presenting the end product as a Community product.[16]

Customs valuation is based on the Brussels Convention adopted by Regulation 803/68[17] which has been substantially altered by Regulation 1224/80[18] and updated by subsequent regulations. These represent a complex and technical code including, what is called, the reasonable means test if the orthodox methods prove to be inapplicable.

Cases before the Community Court include, inter alia, the valuation of spare parts imported into Belgium by the Belgium branch of the Swiss subsidiary of the American Caterpillar Tractor,[19] the pricing of pharmaceutical raw materials imported into France (at a price which suggested a capital transfer) by a French subsidiary of a Swiss Company;[20] the question whether the warehousing charge should be included in the declared value,[1] valuation of pharmaceutical products where the buyer and seller were 'persons associated in business';[2] the question whether 'know-how' (being an intangible property) is part of the 'normal price of a machine';[3] and whether transport costs ought to be included in the valuation of goods.[4]

Subject to certain exceptions of which the 'angels'[5] case is an example, customs duties are computed on an *ad valorem* basis but the rates of duties suggest that there are different price zones in the Community.[6]

15 Case 34/78: *Yoshida Nederland BV v Kamer van Koophandel* [1979] ECR 115, [1979] 2 CMLR 747; Case 114/78: *Yoshida GmbH v Industrie-und Handelskammer Kasse* [1979] ECR 151, 2 CMLR 747.
16 See *Japan v EEC, Re Screwdriver Assembly* [1990] 2 CMLR 639.
17 OJ Sp Edn 1968, (II), p 436 as amended.
18 OJ 1980, L134/1.
19 Case 111/79: *Suisse Caterpillar Overseas v Belgium* [1980] ECR 773, [1980] 3 CMLR 597.
20 Case 65/79: *Procureur de la Republique v Chatain* [1980] ECR 1345.
1 Case 38/77: *Enka v Inspecteur der Invoerrechten* [1977] ECR 2203, [1978] 2 CMLR 212.
2 Case 82/76: *Farbwerke Höechst AG v HZA Frankfurt-am-Main* [1977] ECR 335; [1977] 2 CMLR 565.
3 Case 1/77: *Robert Bosch GmbH v HZA Hildesheim* [1977] ECR 1473; [1977] 2 CMLR 563.
4 Case 290/84: *HZA Schweinfurt v Mainfrucht Obstverwertung GmbH* [1985] ECR 3909, [1987] 1 CMLR 684.
5 Case 248/80: *Firma Glunz v HZA Hamburg-Wattershof* [1982] ECR 197.
6 Case 84/79: *Meyer-Uetze v HZA Reichenhall* [1980] ECR 291, [1981] 1 CMLR 434 (per A-G Reischl).

Goods imported into the Community are released for free circulation on the completion of the requisite formalities governed by directive 79/696.[7] The release is an irrevocable operation.[8] Duties are payable at once but any overcharge may be recovered within three years.[9] The formalities are subject to several Community measures including regulations governing transit through Community territory, free zones, inward and outward processing and duty-free arrangements.

Special provisions apply to Euratom and Coal and Steel products.

COMMON COMMERCIAL POLICY

Whilst the CCP forms the external customs barrier the CCP is meant to integrate the Member States' trade with the outside world into a Community system. However the CCP has to be seen in the broader context of the Community external relations policy[10] dictated not only by economic but also by political considerations.

(i) *Trade agreements*
As part of the Common Market the CCP is concerned with international trading agreements. The EEC in its own right and on behalf of the Member States takes part now in the negotiations within GATT. However it pursues its own policy developing a network of association and trade agreements throughout the world. In this process, as we have observed earlier,[11] the treaty-making power of the Community is used extensively, thus replacing the traditional role of the Member States and projecting the Community as the sole trade unit. By virtue of article 234 of the EEC Treaty the existing trade agreements to which the Member States are parties remain valid but must be adjusted to their obligations within the Community. New agreements negotiated by the Member States in their own right are subject to Community guidelines and regulations but the logic of the Common Market suggests that such activity will be possible only within the 'framework agreements' previously negotiated by the Community or in areas in which the Community competence cannot be, or has not been, exercised.

(ii) *Anti-dumping*
Anti-dumping rules apply to goods originating from third countries

---

7 OJ 1979, L205/19 and Commission Directive 82/57, OJ 1982, L28/28.
8 Regulation 104/79, OJ 1979, L175/1.
9 Regulation 1697/79, OJ 1979, L197/1.
10 Supra, pp 58 et seq, supra.
11 Supra, pp 60 et seq, supra.

imported into the Community and they are, at present, governed by Regulation 2423/88,[12] based on article 113 (1) of the EEC Treaty, and the GATT anti-dumping code.

In the case of dumped imports the Community interests are protected by virtue of anti-dumping procedure and the imposition of an anti-dumping duty. Generally speaking, dumping occurs where the export price of a product is less than its 'normal value' or that of a like product. The normal value is computed according to the rules laid down in the Regulation and there are several reference prices[13] which may be used to establish it.

For the purpose of imposing the anti-dumping duty the 'normal value' is compared with the 'export price' to the Community, ie the ex-factory price of goods intended for export. Where there is no export price or where it appears that there is an association or a compensatory arrangement between the exporter and the importer or a third party, or that for other reasons the price actually paid or payable is unreliable, the export price may be constructed on the basis of the price at which the imported product is first resold to an independent buyer.

Anti-dumping measures may be imposed only if the dumping practice causes or threatens to cause material injury to an established Community industry or materially retards the setting up of planned Community industry. An examination of injury takes into consideration the volume of dumped imports, the prices of such imports and the consequent impact on the industry concerned. The term 'Community industry' is interpreted broadly covering the producers as a whole of the like products or those of them whose collective output constitutes a major proportion of the total Community production.

The anti-dumping procedure starts with a complaint to the Commission or a Member State of a person or body acting on behalf of a Community industry which considers itself injured or threatened. The complaint must be substantiated. Model complaint forms are available at the Commission. Where in the absence of a formal complaint a Member State is in possession of sufficient evidence it must advise the Commission accordingly.

The Regulation provides for consultations within an Advisory Committee to cover the existence of dumping, the extent of the

12 OJ 1988, L209/1.
13 See Cases 260/85 and 106/86: *Tokyo Electric Co v EC Council* [1989] 1 CMLR 169; Cases 273/85 and 107/86: *Silver Seiko v EC Council* [1989] 1 CMLR 249; Cases 113, 118–121/77: *NTN Toyo Bearing Co Ltd v EC Council* [1979] ECR 1185, [1979] 2 CMLR 257. See also Commission decision *Re Anti-Dumping Proceedings concerning Methenamine from Eastern Europe* [1990] 2 CMLR 481.

injury and the link between the dumped imports and injury and the measures which would be appropriate to remedy the position.

Where, after consultation, there appears to be a prima facie case, the Commission will investigate both the dumping practice and the injury, giving the parties an opportunity to make their representations. The Commission is empowered to impose a provisional duty where preliminary examination warrants it.

Where the facts are finally established to the effect that the Community interests have to be protected a definitive anti-dumping duty will be imposed by the Council on a proposal submitted by the Commission.

Provisional or definitive duties are imposed by a regulation which, as a Communty Act, is subject to administrative and judicial review.[14] The duty will be collected by Member States in accordance with the conditions upon which it was imposed and independently of the customs duties, taxes and other charges normally imposed on imports.

During the investigations undertakings may be offered by the parties concerned or suggested by the Commission. Under the undertakings exporters revise their prices or cease exports until such time as the Commission is satisfied that either the dumping margin or the injury is removed. Despite the undertakings the investigation has to be completed. However, the undertaking will lapse if the Commission determines that no injury had been proved.

(iii) *Countervailing measures*

The object of countervailing measures, authorized by article VI of the GATT, is to combat the effect of subsidized exports. These measures run parallel to anti-dumping rules and are comprised at present in Regulation 2423/88 discussed above. Like in dumping situations three conditions have to be present, ie the existence of a subsidy, injury to Community industry and a causal connection linking the two. The annex to the Regulation contains an 'illustrative list of export subsidies' which consist of a variety of governmental measures to boost up exports and thus distort the competitiveness of the product.

The procedural rules applicable to anti-dumping and anti-subsidy are identical and the measures decreed by the Commission are subject to administrative and, ultimately, judicial review within the jurisdiction of the European Court.

As in the case of anti-dumping measures there are two types of anti-subsidy measures, ie the imposition of countervailing duties (provisional and definitive) and the acceptance of undertakings but

14 See in particular Case 191/82: *Fediol v EEC Commission* [1983] ECR 2913, [1984] 3 CMLR 244.

this time by the foreign governments involved. Thus for example, in the case of women's shoes[15] the Brazilian Government informed the Commission that it would impose a tax on exports of the product to equalize the subsidy and that it would not adopt any fiscal or other measures to compensate the exporter.

(iv) *Protective measures*

These measures reflect the escape clause of article XIX of the GATT which enables a party to the Agreement to impose quantitative restrictions on imports of products coming in such increased quantities and such conditions as to cause or threaten serious injury to domestic producers of like or directly competitive products.

At present the protective measures are comprised in three regulations, ie Regulation 1765/82[16] applicable to trade with state-trading countries; Regulation 1766/82[17] applicable to trade with the People's Republic of China; and Regulation 288/82[18] applicable to all other third countries, except Cuba.

Instead of imposing a safeguard measure surveillance may be ordered by virtue of Regulation 288/82, such surveillance to be carried out according to appropriate procedure. Thus the enquiry must focus attention on 'serious injury' and 'Community interests' which cover the whole Community territory as exemplified in the *Quartz Watches* case[19] where France, despite German protests, successfully championed the cause of French (and German) manufacturers in face of the importation of the competing product from Japan and Switzerland.

The protective measures usually take the form of import quotas in volume (quartz watches) or both in volume and value (stoneware from Korea).[20]

Protective measures may be instituted by the Commission, the Council and the Member States according to the procedure laid down in Regulation 288/82. The measures taken are subject to administrative and, ultimately, judicial review by the ECJ. However, the Member States are entitled to request an administrative review. Private parties, whether importers or exporters, have no such right.

15 OJ 1981, L327/29.
16 OJ 1982, L195/1.
17 OJ 1982, L195/21.
18 OJ 1982, L35/1.
19 OJ 1984, L106/31.
20 OJ 1983, L96/8.

(v) *Protection against illicit commercial practice*

Following the example of the US Trade Agreem
(which gave the President the power to respond to fo
restrictions and export subsidies) the Community enac
lation 2641/84[1] (also known as the 'New Commercial Policy
ment') for the purpose of 'strengthening the Common Comm
Policy with regard to protection against illicit commercial pr
tices'. It creates no new substantive remedies but a procedure to
enable the Community to combat illicit practices and to ensure full
exercise of Community rights as an autonomous trade unit. It does
not apply to regulations governing anti-dumping or safeguard and
surveillance but complements the rules applicable to the common
organization of agricultural markets and goods processed from
agricultural products. It does not apply to products covered by the
ECSC Treaty.

The procedure to deal with such practices consists of consultation, examination of complaints and adoption of measures to deal
with the particular situation. It may be initiated by the Commission
upon the complaint of Community producers or the Member
States, but not on its own initiative. Complaints by producers and
referrals of such complaints by Member States must be substantiated.

Like all the regulations concerned with protective measures
Regulation 2641/84 sets up an Advisory Committee consisting of
the representatives of the Member States chaired by a representative of the Commission. The Committee considers the complaint before detailed examination of the facts in co-operation with
the parties concerned which include not only the Member States
but also the third countries involved.

The Regulation provides for the adoption of retaliatory measures
which comprise:

(1) the suspension or withdrawal of any concession resulting
from commercial policy negotiations;
(2) the raising of existing customs duties or the introduction of
any other charge on imports; and
(3) the introduction of quantitative restrictions or any other
measures modifying import or export conditions or otherwise affecting trade with the third country concerned.

(B) MOVEMENT OF PERSONS (EEC ARTICLES 48–50)

The economic object of the freedom of movement of persons is to
create a Common Market in manpower. The political object is to

1 OJ 1984, L252/1.

peoples of the Community through
migration and the promotion of a
technical sense the body of law can
d social security rules.

on between 'workers'[2] which may
s order if their membership con-
and 'self-employed persons'.[4] The
ovement' the latter the 'freedom of
ight of establishment, necessary to
ender a service, is not confined to
companies and bodies corporate which
are treated like individuals.[5] It is common ground that the right of
establishment could not be exercised by individuals without the
right of moving freely within the Community or by bodies corporate without mobility. However the distinction between the
freedom of movement and the right of establishment remains essential to Community law, at least, because the Community continues
to legislate separately in these fields.

Freedom of movement implies the right of entry,[6] residence[7] and
exit. It means in particular the right to accept offers of employment;
move[8] freely within the territory of the host country for this
purpose, reside in a host country for the purpose of employment;
and remain there after the termination of employment in accordance with implementing regulations.[9] Expulsion is also governed

---

2 Arts 48–51.
3 See Case 196/87: *Steymann v Staatssecretaris van Justitie* 1989] 1 CMLR 449.
4 Arts 52–58.
5 EEC, art 58 (1).
6 Case 41/74: *Van Duyn v Home Office* [1975] Ch 358, [1974] ECR 1337. Cf.
   Minister of the Interior v Cohn-Bendit [1980] 1 CMLR 543.
7 Case 118/75: *Re Watson and Belmann* [1976] ECR 1185, [1976] 2 CMLR 552;
   Case 48/75: *Re Royer* [1976] ECR 497, [1976] 2 CMLR 619; *R v Secchi* [1975]
   1 CMLR 383. *Williams v Dutch Secretary of State for Justice* [1977] 1 CMLR
   669, Queen of the Netherlands in Council. Case 8/77: *Sagulo v Public Ministry
   Amtsgericht Reutlingen* [1977] ECR 1495, [1977] 2 CMLR 585; Case 157/79:
   R v Pieck [1980] ECR 2171, [1980] 3 CMLR 220. *Residence of non-Community
   nationals:* Case 2A 72/72: *Re Residence Permit for an Egyptian National* [1975]
   2 CMLR 402 (Admin Court of Appeal, Rheinland). *R v Secretary of State for
   Home Affairs, ex p Tombofa* (deportation of a Nigerian) [1988] 2 CMLR 609:
   Case C-192/89: *Sevince v Staatsecretaris van Justitie* (20 September 1989,
   unreported): *R v Secretary of State for the Home Department, ex p Narin*
   (deportation of Turkish national) [1990] 1 CMLR 682.
8 Case 36/75: *Rutili v Ministère de l'Interieur* [1975] ECR 1219, [1976] 1 CMLR
   140.
9 EEC art 48 (3).

by Community rules. As a corollary the Member States are bound
to abolish any discrimination based on nationality between workers
as regards employment, remuneration and other conditions of work
and employment.[10]

In principle only the citizens of the Member States are entitled
to move freely within the Community but each Member State
defines according to its own law who its citizens are and how the
citizenship is acquired and lost. However the privilege has been
extended to certain categories of persons, ie spouses[11] and dependants of Community citizens, stateless persons and refugees as well
as the inhabitants of certain dependent and associated territories.
Broadly speaking the same principles apply to workers and self-
employed persons who exercise liberal professions or provide services.

The principal Community legislation now in force, that is Regulation 1612/68,[12] is addressed to 'workers' in the sense of Community law[13] rather than national law. The term comprises persons
in actual employment in the host country; persons looking for
employment; unemployed who are capable of working and have
previously been employed; persons incapable of working through
illness or injury sustained during employment in the host country;
as well as retired persons, ie persons who have reached the normal
age of retirement whilst working in the host country. However
the construction of the term 'worker' must bear a relationship to
employment[14] in the sense of activity which in itself is regarded
as genuine work,[15] though it seems a person whose income is
supplemented from public funds may still qualify as a worker.[16]

10 Ibid, p 48 (2); see Case 167/73: *EC Commission v France* [1974] ECR 359,
[1974] 2 CMLR 216.
11 For the interpretation of 'spouse' see Case 9/79: *Wörsdörfer (née Koschniske) v
Raad van Arbeid* [1979] ECR 2717, [1980] 1 CMLR 87; but for purpose of
residence cohabiting foreigners have to be treated as cohabiting citizens: see
Case 59/85: *The State (Netherlands) v Ann Florence Reed* [1987] 2 CMLR
448.
12 JO 1968, L257/2 and Dir 73/148, OJ 1973, L172/14 re self-employed persons.
13 Case 75/63: *Hoekstra (née Unger) v Bestuur der Bedrijfsvereniging voor
Detailhandel en Ambachten* [1964] ECR 177, [1964] CMLR 319; *Levin v
Secretary of State for Justice* [1981] 3 CMLR 663 (Reference from Supreme
Admin Court, Netherlands, ECJ Case 53/81, below, note 13; Case 139/85:
Kempf v Staatssecretaris van Justitie [1987] 1 CMLR 764).
14 See decisions of national courts in *Re a Belgian Prostitute, Queen of The
Netherlands in Council* [1976] 2 CMLR 527; *R v Secchi (International Drifter)*
[1975] 1 CMLR 383.
15 Case 53/81: *Levin v Staatssecretaris van Justitie* [1982] ECR 1035, [1982] 2
CMLR 454.
16 Case 139/85: *Kempf v Staatssecretaris van Justitie* (Re Part-time Music
Teacher) [1987] 1CMLR 764.

Freedom of movement does not include 'employment in the public service'[17] though once so employed the worker is protected from discrimination on the ground of his nationality.[18]

According to the Treaty[19] the Member States may restrict the movement of workers, self-employed persons and providers of services on the grounds of public policy, public security and public health. However, being in the nature of a derogation, this power of the Member States has to be interpreted strictly.[20] Several cases involving refusal of entry[21] and expulsion[22] have highlighted the problem of defining 'public policy', ie whether to allow the Member States to apply their own criteria or whether to formulate a Community concept of public policy. The matter is still to be settled though the Court has stressed on occasions that public policy, allowing a derogation from the principle of free movement, has to be interpreted strictly and that the Member States' discretion has to be applied within the limits of the Treaty. It means, in effect, that the use of derogation is reduced to cases of a particularly repulsive behaviour of the individual concerned,[23] criminal convictions not being per se a ground of expulsion, and that it cannot serve an economic purpose[1] such as to protect the jobs of a Member State's citizens. There must be fair hearing, a right of appeal and the procedure ought not to be more onerous than the procedure in comparable administrative cases of a domestic nature.[2]

The Member States control the movement of people and enforce their immigration laws but criminal sanctions that can be imposed ought to be proportionate[3] to the gravity of the offence whilst

---

17 Article 48 (4) on the meaning of 'public service' see Case 149/79: *EC Commission v Belgium, Re Public Employees* [1980] ECR 388, [1981] 2 CMLR 413; Case 149/79 (No 2): [1982] ECR 1845, [1982] 3 CMLR 539. See also Case 307/84: *EC Commission v France, Re French Nurses* [1987] 3 CMLR 555; Case 225/85: *EC Commission v Italy (Re Employees of National Research Council)* [1987] ECR 2625, [1988] 3 CMLR 635.

18 Case 152/73: *Sotgiu v Deutsche Bundespost* [1974] ECR 153.

19 Article 48 (3), 56 (1), 66.

20 *Van Duyn*, supra; *Rutili*, supra.

21 Eg *Van Duyn*, supra, *Cohn-Bendit*, supra.

22 Eg Case 67/74: *Bonsignore v Oberstadtdirektor der Stadt Köln* [1975] ECR 297, [1975] 1 CMLR 472; Case 30/77: *R v Bouchereau* [1977] ECR 1999, [1977] 2 CMLR 800. See also *R v Escauriaza* [1989] 3 CMLR 281 where the English Court of Appeal justified deportation of a Community national on the authority of Case 30/77.

23 See eg Case 131/79: *R v Secretary of State for the Home Department, ex p Santillo* [1980] 2 CMLR 308, [1981] 2 All ER 897, cf *Astrid Proll v Entry Clearance Officer* (English Immigration Tribunal [1988] 2 CMLR 387.

1 Directive 64/221, OJ S 1952–66, p 117; art 2 (2).

2 Case 98/79: *Pecastaing v Belgian State* [1980] ECR 691, [1980] 3 CMLR 685. Cases 115 and 116/81 *Rezguia Adoui and Dominique Cornuaille v Belgiun State* [1982] ECR 1665.

expulsion cannot be ordered for mere administrative offences such as a failure to apply for automatic renewal of a residence permit[4].

It goes without saying that aliens have to identify themselves and to that end have to produce at the point of entry a valid passport or identity card and acquire a residence permit where appropriate. However, these requirements need not be rigorously enforced since spot checks are permissible. Fines for non-compliance are in order but these ought to be proportional to the offence and do not merit refusal of entry.[5]

Looking towards a 'Europe of Peoples' the Commission, beginning with the White Paper, published a number of proposals to ensure by 1992:

  (a) an improvement of the mobility[6] of workers and their families by amending Regulation 1612/68 and Directive 68/360;
  (b) harmonization of income tax and certain tax[7] reliefs for non-resident workers;
  (c) providing for a right of residence to students;[8]
  (d) providing security of residence of pensioners[9] whether employed or self-employed;
  (e) granting residence[10] rights to nationals of Member States who, at present, do not enjoy the right under other provisions of Community law.

The mobility of corporate providers of services depends upon the harmonization of company law and the implementation of the still unratified Convention on the Mutual Recognition of Companies and Bodies Corporate of 1968.

(ii) *Social security (EEC article 51)*

(a) *Social security or social welfare?* Social security provisions are corollary to immigration rules[11] but there is no Community social security system as such since the primary object of the basic Community legislation[12] is merely to co-ordinate national systems and

---

3 Case 118/75, supra; Case 48/75, supra; Case 8/77: *German Federal Republic v Sagulo, Brenca and and Bakhouche* [1977] ECR1495, [1977] 2 CMLR 585.
4 Case 157/79: *R v Pieck* [1980] ECR 2171, [1980] 3 CMLR 220; Bull EC Supp 2/69.
5 Case 321/87: *EC Commission v Belgium (Re Belgian Passport Controls)* [1990] 2 CMLR 492.
6 COM(88) Final, OJ 1989, C100.
7 COM(797) Final, OJ 1980, C21.
8 COM(89) 275/I Final, OJ 1989, C191.
9 COM(89) 275/II Final, OJ 1989, C191.
10 COM(89) 275/III Final, OJ 1989, C191.
11 Case 10/78: *Belbouab v Bundesknappschaft* [1978] ECR 1915, [1979] 2 CMLR 23.
12 At present reg 1408/71; OJ 1971, L149/1, codified version: OJ 1980, C138/1,

thus provide protection to migrant workers and their families in the host countries. As with the immigration rules the status of a worker[13] or a self-employed person is essential to social security rights since these rights are now available to self-employed persons and their families.[14] However the term 'worker' does not necessarily include persons eligible for employment such as students.[15] Conversely a social benefit may be available to a handicapped person who was never a worker and is incapable of employment but is a child of a worker.[16]

Since affiliation to an insurance scheme is the decisive criterion the distinction between 'workers' and self-employed (ie persons enjoying the right of establishment) has lost its practical significance as far as social security benefits are concerned.[17] However, essential to the system is the classification of benefits into 'social security' and 'social welfare' benefits since, in principle, only the former are covered by the Regulation. Social security benefits are available as of right in consequence of the affiliation to an insurance scheme (national or private) but social welfare benefits depend on the needs of the individual claimant and are in the nature of discretionary grants awarded out of the public purse. Since there is no uniformity in the Community in this respect each Member State has to make a declaration explaining the nature of the benefits available under its system. The ECJ held on several occasions that these declarations were inconclusive since the two categories of benefits overlapped and in such cases found for the claimants[18] but later[19] stated that a declaration must be accepted as proof that the

replaced by reg 2000/83 (OJ 1983, L230) and reg 574/72, OJ 1972 L74/1, codified version: OJ 1980, C138/65, replaced by reg 2001/83 (OJ 1983, L230).

13 Reg 1408/71 art 1; Case 44/65: *Hessische Knappschaft v Maison Singer et fils* [1965] ECR 965, [1966] CMLR 82; Case 75/63: *Hoekstra*, supra.

14 Reg 1390/81 (OJ 1981, L143/1) amended by reg 2000/83 (OJ 2000/83, L230) and reg 2001/83 (OJ 1983, L230).

15 Case 66/77: *Kuyken v Rijksdienst voor Arbeidsvoorziening* [1977] ECR 2311, [1978] 2 CMLR 304 but see Case 93/76: *Liègois v Office National de Pensions pour Travailleurs Salaries* [1977] ECR 543, [1977] 2 CMLR 757 ('post-student'); and Case 84/77: *Caisse Primaire d'Assurance Maladie d'Eure et-Loire v Tessier (née Recq) (au pair girl)* [1978] ECR 7, [1979] 1 CMLR 249.

16 Case 63/76: *Inzirillo v Caisse d'Allocations Familiales de l'Arrondissement de Lyon* [1976] ECR 2057, [1978] 3 CMLR 596.

17 Case 17/76: *Brack v Insurance Officer* [1976] ECR 1429, [1976] 2 CMLR 592 and Reg 1390/81, supra.

18 See Case 24/74: *CRAM de Paris v Biason* [1974] ECR 999, [1975] 1 CMLR 59; Case 39/74: *Costa v Belgium* [1974] ECR 1251; Case 79/76: *Fossi v Bundesknappschaft* [1977] ECR 667.

19 Eg Case 35/77: *Ermin (née Beerens) v Rijksdienst voor Arbeidsvoorziening* [1977] ECR 2249, [1978] 2 CMLR 320; Case 14/72: *Heinze v Landesversicherungsanstalt Rheinprovinz* [1972] ECR 1105, [1975] 2 CMLR 96.

benefits granted on the basis of that law are social security benefits. Even where the national law has not been specified it does not necessarily follow that it does not fall within the scope of the Regulation.[20] Therefore, ultimately the beneficiaries are determined according to the national system which means that a person may enjoy the status of worker when drawing a pension[1] or even when uninsured, provided he complies with the conditions laid down by the relevant social security scheme.[2] These conditions are determined by national legislation, the only concern of the Community being that they are applied without discrimination on the ground of nationality.[3]

However, the problem of classification of benefits persists. In Cases 379–381/85 and 93/86[4] the 'topping-up' of low income to the minimum subsistence level was considered to be available to a worker as of right but it was not so when the applicant was not yet a worker[5] for such benefit could not be claimed through a father as a social advantage available to a worker. The only right the applicant had was the right to equal treatment regarding access to employment. Similarly the 'topping-up' of a pension[6] was classified as social assistance. However, the Algerian-born husband of a French wife was not eligible because of his nationality. He had an invalidity pension in his own right but could not claim a supplementary pension as a member of his wife's family because the wife, having never worked outside France, was not a Community worker and, therefore, the husband could not claim social advantage under Regulation 1612/68.

(b) *Community benefits*   Under Regulation 1408/71 certain benefits can be claimed as of right in all the Member States as 'Community' benefits. These include: sickness[7] and maternity benefits;

---

20 Case 70/80: *Vigier v Bundesversicherungsanstalt für Angestellte* [1981] ECR 229, [1982] 2 CMLR 709.
1 Case 182/78: *Bestuur v Pierik* [1979] ECR 1977, [1980] 2 CMLR 88.
2 Case 39/76: *Bestuur v Mouthaan* [1976] ECR 1901.
3 Case 110/79: *Coonan v Insurance Officer* [1980] ECR 1445.
4 *Caisse Regionale d'Assurance Maladie Rhone-Alpes v Giletti* [1988] 1 CMLR 740.
5 Case 316/85: *Centre Public d'Aide Sociale, Courcelles v Lebon* [1989] 1 CMLR 337.
6 Case 147/87: *Zaoui v Caisse Régionale d'Assurance Maladie de l'Ile de France* [1989] 2 CMLR 646.
7 Arts 18–36; Case 23/71: *Janssen v Alliance Nationale des Mutualités Chrétiennes* [1971] ECR 859, [1972] CMLR 13; Case 117/77: *Bestuur van het Algemeen Ziekenfonds Bestuur van het Algemeen Ziekenfonds Drenthe-Platteland v Pierik (No 2)* [1979] ECR 1977, [1978] ECR 825, [1978] 3 CMLR 343; Case 182/78: *Bestuur van het Algemeen Ziekenfonds Drenthe-Platteland v Pierik (No 2)* [1979] ECR 1977, [1980] 2 CMLR 88; Case 75/63: *Hoekstra*, supra; Case 17/76: *Brack v Insurance Officer* op cit; Case 1/78: *Kenny v Insurance Officer* [1978]

invalidity;[8] old age pension;[9] unemployment benefit;[10] accident at work and occupational diseases;[11] death grants[12] and family benefits[13] which include family allowances[14] and supplementary or special allowances for orphans. The Regulation (article 4 (4)) expressly excludes benefits for victims of war[15] civil servants[16] or persons in a similar occupation, eg military personnel.[17] However in certain grey areas the ECJ, relying on the principle of non-discrimination, extended the protection of national law to migrant workers and their families. These include widows' rights,[18] handicapped persons' allowances;[19] educational[20] grants and facilities (in

ECR 1489, [1978] 3 CMLR 651; Case 41/77: *R v National Insurance Comr, ex p Warry* [1977] ECR 2085, [1977] 2 CMLR 783; Case 69/79: *Jordens-Vosters v Bestuur van de Bedrijfsvereniging voor de Leder-en Leder-verwerkende Industrie* [1980] ECR 75, [1980] 3 CMLR 412 (maternity).

8   Case 7/76: *Re an Absence in Ireland* [1977] 1 CMLR 5; 2/72: *Murru v Caisse Régionale d'Assurance Maladie de Paris* [1972] ECR 333, [1972] CMLR 888.

9   Art 44–51, Case 2/67: *de Moor v Caisse de Pension des Employés Privés* [1967] ECR 197, [1967] CMLR 223; Case 1/72: *Frilli v Belgian State* [1972] ECR 457, [1973] CMLR 386.

10 Arts 67–71; Cases 126/77: *Frangiamore v Office National de l'Emploi* [1978] ECR 725, [1978] 3 CMLR 166; Case 76/76: *Di Paolo v Office National de l'Emploi* [1977] ECR 315, [1977] 2 CMLR 59.

11 Reg 1408/71, art 51 (a) replaced by Reg 2864/72, art 1 (17); Case 173/78: *Villano v Nordwestliche Eisen-und Stahl-Berufsgenossenschaft* [1979] ECR 1851, [1980] 1 CMLR 613; Case 268/78: *Pennartz v Caisse Primaire d'Assurances Maladie des Alpes-Maritimes* [1979] ECR 2411, [1980] 1 CMLR 682.

12 Reg 1408/71 arts 64–66.

13 Ibid arts 72–79; Case 106/76: *Gelders-Deboeck v EC Commission* [1977] ECR 1623, [1978] 2 CMLR 627; Case 134/77: *Ragazzoni v Caisse de Compensation pour Allocations Familiales Assubel* [1978] ECR 963, [1979] 3 CMLR 67; Case 32/76: *Saieva v Caisse de Compensation des Allocations Familiales for the Mining Industry of the Charleroi and Basse-Sambre Coalfields* [1976] ECR 1523, [1977] 2 CMLR 26; Case 115/77: *Laumann v Landesversicherungsanstalt Rheinprovinz* [1978] ECR 805, [1978] 3 CMLR 201.

14 But not educational allowances for children: Case 313/86: *Lenoir v Caisse d'Allocations Familiales des Alpes Maritimes* [1990] 1 CMLR 543.

15 See Case 93/75: *Alderblum v Caisse Nationale d'Assurance Viellesse des Travailleurs Salaries de Paris* [1975] ECR 2147, [1976] 1 CMLR 236; Case 144/78: *Tinelli v Berufsgenossenschaft der Chemischen Industrie* [1979] ECR 757, [1979] 2 CMLR 735; Case 9/78: *Directeur Régional de la Securité Sociale de Nancy v Gillard* [1978] ECR 1661, [1978] 3 CMLR 554.

16 Case 129/78: *Bestuur v Lohmann* [1979] ECR 853, [1977] 3 CMLR 618.

17 Case 207/78: *Ministère Public v Even* [1979] ECR 2019, [1980] 2 CMLR 71.

18 Case 130/73: *Vandeweghe v Berufsgenossenschaft für die Chemische Industrie* [1973] ECR 1329, [1974] 1 CMLR 449.

19 Case 39/74: *Costa v Belgian State* [1974] ECR 1251; Case 7/75: *Fracas v Belgian State* [1975] ECR 679, [1975] 2 CMLR 442; Case 76/72: *Michel S v Fonds National de Reclassement Social des Handicapés* [1973] ECR 457; Case 63/76: *Inzirillo v Caisse d'Allocations Familiales de l'Arrondissement de Lyon* [1976] ECR 2057, [1978] 3 CMLR 596.

20 Case 9/74: *Casagrande v Landeshauptstadt München* [1974] ECR 773, [1974] 2

reliance on article 7 of Regulation 1612/68, which guarantees the same social advantages to foreign as to national workers as well as article 3 of Regulation 1408/71) and special benefits to 'large families'.[1]

(c) *Competent law*   Since the object of Community law is merely to co-ordinate the operation of national systems the Regulation has to designate the competent law to ensure that only one national law applies. The law of the workplace and of residence provide the principal connecting factors. Thus an employed person is subject to the law of his workplace[2] even if he resides in another country or if the registered office or place of business of his employer is situated elsewhere. Similarly, a person self-employed in one Member State is subject to the law of that state even if he resides in another state.[3] There are exceptions in favour of the law of the flag for persons employed on board ships and in favour of the national law for military and civil service personnel. Special provisions apply to frontier and seasonal workers. Residence means 'habitual residence', ie the place where the worker retains the centre of his interests[4] but this is a matter of fact to be determined by national courts.[5]

Normally a frontier worker is attached to the state of his employment as far as his pension rights are concerned but derogation to the state of residence is possible if justified in circumstances.[6] However, a frontier worker who emigrates no longer remains in that category as he joins the labour market in his new country. As he can claim unemployment only in the state of his last employment he cannot draw the benefit in the former place of employment. He can, however, claim in the new state and have his contributions in the previous state accumulated.[7]

CMLR 423; Case 68/74: *Alaimo v Préfet du Rhone* [1975] ECR 109, [1975] I CMLR 262 (Reg 1612/68, art 12).

1 Case 32/75: *Christini (or Fiorini) v Société Nationale des Chemins de Fer Français* [1975] ECR 1085, [1976] I CMLR 573 – railfare concession; Case 237/78 (Reg 1612/68, art 7): *Caisse Régionale d'Assurance Maladie (Lille) v Palermo (née Toia)* [1979] ECR 2645, [1980] 2 CMLR 31 – allowance to elderly mother of a large family (Reg 1408/71, arts 2, 3, 4) and Case 261/83: *Castelli v Office National des Pensions* [1987] I CMLR 465.

2 Case 73/72: *Bentzinger v Steinbruchs-Berufsgenossenschaft* [1973] ECR 283.

3 Case 13/73: *Anciens ELS d'Angenieux v Hakenberg* [1973] ECR 935.

4 Ibid at 951, see also Case 76/76: *Di Paolo v Office National de l'Emploi* [1977] ECR 315, [1977] 2 CMLR 59.

5 Case 1/85: *Miethe v Bundesanstalt für Arbeit* [1988] I CMLR 507.

6 Case 58/87: *Rebmann v Bundesversicherungsanstalt für Angestellte* [1990] I CMLR 17.

7 Case 236/87: *Bergemann v Bundesanstalt für Arbeit* [1990] I CMLR 525.

Article 10 of the Regulation provides that invalidity, old-age or survivors' cash benefits, pensions for accidents at work or occupational diseases and death grants acquired under the legislation of one or more Member States are portable, that is to say, unaffected by change of residence of the beneficiary.[8] Other benefits have to be claimed normally in the country where the worker worked and paid his social security contributions. Subject to certain exceptions he cannot simply move to another country and claim benefits there on the strength of the contributions paid elsewhere.

(d) *Aggregation apportionment and overlapping*   The Community character of the social insurance benefit is emphasised by the principle of aggregation which requires the competent authority of a Member State to take into consideration rights earned in another Member State when computing certain benefits secured by Regulation, ie sickness and maternity, invalidity, old age and death benefits, death grant and unemployment benefits. The relevant periods include periods of insurance, employment and residence as well as periods of involuntary unemployment.[9] It means that the competent authority of a Member State whose legislation makes the acquisition, retention or recovery of the right to benefit conditional upon the completion of periods of insurance, employment or residence must, to the extent necessary, take account of such periods completed in another Member State as if they were periods under its own legislation.

Article 12 of the Regulation provides that it can neither confer nor maintain the right to several benefits of the same kind for one and the same period of compulsory insurance, though cumulation of short-term benefits in respect of invalidity, old age and death pensions, or occupational disease awarded by two or more Member States is not prohibited. However, because of the different levels of benefits in the Member States the actual calculation and apportionment between the States involved may result in lower benefit than that available under a single national law. In such a case, ruled the ECJ,[10] the entitlement under a national law cannot be reduced by the Community rules.

Certain guidelines can be deduced from the case law in this

8 Case 110/73: *Fiege v Caisse d'assurance de Strasbourg* [1974] ECR 1001; Case 27/74, supra; Case 87/76: *Bozzone v Office de Securité Sociale d'Outre-Mer* [1977] ECR 687, [1977] 2 CMLR 604.
9 See Case 58/87, supra.
10 Case 34/69: *Caisse d'Assurance Vieillesse v Duffy* [1969] ECR 597, [1971] CMLR 391 (decided under the previous regulation); Case 22/77: *Fonds National de Retraite des Ouvriers Mineurs v Mura* [1977] ECR 1699, [1978] 2 CMLR 416; Case 37/77: *Greco v Fonds National* [1977] ECR 1711, [1978] 2 CMLR 416.

respect: prohibition of cumulation applies only to benefits of the same kind. Thus family allowances to orphan children payable in one State cannot be demanded in another State where their step-father is already receiving such allowances in that State.[11] In the case of old-age and death pensions where entitlement is conditional upon the aggregation of the insurance periods under different national systems, the benefit will be apportioned pro rata between the Member States involved though the rule should not be applied if, as a result, the benefit would be lower than that granted under the legislation of one State alone.[12] If, on the other hand, the benefit under one national system would be lower the Regulation must be applied.[13] Where invalidity and old-age pensions overlap the beneficiary may opt for the more advantageous one.[14]

The rule against overlapping does not prevent the 'topping-up' of the benefit. Thus it was held where the husband worked in Germany and the wife in Italy the children staying with her, there was no overlapping if the children's allowance was claimed by the husband but not by the wife. The husband was entitled to the allowances in full. However, if the Italian allowances alone were paid the husband would have been entitled to the difference between the lower (Italian) and the higher (German) rate.[15]

(e) *Reimbursement* Corollary to the principle of aggregation is the principle of reimbursement between the Member States involved whereby the paying State will recoup itself from the other State pro rata, ie in proportion to the relevant periods completed in each State.

Having provided the benefit the paying state is entitled to a reimbursement from the other states involved pro rata the insurance periods credited in each of them.[16] Should the liability result from a wrongful act the paying state is, in accordance with article 93 of

---

11 Case 115/77: *Gert and Anja Laumann v Landesversicherungsanstalt Rheinprovinz* [1978] ECR 805, [1978] 3 CMLR 201.
12 Case 26/78: *Institut National d'Assurance Maladie-Invalidité v Viola* [1978] ECR 1771, [1979] 1 CMLR 635.
13 Case 83/77: *Naselli v Caisse Auxiliaire d'Assurance (invalidity pension in Italy and Belgium)* [1978] ECR 683, [1979] 1 CMLR 270.
14 Case 180/78: *Brouwer-Kaune v Bestuur* [1979] ECR 2111, [1980] 2 CMLR 145.
15 Case 153/84: *Ferraioli v Deutsche Bundespost* [1986] ECR 1401, [1987] 2 CMLR 911.
16 Reg 574/72, arts 93/98; Case 793/79: *Menzies v Bundesversicherungsanstalt für Angestellte* [1980] ECR 2085, [1981] 1 CMLR 190.

the Regulation, subrogated to the rights of the beneficiary[17] and may pursue its right of recovery in accordance with the *lex loci injuriae.*[18]

Recently certain imperfections of the system were corrected by the ECJ. In Case 284/84[19] a Dutch retired couple found that their pension was reduced because the wife had not been employed before marriage. There would have been no loss of pension if she was unmarried and resident in the Netherlands at the relevant time. The ECJ held the discrimination an unjustified breach of Regulation 1408/71 as it hindered, inter alia, the husband's mobility as a worker.

In Case 41/84 the ECJ[20] held article 73 (2) of Regulation 1408/71 invalid because the special rules for France allowed discrimination against migrant workers to the extent that French residence for family allowances was required and this denied protection to the family who left the country while the head of the family continued to live and work in France.

Orphans' pensions are normally payable in the state of their residence but if a higher scale applies in the state where they are actually paid the paying state must top up the amount.[1]

The rule against overlapping, which is perfectly justifed, can, however, cause problems, especially in a situation of family dis-integration. After divorce the German father lived in Germany and the Dutch mother in the Netherlands with the children. He received German allowances but did not remit them to the mother. However, his allowances took priority and the rule against over-lapping prevented the mother receiving allowances under Dutch law.[2] This case is difficult to reconcile with a similar situation in which English and Dutch law were involved. Here the English mother was living in England and the divorced father in the Nether-lands. He received the children's allowances under Dutch law. However, the mother, who was originally denied the British child benefit, was held to be entitled to it because her entitlement did

17 Case 27/69: *Caisse de Maladie des CFL Entre'Aide Médicale v Compagnie Belge d'Assurances Générales sur la Vie* [1969] ECR 405, [1970] CMLR 243.
18 Case 72/76: *Landesversicherungsanstalt Rheinland-Pfalz v Töpfer* [1977] ECR 271, [1977] 2 CMLR 121.
19 Case 284/84: *Spruyt v Bestuur van de Sociale Verzekeringsbank* [1989] 1 CMLR 884.
20 Case 41/84: *Pinna v Caisse d'Allocations Familiales de la Savoie* [1986] ECR 1, [1988] 1 CMLR 350. See also Case 359/87: *Pinna v Caisse d'Allocations Familiales de la Savoie* (explanatory judgment) [1989] ECR 585, [1990] 2 CMLR 561.
1 Case 269/87: *Ventura v Landesversicherungsanstalt Schwaben* [1990] 1 CMLR 762.
2 Case 104/84: *Kromhout v Raad van Arbeid* [1987] 3 CMLR 621.

not depend on Community law, and, therefore, there was no over-lapping.[3]

Regarding temporal application of social security law the ECJ ruled that old age pensions granted under Regulations 3 and 4 (the predecessor of Regulation 1408/71) continue to be governed by them at the pensioner's option, but any recalculation because of a change in status (eg the single pensioner's marriage) has to be made according to Regulation 1408/71.[4]

(iii) *Freedom of establishment (EEC articles 52–58)*

(a) *General rules* As mentioned earlier the freedom of movement of persons encompasses, next to 'workers', another group, ie self-employed or professional persons. Immigration rules, broadly the same as for workers, govern their mobility but the full enjoyment of their 'right of establishment' depends upon the recognition of their professional qualifications and this, in turn, depends upon the progress of the harmonization of national laws in this field. There is no definition of the group of persons entitled to the right of establishment. In distinction from 'workers' (who are salaried) article 52 of the Treaty contemplates a group of people who, in principle, pursue activities as self-employed persons or set up and manage undertakings within the meaning of article 58. Such persons belong, as a rule, to recognized professions whose status and membership is regulated by law. Hence the need of har-monizing the national rules and regulations to facilitate their mobility within the Community and, in the first place, to remove restrictions on the ground of nationality and other peculiar national practices established by the professions themselves.

To carry out its mandate the Council adopted in 1962[5] two General Programmes for the Abolition of Restrictions on Freedom to provide Services and on Freedom of Establishments, respect-ively, and in the course of subsequent years embarked on extensive legislation[6] in these fields. However, as recorded in the Commission White Paper,[7] the results as of 1987 were still unsatisfactory. There-

---

3 Case 377/85: *Burchell v Adjudication Officer* [1987] ECR 3329, [1987] 3 CMLR 757.

4 Case 83/87: *Viva v Fonds National de Retraite des Ouvriers Mineurs* [1900] 1 CMLR 220.

5 No 32/62, JO 1962, p 3 and No 36/62, JO 1962, p 7; see Lasok, D, *The Professions and Services in the European Economic Community* (1986), Appendix I and II. Lasok, K P E *Right of Establishment and Freedom to Provide Services* pp 463, et seq. See also Halsbury's Laws of England, vol 51, Law of the European Communities.

6 Ibid, pp 105 et seq.

7 Com (85) 310 Final, in particular paras 54, 55, 58, 81–83, 87, 89–91, 94–95, 152–154.

470 Chapter 13   Community law of the economy: Common Market

fore the Commission recommended action in specific areas including a more efficient policing and enforcement system, resulting, inter alia, in measures to suspend the enforcement of any national legislation which manifestly infringes Community law.

Independently of harmonization of the national rules governing the formation of professions and membership of professional bodies the ECJ was able to remove some of the restrictions in accordance with the principle of non-discrimination. Thus it was held[8] that a Dutch national resident in Belgium with the appropriate Belgian qualifications to practise law could not be debarred from his professional activity on the ground that, according to Belgian law, a lawyer must be a Belgian national. Similarly ruled the Court in the case of a Belgian lawyer[9] and a British architect[10] qualified to practise in France, a Dutch motor insurance claims investigator in Italy.[11]

In this context the judgment of the ECJ in the *Klopp* case complements that of the *Reyners'* case. Klopp, a German lawyer, qualified as lawyer both in Germany and France and wished to open an office in Paris while continuing his practice in Nüremberg, but the Paris Bar, on the basis of French practice that an *avocat* cannot practise simultaneously in more than one area, refused his application. The ECJ ruled in favour of Klopp.[12] This enabled Courts of Appeal in Aix-en-Provence[13] and the *Cour de Cassation*[14] respectively to overrule the rule of practice prohibiting multiple chambers whether in France or in France and overseas. This freedom however does not absolve the foreign lawyers from observing the local rules of conduct[15] but protects them from a local monopoly or restrictive practices.[16] Reverse discrimination does not offend Community law.[17]

8 Case 2/74: *Reyners v Belgian State* [1974] ECR 631, [1974] 2 CMLR 305.
9 Case 71/76: *Thieffry v Conseil de l'Ordre des Avocats à la Cour de Paris* [1977] ECR 765, [1977] 2 CMLR 373.
10 Case 11/77: *Patrick v Ministère des Affaires Culturelles* [1977] ECR 1199, [1977] 2 CMLR 523.
11 Case 90/76: *Van Ameyde v UCL* [1977] ECR 1091, [1977] 2 CMLR 478.
12 Case 107/83: *Ordre des Avocats au Barreau de Paris v Klopp* [1984] ECR 2971; [1985] 1 CMLR 99. The Principle was applied to doctors and dentists in Case 96/85: *EC Commission v France (Re Registration of Foreign Doctors)* [1986] 3 CMLR 57.
13 *Maître Cammarata v Conseil de l'Ordre des Avocats au Barreau de Marseille* [1988] 1 CMLR 243.
14 *Conseil de l'Ordre des Avocats au Barreau de Nice v Raynel* [1990] 2 CMLR 190.
15 Case 292/86: *Gullung v Conseil de l'Ordre des Avocats du Barreau de Colmar* [1988] ECR 111, [1988] 2 CMLR 57.
16 Case 427/85, *EC Commission v Germany (Re Lawyers' Services)* [1988] ECR 1123, [1989] 2 CMLR 677.
17 *Re a German Advocate*, German Federal Supreme Court [1990] 1 CMLR 254.

The principle of non-discrimination on the ground of nationality was extended further when the Court held that residential qualification of a properly qualified person was not a legitimate condition of his exercising the profession.[18]

However conviction for the illegal exercise of the veterinary profession was upheld in the case of a person qualified in Italy who, having become naturalised in France, attempted to practise on his own without first obtaining the requisite French qualifications.[19] Such a bar was justified pending the implementation of the harmonizing directives but no longer thereafter.[20]

In the absence of a Treaty definition of the class of persons entitled to the right of establishment the ECJ was, and is likely to be, confronted with fringe 'professions' including sports activities. So far the Court held that such activities may come under the non-discrimination principle if they entail 'economic activities'.[1] Amateur activities seem unaffected by Community rules.

(b) *Harmonization of the professions* In order to make the right of establishment effective the Community has embarked on a harmonizing process in which the rules governing the formation and exercise of the medical profession have become the example to follow.[2] So far Council directives have been issued in respect of the nursing,[3] dental,[4] midwives[5] and veterinary[6] professions as well

18 Case 33/74: *Van Binsbergen v Bestuur van de Bedrijfsvereniging voor de Metaalnijverheid* [1974] ECR 1299, [1975] 1 CMLR 298 – lawyer; Case 39/75: *Coenen v Sociaal-Economische Raad* [1975] ECR 1547, [1976] 1 CMLR 30 – insurance agent.
19 Case 136/78: *Ministère Public v Auer* [1979] ECR 437, [1979] 2 CMLR 373; and [1981] 1 CMLR 749 (conviction confirmed by the Court of Appeal at Colmar).
20 Case 271/82: (*Auer No 2*) [1985] ECR 2727, [1985] 1 CMLR 123.
1 See Case 36/74: *Walrave and Koch v Association Union Cycliste Internationale* [1974] ECR 1405, [1975] 1 CMLR 320; Case 13/76: *Dona v Mantero* [1976] ECR 1333, [1976] 2 CMLR 578; Case 222/86 *Union Nationale des Entraineurs et Cadres Techniques Professionnels du Football v Georges Heylens* [1989] 1 CMLR 901.
2 Council Directives 75/362, OJ 1975, L167/1 (recognition of qualifications); 75/363, OJ 1975, L169/148 (medical training); 75/364, OJ 1975, L167/17 (advisory committee on medical training); Council Decision 75/365, OJ 1975, L167/19 (advisory committee of senior public health officials); Dir 86/457, OJ 1986, L267 (special training for general medical practitioners).
3 Dir 77/452 and 77/453, OJ 1977, L176/1 and L176/8.
4 Dir 78/686 and 78/687, OJ 1978 L233/1 and L233/10.
5 Dir 80/154; 80/155; OJ 1980, L33/1, L33/8, Decisions 80/156; 80/157; OJ 1980, L33/13; L33/15.
6 Dir 78/1026; 78/1027 and 78/1028; OJ 1978, L362/1; L362/7 and L362/10.

as the exercise of the profession of architect[7] and pharmacist.[8] The harmonization of the rules governing the legal profession began with a Council directive[9] merely to 'facilitate the effective exercise by lawyers of freedom to provide services',[10] but lawyers are now subject to the general harmonizing directive.[11]

Apart from the above the harmonization process covers various other 'sectoral activities'[12] cutting across professions and services such as agriculture, fishery, film industry, mining and quarrying, electricity, gas and sanitary services, food and beverages, manufacturing and processing industries, commerce (wholesale and retail trade), real estate and business, personal services (eg restaurants and the like) in addition to directives[13] abolishing restrictions in certain fields.

Piecemeal legislation, slow and cumbersome, was abandoned in favour of a global solution by Directive 89/48[14] 'on a general system for the recognition of higher education diplomas awarded on completion of professional education and training of at least three year's duration', which came into effect on 4 January 1989. It applies to professions regulated by national laws except those (ie the medical profession and others) already governed by Community legislation. It purports to introduce a general system unrelated as hitherto, to any specific profession relying on comparability of university and such like courses. It is limited to the recognition of foreign qualifications necessary for the exercise of the right of establishment leaving to the Member States the details of implementation. It reserves to the Member States the right to regulate and to ensure respect of the rules of personal conduct and etiquette of the members of the professions. It also provides for the documentation and proof of good character or good repute, etc. Member states may impose an adaptation, or aptitude test but not both cumulatively. This is to ensure that paper qualifications are confirmed by practical experience.

Directive 89/48 is limited to professions based on higher education of university type. Where the professions require a lower educational standard the Commission proposes a harmonization

7 Dir 85/384; OJ 1985, L223/15.
8 Dir 85/432 and Dec 85/434, OJ 1985, L253 (qualifications in pharmacy); Dir 85/433; OJ 1985, L253 (recognition of diplomas in pharmacy).
9 77/249, OJ 1977, L78/17.
10 See Case 138/80R: *Re Borker* [1980] ECR 1975, [1980] 3 CMLR 638; *Public Prosecutor of Cologne v Lischka, Hagen and Heinrichson* [1981] 2 CMLR 189 German Court of Appeal Cologne.
11 Dir 89/48; see p 94, supra and p 473, infra.
12 Lasok, op cit, Ch 6.
13 Lasok, op cit, Ch 5.
14 OJ 1989, L19/16.

scheme based on secondary and post-secondary education. The draft[15] directive follows the same principles as Directive 89/48. However, since it covers two levels of education and training involving occupations, the pursuit of which depends upon the possession of professional or vocational education and training qualifications of secondary level and generally requires manual skills, the draft also provides for the recognition of such qualifications even if they have been acquired solely through occupational experience in a Member State which does regulate such occupations by law.

The Commission,[16] on the other hand, endeavours to see that Member States implement the directives correctly and in time and, as evidenced by the number of enforcement actions, has taken steps to achieve this objective.

(C) FREEDOM TO PROVIDE SERVICES (EEC articles 59–66)

According to article 60 services mean 'services[17] for remuneration' in particular activities of an industrial and commercial character, craftsmanship and exercise of a profession. However the provision of services is often connected with the exercise of a profession and in this respect inseparable from the right of establishment. Provision of services should be separated from the movement of goods as explained by the ECJ which held that copyrights imports are covered by article 36 of the Treaty whereas performing rights constitute services not goods and are, therefore, outside the scope of article 36.[18]

Considerable progress has been achieved in the harmonization of national laws regarding the corporate providers of services, first, in the field of company[19] law (which is absolutely essential to the mobility of corporations) and, secondly, in the extremely important

---

15 COM(89) 372 (final).

16 Lasok, op cit, pp 166–170. See also Case 306/84: *EC Commission v Belgium (Re Specialized Training of Doctors* [1988] 1 CMLR 768.

17 Eg Case 15/78: *Société Générale Alsacienne de Banque SA v Koestler* [1978] ECR 1971, [1979] 1 CMLR 89 (banking); Case 110/78: *Ministère Public and ASBL v Van Wesemael and Poupaert* [1979] ECR 35, [1979] 3 CMLR 87 (agents). Case 155/73: *Italian State v Sacchi* [1974] ECR 409, [1974] 2 CMLR 177 (television advertising); Case 52/79: *Procureur du Roi v Debauve* [1980] ECR 833, [1981] 2 CMLR 362 (television advertising); Case 62/79: *Compagnie Générale pour la Diffusion de la Télévision, Coditel SA v SA Ciné Vog Films* [1980] ECR 881, [1981] 2 CMLR 362 (both cases); Case 279/80: *Re Alfred John Webb* [1982] 1 CMLR 719 (employment agency).

18 See Halsbury's Laws of England, op cit supra; Case 262/81: *Coditel v Ciné Vog* [1983] 1 CMLR 49.

19 Lasok, op cit, Ch 8.

yet politically and economically sensitive banking[20] and insurance[1] sectors. However, a great deal remains yet to be done to achieve the objectives of the Treaty as outlined in the 1985 White Paper (paras 95–107).

(D) FREEDOM OF MOVEMENT OF CAPITAL AND BALANCE OF PAYMENTS (EEC articles 67–73 and 104–109)[2]

Treaty provisions regarding the movement of capital are in the nature of a programme rather than directly applicable measures. Moreover Community legislation is meant to assume a co-ordinating rather than strictly normative rôle. In this respect there is little room for case law to develop, the work being left to the legislator facing a political challenge because the issues, as in taxation, touch the raw nerve of economic control.

In the only case so far decided by the ECJ capital has been defined as 'means of payment' and thus includes foreign gold coins but not silver coins no longer legal tender.[3]

The economic freedoms on which the Common Market is based would be largely illusory without the corresponding liberalization of financial operations whether by a migrant worker, a capital investor or a multinational corporation. To ensure the flow of capital within the Common Market the Member States are committed to 'the abolition as between themselves of all restrictions on the movement of capital belonging to persons resident in Member States and any discrimination based on the nationality or on the place of residence of the parties or on the place where such capital is invested' (article 67 (1)). To that end they must liberalize 'the domestic rules governing the capital market and the credit system' (article 68 (2)).

However, according to articles 104–109, each Member State is responsible for the standing of its currency and its own balance of payments though the rates of exchange as well as the financial stability of each Member State are matters of common concern to all in so far as they affect the functioning of the Common Market. The Treaty[4] provides a machinery for the co-ordination of their economic policy as well as the management of crisis situations.

20 Lasok, op cit, Ch 9.
 1 Lasok, op cit, Ch 10; Ellis, T H *European Integration and Insurance* (1980).
 2 For details see Halsbury's Laws of England, op cit, Part 17, Prout, Sir C and Robinson, A, *Free Movement of Capital*, pp 637 et seq.
 3 *R v Johnson* [1978] 1 CMLR 226, Crown Court; id. on appeal [1978] 1 CMLR 390, CA; on referral Case 7/78: [1978] ECR 2247; [1979] 1 CMLR 47; see also *Allgemeine Gold und Silberscheideanstalt v Customs and Excise Comrs* [1978] 2 CMLR 292; affd [1980] QB 390, [1980] 1 CMLR 488, CA.
 4 Arts 104–109.

Exchange policies of Member States in respect of the movement of capital between them and third countries are to be co-ordinated by Council directives (article 70). As early as 1958[5] a Monetary Committee to review the monetary and financial situation of the Member States had been established and in 1974[6] the Council set up an Economic Policy Committee to link up financial and economic matters. However the most significant development in this field has been the creation of the European Monetary System (EMS) in the late seventies.[7]

The liberalization of capital movement has been slow. The combined effect of the first and the second directive[8] in this field was the elimination of exchange controls in respect of current transactions, transfers of personal funds, investments in real estate and transfers in connection with the movement of goods and the provision of services. However the ECJ found the directive inapplicable to stock exchange dealings. Thus Irish purchasers of shares in Irish companies on the London Stock Exchange had to obtain Irish exchange control permits. These transactions were held to be subject to Irish law.[9]

The third directive[10] standardized the measures to be taken by the Member States to rectify disturbances of the capital markets, control international capital flows and minimize the detrimental effect of these measures upon domestic liquidity. Coupled with the above are the efforts to harmonise the services of banks and other financial institutions[11] in order to remove restrictions imposed on their activities by national legislations.

In the meantime the ECJ had to deal with problems arising from currency restrictions retained by certain Member States. Mr Casati[12] was apprehended whilst leaving Italy in possession of German and Italian currency in excess of the limit permitted by the Italian exchange control legislation. Prosecuted, he claimed that he brought the money into Italy to purchase certain equipment necessary for his restaurant in Germany but was unable to complete the transaction because the factory was closed. The ECJ held, on reference, that article 67 must be interpreted to mean that

---

5 JO 1958, 390; OJ 1952–1958, 60.
6 Decision 74/122, OJ 1974, L63–21.
7 For details see Lasok, *The Law of the Economy*, supra, pp 156 et seq.
8 JO 1960, 921; OJ (Sp edn 1959–62) p 49; and JO 1963, 63; OJ (Sp edn 1963–64) p 5.
9 Case 143/86: *East (trading as Margetts and Addenbrooke) v Cuddy* [1988] 1 CMLR 1.
10 72/156, JO 1972, L91/13; OJ 1972, 296.
11 Council Dir 73/183, OJ 173, L194/1; 77/780, OJ 1977, L322/30; 83/350, OJ 1983, L193/18.
12 Case 203/80: *Guerrino Casati* [1981] ECR 2595, [1982] 1 CMLR 365.

restrictions on the exportation of bank notes may not be regarded as abolished irrespective of the provisions of article 69. The first paragraph of article 71 does not create unconditional rights for the benefit of individuals whilst article 106 (3) does not apply to re-exportation of money previously imported with a view to purchasing goods if such purchase has not in fact materialised. Moreover, with regard to capital movements and transfers of currency which have not been liberalized the Member States retain their power to adopt measures and to enforce these by means of criminal sanction. In the light of the law as it was at that time, Mr Casati's prosecution could not be impeached.

In another case[13] Mrs Luisi and Mr Carbone purchased from Italian banks a quantity of foreign currency in excess of the limit available for use abroad. Mrs Luisi contended that she exported the currency to pay her way as a tourist in France and Germany and to defray the cost of medical treatment in Germany. Mr Carbone used his currency as a tourist. Both were prosecuted and convicted. The ECJ held, on reference, that a distinction should be drawn between 'current payments' which are 'transfers of foreign exchange constituting the consideration within the context of the underlying transaction' and 'movements of capital' which are 'financial operations concerned with the investment of the funds in question rather than remuneration of a service'. Therefore the physical export of bank notes, *in casu*, was not in the nature of a capital movement within the meaning of article 67 but fell within the area of current payments for services covered by article 106 (1). They had a valid defence. Following the judgment of the ECJ the Tribunale of Genoa annulled the fines.[14]

Interpreting the Second Act of Accession the ECJ held that Greece[15] was in breach of article 52 of the Act having blocked the movement of funds out of Greece and insisted that the progressive release required by virtue of article 52 shall be confined to use within Greece only, and thus prohibited transfer to the creditor's home state.

The problem of currency restrictions in Greece[16] led the Commission to enquire into the matter and the ECJ to rule that Greece, by failure to co-operate by giving the required information, was in breach of article 5 of the Treaty.

13 Cases 286/82 and 26/83: *Luisi and Carbone v Ministero del Tesoro* [1984] ECR 377, [1985] 3 CMLR 52.
14 *Luisi v Ministero del Tesoro* [1987] 3 CMLR 455.
15 Case 194/84: *Re Blocked Accounts, EC Commission v Greece* [1989] 2 CMLR 453.
16 Case 240/86: *EC Commission v Greece (Re Foreign Currency Permits)* [1989] 3 CMLR 578.

The real impetus for legislation came from the Commission White Paper 1985[17] which urged greater liberalization of capital movements in the Community, restriction on the use by the Member States of the protective clauses under articles 73 and 108(3) and the creation of a 'financial product' through the harmonization of laws governing financial services. Certain measures have been taken to carry out these plans.

Directive 85/583[18] provided for the liberalization of unit trusts, which is a popular form of investment, and gave investors a more effective protection and uniform safeguards within the Community.

Directive 86/566[19] completes the liberation of capital operations necessary for the proper functioning of the Common Market and for the integration of domestic capital markets. It imposes an obligation upon the Member States to grant authorization and exchange facilities for transactions related to long-term commercial credits, acquisition of securities (shares, bonds and units) which are not dealt with on a stock exchange and admission (ie introduction, issue and placing) of securities to the capital markets.[20]

Directive 88/361[1] purports to remove the remaining restrictions on capital movements between the Member States as part of the completion of the internal market. It imposes an obligation upon the Member States: to abolish restrictions on the movement of capital between persons resident in the Member States and to ensure that capital transfers are made at the same rate of exchange as those applying to current transactions. It also lays down procedures under which the Member States may take protective measures restricting certain capital movements. These are permitted when foreign exchange markets are under the strain of short-term capital movements of exceptional magnitude which may lead to serious disturbances in Member States' monetary and exchange rate policies. Such measures can be applied for six months only.

Finally, Member States should endeavour to apply the same degree of liberalization to operations involving the movement of capital to and from third countries as exists between themselves. Such measures should be taken after consultation between the Member States.

---

17 Paras 95–107.
18 OJ 1985, L372 amending the first directive, supra.
19 OJ 1986, L332.
20 See Case 157/85: *Brugnoni v Cassa di Risparmio de Genoa. (Re ECSC Bonds purchased in Germany)* [1988] 1 CMLR 440.
1 OJ 1989, L178.

It is clear that the freedom of the movement of capital has hardly kept pace with the movement of goods or persons. Though essential to the Common Market a single capital market with a common monetary policy and a common currency is not round the corner.[2]

2 For details see Valaskakis, K, 'La politique monétaire', Lasok and Soldatos, op cit, pp 461 et seq.

The Community law of the economy: Community policies

The progress from the Common Market to the Economic Union of the EEC is marked by the degree of implementation of the various policies laid down in the Treaty. The Treaty provides the legal framework of Community legislation and of Member States' duties to the Community and each other.

Two types of policy can be distinguished, ie the policies laid down in the Treaty and the new policies created out of necessity within the framework of the Treaty.

1. Treaty policies

(A) AGRICULTURE (ARTICLES 38–47)[1]

1. *General principles*
In his report to the Messina Conference which paved the way for the creation of the EEC the Belgian statesman, Henri Spaak, wrote:

> 'On ne peut concevoir l'établissement d'un marché commun général en Europe sans que l'agriculture s'y trouve incluse. C'est l'un des secteurs où le progrès de productivité qui résulteront du marché commun, c'est-à-dire de la spécialisation progressive des productions et de l'élargissement des débouchés, peuvent avoir les effets les plus importants sur le niveau de vie des producteurs aussi bien que des consommateurs. En outre, cette inclusion de l'agriculture dans le marché commun est une condition d'équilibre des échanges entre les différentes économies des États membres ...'[2]

Agriculture, as an absolutely essential sector of the economy, had to be included in the concept of the Common Market together with industry and commerce. Moreover, because of its nature and rôle in the economy of the Member States, agriculture had to be singled out for a special regime. In view of the conflicting interests

---

1 For a fuller account see Bridge, J W, *Agriculture*, Halsbury's Laws of England op cit, pp 189 et seq.
2 Quoted by Olmi, G, 'L'Agriculture', *Les Novelles*, op cit, p 680.

of the Member States, the problem of agriculture in the Community has proved to be not only special, but also the most difficult to solve.

Having been recognized as 'a sector closely linked with the economy as a whole' (article 39(2)(c)) and given its 'particular nature' (article 39(2)(a))[3] the agricultural regime of the Community rests on its own philosophy. This philosophy can be reduced to two principles enshrined in article 38 of the Treaty, ie that the rules governing agriculture derogate from the rules which establish the Common Market (article 38 (2)) and that the operation and development of the Common Market for agricultural products[4] must be accompanied by a Common Agricultural Policy (article 38(4)).

It follows that there can be no common market for agricultural products without a Common Agricultural Policy. Whilst there is no definition of the agricultural policy in the Treaty, article 39 enumerates the objectives of this policy and article 43 gives considerable powers to the organs of the Community, authorizing them to devise and enforce the Common Agricultural Policy. It follows that there is no question of the co-ordination at the Community level of the various national policies but of the one policy for the whole Community.

As for the basic principles of the Common Market in Agriculture, article 42 provides that 'the rules of competition shall only apply to the production of, and trade in, agricultural products, to the extent determined by the Council'. The relevant Common Agricultural Policy Regulation 26,[5] article 2, issued in 1962, exempts agreements essential to an agricultural market organization or the production and sale of agricultural products from the operation of article 85[6] (prohibition of agreements between undertakings which may affect trade between Member States and are designed to stultify free competition) and article 86[7] of the Treaty (prohibition of the abuse of a dominant trade position by one or more undertakings). Furthermore article 92 and 93(2) of the Treaty do not apply to agriculture. Article 92 declares state aids incompatible

---

3 This particular nature 'results from agriculture's social structure and from structural and natural disparities between the various agricultural regions': art 39 (2) (a).
4 Agricultural products comprise the products of the soil, of stock-farming, of fisheries and products of first-stage processing directly related to the foregoing (art 38 (1)). For a list of these see EEC Treaty, Annexe II.
5 JO/993/62 (S. Edn. 1959–62).
6 See pp 501 et seq, infra; Case 71/74: *Frubo v EC Commission* [1975] ECR 563, [1975] 2 CMLR 123 and Cases 40–48/73, etc: *Co-operative Vereniging 'Suiker Unie' UA v EC Commission* [1975] ECR 1663, [1976] 1 CMLR 295.
7 See pp 511 et seq, infra.

with the Common Market and article 93 governs the procedure to be followed by the Commission in cases involving alleged breaches of article 92. It follows that state aids to agriculture are not ruled out as a matter of principle, but, in practice, specific Regulations[8] expressly provide that articles 92–94 of the Treaty shall not be derogated from unless stipulated to the contrary.

2. *Common Agricultural Policy*

Article 39 (1) sets out the objectives of the Common Agricultural Policy as follows:

'(a) to increase agricultural productivity by promoting technical progress and by ensuring the national development of agricultural production and the optimum utilisation of all factors of production, in particular labour;

(b) thus to ensure a fair standard of living for the agricultural community, in particular by increasing the individual earnings of persons engaged in agriculture;

(c) to stabilise markets;

(d) to provide certainty of supplies; and

(e) to ensure supplies to consumers at reasonable prices.'

The Member States are committed to adopt the Common Agricultural Policy gradually during the transitional period. The new members are equally committed.[9] In order to achieve the objectives of the policy the Member States must adopt a Common Organization of Agricultural Markets (article 40 (2)).

3. *Common Organization of Agricultural Markets*

The Common Organisation of Agricultural Markets has not been defined in the Treaty, but article 40 (2) provides that it should take one of the following forms depending on the product concerned:

(a) common rules as regards competition;

(b) compulsory co-ordination of the various national marketing organizations;

(c) a European organization of the market.

---

8 Eg, Regulation 2759/75, on the common organization of the market in pigmeat, art 21, OJ 1975, L282.

9 First Act of Accession 1972, art 50 et seq; Second Act of Accession 1979, art 57 et seq; Third Act of Accession 1985, arts 67 et seq and 233 et seq.

482   Chapter 14   The law of the economy: Community policies

In practice (c) the 'European market organization' model has invariably been followed. This involves the replacement of individual national marketing arrangements for an agricultural product by a single, Community-wide marketing structure for that product. That task has been entrusted to the Community Institutions and in the terms of article 43 (2): 'The Council shall, on a proposal of the Commission and after consulting the Assembly acting unanimously during the first stages and by a qualified majority thereafter, make regulations, issue directives, or take decisions, without prejudice to any recommendations it may also make.' The Commission's proposals emerged from a conference held in July 1958 at Stresa, which defined the guidelines of the Common Agricultural Policy.[10] In June 1960, the Commission, after consulting the Economic and Social Committee, submitted its proposals to the Council in respect of four main considerations: structural, market, commercial and social.[11] Having had the benefit of the views of the Special Committee for Agriculture created in 1960 the Council adopted certain guidelines which were to form the future Common Agricultural Policy, viz free movement of agricultural products within the Community, a joint commercial and agricultural policy, a common price level for agricultural products within the Community and coordination of national structural reform. These guidelines added practically nothing to the existing provisions of the Treaty, but reaffirmed the resolve to tackle the Community agricultural problem and in some respects interpreted the Treaty provisions. The importance of the problem is well reflected in the machinery of Community legislation which involved the cooperation of the Commission, the European Parliament and the Council.

The first regulation issued by the Council concerned the market organization in cereals[12] and applied during the transitional period to wheat, rye, barley, oats, maize, buckwheat, millet, hardwheat, meal and groats of wheat and rye and processed grain products. The current basic rules concerning the market in cereals are now contained in a consolidating regulation made in 1975.[13] This sets up a single Community market based on a common price system within the Community and regulates trade with third countries. The price system comprises a target price, an intervention price and a threshold price.

The *target price* is determined annually before 1 August by the

---

10 See *First General Report*, 1958, ss 97–101.
11 See *Third General Report*, 1960, s. 230 and *Fourth General Report*, 1961, s 103.
12 Regulation of 14 January 1962, No 19, JO 933/62.
13 Regulation 2727/75, OJ 1975, L281.

Council acting on a proposal of the Commission after consulting the Parliament (article 43 (2)). This is not a fixed price, but a price intended to enable the producers to plan their production for the following year; it provides an expectation of the price the product should fetch during the next marketing year (1 August to 31 July). The target price is also designed, inter alia, to encourage trade in cereals from Community surplus areas to Community deficit areas. The target price therefore reflects the transport costs involved in such trade.

The *intervention* or *guarantee price*, determined according to the same procedure as the target price, is the price which the national authorities must pay to producers who are unable to sell their product on the market. It forms a guarantee to farmers. However, whilst the target price is uniform within the Community, the intervention price varies as from area to area according to the circumstances of the area. The intervention price is lower than the target price. The basic intervention price has been fixed by the Council in relation to the market conditions in the area of the Community having the greatest surplus for all cereals.

The *threshold price* is the price fixed by the Community for cereals imported from third countries. It is fixed in respect of the same standard quality as the target price. It is calculated in relation to cereals, notionally imported through Rotterdam to be sold in the area of the Community having the greatest deficit for all cereals. The aim is that cereals thus imported should eventually sell at or above the target price. In other words, the threshold price is the target price less the cost of transport from Rotterdam to the area of greatest deficit.

The threshold price is determined by the Council in accordance with the procedure outlined above every year before 15 March. It is fixed in relation to a system of levies imposed on imported cereals, these levies being equal to the difference between the threshold price and the c.i.f. price at Rotterdam. The levies are fixed by the Commission whilst the c.i.f. prices for Rotterdam are calculated on the basis of the most favourable purchasing possibilities on the world market. It follows that the threshold prices are lower than the Community prices.

Whilst the price system is designed to ensure production within the Community and to guarantee a fair return to Community producers, the system of levies on imports is designed to protect Community producers against competition from third countries. In a sense, this is a Community preference and an example of the economic barrier round the Community. However, the Regulation requires strict control of the quality of the product to preserve not only a high standard of the market, but also an equitable basis of competition.

Target prices, intervention prices and threshold prices are reviewed monthly to take into account the cost of interest and stockpiling. These reviews result in price increases spread out over the marketing year.

In order to encourage exports, the Regulation provides for refunds to exporters from the Community to third countries. These refunds constitute a form of subsidy which is the same for the whole Community, but varies according to the destination of the products and the use to which they are to be put. The refunds are calculated in relation to the difference between the world and Community prices for the given product. This is necessary since world prices are usually lower than Community prices and there is a policy against the accumulation of surpluses within the Community. Exports and imports are under control by means of appropriate certificates.

At the Community level, the system is supervised by a Management Committee set up under the Regulation and consisting of representatives of the Member States presided over by a representative of the Commission. The Chairman refers matters to the Committee either on his own initiative or at the request of the representative of a Member State. The decisions are implemented by the Commission. If there is a difference of opinion between the Committee and the Commission, the latter must submit the matter to the Council which may adopt a different decision from that proposed by the Commission.[14]

In addition to the Regulation for Cereals, the Community has adopted Regulations in respect of other essential sectors of Agriculture, notably Pigmeat,[15] Eggs,[16] Poultry Meat,[17] Fruit and Vegetables,[18] Wine and Vines,[19] Milk and Dairy Products,[20] Beef and Veal,[1] Rice,[2] Vegetable Oils, Fats, Oil Seeds and Olives,[3] Sugar,[4]

---

14 See Chapter 8, ante.
15 Regulation 2759/75, OJ 1975, L282.
16 Regulation 2771/75, ibid.
17 Regulation 2777/75, ibid.
18 Regulation 1035/72, JO 1972, L118 (Sp edn 1972 II).
19 Regulation 337/79, OJ 1979, L54.
20 Regulation 804/68, JO 1968, L148 (Sp edn 1968 I).
 1 Regulation 805/68, ibid.
 2 Regulation 1418/76, OJ 1976, L166.
 3 Regulation 136/66, JO 1966 (Sp edn 1965–66).
 4 Regulation 1785/81, OJ 1981, L177.

Tobacco,[5] Sheepmeat and Goatmeat,[6] certain horticultural products[7] and Fisheries.[8]

As a result of these Regulations, several essential sectors of agriculture have become subject to Community Rules. The organization of these markets differs as from sector to sector, but, broadly speaking, the pattern of the Regulation for Cereals, which we have considered as an example of a Community Market Organization, has been followed.

4. *Structural reorganization*

Alongside the Market Organization the Community postulates a structural reorganization of agriculture. The problem is by no means simple and has, over the years, focused the attention of the Community. In order to solve it, the Commission in 1968 submitted to the Council a 'Memorandum on the Reform of Agriculture in the European Economic Community' (Agriculture 1980)[9] and, in 1971, the Council adopted a resolution[10] based on this Memorandum. The Commission analysed and made recommendations in respect of several aspects of the structural reform of agriculture. In particular it considered the problem of the manpower engaged in agriculture, the size of farms and production methods.

On the first problem, the Commission concluded that in view of high productivity and overproduction fewer people will be needed in the farming industry of the future. This creates a social problem which the Community must alleviate by helping those who wish to leave the land, by assisting farmers over fifty-five years of age who wish to give up their occupation and by providing schemes for retraining and placement of those who wish to find another occupation.

On the second problem, the Commission found that the average farm within the Community was too small to engage in profitable industrial farming and recommended a definite policy for the increase of the size of farms in accordance with the type of production.

On the third problem, the Commission felt that the production methods were not modern enough and that, coupled with the lack of flexibility, this contributed to the relatively low incomes of

5 Regulation 727/70, JO 1970, L94 (Sp edn 1970 I).
6 Regulation 1837/80, OJ 1980 L183.
7 Flax and Hemp, Regulation 1308/70, JO 1970, L146 (Sp edn 1970 II); Flowers, Bulbs and Live Plants, Regulations 234/68, JO 1968, L55 (Sp edn 1968 I).
8 Regulation 3796/81, OJ 1981, L379.
9 See *Second General Report*, 1968.
10 JO 1971, C52.

farmers in the Community. It proposed the modernization of production methods, greater adaptability to market needs and better
marketing.

The Commission costed its recommendation estimating the relative contribution of the Community and the Member States to the
cost of the reform programme.

The Memorandum and the ensuing discussions in the European
Parliament and the Economic and Social Committee led to the
above-mentioned Council Resolution on the subject which, in turn,
paved the way for a new set of proposals by the Commission.[11]
These proposals resulted in the issuing of directives on 17 April
1972 on the modernization[12] of the farming industry, assistance to
farmers leaving the land,[13] professional training and advice.[14] A
further directive concerned with the special problems of farming
in less favoured areas was issued in 1975.[15] Steps have also been
taken to formulate co-ordinated national or regional programmes
for the processing and marketing of groups of agricultural product
as a further means of advancing the economic aims of the Common
Agricultural Policy.[16] Taken together with the Council Resolution,
the emerging picture of agriculture is one of a modernised industry,
manned by well-qualified and efficient farmers, organised into a
competitive market and catering for the social and human problems
involved in the movements of the farming population. In this set-
up, state aids and subsidies authorized under articles 92 and 93 of
the Treaty will have to go as the principles of a Common Market
in agriculture will be implemented. However implementation has
been delayed and problems continue to arise. To deal with these
problems various reforms have been introduced. Initially, in 1981,
steps were taken to enable a greater share of the available Community funding to be applied to the Mediterranean area and to the
west of Ireland. Then, in 1985, a major new initiative was taken to
improve the efficiency of agricultural structures. A new regulation
was made[17] which replaced all existing provisions including those
relating to aid for farming in less favoured areas. This measure
has a tendency to broaden the scope of agricultural policy in the
direction of rural social policy. It enables Member States, with
financial support from the Community, to grant investment aid to
full-time, skilled farmers who submit a technically and economically acceptable improvement plan.

11 [1971] JO C75.
12 72/159, JO 1972, L96 (Sp edn 1972 II).
13 72/160, ibid.
14 72/161, ibid.
15 75/268, OJ 1975, L128.
16 Regulations 355/77, OJ 1977, L51 and 1932/84, OJ 1984, L180.
17 Regulation 797/85, OJ 1985, L93.

5. *Finance and implementation*

In connection with agriculture, two further points have to be mentioned: finance and the machinery for implementing the Community Agricultural Policy.

The financing of the Common Agricultural Policy, although germane to agricultural problems, is really part of the Community budget. Indeed, agriculture figures prominently in the budget, representing in 1986 some 61 per cent of the whole.[18] The underlying philosophy of the financing of the agricultural policy is the principle that since there is a common policy and a common price system, the financial responsibility must be undertaken by the Community. Accordingly, on the basis of article 40(4) of the EEC Treaty, the European Agricultural Guidance and Guarantee Fund[19] was set up and an elaborate system of Community agricultural finance was established.

As for the machinery to implement the Community Agricultural Policy, we have already observed that, at the Community level, the crucial decisions have to be taken by the Council after consulting the Parliament, whilst the background work and the administrative actions stem from the Commission. Agriculture has the constant attention of the highest Community organs. At the national level, the execution of the decisions of the Council has been left to the machinery of the Member States. In particular the Member States assume responsibility for the purchase of the agricultural product at the intervention price determined by the Council. They also operate the system of import and export certificates, collect levies and pay out refunds. Their financial liability to the Community forms part of their contribution towards the Community budget.

The states who became members of the Community in 1973, 1981 and 1986 had to accept the Common Agricultural Policy as a condition of their accession. They were, therefore, committed to a process of adaptation and integration during a transition period as set out in the Act annexed to the relevant Treaty of Accession.[20] For the United Kingdom, this meant a radical change in the system. To implement the Community Policy an Intervention Board for Agricultural Produce has been set up with provision for such consequential changes as appear necessary.[1]

---

18 See *20th General Report* (1987), p 55, Table 1.

19 By Regulation No 25, JO 991/62; the present definitive scheme is laid down by Regulation 729/70, JO 1970 (Sp edn 1970 I).

20 See First Act of Accession, 1972, arts 50 et seq; Second Act of Accession 1979, arts 57 et seq; and Third Act of Accession 1985, arts 67 et seq and 233 et seq.

1 See European Communities Act 1972, s. 6 and the orders and regulations made thereunder.

The implementation of the Common Agricultural Policy requires a uniform body of Community law, as contended on behalf of the Commission:[2]

'... The integral and exclusive nature of the competence of Community institutions in the agricultural sectors formed into "European market organisations" derives from the consistent body of case law of the Court of Justice[3] according to which any lacunæ in a system of organising agriculture cannot be filled by Member States since the institution of a European market organisation has deprived Member States of their original legislative power.'[4]

6. Production disincentives

It can be said that the CAP is a victim of its own success. It has raised the standard of living of farmers but increased the price of food; it has resulted in an unprecedented rise of production but caused surpluses and costly storage problems. It has made the Community not only self-sufficient in food supplies but has not been able to relieve certain overpopulated Third World countries of famine and starvation. For political reasons the CAP has become the bone of contention between agricultural and non-agricultural countries, a hungry sacred cow eating up about two-thirds of the Community budget, leaving little for the development of other well deserving policies. Within the GATT it became a subject of dissension and a stumbling block to the completion of the Uruguay Round. It is evident that, having fulfilled its original function, it is in need of reform but the problem is, politics apart, how to reconcile the contention that the Community is both an economic and social organization. The other problem is that the CAP has become a complex mass of rules and regulations which, because of their complexity, challenge a would-be reformer with a Herculean task.

Since a root and branch reform is not on the agenda various palliatives have been adopted. These, apart from export incentives which extend the Community protectionism to the world market, include production disincentives and measures for the protection of the environment put at risk through intensive farming.

---

2 In Case 31/74: *Filippo Galli* [1975] ECR 47 at 54.
3 Case 159/73: *Hannoversche Zucker AG Rethan-Weetzen v Hauptzollamt Hannover* [1974] ECR 121.
4 Case 131/73: *Re Grosoli* [1973] ECR 1555, [1974] CMLR 40.

(B) COMMON FISHERIES POLICY (CFP)

1. *Establishment of the CFP*
The EEC Treaty provides the basis for a CFP within the framework of the CAP article 38 (1), defining fisheries and products thereof as 'agricultural products'. Indeed, originally, the CFP was regarded as an aspect of the CAP and the first two Council regulations[5] providing respectively for a common structural policy for the fishing industry and a common organization of the market in fishery products, followed the pattern of the CAP legislation.

Conflict of interests of the Member States exacerbated by the first enlargement of the Community delayed the establishment of the CFP. The first Act of Accession accorded certain concessions to the new members as they were allowed, until the end of 1982, to restrict fishing in a six nautical mile sea belt to fishermen exercising traditional rights in those waters and to their fishing zones in certain areas to twelve miles.[6] However the Act[7] gave the Council power to legislate on the management of the fishing industry, and the conservation of sea resources. Pending such enactments the Member States retained their competence to regulate fisheries[8] subject to certain guidelines laid down in the Hague Resolutions of 1976.[9] Eventually, in 1983, a CFP, as a set of regulations, emerged.

2. *Elements of the CFP*

Equal access
In view of the mobile nature of fish no national ownership of them can be claimed. Therefore the CFP accords to Community fishermen equal access to the 'Community pond' delimited by the national limits of 200 nautical miles or a median line. They can fish there without discrimination subject, however, to a negotiated derogation reserving 12-mile national fishing rights, providing for

5 Regulation 2141/70, OJ 1970, L236/1 and Reg 2142/70, OJ 1970, L236/5.
6 Act of Accession 1972, arts 100 and 101.
7 Ibid, arts 102 and 103.
8 See Cases 3, 4, 6/76: *Officier van Justitie v Kramer* [1976] ECR 1279, [1976] 2 CMLR 440.
9 EC Bull 10/1976, item 1502 et seq. See Case 61/77: *EC Commission v Ireland* [1978] ECR 417, [1978] 2 CMLR 466; Case 88/77: *Minister of Fisheries v Schonenberg* [1978] ECR 473, [1978] 2 CMLR 519; Cases 185–204/78: *J van Dam en Zonen* [1979] ECR 2345, [1980] 1 CMLR 350; Case 124/80: *Officier van Justitie v Van Dam* [1981] ECR 1447, [1982] 2 CMLR 93; Case 32/79: *EC Commission v United Kingdom* [1980] ECR 2403, [1981] 1 CMLR 219; Case 804/79: *EC Commission v United Kingdom* [1981] ECR 1045, [1982] 1 CMLR 543; Case 63/83: *R v Kirk* [1984] ECR 2689, [1984] 3 CMLR 522.

a licence for sensitive species and vessels specifications.[10] The conservation and management of fish stocks are controlled by the total allowable catches (TACs) fixed annually. The volume of catches available to the Community are distributed between the Member States.[11] Quotas are exchangeable between the Member States in respect of a species or groups of species allocated to them but these have to be caught in specified fishing zones.[12]

Structural reform
The extension of the fishing rights and extensive overfishing resulted in surplus fishing capacity which had to be reduced within the restructuring of the industry. The basis for action was provided by Regulation 2141/70 and the subsidies by the European Agricultural Guidance and Guarantee Fund.

Marketing organization
The common organization of fishery markets was set up by Regulation 2142/70[13] with the object of rationalizing the development of fisheries, securing a fair deal for fishermen, stabilizing the markets in order to bring supplies of good products to the consumer at reasonable prices. The market organization consists of producers' organizations, common marketing standards and a price support system financed by the European Agricultural Guidance and Guarantee Fund.

Conservation of resources and policing of the CFP
For the conservation of the diminishing sea resources Regulation 2527/80[14] imposed restrictions on mesh sizes, types of gear, by-catches and fishing in closed seasons and certain zones whilst Regulation 753/80[15] introduced a system of reporting catches. Regulation 170/83[16] and Regulation 171/83[17] established a Community system for conservation and management of fishery resources and Regulation 172/83[18] fixed total allowable catches for certain fish stocks and certain zones.

10 Regulation 170/83, OJ 1983 L24/1. See *Rederij L De Boer en Zonen BV v Fish and Fish Products Board* [1987] 2 CMLR 515.
11 See Commission communication on access to fishing quotas [1990] 2 CMLR 97.
12 Regulation 172/83, OJ 1983, L24/30.
13 Amended by Reg 100/76, OJ 1976, L20/1 and revised by Reg 3796/81, OJ 1981, L379/1.
14 OJ 1980, L258/1.
15 OJ 1980, L84/33.
16 OJ 1983, L24/1.
17 OJ 1983, L24/14.
18 OJ 1983, L24/31.

Each Member State is responsible for the application and enforcement of the CFP in the waters under its jurisdiction. In addition to national authorities supervising the system there are also Community fishery inspectors responsible to the Commission.

3. *International aspects*
International aspects of the CFP are now within the competence of the Community.[19] In this capacity the Community has entered into agreements with certain countries (eg Norway, Sweden, Canada and the USA) and international organizations (ie the North Atlantic Fisheries Organization, the North Atlantic Convention on Salmon Conservation and the Convention on Living Resources in the Antarctic).

Fishery products are subject to the Common Customs Tariff and external trade agreements within the Common Commercial Policy.

(C) TRANSPORT POLICY (ARTICLES 74–84)

1. *General principles*
Integrated transport appears to be an indispensible element of the Common Market. Yet the Transport Policy heralded in article 3 (c) of the Treaty has proved to be a difficult task. It should be borne in mind that transport, including transport under the ECSC Treaty (article 70), impinges upon many aspects of economic life,[20] and has, in the Community setting, a distinct international character.[1] It is also relevant to several Community policies, notably, the movement of goods, state aids, taxation, competition, the right of establishment and the freedom to provide services. The fact is that the transport system developed in each Member State was designed to serve the national needs (often military) rather than a wider territorial unit. Hence the problem of integration.

According to article 74 (1) the Transport Policy includes:

(a) common rules applicable to international transport to or from the territory of a Member State or passing across the territory of one or more Member States:

(b) the conditions under which non-resident carriers may operate transport services within a Member State; and

---

19 Sturt, R H B, *Fisheries*. Halsbury's Laws of England, op cit, pp 407 et seq.
20 For a detailed consideration see Close, G, *Transport*, in Halsbury's Laws of England, op cit, pp 667 et seq.
 1 See in particular the *ERTA* Case [1971] ECR 263, [1971] CMLR 335, and Opinion 1/76: *Re Draft Agreement establishing a European Laying-up Fund for Inland Waterways Vessels* [1977] ECR 741, [1977] 2 CMLR 279.

(c) any other appropriate provisions.

Article 84 of the Treaty refers only to 'transport by rail, road and inland waterway' but the Council may extend the policy to transport by air and sea. However, irrespective of the implementation of the policy the ECJ held that job discrimination on board merchant vessels on the ground of nationality could not be maintained.[2]

2. *Initial implementation*
In an attempt to implement the policy the Commission proposed in 1961[3] to establish a 'Common Market in Transport organized according to Community rules, able to respond to the needs of transport in the Community and ensuring elimination of discrimination based on nationality'. This was to be achieved through a uniform approach to the modes of transport, carriers and users; financial independence of carriers; operational freedom; co-ordination of investments and the users' freedom of choice between the modes of transport and carriers. Furthermore[4] the policy was to embrace the principle of sound competition between the various modes of transport and between the carriers. Later[5] further elements reflecting the anxieties of our technological age have been added: regional needs, problems of urbanization, pollution and energy.[6]

However, the lack of tangible progress prompted the Parliament to censure the Council by applying to the Court of Justice for a declaration that the Council has failed to adopt a Common Transport Policy in accordance with article 75 (1) of the Treaty.[7] The Parliament made its point but achieved little since the ECJ, whilst confirming that the Council was remiss, also held that the Parliament failed to indicate what specific measures ought to have been taken.

Subsequently the Commission 1985 White Paper[8] listed the failures in this field and singled out priorities but also warned the Council that if no action is taken regarding the application of competition rules to air and sea transport, the Commission will

2 Case 167/73: *EC Commission v France* [1974] ECR 359, [1974] 2 CMLR 216.
3 Memorandum of 10 April 1961, see also *Ninth General Report*, 1966, item 207 et seq.
4 Council Decision 67/790, JO 1967, 322/4; OJ 1974 (2nd) IV, 23.
5 Commission Memorandum of 24 October 1973, COM (73) 1725 final.
6 See Bull 12/1978; *Twelfth General Report* (1978), 199; *Thirteenth General Report* (1979), 177.
7 Case 13/83: *European Parliament v EC Council* [1985] ECR 1513, [1986] 1 CMLR 138.
8 Supra, at paras 108–112.

record the existing infringements and authorize Member States to take measures as determined by the Commission according to article 89 of the Treaty which defines the powers of the Commission relevant to the enforcement of the Community Competition Policy.

The first steps in the implementation of the Common Transport Policy consisted of attempts to regulate operational, technical and social aspects of transport.

The operational harmonization consists of tariff and non-tariff measures. The former consists of maximum and minimum charges bilaterally agreed between Member States (hence 'bracket tariffs') applicable to transport by rail, road and inland waterways. It was introduced experimentally in 1967[9] for a three-year period, extended until 31 December 1982 and replaced by regulation 3568/83.[10]

Non-tariff measures comprise the rules of competition and the various conditions for the operation of the transport service. Above all it is intended to liberalize transport from the national control and to reorganize the service in response to market forces of supply and demand.

The operation of the service is linked with insurance[11] against civil liability arising from the use of motor vehicles on the road. The exercise of the profession of transport operator, on the other hand, is subject to the freedom of the provision of services and the right of establishment of the operator. Council directives[12] lay down rules regarding the professional formation of road haulage and road passenger transport operators as well as the recognition of professional qualifications. However a Member State may refuse the operator's licence to a person with a criminal record.[13] The directives purport to establish an integrated profession resulting from formal training but allow the Member States to grant licences to persons with adequate practical experience.[14]

Technical harmonization is concerned with the rules governing

9 Reg 1174/68, JO 1969, L194/1; OJ 1968, 411.
10 Reg 2831/77, OJ 1977, L334/22; See Commission arbitration award OJ 1980, L4/14; [1980] 1 CMLR 699. See Case 12/82: *Ministère Public v Trinon* [1982] ECR 4089, [1983] 3 CMLR 85; Reg 3568/83, OJ 1983, L359/1.
11 See Dir 72/166, OJ 1972, 360; Dir 72/430, OJ 1972, 77; Dir 84/5, OJ 1984, L8/17.
12 Dir 74/561, OJ 1974, L308/18; amended by Dir 80/1178, OJ 1980, L350/41; see also Commission Recommendation 77/608, OJ 1977, L248/27, to the United Kingdom; Dir 74/562, OJ 1974, L308/23, amended by Dir 80/1179, OJ 1980, L350/42; see also Commission Recommendation 77/609, OJ 1977, L248/29; Dir 77/796, OJ 1977, L334/37. See Cases 28/81 and 29/81: *EC Commission v Italy* [1981] ECR 2577 and [1981] ECR 2585.
13 Case 21/78: *Delkvist v Anklagemyndigheden* [1978] ECR 2327, [1979] 1 CMLR 372.
14 See Case 145/78: *Augustijn v Staatssecretaris van Verkeer en Waterstaat* [1979]

technical standards of equipment, safety and comfort as well as the control of pollution. Directive 70/156[15] on the approximation of national laws relating to the type-approval of motor vehicles and trailers and Directive 74/150[16] on agricultural and forestry tractors provide a model of legislation in this respect.

Social harmonization consists of Council regulations[17] setting out to establish common standards for working conditions in internal and inter-state transport. These standards apply to drivers irrespective of whether or not they are employees or independent traders;[18] the resting periods laid down by the Regulation apply not only to drivers but also to employers when driving[19] and the penal sanctions cannot be flouted.[20] The Member States[1] are bound to see that the use of certain road transport vehicles both in domestic and inter-state traffic is controlled by means of the recording equipment prescribed by Council Regulation 1463/70.[2]

3. Towards the completion of the policy

(a) *Inland transport*   Measures common to road, rail and inland waterways transport cover such matters as public service taxation, state intervention and state aids[3] and competition.[4]

Proposed legislation includes amendments of Regulation 1191/69 on action by Member States concerning the obligations inherent in the concept of a public service in transport by rail, road and inland waterway,[5] extension of Council Decision 78/174 (setting up a Committee in the field of transport infrastructure to

---

ECR 1025, [1979] 3 CMLR 516; Case 146/78: *Wattenberg v Staatssecretaris van Verkeer en Waterstaat* [1979] ECR 1041, [1979] 3 CMLR 516.

15 JO 1970, L42/1; OJ 1970, 96 amended by dir 78/315, OJ 1978, L81/1.

16 OJ 1974, L84/10, implemented in the UK by the Agricultural or Forestry Tractors (Type Approval) Regulation 1975, SI 1975, No 1475.

17 Reg 543/69, JO 1969, L77/49; OJ 1969, 1970 subsequently amended and modified.

18 Case 65/76: *Re Deryke* [1977] ECR 29, [1977] 1 CMLR 449.

19 Case 76/77: *Auditeur du Travail v Dufour* [1977] ECR 2485, [1978] 1 CMLR 265.

20 Case 97/78: *Re Schumalla* [1978] ECR 2311, [1979] 2 CMLR 176.

1 Case 128/78: *EC Commission v United Kingdom (Tachograph)* [1979] ECR 419, [1979] 2 CMLR 45; see also *Concorde Express Transport Ltd v Traffic Examiner Metropolitan Area* [1980] 2 CMLR 221 (Crown Court, Kingston-upon-Thames). Case 90/83: *Paterson v W Weddell* [1984] ECR 1567, [1984] 2 CMLR 540; Case 133/83: *R v Thomas Scott & Sons* [1984] ECR 2863, [1985] 1 CMLR 188.

2 OJ 1970, L164/1; JO 1970, 482 amended by reg 1787/73, OJ 1973, L181/1; amended by reg 2828/77, OJ 1977, L334/5.

3 Regulation 1191/69, OJ 1969, L156/1 and Reg 1107/70, OJ 1970, L130/1.

4 Regulation 1017/68, OJ 1968, L175/1.

5 COM(89) 563 final, OJ 1990, C34/11.

sea and air transport)[6] and for an action programme with a view to an integrated transport market in 1992.[7]

Measures regulating road transport specifically include provisions for: a Community driving licence;[8] physical inspections and administrative formalities in respect of the carriage of goods between Member States;[9] the approximation of national laws relating to insurance against civil liability in respect of the use of motor vehicles;[10] the use of vehicles hired without drivers for the carriage of goods;[11] amendment of Regulation 543/69 regarding certain social legislation relating to road transport;[12] the weights, dimensions and other technical characteristics of certain road vehicles;[13] standard procedures for the implementation of Regulation 3820/85;[14] the fixing of rates for the carriage of goods between Member States;[15] the conditions under which non-resident carriers may operate national road haulage services within a Member State;[16] the elimination of controls of road and inland water transport at the frontiers of Member States;[17] the harmonization of national laws relating to the tread depths of tyres of certain categories of vehicles and trailers;[18] and vocational training for drivers of vehicles carrying dangerous goods by road.[19]

Proposed legislation includes five provisions related to: the driving licence;[20] permitted blood alcohol concentration for drivers;[1] insurance against civil liability;[2] speed limits for certain vehicles[3] and the introduction of the final regime for the organization of the market for the carriage of goods by road.[4]

(b) *Railway transport* Rail transport has attracted little Community legislation concerning mainly the financial relations

6 COM(88) 577 final, OJ 1989, C34/9.
7 COM(89) 238 final, OJ 1989, C170/10.
8 Directive 80/1263, OJ 1980, L375/1.
9 Directive 83/643, L 359/8.
10 Directive 84/5, OJ 1984, L8/17.
11 Directive 84/647, OJ 1984, L335/72.
12 Regulation 3820/85, OJ 1985, L370/1.
13 Directive 85/3, OJ 1985, L2/14.
14 Directive 88/599, OJ 1988, L325/55.
15 Regulation 4058/89, OJ 1989, L390/1.
16 Regulation 4059/89, OJ 1989, L390/3.
17 Regulation 4060/89, OJ 1989, L390/18.
18 Directive 89/459, OJ 1989, L226/4.
19 Directive 89/684, OJ 1989, L398/33.
20 COM(88) 705 final, OJ 1988, C48/1.
1 COM(88) 707 final, OJ 1988, C25/9 and COM (89) 640, OJ 1990, C 11/18.
2 COM(88) 644 final, OJ 1989, C16/12.
3 COM(88) 706 final, OJ 1989, C33/9.
4 COM(90) 64 final, QJ 1990, C87/4.

between railway undertakings and Member States;[5] uniform costing principles for railway undertakings;[6] rates for the international carriage of goods by rail;[7] the commercial independence of the railways in the management of their international passenger and luggage traffic.[8]

There are on the table proposals for a Council directive on the development of the Community railways[9] and a decision concerning the establishment of a network of high-speed trains.[10]

(c) *Inland waterways*   Legislation on inland waterway transport includes provisions for: reciprocal recognition of navigability licences for vessels;[11] technical requirements for inland waterway vessels;[12] the conditions for access to the arrangements under the revised Convention for the navigation of the Rhine;[13] access to the occupation of carrier of goods by inland waterway and the mutual recognition of professional qualifications;[14] structural improvements in inland waterway transport.[15]

(d) *Maritime transport*   The Council set up a consultation procedure on relations between Member States and third countries in shipping matters and on action relating to such matters in international organizations[16] and issued a regulation concerning the ratification by the Member States of, or their accession to, the UN Convention and a Code of Conduct for Liner Conferences.[17]

Specific legislation includes provisions for: the freedom to provide services to maritime transport between Member States and third countries;[18] the application of the competition rules of articles 85 and 86 of the Treaty to maritime transport;[19] the unfair pricing

---

5 Dec 75/327, OJ 1975, L152/3.
6 Regulation 2183/78, OJ 1978, L258/1.
7 Dec 82/529, OJ 1982, L239/5.
8 Dec 83/418, OJ 1983, L237/33.
9 COM(89) 564 final, OJ 1990, C34/13.
10 COM(89) 564 final, OJ 1990, C34/13.
11 Directive 76/135, OJ 1976, L21/10.
12 Directive 82/714, OJ 1982, L301/1.
13 Regulation 2919/85, OJ 280/5.
14 Directive 87/540, OJ 1987, L322/20.
15 Regulation 1101/89, OJ 1989, L116/25 and Commission Reg 1102/89, OJ 1989, L116/30.
16 Dec 77/587, OJ 1977, L239/23.
17 Regulation 954/79, OJ 1979, L121/1.
18 Regulation 4055/86, OJ 1986, L378/1.
19 Regulation 4056/86, OJ 1986, L378/4; Commission Reg 4260/88, OJ 1988, L376/1.

practices in maritime transport;[20] and the free access to cargoes in ocean trades.[1]

Proposed legislation purports to establish a Community ship register and to provide for the Community flag of sea-going vessels;[2] a common definition of a Community shipowner[3] and to apply the principle of freedom to provide services to maritime transport between Member States.[4]

(e) *Air transport* A rather late start of Community regulation of the transport by air commenced with the setting up of a consultation procedure on relations between Member States and third countries as well as international organizations in this field,[5] followed by a directive on co-operation and mutual assistance in the investigation of air accidents.[6] Further legislation includes measures concerning: the authorization of scheduled inter-regional services;[7] the procedure for the application of competition rules;[8] the application of article 85 (3) of the EEC Treaty to certain categories of agreements and concerted practices in the air transport sector;[9] fares for scheduled air services between Member States;[10] the sharing of passanger capacity between air carriers on scheduled services between Member States and the access for air carriers to scheduled service routes between Member States;[11] the application of article 85 (3) to certain categories of agreements between undertakings, decisions of associations of undertakings and concerted practices concerning joint planning and co-ordination of capacity, sharing of revenue and consultation on tariffs on scheduled services and slot allocations at airports;[12] the application of article 85 (3) to certain categories of agreements between undertakings relating to computer reservation systems for air transport services;[13] the application of article 85 (3) to certain categories of agreements between undertakings, decisions of associations of undertakings

---

20 Regulation 4057/86, OJ 1986, L378/14.
1 Regulation 4058/86, OJ 1986, L378/21.
2 COM(89) 266 final OJ 1989, C263/11.
3 COM(89) 266 final, OJ 1989, C263/17.
4 COM(89) 266 final, OJ 1989, C263/17.
5 Dec 80/50, OJ 1980, L18/24.
6 Dec 80/1260, OJ 1980, L375/32.
7 Directive 83/416, OJ 1983, L237.
8 Regulation 3975/87, OJ 1987, L374/1; and Commission Reg 4261/88, OJ 1988, L376/10.
9 Regulation 3976/87, OJ 1987, L374/9.
10 Directive 87/601, OJ 1987, L374/12.
11 Decision 87/602, OJ 1987, L374/19.
12 Commission Reg 2671/88, OJ 1988, L239/9.
13 Commission Reg 2672/88, OJ 1988, L239/13.

and concerted practices concerning ground handling services;[14] and a code of conduct for computerized reservation systems.[15]

Proposed legislation comprises measures for: consultation and co-ordination between Member States in the field of air traffic services and air traffic flow management;[16] a flexible and efficient use of air space;[17] the regulation of fares for scheduled air services;[18] access for air carriers to scheduled intra-Community air service routes and on sharing of passenger capacity between air carriers on scheduled service between Member States;[19] the application of article 85 (3) to certain categories of agreements and concerted practices in the air transport sector;[1] mutual acceptance of personnel licenses for the exercise of functions in civil aviation; consultation and authorization procedure for agreements concerning commercial aviation between Member States and third countries[2] and the operation of air cargo services.[3]

(D) COMPETITION POLICY (ARTICLES 85–90)

In the Preamble to the Treaty, 'fair competition' is recognized as one of the tenets of the European Economic Community. However, although the Treaty purports to institute a 'system ensuring that competition in the Common Market is not distorted' (article 3 (*f*)), competition, fair or otherwise, has not been defined either by the Treaty or the Community Court.[4] It seems to be treated as a self-explanatory term.

In view of the rich case law and numerous learned treatises on the subject only an outline of the basic principles shall be attempted here.

The Treaty sets out to establish a system of sound competition based on three sets of rules: rules applying to undertakings, rules against dumping and rules governing state aids.

---

14 Commission Reg 2673/88,OJ 1988, L239/17.
15 Regulation 2299/89, OJ 1989, L220/1.
16 COM(88) 577 final, OJ 1988, C34/8.
17 COM(88) 577 final, OJ 1988, C34/10.
18 COM(89) 373 final, OJ 1989, C258/3.
19 COM(89) 373 final, OJ 1989, C258/6.
 1 COM(89) 417 final, OJ 1989, C248/10.
 2 COM(90) 17 final.
 3 COM(90) 63 final.
 4 See the leading case, Cases 56 and 58/64: *Consten and Grundig v EEC Commission* [1966] ECR 299, [1966] CMLR 418.

1. *Rules applying to private undertakings*

In the first set of rules, articles 85 and 86 form the backbone of rules addressed to 'undertakings' in general; article 90 is specifically concerned with 'undertakings' of a public nature. Article 85 prohibits as 'incompatible with the Common Market all agreements between undertakings, decisions by associations of undertakings and concerted practices which may affect trade between Member States and which have as their object or effect the prevention, restriction or distortion of competition within the Common Market'. This does not import prohibitions of *all* combinations or *cartels* but some of them. Article 86, on the other hand, prohibits 'any abuse by one or more undertakings of a dominant position within the Common Market or in a substantial part of it as incompatible with the common market in so far as it may affect trade between Member States'. Here again, the 'dominant position' *as such* is not condemned, but merely its *abuse*.

Since the Treaty contains merely the bare principles, article 87 charges the Council with the task of elaborating detailed Community rules by means of directives or regulations to be designed with the assistance of the Commission and the Parliament. Articles 88 and 89 contain transitory provisions to be in force until the measures envisaged in article 87 have been enacted. In this respect the Council has issued a number of Regulations of which Regulation No 17[5] is the principal one as it lays down procedural rules to complement substantive law.

The provisions of articles 85 and 86 are addressed to 'undertakings', both private and public. The term 'undertakings'[6] has not been defined in the Treaty, but article 58 (2) gives a definition of 'companies or firms' by enumeration earmarking these, however, as profit-making entities. We can say that, by analogy, an 'undertaking' means a legal entity, whether a physical person or corporation or an association of legal entities engaged in a profit-making activity.

The exact legal status of the entity (which is a matter for the national law concerned) seems of secondary importance as long as there are certain characteristics corresponding to the concept of a natural or juristic person.[7] After all, the entity must have a certain standing under the Treaty which implies capacity to enter into

---

5 Of 6 February 1962, JO 204/62, amended by Regulations Nos 59 (JO 1655/62), 118 (JO 2696/63) and 2822 [1971] (JO L285).

6 French: *entreprise*; German: *Unternehmen*; Italian: *impresa*.

7 Cf Cases 42 and 49/59: *SNUPAT v High Authority of the ECSC* [1961] ECR 53.

legal transactions, to sue and be sued;[8] and to own property should a punitive sanction be imposed for contraventions of the rules of competition.

In the light of the Commission's decisions individuals may be involved when engaged in economic activity by themselves[9] or when in control of a firm.[10] Associations of firms acting through a chairman or delegates of the associates[11] and even associations without any formal constitution[12] may also be caught by the rules.

The Community Court on several occasions has had to determine the meaning of the term 'undertaking' and has stated that 'an enterprise is constituted by a unitary organisation combining personal, material and immaterial elements attached to an autonomous juristic subject and pursuing permanently a definite economic objective'.[13] It follows that, for the purpose of articles 85 and 86, an undertaking has to be endowed with a juristic and economic *autonomy* and has to be engaged in the production or distribution of goods or services. It may include a liberal profession within the scope of article 60 of the Treaty,[14] but not purely personal pursuits.[15]

Unlike article 80 of the ECSC Treaty, articles 85 and 86 of the EEC Treaty are not concerned with the geographical situation of the undertakings. They will come, therefore, under the rules even if situated in, or controlled from, a third country.[16]

Some problems have arisen in connection with subsidiaries which, though having a separate legal status from their parent company (*juristic autonomy*), need not be independent (*economic autonomy*). If they are not independent, they cannot be regarded as economic entities in competition with their parent-company. This, in fact, was the conclusion reached by the Commission in *Re Christiani and Nielsen*,[17] where a Dutch subsidiary, wholly owned

---

8 EEC, art 173 (2): 'Any natural or legal person may . . . institute proceedings . . .'
9 Decision 76/29: *AOIP v Beyrard* [1976] 1 CMLR D14.
10 Decision 76/743: *Reuter v BASF A-G* [1976] 2 CMLR D44.
11 Decision 76/684: *Pabst and Richarz KG v Bureau National Interprofessionnel de l'Armagnac* [1976] 2 CMLR D63.
12 Decision 74/431: *Re Groupement des Fabricants de Papiers Peints de Belgique* [1974] 2 CMLR D102; See also Decision 80/234: *Re Rennet* (a co-operative) [1980] 2 CMLR 402; OJ 1980, L51/19.
13 Case 19/61: *Mannesmann A-G v High Authority of the ECSC* [1962] ECR 357.
14 Deringer, A, *Das Wett-Bewerbsrecht der Europäischen Wirtschafts-Gemeinschaft Wirtschaft and Wettbewerb* No 11 (1962), p 794.
15 *Id, Les règles de la concurrence au sein de la CEE* No 12 (1963), p 37.
16 *Re Grossfillex* (decision of the Commission) (1964) 3 CMLRev 257; *Re Kodak* (decision of the Commission) 70/332/EEC, [1970] CMLR D19.
17 69/195/EEC: [1969] CMLR D36. See also *Re Aniline Dyes Cartel* 69/243/EEC [1969] CMLR D23. Cf Case 45/85: *Verband der Sachversicherer v EC*

by its Danish parent company, was held unable to engage in independent economic activity. Therefore, held the Commission, 'the sharing of markets provided for in the agreement is nothing else but a distribution of tasks within a single unit'. In *Re Kodak*[18] the Commission held that a European subsidiary of an American company, acting on instructions from the parent-company, could not behave independently. Therefore, the agreements in question (ie between the parent-company and its subsidiaries) could not restrict competition between the parties although they could do so between one of the parties and third parties. However the existence of a joint[19] subsidiary implies agreement between the parent companies and, consequently, the channelling of sales through such a subsidiary may constitute a concerted practice prohibited by the Treaty. Where a subsidiary operates under the control of the parent organization they constitute a single entity for the purpose of competition and, in appropriate cases, will fall within the scope of article 86.[20]

2. *Practices contrary to article 85*
Article 85 (1) states what kind of agreements, decisions and concerted practices are prohibited. They must exhibit two characteristics, ie they must prevent, restrict or distort competition and they must affect trade between Member States. A textual comparison with article 3 (*f*) which states the general principle reveals that only the word 'distort' occurs in both articles 85 (1) and 3 (*f*). This is the key word and the words 'prevent' and 'restrict' seem purely subsidiary or explanatory of the key word. Thinking in terms of the English terminology 'restrictive practices' may appear narrower than the inelegant phrase 'distortive practices'. As free competition is one of the underlying philosophies of the Common Market, anything affecting that freedom adversely would constitute 'distortion' within the general meaning of the word.

Agreements
Article 85 enumerates agreements and practices which, *in particular*, are considered to have that effect, because they:

Commission [1987] ECR 405, [1988] 4 CMLR 264 where autonomous subsidiary and foreign parent company were involved.
18 *Re Kodak*, supra.
19 Commission decision 80/182: *Re Floral Düngemittelverkaufsgesellschaft mbH* [1980] 2 CMLR 285.
20 Commission Decision: *Re Magill TV Guide Ltd v Independent Television Publications* [1989] 4 CMLR 757; Commission Decision: *Re the Application of Racal Group Services* [1990] 4 CMLR 627.

'(a) directly or indirectly fix purchase or selling prices[1] or any other trading conditions;[2]

(b) limit or control production,[3] markets, technical developments or investments;

(c) share markets or sources of supply;[4]

(d) apply dissimilar conditions to equivalent transactions[5] with other trading parties, thereby placing them at a competitive disadvantage;

(e) make the conclusion of contracts[6] subject to acceptance by the other parties of supplementary obligations which, by their nature or according to commercial usage, have no connection with the subject of such contracts.'

The list is by no means exhaustive, it simply comprises the most usual types of agreement and practices likely to affect the freedom of competition.

The term 'agreement' has to be construed liberally. It does not necessarily mean a binding[7] contract but rather an understanding

1 Commission Decision 69/240: *Re Quinine Cartel* [1969] CMLR D41; Case 45/69: *Boehringer Mannheim GmbH v EC Commission* [1970] ECR 769; Case 48/69: *Imperial Chemical Industries Ltd v EC Commission* [1972] ECR 619, [1972] CMLR 557; Commission Decision 78/163: *Re Distillers Co Ltd* [1978] 1 CMLR 400; see also in *Re Agreements of the Distillers Co* [1980] 1 CMLR 541; Cases 240–242/82, 261–262/82 and 268–269/82: *Stichting Sigarettenindustrie v EC Commission* [1985] ECR 3831, [1987] 3 CMLR 661 but see Commission Decision in *Re Associazione Bancaria Italiana* [1989] 4 CMLR 238; and Commission Decision in *Re the Application of the Nederlandse Bankiersvereniging* [1990] 4 CMLR 768.
2 Commission Decisions in: *Re WEA-Filipacchi Music SA* [1973] CMLR D43; *Re Dutch Book Publishers* [1977] 1 CMLR D2; *Re IFTRA Rules for Producers of Virgin Aluminium* 75/497 EEC [1975] 2 CMLR D20; Commission Decision in *Re Bloemenveilingen Aalsmeer* [1989] 4 CMLR 500 and Commission Decision in *Re BAYO-N-OX* [1990] 4 CMLR 930; Case 27/87: *Erauw-Jacquery Sprl v La Hesbignonne Societé Co-op* [1988] 4 CMLR 576.
3 *Quinine Cartel*, supra.; Case 41/69: *ACF Chemiefarma NV v EC Commission* [1970] ECR 661.
4 *Quinine Cartel*, supra.; Case 63/75: *Fonderies Roubaix SA v Fonderies Roux* [1976] ECR 111, [1976] 1 CMLR 538; Commission Decision 74/292: *Re European Glass Manufacturers* [1974] 2 CMLR D50; Commission Decision 85/618/EEC: *The Community v Fanuc Ltd and Siemens AG* [1988] 4 CMLR 945.
5 Commission Decision in the *Distillers Co*, supra; Commission Decision 74/433: *Re FRUBO* [1974] 2 CMLR D89.
6 *IFTRA*, supra; Case 320/87: *Ottung v Klee and Weilbach: Obligation to pay royalties indefinitely)* [1990] 4 CMLR 915.
7 Case 8/72: *Vereniging van Cementhandelaren v EC Commission* [1972] ECR; 977, [1973] CMLR 7; Joined Cases 209–215, 218/78: *Heintz van Landewyck Sàrl v EC Commission* [1980] ECR 3125, [1981] 3 CMLR 134; Case 123/83:

to act in agreement. Therefore it includes a 'gentleman's agreement',[8] a general unrecorded understanding,[9] an oral agreement,[10] the adoption of common rules,[11] an agreement between two trading associations on behalf of their members,[12] a manufacturer's standard terms of sale,[13] settlement of a claim,[14] or civil action[15] and even a tacit acceptance of a dealer system.[16]

Decisions

Decisions include resolutions by or recommendations of a trade association to its members irrespective of whether or not they are binding[17] and whether or not the association is a legal entity. The very constitution[18] of a trade association and any rules made thereunder may be regarded as decisions for the purpose of influencing the market behaviour of its members. It is immaterial that the association is a non-profit-making and a non-trading body.[19] The following are examples of prohibited decisions: fixing of discounts by an association of undertakings,[20] making rules for exhi-

Bureau National Interprofessionnel du Cognac v Clair [1985] 2 CMLR 430; Commission Decision in *Re Polypropylene Cartel* [1988] 4 CMLR 347; Commission Decision in *Re Italian Flat Glass* [1990] 4 CMLR 535.

8 Case 41/69: *ACF Chemiefarma v EC Commission* [1970] ECR 661.
9 Commission Decision 82/853 (*Re National Panasonic*) [1983] 1 CMLR 497.
10 Case 28/77: *Tepea BV v EC Commission* [1978] ECR 1391, [1978] 3 CMLR 392.
11 Commission Decision 74/292, supra; Commission 75/497 (IFTRA), supra.
12 Commission Decision 74/433 (*Re FRUBO*) [1974] 2 CMLR D89; and Case 71/74 *Nederlandse Vereniging voor fruit v EC Commission* [1975] ECR 563, [1975] 2 CMLR 123; Commission Decision 82/123 (*Re VBBB and VBVB Agreement*) [1982] 2 CMLR 344 and Joined Cases 43, 63/82: *VBVB and VBBB v EC Commission* [1984] ECR 19, [1985] 1 CMLR 27.
13 Commission Decision 78/922 (*Re Zanussi SpA Guarantee*) [1979] 1 CMLR 81.
14 Case 35/83: *BAT Cigaretten-Fabriken GmbH v EC Commission* [1985] 2 CMLR 470.
15 Case 258/78: *L C Nungesser v EC Commission* [1982] ECR 2015, [1983] 1 CMLR 278.
16 Case 107/82: *AEG-Telefunken v EC Commission* [1983] ECR 3151, [1984] 3 CMLR 325.
17 Commission Decision 74/433 (*Re FRUBO*) [1974] 2 CMLR D89; Commission Decision 80/257 (*Re Rolled Steel*) [1980] 3 CMLR 193; Commission Decision 85/75 (*Re Fire Insurance*) [1985] 3 CMLR 246.
18 Commission Decision 78/59 (*Re Central Bureau Voor de Rijwielhandel*) [1978] 2 CMLR 194; Commission Decision 80/234 (*Re Rennet*) [1980] 2 CMLR 402 and Case 61/80: *Cooperative Stremsel en Kluersefrabriek v EC Commission* [1981] ECR 851, [1982] 2 CMLR 240.
19 Joined Cases 209–215, 218/78, supra.
20 Commission Decision 71/23 (*Re German Ceramic Tiles Discount Agreement*) [1971] CMLR D6.

bitions,[1] recommending prices and restrictive contract clauses,[2] collective boycott of a member of an association of manufacturers,[3] arrangement to restrict parallel imports;[4] excluding from fairs foreign firms if not represented in the United Kingdom.[5]

Concerted practices

A concerted practice was defined by the ECJ as 'a form of coordination between enterprises that has not yet reached the point where it is a contract in the true sense of the word but which, in practice, consciously substitutes a practical co-operation for the risks of competition'.[6] In the *Sugar Cartel*[7] cases the Court further amplified this concept by stressing that a concerted practice precludes any direct or indirect contact between competitors, the object or effect of which is to influence the conduct on the market of an actual or potential competitor. It would seem that in order to constitute a concerted practice there must be a conscious effort 'on the part of the undertakers to act in a collective manner'. Thus, eg, members of the Vegetable Parchment Association[8] were held to be involved in a concerted practice by assisting their British members to retain control of the UK and Irish markets and so were manufacturers anxious to maintain an inter-state territorial protection.[9]

Affecting trade

To be contrary to article 85 (1) agreements and practices have to 'affect' trade between Member States. Some problems of the interpretation of this word[10] have arisen in practice and Advocate-

---

1 Commission Decision 71/337 (*Re CEMATEX*) [1973] CMLR D135; also Case 79/37: *Re CECIMO* [1979] 1 CMLR 419.

2 Case 8/72: Joined Cases 209–215, 218/78, supra; Cases 43, 63/82, supra.

3 Commission Decision 74/431 (*Re Groupement des Fabricants de Papiers Peints de Belgique*) [1974] 2 CMLR D102.

4 Cases 96–102/82: *IAZ International v EC Commission* [1983] ECR 3369, [1984] 3 CMLR 276.

5 Commission Decision in *Re the Application of the British Dental Trade Association* [1989] 4 CMLR 1021

6 Case 48/69: *Imperial Chemical Industries v EC Commission* [1972] ECR 619, [1972] CMLR 557 at para 64.

7 Cases 40–48/73: *Cooperative Verniging Suiker Unie v EC Commission* [1975] ECR 1663, [1976] 1 CMLR 295; see also Case 172/80: *Zuchner v Bayerische Vereinsbank* [1981] ECR 2021 at 2031–2032, [1982] 1 CMLR 313 at 324–325.

8 Commission Decision 78/252 (*The Community v Genuine Vegetable Parchment Association*) OJ 1978, 70/54, [1978] 1 CMLR 534.

9 Commission Decision in *ISA France Sarl v Tipp-Ex Vertrieb GmbH & Co KG* [1989] 4 CMLR 425.

10 French: *affecter*; German: *beeintrachtigen*; Italian: *prejudicare*; Dutch: *ongunstig beinvloeden*; Ellis, JJS, 'L'interprétation du mot "affecter" dans l'article 85, par. 1er, du traité de la CEE par rapport aux mots "empêcher", "restreindre",

General Lagrange is on record as saying that one has to approach articles 85 and 86 in their spirit rather than letter.[11]

The word 'affect' has a wide meaning and, it seems, has to be interpreted extensively to give effect to the Community interest in free trade. Indeed, if the Community is to be seen in its federal concept, there is an analogy in this field to the 'interstate commerce' of the United States of America.[12] An allusion to this position can be seen in the decision of the Community Court in the *Ulm* case.[13] Several cases decided by the municipal courts and the Community Court explain the position, but the following two early decisions of the Community Court provide a good illustration of the judicial practice.

In the *Ulm* case[14] there was an exclusive dealing agreement between the German company *Machinenbau Ulm GmbH* and the French company *Technique Minière*, whereby the latter became exclusive dealer for the sale of machinery in France and the French overseas territories. The agreement provided that the French company would buy a specified number of levellers at a fixed price, maintain a stock of spare parts, organize repairs, look after the interests of the sellers and refuse to sell competing products unless authorized by the sellers. A dispute arose in France and the French company argued that the agreement was void under article 85 (1) and (2) of the Treaty, the German company asserted the opposite. The Court of Appeal in Paris sought a preliminary ruling under article 177. In his submissions, Advocate-General Roemer suggested a middle way between the Commission's view that a perceptible interference with competition must take place in order to bring the matter under the rubric of article 85 (1) whilst the German company argued that the application of article 85 (1) should be excluded 'whenever the competition remains in existence notwithstanding the existence of the agreement'. He submitted that 'it would be excessive to place under the rigorous prohibition of article 85 (1) the slightest interference with competition ... and only to grant exemption within the context of article 85 (3).[15] He referred to a risk of divergence in the municipal jurisdiction and concluded that national judges 'must take account of the real or seriously likely repercussions of the agreement on the market and

ou "fausser le jeu de la concurrence"' *Recueil Dalloz* (1963), Ch. XXII, pp 221 et seq.
11 Case 13/61: In *Société Kledingverkoopbedrijf de Geus en Uitdenbogerd v Société de Droit Allemand Robert Bosch GmbH* [1962] CMLR 1 at 23.
12 *Les Novelles*, op cit, p 825.
13 Case 56/65: *Technique Minière v Maschinenbau Ulm GmbH* [1966] CMLR 357 at 375.
14 [1966] CMLR 357.
15 Ibid, at pp 367, 368.

examine in the particular case whether it has interfered with competition to a noticeable extent and trade between Member States
been affected to a noticeable extent'.[16]

In its judgment the Court examined the purpose of article 85 (1)
and held that an agreement must be considered in its economic
context. If the object of the agreement cannot have 'a sufficient
degree of harmfulness with regard to competition' the Court should
consider the possible effect of the agreement, ie whether it is likely
to prevent, restrict or distort competition 'to a noticeable extent'.
In order to determine the extent the court must take into consideration: (1) the nature and quantity of the product, which is the
object of the agreement; (2) the position and size of the parties to
the agreement in the particular market; (3) the isolated nature of
the agreement or its position in a series of similar agreements; (4)
the severity of the clauses which aim at the protection of the
exclusive rights or on the possibilities left for other commercial
currents upon the same products by means of re-exporting and
parallel imports.[17]

In *Consten SA and Grundig-Verkaufs-GmbH v EEC Commission*[18] the German firm, Grundig, concluded with Consten, a
French firm, an agreement for an indefinite period whereby
Consten became the sole representative of Grundig for France, the
Saar and Corsica. Consten undertook to buy Grundig products,
carry out publicity, set up repairs workshops with sufficient spare
parts and to undertake the guarantee and after-sales service.
Consten also undertook not to sell similar products or to compete
with Grundig. Grundig, on the other hand, undertook to retain
sale rights and not to deliver, either directly or indirectly, to other
persons within the area covered by the agreement. Grundig authorized Consten to use the name and emblem of Grundig as registered in Germany and other Member States. Moreover Consten
registered in France, in its own name, the trade mark GINT
(Grundig International).

Since April 1961, the company UNEF had bought Grundig
products from German traders who delivered them in spite of the
export prohibition imposed by Grundig, and UNEF resold these
in France at more favourable prices than those charged by Consten.
Consten brought two actions against UNEF, one for unfair competition and one for infringement of the GINT trademark. The
litigation in France led to a decision by the Commission,[19] which
held the agreement contrary to article 85 (1) and concluded that

16 Ibid, at p 372.
17 Ibid, at p 376.
18 Cases 56 and 58/64: [1966] CMLR 418.
19 *Re Grundig Agreement* 64/599 EEC [1964] CMLR 489; JO 2545/64.

Grundig and Consten 'are required to refrain from any measure tending to obstruct or impede the acquisition by third parties ... of the products set out in the contract, with a view to their resale in the contract territory'.

Both firms brought an action in the Community Court for annulment of this decision and the Governments of Germany and Italy intervened.

Advocate-General Roemer and the Court considered very fully the implication of the Consten-Grundig arrangement and the several points raised by it. The Advocate-General submitted inter alia that to judge the criterion of an agreement capable of affecting trade 'account must be taken of the possible repercussions which it is reasonable to expect *on the market* (and this is so even though the Commission must be held correct in declaring that proof of an *increase* in international trade is not enough in itself to show that trade has not been affected)'.[20]

The Court, considering the effect of the arrangement on inter-state trade, held that:

'... it is necessary ... to know whether the agreement is capable of endangering, either directly or indirectly, in fact or potentially, freedom of trade between Member States in a direction, which could harm the attainment of the object of a single market between states. So the fact that an agreement favours an increase ... in the volume of trade between states is not sufficient to exclude the ability of the agreement to "affect" the trade ... In the present case the contract ..., on the one hand by preventing undertakings other than Consten importing Grundig products into France, and on the other hand by prohibiting Consten from re-exporting those products to other countries of the Common Market, indisputably affects trade between Member States. These limitations on the freedom of trade, as well as those which might follow for third parties, from the registration in France ... of the GINT trademark, which Grundig places on all its products, suffice to satisfy the condition under discussion ...'

Recently the ECJ held reciprocal licensing agreements operative in several Member States capable of affecting inter-state trade even if the parties are situated in the same state.[2]

We should observe that trade need not be *actually* affected. It is sufficient that it *may* be so affected. This was particularly stressed in *Re WEA-Filipacchi Music SA*[3] by the Commission saying that

20 [1966] CMLR 418 at 434.
1 Ibid, at p 472.
2 Case 65/86: *Bayer AG and Maschinenfabrik Hennecke v Süllhöfer* [1990] 4 CMLR 182.
3 Page 502, note 2, supra; see also Commission Decision 74/432: *Re Advocaat Zwarte Kip* [1974] 2 CMLR D79.

'the violation is already complete when an agreement has the object of restricting competition, even if it had not yet had that effect'. The threat to free competition, real or potential, must be 'appreciable'.[4]

However the effect, actual or potential, must not be insignificant since *de minimis non curat lex*. The *de mimimis* doctrine can be traced to the *Machinenbau Ulm* case.[5] It was judicially acknowledged in *Völk v Vervaecke*[6] where the ECJ, considering a contract to sell German washing machines in Belgium and Luxembourg, held that 'to be capable of affecting trade between Member States the agreement must, on the basis of a collection of objective legal or factual factors, permit a reasonable expectation that it could exercise an influence, direct or indirect, actual or potential, on the trade trends between Member States in a direction which would harm the attainment of the objectives of a single market between States'. Therefore an agreement escapes the prohibition of article 85 when it only affects the market insignificantly, account being taken of 'the weak position held by the parties on the market in the product in question ...'.

The principle was affirmed in the Commission Notices[7] concerning Agreements, Decisions and Concerted Practices of Minor Importance. Paragraph 7 of the 1986 Notice provides that:

'The Commission holds the view that agreements between undertakings engaged in the production or distribution of goods or in the provision of services generally do not fall under the prohibition of Article 85 (1) if:

the goods or services which are the subject of the agreement ... together with the participating undertakings' other goods or services which are considered by users to be equivalent in view of their characteristics, price and intended use, do not represent more than 5% of the total market for such goods ... in the area of the common market affected by the agreement and

the aggregate annual turnover of the participating undertakings does not exceed 200 million ECU.'

The present version differs from the previous one in those

---

4 Commission Decisions 68/318: *Re SOCEMAS* [1968] CMLR D28, 68/376: *Re Agreement Johs Rieckermann KG and AEG-Elotherm GmbH* [1968] CMLR D78.
5 Page 505, note 14, supra.
6 Case 5/69: *Völk v Vervaecke* [1969] ECR 295, [1969] CMLR 273. See also Case 107/82: *Allgemeine Elektricitäts-Gesellschaft v EC Commission* [1983] ECR 3151, [1984] 3 CMLR 325.
7 OJ 1970, C64/1 amended by OJ 1977, C313/3 replaced by Notice of 1986, OJ 1986, C 231/2.

respects, ie it includes services, the turnover limit has been increased from 50 to 200 million ECU and the market share is to be calculated in relation to the area in which the agreement is to operate rather than, as hitherto, to a substantial part of the Common Market.

Agreements within the limits need not be notified to the Commission but the Notice does not guarantee immunity from sanctions[8] and does not bind the Court.[9] It provides useful guidelines to business.

3. *Negative clearance*

An undertaking engaged in a practice of a restrictive nature may apply to the Commission for 'negative clearance',[10] that is to say a statement that 'on the basis of the facts in its possession' the Commission sees no grounds for action to be taken under articles 85 (1) and 86 of the Treaty. Such a statement offers no foolproof protection but can be pleaded in mitigation should subsequently an infringement be established. The Commission has power to impose fines upon undertakings supplying incorrect or misleading information.[11]

4. *Exemptions under article 85 (3)*

Restrictive practices may be exempt from the rigour of article 85 (1) if certain conditions can be proved to the satisfaction of the Commission. The onus is on the applicant to show that the agreement or practice in question 'contributes to improving the production or distribution of goods or to promoting technical or economic progress, while allowing consumers a fair share of the resulting benefit, and which does not:

(a) impose on the undertakings concerned restrictions which are not indispensable to the attainment of these objectives;

(b) afford such undertakings the possibility of eliminating competition in respect of a substantial part of the products in question'.[12]

8 Commission Decision 79/68 (*Re Kawasaki Motors*) [1979] 1 CMLR 448.
9 Case 19/77: *Miller International Schallplaten v EC Commission* [1978] ECR 131 at 158, [1978] 2 CMLR 334 at 342 (per A-G Warner).
10 Regulation 17, art 2, of 6 February 1962 as amended, supra p 499, note 5.
11 See Case 28/77: *Tepea BV v EC Commission* [1978] ECR 1391, [1978] 3 CMLR 392.
12 EEC, art 85 (3); See Case 30/78: *Distillers Co Ltd v EC Commission* [1980] 3 CMLR 121; Commission Decision in *Re the Agreement of the Distillers Co Ltd* [1980] 3 CMLR 244, Commission Decision in *Re the Application of Robert Krups & Co* [1980] 3 CMLR 274; Commission Decision in Case 37/79: *Anne*

The system knows two types of exemption, ie *individual exemptions* granted by the Commission in specific cases and *block exemptions* arising from Community legislation.

Individual exemptions are granted or refused by Commission decisions reached in the appropriate process. They are subject to judicial review.[13] The process itself involves notification by the applicant of the practice making a full disclosure to the Commission so much so that mere response to an enquiry instituted by the Commission will not satisfy the requirements.[14]

The burden of proving that the conditions of exemption exist rests upon the applicant.[15] When an application for renewal of an exemption is made the grounds have to be re-examined just in case the position has changed.[16]

Block exemptions have been introduced in order to speed up the process of exemptions. Thus Council Regulation 17/62[17] exempts agreements, decisions and concerted practices where the only parties involved are undertakings from one Member State only and the transactions do not relate either to imports or to exports between Member States.[18] The same Regulation[19] exempts resale agreements between two undertakings but the parties involved need not be in one Member State and the transaction may also relate to imports and exports between Member States. Another exemption under the same Regulation[20] applies to transactions involving no more than two parties which impose restrictions on the rights of the user or assignee of industrial property rights (ie

Marty SA v Estee Lauder SA [1980] ECR 2481, [1981] 2 CMLR 143. *Re the Application by the National Sulphuric Acid Association Ltd* [1980] 3 CMLR 429.

13 See eg Cases 19 and 20/74: *Kali and Salz A-G and Kali-Chemie v EC Commission* [1975] ECR 499, [1975] 2 CMLR 154; Case 30/78, supra.

14 Decision 78/670: *GB-INNO-BM SA v Fedetab* [1978] 3 CMLR 524. *FEDETAB v EC Commission* [1981] 3 CMLR 134; joined Cases 209–215, 218/78, supra ECR at 3243; CMLR at 220.

15 Case 42/84: *Remia BV v EC Commission* [1985] ECR 2545, [1987] 1 CMLR 1.

16 Case 75/84: *Metro-SB-Grossmärkte v EC Commission* [1986] ECR 3021, [1987] 1 CMLR 118.

17 JO 1962, 204; OJ 1959–1962, 87, art 7(2), art 4 (2).

18 See Case 43/69: *Brauerei A Bilger v Jehle* [1970] ECR 127, [1974] 1 CMLR 382; Case 63/75: *Fonderies Roubaix v Soc des Fonderies Roux* [1976] ECR 111, [1976] 1 CMLR 538. Commission Decision 78/155 (*Re BMW Dealers*) [1978] 2 CMLR 126; Commission Decision 82/853 (*Re National Panasonic*) [1983] 1 CMLR 497; Commission 83/400 (*Re Windsurfing International*) [1984] 1 CMLR 1.

19 Art 4 (2), para (2) (a).

20 Art 4 (2), para (2) (b).

patents, trademarks, designs, utility models). Regulation 2349/84[1] provides for a block exemption to certain patent licensing agreements including the transfer of 'know-how'. There is another larger category of block exemptions which includes co-operation[2] agreements among small and medium-sized undertakings where such co-operation enables them to work more rationally and increase their productivity and competitiveness on a larger market, specialisation[3] agreements, exclusive distribution agreements;[4] exclusive purchasing agreements[5] (including beer supply agreements); motor vehicles distribution and servicing agreements;[6] patent licensing agreements;[7] research and development agreements;[8] franchise agreements;[9] know-how licensing agreements[10] and air transport agreements.[11]

Exemption can of course be lost either entirely or partially if the terms under which it has been obtained are not observed.[12]

5. *Practices contrary to article 86*
Whilst article 85 prohibits certain arrangements which may affect inter-state trade and are likely to distort free competition within

---

1 OJ 1984, L219/15, corrected OJ, 1985, L113/34; see Korah, V, *Patent Licensing and EEC Competition Rules* (1985).
2 Commission Notice OJ 1968, C75/3; [1968] CMLR D5.
3 Commission Regulation 2779/72, JO 1972, L292/23 amended by Reg 2903/77, OJ 1977, L338/14 replaced by Reg 3604/82, OJ 1982, L376/33; replaced by Reg 417/85, OJ 1985, L53/1, see Commission Decision 69/242 (*Re Jaz SA's Agreement*) JO 1968, C75/3, [1970] CMLR 129. See also Decision 82/742 (*Re Amersham International and Buchler GmbH Joint Venture*) [1983] 1 CMLR 619 and compare Decision 78/921: (*Re Wano Schwarzpulver GmbH*) [1979] 1 CMLR 403.
4 Reg 1983/83, OJ 1983, L173/1 for interpretative guidelines see Commission Notes OJ 1984, C 101/2 replacing OJ 1983, C 355/7.
5 Reg 1984/83, OJ 1983, L 173/5 Commission guidelines apply also to this reg.
6 Reg 123/85, OJ 1985, L 15/16 and Commission guidelines OJ 1985, C 17/4; see Case 10/86: *VAG France SA v Etablissements Magne SA* [1988] 4 CMLR 98; Commission Decision *Re the Agreements of Automobiles Peugeot SA* (right-hand-drive cars) [1989] 4 CMLR 371; Commission Decision in *The Community v Société Belge des Automobiles Citroën* ibid 338.
7 Reg 2349/84, OJ 1984, L 219/15.
8 Reg 418/85, OJ 1985, L 53/5.
9 Reg 4087/88, OJ 1988, L 359/46, see Commission Decision *Re the Agreements of Pronuptia de Paris SA* [1989] 4 CMLR 355.
10 Reg 559/89, OJ 1989, L 61/1; see Korah, V, 'The Group Exemption for Know-How Licenses' (1989) 4 EIPR 134.
11 Reg 3975/87, OJ 1987, L 374/1; see Commission Decision in *Re London European–Sabena* [1989] 4 CMLR 662; Commission Decision *Re the Joint Venture Agreement between Air France and Air Inter* [1989] 4 CMLR 813; see also Air Transport (Exemption) Reg 2344/90, OJ 1990, L 217/15.
12 See Commission Decision *Re Ecosystem SA v Peugeot SA* [1990] 4 CMLR 449.

the Community, article 86 prohibits abuse of a 'dominant position' which has a similar effect. The two articles are complementary and both can be infringed simultaneously.[13]

The notion of the 'dominant position' is not alien to the Community, as it is well entrenched in the municipal laws of Germany, France, Belgium and the Netherlands.[14] However, it is not defined in the Treaty. A dominant position means, in effect, a monopoly within a sector of the economy. Like cartels, not all the monopolies are prohibited, for they may result from the lack of appreciable competition or from mergers which increase efficiency and do not eliminate competition. On the other hand, as suggested in the *Continental Can* case,[15] market shares in the range of 50% to 55% may constitute a dominant position – a picture somewhat different from a layman's concept of monopoly. 'Abuse' is, therefore, the key word. Article 86 enumerates such abuses as consisting in:

'(a) directly or indirectly imposing unfair purchase or selling prices or other unfair trading conditions;[16]

(b) limiting production, market or technical development to the prejudice of consumers;[17]

(c) applying dissimilar conditions to equivalent transactions with other trading parties, thereby placing them at a competitive disadvantage;[18]

13 Commission Decision *Re Italian Flat Glass: Industria Vetraria Alfonso Cobelli v Societa Italiana Vetro-SIV SpA* [1990] 4 CMLR 535; Commission Decision *Re the Application of Racal Group Services* [1990] 4 CMLR 627.

14 *Les Novelles*, op cit, p 837; see also art 66 of the ECSC Treaty.

15 *Re Continental Can Co Inc* [1972] CMLR D11; see also Commission Decision 81/969: *Bandengroothandel Frieschebrug BV v Nederlandsche Banden-Industrie Michelin NV* [1982] 1 CMLR 643 (60 per cent share of market for tyres considered 'dominant').

16 Case 78/70: *Deutsche Grammophon GmbH v Metro-SB-Grossmärkte GmbH & Co KG* [1971] ECR 487, [1971] CMLR 631; Case 127/73: *BRT v SABAM* [1974] ECR 51, [1974] 2 CMLR 238; Case 22/79: *Greenwich Film Production, Paris v SACEM* [1979] ECR 3275, [1980] 1 CMLR 629. See also Case 26/75: *General Motors NV v EC Commission* [1975] ECR 1367, [1976] 1 CMLR 95; Commission Decision 83/462 (*Re ECS/AKZO*) [1983] 3 CMLR 694.

17 Commission Decision *Re European Sugar Cartel* [1973] CMLR D65; Cases 40-48, 50, 54-56, 111, 113, 114/73: *Co-operative Vereniging Suiker Unce UA v EC Commission* [1975] ECR 1663, [1976] 1 CMLR 295. Case 27/76, supra; Case 126/80: *Salonia v Poidomani* [1981] ECR 1563, [1982] 1 CMLR 64.

18 Commission Decision 71/224 in *Re GEMA* [1971] CMLR D35 and 72/268: *Re Gema (No 2)* [1972] CMLR D115. Case 155/73: *Sacchi* [1974] ECR 409, [1974] 2 CMLR 177; Commission Decision 82/861 (*Re British Telecommunications*) [1983] 1 CMLR 457 and Case 41/83: *Italy v EC Commission* [1985] 2 CMLR 368; Case 322/81: *Nederlansche Banden-Industrie Michelin NV v EC Commission* [1983] ECR 3461, [1985] 1 CMLR 282.

(d) making the conclusion of contracts subject to acceptance by the other parties of supplementary obligations which, by their nature or according to commercial usage, have no connection with the subject of such contracts'.[19]

This list of abuses is illustrative rather than exhaustive. Indeed, in its First Report on the Competition Policy of the Community, the Commission gave notice that it intends to apply article 86 to situations in which consumers are adversely affected as a result of the abuse of a dominant position.[1] In its Third[2] Report on Competition Policy the Commission addressed itself mainly to the problem of 'industrial concentration' as an obstacle to the open market and effective competition threatening the 'unity of the Common Market'. To combat this mischief the Commission drafted, in 1973,[3] a proposal for a regulation to provide control of concentrations between undertakings. After protracted negotiations and several amendments to the draft the Council enacted regulation 2367/90[4] on the procedure for Merger Control and the Commission followed up with interpretative guidelines.[5]

The judicial definition of 'dominant position' is of a rather recent vintage. The Community Court was urged by the Italian Government to apply article 86 in the *Grundig* case[6] and in *Italy v EEC Council and Commission*[7] but the Court refused the temptation, contending that 'the possible application of article 85 to a sole agency agreement should not be excluded merely because the grantor and the concessionaire are not competitors inter se and not on a footing of equality'.[8]

An opportunity to define dominant position arose in the *Sirena* case,[9] where the Community Court held that an undertaking does not enjoy a dominant position by the sole fact of being able to

---

19 Case 85/76: *Hoffmann-La Roche & Co AG v EC Commission* [1979] ECR 461, [1979] 3 CMLR 211; Case 41/83, supra; *Sugar* cases, supra, Commission Decision *Re Iberian Trading UK Ltd v BPB Industries plc* [1990] 4 CMLR 464.
1 *Fifth General Report*, 1971, pp 99 and 103.
2 Annexed to the *Seventh General Report*, 1974, pp 28 et seq. See also Twelfth Report on Competition, p 34; Thirteenth Report, p 96 and Fourteenth Report, p 46.
3 OJ 1973, C92.
4 [1990] 4 CMLR 683.
5 Guidelines on Ancillary Restrictions to Mergers [1990] 4 CMLR 714; Guidelines on Concentration and Co-operation in Merger Control [1990] 4 CMLR 721.
6 Cases 56 and 58/64: [1966] CMLR 418.
7 Case 32/65: [1969] CMLR 39.
8 [1966] CMLR 418 at 470.
9 Case 40/70: *Sirena Srl v Eda Srl* [1971] CMLR 260 at 275.

prevent 'third parties from selling in the territory of a Member State products bearing the same trade-mark; moreover, since article 86 requires that this position covers at least a "substantial part" of the Common Market, it is necessary that it has the power of preventing effective competition within an important part of the market, considering also the possible existence and the position of producers or distributors of similar or substitute products ...'

This passage was substantially repeated in the *DGG v Metro* case[10] where the Community Court held that a price maintenance scheme operating in Germany not only in respect of goods produced in Germany bearing the same trade-mark but also imported from another Member State coupled with the control of supplies constituted an infringement of article 86.

In *Laboratorio Chimico*, etc[11] the Community Court confirmed the finding of the Commission that a company incorporated in a third country but having a substantial presence in the EEC and enjoying a world monopoly in the supply of certain raw materials used in the production of a drug did abuse its dominant position by refusing to supply the necessary material to one of its users in order to eliminate that user from competition in the manufacture of the drug.

In *BRT v NV Fonior*, etc[12] the Belgian Association of Authors, Composers and Publishers, entrusted with the exploitation, administration and management of all copyrights and kindred rights of its members and associates was held to have abused its dominant position by imposing on its members obligations which encroached unfairly upon the freedom of exercising their rights.

The Continental Can case,[13] on the other hand, involved take-overs of companies specialising in various kinds of containers and metal lids for glass jars. As a result of the concentration competition in the field would have been practically eliminated. The Commission, in order to prevent this, initiated a procedure under article 3 (1) of Regulation 17/62 against Continental Can and its subsidiary Europemballage and ordered these companies to divest themselves of the newly-acquired control over other companies. The companies applied for annulment of the Commission decision

10 Case 78/70: *Deutsche Grammophon GmbH v Metro-SB-Grossmärkte GmbH & Co KG* [1971] CMLR 631 at 658.

11 Cases 6–7/73: *Istituto Chemioterapico Italiano SpA and Commercial Solvents Corpn v EC Commission* [1974] ECR 223, [1974] CMLR 309.

12 Case 127/73: *BRT v NV Fonior; SABAM v NV Fonior; BRT v SABAM and NV Fonior* [1974] ECR 51 and 313; [1974] 2 CMLR 238; see also Commission Decision 82/EEC: *Interpar v Gesellschaft zur Verwertung von Leistungsschutzrechten* [1982] 1 CMLR 221.

13 Case 6/72: *Europemballage Corpn and Continental Can Co Inc v EC Commission* [1973] ECR 215, [1973] CMLR 199.

on the ground, inter alia, that the Commission was unable to show in which market or markets these companies were supposed to have abused their dominant position. However the Court clarified an important point saying that:

'Article 86 is not only aimed at practices which may cause damage to consumers directly, but also at those which are detrimental to them through their impact on an effective competition structure, such as mentioned in article 3 (f) of the Treaty. Abuse may therefore occur if an undertaking in a dominant position strengthens such position in such a way that the degree of dominance reached substantially fetters competition, ie that only undertakings remain in the market whose behaviour depends on the dominant one . . .'[14]

In the *Sugar Cartel* case[15] the dominant position consisted in the control of the greater part of sugar production in Belgium and Luxembourg and in the *United Brands* case[16] in the world-wide control of the banana business. *General Motors*,[17] on the other hand, held a legal monopoly to issue certificates of approval for vehicles in its group. A similar position was enjoyed by *Hugin*,[18] a Swedish manufacturer, in the cash registers case as he controlled the market for spare parts which were not obtainable elsewhere and which were not interchangeable. They all were held to have abused their dominant position.

To constitute an abuse of a dominant position the exercise of the economic power must relate to the 'relevant market'. This relates to product[19] which now includes the service sector;[20] product sub-

---

14 Ibid at 245 (para 26).
15 Page 504, note 7, supra.
16 Commission Decision in *Re United Brands Co* [1976] 1 CMLR D28; Case 27/76: *United Brands Co v EC Commission* [1976] ECR 425, [1976] 2 CMLR 147. See also Case 85/76, supra; Case 31/80: *L'Oreal NV v De Nieuwe* [1980] ECR 3775, [1981] 2 CMLR 235; Case 322/81, supra.
17 Commission Decision 75/75: *Re General Motors Continental NV* [1975] 1 CMLR D20; Case 26/75: *General Motors Continental NV v EC Commission* [1975] ECR 1367, [1976] 1 CMLR 95; see also Case 226/84: *British Leyland plc v EC Commission* [1986] ECR 3263, [1987] 1 CMLR 184.
18 Decision 78/68: *Liptons Cash Registers and Business Equipment Ltd v Hugin Kassaregister AB* [1978] 1 CMLR D19; Case 22/78: *Hugin Kassaregister AB v EC Commission* [1979] ECR 1869, [1979] 3 CMLR 345. See also Case 238/87: *AB Volvo v Erik Veng* [1989] 4 CMLR 122 and Case 53/87: *CICRA v Régie Nationale des Usines Renault* [1990] 4 CMLR 265.
19 Eg *United Brands*, supra (bananas); *General Motors*, supra (motor cars); *Lipton and Hugin*, supra (cash registers); Joined Cases 19, 20/74: *Kali und Salz AG v EC Commission* [1975] ECR 499, [1975] 2 CMLR 154 (fertilizers); Case 322/81, supra.
20 See Commission Decision *Re Decca Navigator System*, OJ 1989, L43/27.

stitution[1] and territory.[2] Considering the 'relevant market' not only the volume of the business but also the territorial control has to be taken into account in order to determine whether or not a 'substantial part of the Common Market' has been affected.[3] In a geographical sense a 'substantial part' consisted in the eyes of the ECJ in the Netherlands,[4] Belgium,[5] Belgium with Luxembourg,[6] Germany,[7] Southern Germany[8] and the United Kingdom.[9]

However, as the concept of dominant position implies, the most important factor is the economic strength of the undertakings involved which enables them to dictate terms to the market. More precisely the ECJ considered in the United Brands Case that

> '... the dominant position ... relates to a position of economic strength enjoyed by an undertaking which enables it to prevent effective competition being maintained on the relevant market by affording it the power to behave to an appreciable extent independently of its competitors, customers and ultimately of its consumers'.[10]

As we have seen in most cases some powerful multi-nationals have been before the Commission and the Court. Their market behaviour is another factor and this, in turn, has to 'affect trade' within the Community. 'Trade', in this context, has to be under-

1 Eg Decision 73/457: *Zoja v Commercial Solvents Corpn* [1973] CMLR D50; Cases 6–7/73: *Commercial Solvents Corpn v EC Commission* [1974] ECR 223, [1974] 1 CMLR 309 (basic drug); *Hoffmann-La Roche* supra (vitamins); *Continental Can*, supra (metal lids). Commission Decision *Re BPB Industries plc* (OJ 1989, L10/50). Case 50/89: *BPB Industries plc and British Gypsum v EC Commission* (pending).

2 Eg *United Brands* supra; Decision 76/172: *Re Bayer and Gist Brocades (NV's) Agreement* [1976] 1 CMLR D98; Decision in *Sugar Cartel* [1973] CMLR D65; Cases 40–48, 50, 54–56, 111, 113, 114/73: *Suiker Unie UA etc* [1975] ECR 1663, [1976] 1 CMLR 295; Case 322/81, supra; Case 40/70, supra; Case 78/70, supra; Case 27/76, supra; Case 226/84: *British Leyland v EC Commission* [1986] ECR 3263, [1987] 1 CMLR 185. Case 247/86: *Alsatel v Novasam SA* [1990] 4 CMLR 434; Commission Decision *Re Magill TV Guide/ITP, BBC and RTE* (OJ 1989, L78/43; [1989] 4 CMLR 757; on appeal Case 76/89, *RTE v EC Commission* (pending); *BPB Industries* supra; Commission Decision *Re Hilti AG* (OJ 1988, L65/19, [1989] 4 CMLR 677; on appeal Case 98/88: *Hilti AG v EC Commission* (pending).

3 Case 77/77: *Benzine en Petroleum Handelsmaatschappij v EC Commission* [1978] ECR 1513, [1978] 3 CMLR 174.

4 Case 322/81, supra.

5 Case 26/75, supra.

6 *Sugar* cases, p 504, note 7, supra.

7 Case 7/82: *GVL v EC Commission* [1983] ECR 483, [1983] 3 CMLR 645.

8 *Sugar* cases, supra.

9 Commission Decision 82/861, supra; Commission Decision *Re Napier Brown–British Sugar plc* [1990] 4 CMLR 196.

10 Para 38; see also Commission Decision *Re Michelin*, OJ 1981, L353/33; [1982] 1 CMLR 643 para 35; Commission Decision *Re Brass Band Instruments Ltd v Boosey and Hawkes*, OJ 1987, L286/36; [1988] 4 CMLR 67.

stood in a broad sense as the case law indicates not only trade in the usual sense but also a variety of economic activities such as the manufacture of a product,[11] motor car distribution,[12] advertising,[13] banking,[14] insurance,[15] film[16] distribution, newspaper[17] distribution, telecommunications,[18] flower auctions[19] and funeral services.[20]

6. *Determination of infringements of articles 85 and 86*[1]

The Commission, whilst exercising an exclusive authority in respect of exemptions under article 85 (3) shares, in part, this power with the Member States when dealing with infringements of article 85 (1) and article 86. In other words, the states may deal with the latter as long as the Commission has not initiated proceedings under article 2, 3 or 6 of Regulation 17.[2] This has caused some difficulty in practice and there is no uniformity in this matter in the Community.[3] The disadvantages of concurrent jurisdiction are quite apparent.

The question of the overlap between municipal law and Community law was considered by the Community Court in *Wilhelm v Bundeskartellamt*[4] and it was held that, in principle, both could apply simultaneously subject to the underlying philosophy that Community law has to be implemented by the Member States and that in the case of conflict, Community law prevails.

According to article 3 of Regulation 17, infringements of articles 85 and 86 are dealt with by the Commission either *ex officio* or at the instance of interested parties. The former implies independent investigations of a case which comes to the notice of the Commission informally or in the course of the exercise of its duties as

11 Joined Cases 6, 7/73, supra. Commission Decision *W Burns Tractors Ltd v Sperry New Holland* OJ 1985, L376/21; [1988] 4 CMLR 306.
12 Case 26/75, supra.
13 Case 155/73, supra.
14 Case 172/80.
15 Case 90/76: *Van Ameyde v UCL* [1977] ECR 1091, [1977] 2 CMLR 478. Case 45/85: *Verband der Sachversicherer v EC Commission* [1987] ECR 405, [1988] 4 CMLR 264.
16 Case 22/79, supra.
17 Case 126/80, supra.
18 Case 41/83, supra. Case 247/86: *Alsatel v Novasam* [1990] 4 CMLR 434.
19 Commission Decision *Re Bloemenveilingen Aalsmer* [1989] 4 CMLR 500.
20 Case 30/87: *Bodson v Pompes Funebres des Regions Liberées SA* [1988] ECR 2479, [1989] 4 CMLR 984.
1 Kerse, CS, *EEC Antitrust Procedure* (2nd edn 1988).
2 EEC art 88 and Regulation 17, art 9.
3 *Les Novelles*, op cit, p 844.
4 Case 14/68: [1969] ECR 1, [1969] CMLR 100, cf 'new commercial torts': *Application des Gaz SA v Falks Veritas Ltd* [1974] 2 CMLR 75. See also Case 253/78: *Procurer de la République v Giry* [1981] 2 CMLR 99.

laid down by the Treaty (article 155) and Regulation 17 (article 11). The interested parties who put the Commission on enquiry can be either states or undertakings or individuals who are, but need not be,[5] affected by the alleged infringement. The Commission will use its powers of investigation and follow the prescribed procedure in order to reach a decision.

The Commission has the discretion whether or not to pursue a complaint but must advise the complainant if no action is to be taken.[6] According to case law legitimate interest has been shown by parties affected by a restrictive practice, eg a distributor unable to export;[7] a competitor denied supplies;[8] a wholesaler,[9] a retailer[10] unable to obtain the goods; a consumer[11] unable to purchase goods for export because of the prohibition of export sales by dealers; and a company subject to a takeover bid.[12] However, in practice, it is immaterial whether a complainant has a legitimate interest because, as emphasized by the Court,[13] the Commission has the power to initiate the process on its own initiative and within its discretion. Therefore a decision to do so cannot be invalidated on the ground that the complainant lacked a legitimate interest.

When a search and seizure order under article 14 of Regulation 17 is issued there is no need to give advance warning to the company under investigation. Whilst it is necessary to consult the competent national authorities and act with their co-operation an informal consultation (even over the telephone) will suffice. There is, in such a case, no breach of article 8 of the European Convention on Human Rights.[14] Foreign companies and trade organizations, even if owned by the state, are not entitled to sovereign immunity.[15]

If an infringement has been proved the Commission will take

5 Cases 32/78 and 36–82/78: *BMW Belgium SA v EC Commission* [1979] ECR 2435, [1980] 1 CMLR 370.
6 Case 125/78: *GEMA v EC Commission* [1979] ECR 3173, [1980] 2 CMLR 177.
7 Commission Decision 78/163: (*Re Distillers*) [1978] 1 CMLR 400.
8 Commission Decision 73/457: (*Re Zoja v Commercial Solvents*) [1973] CMLR D50 and Cases 6–7/73, supra.
9 Case 26/76: *Metro-SB-Grossmärkte v EC Commission* [1977] ECR 1875, [1978] 2 CMLR 1.
10 Commission Decision (*Re United Brands*) [1976] 1 CMLR D28 and Case 27/76, supra.
11 Commission Decision 79/68: (*Re Putz v Kawasaki Motors*) [1979] 1 CMLR 448.
12 Commission Decision (*Re Continental Can*) [1972] CMLR D11 and Case 6/72; supra.
13 Cases 36–82/78: *BMW Belgium v EC Commission* [1979] ECR 2435, [1980] 1 CMLR 370.
14 Case 5/85: *AKZO Chemie BV v EC Commission* [1986] ECR 2585, [1987] 1 CMLR 715.
15 Commission Decision in *Re Aluminium Imports from Eastern Europe* [1987] 3 CMLR 813.

appropriate steps to have the offending practice terminated, may make recommendations to the offending party and apply sanctions provided by the Treaty and the Regulation.

Before taking a decision, the Commission must give the parties concerned an opportunity to express their views, give them a hearing (Regulation 17, article 19 (1)) and, where it intends to issue negative clearance, it must publish the essential content of the application or notification, inviting all interested third parties to submit their observations (Regulation 17, article 19). Finally, it must consult the Consultative Committee on Cartels and Monopolies (Regulation 17, article 10).

While the Commission has the power to pass to the complainant against abuse of a dominant position a certain amount of information it must observe the principle of confidentiality and refrain from passing on information covered by professional secrecy.[16]

7. *Sanctions for infringements*[17]

In the case of infringement of article 85 and article 86, the Treaty provides for three different sanctions: nullity of the offending practice, fines and penalties.

According to article 85 (2) any prohibited agreements or decisions are null and void by operation of law, that is void *ab initio*[18] and not from the date of determination. This being a sanction *de plein droit*, there is no discretion in its application. The only exception applies to certain existing agreements, decisions and practices (Regulation 17, article 7).

The question whether nullity taints all has been answered by the Community Court in the *Ulm*[19] and *Grundig*[20] cases in the negative. Only the bad elements are tainted with nullity and these can be severed from the sound body of the contract or decision. The sanction of nullity does not strike activities under article 86 but different sanctions apply.

According to article 15 of Regulation 17, the Commission may inflict heavy fines, ranging from 1,000 to 1,000,000 ECU or a sum in excess of the limit but not exceeding 10 per cent of the turnover,[1] upon undertakings guilty of an infringement of article 85 (1) and article 86, and also for the supply of false or misleading information,

---

16 Case 5/75, supra.
17 Schroth, H-J, *Economic Offences in EEC Law* (1983).
18 Case 48/72: *Brasserie de Haecht SA v Wilkin-Janssen* [1973] ECR 77, [1973] CMLR 287.
19 [1966] CMLR 357 at 376.
20 [1966] CMLR 418 at 475.
1 For meaning of turnover see Joined Cases 100–103/80: *Musique Diffusion Française SA v EC Commission* [1983] ECR 1825 at 1908–1909, [1983] 3 CMLR 221 at 336.

for submission in incomplete forms of the books or other documents required or for refusal to submit to an investigation.[2] These
sanctions are said to have no criminal or punitive character (article
15 (4)) but their severity in certain cases, suggests that they were
meant to have a deterrent effect. For example, in a case[3] involving
the partition of the market the Commission imposed a fine of
7,000,000 ECU which the Court reduced only slightly on account
of certain factual inaccuracies which tainted the Commission
decision. In another case[4] the fines in respect of market-sharing
and price-fixing agreements totalled 57.85 million ECU and in the
Polyethylene[5] case 60 million ECU.

The Commission has power to inflict penalties[6] under article 16
of Regulation 17 in order to oblige the offenders to:

(a) put an end to an infringement of article 85 or 86;

(b) discontinue any action prohibited under article 8 (3) (c) of
    Regulation 17;[7]

(c) supply completely and truthfully any information requested
    under article 11 (5);[8]

(d) submit to any enquiries ordered under the investigative powers
    of the Commission.

The penalties, depending upon the severity of the infringement,
range from fifty to one thousand ECU per day.

The Commission merely fixes the fines and penalties in ECU's
as well as the appropriate national currency.

8. *Judicial control*

At the national level the Community rules are enforced by national
authorities whose decisions are subject to judicial control either by
ordinary courts (eg the United Kingdom) or specialist tribunals

---

2 Commission Decision 80/334: *EC Community v Fabbrica Pisani* [1980] 2 CMLR
  354, OJ 1980, L75/30; Case 28/77, supra.
3 Cases 100–103/80: *Musique Diffusion Française v EC Commission* [1983] ECR
  1825; [1983] 3 CMLR 221.
4 Commission Decision in *Re Polypropylene*, OJ 1986, L230/1; [1988] 4 CMLR
  347. Case 179/86: *Rhones-Poulenc SA v EC Commission* (pending).
5 Commission Decision in *Re PVC*, 1989, L74/1 [1990] 4 CMLR 345 and Ld
  PE, OJ 1989, L74/21 (appeal pending).
6 See 72/457/EEC *Laboratorio Chimico Farmaceutico Giorgio Zoja SpA v
  Commercial Solvents Corpn* [1973] CMLR D50, [1972] JO L299/51.
7 Reference to a decision obtained fraudulently or by false information.
8 See Commission Decision in *The Community v Telos SA* [1982] 1 CMLR 267;
  Commission Decision in *Community v Comptoir Commercial d'Importation*
  [1982] 1 CMLR 440.

(eg Germany). The national authorities may, of course, take advantage of the proceedings for a preliminary ruling under article 177 of the Treaty.

The decisions of the Commission do not rank as *res judicata*. Indeed, decisions made under article 85 (3) may be revoked or amended. However, decisions which impose a pecuniary obligation on persons other than states are enforceable by the authority of article 192 (1) of the Treaty. The procedure of enforcement is left to the municipal law of the Member States.

Decisions of the Commission are subject to judicial review either under proceedings for annulment or the principle of plenary jurisdiction. The former is governed by article 173 (2) of the Treaty, the latter by article 172. We should add that there is also a possibility of a *recours en carence* under article 175 (3) which enables any aggrieved party to complain to the Community Court that the Commission has failed in its duty.

Since the creation of the First Instance Court judicial control of the competition policy has been shared by the two Courts, the CFI having a particular duty to adjudicate in actions for annulment or for failure to act brought by natural or legal persons relating to the implementation of competition rules applicable to undertakings and also to claims for damages by natural or legal persons if damage is alleged to arise from an act or failure to act as aforesaid.

Decisions of the CFI are subject to a right of appeal to the ECJ on points of law only. Such appeals may be brought on any of three grounds: lack of competence of the CFI, a breach of procedure before the CFI which adversely affects the interests of the appellant and infringement of Community law by the CFI.

If an appeal is well founded the ECJ will quash the decision of the CFI. Thereupon the ECJ may either give final judgment itself or refer the case back to the CFI for judgment.

The ECJ has unlimited jurisdiction in respect of Commission decisions which it can affirm or annul in entirety[9] or in part.[10] It may also cancel, reduce[11] or increase fines and penalties imposed by the Commission.

9. *Extra-territorial effect*

The long arm of Community law may reach offenders established outside but involved in economic operations having effect inside

---

9 Eg *Continental Can*, supra Case 17/74: *Transocean Marine Paints Association v Commission* [1974] ECR 1063, [1974] 2 CMLR 459.
10 Eg *Consten and Grundig*, supra.
11 Eg *Re Sugar Cartel*, supra; *United Brands*; Reg 17, art 17.

the Community.[12] The Community jurisdiction to deal with such cases is, in the eyes of the Commission, based on the so-called effects doctrine. However, the ECJ takes a more pragmatic view of the situation. In the *Wood Pulp*[13] case the Commission, having found that there was a concerted practice between undertakings operating in several non-Community countries, was anxious to establish jurisdiction on the basis of the effects of the concerted practice in the Common Market. The ECJ, however, took the view that since the agreement in question was implemented in the Community, it was sufficient to rely on the classical principle of public International Law, ie the principle of territoriality, rather than the more controversial effects doctrine.

The Court did not have to speculate on the position which would arise if the agreement had been made and implemented outside the Community but had an effect on intra-Community trade. Such a situation may arise in the future and revive interest in the effects doctrine.

There are no special rules regarding communications with undertakings whose seat is outside the Common Market. If the foreign-based undertaking has a commercial presence in the Community, such as a branch or even only showrooms, service can be effected at these premises[14] and there is no need, as has been claimed,[15] to use diplomatic channels for the purpose. A postal communication will suffice.[16] The Commission has no power to investigate cases outside the Community though it may request a Member State to conduct investigations abroad with the consent of the third country concerned. Failure to co-operate on the part of the foreign undertaking will result in penalties which, of course, can be executed only against assets within the territory of the Community. Sanctions for breaches of Community law, such as fines or orders to discontinue the prohibited practice, can be executed within the Community against the offender or its subsidiaries. An order to comply with the rules within the Com-

---

12 Case 48/69: *Imperial Chemical Industries Ltd v EC Commission* [1972] CMLR 557; Cases 52 and 53/69: *Geigy and Sandoz v EC Commission* [1972] CMLR 637; Dec. 76/642: *Community v Hoffmann-La Roche* [1976] 2 CMLR D25.

13 Commission Decision *Re Wood Pulp Cartel* OJ 1985, L85/1; [1985] 3 CMLR 474; Cases 89/85, 104/85, 114/85, 116–117/85, 125–129/85: *A Ahlstrom v EC Commission* [1988] 4 CMLR 901.

14 Case 8/56: *ALMA v High Authority* [1957] ECR 95 at 99.

15 See Case 48/69, supra; Case 52/69: *Geigy AG v EC Commission* [1972] ECR 787, [1972] CMLR 557; Case 6/72, supra; Cases 60/81 R and 190/81 R: *International Business Machines Corpn v EC Commission* [1981] 3 CMLR 93 at paras 9 and 10.

16 See Case 48/69, supra; Joined Cases 6, 7/73, supra.

munity[17] may be made to an offender operating from a foreign base but it is doubtful whether an order affecting its conduct outside the Community can be made.

Proceedings within the Community will not absolve the offender from proceedings outside the Community. This may lead to double jeopardy and double sanction.[18] The problem can be solved only by international agreements.

10. *Rules applying to public undertakings*
Modern states are involved in trade and industry through the instrumentality of public undertakings. The forms and the degree of government control of these bodies differ considerably as from country to country and so does the area of their operation. They have, however, a common tendency towards monopolies and in that sense enjoy a 'dominant position' – the very negation of the idea of the Common Market. The Treaty attacks the problem from two angles. By article 37 the Member States are committed to a policy of progressive adjustment of state monopolies 'so as to ensure that ... no discrimination regarding the conditions under which goods are procured and marketed exists between nationals of Member States'. Rather than 'adjusting' their monopolies the Commission recommended[19] that states should bring about their abolition. Indeed a certain amount of progress has already been made in that direction though the end of state monopolies is not in sight yet.[20]

The second angle of attack is expressed in article 90 of the Treaty, which is addressed specifically to two types of undertakings, viz 'public undertakings' and 'undertakings to which Member States grant special or exclusive rights' – a classification rather difficult to substantiate in the light of the law of the Member States, but corresponding to article 17 of the GATT. Accordingly, Member States are obliged to 'neither enact nor maintain in force any measure contrary to the Treaty, in particular article 7 and articles 85 to 94'. The gist of the provisions, as far as the rules of competition are concerned, is that a state enterprise is, in principle,

---

17 But see Case 22/79: *Greenwich Film Production v SACEM* [1979] ECR 3275, [1980] 1 CMLR 629 which suggests that it can be done.
18 Case 45/69: *Boehringer Mannheim GmbH v EC Commission* [1970] ECR 769; Case 7/72: *Boehringer Mannheim GmbH v EC Commission* [1973] CMLR 864; see also Commission Decision 80/1283 in *Eurim Pharm GmbH v Johnson and Johnson Inc* [1981] 2 CMLR 287.
19 [1970] JO L6 and L31.
20 See eg Case 90/82: *EC Commission v France* [1983] ECR 2011; [1984] 2 CMLR 516; Case 78/82: *EC Commission v Italy* [1983] ECR 1955; Case 161/82: *EC Commission v France* [1983] ECR 2079; [1984] 2 CMLR 296.

reduced to an equal status with a private[1] enterprise provided
it carries on normal commercial activities. This is not without
significance in view of the rôle played by state enterprises in the
national economy and the traditional (especially on the Continent)
preference accorded to 'public' interest. The privilege had to be
sacrificed on the altar of the Common Market. Thus, according to
the Commission[2] the precise status of the entity in question under
national law is immaterial as long as it is engaged in trade. In this
respect it is interesting to have the ruling of the ECJ[3] on the status
of the French *Pompes Funèbres* and the legality of the exclusive
franchises granted by municipal authorities, *qua* public authorities,
to perform funeral services by these undertakings. The Court
found that article 37 of the Treaty refers to trade in goods and
cannot relate to a monopoly over the provision of services; that the
franchises were not 'agreements' within the terms of article 85 (1)
but article 86 applies where a number of communal monopolies
are granted to a single group of undertakings whose market strategy
is dominated by the parent company. Article 90 (1) must be interpreted as precluding public authorities from imposing on undertakings to which they have granted exclusive rights any conditions
which are contrary to articles 85 and 86.

However, not all was sacrificed because article 90 (2) provides
an exception in the case of 'undertakings entrusted with the operation of services of general economic interest or having the character of a revenue-producing monopoly'. In the first category one
can place undertakings procuring public utility services such as
water, gas, electricity[4] or transport where the elements of manufacture and trade are, in a sense, in the background and 'service'
to the public at large[5] (having incidentally an economic value) is
the primary function of the undertaking. In the second category
fall the revenue-raising undertakings engaged in the manufacture
and marketing of certain products of everyday use (eg salt in Italy,

---

1 See Case 10/71: *Ministère Public Luxembourgeois v Müller* (dredging operations)
   [1971] ECR 723; Commission Decision 82/861 (*Re British
   Telecommunications*) [1983] 1 CMLR 417 and Case 41/83: *Italy v EC
   Commission* [1985] 2 CMLR 368.
2 Commission Decision 85/206 (*Re Aluminium Imports from Eastern Europe*) OJ
   1985, L89/1.
3 Case 30/87: *Bodson v Pompes Funèbres des Regions Liberées SA* [1988] ECR
   2479, [1989] 4 CMLR 984.
4 Eg Case 6/64: *Costa v ENEL* [1964] ECR 585, [1964] CMLR 425.
5 Eg Case 155/73: *Re Sacchi* (television advertising) [1974] ECR 409 at 431,
   [1974] 2 CMLR 177 at 204; see also Case 52/79: *Procureur du Roi v Debauve*
   [1980] ECR 833, [1981] 2 CMLR 362 and Case 62/79: *Compagnie Générale
   pour la Diffusion de la Télévision SA, Coditel v Ciné Vog Films SA* [1980] ECR
   881, [1981] 2 CMLR 362.

matches in France and Italy) or luxuries (eg alcohol in France and Germany, tobacco in France and Italy). However, even these exempted undertakings are subject to the Treaty, notably the rules of competition, in so far as the application of these rules does not obstruct the performance of their specific tasks. And for good measure the Treaty adds: 'The development of trade must not be affected to such an extent as would be contrary to the interests of the Community' (article 90 (2)).

(E) DUMPING (ARTICLE 91)

To combat dumping (that is exporting goods unsaleable at high prices in home markets to foreign markets for sale at low prices in order to capture a new market or maintain high prices in the home market) in the Common Market, during the transitional period article 91 authorized the Commission to investigate allegations of dumping and to address recommendations to the perpetrators with a view to bringing such practices to an end. By the end of the transitional period article 91 ceased to apply since dumping of goods has no place in the internal market governed by the free movement of goods. However, anti-dumping rules form an important part of the Community protective mechanism in external trade governed by Common Commercial Policy[6] and have been discussed in that context.

(F) AIDS GRANTED BY STATES (ARTICLES 92–94)

Article 92 (1), in general terms, declares incompatible with the Common Market 'any aid granted by a Member State or through state resources in any form whatsoever which distorts or threatens to distort competition by favouring certain undertakings or the production of certain goods'. According to the Commission a whole range of economic activities constitute aids viz: direct subsidies, tax exemptions, preferential interest rates, guarantees of loans on especially favourable terms, acquisition of land or buildings either gratuitously or on favourable terms, provision of goods and services, on preferential terms, indemnities against losses and other measures of similar effect.[7] This list was further extended to include reimbursement of costs in case of success, direct or indirect state guarantees of grants or credits, preferential application of discount rates, preferential settlement of public accounts, deferred collection of fiscal and social contribution.[8] State aid may also consist of the

6 See pp 453 et seq, supra.
7 OJ 1963, 2235.
8 Doc 20.502/IV/68.

purchase of company's shares[9] where the Government effectively assists in this way an ailing enterprise. The list is by no means exhaustive[10] as indicated by the variety of cases decided by the Commission and the ECJ. We should note that not *all* the aids are prohibited and that the prohibition, applying to selected undertakings and goods, starts from the premise that such aids would affect trade between Member States.[11]

As an exception to the rule article 92 (2) regards certain state aids compatible with the Common Market, viz. those which:

(a) have a social character granted to individual consumers without discrimination as to the origin of the products concerned;[12]

(b) are intended to alleviate hardship resulting from natural disasters or other extraordinary events;[13]

(c) are provided for certain regions of Germany to relieve the hardship resulting from the division of Germany.

A further exception to the rule may, in appropriate circumstances, be considered in respect of:

(a) aids intended to promote the development of regions afflicted by a low standard of living or serious unemployment;

(b) aids intended to promote an important European project (though the manufacture of cigarettes is not such a 'project')[14] or remedy a serious disturbance in the economy of a Member State;

(c) aids intended to facilitate the development of certain economic activities or regions;

(d) aids specified by the Council on a proposal from the Commission.

In the spirit of article 92 (3) the Commission saw no objection

---

9 Case 40/85: *Belgium v EC Commission (Re Aid to Bosch SA)* [1988] 2 CMLR 301; Case 234/84: *(Re Aid to Meura SA) Belgium v EC Commission* [1988] 2 CMLR 331.
10 See Sharpe, T, *State Aids and Regional Policy in Halsbury's Laws of England*, op cit, pp 701–702.
11 See Case 730/79: *Philip Morris Holland BV v EC Commission* [1980] ECR 2671 at 2688, [1981] 2 CMLR 321 at 339; Joined Cases 296, 318/82: *Netherlands and Leeuwarder Papierwarenfabriek BV v EC Commission* [1985] 3 CMLR 380.
12 See Case 52/76: *Benedetti v Munari* [1977] ECR 163 at 190.
13 See Commission Fifth Report on Competition Policy, point 164.
14 Case 730/79, supra.

to various measures for the promotion of artisanship in Sicily,[15] or the development of the machine-tools sector in the United Kingdom[16] (subject to reservation regarding stockpiling), but objected to a Belgian project in aid of the production of tractors by the Ford Company;[17] French aids to the textile industry;[18] a preferential rediscount rate for export credits introduced by France to support her exporters;[19] a subsidy to Dutch Cigarette Manufacturers;[20] a subsidy to British pig producers[1] and statutory rates on loans and special rebates for exporters.[2]

It is immaterial whether aid is granted to private or public enterprise or whether the latter is separate from the state administration. *A fortiori* a public enterprise being subject to Directive 80/723 on transparency of accounting cannot shelter behind the veil of its status. Thus the Italian state tobacco monopoly was held not to be immune from the prohibition of state aids.[3]

As we have seen, state aids cover a variety of matters and these include parafiscal taxes[4] and preferential low prices of public power utility to a particular sector of national industry (horticulture, *in casu*).[5]

In future state aids are likely to be administered according to Community guidelines. Thus, eg in its Practice Notice on State Aids for Dairy Products[6] the Commission established a framework for investment aids in support of the manufacture and marketing of certain dairy products and their substitutes and in another Practice Notice[7] on State Aids for Agricultural Advertising. Com-

---

15 *Les Novelles*, op cit, p 865.

16 *Europe*, No 1946 (22–23 March 1976), p 7.

17 Case 64/651/EEC: *Re Subsidies to Ford Tractor (Belgium) Ltd* [1965] CMLR 32, JO 3257/64.

18 Case 47/69: *Re Aids to Textile Industry, France v EC Commission* [1970] CMLR 351.

19 Cases 6/69 and 11/69: *EC Commission v France* [1969] ECR 523, [1970] CMLR 43.

20 Decision 79/743 [1980] 1 CMLR 453, OJ 1979, L217/17.

1 Cases 31/77 and 53/77: *EC Commission v United Kingdom* [1977] ECR 921, [1977] 2 CMLR 359.

2 Case 57/86: *Re Export Interest Rebates, Greece v EC Commission* [1990] 1 CMLR 65.

3 Case 118/85: *EC Commission v Italy, Re the Amministrazione Autonoma Dei Monopoli Di Stato* [1988] 3 CMLR 255.

4 Case 259/85: *France v EC Commission, Re Parafiscal Tax on Foreign Textiles* [1989] 2 CMLR 30.

5 Cases 67–68/85 and 70/85: *Kwekerij Gebroeders Van der Kooy BV v EC Commission* [1989] 2 CMLR 804.

6 (1988) 1 CMLR 275.

7 (1988) 1 CMLR 545.

mission Communication on the Method of the Application of
Article 92 (3) (c) to Regional Aid[8] is also of interest in this context.

To examine the aid system and bring about the elimination of
aids incompatible with the Common Market, articles 93 and 94
define the powers of the Commission and the Council and determine the procedure to be followed in such cases. However, it should
be borne in mind that these provisions are addressed to the Member
States and create no rights enforceable by individuals.[9]

Where approved a state aid has to be administered according
to the terms of the approval.[10] On finding an illegal state aid
the Commission will issue an order to cease and desist and
will allow the state concerned a time limit within which to
advise the Commission of the steps undertaken to bring the
illegality to an end. The aid must be discontinued within the set
time.[11]

The control of state aids by the Commission and Council is
subject to judicial review for regularity in substance and procedure.
In such review both the grantor and the recipient have a *locus
standi*.[12]

Illegal aids have to be repaid as ordered by the Commission.[13]
Failure to heed a repayment order or to take the necessary measures
and notify the same to the Commission amounts to a breach of the
Treaty.[14]

As a by-product of the problem arising from state aids, certain
Community policies began to emerge. These are the regional
policy[15] and industrial policy.[16] Irrespective of these, as a result of

8 (1989) 2 CMLR 901.
9 Case 6/64: *Costa v ENEL* [1964] ECR 585, [1964] CMLR 425.
10 Case 8/87: *Omada Paragogon v The Republic* [1989] 3 CMLR 50.
11 Case 213/85: *EC Commission v Netherlands, Re Cheap Gas for Dutch Horticulturalists* [1988] 2 CMLR 287.
12 Cases 62/87 and 72/87: *Executif Regional Wallon and Glaverbel SA v EC Commission* [1989] 2 CMLR 771.
13 Case C-74/89: *EC Commission v Belgium, Re a State Shareholding in Synthetic Fibres* [1990] 2 CMLR 393.
14 Case 5/86: *EC Commission v Belgium, Re Aid for Polypropylene* [1988] 2 CMLR 258.
15 *Third General Report*, 1969, p 277. Draft regulations regarding regional developments: 1971, JO C90; 1973, Report on Regional Problems in the Enlarged Community, *Bulletin of the European Communities*, Supp 8/73; Regional Development Fund, 1973, OJ C86; *Bulletin of the European Communities*, 12/74; Council adoption of regulation to set up the Regional Fund on 18 March 1975. See *Eighth General Report* 1975, pp 105 et seq.
16 *Fourth General Report*, 1970, p 167. Commission memorandum, 1970, *Fourth General Report*, para 205; Commission communication to Council, 1973, *Bulletin of the European Communities*, 5/73, para 1101 and Supp 7/73; *Eighth General Report*, 1975, pp 169 et seq.

practice, a Community State Aids regime has developed.[17] However, whilst pertinent to State duties inter se, aids to industry tend to distort the competitiveness between undertakings involved in the internal trade of the Community. This, no doubt, is the reason why the provisions to control state aids form part of the Community competition policy.

(G) TAX PROVISIONS (ARTICLES 95–99)

(1) *Discriminatory taxes*

It should be stated from the outset that uniform taxation throughout the Community is not the object of the Treaty, but a harmonization of the tax system relevant to the Common Market. Therefore the tax provisions of the Treaty should be seen in that perspective, that is, as relative to the free movement of goods, persons, services and capital. In so far as taxation is relevant to these objectives, it is a proper concern of the Community. Thus, with the abolition of customs duties and charges having equivalent effect, it is necessary to ensure that internal taxation will not replace the abolished customs duties.

Article 95 (1), which the Community Court has held to be directly enforceable in the Member States,[18] prohibits the imposition on the products of other Member States of internal taxation of any kind in excess of the tax imposed upon similar domestic products. Consequently the ECJ[19] held incompatible with article 95 (1) the Irish system which made excise duty payable by importers immediately on import whilst allowing domestic traders time to pay.

Further examples of discriminatory taxes include tax rebates[1] to the disadvantage of competing imported products; tax on imported drinks to support a national spirits monopoly;[2] and taxes on imported motor cars. Comparability of the products involved provides a decisive criterion.

Article 95 (2) prohibits any internal taxation intended to afford protection to domestic products. The principle has been dem-

---

17 See Sharpe, T, 'State Aids and Regional Policy', in Halsbury's Laws of England, op cit, pp 697 et seq.
18 Case 57/65: *Lütticke GmbH v Hauptzollamt Saarlouis* [1966] ECR 205, [1971] CMLR 674.
19 Case 55/79: *EC Commission v Ireland* [1980] ECR 481, [1980] 1 CMLR 734; see also Case 26/80: *Schneider-Import GmbH v HZA Mainz* [1980] ECR 3469, [1981] 3 CMLR 562.
 1 Case 277/83: *EC Commission v Italy, Re Marsala Liqueur Wine* [1987] 3 CMLR 324.
 2 Case 253/83: *Sektkellerei Kupfenberg Cie KG v HZA Mainz* [1985] ECR 157, [1987] 1 CMLR 36.

onstrated in the enforcement actions against four Member States[3] charging discriminatory indirect taxes on imported alcoholic beverages with a clear intention of protecting similar national products. Thus article 95 imports the principle of non-discrimination into the field of taxation of imported goods. Taxes on such goods can be levied, but only in the same measure as the internal taxes on similar goods. The principle has been applied (by analogy) to exports.[4]

Article 95 is complemented by article 96, which provides that 'any refund of internal tax in respect of exported goods shall not exceed the internal tax imposed upon such goods whether directly or indirectly'. 'Direct' taxes are taxes charged upon finished products; 'indirect' taxes are charges upon the product at the various stages of production. Article 96 covers, therefore, both eventualities. However, from a practical point of view, a line has to be drawn between taxes affecting the undertaking and those which fall upon the product. The Community Court has held that a refund of taxes which are charged to the undertaking as a taxable entity to encourage exports was inconsistent with article 96.[5] Should this not be so, the undertaking would enjoy an advantage over another exporter and this, in turn, would affect free competition and trade between Member States. This case is also important in so far as it provided an opportunity for an examination of tax refunds. The Community Court found the Italian system incompatible with the Treaty, especially that customs duties were included in the computation of the refunds.[6]

Article 97, which is not directly applicable,[7] purports to bring about a simplification of the multi-stage turnover tax by introducing a single tax on imports according to products or groups of products. By the same token, tax refunds on exports should be subject to uniform average rates. In order to ensure that there is no infringement of articles 95 and 96, the Commission is authorized to issue directives or decisions to the state concerned (article 97).

3 Case 168/78: *EC Commission v France* [1980] ECR 347, [1981] 2 CMLR 631; Case 169/78: *EC Commission v Italy* [1980] ECR 385, [1981] 2 CMLR 673; Case 171/78: *EC Commission v Denmark* [1980] ECR 447, [1981] 2 CMLR 688; see also Case 106/84: *EC Commission v Denmark, Re Taxation of Wine* [1986] ECR 833, [1987] 2 CMLR 278; Case 170/78: *EC Commission v United Kingdom* [1980] ECR 417, [1980] 1 CMLR 716; Case 170/78: *EC Commission v United Kingdom* [1983] ECR 2265, [1983] 3 CMLR 512.
4 Case 51/74: *Van der Hulst Zonen v Produktschap voor Siergewassen* [1975] ECR 79, ECR 79, [1975] 1 CMLR 236.
5 Case 45/64: *EEC Commission v Italy* [1965] ECR 857, [1966] CMLR 97.
6 Case 45/64: *EC Commission v Italy* [1969] ECR 433.
7 Case 28/67: *Molkerei-Zentrale Westfalen-Lippe GmbH v Hauptzollamt Paderborn* [1968] ECR 143, [1968] CMLR 187 at 221.

In pursuance of this provision, the Council issued a directive to provide a uniform system of calculating the average rates.[8]

Article 98 purports to control charges 'other than turnover taxes, excise duties and other forms of indirect taxation'. More specifically, it prohibits exemptions and repayments in respect of exports and the imposition of countervailing duties in respect of imports from Member States, unless approved by the Council.

Taking articles 95–98 together, we can see the overall concern with the complexities of the national tax systems and the desire to remove the obstacles to free movement of goods concealed in the technicalities of fiscal policies designed to promote export of national products and restrict import of foreign goods on a competitive basis of equality. Rationalization of the tax provisions necessitates a Community policy in this respect aiming, first, at the removal of fiscal obstacles to the establishment of the Common Market and, thereafter, at a modicum of uniformity corresponding to the objectives of the Economic Union. In this process budgetary considerations cannot be ignored simply because a proportion of taxes forms a source of the Community's 'own resources'. Since, at this stage, a uniform tax system appears unattainable, a modicum of order appears possible through harmonization of national tax systems.

(2) *Harmonization*

A general scheme for the harmonization of tax systems is provided in article 99, replaced by article 17 of the Single European Act, which provides that the Council shall, acting unanimously on a proposal from the Commission and after consulting the European Parliament, adopt provisions for the harmonization of legislation concerning turnover taxes, excise duties and other forms of indirect taxation to the extent that such harmonization is necessary to ensure the establishment and the functioning of the internal market. Harmonization does not mean uniformity, but a tolerable state of affairs which permits diversity within the ideal of the Common Market. Moreover, in relation to article 95 which is fundamental to the Common Market, directives adopted under article 99 cannot create derogations from the principles embodied in the former.[9]

The Council, on the proposals of the Commission, issued a number of directives. Of the numerous directives issued or proposed so far the most important are the two directives of 1967

8 Directive 68/221, 30 April 1968; OJ (Sp edn), 1968 (I) 114; JO L115.
9 See Case 21/79: *EC Commission v Italy* [1980] ECR 1, [1980] 2 CMLR 613; Case 15/81: *Gaston Schul v Inspecteur der Invoerrechten en Accijnzen, Roosedaal* [1982] ECR 1409 at 1434, [1982] 3 CMLR 229 at 253.

intended to introduce a common value added tax system (VAT).[10] The first directive consists of a general outline of the principles, definition of the value added tax and the timetable according to which it should become part of a reformed tax system of the Member States. The second directive replaced by the sixth directive established a uniform basis of assessment. Whilst members are committed to apply the principles, they are free to determine the rates of tax and exceptions but are not allowed to frustrate the operation of article 95 of the treaty.[11]

Thus in Case 112/84[12] the ECJ condemned the special tax applied only to imported luxury cars and also in another case[13] on imported cars with a taxable horsepower rating exceeding the largest cylinder capacity of cars manufactured in France. Such taxes are illegal and, if already paid, have to be repaid.[14] There is, of course, nothing to prevent Member States from imposing a luxury rate on high capacity cars provided it is not discriminatory.[15]

Zero-rating is allowed for clearly defined social reasons[16] and exemptions[17] too are subject to Community rules. It follows that the VAT system can be described, in principle, as a common Community tax.

No import VAT is chargeable on illegally imported narcotics[18] for these are outside the commercial sector. Drugs imported for strictly controlled medical purposes are in a different category but they are not subject to VAT.

The Community VAT system applies to the supply of goods, ie

---

10 67/227, JO 1967, 1301; OJ 1967, 14 and 67/228, JO 1967, 1303; OJ 1967, 16 replaced by dir 77/388 (sixth dir), OJ 1977, L145/1.

11 Case 319/81: *EC Commission v Italy (Re VAT on Spirits)* [1983] ECR 601, [1983] 2 CMLR 517.

12 Case 112/84: *Humblot v Directeur des Services Fiscaux* [1985] ECR 1367, [1986] 2 CMLR 338.

13 Cases 76, 86–89 and 149/87: *Segnela v Administration des Impots* [1988] ECR 2397; [1989] 3 CMLR 225.

14 *Directeur General des Impôts v Dubois,* Cour de Cassation [1990] 2 CMLR 823.

15 Case 200/85: *EC Commission v Italy, Re VAT on Diesel Cars* [1988] 1 CMLR 97.

16 Case 415/85: *EC Commission v Ireland* [1988] 3 CMLR 189; Case 416/85: *EC Commission v United Kingdom* [1988] 3 CMLR 169; Case 203/87: *EC Commission v Italy, Re Zero-rating for Earthquake Victims* [1989] 2 CMLR 461.

17 Directive 83/181, OJ 1983, L105/38; Case 252/86: *Bergandi v Directeur General des Impots (Re Tax on Amusement Arcade Machines)* [1989] 2 CMLR 933; Case 122/87: *EC Commission v Italy, Re VAT on Veterinary Services* [1989] 3 CMLR 844 (unlike medical services, veterinary services are not exempted).

18 Case 269/86: *Mol v Inspecteur der Invoerrechten en Accijnzen* [1989] 3 CMLR 729 and Case 289/86: *Vereniging Happy Family v Inspecteur der Omzetbelasting* [1989] 3 CMLR 743.

the transfer of the right to dispose of tangible property *qua* owner,[19] or services which cover any transaction other than a supply of goods within the scope of the sixth directive[20] and the importation of goods, ie the entry of goods into the territory of a Member State.

VAT is chargeable within the territory of a Member State to 'taxable persons',[1] that is, persons or bodies who carry out 'independently'[2] certain economic activities. These activities include all activities of producers, traders, suppliers of services including agricultural, mining and professional activities as well as the exploitation of property for continuous income.[3] Member States may also include among taxable persons anyone who performs on an occasional basis transactions related to the foregoing, in particular the supply of buildings or parts of buildings before first occupation and of the building land.[4] States, regional and local government authorities and other bodies governed by public law are not regarded as taxable in respect of the activities within their public competence.[5]

There is no doubt that the introduction of the Community VAT system is an important step not only towards the elimination of fiscal frontiers but also towards uniform taxation within the Community. The income it produces forms part of the Community's own resources.[6]

(3) *Tax offences*
Tax offences are subject to national law. However, criminal sanctions which can be imposed by national authorities may be mitigated by the Community principle of proportionality.[7]

(4) *Repayment of undue taxes*
Discriminatory taxes are treated like charges having equivalent effect to customs duties.[8] Being illegal they have to be repaid, but repayment follows the rules governing the return of taxes unduly

---

19 The Sixth Directive (77/388, OJ 1977, L145/1) art 5 (1).
20 Ibid, art 6 (1).
1 Ibid, art 5 (4) (b) (c).
2 Ie otherwise than as employed persons.
3 Ibid, art 4 (2); see Case 89/81: *Staatssecretaris van Finanzien v Hong Kong TDC* [1982] ECR 1277, [1983] 1 CMLR 73. See also Case 230/87: *Naturally Yours Cosmetics Ltd v Commissioners of Customs and Excise*, (*Re Taxation of Free Gifts to Hostesses*) [1989] 1 CMLR 797.
4 Ibid, art 4 (3).
5 Ibid, art 4 (5).
6 Council Decision 70/243, (OJ 1970, L94/19) and Council Decision 85/257 (OJ 1985, L128/15).
7 Case 299/86: *Italy v Drexl* [1989] 2 CMLR 241.
8 Case 199/82: *Amministrazione delle Finanze dello Stato v San Giorgio SpA* [1983] ECR 3595; [1985] 2 CMLR 658.

collected.[9] However, the taxpayer will not recover if the undue tax was incorporated in the price of the goods and passed on to the purchasers.[10]

(H) APPROXIMATION OF LAWS (ARTICLES 100–102)

1. *General principles*
It is common ground that the approximation of laws of the Member States is necessary for the proper functioning of the Common Market (EEC Treaty, article 3 (*h*)). This we have already observed since the implementation of the economic freedoms of the Community depends on the degree of harmonization of national laws affecting trade and the movement of persons and services. Approximation (*rapprochement, Angleichung*) represents, by definition, a more intensive process of integration than harmonisation. The problem was well understood from the inception of the Community and the difficulties of changing laws, like changing the ways of life or forsaking the national heritage, were never underestimated. There is a Community policy in this field and there is no lack of ideas or projects. The aims were thus summarized by the Commission:[11]

'... the object is not the creation of a vast European law of a unique character, but of a system of a federal type which would draw its force and authority of the conviction of history and at the same time of the plurality of the living nature of the laws of the Member States, of the common juristic heritage and of the necessity of an economic concentration'.

Community law, because of its nature and origin, should reflect the legal philosophy of the Member States and their experience. It should, at the same time, contribute towards political and economic integration by building up a federal system of law. In this respect, the objectives are limited for they are centred, at this stage, on the concept of the Common Market. In other words the mechanism of harmonization must be used for the removal of obstacles to the establishment of the Common Market. Whilst there is a challenge

9 Case 33/76: *Rewe-Zentralfinanz GmbH v Landwirtschaftskammer für Saarland* [1976] ECR 1989; [1977] 1 CMLR 533; Case 68/79: *Hans Just I/S v Ministry for Fiscal Affairs* [1980] ECR 501; [1981] 2 CMLR 714; Case 811/79: *Amm. delle Finanze v Ariete SpA* [1980] ECR 2545; [1981] 1 CMLR 316; Cases 66, 127, 128/79: *Amm. delle Finanze v Meridionale Industria Salumi Srl* [1980] ECR 1237; [1981] 1 CMLR 1; Case C-175/88: *Biehl v Administration des Contributions du Grand-Duche de Luxembourg* [1990] 3 CMLR 143.
10 Case 199/82: supra; Case 68/79, supra; Cases 142, 143/80: *Amm. delle Finanze v Essevi SpA* [1981] ECR 1413.
11 *Eighth General Report of the EEC*, 1965, para 83.

to comparative lawyers at the national and Community level, the Community organs, especially the Commission being entrusted with the task, must adopt a functional approach.

The guidelines can be found in articles 100–102 of the Treaty complemented by the provisions of the Single European Act. Article 100 refers to 'such provisions laid down by law, regulation or administrative action ... as directly affect the establishment or functioning of the Common Market'. This is both a programme and its limitation. Moreover, laws are to be enacted by the Member States on the basis of directives[12] issued according to the Community procedures involving consultations with the European Parliament and the Economic and Social Committee. The power of the Council to issue such directives under article 100 is limited because unanimity is required and so a Member State can veto the proposals of the Commission. Where, however, the Commission finds a distortion of the conditions of competition arising from the laws of the offending state, the Commission shall, through consultation, eliminate such distortion, but should this effort fail, the Council may be called in (article 101). The Council must be unanimous during the first stage but thereafter may issue appropriate directives by a qualified majority. Where there is reason to fear that a state will create distortions through taking certain legislative or administrative measures, the Commission alone is empowered to act and shall issue appropriate recommendations (article 102). The sanction for ignoring the recommendation is that the other Member States may disregard article 101 in relation to the offending state.

It appears that the above provisions proceed from the principle of the sovereign law-making power of the Member States modified by the Treaty obligation. Nevertheless there is implied coercion and sanction since failure to enact a directive into national law correctly would, as in the case of a regulation, expose the Member States to enforcement proceedings.[13] In fact several such actions

12 See Case 32/74: *Firma Friedrich Haaga GmbH v Rechtspfleger* [1974] ECR 1201, [1975] CMLR 32, in which for the first time the Court had to interpret an article in a directive (ie 68/151 of 9 March 1968 (OJ L65)) on harmonization of company law.

13 Eg Case 95/77: *EC Commission v Netherlands (Re Directive on Meteorology)*, [1978] ECR 863; Case 100/77: *EC Commission v Italy (Re Directive on Meteorology)* [1978] ECR 879, [1979] 2 CMLR 655; Case 147/77: *EC Commission v Italy (Re Slaughter of animals)* [1978] ECR 1307, [1978] 3 CMLR 428; Case 69/77: *EC Commission v Italy (Re Agricultural tractors)* [1978] ECR 1749; Case 93/79: *EC Commission v Italy (Re Weighing Machines for Conveyor Belts)* [1979] ECR 3837, [1980] 2 CMLR 647; Case 42/80: *EC Commission v Italy (Re Wire-Ropes, Chains and Hooks)* [1980] ECR 3635, [1981] 2 CMLR 532; Case 133/80: *EC Commission v Italian Republic (Re Public*

have been initiated and withdrawn when the state in default decided to implement the measure.

However the results, after thirty years of the existence of the Community, have proved disappointing mainly because of the cumbersome procedure and the requirement of unanimity for the enactment of directives. Therefore a new impetus is to be given by article 19 of the Single European Act which provides that during 1992, the Commission shall, together with each Member State, draw up an inventory of national laws, regulations and administrative provisions which affect the establishment and functioning of the internal market and charges the Commission with the making of proposals in good time to allow the Council to act before the end of 1992.

The Single Act, without changing the wording of articles 100–102, provides nevertheless an improved machinery for legislation. In supplementing article 100 it provides, by way of derogation from it, that save where otherwise provided in this Treaty, the Council shall, acting by a qualified majority on a proposal from the Commission in co-operation with the European Parliament and after consulting the Economic and Social Committee, adopt the measures for the approximation of the provisions laid down by law, regulation or administrative action in Member States which have as their object the establishment and functioning of the internal market. This derogation is limited, in particular, to the objectives which focus attention on the shortcomings of the internal market and recommends tackling problems inherent in the incomplete implementation of articles 28 (Common Customs Tariff); 57 (2) (activities of self-employed persons); 59 (services); 70 (1) (exchange restrictions on the movement of capital); 84 (transport); and 99 (taxation) of the EEC Treaty. Furthermore the derogation does not apply to fiscal provisions, to those relating to the free movement of persons nor to those relating to the rights and interests of employed persons. It preserves the Member States' rights of derogation under article 36 of the Treaty subject to a Community control procedure.

The improved legislative machinery has been matched by improved enforcement machinery since, by way of derogation from the procedure laid down in articles 169 and 170, the Commission or any Member State may bring a complaint directly before the Court of Justice if it considers that another Member State is making

Supply Contracts Directive) [1981] ECR 457, [1981] 3 CMLR 456; Case 163/78: *EC Commission v Italy (Re aerosol dispensers)* [1979] ECR 771, [1979] 2 CMLR 394; Case 43/80: *EC Commission v Italy (Re non-automatic weighing machines)* [1980] ECR 3643, [1981] 2 CMLR 532 and many subsequent cases.

improper use of the powers provided in this respect by the Single Act (article 18, article 100A (41)).

2. *The area of approximation*

At first sight, articles 100–102 may appear rather narrow in scope, but, if one considers that they are concerned not only with the 'establishment' but also with the 'functioning' of the Common Market, the scope widens considerably and is as wide as the concept of the Common Market itself. The same applies to the mechanism of approximation with its increased potential under the Single Act. Although these articles are framed to emphasize the sovereign law-making power of the Member States and, if interpreted narrowly, articles 101 and 102 would suggest that the Community organs will intervene only in a remedial capacity, there is ample authority for positive initiatives. Greater legislative activity is expected if harmonization of the laws necessary for the completion of the internal market is to be achieved, as planned, by the end of 1992.

(I) ECONOMIC POLICY (ARTICLES 103–109)

Generally speaking the Community economic policy ought to embrace all matters economic but in the terms of the Treaty it consists of three elements: ie conjunctural policy, balance of payments and commercial policy.

1. *Conjunctural policy*

As the economy of a country or a group of countries (eg the European Community) is subject to fluctuations resulting in booms and depressions, it was thought necessary to deal with the problem on a Community basis. In other words, there ought to be a Community 'conjunctural policy' (*politique de conjoncture, Konjungturpolitik*).

Accordingly, article 103 (1) is addressed to the Member States who should consult with each other and the Commission in matters affecting economic trends and should regard these problems as Community problems. However in economic matters regulated by the Community the Member States can no longer enact unilateral measures.[14]

By virtue of article 103 (2) the Council may, acting unanimously on a proposal from the Commission, decide upon the measures appropriate[15] to the situation, without prejudice to any other pro-

---

14 See Case 31/74: *Re Galli* [1975] ECR 47 at 63–64; [1975] 1 CMLR 211 at 228–229.
15 See Case 5/73: *Balkan Import-Export GmbH v HZA Berlin-Packhof* [1973] ECR 1091.

cedures provided for in the Treaty. The power is discretionary and designed to meet a particular crisis (as eg the energy crisis of 1973–1974) or to mitigate a particular hardship such as, eg, the effects of currency fluctuations upon importers and exporters of agricultural products. It is exercised as a matter of common Community concern and not for private interest of a particular section of trade.[16]

In order to assist the Member States and the Community, a Committee on Policy relating to Economic Trends was set up in 1960. Two other Committees, ie Medium Term and Budgetary, were added in 1964. All three were replaced by the Economic Policy Committee in 1974.[17]

2. *Balance of payments*

The realization that balance of payments problems have a chain reaction and may endanger the working of the Common Market is behind the provisions of the Treaty. Article 104 proceeds from the principle that the Member States are responsible for their own balance of payments, whilst maintaining a high level of employment and the stability of prices. In order to achieve these objectives, article 105 counsels co-ordination of the economic policies of the Member States and sets up the appropriate machinery. Accordingly, an advisory and co-ordinating body has been established. This is the Monetary Committee[18] consisting of representatives of the governments and central banks of the Member States. Its function is 'to keep under review the monetary and financial situation of the Member States and of the Community and the general payments system of the Member States and to report regularly thereon to the Council and the Commission' (article 105 (2)). It can also deliver opinions at the request of the Council or the Commission or on its own initiative.

Article 106 gives effect to the basic policies of the Common Market as it obliges the Member States to remove restrictions on the outflow of currency in connection with the movement of goods, persons, services and capital. Moreover, the Member States undertake to refrain from introducing as between themselves any new restrictions on transfers of currency in respect of the invisible transactions listed in Annexe III to the Treaty.[19]

---

16 See Case 43/72: *Merkur-Aussenhandels-GmbH v EC Commission* [1973] ECR 1055.
17 By Council decision 74/122, OJ 1974, L63/21.
18 Set up in 1958, JO 1958, 390; OJ 1952–1958, 60.
19 The list comprises some 60 items, including earnings from transport, warehousing, repairs, technical assistance relating to the production and distribution of goods, commissions, travel and tourism, films, repair and maintenance of property, customs duties and taxes, fines, salaries and wages,

Article 107 refers to the rates of exchange which each Member State is free to determine for its own currency bearing in mind the interest of the Community and the objectives of article 104. Should an alteration of its rate of exchange result in distortion of the conditions of competition, the Commission may step in and, after consulting the Monetary Committee, authorize other Member States to take appropriate measures.

Article 108 purports to deal with balance of payments difficulties which may endanger the economy of a Member State. The underlying philosophy is that no member of the Community should suffer and, in order to alleviate the resulting hardship, the Commission ought to assist the member facing such difficulties. In particular, the Commission is bound to investigate the problem and recommend appropriate measures. If necessary, the Council may authorize mutual assistance recommended by the Commission but, should this prove insufficient, the state concerned may be authorized to take protective measures. Such measures may, in accordance with article 226, derogate from the Treaty obligations, but should cease when no longer necessary.

The French crisis of 1968 provides an illustration of the practical application of article 108. The Commission investigated the difficulties facing the French economy at that time and recommended that mutual assistance be granted. The Council issued a directive to that effect[20] and the Commission decided that France may adopt emergency measures including exchange controls of certain capital transactions, restrictions of certain imports and aid to exports.[1]

Finally, article 109 authorizes the Member States to take provisional emergency measures when faced with a sudden crisis in the balance of payments. These measures must take into consideration possible repercussions within the Community, they should be appropriate to the emergency and the least harmful to the Common Market. The Commission and the other Member States must be informed. The Commission may then recommend action under article 108 and the Council may decide, by a qualified majority, that the protective measures be amended, suspended or terminated.

These procedures were in 1974 applied in respect of Italy in order to assist that country to solve its financial difficulties. The Commission authorized[2] Italy to take protective measures, includ-

---

dividends, interest, rents, royalties, pensions, maintenance, inheritances and dowries.
20 On 20 July 1968, [1968] JO L189.
1 See *Second General Report*, 1968, p 110 but see Joined Cases 6, 11/69: *EC Commission v France* [1969] ECR 523, [1970] CMLR 43.
2 (1974) OJ L152.

ing restrictions on the supply of money, and agreed that aid should be provided for, but the Council opposed the latter.

3. *Commercial policy (articles 110–116)*

A common commercial policy, as one of the basic principles of the Common Market (article 3 (*b*)) is the necessary corollary to the establishment of a common customs tariff.[3] It means, in effect, a common attitude to the outside world, the Community acting virtually as one commercial unit. Article 111 regulates the position during the period of transition providing for a co-ordination of the commercial relations of the Member States with third countries. Article 112 is concerned with export aids to third countries and article 113 regulates the position after the expiry of the period of transition. Article 114 connects article 111 (2) and article 113, providing that customs agreements and commercial treaties with third countries shall be concluded by the Council on behalf of the Community, acting unanimously during the first two stages and thereafter by qualified majority. Article 115 deals with the difficulties individual states may experience as a result of the common commercial policy and authorizes such states to take protective measures under the guidance of the Commission. During the period of transition, in emergency situations, states may take unilateral measures but have to notify these to the other Member States and the Commission. In choosing these measures, they must cause least disturbance to the operation of the Common Market. Finally, article 116, with reference to the end of the transitional period, brings the principle of co-ordination and common commercial policy into operation with regard to the participation of the states in international organizations of an economic character. At present transitional provisions apply only to Spain and Portugal[4] but they shall remain in reserve as long as the Community continues to expand.

In the seventies there began a process of *convergence of policies* leading to a concept of a unified Community Economic Policy.[5]

(J) SOCIAL POLICY (ARTICLES 117–128)

1. *Social provisions*

In the blueprint of the Community one can see a close connection between economics and social problems expressed in the general principles of the Treaty (articles 2 and 3 (i)) and the specific 'social

---

3 See pp 449 et seq.
4 OJ 1985 L302; Act of Accession arts 379 and 380.
5 For further details see Lasok, *The Law of the Economy*, op cit, pp 339 et seq.

provisions'. In this way, the Community law of the economy has been linked with social policy.

It seems, at this stage, premature to speak of a 'social law'[6] of the Community, as article 117 merely expresses an agreement between the Member States 'upon the need to promote improved working conditions and an improved standard of living for workers' and their belief that 'such a development will ensue not only from the functioning of the Common Market, which will favour the harmonisation of social systems, but also from the procedures provided for in this Treaty and from the approximation of provisions laid down by law, regulation or administrative action'. A great deal of effort, both domestically and at the Community level, will be required to implement this programme.

Whilst social services and welfare state benefits are essentially a matter for the domestic concern of the Member States, the Community is also interested not only because of its professed aim of a 'better Europe', but more practically because of the social problems consequent upon the movement of labour.[7] Hence the special concern with 'workers'. As the scope and standards of the social security systems differ as from country to country, it is essential to improve some and harmonise all into a system where the migrant worker and his family would find an adequate level of protection whether at home or in another Member State. The long-term policy of the Community seems to have this object in mind.

It follows that, in accordance with the general pattern of the Treaty, the Commission, assisted by the Economic and Social Committee, must address itself to certain specific tasks enumerated in article 118, viz employment, labour law and working conditions, basic and vocational training, social security, prevention of occupational accidents and diseases, occupational hygiene, the right of association and collective bargaining between employers and workers. This may be the broad outline of the European social law.

Whilst it may be taken for granted that the Member States are, within the general terms of the Treaty, committed to work towards an improvement of their social security system, article 119 specifically enjoins the Member States to 'ensure and maintain the application of the principle that men and women shall receive equal pay for equal work'.[8] This reflects the trend towards the equality of the

---

6 But see Lyon-Caen, G, *Droit Social Européen* (1969); Ribas, J J *Droit Social Européen* (1973); Leaper, R A B, 'Social Policy' in Lasok and Soldatos, op cit, pp 273 et seq.

7 See pp 457 et seq.

8 Council directive 75/117 of 10 February 1975 OJ 1976, L39; Case 80/70: *Defrenne v Belgian State* [1971] ECR 445, [1974] CMLR 494 at 509; Cases 43/75: *Defrenne v SABENA* [1976] ECR 455, [1976] 2 CMLR 98; Case 149/77:

sexes and the specific recommendations of the Convention of 24 June 1951 sponsored by the International Labour Organisation.

Article 120 is concerned with the maintenance of the existing equivalence between paid holiday schemes. Articles 121 and 122 are concerned with the function of the Council and Commission, and with studies and reports on social developments within the Community.

2. Draft Charter of Social Rights

Encouraged by the provisions of the Single European Act (Subsection III – Social Policy) the Commission presented to the Heads of State or Government a Draft Community Charter of Fundamental Social Rights[9] comprising twelve items, ie rights to: free movement; employment and remuneration; improved living and working conditions; social protection; freedom of association and collective bargaining; vocational training; equal treatment for men and women; information, consultation and participation in the management of companies; health protection and safety of the workplace; protection of children and adolescents; protection of the elderly and of the disabled.

The Member States are enjoined to take the necessary measures and the Commission is obliged to work out an action programme in order to implement the Charter.

Despite the British opposition the Charter was adopted by the European Council at its Madrid meeting in the summer of 1989. This rather innocuous declaration of intent was denounced by the British Government as an instrument of socialism and opposed as such.

3. The European Social Fund

The Treaty sets up a European Social Fund to be administered by a Committee under the supervision of the Commission and governed by its own statute.[10] The title is rather misleading because the scope of the Fund is limited to 'the task of rendering the employment of workers easier and of increasing the geographical and occupational mobility within the Community' (article 123). The real purpose is to provide financial assistance, that is, to provide fifty per cent of the expenditure incurred by a state or a body governed by public law for the purpose of re-employment of workers or relief of temporary unemployment resulting from the

---

Defrenne v SABENA [1978] ECR 1365, [1978] 3 CMLR 312; See also British cases, p 187, supra.

9   COM(89) 248 final (30 May 1989).

10 For the Statute, see JO 1201/60, 31 August 1960.

conversion of an undertaking to another type of production (article 125 (1)).

The Fund has been reformed in 1971[11] in accordance with article 126 to undertake two different functions, ie to implement the Community policies and to deal with difficulties which impede the smooth working of the Common Market.

Article 128 gives the Council authority to lay down general principles for implementing a common vocational training policy capable of contributing to the harmonious development both of the national economies and the Common Market.[12]

In accordance with Council Decision 83/516[13] the present tasks of the Fund focus attention on the unemployment problem especially job creation and skills for stable employment. Therefore the Fund ought to help to implement policies capable of creating employment opportunities and to help finance vocational training, recruitment and wage subsidies as well as the resettlement and social integration of the workforce.

Clearly, the rudiments of social policy and its implementation are too fragmentary to provide more than a modest beginning of what may become in the future a body of rules complementary to the economic and commercial policies of the Community.

II. Consequential policies

As the Community develops and the programme of action laid down in the Treaty is being implemented new policies emerge either in consequence of the developments or in response to necessity.

1. *Energy*[14]

A continuous supply to meet the ever growing demand for energy is one of the imperatives to sustain the industrial economy and the standard of living of the peoples of the Community. This was well understood during the 1958 crisis in the coal industry. Some initial steps to develop a Community energy policy had been taken at that time[15] and efforts continue but, so far, apart from a statement of

---

11 JO [1971] L28.
12 Cf 'General Guidelines for a Community-level Programme on Vocational Training', JO C81, 12 August 1971.
13 OJ 1983, L289/38.
14 For a detailed treatment see Thomas, H M, Grazebrook, D and Brebner G D A 'Energy other than Coal', Halsbury's Laws of England, op cit pp 947 et seq.
15 Agreement of the Council of Ministers and the High Authority of the ECSC, JO 7 December 1958, 574.

policy objectives[16] and exhortations at the highest level[17] little has been achieved. The 1973–74 energy crisis caused by the quadrupling of oil prices by the OPEC countries[18] found the Community in disarray, each Member State endeavouring to further its own interest. At that time the Commission issued a Memorandum[19] recommending a strategy consisting in a reduction of the Community dependence on imported oil by energy saving, development of nuclear energy, stabilization of the production of solid fuels and greater security of supply. The Council[20] approved the scheme.

The Commission issued further communications on the subject, the most recent one 'On energy objectives for 1990 and convergence of policies of Member States'[1] and again on 'Energy and economic policy,'[2] the latter being concerned mainly with pricing policy. The Council, on the other hand, adopted in 1980 two resolutions[3] dealing with energy objectives and convergence of the policies of Member States, and with energy saving, respectively. The Member States are to submit to the Commission their annual energy programmes and the Commission is to report annually making also proposals to improve the convergence of Member States' energy policies. It is expected that by 1990 each Member State shall have a programme covering the main sources of energy and an energy use and pricing policy. In this sector the Community seems content with mere co-ordination of national policies.

2. *Environment*

Industrial countries have paid a heavy price for their prosperity in the damage inflicted upon their physical environment. Technological development in the area of nuclear energy has added a further hazard to the present and the future generations. Thus concern for the conservation and protection of the environment, apart from the preamble to the EEC Treaty, has become the prime mover of the Community environmental policy. This reflects not only the world-wide interest in the protection of natural resources and amenities but also purely Community interests. International nuisance affects relations between the Member States[4] and leads

---

16 EEC Bull Supp 4/74.
17 Dublin communique of the meetings of the Heads of State or Government, *The Times*, 1 December 1979.
18 Organization of Petroleum Exporting Countries.
19 EC Bull Supp 1/74.
20 OJ 1975, C153.
 1 Communication 79/7662.
 2 EC Bull 10–1980, points 1.2.2–1.2.4.
 3 OJ 1980, C149.
 4 Eg the Franco-Dutch dispute over the discharge of sulphur into the Rhine, Europe, 6 December 1979, p 5.

to litigation[5]. Moreover disregard of the environment has wider repercussions in the areas of energy, consumer protection, industrial and regional policies as well as competition since manufacturing costs can be reduced at the expense of the environment.

The Community Policy for the Environment can be summarized as follows:

(a) *First Programme*[6] *(1973–1977)* The main objectives of the first programme included:

  (aa) the protection of the aquatic environment by controlling pollution through discharge of certain dangerous substances and establishing a common procedure for the exchange of information on the quality of surface water;

  (bb) the measures to combat atmospheric pollution by controlling, in particular, air quality standards for lead, air quality standards for sulphur dioxide and the use of fuel oils;

  (cc) the control of noise pollution by laying down maximum permitted noise levels for different types of motor vehicles, construction equipment and domestic appliances;

  (dd) the control of chemicals in the environment and the management of water disposal;

  (ee) action at international level by bi-lateral treaties and multi-lateral conventions;

  (ff) the promotion of scientific research and improvement of information, training and awareness of environmental problems.

Several directives were enacted during that period but the most important guideline[7] was that 'the polluter pays for the prevention and elimination of environmental nuisance'.

(b) *Second Programme*[8] *(1977–1983)* was devoted to the implementation of the first programme with an emphasis on the protection of the marine environment following the pollution caused by the *Amoco Cadiz* disaster and other oil spills.[9] The emphasis also shifted to the improvement of the environment with

5 Cf Case 21/76: *Handelskwekerij GJ Bier BV and Stichting Reinwater (Reinwater Foundation) v Mines de Potasse d'Alsace* [1976] ECR 1735, [1977] 1 CMLR 284.
6 OJ 1973, C112/1.
7 OJ 1975, L194.
8 OJ 1977, C139/1.
9 OJ 1978, C162.

a view to assessing the environmental impact of major industrial and infrastructure projects.[10] This concern led to measures for the protection of wildlife, the preservation of the natural habitat of endangered species affecting hunting, farming and the use of land generally.

(c) *Third Programme*[11] *(1983–1987)*   The main achievement of this period was the international co-operation in respect of the protection of the aquatic environment resulting in a number of international conventions and Community directives including a directive to ensure that the movement of hazardous waste to non-Community countries is supervised and controlled.

Community legislation was also targeted on air pollution, noise abatement, control of chemicals, dangerous substances and preparations.

(d) *Fourth Programme*[12] *(1988–1992)*   The present programme has been influenced by the objectives of the Commission White Paper on the completion of the internal market and article 25 of the Single European Act which put the environment firmly on the agenda of the forthcoming legislative process.

The measures enacted so far are concerned primarily with the improvement and extension of the existing Community legislation with the addition of several new instruments on air pollution, disposal of waste, the protection of animals used for experimental purposes and the protection of forests from atmospheric pollution and fires. Further international agreements involving the Community include the protection of the ozone layer, the protection of wildlife in Europe and elsewhere and of the tropical forests.

In order to ensure the execution of the environmental programme the Commission has taken up a position to step up the monitoring of its implementation by the Member States and to take enforcement action against the defaulting states.

To progress further the Community established the European Foundation for the Improvement of Living and Working Conditions at Dublin,[13] a Committee on Waste Management[14] and a Scientific Advisory Committee on the Toxity and Ecotoxity of Chemical Compounds.[15] It also became engaged in active co-oper-

10 Directive 85/337, implemented in the UK by the Town and Country Planning (Assessment of Environmental Effects) Regulation 1988 (SI No 1199) and 14 other Regulations: (Environmental Assessment, HMSO 1989, App 8).
11 OJ 1983, C46.
12 OJ 1988, L324.
13 Council Regulation 1365/75, OJ 1975, L139.
14 Commission Decision 76/431, OJ 1976, L115.
15 Commission Decision 78/618, OJ 1978, L198.

ation with non-Member States[16] and international organizations such as the UNEP, OECD, WHO and FAO leading, among others, to the signing of the Helsinki Convention on the Protection of the Marine Environment of the Baltic Sea Area,[17] the European Convention on Wildlife and Natural Habitats and the Convention on Long-range Transboundary Air Pollution.[18] It concluded for the Community the Barcelona Convention for the Protection of the Mediterranean Sea against Pollution[19] and the Bonn Convention for the Protection of the Rhine against Chemical Pollution.[20]

3. *Consumer protection*

European consumerism owes a great deal to the developments in the USA but has taken a different turn from the legal confrontation between the manufacturers and the public which seems to dominate the American scene. Consumer protection is to be achieved in the context of the Common Market by means of harmonizing legislation effected according to a continuing action programme.

(a) *First Programme (1975–1981)*

The First Programme[1] expressed consumer interests in terms of five basic rights to be implemented by Community legislation, ie the right to protection of health and safety; the right to protection of legal and economic interests; the right of redress; the right of information and the right of representation.

Consumer health and safety

By the end of 1976[2] some 80 directives had been issued to protect consumers' health and safety. These cover a wide range of products but mainly in the context of the CAP, ie foodstuffs, fruit and vegetables and animal health. In the context of the free movement of goods some 18 directives have been adopted in July 1976[3] under the general programme for the removal of technical barriers to trade, which concern consumers directly. Of these, of particular interest are the measures applicable to motor vehicles,[4] chemical substances such as solvents, paints and varnishes and household goods and cosmetics.

16 Ie Austria, Canada, Japan, Sweden, Switzerland and the USA.
17 EC Bull 6/1977, point 2.1.70.
18 Thirteenth General Report, point 284.
19 Council Decision 77/585, OJ 1977, L240.
20 Council Decision 77/786, OJ 1977, L240.
 1 Annex to Council Resolution of 14 April 1975; OJ 1975, C92.
 2 See First Report on Consumer Protection and Information Policy (1977).
 3 Tenth General Report (1976); item 116 et seq.
 4 Ibid, items 121 and 122.

Cosmetics present a continuing problem. In 1978[5] a Scientific Committee on Cosmetology was set up with the object of providing the Commission with opinions on the toxilogical effects of the use of cosmetics and thus providing a sound scientific background to further legislation.

Toy safety too has been considered and, to protect children from the dangers inherent in certain toys, the Commission drafted a directive[6] which was enacted by the Council in 1988.

Legal and economic interests

The Programme[7] envisaged that 'purchasers of goods should be protected against the abuse of power by the seller, in particular against one-sided standard contracts, the unfair exclusion of essential rights in contracts, harsh conditions of credit, demands for payment for unsolicited goods and against high-pressure selling methods'. Moreover, the consumer ought to be protected against damage to his economic interests caused by defective products or unsatisfactory services.

Redress

The Programme[8] postulated that consumers should receive advice and help in respect of complaints arising from purchase or use of defective goods or unsatisfactory services. They should be entitled to proper redress for injury or damage by means of prompt, effective and inexpensive procedures. No measures have as yet been enacted to attain this objective.

Information and education

According to the Programme[9] sufficient information should be made available to the purchaser of goods or services to enable him to assess the basic features of the goods or services offered; make a rational choice between competing products and services; use these products and services safely and to his satisfaction; and claim redress for any resulting injury or damage. Consumer education ought to begin at school.

Several proposals have been made by the Commission to attain these objectives but so far only a directive on the indication by labelling of the energy consumption of domestic appliances has been adopted by the Council.[10]

---

5 OJ 1978, L13.
6 OJ 1980, C228 amended OJ 1983, C203; enacted OJ 1988, L187.
7 OJ 1975, C92 art 19.
8 OJ 1975, C92, art 32.
9 Ibid, art 34.
10 OJ 1979, L145.

Representation
Consumers should be consulted and allowed to express their views, in particular through organizations representing their interests.[11] The Commission itself consults the Consumers' Consultative Committee established in 1973 and financially supports major European consumer organizations but has as yet produced no legislation in this field.

(b) *Second Programme (1981–1985)*
In 1981 the Council approved the Second Programme[12] which reiterated the objectives of the First Programme but underlined priorities for legislative action and added a new dimension, ie consumer protection in the field of services.[13]

The legislative activity under the Second Programme comprises several amendments to the 1976 directive on cosmetics;[14] a proposal to improve the 1978 directive on alcoholic beverages by indicating on the labels their alcoholic strength;[15] a directive on the labelling of foodstuffs;[16] a directive on misleading and unfair advertising;[17] a discussion paper on unfair contract terms;[18] and a directive to establish an information procedure for technical standards.[19]

(c) *Third Programme (1985–1988)*
A Third Programme,[1] submitted to the Council in 1985, reviewed critically the progress to date and recommended vigorous legislative action to deal with the outstanding problems in three areas, ie health and safety, economic interests and co-ordination of consumer protection with other Community policies. It singled out the reasons for the slow pace of the Community action, of which the principal one is the unanimity requirement for the enactment of harmonizing directives. It is hoped that the Single European Act,[2] by derogating from the principle and expressly giving a high profile to consumer protection, will remedy the position.

Perhaps the most important development lies in the field of Community standards aiming at the quality of products, ensuring

11 OJ 1975, C92, art 46.
12 OJ 1981, C133.
13 Ibid, arts 34–37.
14 OJ 1982, L167; OJ 1982, L63; OJ 1982, L185; OJ 1983, L332; OJ 1983, L291; OJ 1984, L228.
15 OJ 1978, L33; proposal OJ 1982, C281.
16 OJ 1983, L255.
17 OJ 1984, L250.
18 COM(84)55, Final, EC Bull Supp 2/1984, point 2.1.94.
19 OJ 1983, L109.
1 'A New Impetus for Consumer Protection Policy', COM(83) 314, Final.
2 Single European Act, art 18 (1), (3).

thereby a degree of consumer protection. The task of laying down Community standards has been given to independent bodies consisting of industry experts and representatives of consumer organizations. Thus consumers have become directly involved.

The Community has abandoned the piecemeal approach to standardization which required legislation for every product. Instead it intends to harmonize only what is 'essential', leaving the rest to the discretion of the Member States. However, Member States are obliged to notify the Commission in advance of any newly proposed technical standards. The Commission has the power to prevent the implementation of such proposals until satisfied that they will not create any new barriers to intra-Community trade.

The programme of 'essential' harmonization is, at present, directed at the telecommunication sector, pharmaceutical sector, civil engineering and construction sector, and above all, at the food sector, which is extremely complex.

The major legislation comprises directives on doorstep selling,[3] consumer credit, correct description of products,[4] unfair terms in contracts[5] and product liability.[6] In order to overcome the difficulty of reconciling national differences and thus speed up the process of harmonization the Community legislation seems to be enacted on the basis of the lowest common denominator which allows for derogations and the recognition of particular national susceptibilities. Only time can tell whether this method shall prove satisfactory.

(d) *Fourth Programme (1988–1992)*

The Fourth Programme represents a continuation of the process in the context of the completion of the internal market with an emphasis on the greater awareness of the protection of economic interests generally and on the greater consumer involvement in standardization, in particular.[7] In 1989 the Consumer Policy Service was set up with the object of promoting consumer interests and the Commission organized a publicity campaign on child safety. The Commission set up guidelines for the promotion of Community policy on food product quality. The Council adopted a resolution on consumer education in primary and secondary schools.[8]

3 Bull EC 12-1985.
4 OJ 1987, L192.
5 OJ 1987, L42.
6 Dir 85/374, OJ 1985, L210/29.
7 Council Resolution OJ 1988, C293/1.
8 Council Resolution OJ 1986, C184/21; see 23rd General Report, point 554.

The legislation activity includes directives on trade in animals treated with substances having an hormonal action, foodstuffs, food labelling, cosmetics, detergents and cleaning substances, aerosol dispensers, and package holidays.

4. *Industry*[9]

The Community, because of its nature and objectives, seems unthinkable without an industrial policy linked to economic policy and State involvement in the economy. Yet, perhaps because of the industrial nature of West European societies, the formulation and implementation of such a policy has been fraught with difficulties. An Industrial Policy implies a change of entrenched attitudes in the face of technological advancement and a Community approach to sectoral interests. It means, in effect, an adaptation and sometimes a drastic revision of national capacity (eg in steel, textiles, shipbuilding) to accommodate the European and world markets. Social consequences inevitably call for reflection and prudence.

There is at present a framework of industrial policy proposed in 1970[10] and further elaborated in 1973[11] with the object of establishing ... 'a single industrial base for the Community as a whole'.[12]

Industrial policy is closely connected with the establishment of the internal market, activities of undertakings, investments, State and Community aids to industry as well as scientific research and development. It requires co-ordination of policies and Community initiatives.

Due to economic recession, competition from abroad and technological changes the industrial pattern of Western Europe has been subject to revolutionary change. Certain traditional industries (eg coal and steel, shipbuilding, textiles, footwear etc.) have to face the problem of restructuring and adaptation. Growth industries (eg data processing, aerospace, telecommunications, pharmaceuticals, new energy sources etc) face the problem of investments, research, development and foreign competition. A coherent Community action pooling the national resources seems the rational answer to these problems but progress to date does not seem to match the challenge.

9 For a detailed treatment see Hunnings, N M 'Industrial Policy and Internal Market', Halsbury's Laws of England, op cit, pp 631 et seq.
10 Commission Memorandum to the Council, Fourth General Report, 1970, item 205 et seq.
11 OJ 1973, C117/1.
12 Sixth General Report, 1972, p 12.

5. *Regionalism*[13]

There is much in the EEC Treaty, beginning with article 2, to promote a regional policy not only to eliminate disparities between regions but also to promote a harmonious development of the Community as a whole.

The policy was initiated in 1969 but got off the ground as late as 1975 with the setting up by the relevant Regulations of the Regional Policy Committee and the Regional Development Fund.

The Committee[14] is a consultative body consisting of representatives of the Member States and the Commission with an observer from the European Investment Bank. Its function, in particular, is to investigate the regions, their needs and aspirations, vet their development programmes and fix priorities taking into account the Community interest and other policies. It reports to the Council and the Commission, the latter informing the Parliament in its annual report.

The Regional Development Fund[15] is intended to correct the principal regional imbalances resulting, in particular, from agricultural preponderance, industrial change and structural underemployment. It is financed out of the Community general budget. It does not finance projects entirely but makes a contribution to their cost supported by national resources. It does not entertain direct applications for grants. Such applications have to be made by the national governments in accordance with their priorities. When grants are made they are either passed by the government to the grantee or used as a part reimbursement of the national contribution to the project from public funds.

The Fund was reformed[16] in 1984 with the object of a better co-ordination of Community policies and of the Community regional policy and national regional policies; of an equitable allocation of funds and of an efficient monitoring of the application of grants.

Much has been done to establish a comprehensive system of analysis of the problems to be remedied and policy formulation to carry out the remedy.[17] This process has to take into account not only the situation as presented but also the evaluation of the policy decisions on future developments and co-ordination at a national and international level. Though concerned primarily with economic and social problems the regional policy has far-reaching political implications. Operating on a geographical rather than strictly

13 For a detailed treatment see Sharpe, T, 'State Aids and Regional Policy', Halsbury's Laws of England, op cit, pp 697 et seq.
14 Council Decision 75/185, OJ 1975, L73/47.
15 Council Regulation 724/75, OJ 1975, L73/1.
16 Council Regulation 1787/84, OJ 1984, L169/1.
17 Commission Communication to the Council, JO 1969, C152.

national basis the policy, when fully implemented, would tend to ignore political frontiers and territorial divisions and thus promote the unity of the Community at the expense of the national state.

The policy will be developed further in the light of the economic and social cohesion brought about by the completion of the internal market as envisaged by the Single European Act Title V (Articles 130A–130E).

6. *Science and technology*

The roots of a Community policy for science and technology are in the ECSC and EAEC Treaties.[18] The EEC Treaty refers somewhat obliquely to 'technical progress' and research in agriculture.[19] However overall Community policy began emerging only from the exhortations of the Summit Conferences culminating in the four guidelines adopted in 1974.[1] These four guidelines include the co-ordination of national policies, the participation in the European Science Foundation, elaboration of a Community programme of research in science and technology and a programme of research for forecasting, assessment and methodology. The resulting policy should, in particular, focus attention on the supply of resources (ie raw materials, energy, food and water), the competitiveness of the Community as a whole, the improvement of the standards of living within the Community and the protection and conservation of the environment.

To carry out these objectives the Commission is advised by specialist committees of eminent scientists concerned both with general and specific programmes in addition to a committee of senior civil servants from the Member States and management and co-ordination advisory committees to deal specifically with atomic energy research and storage of radioactive waste.

In the course of time, especially during the recent decade, a number of programmes covering a wide range of scientific and technological research came into being. These include a programme in the field of science and technology for development (1983–86);[2] a programme for the transnational development of the supporting infra-structure for innovation and technology transfer (1983–85);[3] the European Strategic Programme for Research and Development in Information Technologies (ESPRIT);[4] Research and Development in Advanced Communication Technologies in

---

18 Art 55 and 411 respectively.
19 Arts 39 (1) and 41 (a).
 1 JO 1974, C7/4.
 2 Council Decision 82/837, OJ 1982, L352/24.
 3 Council Decision 83/624, OJ 1983, L353/15.
 4 Council Decision 84/130, OJ 1984, L67/54.

Europe (RACE);[5] Research and Development Programme in Raw
Materials Sector;[6] and Multiannual Research Action Programme in
Biotechnology (1985–89).[7] The expenditure on research constitutes
now a separate item in the Community budget.

The policy for science and technology is likely to develop further
in the light of the Single European Act Title VI (articles 130F–
130Q) which extends the scope of the EEC Treaty and enjoins the
Council to adopt appropriate programmes of action.

7. *Education and culture*

A policy for education appears necessary not only to carry out
certain Treaty provisions but also to promote the general well-
being of the population of the Community. The EAEC[8] envisages
specifically the setting up of an institution of nuclear science and
technology whilst the other treaties refer to the vocational training
for workers[9] and farmers[10] as well as the recognition of diplomas[11].
Despite these desiderata progress towards a coherent policy has
been slow and uninspiring. At last in 1976 the Council of Ministers
adopted an action programme[12] comprising the following: cultural
and vocational training for migrant workers and education of their
children; vocational training of the young; education at a higher
level (including the creation of the European University Institute
at Florence); language teaching, teachers' and students' mobility;
and dissemination of information and co-operation between the
national educational systems. Since education affects all aspects of
life a great deal remains yet to be done to establish a Community
policy for education.

The movement towards West European unity, apart from its
political and economic aspects, remains largely an act of faith in
the future of the Continent sustained by common cultural heritage.
Logic suggests that materialistic aspirations of the Community
ought to be matched by cultural activities. This no doubt was
behind the Commission's memorandum[13] to the Council on 'Community action in the cultural sector'. In the Commission's view
this sector comprised 'the socio-economic whole formed by persons
and undertakings dedicated to the production and distribution
of cultural goods and services'. This curious definition can be

5 Notice OJ 1985, C105/2.
6 Council Decision 82/402, OJ 1982, L174/23.
7 Council Decision 85/195, OJ 1985, L83/1.
8 Art 9.
9 ECSC Art 56; EEC Art 118.
10 EEC Art 41.
11 EEC Art 57 see pp 405 et seq, supra.
12 JO 1976, C38/1.
13 EC Bull Supp 6/77, p 5.

understood perhaps in the light of what the Commission considered appropriate for Community action, ie freedom of trade in cultural goods, eliminating theft of cultural goods, movement of cultural workers, training of cultural workers, harmonization of laws on copyright and related intellectual rights, preservation of the architectural heritage, development of cultural exchanges, co-operation between the cultural institutes of the Member States and promotion of socio-cultural activities at European level. The difficulties in moulding such an enterprise into a programme of action and, indeed, a legally enforceable policy are more than apparent. However the desire of complementing the 'European Economic' Community with a 'Cultural' Community provides a promising starting point.

Appendix

Lists of further reading

Chapter 1

ANDERSON, S.V, *The Nordic Council. A Study of Scandinavian Regionalism* (1967)

AUBREY, H G, *Atlantic Economic Cooperation. The Case of the OECD* (1967)

BRUGMANS, H, *L'idée européenne 1920–1970* (1970)

CAMPS, M, *Britain and the European Communities, 1955–63* (1964)

CAPOTORTI, FR, et al., *Le Traité d'Union Européenne* (1985)

COONEY, J, *EEC in Crisis* (1979)

ESMAN, J, & CHEEVER, D S, *The Common Aid Effort. The development assistance activities of the Organisation for Economic Cooperation and Development* (1967)

FORSYTH, M, *Unions of States: The Theory and Practice of Confederation* (1981)

GALTUNG, J, *The European Community: A Superpower in the Making* (1973)

GLADWYN, LORD, *The European Idea* (1966)

GROSSER, A, *Les Occidentaux, les pays d'Europe et les Etats-Unis depuis la guerre* (1978)

GRZYBOWSKI, K, *The Socialist Commonwealth of Nations* (1964)

JACOBS, F G, *The European Convention on Human Rights* (1975)

JANSEN, M, *History of European Integration* (1975)

JOHN, I G (Editor), *EEC Policy towards Eastern Europe* (1975)

JOLIET, R, *Le Droit Institutionnel des Communantés Européennes* (1983)

KITZINGER, U, *Diplomacy and Persuasion* (1973)

KITZINGER, U, *The European Common Market and Community* (1967)

KITZINGER, U, *The Second Try* (1968)

Manual of the Council of Europe, Structures, Functions and Achievements (1970)

LOUIS, J-V, *L'Ordre Juridigue Communantaire* (2nd edn 1983)

PALMER, M, & LAMBERT, J, et al, *European Unity, A Survey of the European Organisations* (1968)

PATIJN, S (Editor), *Landmarks in European Unity* (1970)

PHILIP, C, *Les Institutions Européennes* (1981)

POLLARD, S, *The Integration of the European Economy Since 1815* (1981)

PRYCE, R, *The Politics of the European Community* (1973)

RANSOM, C, *The European Community and Eastern Europe* (1973)

ROBERTSON, A H, *European Institutions, Co-operation, Integration, Unification* (Third edn 1973)

SPINELLI, A, *The European Adventure* (1972)

The European Free Trade Association and the Crisis of European Integration An aspect of the Atlantic crisis? (1965)

TORELLI, M, *Great Britain and the Europe of the Six: the Failure of Negotiations* (1969)

URWIN, D W, *Western Europe Since 1945* (1968)

VAUGHAN, R, *Twentieth Century Europe* (1979)

WALLACE, W (Editor), *Britain in Europe* (1980)

SPAAK, H-P, *Combats Inachevés* (1969)

Chapter 2

ALTING VON GEUSAU, F A M, *European Organisations and Foreign Relations of States* (2nd edn 1964)

AXLINE, A W, *European Community Law and Organisational Development* (1968)

BATHURST, M, et al. (Editors), *Legal Problems of an Enlarged European Community* (1972), Part IV

BOURRINET, J, *et* TORRELLI, M, *Les relations extérieures de la Communauté économique européenne* (1980)

CARDIS, F, *Fédéralisme et intégration européene* (1963)

COFFEY, P, *The External Relations of the EEC* (1976)

GROUX, J & MAXIM, P, *The European Communities in the International Order* (1985)

HALLSTEIN, W, *Europe in the Making* (1972)

HARTLEY, T C, *The Foundations of European Community Law* (2nd edn 1989), Chapters 5, 6

HAY, P, *Federalism and Supranational Organisations* (1965)

HENIG, S, *External Relations of the European Community* (1971)

HOUSE OF LORDS SELECT COMMITTEE ON THE EUROPEAN COMMUNITIES, *External Competence of the European Communities* (HL 236, 1984/85)

L'acte unique européen, Bruxelles, Institut d'études européennes (1986)

L'association à la Communauté économique européene Aspects juridiques, Bruxelles, Institut d'études européennes (1970)

Les Communautés européennes et les relations Est-Ouest, Colloque des 31 mars-1er avril, 1966 (1967)

NERI, S, *De la nature juridique des Communautés européennes* (1965)
PUISSOCHET, J-P, *The Enlargement of the European Communities: A Commentary on the Accession of Denmark, Ireland and the United Kingdom* (1975)
RAUX, J, *Les relations extérieures de la CEE* (1966)
SCHONFIELD, A, *Europe: Journey to an Unknown Destination* (1973)
SJÖSTEDT, G, *The External Role of the European Community* (1977)
TIMMERMANS, C W A, & VÖLKER, E L M, *Division of Powers between the European Communities and their Member States in the field of External Relations* (1981)

ALTING VON GEUSAU, F A M, 'The External Representation of Plural Interests', (1967), *Journal of Common Market Studies*, 426
COSTONIS, J J, 'Treaty making power of the EEC', [1967] *European Yearbook*, 31
LEOPOLD, P, 'External Relations power of the EEC in theory and in practice', (1977) 26 ICLQ 54
MCMAHON, J, 'The Renegotiation of Lomé: Inventing the future?' (1989) 14 EL Rev 140
RAUX, J, & FLAESCH-MOUGIN, C, 'Les accords externes de la CEE', (1975) *Rev Trim de Droit Européen*, 227
SCHERMERS, H, 'Community Law and International Law', (1975) 12 CML Rev 77
Thirty Years of Community Law, Commission Publication (1983)
USHER, J, 'The influence of national concepts on decisions of the European Court', (1976) 1 EL Rev 359
WAELBROECK, M, *Traités internationaux et juridictions internes dans les pays du marché commun* (1969)

Chapter 3

AKEHURST, M, 'Preparing the authentic text of the EEC Treaty', in Wortley, B (Editor), *An Introduction to the Law of the EEC* (1972), at p 20
BRINKHORST, L J, & MITCHELL, J D B, *European Law and Institutions* (1969)
CAPPELLETI, M (Editor), *New Perspectives for a Common Law of Europe* (1978)
CARSTENS, K, et al, *Der Beitrag des Rechts zum europäischen Einigungsprocess* (1984)
DAGTOGLOU, P D (Editor), *Basic Problems of the European Community* (1975)
DONNER, A M, *The Role of the Lawyer in the European Community* (1968)

HÉRAUD, G, 'La Communauté Européenne et la Question Lin-
guistique', (1981) 5 *Rev d'Integration Européenne*, 5
JACOBS, F G, *European Community Law and Public International
Law—Two Different Legal Orders?* (1983)
LASOK, D, & STONE, P A, *Conflict of Laws in the European Community*
(1987)
LECOURT, R, *Le juge devant le Marché Commun* (1970)
USHER, J, *European Law and National Law: The Irreversible Trans-
fer?* (1981)
MITCHELL, J D B, 'Lawyers and the European Communities', (1971)
22 NILQ 149
PESCATORE, P, *The Law of Integration* (1974)
BROWN, L N, 'Two legal traditions', (1980) 18 *Journal of Common
Market Studies*, 246

BROWN, L N, 'The linguistic regime of the European Communities',
(1981) 15 *Valparaiso University L Rev*, 319
POLACH, J G, 'Harmonization of Laws in Western Europe', [1959]
American Journal of Comparative Law, 148
SIEDL-HOHENVELDERN, I, 'Harmonization of Legislation in the
Common Market', [1962] *Journal of Business Law*, 247 and 363
SCHNEIDER, H H, 'Towards a European Lawyer', (1971) 8 CML Rev
44
STEIN, E, 'Assimilation of National Laws as a Function of European
Integration', (1964), 58 *American Journal of International Law*,
1
THOMPSON, D, 'Harmonization of Laws', (1965), 3 *Journal of
Common Market Studies*, 302
WELLENS, K, & BORCHARDT, G, 'Soft Law in European Community
Law', (1989) 14 EL Rev 267
WYATT, D, 'New Legal Order, or Old?' (1982) 7 EL Rev 147

Chapter 4

DETTER, L, *Law Making by International Organisations* (1965)
ECONOMIDES, C E, *Le pouvoir de décision des organisations inter-
nationales européenes* (1964)
EHLERMANN, C-D, *The Role of the Legal Service of the Commission
in the Creation of Community Law* (University of Exeter, 1981)
HARTLEY, T C, *The Foundation of European Community Law* (2nd
edn 1989), Chapters 3, 4
EDESON, W R & WOOLDRIDGE, F, 'European Community Law and
Fundamental Human Rights', LIEI 1976/1, 1
*Institut d'études européenes, La Décision dans les Communautés euro-
péenes* (1969)

KUTSCHER, K, *Methods of Interpretation as seen by a Judge at the Court of Justice* (1976)

LAUWAARS, R H, *Lawfulness and Legal Force of Community Decisions* (1973)

Les Novelles: Droit des Communautés européenes (1969), Nos 483–806, 1134–1172

LOUIS, J-V, *Les réglements de la Communauté économique européenne* (1969)

MACKENZIE STUART, A J, *The European Communities and the Rule of Law* (1977)

MATHIJSEN, P S R F, *A Guide to European Community Law* (5th edn 1990)

MITCHELL, J D B, 'Community Legislation' in Bathurst, M E, et al., *Legal Problems of an Enlarged Community* (1972), 100

MORAND, C-A, *La législation dans les Communautés européenes* (1968)

NOEL, E., & NUTTALL, S., 'The Functioning of the Commission of the European Communities' in Bates, St J. et al. (Eds). *In Memoriam J D B Mitchell* (1983) at p 107

PESCATORE, P, *L'Ordre juridique des Communautés européenes* (2nd edn 1973)

RIDEAU, J, et al *Droit Institutionnel des Communautés européennes* (1974)

SCHMITTHOFF, C M, 'The Doctrines of Proportionality and Non-Discrimination' (1977) 2 EL Rev 329

ZULEEG, 'Fundamental Rights and the Law of the European Communities' (1971) 3 CML Rev 446

BEBR, G, 'Acts of representatives of governments of the member states', [1966] *Sociaal-economische Wetgeving*, 529

DAUSES, M A, 'The Protection of Fundamental Rights in the Community Legal Order', (1985) 10 EL Rev 398

RASMUSSEN, H, 'A new generation of Community law?' (1978) 15 CML Rev 249

SCHWARTZ, I E, 'Article 235 and law-making powers in the European Community', (1978) 27 ICLQ 614

Chapter 5

BRAUN, N C, *Commissaires et juges dans les Communautés européennes* (1972)

La Commission des Communautés Européennes et l'Elargissement de l'Europe, Bruxelles, Institut d'études européennes (1974)

COOMBES, D, *Politics and Bureaucracy in the European Community* (1970)

HENIG, S, *Power and Decision in Europe* (1980), Chapter 4

LINDBERG, L, *Political Dynamics of European Economic Integration* (1963)
MAYNE, R, *The Institutions of the European Community* (1968)
SASSE, C, et al, *Decision Making in the European Community* (1977), Part 2
SPINELLI, A, *The Eurocrats* (1966)
VON DER GROEBEN, H, et al, *Die Europäische Union als Prozess* (1980)
HALLSTEIN, W, 'The EEC Commission: a new factor in international life', (1965) 14 ICLQ 727
NOEL, N, 'The Commission's Power of Initiative', (1973) 10 CML Rev 123
WEILER, J, 'The Community System: The Dual Character of Supranationalism', (1981) 1 YEL 267

Chapter 6

CAMPS, M, *European Unification in the Sixties* (1967)
CONSTANTINESCO, V, *Compétences et pouvoirs dans les Communautés européennes* (1974)
EC Commission, *An Ever Closer Union* (1985)
ECONOMIDES, C E, *Le pouvoir de décision des organisations internationales européenes* (1964)
HENIG, S, *Power and Decision in Europe* (1980), Chapter 3
HOUBEN, P H J M, *Les Conseils de Ministres des Communautés européenes* (1964)
Institut d'études européennes, La décision dans les Communautés européenes (1969)
Institut d'études juridiques européenes, La fusion des Communautés Européennes au lendemain des Accords de Luxembourg (1967)
JAUMIN-PONSAR, A, *Essai d'interprétation d'une crise* (1970)
LOUIS, J-V, *Les règlements de la Communauté économique européene* (1969)
NEWHOUSE, J, *Collision in Brussels* (1968)
SASSE, C, et al., *Decision Making in the European Community* (1977), Part 1
SASSE, C, 'Kommission und Rat' (1972) EuR, 341
TORELLI, M, *L'Individu et le Droit de la CEE* (1970)
VON LINDEINER-WILDAU, K, *La Supranationalité en tant que Principe de Droit* (1970)
WALLACE, H, *National Governments and the European Communities* (1973)

ESCH, B VAN DER, 'Legal policy in an enlarged European Community', (1973) 10 CML Rev 56
GLAESNER, H-J, 'Single European Act' (1986) 6 YEL 283

KRANZ, J, 'La vote dans la pratique du Conseil des ministres des Communautés européennes' (1982) RTDE 403

LAUWAARS, R H, 'The European Council', (1977) 14 CML Rev 25

MORTELMANS, K J, 'The Extramural Meetings of the Ministers of the Member States of the Community', (1974) 11 CML Rev 62

NUTTALL, S, 'European Political Cooperation and the Single European Act' (1985) 5 YEL 203

NUTTALL, S, 'Interaction between European Political Cooperation and the European Community', (1987) 7 YEL 211

Chapter 7

ALLOTT, P, 'The Democratic Basis of the European Communities,' (1974) 11 CML Rev 298

COOMBES, D, *The Power of the Purse in the European Communities* (1972)

EUROPEAN PARLIAMENT, *The Case for elections to the European Parliament by direct Universal Suffrage* (1969)

HENIG, S (Editor), *European Political Parties* (1969)

HENIG, S, *Power and Decision in Europe* (1980) Chapter 5

HERMAN, U, & HAGGER, M, *The Legislation of Direct Elections to the European Parliament* (1980)

HERMAN, V, & LODGE, J, *The European Parliament and the European Community* (1978)

HOUBDINE, A M, & VERGES, R, *Le Parlement Européen dans la Construction de l'Europe des Six* (1966)

JACKSON, R, & FITZMAURICE, J, *The European Parliament: A Guide to Direct Elections* (1979)

LASALLE, C, *Les rapports institutionnels entre le Parlement européen et les Conseils de Ministres des Communautés* (1964)

LOUIS, J V & WAELBROECK, D, *Le Parlement Européen dans l'Evolution Institutionnelle* (1986)

MARQUAND, D, *Parliament for Europe* (1979)

SASSE, C, et al., *Decision Making in the European Community* (1977), Part 3

SCALINGI, P, *The European Parliament* (1980)

SCHERMERS, H G, 'The Powers of the European Parliament' in Bates, St J et al. (Eds) *In Memoriam J D B Mitchell* (1983) at p 128

TUGENDHAT, C, *European Community Budgetary Issues* (University of Exeter, 1980)

TYRELL, A R, *The Parliamentary Challenge to the Community Law Making Process* (University of Exeter, 1983)

VINCI, E, *Il Parlamento Europeo* (1980)

WALLACE, H, *Budgetary Politics* (1980)

WESTLAKE, M, The Origin and Development of the Question Time

Procedure in the European Parliament (EUI Working Paper, EPU No 90/4)

BIEBER, R, 'Legal Developments in the European Parliament' (1986) 6 YEL 357

DRUNKER, I E, 'Strengthening democracy in the EEC', (1964) 2 CML Rev 168

EHLERMANN, C-D, 'Applying the new budgetary procedure for the first time', (1975) 12 CML Rev 325

Chapter 8

BECKER, M, *La Banque européenne d'investissement* (1973)

BERNARD, N, et al., *Le Comité Economique et Social* (1972)

CEREXHE, E, *Le Droit Européen, Les Institutions* (1979)

ECONOMIC & SOCIAL COMMITTEE, *The Right of Initiative of the Economic and Social Committee* (1977)

European Interest Groups and their Relationships with the Economic & Social Committee (1980)

EUROPEAN INVESTMENT BANK, *Investing in Europe's Future* (1983)

Institut d'études européennes, La Décision dans les Communautés européennes (1969), 127–132

MENAIS, G P, *La Banque européenne d'investissement* (1968)

BERTRAM, C, 'Decision making in the EEC: The Management Committee Procedure', (1967–68) 5 CML Rev 246

GENTON, J, 'La représentation et l'influence des opérateurs économiques dans la Communauté européenne', [1968] *Institutions Communautaires et Institutions Nationales* 75

KÄSER, J, 'The European Investment Bank: its Role and Place within the European Community System' (1984) 4 YEL 303

PRICE, SIR N, 'The Court of Auditors of the European Communities' (1982) 2 YEL 239

SCHINDLER, P, 'Problems of decision making by way of the Management Committee Procedure in the EEC', (1971) 8 CML Rev 184

ZELLENTIN, G, 'The Economic and Social Committee', (1962), 1 *Journal of Common Market Studies*, 22

Chapter 9

AUDRETSCH, H A H, *Supervision in European Community Law* (2nd edn 1986)

BEBR, G, *Development of Judicial Control of the European Communities* (1981)

BRAUN, N C, *Commissaires et juges dans les Communautés européennes* (1972)

BREDIMAS, A, *Methods of Interpretation and Community Law* (1978)

BROWN, L N, & JACOBS, F G, *The Court of Justice of the European Communities* (3rd edn 1989)

COLIN, J P, *Le Gouvernement des Juges dans les Communautés européennes* (1966)

DONNER, A M, *The Role of the Lawyer in the European Communities* (1968)

DONNER, A M, *The Court of Justice as a Constitutional Court of the Communities* (University of Exeter, 1978)

EVERLING, V, 'The Member States of the European Community before their Court of Justice', (1984) 9 European LP 215

FELD, W, *The Court of the European Communities: new dimension in international adjudication* (1964)

FERRIERE, G, *Le controle des actes étatiques par la Cour de Justice des Communautés européennes* (1968)

HARTLEY, T C, *The Foundations of European Community Law* (2nd edn 1988), Chapters 2, 10, 11, 12, 13, 14, 15, 16 and 17

JACOBS, F, *Judicial Process in the European Court and the Role of the Advocate-General* (University of Exeter 1990)

LASOK, K P E, *The European Court of Justice: Practice and Procedure* (1984)

LAUWAARS, R H, *Lawfulness and Legal Force of Community Decisions* (1973)

MANN, C J, *Function of Judicial Decision in European Economic Integration* (1972)

MACKENZIE STUART, A J, *The European Communities and the Rule of Law* (1977)

MILLETT, T, *The Court of First Instance of the European Communities* (1990)

PAVLOPOULOS, A J, *The Advocate General's Office and its Contribution to the Development of the Law and the Judicial Machinery of the European Communities* (1986)

PLENDER, R O, 'The European Court as an International Tribunal' (1983) Cambridge LJ 279

RASMUSSEN, H, *On Law and Policy in the European Court of Justice* (1986)

Reports presented to a Judicial and Academic Conference, Court of Justice, Luxembourg (1976)

SCHEINGOLD, A, *The Rule of Law in European Integration* (1965)

SCHERMERS, H G, *Judicial Protection in the European Communities* (4th edn 1987)

SLYNN, SIR G, *Judicial Review of Community Administrative Acts* (University of Exeter, 1985)

TOTH, A G, *The Protection of Individuals in the European Communities* (1978)

USHER, J A, *European Court Practice* (1983)

WARNER, J-P, *The Evolution of the Work of the Court of Justice* (1976)

Chapter 10

BARAV, A, 'Some Aspects of the Preliminary Rulings Procedure in EEC Law', (1977) 2 EL Rev 3

BATHURST, M (Editor), *Legal Problems of an Enlarged European Community* (1972), Parts II and IV

BEBR, G, 'Article 177 of the EEC Treaty in the Practice of National Courts', (1977) ICLQ 241

CONSTANTINIDES-MEGRET, C, *Le droit de la Communauté économique européenne et l'ordre juridique des Etats membres* (1967)

DE RICHEMONT, J, *Integration of Community Law within the Legal Systems of the Member States* (1978)

DONNER, A M, *Le juge national et le droit communautaire* (1966)

Droit communautaire et droit national, Semaine de Bruges, Colloque 8–10 avril 1965, Bruges (1965)

HARTLEY, T C, *The Foundations of European Community Law* (2nd edn 1989), Chapters 7, 9

JACOBS, F G, & DURAND, A, *References to the European Court* (1975)

JALLES, J, *Implications juridico-constitutionnelles de l'adhesion aux Communautés Européennes: Le Cas du Portugal* (1981)

PESCATORE, P, *L'ordre juridique des Communautés européennes* (1971)

RIDEAU, J, et al, *La France et les Communautés Européennes* (1975)

SAINT-ESTEBEN, R, *Droit communautaire et droits nationaux* (1967)

BEBR, G, 'How Supreme is Community Law in the National Courts?' (1974) 11 CML Rev 3

BIEBER, R, 'On the Mutual Completion of Overlapping Legal Systems: The Case of the European Communities and the National Legal Orders,' (1988) 13 EL Rev 147

DASHWOOD, A, 'The principle of direct effect in European Community law', (1978) 16 *Journal of Common Market Studies*, 229

IPSEN, H P, 'Relationship between the law of the European Communities and National Law', (1965) 2 CMLR Rev 379

PESCATORE, P, 'The Doctrine of Direct Effect: An Infant Disease in Community Law', (1983) 8 EL Rev 155

WINTER, J, 'Direct applicability and direct effect: two distinct and different concepts in Community law', (1972) 9 CML Rev 425

Chapter 11

ADAMS, J C, & BARILE, P, *The Government of Republican Italy* (1972)

BERGSTEN, E E, *Community Law in French Courts* (1973)

CONSTANTINIDES-MEGRET, C, *Le droit de la Communauté économique européenne et l'ordre juridique des Etats-membres* (1967)

DONNER, A M, et al, *Le juge national et le droit communautaire* (1966)

DONNER, A M, *Le rôle de la Cour de Justice dans l'élaboration du droit européen* (1964)

FORRESTER, I S, & ILGEN, H M, *The German Legal System* (1972)

GAUDET, M, *Conflits du droit communautaire avec les droits nationaux* (1967)

HARTLEY, T C, *The Foundations of European Community Law* (2nd edn 1989), chapter 8

HAURIOU, A, *Droit Constitutionnel* (1970)

HERLITZ, N, *Elements of Nordic Public Law* (1969)

HOLBORN, L W, et al., *German Constitutional Documents since 1871* (1970)

HOLT, S, *Six European States The Countries of the European Community* (1970)

Institutions communautaires et institutions nationales dans le développement des Communautés (1968)

WARNER, J-P, 'The Relationship between European Community Law and the National Laws of the Member States', (1977) LQR 349

MAJERUS, P, *L'Etat Luxembourgeois* (1970)

MCMAHON, B M E, & MURPHY, F, *European Community Law in Ireland* (1989)

PEASELEE, A, *Constitutions of Nations*, 3rd edn, Vol. III Europe (1963)

SENELLE, R, *Revision of the Constitution 1967–1971* (1972)

WAELBROECK, M, *Traités internationaux et juridictions internes dans les pays du Marché commun* (1969)

BOULOUIS, J, 'L'applicabilité directe des directives. A propos d'un arrêt Cohn-Bendit du Conseil d'Etat', (1979) RMC 104

CONSTANTINESCO, V, SIMON, D, & SOLER-COUTEAU, P, 'Jurisprudence administrative française intéréssant le droit communautaire', [1988] RTDE 87 and [1989] RTDE 685

DAGTOGLOU, P D, 'European Communities and Constitutional Law', [1973] C.L.J. 256

DONNER, A M, 'Les rapports entre la compétence de la Cour de Justice des Communautés et les tribunaux internes', (1965) 115 *Recueil des Cours de l'Académie de la Haye*, 5

HAY, P, 'Supremacy of Community Law in National Courts', (1968) 16 AJ Comp L 524

KELLERMANN, A, 'Supremacy of Community Law in the Netherlands', (1989) 14 EL Rev 175

PETRICCIONE, R, 'Italy: A new mechanism for the implementation of Community Law', (1989) 14 EL Rev 456

SIMON, M, 'Enforcement by French Courts of European Community law', (1974) 90 LQR 467 and (1976) LQR 85 and 357

SIMON, M, & DOWRICK, F E, 'Effect of EEC Directives in France', (1979) 95 LQR 376

Chapter 12

BATHURST, M, et al., *Europe and the Law* (1968)

BRIDGE, J W, 'Abstract Law and Political Reality in the Post-European-Accession British Constitution' (1987)

COLLINS, L, *European Community Law in the United Kingdom* (4th edn 1990)

DE SMITH, S A, *Constitutional and Administrative Law* (6th edn 1989), chapters 4, 5

FURMISTON, M P, KERRIDGE, R, & SUFRIN, B E (Eds), *The Effect on English Domestic Law of Membership of the European Communities* (1983)

GORMLEY, L, 'The Application of Community Law in the United Kingdom, 1976–1985', (1986) 23 CML Rev 287

HOOD PHILLIPS, O, *Constitutional and Administrative Law* (7th edn 1987), chapters 3, 4, 5

KEETON, G W, & SCHWARZENBERGER, G, *English Law and the Common Market* (1963 Current Legal Problems)

LANG, J T, *The Common Market and Common Law: Legal Aspects of Foreign Investment and Economic Integration in the European Community, with Ireland as a Prototype* (1966)

LASOK, D, 'The United Kingdom before the European Court', in Luke, Ress, Will (Eds), *Rechtsvergleichung, Europarecht und Staatenintegration* (1983)

Legal and Constitutional Implications of United Kingdom Membership of the European Communities, Cmnd 3301 (1967)

MUNRO, C R, *Studies in Constitutional Law* (1987) Chapter 6

PISANI, E, et al., *Problems of British Entry into the EEC* (1969)

The United Kingdom and the European Communities, Cmnd 4715 (1971)

WALL, E A, *European Communities Act 1972* (1973)

BRIDGE, J W, 'Abstract Law and Political Reality in the Post-Euro-

pean-Accession British Constitution' [1987] Denning Law
Journal 23

BRIDGE, J W, 'Community Law and English Courts and Tribunals:
General Principles and Preliminary Rulings', (1975–76) I *European Law Review*, 13

DE SMITH, S A, 'The Constitution and the Common Market: a tentative appraisal', (1971) 34 MLR 597

FORMAN, J, 'The European Communities Act 1972', (1983) 10 CML
Rev 39

GREMENTIERI, V, & GOLDEN, C J, 'The United Kingdom and the
European Court of Justice: an Encounter between Common and
Civil Law Traditions', (1973) 21 AJCL 464

HUNNINGS, N M, 'Constitutional Implications of Joining the
Common Market', (1968–69) 6 CML Rev 50

MARTIN, A, 'The Accession of the United Kingdom to the European
Communities: Jurisdictional Problems', (1968–69) 6 CML Rev
7

MITCHELL, J D B, 'What do you want to be inscrutable *for* Marcia?'
(1967–68) 5 CML Rev 112

MITCHELL, J D B, et al., 'Constitutional aspects of the Treaty and
Legislation relating to British membership', (1972) 9 CMLR
Rev 134

OLIVER, P, 'Enforcing Community Rights in English Courts' (1987)
50 MLR 881

SIMMONDS, K R, '*Van Duyn v Home Office*: the Direct Effectiveness
of Directives', (1975) 24 ICLQ 419

THOMPSON, D, & MARSH, N S, 'The United Kingdom and the Treaty
of Rome: some preliminary observations', (1962) 2 ICLQ 73

TRINIDADE, F A, 'Parliamentary Sovereignty and the Primacy of the
Community Law', (1972) 35 MLR 375

WADE, H W R, 'Sovereignty and the European Communities', (1972)
88 LQR I

Chapter 13

BERR, C L, ET TREMEAU, H, *Le Droit Douanier* (1975)

BERTHAUD, C, *Le Marché Commun* (1975)

BURROWS, F, *Free Movement in the European Economic Community*
(1987)

CEREXHE, E, *Le Droit Européen: La Libre Circulation des Personnes
et des Entreprises* (1982)

DAINTITH, T, *Report on the Economic Law of the United Kingdom*
(1974)

FROMONT, M, *Rapport sur le droit économique français* (1973)

GRISOLI, A, *L'Europa del Mercato Comune* (1983)

HARTLEY, T C, *EEC Immigration Law* (1978)

JAQUEMIN, A, & SCHRANS, G, *Le droit économique* (1970)

LASOK, D, *The Law of the Economy in the European Communities* (1980) chapters 1, 3

LASOK, D, *The Professions and Services in the European Economic Community* (1986)

LASOK, D, *The Customs Law of the European Economic Community* (2nd edn 1990)

MAESTRIPIERI, C, 'Freedom of Establishment and Freedom to Supply Services', (1973) CML Rev 150

MORSIANI, G S, *Rapport sur le droit économique italien* (1973)

OLIVER, P, *Free Movement of Goods in the EEC* (2nd edn 1988)

PROUDHON, P J, *De la capacité politique des classes ouvrières* (1865)

SALIN, P, *L'unification monétaire européene* (1974)

SLOT, P J, *Technical and Administrative Obstacles to Trade in the EEC* (1975)

SVOBODA, K, *La Notion de Droit Economique* (1966)

TIZZANO, A, et al., *Professioni e Servizi nella CEE* (1985)

VERLOREN VAN THEMAAT, P, *Le droit économique des Etats membres des Communautés européennes dans le cadre d'une Union économique et monétaire* (1973)

VERLOREN VAN THEMAAT, P, *Rapport sur le droit économique néerlandais* (1973)

ZACHER, H F, *Rapport sur le droit économique en république fédérale d'Allemagne* (1973)

CHAMPEAUD, C, 'Contribution à la définition du droit économique', [1967] *Dalloz Chron* 215

DAINTITH, T, 'Public Law and Economic Policy', [1974] JBL 9

KIRALY, F DE, 'Le droit économique, branche indépendente de la science juridique', *Recueil d'études sur les sources du droit en honneur de F Geny*, (1935) Vol 3

LIMPENS, J, 'Contribution à l'étude de la notion de droit économique', (1966) *Il Diritto dell' Economia*, No 6

SCHMITTHOFF, C M, 'The Concept of Economic Law in England', [1966] *Journal of Business Law*, 309

WILBERFORCE, LORD, 'Law and Economics', [1966] *Journal of Business Law*, 301

Chapter 14

ADAMS, J, et al., *Essays for Clive Schmitthoff* (1983)

BALEKJIAN, W H, *Legal Aspects of foreign investment in the European Economic Community* (1967)

BATHURST, M, et al. (Editors), *Legal Problems of an Enlarged European Community* (1972), Parts V, VI and VII

BELLAMY, C, & CHILD, D G, *Common Market Law of Competition* (3rd edn 1987)

BLAKE, H M, *Business Regulations in the Common Market Nations,* Vols 1, 2 and 3 (1969), Vol 4 (with J A RAHL), *Common Market and American Antitrust: Overlap and Conflict* (1970)

CAWTHRA, B T, *Industrial Property Rights in the EEC* (2nd edn 1986)

CLOSE, G, 'Harmonization of Laws: Use or Abuse of the Powers under the EEC Treaty?' (1978) EL Rev 461

DE RIPAINSEL-LANDY, D, et al., *Les instruments du rapprochement des législations dans la Communauté économique européenne* (1976)

DESPICHT, N, *The Transport Policy of the European Communities* (1969)

EASSON, A J, *Tax Law and Policy in the EEC* (1980)

EC COMMISSION, *The Agricultural Policy of the European Community* (European Documentation, 6/1982)

ELLIS, T H, *European Integration and Insurance* (1980)

European Competition Policy, European Aspects Law Series No 12 (1973)

FENNELL, R, *The Common Agricultural Policy of the European Communities* (1979)

GOLDMAN, B, *European Commercial Law* (2nd edn 1975)

GOYDER, D, *EEC Competition Law* (1988)

GREAVES R, *Transport Law of the European Community* (1991)

GUY, D, & LEIGH, G. I F, *The EEC and Intellectual Property* (1981)

JOHNSON, S, & COURCELLE, G, *Environmental Policy of the EEC* (1989)

JOLIET, R, *Monopolization and Abuse of Dominant Position* (1970)

JOLIET, R, *The Rule of Reason in Antitrust Law* (1967)

KORAH, V, *Competition Law of Britain and the Common Market* (3rd edn 1982)

KORAH, V, *An Introductory Guide to EEC Competition Law and Practice* (4th edn 1990)

LASOK, D, *The Law of the Economy in the European Communities* (1980)

LASOK, D, & SOLDATOS, P, *The European Communities in Action* (1981) Part 3

LASOK, K P E, State Aids and Remedies under the EEC Treaty, 7 ECLR (1986) 53

LYON-CAEN, G, *Droit social européen* (1969)

MARSH, J S, & SWANNEY, P J, *Agriculture and the European Community* (1980)

MCLACHLAN, D L, & SWANN, D, *Competition policy in the European Community* (1967)

MERKIN, R, & WILLIAMS, K, *Competition Law: Anti-Trust Policy in the United Kingdom and the EEC* (1984)

PARRY, A, & HARDY, S, *EEC Law* (2nd edn 1981)

PENNINGTON, R R, & WOOLDRIDGE, F, *Company Law in the European Communities* (3rd edn 1982)

PERRET, F, *Coordination du droit des sociétés en Europe* (1970)

PRECHAL, S, & BURROWS, N, *Gender Discrimination Law of the European Society* (1990)

RIBAS, J J, *La politique sociale des Communautés Européennes* (1969)

RIES, A, *L'ABC du Marché Commun Agricole* (1978)

SCHINA, D, *State Aids under the EEC Treaty: Articles 92 to 94* (1986)

SCHMITTHOFF, C M, *The Harmonisation of European Company Law* (1973)

SEMINI, A, *La CEE Harmonisation des législations* (1971)

SHOUP, C (Editor), *Fiscal Harmonization in the Common Market,* 2 Vols (1967)

SNYDER, F G, *Law of the Common Agricultural Policy* (1985)

STEIN, E, *Harmonization of European Company Laws* (1971)

STONE, P, *Copyright Law in the United Kingdom and the European Community* (1990)

SUNDBERG-WEITMAN, B, *Discrimination on Grounds of Nationality* (1977)

THOMPSON, D, *The Proposal for a European Company* (1969)

USHER, J, *Legal Aspects of Agriculture in the European Community* (1988)

VAN BAEL, J, & BELLIS, J-F, *International Trade Law and Practice of the European Community: EEC Anti-Dumping and Other Trade Protection Laws* (1985)

WALLACE, H, et al. (Editors), *Policy Making in the European Communities* (1977)

WATSON, P, *Social Security Law of the European Communities* (1980)

WISE, M, *The Common Fisheries Policy of the European Community* (1984)

WOOLDRIDGE, F, *Company Law in the United Kingdom and the European Community* (1991)

WYATT, D, & DASHWOOD, A, *The Substantive Law of the EEC* (2nd edn 1987)

Index